ENDORSEMENTS

"Man and Woman, One in Christ subjects every Pauline text that deals with women to careful scrutiny; this means this book is a must-read for anyone doing serious study or preaching about these texts. Simply put, this is the most technically proficient study ever published on women in the Pauline texts."

> Professor Scot McKnight, North Park University, Jesus Creed

"The most comprehensive and well-reasoned contribution by an individual evangelical scholar in the modern history of the debate."

> Professor Ron Pierce, Biola University

"A masterpiece. Payne's research is comprehensive and fair-handed, biblically faithful, historically responsible, and culturally insightful. It contains some of the most important findings to date. Chapter 7 on 'Head/Source Relationships' is worth the price of the book many times over. Quite simply, this is the best treatment today."

> Paul D. Adams blog (in Christ Jesus){TXB1}

"As a long time adherent to CBMW's Danver's Statement, I had assumed the exegetical and theological issues to be well and truly settled by Wayne Grudem's research and responses on kephalē, along with Schreiner, Köstenberger, et al's latest tome on 1 Timothy 2. However, this meticulous study of the relevant passages in the Pauline corpus has given me much food for thought and stirred afresh certain reservations I still held regarding CBMW's position. From the purely

1

exegetical perspective this book is the best I have read to date. The analysis of kephalē was for the most part clear and persuasive. This book has won me over with regards to ministry roles. A fruitful and stimulating paradigm-changing challenge."

David R. Booth, Balcatta, Western Australia

"Man and Woman, One in Christ represents a massive amount of research and careful thinking! What an important contribution to the church! It should shape the discussion for some time to come. The book is carefully researched and argued, a significant piece of work."

Harold Netland, professor of philosophy of religion and chair of missions, Trinity Evangelical Divinity School

"Philip Payne's new book is an extraordinarily well-done study of Paul's teachings on women's roles in the church. Payne's knowledge of the first-century AD background, of New Testament Greek, of textual criticism, and of the theological issues is extensive. His discussion of 1 Corinthians 14:34–35 is outstanding, demonstrating that these two verses are almost certainly an interpolation. I highly recommend this marvelous book. Definitely five stars."

Shirley L. Barron, Richmond, Kentucky

"I can't adequately express how much this book has meant to so many within my family, dear friends, and others in leadership. Philip is a first-class scholar who has gone the third and fourth mile to research and write on each point in detail. A rock-solid, monumental work."

David Sanford, Credo Communications

"This is a monumental gift that we are thoroughly enjoying. Philip's diligent work and valuable contribution are needed for our times."

Roy and Ethel Anderson, Edmonds, WA

"Thank you for searching the Word, thorough research, and listening to the Spirit in writing this great book."

Nancy Boote, Columbia, MO

MAN AND WOMAN,
ONE IN CHRIST

You are welcome to email *Philip B. Payne* directly at **philip.b.payne@gmail.com** with corrections, questions, and other feedback regarding this book. Emailing here constitutes your permission for Payne to quote from your message (not your contact information) on the **www.pbpayne.com** website. You are welcome to see *Philip B. Payne's* interaction with questions raised about this book, supplemental information about the book, including the complete, up-to-date bibliography, and free downloads of articles by *P. B. Payne* at **www.pbpayne.com**.

MAN AND WOMAN,
ONE IN CHRIST

An Exegetical and Theological Study of
PAUL'S LETTERS

PHILIP B. PAYNE, PhD

ZONDERVAN ACADEMIC

Man and Woman, One in Christ
Copyright © 2009 by Philip B. Payne

Published in Grand Rapids, Michigan, by Zondervan. Zondervan is a registered trademark of The Zondervan Corporation, L.L.C., a wholly owned subsidary of HarperCollins Christian Publishing, Inc.

Requests for information should be addressed to customercare@harpercollins.com.

Zondervan titles may be purchased in bulk for educational, business, fundraising, or sales promotional use. For information, please email SpecialMarkets@Zondervan.com.

ISBN 978-0-310-52532-5 (ebook)

Library of Congress Cataloging-in-Publication Data

Payne, Philip Barton.
    Man and woman, one in Christ : an exegetical and theological study of Paul's Letters / Philip Barton Payne.
       p. cm.
    Includes bibliographical references and indexes.
    ISBN 978-0-310-21988-0 (softcover)
    1. Bible. N.T. Epistles of Paul—Criticism, interpretation, etc. 2. Sexism—Biblical teaching. 3. Equality—Biblical teaching. I. Title.
BS2650.52.P39 2009
261.8'357—dc22
                                         2009022466

The Greek, Hebrew, and transliteration fonts used in this book are available at www.linguistsoftware .com

Interior design: Melissa Elenbaas

Printed in the United States of America

HB 06.24.2024

To my father, J. Barton Payne, who inspired in me the love of life, truth, scholarship, and God's Word; who taught me to think biblically and critically; who had a song for every occasion; and who lived both his personal and professional life in the joy of the Lord.

To my family: my wife, Nancy, and my children, David, Kimi, and Brendan, whose love and support over the past decades made this book possible. The wait is finally over. Special thanks to Brendan, whose probing questions, keen insights, and exacting editorial revisions have brought clarity of expression throughout the book.

CONTENTS

❧ PART I ❧

Exegesis of Paul's Statements about Woman: Earlier Letters

PART 2

Exegesis of Paul's Statements about Woman: Later Letters

ACKNOWLEDGMENTS

I am grateful to teachers who prepared me for this, especially Gerald Hawthorne, Arthur Rupprecht, Merrill Tenney, Richard Longenecker, Kenneth Kantzer, John Stott, Walter Liefeld, Murray Harris, Peter Stuhlmacher, Martin Hengel, J. P. M. Sweet, and C. F. D. Moule.

I thank my students at Cambridge University, Trinity Evangelical Divinity School, Gordon-Conwell Theological Seminary, Bethel Seminary, and Fuller Seminary for their questions and encouragement.

Thanks to David Sanford and Sanford Communications, Inc., for their work in polishing each chapter.

I am deeply grateful to my children, David, Kimi, and Brendan, for all of their insights, Brendan for critiquing my text, and most of all to my wife, Nancy, who has enabled this work and who sacrificed more than anyone else to make this book possible.

Soli Deo gloria.

Abbreviations

BAR	*Biblical Archaeology Review*
BBR	*Bulletin for Biblical Research*
BDAG	Bauer, W., F. W. Danker, W. F. Arndt, and F. W. Gingrich. *Greek-English Lexicon of the New Testament and Other Early Christian Literature.* 3d ed. Chicago, 1999
BDB	Brown, F., S. R. Driver, and C. A. Briggs. *A Hebrew and English Lexicon of the Old Testament*
BDF	Blass, F., A. Debrunner, and R. W. Funk. *A Greek Grammar of the New Testament and Other Early Christian Literature*
BETL	Bibliotheca ephemeridum theologicarum lovaniensium
BETS	*Bulletin of the Evangelical Theological Society*
BGU	*Aegyptische Urkunden aus den Königlichen Staatlichen Museen zu Berlin, Griechische Urkunden.* 15 vols. Berlin, 1895–1983
BJRL	*Bulletin of the John Rylands University Library of Manchester*
BKAT	Biblischer Kommentar, Altes Testament
BNTC	Black's New Testament Commentaries
BR	*Biblical Research*
BSac	*Bibliotheca sacra*
BT	*The Bible Translator*
BTB	*Biblical Theology Bulletin*
BWANT	Beiträge zur Wissenschaft vom Alten (und Neuen) Testament
BZ	*Biblische Zeitschrift*
CBC	Cambridge Bible Commentary
CBQ	*Catholic Biblical Quarterly*
CBQMS	Catholic Biblical Quarterly Monograph Series
Chm	*Churchman*
CIG	*Corpus inscriptionum graecarum*
CSEL	Corpus scriptorum ecclesiasticorum latinorum
CT	*Christianity Today*

CTQ	*Concordia Theological Quarterly*
EBib	*Études bibliques*
EDNT	*Exegetical Dictionary of the New Testament*
EF	*Evangelical Feminism & Biblical Truth: An Analysis of More Than One Hundred Disputed Questions.* Edited by Wayne Grudem. Sisters, Ore.: Multnomah, 2004
EKKNT	Evangelisch-katholischer Kommentar zum Neuen Testament
EvQ	*Evangelical Quarterly*
ExpTim	*Expository Times*
FBBS	Facet Books, Biblical Series
FC	Fathers of the Church
FoiVie	*Foi et vie*
GCS	Die griechische christliche Schriftsteller der ersten [drei] Jahrhunderte
GKC	*Gesenius' Hebrew Grammar*
HALOT	*The Hebrew and Aramaic Lexicon of the Old Testament*
HNT	Handbuch zum Neuen Testament
HNTC	Harper's New Testament Commentaries
HR	*History of Religions*
HTR	*Harvard Theological Review*
HvTSt	*Hervormde teologiese studies*
IB	*Interpreter's Bible*
IBC	Interpretation: A Bible Commentary for Teaching and Preaching
ICC	International Critical Commentary
IDB	*The Interpreter's Dictionary of the Bible*
IDBSup	*Interpreter's Dictionary of the Bible: Supplementary Volume*
IG	*Inscriptiones graecae*
Int	*Interpretation*
JAAR	*Journal of the American Academy of Religion*
JBL	*Journal of Biblical Literature*
JES	*Journal of Ecumenical Studies*

JETS	*Journal of the Evangelical Theological Society*
JRE	*Journal of Religious Ethics*
JSJ	*Journal for the Study of Judaism*
JSNT	*Journal for the Study of the New Testament*
JSNTSup	Journal for the Study of the New Testament Supplement Series
JSOT	*Journal for the Study of the Old Testament*
JSOTSup	Journal for the Study of the Old Testament Supplement Series
JTS	*Journal of Theological Studies*
K&D	Keil, C. F., and F. Delitzsch, *Biblical Commentary on the Old Testament*
Kairós	*Kairós*
KBL	Koehler, L., and W. Baumgartner, *Lexicon in Veteris Testamenti libros*
L&N	*Greek-English Lexicon of the New Testament: Based on Semantic Domains*. Edited by J. P. Louw and E. A. Nida
LCL	Loeb Classical Library
LEC	Library of Early Christianity
LLA	Library of Liberal Arts
LSJ	Liddell, H. G., R. Scott, H. S. Jones, *A Greek-English Lexicon*
MM	J. H. Moulton and G. Milligan. *The Vocabulary of the Greek Testament*
MNTC	Moffatt New Testament Commentary
NA	Nestle-Aland, *Novum Testamentum*
NCBC	New Century Bible Commentary
NCV	New Century Version
NEchtB	Neue Echter Bibel
NIBCNT	New International Biblical Commentary on the New Testament
NICNT	New International Commentary on the New Testament
NICOT	New International Commentary on the Old Testament

NIDCC	*New International Dictionary of the Christian Church*, ed. J. D. Douglas
NIDNTT	*New International Dictionary of New Testament Theology*
NIGTC	New International Greek Testament Commentary
NIVAC	NIV Application Commentary
NovT	*Novum Testamentum*
NPNF¹	*Nicene and Post-Nicene Fathers*, Series 1
NPNF²	*Nicene and Post-Nicene Fathers*, Series 2
NRTh	*La nouvelle revue théologique*
NS	New Series
NTL	New Testament Library
NTM	New Testament Message
NTS	*New Testament Studies*
NTTS	New Testament Tools and Studies
OCD	*Oxford Classical Dictionary*
OTP	*Old Testament Pseudepigrapha*
PG	Patrologia graeca [= Patrologiae cursus completus: Series graeca]
PGL	*Patristic Greek Lexicon*
PL	Patrologia latina [= Patrologiae cursus completus: Series latina]
PNTC	Pillar New Testament Commentaries
PTS	Patristische Texte und Studien
PW	*Paulys Realencyclopädie der classischen Altertumswissenschaft*
RAC	*Reallexikon für Antike und Christentum*
RB	*Revue biblique*
RBMW	*Recovering Biblical Manhood and Womanhood: A Response to Evangelical Feminism.* Edited by John Piper and Wayne Grudem. Wheaton, Ill.: Crossway, 1991
ResQ	*Restoration Quarterly*
RevExp	*Review and Expositor*
RGG	*Religion in Geschichte und Gegenwart*

SBLSCS	Society of Biblical Literature Septuagint and Cognate Studies
SBLSP	*Society of Biblical Literature Seminar Papers*
SBT	Studies in Biblical Theology
SE	*Studia evangelica I, II, III* (= TU 73 [1959], 87 [1964], 88 [1964]. etc.)
SIG	*Sylloge inscriptionum graecarum.* Edited by W. Dittenberger.
SNTSMS	Society for New Testament Studies Monograph Series
SP	Sacra pagina
StPatr	Studia patristica
Str-B	Strack, H. L., and P. Billerbeck, *Kommentar zum Neuen Testament aus Talmud und Midrasch*
SVTP	Studia in Veteris Testamenti pseudepigraphica
TDNT	*Theological Dictionary of the New Testament*
Them	*Themelios*
ThEv	*Theologia evangelica*
ThTo	*Theology Today*
TJ	*Trinity Journal*
TJT	*Toronto Journal of Theology*
TLG	*Thesaurus linguae graecae: Canon of Greek Authors and Works*
TQ	*Theologische Quartalschrift*
TSF Bulletin	*Theological Students Fellowship Bulletin*
TTKi	*Tidsskrift for Teologi og Kirke*
TU	Texte und Untersuchungen
TynBul	*Tyndale Bulletin*
UBS[4]	United Bible Societies, *The Greek New Testament*, 4th ed. revised
USQR	*Union Seminary Quarterly Review*
VC	*Vigiliae christianae*
VE	*Vox evangelica*
WBC	Word Biblical Commentary
WCA	*Women in the Church: An Analysis and Application of 1 Timothy 2:9–15.* Edited by Andreas

	J. Köstenberger and Thomas R. Schreiner. 2nd ed. Grand Rapids: Baker, 2005
WCFA	*Women in the Church: A Fresh Analysis of 1 Timothy 2:9–15.* Edited by Andreas J. Köstenberger, Thomas R. Schreiner, and H. Scott Baldwin. Grand Rapids: Baker, 1995
WMANT	Wissenschaftliche Monographien zum Alten und Neuen Testament
WTJ	*Westminster Theological Journal*
WUNT	Wissenschaftliche Untersuchungen zum Neuen Testament
WZKM	*Wiener Zeitschrift für die Kunde des Morgenlandes*
ZNW	*Zeitschrift für die neutestamentliche Wissenschaft und die Kunde der älteren Kirche*

CLASSICAL WORKS

Aristotle

Gen. an.	*Generation of Animals*
Hist. an.	*History of Animals*
Mot. an.	*Movement of Animals*
Mund.	*De mundo*
Part. an.	*Parts of Animals*
Pol.	*Politics*

Artemidorus Daldianus

Onir.	*Onirocritica*

Athenaeus

Deipn.	*Deipnosophistae*

Callamachus

Hymn. Cer.	*Hymn to Ceres or Demeter*

Diogenes Laertius

Vit. Phil.	*Lives and Opinions of Eminent Philosophers*

Dionysius of Halicarnassus

Ant. rom.	*Antiquitates romanae*

Euripides

Bacch.	*Bacchanals*
Hec.	*Hecuba*
Hipp.	*Hippolytus*

Herodotus

Hist.	*Histories*

Hippocrates

Coac.	*Praenotiones coacae*
Nat.	*De natura hominis*

Hippolytus

Haer.	*Refutation of All Heresies*

Horace

Sat.	*Satires*

Joannes Philoponus

Comm. De an.   Commentary on Aristotle's *De anima*

Juvenal

Sat.	*Satirae*

Lactantius

Inst.	*The Divine Institutes*

Lucian

[Am.]	*Affairs of the Heart*
Bis acc.	*The Double Indictment*
Syr. d.	*The Goddess of Syria*

Malalas, John

Chron.	*Chronographia*

Nonnus

Dion.	*Dionysiaca*

Ovid

Ars am.	*Ars amatoria*

Pausanias

Descr.	*Description of Greece*

Philostratus
  Imag.   *Imagines*

Plato
  Prot.   *Protagoras*
  Resp.   *Republic*
  Tim.   *Timaeus*

Pliny the Elder
  Nat.   *Natural History*

Pliny the Younger
  Ep.   *Letters*

Plutarch
  Arist.   *Aristides*
  Brut. an.   *Bruta animalia ratione uti*
  Caes.   *Caesar*
  Comm. not.   *De communibus notitiis contra stoicos*
  Def. orac.   *De defectu oraculorum*
  Mor.   *Moralia*
  Pomp.   *Pompeius*
  Quaest. rom.   *Quaestiones romanae et graecae (Aetia romana et graeca)*
  Them.   *Themistocles*
  Tranq. an.   *De tranquillitate animi*
  Vit. Alexander   *Life of Alexander*

Sophocles
  Oed. col.   *Oedipus coloneus*

Stobaeus
  Ecl.   *Eclogae*

Strabo
  Geogr.   *Geography*

Tacitus
  Germ.   *Germania*

OLD TESTAMENT PSEUDEPIGRAPHA

Apoc. Mos.	Apocalypse of Moses
2 Bar.	2 Baruch (Syriac Apocalypse)
1 En.	1 Enoch (Ethiopic Apocalypse)
2 En.	2 Enoch (Slavonic Apocalypse)
Jos. Asen.	Joseph and Aseneth
Jub	Jubilees
L.A.E.	Life of Adam and Eve
Odes Sol.	Odes of Solomon
Pss. Sol.	Psalms of Solomon
Sib. Or.	Sibylline Oracles
T. Reu.	Testament of Reuben
T. 12 Patr.	Testaments of the Twelve Patriarchs

JEWISH LITERATURE

ʾAbot	ʾAbot
b.	Babylonian Talmud
Ber.	Berakot
ʿErub.	ʿErubin
Giṭ.	Giṭṭin
Ḥag.	Ḥagigah
Ketub.	Ketubbot
m.	Mishnah
Meg.	Megillah
Midr.	Midrash
Menaḥ.	Menaḥot
ʿOr.	ʿOrlah
Pirqe R. El.	Pirqe Rabbi Eliezer
Qidd.	Qiddušin
Rab.	Rabbah
Roš Haš.	Roš Haššanah
S. Eli. Rab.	Seder Eliyahu Rabbah
Soṭah	Soṭah
t.	Tosefta
Tanḥ.	Tanḥuma
y.	Jerusalem Talmud

Yebam.	*Yebamot*

Josephus

Ant.	*Jewish Antiquities*
Ag. Ap.	*Against Apion*
Vita	*Life*

Philo

Alleg. Interp. 1, 2, 3	*Allegorical Interpretation 1, 2, 3*
Creation	*On the Creation of the World*
Dreams 1, 2	*On Dreams 1, 2*
Drunkenness	*On Drunkenness*
Embassy	*Embassy to Gaius*
Flacc.	*Against Flaccus*
Her.	*Who Is the Heir?*
Plant.	*On Planting*
Prelim. Studies	*On the Preliminary Studies*
QG 1, 2, 3, 4	*Questions and Answers on Genesis 1, 2, 3, 4*
Rewards	*On Rewards and Punishments*
Spec. Laws 1, 2, 3, 4	*On the Special Laws*

APOSTOLIC FATHERS

1–2 Clem.	*1–2 Clement*
Did.	*Didache*
Herm. Sim.	*Shepherd of Hermas, Similitudes*
Eph.	*Ignatius, To the Ephesians*
Trall.	*Ignatius, To the Trallians*

CHURCH FATHERS

John Chrysostom

Hom. in ep. 1 ad Cor.	*Homilies on the First Letter to the Corinthians*
Hom. in ep. ad Col.	*Homilies on the Letter to the Colossians*
In ep. ad Romanos	*On the Letter to the Romans*
In Genesium	*On Genesis*
In Joannen	*On the Gospel of John*

Clement of Alexandria

Const. ap.	*Apostolic Constitutions*

Paed.	Christ the Educator
Protr.	Exhortation to the Greeks
Strom.	Miscellanies

Eusebius

Chron.	Chronicle
Hist. eccl.	History of the Church
Praep. ev.	Preparation for the Gospel

Irenaeus

| Demonstration | Demonstration of Apostolic Preaching |
| Haer. | Against Heresies |

Origen

| Orat. | De oratione [Prayer] |

Tertullian

Bapt.	Baptism
Marc.	Against Marcion
Virg.	The Veiling of Virgins

VERSIONS AND MODERN EDITIONS OF THE BIBLE

Amplified	The Amplified Bible
ASV	American Standard Version
Beck	The New Testament in the Language of Today (William F. Beck)
Berkeley	Berkeley Version in Modern English
CEV	Contemporary English Version
ESV	English Standard Version
Fenton	The Holy Bible in Modern English: Translated into English Direct from the Original Hebrew, Chaldae, and Greek (F. Fenton, 1903)
Goodspeed	The Complete Bible: An American Translation (E. J. Goodspeed)
HCSB	Holman Christian Standard Bible
GWT	God's Word Translation
JB	Jerusalem Bible
JBCerf	French edition of Jerusalem Bible

JND	J. N. Darby Bible: A *New Translation from the Original Languages*
KJV	King James Version
LB	Living Bible
LXX	Septuagint (the Greek OT)
Moffatt	A *New Translation* (James Moffatt)
MT	Masoretic Text (of the OT)
NA[27]	Nestle-Aland, *Novum Testamentum Graecae*
NAB	New American Bible
NASB	New American Standard Bible
NEB	New English Bible
New Berkeley	The New Berkeley Version in Modern English
NIV	New International Version
NRSV	New Revised Standard Version
Phillips	*The New Testament in Modern English* (J. B. Phillips)
REB	Revised English Bible
REV	Revised English Version
RSV	Revised Standard Version
RV	Revised Version
TEV	Today's English Version (= Good News Bible)
TNIV	Today's New International Version
TNT	*The New Translation* (edited by Kenneth N. Taylor, 1990)
UBS[4]	*The Greek New Testament*, United Bible Societies, 4th ed.
Way	*The Letters of Paul* (A. S. Way, 1935)
Weymouth	*The New Testament in Modern Speech* (R. F. Weymouth)
Williams	*The New Testament: A Translation in the Language of the People* (C. B. Williams)

GENERAL ABBREVIATIONS

c.	century
ca.	circa
cf.	compare

ch(s).	chapter(s)
d.	died
e.g.	for example
esp.	especially
et al.	and others
frg.	fragment
FS	Festschrift
ibid.	in the same place
ibid.	in the same place
idem.	the same author just mentioned
MS(S)	manuscript(s)
n(n).	note(s)
NT	New Testament
OT	Old Testament
pace	contrary to
passim	here and there
pl.	plural; plate
p(p).	page(s)
re	regarding
rev.	revised
sub	under
s.v.	under the word
v(v).	verse(s)

My Odyssey

M y belief in both inerrancy[1] and the equality of man and woman may seem absurd to many on each side of the egalitarian/complementarian divide. How can a thinking textual critic with an enlightened egalitarian view still cling to the notion of biblical inerrancy? Conversely, how can someone who believes everything taught by God's inspired Word come to the position that the Bible permits women to teach and exercise authority over men in the church? I offer a sketch of my journey to help explain.

My father, J. Barton Payne, instilled in me a love for Scripture in its original languages and a devotion to its truth. After every breakfast and dinner he gave us a fresh translation either from a chapter of the Hebrew OT or from the Greek NT. We had many spirited discussions as we repeatedly read through the Bible. Dad was one of the founding fathers and past president of the Evangelical Theological Society, a contributor to the Chicago Statement on Biblical Inerrancy, a translator of the New American Standard Bible and the chairman of the New International Version's final exegetical committee for the OT. Although strong in his convictions, my father taught me to love and respect people whose views of Scripture differ widely from my own and to appreciate the reasons for and potential benefits of differing interpretations.

My own commitment to inerrancy grew at Trinity Evangelical Divinity School, but I was unable to answer Joachim Jeremias's seemingly irrefutable arguments that the interpretation of the parable of the sower in Mark

---

1. As defined in "The Chicago Statement on Biblical Inerrancy," *JETS* 21 (1978): 289–96.

could not have been by Jesus. This was the greatest challenge I had yet encountered to biblical inerrancy. Although I may not be able to provide a satisfying answer to every objection to the reliability of Scripture, I felt I had to face this challenge honestly or I could not in good faith continue to affirm inerrancy. Consequently I made this a focus of my doctoral dissertation at Cambridge University. To make a long story short, at point after point, the very anomalies Jeremias depicts as undermining the reliability of the parable's interpretation give evidence it had an Aramaic source. This supports both its originality to Jesus and its consistency with the parable.[2] This taught me a key lesson: Beginning with the assumption of the reliability of the Scriptures can lead to the discovery of new insights that elucidate the meaning of the original text and resolve apparent contradictions. This stands in sharp contrast to the common belief that only a higher critical view of the Scriptures leads to valuable intellectual contributions.

Although I affirm the value of historically critical analysis of the biblical text and find it a vital help to a culturally sensitive understanding of the text, I challenge what I believe to be the incorrect and intellectually dangerous belief that only a skeptical view of the reliability of the Scriptures is worthy of scholars. My belief in the inerrancy of Scripture has led to many of the insights in this book, which in turn have brought me to the conviction that, properly understood in their original context, all of Paul's teachings on man and woman are internally consistent. My view stands in contrast to those who affirm the authority of Paul's worthy insights on the equality of man and woman but reject as misogynist, culturally conditioned, and unauthoritative his statements that they interpret as limiting the leadership of women in the churches.

In 1973 at a New Testament Seminar in Cambridge, England, my assumption of male headship was challenged when a scholar stated that no passage of Scripture properly understood in its context excludes women from any form of Christian ministry. Could this be true? What of 1 Cor 14:34–35 and especially 1 Tim 2:12? To check this, I read 1 Timothy in Greek daily for several months. Soon I felt with Paul the urgency of counteracting the false teaching that was threatening the life of the church in

---

2. Cf. Philip B. Payne, "The Seeming Inconsistency of the Interpretation of the Parable of the Sower," *NTS* 26 (1979–80): 564–68; idem, "The Authenticity of the Parable of the Sower and Its Interpretation," in *Gospel Perspectives: Studies of History and Tradition in the Four Gospels* (ed. R. T. France and D. Wenham; Sheffield: JSOT Press, 1980), 1:163–207.

Ephesus. Key word studies in 1 Tim 2:12 and some shocking discoveries (such as how English translations have introduced a dozen or more masculine pronouns into 1 Tim 3's list of qualifications for overseer and deacon, where the Greek text has none), convinced me that 1 Tim 2–3 is not a solid foundation for restricting women's ministry.

Nevertheless, I was keen that my wife include in her vows: "By God's grace I promise to submit to your leadership." My ongoing research, however, of the Corinthian passages, then Ephesians, Genesis, and finally Galatians forced me to conclude that Scripture does not support a hierarchy of male authority in marriage, either. During our two terms as Evangelical Free Church missionaries in Japan, Dad and Mom visited us following six months in India, where Mom taught the gospel of John at a seminary. Dad argued in a special annual lecture that the Bible does not exclude women from any church office or ministry. He chuckled that their journal would not publish it since they had no contrasting perspective, yet that journal had published a lecture the previous year advocating male headship with no contrasting perspective.

For over seven years I did not publish my research out of a desire not to cause division in the church. Then I prayed that the Lord would make it clear if he wanted me to make my research known. Within two days of that prayer, the EFCA president urged me to publish my findings, the EFCA Ministerial Association asked me to write a position paper on women in ministry, and I was given an article that argued on the basis of 1 Tim 2:11–15 that woman's "susceptibility to deception bars them from engaging in public teaching ... there are some activities for which women are by nature not suited" (cf. above, pp. 323, 411–12). I took this as clear guidance and began the writing and distilling of my research findings, culminating in this work. I have put my exegetical chapters in what I consider to be the chronological order of Paul's letters, in order to show as clearly as possible how he remained faithful to his own principles regarding man and woman in Christ throughout his varied applications of them. It is my prayer that this distillation of my last thirty-six years of research will encourage and enlighten many.

1

Backgrounds to Paul's Teaching regarding Man and Woman

Before analyzing Paul's teachings on women, it is fitting first to examine influences on his view of women, his women colleagues, and his theological axioms, since it is reasonable to expect a correlation among these. This chapter begins with Paul's Hellenistic and Jewish cultural context, including his teacher, Gamaliel. It then examines the most profound influences on Paul's view of women: the Holy Scriptures and Jesus.

Hellenistic Culture

The apostle Paul was born in Tarsus of Cilicia. His travels and the bulk of his ministry were in the Gentile, Greek-speaking world, so it is inevitable that he had extensive contact with Hellenistic thought and practice. The treatment of Hellenistic women varied dramatically from region to region; from Sparta and Rome, where women had political responsibilities, to Athens, where wives of the wealthy were essentially imprisoned.[1] Women tended to have more freedom in the western portions of the Hellenistic world[2] and in Egypt. The first-century BC Greek historian Diodorus Siculus 1.27.2 wrote that in Egypt "it was ordained that the queen should have greater power and honour than the king and that among private persons

---

1. Johannes Leipoldt, *Die Frau in der antiken Welt und im Urchristentum* (3rd ed.; Leipzig: Koehler und Amelang, 1965); Markus Barth, *Ephesians* (AB; Garden City, N.Y.: Doubleday, 1974), 2:655–61; A. Oepke, "γυνή," *TDNT* 1:777–84; and the articles on woman and marriage in *RGG*, *RAC*, *PW*, and *IDB* summarize the spectrum.
2. Cf. Oepke, "γυνή," 1:777.

the wife should enjoy authority over her husband, the husbands agreeing in the marriage contract that they will be obedient in all things to their wives."[3] In Paul's day Musonius Rufus (*frag.* 13A and 14.94.2–19) praised marital love and the deep union between husband and wife.[4]

Hellenism, however, had a broad misogynist streak, as has been demonstrated in many studies.[5] Euripides' (ca. 479–406 BC) *Hippolytus* calls women "this bane to cheat mankind" (616–17), "a great bane" (627), and "this creature of ruin," and he wishes that men could just buy sons for gold at the temple (620–23);[6] "I shall never take my fill of hating women" (664–65).[7]

Even Plato (ca. 437–347 BC), who occasionally affirms the virtue of particular women (a woman could be a guardian, though not a philosopher-king in his republic), calls men superior to women (*Tim.* 42a). He writes, "Do you know, then, of anything practiced by mankind in which the masculine sex does not surpass the female on all these points?... [The] one sex is far surpassed by the other in everything, one may say ... the woman is weaker than the man"[8] (*Resp.* 5.455c–e). He warns that "whoso has failed therein [in life] shall be changed into woman's nature at the second birth"[9] (*Tim.* 42b).

Aristotle (384–322 BC), too, says, "the male is by nature superior and the female inferior, the male ruler and the female subject"[10] (*Pol.* 1254.b.13–15), "for the male is by nature better fitted to command than the female"[11] (*Pol.* 1259.b.2–3, b.10), since man is rational and woman irra-

---

3. *Diodorus of Sicily* 1:84–87 (C. H. Oldfather, LCL). Cf. Herodotus, *Histories* 2.35, 60; Barbara S. Lesko, *The Remarkable Women of Ancient Egypt* (Berkeley: B. C. Scribe Publications, 1978), 30–31.

4. Musonius Rufus, *frag.* 3, 42.33, 23, also encouraged women to study Stoic philosophy, which emphasized self-control. Wayne A. Meeks, *The Moral World of the First Christians* (LEC 6; Philadelphia: Westminster, 1986), 46, however, writes, "there is no record of any women among his own pupils." Cf. R. B. Ward, "Musonius and Paul on Marriage," *NTS* 36 (1990): 281–89; Craig S. Keener, *Paul, Women & Wives: Marriage and Women's Ministry in the Letters of Paul* (Peabody, Mass.: Hendrickson, 1992), 97.

5. E.g., Evelyn and Frank Stagg, *Woman in the World of Jesus* (Philadelphia: Westminster, 1978), 56–78; John T. Bristow, *What Paul Really Said about Women* (San Francisco: Harper & Row, 1988), 1–30; Alvin J. Schmidt, *Veiled and Silenced: How Culture Shaped Sexist Theology* (Macon, Ga.: Mercer Univ. Press, 1989), 1–129.

6. Its continuing influence is evident in its quotation after the second century AD by Pseudo-Lucian, *Affairs of the Heart* 38.

7. Euripides, *Children of Heracles, Hippolytus, Andromache, Hecuba* 184–89 (D. Kovacs, LCL).

8. Plato, *Resp.* 1:447 (P. Shorey, LCL).

9. Plato, *Tim.* 7:90–93 (R. G. Bury, LCL).

10. Aristotle, *Pol.* 20–21 (H. Rackham, LCL).

11. Ibid., 58–59.

tional (*Pol.* 1260.a.5–9). Consequently, "for the two parties to be on an equal footing or in the contrary positions is harmful in all cases"[12] (*Pol.* 1254.b.9–10). Even their virtues are qualitatively different. Man has "the courage of command, and the other [woman] that of subordination"[13] (*Pol.* 1260.a.23–24). He describes "the female is as it were a deformed male"[14] (*Gen. an.* 737a and 775a).

Menander (ca. 343–291 BC) calls woman "nature's greatest misfit" (*Fr.* 488) and writes, "where woman is, there is all evil" (*Fr.* 804) and "to instruct a woman is simply to increase the poison of a dangerous serpent"[15] (*Fr.* 702). Democritus (a.k.a. Democrates) states, "To be ruled by a woman is the worst insult for a man" (*Saying* 111).[16] In Hellenistic Judaism, *2 En* 30.18 (written between 30 BC and AD 70) describes God's purpose in creating a wife for Adam, "that death should come to him by his wife." After the second century AD, Pseudo-Lucian states, "Let women be ciphers and be retained merely for child-bearing; but in all else away with them,"[17] "perfect virtue grows least of all among women,"[18] and "all the gods, methinks, hate what he [Promethus] did in fashioning females, a cursed brood."[19]

In first-century Hellenism, women were generally treated as their husband's property. In order not to dishonor their husbands, faithful observance of social conventions was expected, particularly in avoiding the appearance of an adulteress or prostitute. Plutarch (ca. AD 46–120), in *Advice to the Bride and Groom*, describes harmonious marital life: "The wife ought to have no feeling of her own, but she should join with her husband in seriousness and sportiveness and in soberness and laughter" (14, *Mor.* 140a). "A wife ought not to make friends of her own, but to enjoy her husband's friends in common with him" (19, *Mor.* 140d). "And control ought to be exercised by the man over the woman, not as the owner has control of a piece of property, but, as the soul controls the body, by entering into her feelings and being knit to her through goodwill" (31, *Mor.*

---

12. Ibid., 20–21.
13. Ibid., 62–63.
14. Aristotle, *Gen. an.* 175 (A. L. Peck, LCL).
15. Oepke, "γυνή," 1:777.
16. C. C. W. Taylor, *The Atomists, Leucippus and Democritus: Fragments: A Text and Translation with a Commentary* (Toronto: Univ. of Toronto Press, 1999), 238; cf. pp. 44–45, Fr 137 (IV.22.199), "A woman is much more impetuous in foolish speech than a man"; Fr. 138, "Having little to say is an ornament for a woman."
17. Lucian, *[Am.]* 38 8:210–11 (M. D. Macleod, LCL). Cf. TLG 248.
18. Ibid., 51 8:228–29.
19. Ibid., 43 8:216–17, quoting Menander; cf. similarly, *[Am.]* 9.

142d).[20] Plutarch said that married people "should pour all their resources into a common fund.... [The] property and the estate ought to be said to belong to the husband even though the wife contribute the larger share"[21] (20, *Mor.* 140–41). This attitude continued after Paul's time, as seen in Aelius Aristides's affirmations about husband and wife:

> ... not waiting to listen to his wife, he will tell his wife what must be done; nor does he attend to her words ... he will make his wife conform as closely as possible to his own nature, as a better person would treat an inferior one.... God is superior and more perfect than man, and the ruler than the private citizen, and the master than the slave and the husband than the wife ... or everything would be topsy-turvy.[22]

Yet in Paul's day, new roles were appearing for women. Various philosophical, political, financial, religious, poetic, and romantic forces promoted equal rights or greater equality for women.[23] The Isis cult taught, "Thou [Isis] gavest to women the same power as to men."[24] Women of status could study, organize meetings, and participate in religious ceremonies and demonstrations. By staying at least three days in her parents' home each year, a Roman woman avoided becoming the property of her husband.[25] First-century AD Roman law permitted women to hold political and religious offices, own and dispose of property, make a will, give testimony, terminate a marriage, and other things, such as sue for child support and custody.[26]

Many of the pagan roles for women, however, were repugnant to Christian morality, not just because they were sexually immoral, but because they did not treat women as full persons. This left Paul with a thorny problem: How could women demonstrate Christian liberty and equality in

---

20. Plutarch, *Mor.* 2:308–9, 310–11, 320–23 (F. C. Babbitt, LCL). Cf. below, pp. 217–18.
21. Plutarch, *Mor.* 2:312–13 (Babbitt, LCL).
22. *In Defense of Oratory* 129 (41D), written between AD 145 and 147; Plutarch, *Arist.* 354–57 (C. A. Behr, LCL).
23. Barth, *Ephesians,* 2:656; Linda L. Belleville, "'Ιουνιαν ... ἐπίσημοι ἐν τοῖς ἀποστόλοις: A Re-examination of Romans 16.7 in Light of Primary Source Materials," *NTS* 51 (2005): 248–49.
24. *P.Oxy.* 1380, 214–215 in *The Oxyrhynchus Papyri* (ed. Bernard P. Grenfell, et al.; London: Egypt Exploration Fund/Graeco-Roman Branch, 1915), 11:200; cited in Barth, *Ephesians,* 2:656–57.
25. Cf. below, pp. 315, 392–93.
26. Linda L. Belleville, *Women Leaders and the Church: Three Crucial Questions* (Grand Rapids: Baker, 2000), 71–96; Belleville, "'Ιουνιαν," 248–49.

Christ without bringing offense to the gospel?[27] He does this by honoring women as fully human even though this clashed with cultural conventions, and he affirms prophecy by women if done with modest deportment (1 Cor 11:4–5).

Most women lacked formal education, resulting in their widespread disdain.[28] This disdain was furthered by the prominence of homosexual relations between men and teenagers in educational circles, particularly in the gymnasia and the symposia. Many of the pillars of Greek literature, including Plato, Aristotle, Euripides, Aeschylus, and Hesiod, were critical of the abilities of women and wrote highly of homosexual relationships. The pederasts described in Plutarch, Achilles Tatius, and Lucian viewed woman as "vicious, lazy, and vain."[29] Achilles Tatius (2.38) describes the character of a youthful male as noble, unaffected, and soul-satisfying, but all a woman "says and all her actions too are figments for the occasion."[30]

Gamaliel and Contrasting Jewish Culture

Acts 22:3 reports that Paul (Saul) had the highest possible credentials in Pharisaic rabbinic education: "brought up in Jerusalem, at the feet of Gamaliel, I was thoroughly trained in the law of our fathers and was just as zealous for God as any of you are today." Paul's teacher was none other than the famous Rabban Gamaliel I (the Elder) who, like his grandfather (or possibly father) Hillel, was held in high esteem, so high that *m. Soṭah* 9:15 states, "When Rabban Gamaliel the Elder died, the glory of the Law ceased and purity and abstinence died." He is the Gamaliel described in Acts 5:34 as "a teacher of the law, who was honored by all the people." His learning and character earned him the title "Rabban," given to only seven Jewish doctors.

27. E. A. Judge (*Rank and Status in the World of the Caesars and St. Paul* [University of Canterbury Publications 29; Christchurch, New Zealand: University of Canterbury, 1982], 9) argued that Paul accepted recognized social ranking but repudiated conventions of status used for exploitation; cf. his "Cultural Conformity and Innovation in Paul: Some Clues from Contemporary Documents," *TynBul* 35 (1984): 12. Based on this, Timothy J. Harris, "Why Did Paul Mention Eve's Deception? A Critique of P. W. Barnett's Interpretation of 1 Timothy 2," *EvQ* 62 (1990): 337, argues that Paul would accept today's equal professional and social ranking for women and men.

28. Bennett Simon, *Mind and Madness in Ancient Greece: The Classical Roots of Modern Psychiatry* (Ithaca, N.Y.: Cornell Univ. Press, 1978), 250.

29. Richard C. Kroeger and Catherine C. Kroeger, "St. Paul's Treatment of Misogyny, Gynephobia, and Sex Segregation in First Corinthians 11:2–16," in *SBLSP* (Missoula, Mont.: Scholars Press, 1979), 215.

30. Achilles Tatius, 130–31 (S. Gaselee, LCL).

Gamaliel emphasizes the sovereignty of God in his address to the Sanhedrin recorded in Acts 5:35–39. When the Sanhedrin wanted to put the apostles to death, Gamaliel warns them, "For if their purpose or activity is ... from God, you will not be able to stop these people" (5:38–39). Paul, like his teacher Gamaliel, lays strong emphasis on God's sovereignty (e.g., Rom 8–9). Gamaliel's references to "the kingdom of heaven" (e.g., m. Ber. 2.5) are reflected in Paul's fourteen references to the kingdom of God and of Christ.[31] Gamaliel claims that he "saw directly by the holy spirit" (t. Soṭah 9.15).[32] The Holy Spirit is also a key theme in Paul's letters, with "spirit" (πνεῦμα) occurring 143 times, including its occurrence in each of the Pastoral Epistles. Both Gamaliel and Paul exemplify care for particular slaves. "Like Tabi before him, Onesimus could hope for a better deal than most in his station."[33]

The surviving sayings of Rabban Gamaliel I indicate a favorable attitude toward women in sharp contrast to the rabbinic tradition as a whole. All but two (m. ᾿Abot 1:16; m. ῾Or. 2:12, neither mentioning women) of the six sayings of Rabban Gamaliel I in Danby's index of the Mishnah[34] explicitly treat women and men equally (m. Roš Haš. 2:5, freedom to walk; m. Yebam. 16:7, to testify in court; m. Giṭ 4:2, in recording divorce) or promote the welfare of women (m. Roš Haš. 2:5; m. Yebam. 16:7; m. Giṭ 4:3), and none are derogatory to women. Gamaliel is considerate of the practical needs of women, as in freeing midwives to go anywhere to help a delivery (m. Roš Haš. 2:5) and allowing "a woman to marry again on the evidence of one witness [that her husband had died, including evidence] ... from a slave or from a woman or from a bondwoman" (m. Yebam. 16:7). Paul also grants women freedom to remarry in Rom 7:1–3 and 1 Cor 7:15: "If the unbeliever divorces, let him divorce. A believing man or woman is not bound in such circumstances."

Gamaliel ordains that a widow may make a vow to collect payment for her Ketubah (m. Giṭ 4:3). Similarly, Paul defends women's marital rights

---

31. Rom 14:17; 1 Cor 4:20; 6:9, 10; 15:24, 50; Gal 5:21; Eph 5:5; Col 1:13; 4:11; 1 Thess 2:12; 2 Thess 1:5; 2 Tim 4:1, 18.
32. Cf. W. D. Davies, Paul and Rabbinic Judaism: Some Rabbinic Elements in Pauline Theology (London: SPCK, 1948), 331.
33. Bruce D. Chilton and Jacob Neusner, "Paul and Gamaliel," BBR 14.1 (2004): 41.
34. Herbert Danby, The Mishnah, Translated from the Hebrew with Introduction and Brief Explanatory Notes (Oxford: Oxford Univ. Press, 1933), 822. All subsequent citations from the Mishnah are from this edition.

(1 Cor 7:3–40). *Y. Ber.* 9.1 (136b), which says that a man should bless God every day that he was not created a woman, also says: "R. Gamaliel once pronounced the formula of blessing on seeing a very pretty pagan woman. Is it possible? cried the doctors. [Have not six rabbis, each named, said] … that one must not attribute the gift of beauty to pagans?"[35]

Gamaliel's affirmations of woman pave the way for *Midr. Rab. Exod.* 14, 15: "Before God all are equal: women and slaves, poor and rich"; and *Tanna Elialm R.* 9: "Whether Israelite or Gentile, man or woman, male or female slave — according to their works the Holy Spirit dwells also upon him."[36] Paul develops Gamaliel's positive assessment of women, slaves, and Gentiles (e.g., Gal 3:28). Paul, too, takes women seriously; so seriously that he testifies, "I persecuted this Way to death, binding and putting both men and women into prisons" (Acts 22:5; cf. 8:3; 9:2). In rejecting the petty limits of legalistic Pharisaism and championing freedom and equality, Paul extends the trajectory of his teacher, particularly as regards women.

Gamaliel's affirmations of women and his unusually free spirit, combined with the affinities of Paul to his great teacher, should caution against assuming that Paul shared the lowly view of women that characterized much of Pharisaic Judaism. Many commentators dismiss Paul's view of women as "the point of view of first-century Judaism, which he did not leave behind when he became a Christian."[37] P. K. Jewett argues that Paul's Jewish perspective was incompatible with his Christian insight into the equality of man and woman and that "Paul himself sensed that his view of the man/woman relationship, inherited from Judaism, was not altogether congruous with the gospel he preached."[38] On the next page Jewett notes, "one can only suppose that the apostle's remarks in I Corinthians 14:34–35 reflect the rabbinic tradition which imposed silence on the woman in the synagogue as a sign of her subjection." But surely, if Paul himself taught male-female equality in Christ, one should examine carefully what Paul does say about man and woman before jumping to

---

35. Moses Schwab, *The Talmud of Jerusalem. Translated for the First Time Vol. I Berakhoth* (1886; repr., New York: Hermon Press, 1969), 156.
36. Translation cited from Barth, *Ephesians*, 2:660 n. 212.
37. Kenneth J. Foreman, *The Layman's Bible Commentary*, vol. 21: *The Letter of Paul to the Romans, The First Letter of Paul to the Corinthians, The Second Letter of Paul to the Corinthians* (Atlanta: John Knox, 1961), 94.
38. Paul K. Jewett, *Man as Male and Female: A Study in Sexual Relationships from a Theological Point of View* (Grand Rapids: Eerdmans, 1975), 113.

the conclusion that he is promoting the common Jewish view — and thus contradicting himself.

With few exceptions, such as the adulation of Sir 26:13 – 18, the overall picture of Jewish tradition from around the time of Paul is fairly consistent in its low view of women. Josephus asserts, "The woman, says the Law, is in all things inferior to the man. Let her accordingly be submissive, not for her humiliation but that she may be directed; for the authority [τὸ κράτος] has been given by God to the manspirit" (Ag. Ap. 2.201).[39] He writes that the Essenes disdain marriage because "they wish to protect themselves against women's wantonness, being persuaded that none of the sex keeps her plighted troth to one man" (Ant. 2.121).[40]

Philo declares, "The woman, being imperfect and depraved by nature, made the beginning of sinning and prevaricating; but the man as being the more excellent and perfect creature, was the first to set the example of blushing and of being ashamed, and indeed of every good feeling and action" (QG 1.43). He writes that "mind corresponds to man, the senses to woman"[41] (Creation 165; cf. 167) and that woman is "irrational" (Alleg. Interp. 3.50; cf. 2.38). He calls woman "the weaker and more effeminate soul. For nature is of men, and to follow nature is the mark of a strong and truly masculine reason"[42] (Drunkenness 55; cf. Embassy 319). He teaches that "woman is not equal in honor with man" (QG 1.27) and that women are easily deceived (QG 1.23, 33, 46). Moreover, "virgins and wives are not allowed full control of their vows by the law ... [since that] would not be to their husband's advantage"[43] (Spec. Laws 2.24).

Sirach says, "A man's spite is preferable to a woman's kindness; women give rise to shame and reproach" (Sir 42:12b – 14 JB). "Any spite rather than the spite of woman! ... No wickedness comes anywhere near the wickedness of a woman, may a sinner's lot be hers!" (25:13, 19).[44] In T. Reu. 5:1, 3 the author even states, "Women are evil ... women are overcome by the

39. Josephus, 1:372 – 73 (Thackeray, LCL).
40. Ibid., 2:368 – 69.
41. Philo, 1:130 – 31 (F. H. Colson and G. H. Whitaker, LCL); cf. Dorothy Sly, Philo's Perception of Women (Atlanta: Scholars, 1990).
42. Philo, 3:344 – 45 (Colson and Whittaker, LCL).
43. Philo, 7:320 – 2 (F. H. Colson, LCL).
44. Barth (Ephesians 2:658 n. 208) cites "a warm attitude toward woman" in Sir 26:1ff., which does praise a "good wife," but contrast 26:7 – 12! For Sirach, "A silent wife is a gift from the Lord" (26:14). In his desire to counter "traditional, popular, and scholarly anti-Semitism fostered in the Christian church" (2:660), Barth minimizes the extent of misogyny in the Jewish tradition, as he also does of the Hellenistic tradition (cf. 2:656).

spirit of fornication more than men, and in their heart they plot against men" (cf. 3:10; 4:1; 6:1 – 2). Rabbinic writings, which though conserving earlier traditions are generally later than Paul, are particularly misogynistic: "Ten portions of empty-headedness have come upon the world, nine having been received by women and one by the rest of the world" (b. Qidd. 49b). R. Joshua says: A woman has more pleasure in one *kab* [measure] with lechery than in nine *kabs* with modesty" (m. Soṭah 3.4). "Women are greedy, inquisitive, lazy, vain" (Gen. Rab. 45b). "Woe to him whose children are females" (b. Qidd. 82b).

Based on this view of woman, Jose ben Johanan of Jerusalem, one of the earliest scribes of the rabbinic tradition (ca. 150 BC) counsels: " 'Talk not much with womankind.' They said this of a man's own wife: how much more of his fellow's wife! Hence the sages have said: He that talks much with womankind brings evil upon himself and neglects the study of the Law and at the last will inherit Gehenna" (m. ʾAbot 1:5; cf. b. ʿErub. 53b). B. Qidd. 70a – b forbids giving a woman a greeting, and b. Ber. 43b says it is disgraceful for a scholar to speak with a woman in the street. M. Ketub. 7:6 states a wife who "speaks with any man" may be divorced without payment of her dowry. Philo says that assemblies are for men and that "women are best suited to the indoor life which never strays from the house, within which the middle door is taken by the maidens as their boundary, and the outer door by those who have reached full womanhood.... A woman ... should seek a life of seclusion"[45] (Spec. Laws 3.169 – 171). The "middle door" identifies this as a description of the wealthy of Jerusalem.

The social status of women is summed up in the common phrase, "woman, slaves, and children" (m. Ber. 3:3; 7:2), for all three have over them a man who is their master. Legally, women lacked many normal human rights. They were almost entirely at the disposal of their father or husband. During the first century AD, however, women did have various legal and property rights paralleling those granted in Roman law.[46]

The inferiority of women was particularly evident in religious matters (Str-B 3:558 – 62). A prayer recommended for daily use says, "Blessed be

---

45. Philo, 7:580–83 (Colson, LCL).
46. Belleville, *Women Leaders*, 71 – 96; Belleville, "Ἰουνιαν," 248–49.

God that hath not made me a woman."[47] This may have been adopted from Hellenistic writers who attribute similar statements to Thales, Socrates, and Plato.[48] In religious standing, women were almost "non-persons." According to *m. Ber.* 7:2, "Women or slaves or minors may not be included (to make up the number needed) for the Common Grace." Nor was it customary[49] for women to lay their hands on the head of the sacrificial victims or to wave the portions of the sacrifice. Women apparently desired to participate more as evidenced in *b. Ḥag.* 16b, where women laid their hands on the victim, for this is added: "Not that that was customary for women, but was to appease the women." Rabbis even debated whether fathers should teach their daughters the Law (*m. Soṭah* 3:4), and *m. Qidd.* 4:13 forbids women to teach even children.

Josephus describes "the two sections of a synagogue mentioned in the law of Augustus, σαββατεῖον and ἀνδρών (*Ant.* 16.164), the first, where the liturgical service took place, was open to women too; but the other part, given over to the scribes' teaching, was open only to men and boys as its name suggests."[50] *T. Meg.* 4.11, 226 reads: "All are qualified to be among the seven (who read the Torah in the synagogue on Sabbath mornings), even a minor and a woman. But a woman should not be allowed to come forward to read (the Torah) in public." Although the evidence suggests a variety of practice in Palestine and the Diaspora, where women were more involved,[51] in general, during the liturgical service women were simply to listen. They were not considered part of the assembly or regular or full participants. Thus, they were not included in the quorum required to establish a new synagogue or to worship. In gatherings for worship, the ancient synagogue forbade women to speak in practice as well as principle (Str-B 3:467). In every case where we have records, the rabbinic schools were solely for boys, never girls.[52]

---

47. Cf. below pp. 84–85 for citations.
48. Cf. Oepke, "γυνή," 1:777; Barth, *Ephesians*, 2:656 n. 198; below p. 84 for citations.
49. *T. Menaḥ.* 10.13, 528. *m. Menaḥ.* 9:8 says it was not permitted.
50. Joachim Jeremias, *Jerusalem in the Time of Jesus: An Investigation into Economic and Social Conditions during the New Testament Period* (trans. F. H. and C. H. Cave; Philadelphia: Fortress, 1969), 373.
51. Lee I. Levine ("Women in the Synagogue," in *The Ancient Synagogue* [2nd ed.; New Haven: Yale Univ. Press, 2005], 499–518) notes inscriptional evidence for women elders (*presbytera*) and women given the title *archisynagōgēs*, ruler of the synagogue.
52. Moses S. Zuckermandel, *Die Befreiung der Frauen von bestimmten religiösen Pflichten nach Tosefta und Mischna: Ein Beitrag zur Entwicklung der Halacha im Anschluss an meine Darstellung in dem Buche: Tosefta, Mischna und Boraitha* (Breslau: M&H Marcus, 1911), 22.

HOLY SCRIPTURE

According to Paul, in Christ believers stand in a new relationship to the law. Particularly in contrasting the law and faith, Paul makes statements that stand in stark contrast to anything from his Jewish contemporaries, such as: "Christ is the end of the law" (Rom 10:4); "Christ redeemed us from the curse of the law" (Gal 3:13); "we are no longer under the supervision of the law" (Gal 3:25); and "Christ abolished in his flesh the law with its commandments and regulations" (Eph 2:15).

Nevertheless, Paul teaches that the God who revealed his ethical requirements in the past is the same today. Thus, Paul encouraged Christians to submit their minds to God's law (Rom 8:5–7). He affirms that "the law is holy, and the commandment is holy, righteous and good" (Rom 7:12) and "that the law is spiritual" (7:14) and "good" (7:16). He says, "in my inner being I delight in God's law" (7:22). He taught in Rom 8:4 that Christ came so "that the righteous requirements of the law might be fully met in us." Acts 24:14 records Paul's statement to Governor Felix, "I believe everything that agrees with the Law and that is written in the Prophets." In 2 Tim 3:16, Paul[53] affirms, "All Scripture is inspired by God." In 1 Tim 1:8, Paul suggests the resolution between his critique of the law and his affirmation of it, "the law is good if one uses it properly." The goal of the law is love (1 Tim 1:5; Gal 5:14; Rom 13:9–10), and its proper interpretation must center on Christ, the fulfillment of the law (1 Tim 1:11, 14–16; 2:4–6; Rom 10:4). Thus, the OT was a key influence on Paul. His teaching about women sometimes refers to the law, particularly its account of the creation and fall.

1. The Creation and Fall of Man and Woman in Genesis 1–3

The creation of man and woman is summarized at the end of the grand overview of the whole of creation: "Then God said, 'Let us make man in our image,[54] according to our likeness;[55] and let them have dominion over

---

53. Cf. below, pp. 291–95 on Pauline authorship of the Pastoral Epistles (1 Tim backgrounds).
54. צֶלֶם means "*likeness, image*," *HALOT* 3:1029, as does LXX εἰκόνα. Gen 9:6 states, "Whoever sheds the blood of man, by man shall his blood be shed; for in the image of God has God made man." Thus, the image of God is a basis for respect for the value of each individual human life after the fall. This also indicates that part of what it means to be in the image of God is that human beings have moral responsibility and have been granted authority to defend what is right morally. Cf. Victor P. Hamilton, *The Book of Genesis Chapters 1-17* (NICOT; Grand Rapids: Eerdmans, 1990), 138–39.
55. "Likeness" (דְּמוּת) "is an abstract formation from the verb 'to be like'... and means 'that which is like something, likeness, representation'.... The word is used in Hebrew only when something

... all the wild animals of the earth....' So God created man in his image, in the image of God he created him;[56] male and female he created them" (Gen 1:26–27). "Man" (Heb. אָדָם) is explained as "them"[57] and as "male and female," and Gen 5:2 explicitly states, "he called their name 'man' [אָדָם] in the day he created them [male and female]"; thus, אָדָם in these verses clearly refers to "human beings" (TNIV, NCV), "humans" (CEV), or "humankind" (NRSV). It is only later in the text that this name is applied to the first male human being, Adam. God's image is not restricted to the male, nor does the text imply any difference between the image of God in man and woman.

God's repeated references to himself as "us" in 1:26 highlight the relational interpersonal aspects of God and implies that there is a relational interpersonal aspect to male and female being "in the image of God."[58] There is an analogy between God in community ("let us make")[59] and man in community ("male and female"). It is not that God, who is spirit, is sexual, but that personal relationships are essential to the being of God and of humankind. "God is, according to this bold affirmation ... mirrored ... as a community."[60] Correspondingly, the revelation of Jesus Christ, the image of God (2 Cor 4:4; Col 1:15), "embodies *a call for a new human community*."[61] Ephesians 4:24–25 reflects this: "put on the new self, created to be like God [τὸν κατὰ θεὸν κτισθέντα] in true righteousness and holiness. Therefore each of you must ... speak truthfully to his neighbor, for we are all members of one body."

God's blessings in Gen 1:28 encompass both man and woman and highlight their intimate personal relationships: "God blessed them, and God

---

is compared with something else." Claus Westermann, *Genesis 1–11* (trans. John J. Scullion; Minneapolis: Augsburg, 1984; London: SPCK, 1984), 146. Consequently, mankind "is the only creature ... which discloses to us something about the reality of God ... where power is received, decisions are made" (Walter Brueggemann, *Genesis* [Atlanta: John Knox, 1982], 32).

56. The singular "him" accords with "the man [הָאָדָם]," in 1:27, where the article is used "to denote the sum total of individuals belonging to the class" (GKC §126m), referring back to אָדָם in 1:26: "The masculine as *prior gender* includes the feminine" (GKC §122g; cf. §132d). This also applies to "him" in Gen 5:1.

57. Verse 26 describes "man" using the plural verb "let them have dominion," and in v. 27 the suffix "them" identifies "man" as plural: "male and female he created them," with no punctuation in Hebrew separating this from the affirmation that man is in God's image. "Them" occurs twice in v. 28, where God addresses them with five plural verbs, including the same verb "have dominion" over animals in v. 26. This shows that אָדָם in v. 26 identifies the same group as הָאָדָם in v. 27. God gives "you" (plural twice) seed-bearing plants and fruit in v. 29.

58. This affirmation that humankind reflects God is particularly striking in light of Judaism's absolute prohibition of images of God (Exod 20:4–5).

59. Cf. Gregory T. Armstrong, *Die Genesis in der alten Kirche: die drei Kirchenväter* (Tübingen: Mohr, 1962), 39, 69–70, 132 n. 1; Karl Barth, *Church Dogmatics*, III/1 (trans. J. W. Edwards, O. Bussey, and H. Knight; Edinburgh: T&T Clark, 1958), 191ff.

60. Brueggemann, *Genesis*, 34.

61. Ibid., 34.

said to them, 'Be fruitful and multiply, and fill the earth and subdue it; and have dominion over ... every living thing that moves upon the earth'" (NRSV). The surrounding pagan creation myths say nothing about God granting both man and woman authority over the earth and its creatures.[62] This blessing in Genesis gives no hint that God gave man more authority than woman or that God subjected woman to man. God's granting of authority to man and woman without differentiation supports that they are equally created "in his image."[63] In Gen 1:29, God grants man and woman together all plants for food. Nothing in the first chapter of Genesis grants man priority in status or authority over woman.

Genesis 2 focuses on the creation of man and woman. Its narrative structure climaxes in the creation of woman. In contrast to the refrain, "it was good," for every other stage of creation, it highlights man's need for woman by stating: "It is not good for the man to be alone; I will make a partner for him" (Gen 2:18, 20 NEB). Some argue that Gen 2–3 describes man in a position of authority over woman so that it is a Christian duty for women to be subordinate to men. Although nothing in Gen 2–3 teaches this directly, they argue that certain elements in the story imply that God put man in a position of authority over woman. Various proponents of this view give eleven arguments to support it, just as some feminists point to various elements in the text that might suggest that God put woman in a position of authority over man. The following examination of these points shows that neither assertion is justified. Instead, the dominant focus of the text is on the equal status and mutual responsibility of man and woman.

1. *Man was created before woman, and therefore should have authority over woman.* For instance, K&D 1:89 states, "By this [the creation of the man first, then the woman] the priority and superiority of the man, and the dependence of the woman upon the man, are established as an ordinance of divine creation." This logic, when applied to Genesis, would imply that the creatures of the sea and the birds of the air created in the fifth day should have authority over the land animals — and all of these should have

---

62. Cf. ibid., 37.
63. David J. A. Clines ("What Does Eve Do to Help? and Other Irredeemably Androcentric Orientations in Genesis 1–3," pp. 1–22 in *What Does Eve Do to Help? and Other Readerly Questions to the Old Testament* [JSOTSup 94; Sheffield: JSOT Press, 1990], 18) affirms that the image of God is related "to humankind's having rule over the animals," yet writes, "to say ... that women as well as men are created as the image of God is to move beyond the horizon of the text." This does not do justice to the definition of humankind as "male and female" in Gen 1:27.

authority over the human race since they were created prior. This logic is contradicted by God explicitly granting authority to both man and woman over animals and plants in Gen 1:26, 28–29.

Furthermore, in context, the significance of the woman being created second is to highlight man's need for a partner corresponding to him, not to man's authority over woman. The primary message of Gen 2:18–20 is that no animal is a suitable partner for man. Nothing in the context implies that man has authority over woman. Only after humankind's disobedience does God predict, "he will rule over you" (Gen 3:16).

2. *Man should have authority over woman because God said in 2:18, "I will make a helper suitable for him."* Not only is this translation in doubt, it depends on the assumption that helpers are naturally under the authority of those they help. The noun used here, however, throughout the OT does not suggest "helper" as in "servant," but "help, savior, rescuer, protector" as in, "God is our help." In no other occurrence in the OT does this noun refer to an inferior, but always to a superior or an equal.[64] Sixteen times it describes God as the rescuer of his people, their strength or power; the remaining three times of a military protector.[65] "Help" expresses that woman is a help/strength[66] who rescues or saves man.

The expression following "help," "as in front of him," כְּ = as + נֶגֶד = in front of/before + וֹ = him, is explained by *HALOT* 2:666, "like his opposite > proper for him." Both the LXX of Gen 2:20 and Tob 8:6 translate this verse, "Let us make a helper [βοηθός, as in Heb 13:6, 'the Lord is my helper'] like unto [ὅμοιος] him." The LXX of Gen 2:18 similarly translates it "corresponding to [κατ']"[67] him." The expression "in front of" man is more appropriate for a superior or equal than for a subordinate.[68] Freedman translates this phrase, "a power (or strength) equal to him."[69] The etymologically

---

64. When describing God it does not imply that God is subordinate to man, *pace* Raymond C. Ortlund Jr., "Male-Female Equality and Male Headship: Genesis 1–3," *RBMW* 95–112, 104.
65. Of God: Exod 18:4; Deut 33:7, 26, 29; Ps 20:3; 33:20; 70:6; 89:20; 115:9, 10, 11; 121:1, 2; 124:8; 146:5; Hos 13:9. Of a military protector: Isa 30:5; Dan 11:34; Ezek 12:14. For more on the background of this expression, see Aída B. Spencer, *Beyond the Curse: Woman Called to Ministry* (Nashville, Tenn.: Nelson, 1985), 23–29.
66. On the meaning "strength, might," see *HALOT* 2:812, citing Deut 33:26; Ps 33:20; 115:9, 10, 11. Cf. Ps 89:20.
67. BDAG 512 (κατά 5): "similarity or homogeneity, *according to, in accordance with, in conformity with.*"
68. Though it can refer simply to something in the presence of another, as in Ps 119:168.
69. R. David Freedman, "Woman, a Power Equal to Man: Translation of Woman as a 'Fit Helpmate' for Man is Questioned," *BAR* 9, no. 1 (January–February 1983): 56–58.

related noun נָגִיד refers to the person in front and according to *HALOT* 2:667–68 means, "the one declared (by Yahweh) to lead ... chief, leader, prince ... officer ... governor of a town ... court official ... head of a family ... eminent person ... cult official ... the high priest ... overseer ... supervisor ... the leader of Israel, appointed by Yahweh." It is used of David's and Solomon's rule over Israel in 1 Sam 9:16; 13:14, and 1 Kgs 1:35. Consequently, this expression highlights the role of the woman as the rescuer of the man, "a strength corresponding to him," and hence no less than an equal. Only with her is he able to fulfill his command to multiply and fill the earth, and together, they "rule over all the creatures." Consequently, nothing in the lexical background of "help meet" implies that the woman is to be under the authority of the man.[70]

3. *The man must have authority over the woman since he has a more active role than the woman. He names the animals, rejoices over the woman, names her, leaves father and mother, and cleaves to his wife.* Each of these arguments fails to stand up to scrutiny. The point of naming the animals is made clear by the statements that bracket this passage, "It is not good for the man to be alone. I will make a partner corresponding to him.... But for man no partner corresponding to him was found" (Gen 2:18, 20). The following verse, "So God caused the man to fall into a deep sleep," confirms that the primary message of verses 18–20 is not that man names the animals, but that no animal is a suitable partner for man. At the crucial point of the creation of woman, man is entirely passive. God is the active creator, who "took one of the man's ribs and closed up the place with flesh. Then the LORD God made a woman from the rib[71] ... and he brought her to the man" (2:21–22). The man's joyful exclamation, "Finally[72] bone of my bones and flesh of my flesh" (2:23), emphasizes the man's recognition that man and woman share the same essence. Throughout Scripture, "bone of my bones and flesh of my flesh" identifies shared standing or kinship, never subordination.

---

70. *Pace* Clines, who correctly identifies the crucial role of woman in procreation ("Eve," 10–11), but contrary to Gen 1:28, associates this role solely with the woman and without textual warrant reads subordination into it. In implying on p. 12 that "procreation is the sole purpose ... of women," he ignores God's purpose that she subdue the earth and have dominion over every living thing (Gen 1:28–30) and for her personal relationships (Gen 2:23–25).

71. The correctness of this meaning, which is given by all the ancient versions, is evident from the words, "God took one of his ribs (מִצַּלְעֹתָיו)," implying he had several of them. This is further confirmed by the man's response in 2:23.

72. *HALOT* 3:952, sub פַּעַם (5).

Complementarians[73] like Raymond C. Ortlund Jr. assert the man's "sovereign act" in naming woman: "he also names her ('she shall be called Woman').... [In] naming the creatures ... Adam brought the earthly creation under his dominion. This royal prerogative extended to Adam's naming of his helper ... [God] allowed Adam to define the woman."[74] According to Gen 1:26, 28, however, God, not the man's naming, grants humankind (not just man) rule over the animals. Nothing in the text implies that God allowed the man to define woman.[75] The use of "the woman" (הָאִשָּׁה) three verses later (3:1) proves that "woman" is not being used here as a proper name. The man names Eve only after the fall (Gen 3:20). There, but not in 2:23, is the Hebrew naming formula: to call + name (שֵׁם) + a proper name. Only one of these three parts of the formula is in 2:23, the verb to call. In Gen 2:23, the name woman (אִשָּׁה) is merely a derivative from the word for man (אִישׁ) with a feminine ending. Their corresponding names reinforce their oneness of essence, also implied by woman's origin in man. Since these words mean "male and female" twice in Gen 7:2 (HALOT 1:43, 93), it is clear that the feminine ending identifies woman as the man's female sexual counterpart.[76] Since that is its obvious function, it is arbitrary and unsupported by the text also to read dominion into this recognition.

Genesis does not say that Adam left father and mother and cleaved to his wife. Adam, after all, had no father or mother, so this is not about his initiative or action. Instead, leaving and cleaving stresses the independence of the new family begun by marriage and its priority over all other human relationships. Strikingly, this statement is the opposite of Hebrew experience, where the woman typically left her father and mother to live with her husband. If the text had read, "For this reason shall a woman leave her father and mother and be united to her husband," doubtless complementarians would interpret this as the perfect confirmation that a woman must

---

73. Since both egalitarians and complementarians believe men and women complement each other, the designation "complementarian," though politically convenient to hide the true difference, is unhelpful to distinguish the views.
74. Ortlund, "Male Headship," RBMW 102–3.
75. Cf. George W. Ramsey, "Is Name-Giving an Act of Domination in Genesis 2:23 and Elsewhere?" CBQ 50 (1988): 24–35, who argues that name-giving is an act of discernment, not domination. Cf. also Phyllis Trible, God and the Rhetoric of Sexuality: Overtures to Biblical Theology (Philadelphia: Fortress, 1978), 100.
76. Pace Clines ("Eve," 13), who acknowledges, "if he called her 'female' because she was taken out of 'male,' there would be no naming."

always be under the authority of a man, leaving her father's covering to come under her husband's covering. The text, however, does not endorse this normal pattern of Hebrew patriarchial society.

Instead, the man leaving father *and mother* suggests the equal standing of father and mother. This equal standing is immediately reinforced both by "and be united to his wife"[77] and "they will become one flesh."[78] Jesus confirms the Gen 2:24 definition of marriage in Matt 19:5.

4. *Woman is morally inferior to man or less discerning because woman first took of the fruit of the forbidden tree and then gave to the man.* James Hurley states, "Satan through the serpent led Eve to persuade her husband that God had lied about the fruit for selfish reasons."[79] Genesis 3:6, however, states, "She also gave some to her husband, who was with her, and he ate it." This passage says nothing about the woman (who was not yet named Eve) persuading her husband that God had lied about the fruit, but rather states that he was with her, and so he probably heard (or overheard) the dialogue with the serpent and desired to be like God, knowing good and evil. His being with her shows that he shared moral culpability with her. This is underscored by God's separate statements of the consequences of their acts directed first to the woman and then to the man. Paul confirmed Adam's disobedience and culpability in Rom 5:12–19 and 1 Cor 15:21–22.

5. *Eve usurped the man's headship when "she took some and ate it. She also gave some to her husband, who was with her, and he ate it" (Gen 3:6b).*[80] The sin, however, is identified in Gen 3:11 as disobedience to God's command. The text nowhere mentions male headship or states that women taking initiative would be usurping the man's authority.

6. *God's question to the man in 3:9, "Where are you?" implies that the man was the "God-appointed head . . . [who] bore primary responsibility to lead their partnership." Otherwise, "Why doesn't God summon both Adam and Eve to account together?"*[81] First of all, God did call them to account together, as

77. This points to mutuality, the "deepest corporeal and spiritual unity of man and woman" (K&D 1:90).
78. Paul interprets "one flesh" as conjugal union: "he who unites himself with a prostitute is one with her in body? For it is said, 'The two will become one flesh'" (1 Cor 6:16).
79. James B. Hurley, *Man and Woman in Biblical Perspective* (Grand Rapids: Zondervan, 1981), 220–21. Cf. pp. 215–16, "Eve was deceived by the serpent about the central theological issue of the truthfulness of God. Adam was not."
80. Ortlund, "Male Headship," *RBMW* 107, where he also identifies this as "sex role reversal" without evidence.
81. Ibid., 108.

the waw consecutive[82] implies in God's question to the woman in verse 13, "Then the LORD God said to the woman, 'What is this you have done?'" The order of the questions introduces a chiastic review of the events in reverse that exposes the sin and traces it back to the serpent's deception. This in turn is followed by a recapitulation of the consequences for the participants in their original order: serpent, woman, man. This literary structure would be broken if the order of the questioning were changed. Furthermore, this order exposes the man's passing the buck in verse 12[83] and the woman's admission that the serpent had deceived her.

The chiastic structure of Gen 3:1–19 is as follows:

A The Serpent deceived the woman (3:1–5).
  B The woman ate the forbidden fruit (3:6a).
    C The woman gave to the man the forbidden fruit, and he ate it (3:6b)
      D They realized they were naked (3:7).
        E They heard the sound of God in the garden and hid (3:8).
          F "The LORD God called to the man" (3:9a).
        E′ Qn./Ans. "I heard your sound in the garden and hid" (3:9b–10).
      D′ Qn. "Who told you that you were naked?" (3:11a).
    C′ Qn./Ans. "She gave to me from the tree, and I ate." (3:11b–12).
  B′ Qn./Ans. "The serpent deceived me, and I ate." (3:13).
A′ God identifies the Serpent's deception as the reason he will face judgment (3:14a).
A″ God curses the Serpent (3:14b–15).
  B″ God identifies consequences of the woman's disobedience (3:16).
    C″ God identifies consequences of the man's disobedience (3:17–20).[84]
      D″ God provided a solution to their nakedness (3:21).
        E″ God banished them from the garden (3:22–24).[85]

82. The Hebrew "and" used to introduce a series of past events occurring consecutively. Cf. GKC §49.
83. Ironically, Ortlund concludes from this that Adam bears the final responsibility ("Male Headship," RBMW 108).
84. As in C′, Adam reacts to God's pronouncement by shifting attention to his wife. His naming her Eve reminds the woman of both aspects of her punishment: that he will rule over her (by naming her) and that she will bear children in pain (as mother of all the living).
85. Banishment echoes hiding (in E and E′) because both show man's separation from God. The shift from hiding to banishment signifies the movement of the text from man's sin to God's

A question from God introduces each of the chiastic reversals from E′ through B′. These questions confirm the steps of this chiastic structure. God explains his curse on the Serpent, but the Serpent apparently does not deserve the platform that a question would provide.

7. *Beginning in Gen 3:9, "it is the man who is addressed and questioned. . . . The exchange between God and the couple suggests throughout that the husband was presumed to be the one responsible for religious decisions and the spokesman for the couple with God."*[86] The woman, however, *is* addressed directly by God in 3:13, showing she needs no spokesman. And what is the evidence that the husband was presumed to be the one responsible for religious decisions? That is a huge jump from God simply calling to him, "Where are you?" But Hurley goes even further, stating, "Adam functions as priest, husband, and perhaps as head of the social unit."[87] Nothing in Gen 1 – 3 implies Adam's religious or social leadership. The allegation that the Genesis creation narrative teaches "headship"[88] is without clear basis in the text. Contrast the clear hierarchical message of the Slavonic *Books of Adam and Eve* (32:1): "The archangel Joel said to Adam: 'Thus saith the Lord; I did not create thy wife to command thee, but to obey; why art thou obedient to thy wife?' "[89] Current hierarachical understandings of roles in marriage clearly reflect pseudepigraphical writings in a way that has no clear analogy in the Genesis account of creation.

8. *God's prophecy to the woman in Gen 3:16, "he will rule over you," is a command; that is: "he should rule over you."*[90] Since the text identifies this as a consequence of the fall, it must describe something new and not preexisting, just like all the other results of the fall in 3:14 – 19. Furthermore, all the other results of the fall are future; none are obligatory ("should"). Even Piper and Grudem agree that this "is not a prescription of what should be."[91] Grudem argues that 3:16 "should never be used as

---

judgment. Initially man willingly separated himself from God by hiding. By banishing man from the garden, God took away not only access to the tree of life but also the unbroken relationship with God that man had previously enjoyed in the garden but had rejected.

86. Hurley, *Man and Woman*, 216, 219.
87. Ibid., 219.
88. Ibid., 212; Ortlund, "Male Headship," *RBMW* 107 – 12; Grudem, *EF* 42.
89. *APOT* 2.134.
90. Ortlund, "Male Headship," *RBMW* 109. Ortlund does not even acknowledge the grammatically most obvious reading, "he will rule over you," namely the use of "rule" as something new, acknowledged by Hurley (*Man and Woman*, 192).
91. John Piper and Wayne Grudem, "Charity, Clarity, and Hope: The Controversy and the Cause of Christ," *RBMW* 403 – 22, 409.

a direct argument for male headship in marriage."[92] Virtually all versions of the Bible translate this as future, just like the other effects of the fall.[93] Everything in 3:14–19 is disastrous news for the party addressed, and every other result of the fall for humankind is something people should try to overcome, such as pain in childbearing (through medical techniques) and removal of thorns and thistles (through weeding and farming). People should not foster, but rather alleviate, the consequences of the fall, including the husband's rule over his wife. Claus Westermann astutely concludes that "the domination of the husband and the consequent subordination of the wife is seen as something which is not normal (hence as punishment)."[94]

The woman receives bad news: "I will greatly increase your pains in childbearing; with pain you will give birth to children. Your desire [will be] toward your husband, and he will rule over you" (Gen 3:16). K&D 1:103 notes, "she was punished with a desire bordering upon disease" (תְּשׁוּקָה from שׁוּק, run, "to fill with longing, desire, craving").[95] The meaning of the Hebrew in 3:16b, "towards [אֶל] your husband [is] your desire [תְּשׁוּקָה], and/but [וְ][96] he will master [מָשַׁל] over [בְּ] you," closely parallels Gen 4:7, "towards [אֶל] you [is] sin's desire [תְּשׁוּקָה], but [וְ] you must master [מָשַׁל] over [בְּ] it." The imperfect verb can be either future, "you will master," or modal, "you must master" over it, but since Cain then killed Abel, Cain clearly did not master over sin, so in this instance it makes more sense as modal. God tells Cain he must fight back to master sin and its desire to dominate him. "Sin's desire [is] towards you" means that sin desires to master or manipulate Cain. Analogously, "your desire will be for your husband" means "your desire will be to master or manipulate your husband," but he will master you. Every other result of the fall is future, so

---

92. "We should *never* try to perpetuate the elements of the curse!" (*EF* 40).
93. Benjamin Davidson identifies this as future (*Analytical Hebrew and Chaldee Lexicon of the Old Testament* [London: Paternoster, n.d.], 322).
94. Westermann, *Genesis 1–11*, 262. He argues that there is no subordination of woman to man in Genesis 2 (*Genesis* [BKAT; Neukirchen-Vluyn: Neukirchener, 1966], 311–16).
95. HALOT 4:1448. Song 7:11 later uses this word positively to mean romantic attraction, "I am my beloved's and his desire is for me," but how would this describe a new situation caused by the fall? It could if the newness comes in "*but* he will rule over you." This nuance, however, does not fit the context of Gen 3:16 as naturally, and the other elements of this construction are missing from Song 7:11: אֶל + וְ + a future sense of מָשַׁל + over [בְּ] you.
96. וְ is usually coordinative ("and" sixteen other times in 3:14–19) but can be adversative ("but," as in the 4:7 parallel).

in this context the imperfect naturally has its future sense, just as rendered in virtually all versions.

The fall transformed the relationship of Adam and Eve from equality into a power struggle. "Far from being a reign of coequals over the remainder of God's creation, the relationship now becomes a fierce dispute, with each party trying to rule the other. The two who once reigned as one attempt to rule each other."[97]

Hebrew has many words for "rule" and some of them imply bad rule or oppression. The word used in Gen 3:16, however, is by far the most common word for "rule" and for God's rule in the Hebrew Bible. *HALOT* 2:647–48 and BDB 605 analyze every OT instance of מָשַׁל and list no negative meaning for this word. It does not imply bad rule;[98] rather, it is simply that due to the fall, man will rule over woman. Since man's ruling over woman is a result of the fall, man must not have ruled over woman before the fall. It would be out of harmony with every other consequence of the fall to interpret man's rule over woman as something good that should be fostered. This passage no more teaches this than it teaches that women ought to have pain in childbirth.

9. *"Because you listened to your wife"* in 3:17 *implies Adam "abandoned his headship" and "this moral failure . . . led to his ruination."*[99] Ortlund misses the obvious reason why God addresses the man in this way. It is specifically because he blames his eating the fruit on "the woman you put here with me" for giving him the fruit to eat (v. 12) that God rebukes him for listening to his wife and eating it. Unlike the woman, who admitted she was deceived in verse 13, the man blamed the woman and blamed God for putting her with him. The man was fully culpable for eating the fruit. He knew this was in direct disobedience to God's command. If the fruit had been from any other tree, it would not have been a sin for the man to listen

---

97. Cf. Hamilton, *Genesis Chapters 1–17*, 202.
98. *Pace* George W. Knight III's assertion that this is "'rule' in an autocratic, unloving way" ("The Family and the Church: How Should Biblical Manhood and Womanhood Work out in Practice?" *RBMW* 345–57, 346), and Piper and Grudem's assertion that this is "fallen 'rulership'" not "God-ordained headship" ("Charity," *RBMW* 409), and Grudem's defining this verb, "a rule that was forceful and at times harsh" (*EF* 40; cf. 43, 123). Grudem rightly corrects assigning a negative "meaning" to a different word (p. 38 n. 27), so he should know that it is wrong to assign a negative meaning to a verb simply because other words describe its subject negatively in other passages (Neh 9:37; Isa 19:4).
99. Ortlund, "Male Headship," *RBMW* 110.

to his wife and eat. God's rebuke highlights both his disobedience and his refusal to take responsibility.

10. *The statement to Adam in 3:17, "Cursed is the ground because of you," teaches that "Adam was the head, the finally responsible member of the partnership. His disobedience, not Eve's, was the pivotal factor in the fall."*[100] *"The woman is not told that her curse flows from her deed."*[101] In 3:13, however, God says to the woman, "What is this you have done?" proving that God *was* concerned with *her* deed. Paralleling the man's acknowledgment "I ate," the woman, too, says, "I ate," acknowledging *her* deed. God's statement of consequences for the woman precedes the consequences for the man, which shows just how dubious is the speculation that she is cursed for the man's sin rather than or as well as for her own. If both sets of effects were a result of the man's disobedience, the text should have included both after God's statement to the man rather than separating them and having the effects on the woman stated directly to her first.

11. *God's naming the human race "man" in Gen 5:2 implies male leadership.*[102] It is precisely Gen 5:2's identification of "man" [אָדָם] as "male and female" "in the day he created them" that most clearly shows that the "man" [אָדָם] created in God's image in Gen 1:26–27 and 5:1 refers to man as "male and female." God's giving "male and female" humanity the same name highlights their oneness and supports their equality.

In summary, none of the eleven alleged indications that God put man in authority over woman stand up to scrutiny, and several of them are, if anything, more likely to suggest the opposite. The description of the creation of man and woman in Gen 1 does not contradict Gen 2–3, and neither shows that the man should have authority over woman. Genesis 1–3 consistently depicts the unity of the man and the woman as equal partners, not woman under man. Twenty statements in Gen 1–3 depict man and woman equally:

   1. God creates both male and female in God's image and likeness (1:26–27; cf. 5:1–2).

---

100. Ibid.
101. Hurley, *Man and Woman*, 218.
102. E.g. Grudem, *EF* 34–36.

2. God gives both male and female rule over animals and all the earth (1:26b, 28).

3. God gives both male and female the same blessing and tells them together to be fruitful and increase in number, fill the earth, and subdue it (1:28–29; cf. 5:2).

4. God speaks directly to both man and woman (1:28–29 "to them," "to you" plural twice).

5. God gives male and female together all plants for food (1:29 "to you" plural).

6. Woman is a "help" to man, a noun the OT never elsewhere uses of a subordinate (2:18, 20).

7. Woman "corresponds to" man, literally "in front of" man, face-to-face, not below (2:18, 20).

8. God makes woman from the man's rib, so she is made of the same substance as he (2:21–23).

9. The man recognizes, "This is now bone of my bones and flesh of my flesh" (2:23).

10. "Father and mother" are identified without hierarchical distinction (2:24).

11. A man is "united" to his wife, implying oneness (2:24).

12. A man becomes "one flesh" with his wife, implying unity (2:24).

13. Both the man and woman are naked[103] and feel no shame, sharing moral sensibility (2:25).

14. The woman and the man are together at the temptation and fall (3:6); both faced temptation.

15. Both the woman and man eat the forbidden fruit (3:6), both exercising a (bad) moral choice.

16. The eyes of both are opened, they realize they are naked, and sew coverings (3:7).

17. Both hide from God (3:8), showing they both experience guilt.

18. God addresses both directly (3:9–13, 16–19), showing both have access to God.

19. Both pass the blame (3:12–13), showing both have this weakness.

---

103. Naked (עֲרוּמִּים) is a play on the word עָרוּם, the serpent's cunning, craftiness in the next verse. It contrasts the transparency of humanity and the cunning of the serpent, who is bent on evil—getting humankind to disobey God. Thus, the purpose of this narrative is not to describe the origin of evil, but the origin of evil choices by humans.

20. God announces to both specific consequences of their sin
    (3:16–19); both are responsible.

In the curse against "the serpent,"[104] God affirms the seed of the woman "will crush your head" (Gen 3:15).[105] K&D 1:102 notes, "as it was through the woman that the craft of the devil brought sin and death into the world, so it is also through the woman that the grace of God will give to the fallen human race the conqueror of sin, of death, and of the devil ... [Christ] the destroyer of the serpent was born of a woman (without a human father)." In 1 Cor 15:21–26 and 1 Tim 2:14–15 Paul implies Christ's fulfillment of the Gen 3:15 *Protoevangelium*, the earliest prediction of the costly victory of Christ over Satan.[106]

2. Woman's Marital Position in Holy Scripture

OT descriptions of how women were treated should not be confused with prescriptions of how women *ought* to be treated. The OT says little about how marital relations ought to be structured. Proverbs criticizes bad wives and praises good wives (e.g., Prov 12:4; 19:13–14), but affirms, "He who finds a wife finds what is good and obtains favor from the LORD" (18:22).

The most extensive passage on the position of a wife and her activities is the description of an excellent wife in Prov 31:10–31. Its final position in the book gives it prominence. Though not an exhaustive description or even a normative pattern that all women must follow, it clearly encourages emulation. The "excellent wife" is an efficient executive with a well-ordered domestic staff. She deals in real estate, carries on a clothing concession, and cares for the poor as well as her own household. She has her own earnings and seems to be the primary income earner in the family. She is a wise and kind teacher. The prominent position of this passage in the canon of

---

104. The article with every reference to the serpent (cf. GKC § 126.2[d] on its use to restrict reference to a particular individual), the description of the serpent as "more cunning than any of the wild animals the LORD God had made," the words of the temptation, undermining the truth of God's word and epitomizing the causes of sin, and the sweeping consequences of the temptation all demand a more serious purpose to the story than "why snakes crawl on their bellies" or "why women hate snakes." Together these factors imply that the serpent represents ultimate moral temptation, namely the Tempter, Satan.
105. "He will crush" is a third person singular verb, and "his" in "you will strike his heel" is a third person singular suffix. Both are appropriate for a particular descendant. Cf. pp. 420–24 and 434–40 on the seed of the woman and 1 Tim. 3:15.
106. Cf. below pp. 417–42.

Hebrew Scripture implies that the kind of roles it mentions for a wife were not offensive either to Jews of that day or to God, who inspired it to be written as Scripture.

3. Woman's Social Position in Holy Scripture

Various passages describe women in public places and attending festivals (Gen 24:13–28; Exod 2:16–21; Judg 21:9–23), but what is particularly striking are women who held political leadership. The prophetess Miriam is sent by God "to lead" Israel (Mic 6:4; cf. Exod 15:20–21). Deborah is one of the judges whom "the LORD raised up" and who "saved Israel from the hands of their enemies" (Judg 2:16, 18), the highest leader in all Israel in her day (4:4). She is gifted by God for her administrative and prophetic role and is richly blessed in her position of authority over all the men of Israel. She delivers Israel from Canaanite rule (4:10, 14, 24; 5:1–31). Judges 4:4–5 states, "Deborah, a prophetess, the wife of Lappidoth, was leading Israel at that time. She held court under the Palm of Deborah between Ramah and Bethel in the hill country of Ephraim, and the Israelites came to her to have their disputes decided." She has authority to command Barak, the military commander of Israel, "Go!" (4:6, 14) and he goes. Her power to unite the people is compatible with her being a wife and mother (5:7).

Queen Esther has sufficient influence to bring about the destruction of the house of Haman along with 75,000 enemies of the Jews (Esth 7:1–10; 9:1–32). She, along with Mordecai, "wrote with full authority ... decreed ... established for themselves and their descendants.... Esther's decree confirmed these regulations" (9:29–32).

The records of the kings of Judah always note or name the queen mothers (cf. Jer 13:18; 29:2; 2 Kgs 24:15). They include Bathsheba (1 Kgs 2:17–19), Maacah (10:13, 15),[107] and Nehushta (2 Kgs 24:8), who is enthroned and crowned. Queen Athaliah "ruled the land" for six years (2 Kgs 11:1–3; 2 Chr 22:10–12). Although Athaliah and Jezebel (1 Kgs 18:4), like most of Israel's kings, were wicked, neither they nor any other woman leader of Israel is criticized in Scripture for being in authority on the grounds that this is an inappropriate role for a woman.

---

107. She is queen mother with both her son Abijam and her grandson Asa, 1 Kgs 15:2, 10, 13; 2 Chr 15:16.

4. Woman's Religious Position in Holy Scripture

The OT never commands that women be silent in religious gatherings. To the contrary, Isa 40:9 commands, "O woman who brings good tidings to Zion, go up on a high mountain. O woman who brings good tidings to Jerusalem, lift up your voice with a shout, lift it up, do not be afraid, say to the towns of Judah, 'Here is your God!'" Psalm 68:11 (12 MT) reads, "The Lord announced the word; the women proclaiming [feminine plural][108] it are a great company." Various passages describe women in public religious events (Deut 12:12; 2 Sam 6:5, 15, 19–22).

The priests consult the prophetess Huldah when they find the lost book of the Law. The king, the elders, the prophets, and the people accept her word as divinely revealed (2 Kgs 22:14–23:3; 2 Chr 34:22–32), and their obedience to her word sparks what is probably the greatest revival in the history of Israel (2 Kgs 22:14–20; 23:1–25; 2 Chr 34:29–35:19). Marriage does not hold her back from ministry. The priests choose to consult her rather than her contemporaries, Jeremiah (1:2) and Zephaniah (1:1).[109]

Joel predicts a future, greater prophetic role for women: "afterward, I will pour out my Spirit on all people. Your sons and daughters will prophesy.... Even on my servants, both men and women, I will pour out my Spirit in those days" (Joel 2:28–29; cf. Acts 2:14–21).

God uses women to communicate several key portions of inspired Scripture: the song of the prophetess Miriam (Exod 15:21), the song of the judge Deborah (Judg 5:2–31), the prayer of Hannah (1 Sam 2:1–10), and in the NT, the Magnificat of Mary (Luke 1:46–55).

Complementarians typically describe these as exceptional cases that establish the rule. If this is the case, however, the rule is not an absolute established by God's creative will, but must be reduced to a "general rule" or observed cultural pattern. These examples of God appointing women to leadership positions prove that God does approve women to exercise authority over men, at least in certain circumstances. Furthermore, none

---

108. Davidson, *Analytical Hebrew*, 191.
109. Note also Noadiah (Neh 6:14 = 2 Esd 16:14), who is called "the prophetess" in Hebrew but in the LXX is called "the prophet" (τῷ προφήτῃ), from the masculine word for prophet, not the feminine word for prophetess (προφῆτις). Rabbinic tradition includes Sarah, Hannah, Abigail, and Esther as prophetesses. E.g., Str-B 2:140; Abel Isaksson, *Marriage and Ministry in the Temple: A Study with Special Reference to Mt. 19:3–12 and 1 Cor. 11:3–16* (trans. N. Tomkinson et al.; ASNU 24; Lund, Sweden: C. W. K. Gleerup, 1965), 159. Just as there were good prophets and prophetesses, there were evil prophets and prophetesses, e.g., Ezek 13:1–16, 17–23.

of these texts says that God gives women social and/or religious authority over men only because of special circumstances, nor do they describe these cases as exceptions to a "general rule." In fact, Paul identifies such a high proportion of women in his circle of ministry that "general rule" becomes merely a slightly higher proportion of men than women, if that.[110]

The only social or religious position of significance that women are not recorded in the OT as holding the office of priest. The most obvious reason for this is the association of priestesses in some heathen cults with prostitutes, which Deut 23:17 prohibits. God repeatedly forbade his people from giving an appearance of following the immoral practices of the surrounding nations,[111] and to have women priestesses would give that appearance. The history of Israel supports the legitimacy of this concern.

JESUS CHRIST

Paul affirms "I follow the example of Christ" (1 Cor 11:1). Christ's example in all his deeds and words was to treat women as persons equal with men. He respected their intelligence and spiritual capacity as is evident in the great spiritual truths he originally taught to women. To the Samaritan woman he said, "The water I give will become a fountain of water springing up to eternal life ... salvation is from the Jews ... true worshipers will worship the Father in spirit and truth.... God is spirit.... I who speak to you am [the Messiah]" (John 4:14–26). To Martha he taught, "I am the resurrection and the life. He who believes in me will live, even though he dies; and whoever lives and believes in me will never die" (John 11:25–26).

Although a woman's testimony was generally not recognized in the courts, Jesus demonstrated his respect for their testimony by appearing first to Mary Magdalene after his resurrection (John 20:14–18) and instructing her to tell the others. After Jesus taught the Samaritan woman, she acted as the first missionary to her people, and many of her people believed (John 4:39–42).

Jesus seems to be unconcerned with gender differences in the kingdom of God. When a woman in the crowd says, "Blessed is the womb that bore you, and the breasts you nursed," Jesus responds, "On the con-

---

110. Cf. below, pp. 61–68, especially 68.
111. E.g., Lev 18:3; 20:23; Ps 106:35.

trary, blessed are those who hear the word of God, and keep it" (Luke
11:27–28). Jesus affirms that those who do the will of God are his brother
and sister and mother in Mark 3:34–35; Matt 12:49–50; and Luke 8:21,
showing that obedience, irrespective of gender, is more important than
kinship. Elsewhere, Jesus explains that in heaven there will be no marriage, but those who rise from the dead will be like angels (Luke 20:34,
35).[112] Significantly, Jesus does not rebuke the mothers at the feeding of
the four thousand for leaving their domestic duties for three days to listen
to his teaching (Matt 15:38). Similarly, when Mary was "listening to the
Lord's word, seated at his feet," the posture and position of a disciple, Jesus
affirms her: "Mary has chosen what is better, and it will not be taken away
from her" (Luke 10:38–42).

Jesus gives no hint that the nature of God's will for women is different
than for men. He made no distinction in the righteousness demanded
of both. The issues facing all people at the last judgment apply equally
to men and women: giving food and drink to the hungry and thirsty,
welcoming strangers, clothing the naked, and visiting those sick and in
prison (Matt 25:31–46).

The equality of the sexes is evident in Jesus' vocabulary. He calls a
crippled woman a "daughter of Abraham" (Luke 13:16), a linguistic usage
seventy years prior to the first recorded rabbinic equivalent (Str-B 2:200).
He says, "You are all brothers" (Matt 23:8), and he treats obligations to
father and mother equally (Mark 7:10–12). Jesus occasionally breaks social
customs, causing consternation, as when he speaks alone with the Samaritan woman at the well and allows a sinful woman to touch him. He also
touches many women with his healing hands.[113]

Jesus is sensitive to the social structures oppressing women. He attacks
the divorce customs of his day that allow only the husband to file for
divorce—and for practically any reason (Matt 19:3). Similarly, he denies
the common view that a man cannot commit adultery against his own
wife, only against another man.[114] Jesus attacks traditions in a way that
includes a significant change in the status of women in Israel. There is no

---

112. Matt 22:30; Mark 12:25; Luke 20:35–36.
113. Matt 8:15; 9:25; Mark 1:31; 5:41; Luke 4:40; 8:54; 13:13.
114. Mark 10:10. Cf. Jeremias, Jerusalem, 370–71; T. W. Manson, The Sayings of Jesus as Recorded in
    the Gospels according to St. Matthew and St. Luke Arranged with Introduction and Commentary
    (London: SCM, 1949), 136 (first published as Part II of the Mission and Message of Jesus in
    1937).

close parallel to Jesus' overall treatment of women as equal to men in the records of any of his Jewish contemporaries.

Although nothing in Jesus' teachings advocates male/female role distinctions or the subordination of women, Jesus' choice of the twelve disciples has been thought by some to imply these. Practical issues related to the "supremely personal union" (*TDNT* 4:442) of Jesus and his disciples, however, explain this. It is one thing for a number of women to be mentioned as following Jesus from time to time in his preaching in the towns (Mark 15:40–41; Luke 8:1–3), but traveling full time for three years with late night meetings such as at the Garden of Gethsemane and spending periods of time in the wilderness are quite another thing. Strong cultural objections and moral suspicions would undoubtedly be raised not only about Jesus, but also about the men whom he chose to be with him. Married women could hardly leave their families for such a long period, and single women would have been even more suspicious. To have chosen women disciples would have raised legitimate suspicion undermining the gospel.

Neither Jesus nor Paul says why Jesus chose only Jewish free men for the Twelve. The church should no more exclude women from its leadership simply because none of the Twelve were women than it should other social groups since they were not among the Twelve, including Gentiles, slaves, and freed slaves. Why exclude based on silence?

This survey of the influences on Paul reveals a stark contrast between the low view of women that pervaded both Hellenism and Judaism and the respect for women espoused by the primary guiding influences on Paul: Holy Scripture, Gamaliel, and Jesus. Awareness of this contrast enriches analysis of Paul's teachings about women, as does the following study of what Paul wrote about his female colleagues in ministry.

2

WOMEN PAUL NAMES AS
MINISTRY LEADERS

For centuries, the apostle Paul has been castigated as a stone-faced misogynist with a particular dislike for women. Yet reading his letters reveals, instead, a man deeply invested in relationships with both men and women. He accepts women as ministry leaders and respects and honors women who labor for the Lord, not as his subordinates, but as his partners and equals.

PHOEBE

In Rom 16:1, Paul commends "our sister Phoebe, who is [οὖσαν] a deacon [διάκονον] of the church of Cenchrea."[1] Each of the other three occurrences of διάκονος in Romans (13:4 twice; 15:8) refers to a leader and in context is better translated "minister" than "servant." If Paul had intended merely a regular pattern of service, a verbal form such as "who serves" (e.g., Rom 15:25) or the more general "ministry" (διακονία, e.g., 1 Cor 16:15) would have been more appropriate than the noun διάκονος.[2] The

---

1.   Cenchrea is Corinth's eastern harbor city on the Saronic Gulf. Cf. Strabo, 8.6.22; Philo, *Flacc.* 155. Καί in 𝔓⁴⁶ A² B C* 81 pc bo emphasizes that Phoebe is "also" a deacon, reinforcing her credentials, cf. C. E. B. Cranfield, *The Epistle to the Romans* (ICC; Edinburgh: T&T Clark, 1979), 2:781, and below, pp. 452–53, 457.
2.   James D. G. Dunn, *Romans 9–16* (WBC; Dallas: Word, 1988), 886. LSJ 398 lists it as a masculine noun, "διάκονος, ὁ," that can be used of women, in which case it can be feminine, e.g., *CIG* 3037, "fem. *deaconess, Ep. Rom.* 16.1." Patristic literature uses the feminine form, "διάκονος, ἡ," for "teacher and evangelist among women ... intermediary between lay women and deacon or bishop, compared with [the Holy] Ghost in relation to Christ and believers, *Const. App.* 2.26.6 ... regular minister of Church" (*PGL* 1:353); G. H. R. Horsley, ed., *New Documents Illustrating*

participle οὖσαν, specifying Phoebe to "be" a deacon, and the qualifier, "of the church in Cenchrea," seems to imply a recognized office. C. E. B. Cranfield concludes it is "virtually certain that Phoebe is being described as 'a (or possibly "the") deacon' of the church in question, and that this occurrence of διάκονος is to be classified with its occurrences in Phil 1.1 and 1 Tim 3.8 and 12."[3]

Phoebe's leadership role is evident in Paul's request in Rom 16:2, "receive her in the Lord in a way worthy of the saints, and give her support in whatever matters[4] she may have need from you, for she has been a leader [προστάτις, "leader, chief," "president or presiding officer," "one who stands before," LSJ 1526] of many and of myself as well." "Receive her," in contrast to all the other people to whom he conveys "greetings," indicates that Phoebe was the bearer of Romans, Paul's most theologically comprehensive epistle. He must, therefore, have held her in the highest trust.

Since Paul includes himself as having been under Phoebe's leadership, this was not simply a leadership role over other women. It should not be thought strange that Paul, who commanded all Christians to "be subject to one another" (Eph 5:21), should himself be subject to others, at least in certain situations, such as submitting to the local church leadership in the churches he visited. Herman Ridderbos concludes there is no "argument whatsoever to be derived from Paul's epistles that it was only the non-official *charisma* that was extended to the woman and not regular office."[5]

Every meaning of every word in the NT related to the word Paul has chosen to describe Phoebe as a "leader" (προστάτις) that could apply in Rom 16:2 refers to leadership. This includes the usage shortly before in Rom 12:8, "The one in leadership [ὁ προϊστάμενος], let him govern diligently."[6] G. H. R. Horsley identifies citations of προστάτης, including

---

Early Christianity: A Review of the Greek Inscriptions and Papyri Published in 1977/79 (Macquarie University, N.S.W., Australia: The Ancient History Documentary Research Centre, 1982/87), 2.193–95; 4:239–41. LSJ 398 and PGL 1:352 list a separate word for "deaconess," διακόνισσα, e.g., IG 3:3527.

3.   Cranfield, *Romans*, 2:781.

4.   "Matters" covers all kinds of business and legal affairs, e.g., 1 Thess 4:6; cf. Peter Stuhlmacher, *Paul's Letter to the Romans: A Commentary* (trans. S. J. Hafemann; Louisville, Ky.: Westminster/John Knox, 1994), 246.

5.   Herman Ridderbos, *Paul: An Outline of His Theology* (Grand Rapids: Eerdmans, 1975), 461.

6.   E.g., 1 Thess 5:12, "respect those who ... who have charge over you [προϊσταμένους] in the Lord"; 1 Tim 5:17, "The elders who rule [προεστῶτες] well are worthy of a double honor." Used in relation to the family, it means "ruling one's household" (1 Tim 3:4, 5, 12). The only other NT usage, "busy oneself with," does not fit Rom 16:2.

O. Tebt. Pad. 67 and *I. Eph.* III.668a, that identify the president of an association.[7] Horsley also cites "Sophia, 'the second Phoibe' "[8] and six other inscriptions or papyri about "female deacons and office-holders" published in 1979 alone. Προστάτις can also, like the Latin *patrona* ("patroness"), denote the legal representative of strangers and their protector; for as aliens they were deprived of civil rights. This meaning does not fit Rom 16:2, however, since "Phoebe cannot have stood in this relation to Paul since he was born free, Acts 22:28."[9] Even Charles Ryrie, who teaches that woman's role in church is "not a leading one," acknowledges that προστάτις "includes some kind of leadership."[10] This term almost always refers to an officially recognized position of authority.[11]

Translations such as the NIV, which repeat the word "give her any *help* . . . for she has been a great *help*," hide the fact that the Greek verb translated as "help [her]" (παραστῆτε from παρίστημι, "to help") is almost opposite in meaning to the word describing Phoebe as a προστάτις. If Paul had intended to say simply that Phoebe had "helped" others, it would have been natural for him to repeat παρίστημι to make his reason parallel his request. The NRSV "for she has been a *benefactor* of many and of myself as well" has the disadvantage that this meaning is not listed by LSJ or BAG,[12] and that Paul's companion Luke uses a different word that LSJ, BDAG, and BAG identify as meaning "benefactor," "those in authority over them are called benefactors [εὐεργέται]" (Luke 22:25). Thus, the linguistic evidence and the context of Phoebe's standing in the church strongly favor the normal meaning of the term, προστάτις, namely, "leader."[13] Since her leadership was in the church it would entail spiritual oversight.

---

7. G. H. R. Horsley, "Sophia, 'the second Phoibe,' " *New Documents* 4:239–44, 242.
8. Ibid.
9. Barrett, *Romans*, 283.
10. Charles C. Ryrie, *The Role of Women in the Church* (Chicago: Moody Press, 1958), 140 and 88.
11. Cf. examples in Philip B. Payne, "Libertarian Women in Ephesus: A Response to Douglas J. Moo's Article, '1 Timothy 2:11–15: Meaning and Significance'," *TJ* 2 NS (1981): 169–97, 195; Leonard Swidler, *Biblical Affirmations of Woman* (Philadelphia: Westminster, 1979), 310–11; Dunn, *Romans 9–16*, 888–89.
12. BDAG (885), does, however, list "a woman in a supporting role, *patron, benefactor,*" citing Horsley, "Phoibe," 4:242–44, but Horsley cites instances not only of the meaning "benefactor" but also of "guardian" (a person with legal authority) and "president." Lucian, in *Bis acc.* 29, uses προστάτις to mean "patroness," according to A. M. Harmon (3:140–41 [LCL]).
13. LSJ 1526–27 identifies προστάτις as the femine form of προστάτης, for which it gives only the following meanings: "*one who stands before, front-rank man . . . leader, chief . . . ruler . . . chief authors . . . administrator . . . president or presiding officer . . . one who stands before and protects, guardian, champion . . . patron . . . suppliant . . . prostate gland.*"

PRISCILLA

Paul ministered extensively with Priscilla and Aquila. He lived and worked with them for at least one and a half years in Corinth (Acts 18:1–3, 11, 18) before traveling with them to Ephesus (Acts 18:18), where a church met in their house (1 Cor 16:19). Paul left them in Ephesus to oversee the work there, where "Priscilla and Aquila ... explained [plural verb] to [Apollos] the way of God more accurately" (Acts 18:26). Priscilla's name is listed first before her husband's, contrary to Greek and Hebrew custom, as it is in every context mentioning their active ministry (Acts 18:18, 26; Rom 16:3). This makes it virtually certain that she played a significant, if not the dominant, role in these actions.[14] Luke, Paul's long-term co-worker, gives no hint that Priscilla's instruction of Apollos was in any way inappropriate for a woman, but rather praises her instruction's accurate content (Acts 18:26) and its results (18:27–28).

Apollos was "an eloquent man ... mighty in the Scriptures ... instructed in the way of the Lord ... fervent in spirit ... speaking and teaching accurately the things concerning Jesus ... speaking out boldly in the synagogue" (Acts 18:24–26a). Since Scripture speaks with approval of a woman instructing him, it is hard to imagine any man who would be above being taught by a woman or any theological topic that would be out of bounds for a woman. Even Ryrie acknowledges, "She could hardly be excluded from the ranks of a teacher."[15]

Paul always refers to her as "Prisca," the more respectful form of her name; Luke always adds the diminutive ending in "Priscilla." Paul also shows his respect by greeting Prisca first in both of his two most extensive lists of his colleagues: 2 Tim 4:19, when they were in Ephesus, and Rom 16:3–5, when they were in Rome: "Greet Prisca and Aquila, my fellow workers in Christ Jesus. They risked their necks for me. Not only I, but all the churches of the Gentiles are grateful to them. Greet also the church that meets at their house." "Fellow worker" connotes "one who labors with Paul as commissioned by God in the shared work of mission preaching."[16]

---

14. Both Luke in Acts 18:2 and Paul in 1 Cor 16:19 introduce them listing Aquilla's name before his wife's, proving that something like her wealth or social status did not necessitate this reversal of convention.

15. Ryrie, *Women*, 55.

16. W. H. Ollrog, *Paulus und seine Mitarbeiter* (WMANT 50; Neukirchen: Neukirchener, 1979), 63–72, esp. 67; cf. Dunn, *Romans 9–16*, 892.

JUNIA

Although many careful studies come to the same central conclusion that Junia is a woman apostle,[17] Eldon Jay Epp's masterful study, *Junia: The First Woman Apostle*, has untangled the convoluted web of how most recent Greek texts up until the 1998 printings of NA[27] and USB[4] and English versions changed this clear affirmation of the woman Junia into a man. Romans 16:7 reads, "Greet Andronicus and Junia, my relatives who have been in prison with me. They are outstanding among the apostles and became Christians before I did." Epp argues that the unanimous credible testimony of the church's first millennium identifies Junia as a woman (pp. 31–36, 57),[18] that no surviving Greek MS unambiguously identifies the partner of Andronicus as a man (pp. 45–49), that no early translation gives any positive sign that this is a masculine name (pp. 23–24), that Junia was a common Latin woman's name (pp. 54, 57), and that no bona fide instance of Junias has ever been found (pp. 24, 27, 34, 44, 57), nor is it likely to be found since the very similar Iunius was such a common name (p. 43).[19]

Epp goes on to show that Aegidius of Rome (ca. AD 1243/47–1316) is the first reliably documented instance treating this as a man's name (Juliam! p. 35), and that the male name Junias first become popular with Luther's translation (p. 38). It was first published this way in a Greek NT in the 1852 edition by Alford (p. 23), and first published in English in 1833 (pp. 24, 66). The Junianus name contraction theory is not only unattested, but standard contraction conventions would not result in the NT spelling (pp. 23–31, 39–44),[20] and the identity in form with the

---

17. E.g., Cranfield, *Romans*, 2:788–90; Dunn, *Romans 9–16*, 894; John Thorley, "Junia, a Woman Apostle," *NovT* 38 (1996): 18–29; Peter Lampe, "Junias," *ABD* 3:1127; Peter Lampe, "Iunia/Iunias: Sklavenherkunft im Kreise der vorpaulinischen Apostel (Röm 16,7)," *ZNW* 76 (1985): 132–34; Peter Lampe, *From Paul to Valentinus: Christians at Rome in the First Two Centuries* (trans. M. Steinhauser; ed. M. D. Johnson; Minneapolis: Fortress, 2003), 153–83; Richard S. Cervin, "A Note Regarding the Name 'Junia(s)' in Romans 16.7," *NTS* 40 (1994): 464–70; Belleville, "'Ιουνιαν," 231–49. See the extensive bibliography in Eldon J. Epp (*Junia: The First Woman Apostle* [Minneapolis: Fortress, 2005], 110–21) and Richard Bauckham (*Gospel Women: Studies of the Named Women in the Gospels* [Grand Rapids: Eerdmans, 2002], 165–86).
18. Epiphanius identifies both Junias and Prisca as men, so is not a credible instance. Cf. Epp, *Junia*, 34.
19. Thorley ("Junia," 24), "So it seems that Ἰουνίαν cannot be a male name." Cervin ("Junia(s)," 470) writes that the accusative of Ἰούνιος (the equivalent of Iunius, masculine Iunia) should be Ἰούνιον, not Ἰουνίαν.
20. Thorley ("Junia," 24–25) shows that the shorted form of Junianus would drop the final iota in the stem to form Ἰουνᾶς not Ἰουνιᾶς, just as the Oxyrhynchus Papyri (3:502, line 6) has Ἰουλᾶς, presumably a short form of Julianus.

common woman's name tells heavily against this theory. There simply is no basis for the seemingly arbitrary change from "Junia" to "Junias" (p. 39).

'Ιουνίαν's only textual variant is 'Ιουλίαν (𝔓⁴⁶ 6 ar b vgmss bo), an even more common woman's name. It is unlikely that anyone who thought that 'Ιουνίαν was a man's name would insert a woman's name in its place. Thus, this variant is evidence for the very early (Comfort and Barrett date 𝔓⁴⁶ to a mid-second century)[21] understanding that Junia was a woman.

Paul repeatedly defines an apostle as one who encounters the risen Christ (1 Cor 9:1; 15:8; Gal 1:1, 15–17), receives a commission to preach the gospel, and endures the labors and sufferings of missionary work (Rom 1:1–5; 1 Cor 1:1; 15:10, as their imprisonment with Paul attests) that bears fruit (1 Cor 9:1; 15:10) and is certified by "signs, wonders and miracles" (2 Cor 12:11–12). Paul identifies as apostles: himself, Silvanus, and Timothy (1 Thess 1:1; 2:7), Barnabas (1 Cor 9:1–6; cf. Acts 14:4, 14), Peter and James the brother of the Lord (Gal 1:18–19; cf. Gal 2:8–9), and probably John (Gal 2:8–9), Apollos (1 Cor 4:6, 9), and Epaphroditus (Phil 2:25). "Outstanding among the apostles"[22] implies that Adronicus and Junia were revered missionaries recognized in the churches as having authority as ministers of the gospel (cf. *Did.* 11:3–6).

Chrysostom (ca. AD 344–407), even though he typically disparages women in church leadership, confirms that Junia was an apostle: "Even to be an apostle is great, but also to be prominent among them [ἐν τούτοις ἐπισήμους] —consider how wonderful a song of honor that is. For they were prominent because of their works, because of their successes. Glory

---

21. Philip W. Comfort and David P. Barrett, *The Text of the Earliest New Testament Greek Manuscripts* (Wheaton, Ill.: Tyndale, 2001), 203–6.
22. This "can only mean 'noteworthy among the apostles.'" Cervin, "Junia(s)," 463; and similarly, e.g., Epp, *Junia*, 69–78; Cranfield, *Romans*, 2:789; Dunn, *Romans 9–16*, 894–95. This is the way it was understood by the patristic commentators, apparently without exception. Paul of all people was not impressed with name dropping. He is not the type to encourage status based on: "even the *apostles* think they are outstanding, e.g. Gal 2:6, 'what they were makes no difference to me.'" Furthermore, the meaning of ἐπίσημος as "*notable, remarkable*" (LSJ 656), "of exceptional quality, *splendid, prominent, outstanding*" (BDAG 378), applies naturally to those distinguished among the wider group of apostles in the early church, but it is not natural to suppose that the apostles were known to have a consensus of judgment that particular people, including Andronicus and Junia, were outstanding (cf. Sanday and Headlam, *Romans*, 423). Every example of ἐν meaning "in the eyes of" listed in BAG (258, I. 3) follows the set phrase, ἐν ὀφθαλμοῖς (αὐτῶν), and there is no mention of "their eyes" in Rom 16:7. The "in the eyes of" defense by Michael H. Burer and Daniel B. Wallace ("Was Junia Really an Apostle? A Re-examination of Rom 16.7," *NTS* 47 [2001]: 76–91), has been thoroughly answered by Epp (*Junia*, 69–78); Bauckham (*Gospel Women*, 165–80); and Belleville ("Romans 16.7," 231–49).

be! How great the wisdom of this woman that she was even deemed worthy of the apostle's title."[23]

MARY, TRYPHENA, TRYPHOSA, AND PERSIS

Paul praises "Mary, who worked very hard among you" (Rom 16:6), "Tryphena and Tryphosa, those women who work hard in the Lord ... [and] my dear friend Persis, another woman who has worked very hard in the Lord" (16:12). Ridderbos notes that the Greek word for "worked hard" (κοπιάω) describing each of these four women is "a word that specifically denotes work in the gospel and in the church."[24] These four women are the only people in this chapter to whom Paul gives this commendation.[25] He repeatedly describes his own ministry with this word (1 Cor 4:12; Gal 4:11; Phil 2:16) and entreats the Corinthians to submit to everyone who works with him and labors at it (κοπιῶντι, 1 Cor 16:16). In 1 Thess 5:12–13, he associates those who so labor with those in authority, "Now we ask you, brothers, to respect those who work hard [κοπιῶντας] among you, who are over you [προϊσταμένους] in the Lord and who admonish you. Hold them in the highest regard in love because of their work."

EUODIA AND SYNTYCHE

In Phil 4:2–3, Paul writes, "I plead with Euodia and I plead with Syntyche to agree with each other in the Lord. Indeed, true comrade, I ask you also to assist these women inasmuch as they have contended at my side in the cause of the gospel [ἐν τῷ εὐαγγελίῳ] along with [μετὰ καί] Clement and the rest of my fellow workers, whose names are in the book of life." Paul specifically classifies them with "Clement and the rest of my fellow workers [συνεργῶν]," confirming that Paul associates them not simply with other devout women, but with his own fellow ministers of the gospel. The words "along with" and especially by "and the rest of my fellow workers" indicate their equality in standing with Paul's male fellow workers in the gospel. This is a group whose stability in the faith and final commitment to Christ is unquestioned, as "whose names are in the book of life" demonstrates. Paul considered their ministry in the gospel too important to let

---

23. Chrysostom, *In ep. ad Romanos* 31, 2 (PG 60:669–70). Translation from Epp, *Junia*, 79.
24. Ridderbos, *Paul*, 461; cf. Hauck, "κόπος, κοπιάω," *TDNT* 3:829: "missionary and pastoral work ... of the highest esteem."
25. Dunn, *Romans 9–16*, 900.

their energies be sidetracked over their issue of contention, so he enlists his true "comrade" (or possibly "Syzygus") to assist them in resolving it.

OTHER NOTABLE WOMEN

Many other women were in Paul's circle, such as: Lydia of Thyatira, the first recorded European believer, in whose home Paul and Barnabas stayed (Acts 16:14–15); the leading women of Thessalonica and Berea, who were among the founding pillars of those churches (Acts 17:4, 12); Damaris, "follower of Paul" (Acts 17:34); Nympha (Col 4:15) and Apphia (Phlm 2), in whose homes churches met; the mother of Rufus, "who has been a mother to me" (Rom 16:13); and the four virgin daughters of Philip the evangelist, "who had the gift of prophecy" (Acts 21:8–9). Their virginity suggests special consecration to the work of the Lord (1 Cor 7:34).

SUMMARY

The titles that Paul gives to the women he mentions imply leadership positions: "deacon" (Rom 16:1), "leader" (Rom 16:2), "my fellow worker in Christ Jesus" (Rom 16:3; Phil 4:3), and "apostle" (Rom 16:7). Furthermore, Paul describes them as fulfilling functions associated with church leadership: they "worked hard in the Lord" (Rom 16:6, 12) and "contended at my side in the cause of the gospel" (Phil 4:3). Over two-thirds of the colleagues whom Paul praises for their Christian ministry in Rom 16:1–16—seven of the ten—are women.[26] His partner Luke adds that women "prophesied" (Acts 21:9) and Priscilla "explained the way of God more accurately" (Acts 18:26).

The extent of Paul's affirmations of women in his circle of ministry stands in stark contrast with the typical attitude toward women in Paul's day. Paul's teachings about women in the church ought to be interpreted in harmony with Paul's actual practice. Since Paul's own affirmations of colleagues who are women are so extensive and their range of ministries is so broad, one ought to expect corresponding affirmations of women in his teaching.

The primary guiding influences on Paul (the Holy Scriptures, Gamaliel, Jesus, and the Holy Spirit) and his many respectful relationships with women colleagues in ministry go hand in hand with an egalitarian understanding of Paul's teachings on man and woman, as do his theological axioms, which the next chapter analyzes.

---

26. The seven are listed above. The men are Aquila, Andronicus, and Urbanus.

3

PAUL'S THEOLOGICAL AXIOMS IMPLY THE EQUALITY OF MAN AND WOMAN

Paul's theological axioms provide the framework for understanding his teachings about man and woman. Steeped as he was in the Hebrew Scriptures, many of his principles are drawn directly from the OT and firmly imply the equal standing of men and women.

1. MALE AND FEMALE ARE EQUALLY CREATED IN GOD'S IMAGE

Paul writes that all believers are created in God's image: their new self in Christ is "being renewed in knowledge in the image of its Creator" (Col 3:10; cf. 2 Cor 3:18). Paul argues for the equal standing of man and woman in Christ in 1 Cor 11:11–12 since from the creation each has its source in the other.[1] In Col 2:10–11, he affirms that all Christians, female as well as male, "have this fullness [of the Godhead] in Christ ... in whom you were also circumcised." Paul depicts females as having the fullness of the Godhead and being "circumcised," and he depicts males as members of the bride of Christ (Eph 5:22–27) because their gender is irrelevant to their being in the image of God and their being in Christ.

Since humanity as male *and female* is in God's image, God cannot be exclusively male. Indeed, God as spirit cannot be male at all. Accordingly,

---

1. Cf. below, pp. 189–98.

Paul's reflection on the person and work of Jesus typically uses the inclusive word ἄνθρωπος (man/human; e.g., Rom 5:12, 15; Phil 2:7; 1Tim 2:5).[2]

2. MALE AND FEMALE EQUALLY RECEIVED THE CREATION MANDATE AND BLESSING

Paul reflects the creation mandate and blessing given to man as male and female (Gen 1:26–30) in his affirmation in 1 Tim 6:17, "God richly provides us with everything for our enjoyment." Similarly, Paul's repeated affirmations of freedom and of food as gifts from God and his rejection of dietary restrictions (e.g., 1 Cor 10:23–30), each without gender distinction, is based on woman's, as well as man's, authority over all other earthly creatures.

3. THE REDEEMED—MALE AND FEMALE—ARE EQUALLY "IN CHRIST"

At the heart of Paul's theology is the unity of redeemed humanity "in Christ." There is no requirement for salvation that distinguishes men from women.[3] "There is no distinction [διαστολή].... Everyone who calls on the name of the Lord will be saved" (Rom 10:12–13). In one's standing in Christ, too, it makes no difference whatsoever whether someone is male or female (Gal 3:28). Paul affirms "woman is not separate from man, nor is man separate from woman in the Lord" (1 Cor 11:11).[4] This entails women's equal standing with man in Christ.

4. THE NATURE OF CHURCH LEADERSHIP AS SERVICE APPLIES EQUALLY TO MALE AND FEMALE

The nature of Christian leadership and authority entails humble service.[5] Christian leadership is based on love, willingness to serve, and spiritual gifts, not on wisdom, strength, or influence as the world sees these (1 Cor 1–2). Indeed, "deacon" means "servant," and "slave" (δοῦλος) is one of Paul's favorite self-designations (Rom 1:1; 1 Cor 9:19; Gal 1:10; Titus 1:1)

---

2. The only possible exception using ἀνήρ ("man/male") is Eph 4:13, "grow up into full manhood," but even this command is specifically given to *all* believers, female as well as male, and so is translated "mature" in the NRSV and NIV.
3. Cf. below, pp. 425–27, 440–42.
4. Cf. below, pp. 189–98.
5. Cf. Efrain Agosto, *Servant Leadership: Jesus and Paul* (St. Louis: Chalice, 2005).

and an accolade to others (1 Cor 7:22; Col 4:12) following Christ's example (Matt 20:25–28; Luke 22:25–27).

No "overseer" except Christ is named in the NT, which depicts church leadership by a group of overseers. In any event, the churches' authority is anchored in the Scriptures, not in ministers per se. The prophets' messages are to be "judged" carefully (1 Cor 14:29) to ensure conformity with the apostolic message and the Scriptures. Paul even applies this to himself: "Even if we or an angel from heaven should preach a gospel other than the one we preached to you, let him be eternally condemned!" (Gal 1:8).

Consequently, church leaders' authority is not intrinsic to themselves or their office, but is derived. Their authority comes from the faithful expounding of Scripture. Their words have no authority if they go against Scripture (Acts 17:11), and their deeds are subject to Scripture. Their authority is inextricably tied to the work of the Holy Spirit, who gives the necessary gifts for leadership and who guides the leader (Acts 20:28). The way Paul describes his women colleagues, analyzed in chapter 2, shows that he believes the Spirit gifts and guides women as well as men for church leadership.

5. MUTUAL SUBMISSION IN THE CHURCH PRESUPPOSES THE EQUAL STANDING OF WOMEN AND MEN

"Submitting to one another out of reverence for Christ" is a natural outgrowth of being "filled with the Spirit" (Eph 5:18–21; cf. 1 John 4:13, 16). The theme of mutual submission[6] permeates Paul's "one another" statements such as Gal 5:13, "Serve one another in love"; Rom 12:10, "Honor one another above yourselves"; and Eph 4:2, "Be completely humble and gentle; be patient, bearing with one another in love." Paul does not limit any of these to only one gender. If only one party does all the submitting, it is not mutual but hierarchical. The bidirectional nature of mutual submission presupposes the equal standing of the persons submitting to each other. This undergirds the nature of Christian leadership as humble service.

6. MUTUAL SUBMISSION IN MARRIAGE PRESUPPOSES THE EQUALITY OF MEN AND WOMEN

Ephesians 5:21–22 applies Paul's general command for believers to submit to one another specifically to the relationship between wives and

---

6.   Cf. below, pp. 271–83.

husbands. Paul's following explanation of mutual husband–wife obligations bears this out, particularly as Paul explains his "head" metaphor.[7] Paul gives Christ's self-sacrifice as a model for husbands to follow in loving, nourishing, and caring for their wives. The parallel passage (cf. Col 3:18–19) calls for "humility" (3:12) and exhorts believers to "bear with each other" and "forgive one another" (3:13).[8]

In 1 Cor 7:1–16, Paul speaks of the mutual submission of husband and wife, repeatedly describing both sides of the relationship using exact parallelism.[9] In verse 5, Paul requires that there be "mutual consent" between husband and wife to abstain from sexual relations. Then in verses 14 and 16, Paul affirms mutuality in spiritual relations. Paul also affirms woman's capacity for leadership in the home in 1 Tim 5:14, calling younger women to marry and "to manage the household" (οἰκοδεσποτεῖν, from the roots meaning "house" and "despot").

Side by side with Paul's teaching of mutual submission, he calls wives to submit to their husbands, children to parents, and slaves to masters. Comparison with secular "house tables" shows that Paul is giving these conventions a decidedly egalitarian twist, as chapter 15 shows. Following Christ's model, the husband should give himself in love for his wife. This gives his wife security and kindles her respect (Eph 5:33) and love (Titus 2:4). As husband and wife mutually submit to the other's desires, they experience a deeper and deeper unity (Eph 5:28, 30, 31)—not the unity of ruler and subordinate, but of coequals, each free to take initiative, neither with final say. The husband's self-giving love and the wife's submission cause the relationship to flourish. Ephesians 5:21–33 is thus a grand charter for a marriage relationship modeled after Christ's love and self-giving.

7. THE ONENESS OF THE BODY OF CHRIST PRESUPPOSES THE EQUALITY OF MEN AND WOMEN

The church is the "body of Christ." Paul insists in 1 Cor 12:25 "that there should be no division in the body ... its parts should have equal concern for each other." Since Paul explains that different parts of the body have different functions, it is clear he is not advocating that all believers

---

7.   Cf. below, pp. 279–90.
8.   Cf. below, pp. 271–77.
9.   Cf. below, pp. 105–8.

are the same or all do the same thing. Rather, the division he opposes is for one part to put itself over other parts, namely, competitive ranking. Stratification of status is antithetical to the oneness of the body. Furthermore, according to Eph 4:12, all members—women and men—should be involved in ministering and building up the body of Christ.

8. THE PRIESTHOOD OF ALL BELIEVERS PRESUPPOSES THE EQUALITY OF MEN AND WOMEN

In affirming the direct access of believers to God in 2 Cor 3:12–18, Paul implies the universal priesthood of believers. Paul's prayer in Col 3:16 is that all Christians, women as well as men, will have a teaching ministry, "Let the word of Christ dwell in you richly as you teach and admonish one another with all wisdom." Similarly, 1 Cor 14:26 affirms, "When you assemble, each one has … a teaching." The priesthood of all believers is incompatible with excluding women from the priesthood, but rather presupposes the equal standing and priestly privileges of men and women.

9. THE GIFTS OF THE SPIRIT MANIFEST THE EQUALITY OF MEN AND WOMEN

For Paul, the order of church worship and the structure of church authority are intimately connected with the gifts of the Spirit. He states: "to each the manifestation of the Spirit is given for the common good" (1 Cor 12:7; cf. Rom 12:6–8), and in 1 Cor 12:11: "the Spirit gives to each one, just as he determines." Thus, all women, just as all men, have spiritual gifts and are responsible to use them not in seclusion but "for the common good." Indeed, in 1 Cor 12:31 and 14:1, Paul urges all believers, women as well as men, "Eagerly desire the greater gifts [i.e., to be apostles, prophets, teachers] … especially the gift of prophecy." To restrict women from such forms of ministry is not simply to deprive the church; it is to impede their obedience to God's command.

Following the OT tradition of women prophets such as Miriam, Huldah, and Deborah, and other NT prophets such as Anna and the four daughters of Philip, Paul permitted women to prophesy. He states clearly in 1 Cor 11:5 and 14:31, "you can all prophesy." Announcing the advent of the age of the Spirit, Peter also declared, "Your … daughters will prophesy.... Even on my servants, both men and women, I will pour out my Spirit in those days" (Acts 2:17). Believers should recognize gifts in women in exactly the same way they do in men, by testing the gift in practical ministry and seeing whether the Spirit blesses. Who dares to oppose the Spirit giving women gifts and guiding women into ministry as he chooses?

10. LIBERTY IN CHRIST PRESUPPOSES THE EQUALITY OF MEN AND WOMEN

Paul, the "Apostle of Liberty," never distinguished the freedom of men from that of women. Shortly after his affirmation that there is neither "male nor female, for you are all one in Christ Jesus" (Gal 3:28), he wrote, "It is for freedom that Christ has set us free. Stand firm, then, and do not let yourselves be burdened again by a yoke of slavery" (5:1). This is addressed to all the congregations in Galatia and cannot be restricted to men alone. For Paul, arbitrarily stratified status is repugnant, whether determined by race, nationality, economics, or gender.

Paul himself was remarkably free from the restraints of male stereotypes. In 1 Thess 2:7, he depicts himself yearning over the Thessalonians with the tender affection of a nursing mother holding her child to her breast (MM 643). He was no chauvinist who needed to protect a fragile male ego. Rather, because his identity was secure in Christ, he was free to identify with women.

11. INAUGURATED ESCHATOLOGY REQUIRES THE EQUALITY OF MEN AND WOMEN WHILE AFFIRMING THAT THE SEXES COMPLEMENT EACH OTHER

Paul affirms inaugurated eschatology but denies that it is already consummated. He emphatically rejects the consummated eschatology of those who, under Gnostic or proto-Gnostic influence, proclaim the abolition of sexual distinctives and prohibit marriage (e.g., 1 Cor 7; 1 Tim 4:3). Rather, he affirms that the new age of the kingdom has dawned in the life of the church, where the old relationship barriers such as race, nationality, economic status, and gender are overcome. Ephesians 2:11–22 argues for one new humanity where Jews and Gentiles share equal citizenship, "For he himself is our peace, who has made the two one and has destroyed the bar-

rier, the dividing wall of hostility" (2:14). Therefore, Paul calls believers in
Col 3:10–11 to "put on the new self, which is being renewed in knowledge
in the image of its Creator. Here there is no Greek or Jew, circumcised or
uncircumcised, barbarian, Sythian, slave or free, but Christ is all, and is in
all" (cf. 1 Cor 12:12–13). Galatians 3:28 adds male and female.

In place of the former hostility, in the new order reconciliation, love,
and humble service to one another should characterize all personal relationships. Accordingly, Eph 5:21 calls all believers to mutual submission.
Christ by the Spirit (Rom 8:23) gives those who put off the old self a new
heart and attitudes, indeed, a "new self" (Rom 6:6; Eph 4:22–24; Col
3:9–10; cf. 2 Cor 5:17) to enable them truly to live in the new order.

Because Satan has been cast down and the last Adam, Christ, has
begun the new creation, life in Christ's kingdom should not perpetuate
the curse of the fall, "he will rule over you" (Gen 3:16), just as it should
not foster any of the sinful and unfair tendencies of fallen human nature.
Rather, in male–female relations, just as in relations between the races
and between slaves and masters, the church is to model the new order of
the kingdom, where these distinctions are irrelevant to standing (1 Cor
11:11; Gal 3:28). Consequently, Paul appeals to all believers to manifest
the new creation in Christ in transformed relationships characterized by
love and mutual self-giving. In marriage, sexual identity is not dissolved
but is affirmed in such a way that husband and wife stand together as true
complements with equal rights and privileges (1 Cor 7).

12. IN CHRIST, MALE AND FEMALE ARE EQUAL

"There is neither Jew nor Gentile, slave nor free, male nor female, for
you are all one in Christ Jesus" (Gal 3:28) demands equal status and privileges for women as for men,[10] just as Jas 2:1–13 does for economic status.
In Christ, these groups do not stand on different levels but as equals. This
was not just a theoretical comment about the question of individual salvation. Paul did everything he could to realize its implications in the social
dimensions of the church, as his conflict with Peter in Gal 2:11–14 shows.
The high proportion of women in Paul's circle of ministry and the many
Gentiles, slaves, and women in Paul's churches confirms this. Surely Paul

---

10. Cf. below, pp. 79–104.

would object vehemently to the idea that Gentiles, slaves, and women can be saved but may not hold offices of leadership in the church. While not denying sexual differences, Gal 3:28 does repudiate any second-class status or reduced privileges for women in Christ.

Similarly, 1 Cor 11:11–12 affirms, "Neither is woman separate from man, nor is man separate from woman in the Lord."[11] This repudiates any separate treatment or status for women from men, such as excluding women from teaching or leadership positions in the church. Paul's theology of man and woman is grounded in these twelve theological axioms, each of which presupposes the equality of woman and man: creation in God's image, the creation mandate and blessing, being in Christ, servant leadership, mutual submission in both marriage and church life, the oneness of the body of Christ, the priesthood of all believers, the gifts of the Spirit, liberty in Christ, inaugurated eschatology, and equal status in Christ. These axioms provide the central theological context for understanding each of Paul's teachings about women.

---

11. Cf. below, pp. 189–98.

PART ONE

Exegesis of Paul's
Statements about Woman:
Earlier Letters

4

GALATIANS 3:28:
MAN AND WOMAN: ONE IN CHRIST

The classic statement repudiating ethno-religious, socioeconomic, and gender discrimination in the church is Gal 3:28: "There is neither Jew nor Greek, slave nor free, male nor female, for you are all one in Christ Jesus." Ethno-religious background (Jew/Greek), socioeconomic status (slave/free), and gender (male/female) have no bearing on one's standing in Christ and in his body, the church. This verse states an accomplished fact; in Christ, believers *are* one, as Jesus prayed in John 17:21 that they would be, with the result that the world will believe. Galatians 3:28 has been called the "Magna Carta of Humanity"[1] since it affirms equality in Christ that transcends each of the three major social barriers to privilege. The ancient world offers no parallel to the verse.[2] Its message is echoed in 1 Cor 11:11–12 specifically regarding men and women, which is also without precedent.

Some have tried to evade the practical consequences of all believers being "one in Christ" by interpreting Gal 3:28 to mean merely that Greeks, slaves, and women can also become sons of God through faith in Christ. Paul, however, has just entailed this two verses earlier in Gal 3:26. If that is all 3:28 means, it is redundant. Furthermore, no one held the view that Greeks, slaves, and women could not be saved, so what is the point of the affirmation in that case?

---

1. Jessie Penn-Lewis, ed., The *"Magna Charta" of Woman "According to the Scriptures" Being Light upon the Subject Gathered from Dr. Katherine Bushnell's Text Book, "God's Word to Women"* (3rd ed.; Bournemouth, England: Overcomer Book Room, 1948; repr., Minneapolis: Bethany, 1975).
2. Han Dieter Betz, *Galatians* (Philadelphia: Fortress, 1979), 196–97.

In verse 28, Paul goes beyond verse 26 to state that in Christ "there is neither Jew nor Greek, slave nor free, male nor female." This explicitly affirms, without any qualification, that these divisions do not exist in the body of Christ. They are irrelevant to one's standing in Christ. The explanatory "for" (γάρ) in 3:28b proves that the three negations deal with the "you all" who are now one. "You all" includes all members of the Galatian churches. "Are one" implies a social unit and so should not be limited to the spiritual state of individuals before God. Paul's conclusion, "for you are all one in Christ Jesus," states that these barriers do not divide the social community of the church. The following study highlights factors in Gal 3:28, its context, and its parallel passages that repudiate views that divorce this verse from life in the church.

PARALLEL PASSAGES: COLOSSIANS 3:11 AND 1 CORINTHIANS 12:13

Paul repeats Gal 3:28's principle of equality over traditional barriers in two closely parallel passages, Col 3:11 and 1 Cor 12:13. Both apply this principle to practical issues in church life. Colossians 3:11 teaches that oneness in Christ across traditional barriers is incompatible with such things as greed (3:5) and malice (3:8). Its context makes it unmistakable that this principle applies to practical life in the church:

> Do not lie to each other, since you have taken off your old self with its practices and have put on the new self, which is being renewed in knowledge in the image of its Creator. Here there is no Greek or Jew, circumcised or uncircumcised, barbarian, Scythian, slave or free, but Christ is all and is in all. Therefore, as God's chosen people, holy and dearly beloved, clothe yourselves with compassion, kindness, humility, gentleness and patience. (Col 3:9–12)

Verses 10–11 here closely parallel Gal 3:27–28:

Gal 3:27–28: ἐνεδύσασθε.   οὐκ ἔνι Ἰουδαῖος οὐδὲ Ἕλλην,
                          οὐκ ἔνι δοῦλος   οὐδὲ ἐλεύθερος,
Col 3:10–11: ἐνδυσάμενοι ... οὐκ ἔνι Ἕλλην καὶ Ἰουδαῖος ...
                          δοῦλος,   ἐλεύθερος,

Gal 3:28:   πάντες γὰρ ὑμεῖς εἷς ἐστε ἐν Χριστῷ Ἰησοῦ.
Col 3:11: ἀλλὰ [τὰ] πάντα καὶ   ἐν πᾶσιν Χριστός.

Manuscripts D* F G 629, the Old Latin witnesses, the Vulgates and its citation by Hilary (d. 367) and Ambrose (d. 397) begin Col 3:11: "there is no male and female" (οὐκ ἔνι ἄρσεν καὶ θῆλυ). It is often said that this was done to bring Col 3:11 into conformity with Gal 3:28, but if that had been the goal, it is surprising that this pair was put at the head of the list rather than following the others. Given the widespread male chauvinism of that time, it is possible that a scribe dropped "there is no male and female" from Col 3:11. If, as is more likely, this clause was added later, its use in so many Western MSS to identify transformed life demonstrates that in the early church, especially the church centered in Rome, "there is no male and female" entailed practical life consequences in the church and was not restricted to spiritual status.

The baptismal statement in 1 Cor 12:13 also applies the bridging of traditional barriers to the practical life of the church and has close verbal parallels to Gal 3:27–28:

1 Cor 12:13: "For we were all baptized by one Spirit into one
             body—whether Jews or Greeks,

1 Cor 12:13a: γὰρ ... εἰς ἓν σῶμα ἐβαπτίσθημεν, εἴτε Ἰουδαῖοι
             εἴτε Ἕλληνες

Gal 3:27–28a: γὰρ εἰς Χριστὸν ἐβαπτίσθητε ... οὐκ ἔνι Ἰουδαῖος
             οὐδὲ Ἕλλην,

1 Cor 12:13: slave or free—and we were all given the one Spirit to
             drink."

1 Cor 12:13b: εἴτε δοῦλοι εἴτε ἐλεύθεροι ... πάντες ἓν πνεῦμα ...

Gal 3:28b: οὐκ ἔνι δοῦλος οὐδὲ ἐλεύθερος ... πάντες γὰρ ὑμεῖς
             εἷς...

This passage supports Paul's assertion of the unity of the body in 1 Cor 12:12–27. His goal is "that there should be no division in the body, but that its parts would have equal concern for each other" (12:25). To exclude any of these groups from full participation and ministry opportunities in the church would be to create just such a division in the body. Thus, in both Col 3:11 and 1 Cor 12:12 these expressions specifically refer to the practical life of the church to show that social barriers are broken. Consequently, the closely parallel words in Gal 3:28 must not be divorced from the practical life of the church. The evidence that these sayings are variants on a baptismal liturgical formula[3] reinforces this argument since liturgical formula carry standardized implications. The reference to baptism in 3:27 and "you are all one in Christ" in verse 28 implies that this inheritance (3:29–4:7) and freedom (4:8–5:1) is experienced in church life.

GALATIANS 3:28 IN LIGHT OF THE JEW–GENTILE CONFLICT OVER SPECIAL PRIVILEGES

The argument of Galatians focuses on the conflicting practices of Paul and the Judaizers. Paul, the apostle of liberty, opposed the Judaizers' contention that the Jewish ceremonial law must be fulfilled by Gentile Christians in order for them to have full standing in the church. They demanded that Gentiles be circumcised; Paul prohibited this. The Judaizers prohibited Jews from having table fellowship with Greeks who broke Jewish dietary laws.[4] Paul responds in Gal 2:11–13:

> When Peter came to Antioch, I opposed him to his face, because he was in the wrong. Before certain men came from James, he used to eat with the Gentiles. But when they arrived, he began to draw back and separate himself from the Gentiles because he was afraid of those who belonged to the circumcision group. The other Jews joined him in his hypocrisy, so that by their hypocrisy even Barnabas was led astray.

The Judaizers demanded observance of special days, months, seasons, and years (Gal 4:10). Paul regarded this as a return to the slavery of legalism and a denial of the heart of the gospel (4:8–11). These requirements had the practical effect of elevating the Jews to a status with special privileges over the Gentiles, who were being treated as second-class citizens in the church. The entire book of Galatians is a frontal attack against favored status or privileges being granted to Jews over Gentiles. In 3:28, Paul states the core theological argument against the Judaizers and intro-

---

3.   E.g., C. F. D. Moule, *Worship in the New Testament* (Richmond, Va.: John Knox, 1961), 52, notes that "this metaphor [fits] with the actual movements of the baptized"; cf. F. F. Bruce, *The Epistle to the Galatians* (Exeter, England: Paternoster, 1982), 186–87; G. R. Beasley-Murray, *Baptism in the New Testament* (Grand Rapids: Eerdmans, 1962), 148–49; Otto Michel, "Σκύθης," *TDNT* 7:450; R. Scroggs, "Woman in the NT," *IDBSup* 966; Robin Scroggs, "Paul and the Eschatological Woman," *JAAR* 40 (1972): 291–92; J. Louis Martin, *Galatians* (AB; New York: Doubleday, 1997), 375–80.

4.   Paul's complaint in 2:14, "you force Gentiles to follow Jewish customs," seems to imply that if the Gentiles followed Jewish customs, then they could have table fellowship with Jews. Cf. Ernest de Witt Burton, *A Critical and Exegetical Commentary on the Epistle to the Galatians*, (ICC; Edinburgh: T&T Clark, 1921), lix.

duces his opposition to circumcision of Gentiles: "There is neither Jew nor Greek ... in Christ Jesus." Consequently, all believers are "children of Abraham" (3:7), "blessed along with Abraham" (3:9, 14), "Abraham's offspring and heirs according to the promise" (3:29), "children of the free woman [Sarah]" (4:31), and "the Israel of God" (6:16).

In the context of the letter's argument, Gal 3:28 is not merely saying that Gentiles, too, can be saved. Even Judaizers accepted that. Paul clearly intended 3:28 to prohibit excluding Gentiles as a group from any privilege or position in the church. Not only must Jews accept believing Gentiles as members of the community of faith, they must treat them as equals and must not discriminate against them. They must welcome them to table fellowship. They must not force them to follow Jewish ceremonial or dietary laws as a condition for acceptance.[5]

"For" (γάρ) in both Gal 3:26 and 27 shows that Paul intended to give reasons why believers are no longer under the law (vv. 23–25) but are sons of God through faith (v. 26). This has immense practical implications for life in the church, including freedom from observing dietary and separation laws (2:11–16), from circumcision (5:1–12; 6:12–15), and from observing the Jewish festival calendar (4:10). Galatians 3:28 repudiates Jewish exclusivism with its demand for observance of the law (chs. 2–3) and delineates key implications of freedom from the law experienced in Christ. "There is no slave nor free" introduces Paul's argument from slavery[6] in 4:1–5:1 against being bound by ceremonial customs of the law, particularly circumcision. Galatians 3:29 assures that all in Christ are "Abraham's seed and heirs according to the promise." Paul develops this imagery in Gal 4 by contrasting the sons of Hagar and Sarah to explain that Abraham's heirs in Christ inherit the promise of freedom as sons rather than slaves to the law. "There is no male and female" undermines the law's purity regulations that kept women from full participation in worship. The barriers in the law separating Jews and Greeks, slaves and free, male and female, are done away in Christ, freeing them all from the bondage of the law.

---

5. Ben Witherington III (*Grace in Galatia: A Commentary on Paul's Letter to the Galatians* [Grand Rapids: Eerdmans, 1998], 278) argues that Paul in this verse "is trying to hammer home to his own converts that they do not have to become Jews, submitting to circumcision and the Mosaic Law."

6. The verb καταδουλόω, "enslave," in Gal 2:4 also anticipates this.

THE CULTURAL BACKGROUND TO GALATIANS 3:28

The affirmations of Gal 3:28 are the opposite of typical Greek and Jew-ish attitudes, by which ethnic background, economic standing, and gender were three of the major barometers for social standing and privilege. There are several famous Greek and Jewish thanksgivings that affirm practi-cally the opposite of Gal 3:28. Diogenes Laertius (*Vit. Phil.* 1.33) records a thanksgiving that he attributes variously to Socrates and to Thales (sixth century BC) as reported by Hermippus: "that I was born a human being and not a beast, next, a man and not a woman, thirdly, a Greek and not a barbarian." Lactantius (*Inst.* 3.19.17) attributes this saying to Plato.

A famous Jewish prayer says, "Blessed art Thou, O Lord our God, King of the Universe, who hast not made me a heathen ... a bondman ... [or] a woman."[7] According to rabbinic tradition, these three groups were exempt from the study of the law, so the prayer's focus is on the privilege of study-ing the law—and their exclusion from this privilege.[8] The conservative nature of Jewish oral tradition and the extensive citations of this prayer make it probable that Paul knew it.[9] Some scholars have suggested that this prayer was modeled on the Greek version,[10] but Gal 3:28 more closely resembles the Jewish version of the prayer,[11] which follows the same order: Gentile, slave, then woman.

In light of Paul's rabbinic upbringing it is more likely that he would have been familiar with this thanksgiving than its Greek parallels.[12] Since

----

7. George S. Duncan, *The Epistle of Paul to the Galatians* (London: Hodder and Stoughton, 1934), 123. This prayer occurs with slight variations in *t. Ber.* 7.18; *b. Menaḥ.* 43b (both with "brutish man" for "slave"); *y. Ber.* 9.1 (136b), 13b (3, 3), 57ff. (7, 2); Cf. also *Gen. Rab.* 8.9; 22.2; *S. Eli. Rab.* 7, 10 and 14; Str-B, 3:559–63; Oepke, "γυνή," 1:777 n. 4.
8. This prayer is still in *The Standard Prayer Book.* See Simeon Singer, ed., *The Standard Prayer Book* (New York: Bloch, 1943), 6. Women substitute, "who has made me according to thy will."
9. One version of the prayer is in the Tosefta (*t. Ber.* 7.18), which according to Johanan "is based on the lectures of Nehemiah, a contemporary of Meir" (ca. AD 140–65); see Hermann L. Strack, *Introduction to the Talmud and Midrash* (New York: Atheneum, 1980), 75; as dated by Danby, *Mishnah*, 800. The prayer is associated with Rabbis Judah b. Elai and Meir, both active during this time.
10. Bruce, *Galatians*, 187; Wayne A. Meeks, "The Image of the Androgyne: Some Uses of a Symbol in Earliest Christianity," *HR* 13 (1974): 167–68. But see David Kaufmann, "Das Alter der drei Benedictionen von Israel, vom Freien und vom Mann," *Monatsschrift für Geschichte und Wis-senschaft des Judentum* N.F. 1 (1893): 14–18. Spencer (*Beyond the Curse*, 65) suggests that this prayer may have been a Jewish response to Gal 3:28.
11. Some have argued against this allusion because the Jewish prayer uses "woman" instead of "female," but the shift from "or" to "and" (καί) and the wording identical to the LXX, "male and female" (ἄρσεν καὶ θῆλυ, Gen 1:27; 5:2), indicate that this pair is a deliberate allusion to the LXX, which adequately explains this difference.
12. Cf. Leonard Swidler, *Women in Judaism: The Status of Women in Formative Judaism* (Metuchen, N.J.: Scarecrow, 1976), 81; Spencer, *Beyond the Curse*, 64–65.

the Jewish prayer identifies groups excluded from the privilege of studying the law, Paul's repudiation of it must entail the opposite, namely, inclusion of those groups into the full life of the church. Even if Gal 3:28 was not worded deliberately in antithesis to this prayer, Paul almost certainly intended it to reject such stratification and to grant equal status and privilege to Gentiles, slaves, and women in the church.

THE CONTINUING REALITY OF THESE DISTINCTIONS IN THE CHURCH

Paul repeatedly acknowledges that there were Jews and Greeks in the church (e.g., Rom 9–11). He acknowledges the reality of slavery and so urges believers, "do not become slaves of men" (1 Cor 7:23). Paul acknowledges the biological reality of male and female and repeatedly stresses the mutual obligations of husbands and wives (e.g., 1 Cor 7). Clearly, then, he is not denying or ignoring the reality of these distinctions. Furthermore, he emphasizes that the gospel transforms all aspects of human life. It speaks to each of these groups with messages that are particularly relevant to them and makes specific demands on them.

Consequently, the irrelevance of the social distinctions listed in Gal 3:28 for standing in Christ does not mean that the church should simply ignore these distinctions. The body of Christ does not exist solely for believers. It interacts with the world as salt and light. In the world and in the church, biological, racial, social, economic, and ethnic differences have not ceased to exist, but form fundamental structures within which humans relate to each other. Standards of decency must be upheld and stumbling blocks avoided (1 Cor 8:9–13; cf. 11:2–16). Acknowledgment of these realities, however, must not become an excuse to deny any group privileges or status in the church or to exclude any group from church office based on ethno-religious background (Jew/Greek), socioeconomic factors (slave/free), or gender (male/female).

Paul celebrates the different gifts given as the Spirit determines (1 Cor 12:4–11) and the contributions of the different members of the body. All are to be affirmed as important. Just like the parts of a body, each member of the church has his or her own work to do (Eph 4:16). All have the opportunity and the responsibility to minister as God calls and gifts them. Equality of opportunity does not entail uniformity, but it does prohibit discrimination or ranking by class.[13] Paul is not asking believers to repudiate their differences. First Corinthians 7:17–27 discusses the Jew/Gentile, slave/free, and male/female pairs following the same order he gives in Gal 3:28.[14] In each case Paul encourages believers to be content with their status whether they are circumcised or uncircumcised, slave or free, married or unmarried. Paul, however, denies their relevance to status in the church. He does not attach value to them such that one ranks higher or has special privileges. Christ removes these distinctions as barriers and demands such radical changes in attitude and relationships that *in Christ* they do not exist.

The prominence of Gentiles, slaves, and women in the leadership of Paul's churches shows that Gal 3:28 is not just a theoretical comment about individual salvation. Paul fought to actualize the social implications of Gal 3:28 in the church. His conflict with Peter over equal treatment of Gentiles in 2:11–14 proves this. His praise of women coworkers in the gospel, as in Rom 16:1–16,[15] shows that he was not content with lip service to the ontological equality of men and women[16] while perpetuating social stratification by restricting special privileges to males.

THE STATEMENT ITSELF

Structurally, Gal 3:28 is a triple negation followed by an explanatory affirmation:

There is no Jew nor Greek   οὐκ ἔνι Ἰουδαῖος οὐδὲ Ἕλλην

There is no slave nor free   οὐκ ἔνι δοῦλος οὐδὲ ἐλεύθερος

These is no male and female οὐκ ἔνι ἄρσεν καὶ θῆλυ

for you are all one in Christ Jesus

     πάντες γὰρ ὑμεῖς εἷς ἐστε ἐν Χριστῷ Ἰησοῦ.

Ἔνι ("there is")

Ἔνι ("there is ...") occurs five times in the Pauline letters, always translatable "there is" and always functioning as a present active indicative verb. In each occurrence it follows οὐκ. It occurs in 1 Cor 6:5: "*is there*

---

13. Cf. Scroggs, "Eschatological Woman," 288.
14. Cf. Ibid., 293.
15. Cf. above, pp. 61–68, which discuss Paul's women colleagues.
16. Although he does affirm this in 1 Cor 11:11–12, cf. below, pp. 189–98.

not [οὐκ ἔνι][17] among you even one person wise enough to judge a dispute between believers?" It also occurs in the closely parallel passage Col 3:11, "Here *there is* no Greek and Jew" (οὐκ ἔνι Ἕλλην καὶ Ἰουδαῖος). In its one other occurrence in the NT outside Paul's letters (Jas 1:17), οὐκ ἔνι affirms that with God, "*there is* no change or shifting shadow." In each case, as it is defined by BDAG (336), it means "to be or exist in a certain context," in this case, "in Christ."

Although grammarians generally agree on how ἔνι functions and that it is equivalent to ἔνεστι, there are two reasonable explanations of its etymology. Most of the ancient grammarians regarded it as a contracted form of ἔνεστι from the verb ἔνειμι, "to be in."[18] This contracted form occurs frequently in classical, Hellenistic, medieval, and modern Greek.[19] But most recent commentators follow George Benedict Winer's analysis and regard ἔνι to be derived from a poetic form of the preposition ἐν ("in") used in Epic and Attic Greek and in Ionic prose, ἐνί, "strengthened by a more vigorous accent" (MM 215) with the substantive verb "to be" omitted by ellipsis.[20] Analogously, ἔπι (from ἐπί), πάρα (from παρά), ἄνα (from ἀνά) and μέτα (from μετά) were used with the force of ἔπεστι, πάρεστι, ἄνεστι, and μέτεστι.[21]

Either explanation of the origin of ἔνι is plausible. Since "to be" is understood elliptically in the second, both explanations result in the same meaning. The first results in, "In [Christ] there is no...." The second results in, "In [Christ there is] no...." The variant reading of Gal

---

17. BDF §98 notes that MSS D, F, and G substitute ἐστιν. Some manuscripts of 1 Cor 6:5 also have ἐστίν instead of ἔνι, including 𝔓[11] D F G 6 104 365 630 1739 1881. These variant readings confirm the meaning "there is."

18. LSJ 562; BDAG 336; Heinrich A. W. Meyer, *Critical and Exegetical Hand-book to the Epistle to the Galatians* (trans. G. H. Venables; 6th ed.; New York: Funk & Wagnalls, 1884), 157; A. T. Robertson, *A Grammar of the Greek New Testament in the Light of Historical Research* (Nashville: Broadman, 1934), 313; BDF §98.

19. James H. Moulton and Wilbert F. Howard, *A Grammar of New Testament Greek; Vol. II Accidence and Word-Formation* (Edinburgh, T&T Clark, 1979), 2:306; LSJ 562 ἔνειμι.

20. George B. Winer and Gottlieb Lünemann, *A Grammar of the Idiom of the New Testament* (7th ed.; Andover: Draper, 1893), §14.2, 80; Moulton and Howard, *Grammar*, 2:306; J. B. Lightfoot, *The Epistle of St. Paul to the Galatians* (Grand Rapids: Zondervan, 1957), 150; Herman N. Ridderbos, *The Epistle of Paul to the Churches of Galatia* (NICNT; Grand Rapids: Eerdmans, 1953), 148 n. 10; Bruce, *Galatians*, 187.

21. Burton, *Galatians*, 207; Joseph H. Thayer, *Greek-English Lexicon of the New Testament Being Grimm's Wilke's Clavis Novi Testamenti Translated Revised and Enlarged* (Grand Rapids: Zondervan, 1982; orig., 1889), 216; Frederic Rendall, *The Epistle to the Galatians* (vol. 3 of *Expositor's Greek Testament*; W. R. Nicoll, ed.; Grand Rapids: Eerdmans, 1970), 3:174–75. Thayer (*Lexicon*, 216), in defense of this etymology states that πάρα and ἄνα "can hardly be supposed to be a contraction from πάρεστι, ἄνεστι"; cf. Winer, *Grammar*, 80.

3:28 in $\mathfrak{P}^{46}$, οὐκέτι, means "no more, no longer, no further"[22] and also presupposes ellipsis of "there is." Both readings emphasize the change in status of Greeks, slaves, and women in Christ.

Whether ἔνι is derived from a poetic form of the preposition ἐν, "in," or is a contracted form of ἔνεστι, "to be in," the sense of being "in" is normally understood if it fits the context, which it does in Gal 3:28, namely "in [Christ]."[23] The explanatory conclusion of the sentence, "for you are all one in [ἐν] Christ Jesus" makes it clear that Paul is speaking specifically about life "in Christ." The two preceding verses also identify the sphere of Paul's concern to be "in Christ": "You are all sons of God through faith in [ἐν] Christ Jesus, for all of you who were baptized into [εἰς] Christ have clothed yourselves in [with the prefix ἐν] Christ." This understanding fits Paul's "in Christ" theme.

This same understanding is given in Gal 5:6, "For in [ἐν] Christ neither circumcision nor uncircumcision has any value." The Col 3:10–11 parallel also makes it clear that it is specifically in the sphere (ὅπου, "where") of the new creation in Christ that "there is no Greek and Jew." Thus, whether "in Christ" is understood to be implied by ἔνι ("there is in [Christ]") or by the explanatory clause in Gal 3:28b and the rest of the context, virtually all exegetes agree that Paul is stating that in Christ these divisions do not exist.[24]

Some commentators following J. B. Lightfoot say that οὐκ ἔνι negates "not the fact only, but the possibility."[25] Lightfoot explains, "Every barrier is swept away. No special claims, no special disabilities exist in Him, none *can* exist."[26] Although not excludable lexically, the entire context is clearly about the state that exists in Christ: Gal 3:25–29, "we are [ἐσμεν] no longer under the supervision of the law ... you are [ἐστε] sons of God ...

---

22. BDAG 736; BDF §98.
23. Burton, *Galatians*, 207; Thayer, *Lexicon*, 216: "*is in, is among, has place, is present.*"
24. MM 215; cf. BDAG 336, ἔνι "*there is.*" Most commentators who affirm ἔνι to mean "there is" explain that this applies to those in Christ. E.g., Meyer, *Galatians*, 157–58; Rendall, *Galatians*, 174; John R. W. Stott, *The Message of Galatians* (London: Inter-Varsity Press, 1968), 99–100; Duncan, *Galatians*, 123–24; R. A. Cole, *The Epistle of Paul to the Galatians* (Grand Rapids: Eerdmans, 1965), 110–11; James M. Boice, *Galatians* (vol. 10 of *The Expositor's Bible Commentary*; ed. F. E. Gaebelein; Grand Rapids: Zondervan, 1976), 5:468–69.
25. Lightfoot, *Galatians*, 150; cf. Ridderbos, *Galatians*, 148: "there can be neither Jew nor Greek," but he explains it as "this gulf does not exist in Christ." The RV adopts this consistently, even 1 Cor 6:5. James 1:17, however, is the only passage for which this translation makes sense, and even here it makes equally good sense translated "there is not." The meaning "there is" makes sense in every NT passage and seems to be required in 1 Cor 6:5 and Sir 37:2.
26. Lightfoot, *Galatians*, 150.

baptized into Christ … clothed in Christ … for you are [ἐστε] all one in Christ Jesus. If you belong to Christ, then you are [ἐστέ] Abraham's seed and heirs according to the promise." Nothing in this context indicates that Paul shifts from his focus on what is in Christ to what is not possible in Christ. Consequently, the translation "there can be no Jew or Greek" is less appropriate to the context of Gal 3:28. "There is" focuses on present existence in Christ, not on baptism or on who is eligible for baptism, though it has implications for both

"There is no Jew or Greek"

The first barrier that is overcome in Christ is "there is neither Jew nor Greek [Ἰουδαῖος οὐδὲ Ἕλλην]." Paul's eleven uses of "Gentiles" in Gal 1–3 establishes his focus on them, but "Greek" is more appropriate in a baptismal liturgy since it carries none of the pejorative associations of "Gentile." It is an appropriate term to use with the sense of "Gentile" both because Greeks were Gentiles and because the vast majority of those reached by Paul's ministry were Greeks in language and culture if not race. The Gentile mission is the natural setting for a baptismal formula like this, and Paul was the pioneer of the Gentile mission, so it may well have originated in Paul's own baptismal practice.[27]

Paul's own teaching and practice exemplified the full acceptance of Gentiles, slaves, and women[28] into the life and ministry of the church. Even if these liturgical words were not originally from Paul, his life championed their truth. Baptism for Paul not only symbolizes entering a new spiritual status, it begins a new life here on earth. Romans 6:3–4 states, "all of us … were baptized … to live a new life." The uniting of Jew and Greek and slave and free in this and parallel baptismal passages stresses equality in the life of the church.

The first word of this paragraph is the inclusive, "All [πάντες] of you are sons of God" (Gal 3:26). Its initial stress position highlights the universality of Paul's intent. This focus on universality is sustained by the "all [ὅσοι, 'as many as'] of you who were baptized" (Gal 3:27). The meaning "Gentile" focuses on religious difference and so reinforces Paul's concern to nullify the importance of circumcision, his central practical concern in

---

27. Cf. Bruce, *Galatians*, 187.
28. Cf. above, pp. 61–68 and below, pp. 90–92 and 102–4.

Galatians. Paul often uses "Greek" to signify Gentiles, frequently alongside uses of ἔθνος, also meaning "Gentiles." Paul's use of the pair "Jew and Greek" in Rom 1:16; 2:9, 10; 3:9; 10:12; and 1 Cor 12:13 must signify "Jew and Gentile"[29] since these two groups encompass "everyone" (1:16; 2:10), "every human being" (2:9), and "all" (3:9; 10:12; 1 Cor 12:13). Similarly, Paul alternates his use of "Greek" and "Gentile" in 1 Cor 1:22–24, using "Greek" twice to identify the same group as "Gentiles."

Galatians 5:6 and 6:15 parallel the grammatical construction of 3:28: "For in Christ Jesus neither circumcision nor uncircumcision has any value, but faith expressing itself through love" (5:6). "For neither circumcision nor uncircumcision means anything, but a new creation" (6:15). "Faith expressing itself in love" and "a new creation" both express an ongoing state and practical implementation. Like all the previous factors cited above, these strongly favor that Paul intended Gal 3:28 to result in practical implementation of Jew–Gentile equality in the church. In Gal 2:6, Paul affirms that God does not show favoritism, confirming his commitment to equality. The practical implications of the breach of the Jew–Gentile division are explicated in Eph 2:14, 19–22: Christ "has made the two one and has destroyed the barrier, the dividing wall of hostility.... Consequently, you are no longer foreigners and aliens, but fellow citizens with God's people and members of God's household ... a holy temple in the Lord ... in which God lives by his Spirit." Gentiles are at last full citizens in a community guided by the Spirit indwelling all God's people.

"There is no slave nor free"

The second barrier that is broken in Christ is the socioeconomic barrier between slaves and free persons. This slave and free imagery introduces the theme of the second half of Galatians. Galatians 4:1 picks up the theme that unlike a slave, the heir "owns the whole estate." To Greeks the essence of freedom was not to belong to another (TDNT 2:261–64; OCD 994–996). For Paul "there is no slave nor free" implies enormous practical consequences. The breaking of the barrier of slavery reflects the deliverance experienced by all who are in Christ: "we were in slavery under the basic principles of the world. But ... you are no longer a slave, but a son;

29. H. Windisch, "Ἕλλην, Ἑλλάς, Ἑλληνικός, Ἑλληνίς, Ἑλληνιστής, Ἑλληνιστί," TDNT 2:516, argues this; cf. NIV's "Gentile(s)." Cf., similarly, Josephus, Ant. 20. 262 (11,2).

and since you are a son, God has made you also an heir" (Gal 4:3, 7). Paul stresses the importance of freedom in Gal 5:1: "It is for freedom that Christ has set us free. Stand firm, then, and do not let yourselves be burdened again with a yoke of slavery."

One of the most striking explications of this theme comes when Paul urges believing couples not to divorce. To keep their marriages together, Paul appeals to "the rule I lay down in all the churches" that "each person should walk in the place in life that the Lord assigned" (1 Cor 7:17, cf. 20 and 24, where "walk in" is replaced by "remain in"). The rule to "remain in one's place in life" also provides a theological basis for freeing Gentiles from following all the trappings of Jewish Christianity. Thus, although in its wording this rule appears conservative, in practice it was a key buttress for Paul's message of freedom in Christ for the Gentiles

Paul's statements about slavery here show that his underlying goal is liberty: "Were you a slave when you were called? Don't let it trouble you—although if you can gain your freedom, do so. For he who was a slave when he was called by the Lord is the Lord's freedman; similarly he who was a free man when he was called is Christ's slave. You were bought at a price; do not become [imperative μὴ γίνεσθε] slaves of men" (1 Cor 7:21–23). Even "Don't let it [being a slave] trouble you" (7:21) has a libertarian ring since the justification for this contentment is their knowledge that in Christ they are free men. Paul applies "there is no slave or free" in Col 3:11 by commanding masters to give their slaves "justice and equality [ἰσότης, BDAG 481, entailing at least fairness], because you know that you also have a Master in heaven" (Col 4:1). Paul even risks all his "capital" to pressure Philemon to receive his slave Onesimus back "forever [αἰώνιον, hence no reinstatement to slavery is allowed] no longer [οὐκέτι] as a slave, but better than a slave, as a dear brother ... both in the material [ἐν σαρκί] and spiritual [ἐν κυρίῳ] realms" (Phlm 15–16).[30] It is a testimony to Paul's commitment to freedom that, in the midst of promoting the principle of retaining the situation in life to which God has called one, he would command slaves to gain their freedom if they can.[31]

---

30. See www.pbpayne.com for evidence that Paul pressured Philemon to grant Onesimus manumission.
31. See www.pbpayne.com for twelve key factors that support this to be a call to gain freedom, if possible.

Slaves who became church leaders exemplify the equal standing of slaves in the church. Within a half century of Paul's writing the letter of Philemon,[32] Ignatius in *Eph.* 1:3 speaks highly of "Onesimus, a man of inexpressible love and your bishop." Onesimus was a common slave name and so exemplifies this, whether or not this bishop of Ephesus was formerly Philemon's slave. The Muratorian Canon (lines 73–77) identifies Pius I, bishop of Rome, either as a slave or the brother of the slave Hermas, the author of the *Shepherd.* Similarly, Hippolytus in *Haer.* 9.11–12 says that Callixtus, bishop of Rome (AD 217–222), was an ex-slave. All of these contextual factors, parallel passages, and historical application, make an extraordinarily strong case that Paul intended his statement "there is no slave or free" (Gal 3:28) to be implemented in practice in the church.

"There is no male and female"

The conjunction joining "male and [καί] female" is different from the previous two pairs. As the Col 3:11 parallel demonstrates, the change in conjunction entails no substantive change in meaning.[33] This change is generally understood as an allusion to Gen 1:27, "male and female he created them," since ἄρσεν καὶ θῆλυ is a set phrase that in every other passage referring to humans in the LXX and the NT refers to the creation of male and female (Gen 1:27; 5:2; Matt 19:4; Mark 10:6).[34] The purpose of this allusion to the creation is to contrast the creation of Gen 1 to the new creation. The new creation is a key theme in Galatians—always pointing to the new life in Christ lived through the Spirit.[35]

Galatians 3:28 teaches that in Christ there is no male and female. It is not that Christ is irrelevant to the relations between male and female, but that gender, just as ethnicity and socioeconomic status, is irrelevant to status in Christ. The barriers that separate male and female in society do not exist in the new reality of their relations *in Christ*. In Christ, gender divisions do not exist, just as the divisions between Jew and Gentile and

---

32. Philemon was written about AD 61 or 62. Eusebius's *Chronicle* dates the martyrdom of Ignatius in AD 108.
33. The parallel passages use a variety of conjunctions. Col 3:11 uses καί to join both "Greek and Jew" and "circumcision and uncircumcision." 1 Cor 12:13 uses εἴτε ... εἴτε ("whether ... or") for these same groups. Rom 10:12 uses τε καί to join "Jew and Greek."
34. The only other occurrence of both of these words in the NT is Rom 1:26–27, although those verses do not use this phrase. They do, however, follow immediately after a reference to the Creator in 1:25.
35. See below, pp. 103–4, 193–95.

slave and free do not exist. In Christ, these ethnic, socioeconomic, and biological divisions have been replaced with a new oneness. Consequently, discrimination and special privilege based on these external factors is contrary to the unity of Christ's body.[36]

Paul was concerned not to denigrate the body or sexuality.[37] First Corinthians repeatedly affirms that the acts of the body must not be excused as irrelevant to one's spiritual life. Galatians 3:28 does not deny the reality of sexuality, but affirms that discrimination based on gender is overcome in Christ, just as discrimination against Gentiles and slaves is overcome in Christ. It is precisely because of their spiritual oneness, their equal standing in Christ, that discrimination against Gentiles, slaves, or women was repugnant to Paul.[38]

Ephesians 2:14 asserts that Christ "has made the two one and has destroyed the barrier, the dividing wall of hostility" between Jew and Gentile. The court of the women with its own dividing wall lay between the court of the Gentiles and the temple. Galatians 3:28 implies the spiritual abolition of both of these walls and the consequent opening of temple-fellowship status to women as well as Gentiles. Similarly, the abolition of the necessity of circumcision (e.g., Eph 2:11–13) opens the door to full participation by women as well as Gentiles in Christian worship.

The barrier metaphor Paul chose implies not just equal spiritual standing but equal access and privileges within the church. Ephesians 2:15 confirms what this implies: "abolishing in his flesh the law with its commandments and regulations. His purpose was to create in himself one new man out of the two, thus making peace ... he put to death their hostility."

---

36. This principle is also evident in 1 Cor 7, see below, pp. 105–8, and 1 Cor 11:11, see below, pp. 189–98.

37. So he cannot be adopting a Gnostic "baptismal reunification formula" about the restoration of a primordial androgynous unity according to which Adam originally was both male and female as suggested by Meeks ("Androgyne," 165–208). Betz (*Galatians*, 196 n. 122) cites Meeks favorably. Such a formula is evidenced by Clement, *Strom.* 3.13.92; 2 *Clem.* 12.2; cf. *Gos. Thom.* 22b; Hippolytus, *Haer.* 5. 7, of the Ophites, and Philo's concept of the original man made after God's image being "incorporeal [ἀσώματος] neither male nor female [οὔτε ἄρρεν οὔτε θῆλυ], incorruptible by nature" *Creation* 134; cf. *Alleg. Interp.* 1.53, 88–92; *Plant.* 44; *Her.* 57; *QG* 1.4, 8; 2.56; 4.160. There is no solid evidence that Paul knew such a formula or regarded it as dominical, *pace* the speculation of Dennis R. MacDonald, *There Is No Male and Female: The Fate of a Dominical Saying in Paul and Gnosticism* (Philadelphia: Fortress, 1987), 127–28. The Gnostic formula, however, whose attestation is much later, may have drawn from Gal 3:27–28, as suggested by Bruce (*Galatians*, 189).

38. Cf. Ridderbos (*Paul*, 337), who says that Gal 3:28 "signifies a breaking through of the boundaries that obtained till now, a universalizing of salvation and with it of the church as the people of God."

The cleanliness code of the law and the court of the women limited women's participation in Jewish worship. Christ destroyed these barriers and overcame the hostility and discrimination associated with them. Women, like Gentiles, are no longer second-class citizens but are blessed with the same privileges as men in a community guided by the Spirit indwelling all God's people.

Each of these pairs identifies a social division. To say that they do not apply to the social realm is to miss their most apparent application. Consequently, Paul's denial of their existence in Christ must apply at least to social status. These three pairs were universally viewed as antagonistic; their very nature demands that Gal 3:28 deny their relevance for social status in Christ. The negation of these divisions implies that discrimination based on these social divisions is also rejected. Since the natural meaning of Paul's words carries its full weight for the first two contrasted pairs, the same must be true of the third pair, that there is "neither male nor female," especially since it is conjoined with the other two pairs by the affirmation, "for you are all one in Christ Jesus."

"For you are all one in Christ Jesus"

The concluding clause makes explicit what was anticipated in the three previous ἔνι ("to be in") statements, namely, that it is "in Christ" that these barriers no longer exist. Paul emphasizes "you" (plural) by adding the pronoun ὑμεῖς even though it is implicit in the verb. This highlights that these negations apply to the actual Galatian churches. The "all" emphasizes that there are no exceptions. The word Paul uses for "one," εἷς, is a masculine[39] singular pronominal adjective. Since "one" is an adjective, it implies a corresponding noun such as the ASV translation, "one man," or the NEB, "one person." Use of the masculine was simply conventional in Greek when referring to a body of people that included men.[40] It does not

---

39. In light of Paul's extensive use of "the body" (τὸ σῶμα, neuter) as a metaphor for the church (e.g., Rom 12:4–5; 1 Cor 10:16–17; 12:12–27; Eph 1:23; 4:4–16; 5:23, 30; Col 1:18, 24; 2:19; 3:15) that fits this context, it is surprising that he used the masculine form rather than the neuter form of the adjective "one" unless it was later that he created this metaphor to express the unity of the church. The earliest writings of Paul, including 1 and 2 Thessalonians and Galatians, do not use "body" as a metaphor for the church. If the south Galatian hypothesis is correct, as many scholars have accepted since the careful work on historical geography by W. M. Ramsay, Galatians was one of the earliest, if not the earliest, of Paul's surviving letters. His arguments are analyzed by Bruce (Galatians, 3–18).
40. Cf. Cervin, "Junia(s)," 469 and n. 28.

exclude females, as the inclusion of "male and female" demands in any case. The vast majority of versions appropriately translate it, "You are all one in Christ Jesus."

Ernest de Witt Burton notes that it may be taken either distributively or inclusively. "In the former case the meaning is: once in Christ Jesus, whether you be Jew or Gentile, slave or master, man or woman, all these distinctions vanish (there is no respect of persons with God).... In the latter case the thought is that all those in Jesus Christ merge into one personality."[41] The distributive sense fits Paul's theology, whereas the idea that individual believers merge into one personality in Christ is foreign to Paul's theology. Paul's development of the idea of the body of Christ consistently focuses on a diversity of members working together. It is not the absence of diversity but the presence of harmony in the midst of diversity that distinguishes the body. Individuals do not lose their personalities or gifts. They use their individual gifts for the good of the body. There is no "corporate personality" in the sense that all Christians look and act alike or that their individual personalities and gifts are suppressed. Here in Gal 3:28, the focus on the absence of barriers in Christ implies an equality of opportunity to become part of the body and to participate in it unimpeded by ethnic, economic, or gender discrimination.

A close parallel is the use of "one new man" (ἕνα καινὸν ἄνθρωπον) in Eph 2:15. Although the "one new man" is inclusive since it stands for the church, the "destruction of the barrier" in 2:14 shows that Paul intends "one new man" to stress the equal standing of Gentiles and Jews. To accomplish this oneness and open full participation to Gentiles, Christ "abolished in his flesh the law with its commandments and regulations" (2:15). Thus, even when Paul does use "one man" inclusively, he uses it to stress that Christ destroyed barriers separating believers.

The association of this "one new man" with the expression "one body" (ἐνὶ σώματι) in Eph 2:16 and the explication of the body of Christ in Eph 4:1–16 make it clear that the oneness of the body is not just a spiritual oneness but a oneness that affects personal relationships. "Be completely humble and gentle; be patient, bearing with one another in love. Make every effort to keep the unity of the Spirit through the bond of peace. There is one body and one Spirit" (Eph 4:2–4). The distributive sense

---

41. Burton, *Galatians*, 207–8.

of individual participation in this oneness is emphasized, "to each one of us grace has been given" (4:7) and "each part does its work" (4:16). Paul is typically concerned with practical consequences when he refers to "the body of Christ." The parallel "you are all one" in Gal 3:28 naturally also implies practical consequences.

CAN ONE LEGITIMATELY RESTRICT THE MEANING OF GALATIANS 3:28 TO SPIRITUAL STANDING?

Some interpret the oneness of Gal 3:28, or at least the male–female part of it, to be limited to each individual believer's personal relationship to God and spiritual standing only. They say it does not also apply to life in the church or to interpersonal relations but is only about relationships with God, the *coram deo*. They treat it as having no bearing on whether any of these groups are treated as second-class citizens or are excluded from any church ministry.

S. Lewis Johnson Jr. insists that Paul's reference to "male and female" in Gal 3:28 "is not speaking of relationships in the family and church, but of standing before God in righteousness by faith."[42] Many of Johnson's statements, however, show that he was aware of contextual evidence of the practical implications of this statement. He admits that these three distinctions are "invalid in Christ" and acknowledges that Paul was rejecting the common Jewish view that Gentiles, slaves, and women are "limited in certain spiritual privileges open to Jewish males."[43] He acknowledges that Gal 3:28 affirms "the irrelevancy of the institution of slavery for status and relationship within the church"[44] and even cites approvingly Augustine, that "man and woman are one in the one Man. He is no longer man or woman who lives in Christ."[45] Johnson's refusal to apply this principle to the equal standing of women in church life, therefore, is inconsistent with his treatment of the rest of the verse.

---

42. S. Lewis Johnson Jr. ("Role Distinctions in the Church: Galatians 3:28," *RBMW* 154–64, 160, 163) cites with approval Ronald Y. K. Fung (*The Epistle to the Galatians* [Grand Rapids: Eerdmans, 1988], 176), "Paul's statement is not concerned with the role relationships of men and women within the Body of Christ but rather with their common initiation into it through (faith and) baptism."

43. Johnson, "Galatians 3:28," *RBMW* 158.

44. Ibid., 159.

45. Ibid., 156.

Galatians 2:11 – 14 shows how strongly Paul would have reacted if anyone had used "role distinctions" to exclude Gentiles or slaves from leadership roles in the church.[46] It is Paul himself who in Gal 3:28 draws the analogy from discrimination against Gentiles and slaves to discrimination against women. Galatians 3:28 opposes the exclusion of all members of a class of people from full participation in the church simply because they are Gentiles, slaves, or women. Such exclusion is discrimination and is a denial of equality in Christ.

Perhaps realizing that the social implications of there being no Jew or Gentile in Christ are inescapable, Johnson attempts to separate the male and female pair so that it alone avoids the implication of equal standing and privilege in the church. This attempt fails for three reasons. First, because the identical expression "there is no ..." introduces each pair, and, second, because each of the three statements is absolute with no qualification.[47] Paul did not add "as an entry requirement" or "as regards their spiritual status only" or any other qualifier that could have limited the meaning. Third, the "all" in the summarizing statement, "You are all one in Christ Jesus," must apply to all three of the prior pairs and reinforces their parallel significance. Furthermore, the immediate and wider context in Galatians explicitly refers to the practical implications of Gal 3:28 in the life of the church.

Galatians 3:23 states, "we were held prisoners by the law, locked up until faith should be revealed." This imagery of the barriers of prison contrasts directly with the negation of barriers in Gal 3:28. Since the barriers of the law did severely restrict access of Gentiles and women, and to some degree of slaves, from full participation in the social life of the people of God, this contrast implies that the removal of those barriers in Christ will result in freedom to participate fully in the social life of the church.

Galatians 3:25 affirms that believers "are no longer under the supervision of the law." The law is filled with social and interpersonal regulations

---

46. Leon Morris (*Galatians: Paul's Charter of Christian Freedom* [Downers Grove, Ill.: InterVarsity Press, 1996], 123 n. 77) approvingly quotes F. F. Bruce that women "may exercise spiritual leadership in church ... as freely as a man." So, too, Richard N. Longenecker, *New Testament Social Ethics for Today* (Grand Rapids: Eerdmans, 1984), 70–93; James D. G. Dunn, *The Epistle to the Galatians* (BNTC; Peabody, Mass.: Hendrickson, 1993), 207–8, and his *The Theology of Paul's Letter to the Galatians* (Cambridge: Cambridge Univ. Press, 1993), 127 n. 12; G. Walter Hanson, *Galatians* (Downers Grove, Ill.: InterVarsity Press, 1994) 112–13; Scot McKnight, *Galatians* (NIVAC; Grand Rapids: Zondervan, 1995), 202.

47. "An axiom with no qualification" (Dunn, *Galatians*, 204).

that people must "do" (Gal 3:12) in order to live. Galatians 3:2, 5, and 10 speak of "observing the law" and "continue to do everything written in the Book of the Law." The Gal 3:28 principle proclaims the breakdown of barriers that were enshrined in the law. Since the law enumerates regulations restricting the social life of Gentiles and women in particular, it would not make sense for the removal of these regulations and the barriers they erected to have no social application.

Paul's concluding argument against treating Gentiles as second-class citizens is Gal 3:28–29. Here he gives theological justification for the full inclusion of the Gentiles without requiring them to live by the law in order to participate in table fellowship. Galatians 3:28 also gives theological justification why circumcision will be judged irrelevant in the second half of the letter. An exclusively spiritual interpretation is contrary to what Paul demands regarding Jew–Gentile relations in particular and interpersonal relations in the church in general. In this context, Gal 3:28's absolute and unqualified assertions regarding social categories demand social application to remove barriers between Jew and Gentile.

It is against Paul's normal usage to divorce "in Christ" from relationships in the family and church, and no such divorce is supported in Gal 3:28. "The churches of Judea that are in Christ" (Gal 1:22) specifically associates "in Christ" with the churches. Galatians 2:4 states, "some false brothers had infiltrated our ranks to spy on the freedom we have in Christ Jesus and to make us slaves." Here, being "in Christ Jesus" is linked to freedom from the requirement of circumcision. In Gal 5:6 Paul says that what counts "in Christ Jesus ... is faith expressing itself through love." Being "in Christ" in Paul's letters is not divorced from the life of the church but is a key description of life in the church, and should be so interpreted in Gal 3:28.

Galatians 3:29 affirms that all of these groups who are one in Christ "are Abraham's seed, heirs according to the promise." The promise to Abraham includes many practical and social blessings. Its classical expression in Gen 12:2–3 contains seven blessings, and all seven are about Abraham and his descendents' relationships with other people; none of the seven mention a spiritual relationship with God. Galatians 3:28–29 associates the overcoming of these three barriers with being heirs of the promise to Abraham. Being heirs of Abraham entails not only what they receive, including freedom, status, and standing in the church, but also in what they contribute to fulfilling the Abrahamic blessing to all nations.

If all women are excluded from positions of leadership in the church, then their blessing is limited in a way that the men's blessings are not. It would be incompatible with the promises to Abraham to restrict Gal 3:28 only to the spiritual realm. Indeed, the Abrahamic blessings cannot be fulfilled either in the church or to all nations if the blessings are restricted to individual salvation. Johnson states that Gal 3:29 teaches that "every believer in Christ inherits fully the Abrahamic promises."[48] Inconsistently, however, he questions whether women may hold church offices or teach in church. Those excluding women from church leadership either assume that God never gives women certain gifts of the Spirit such as teaching and administration, or they restrict the use of those gifts even though Paul explains that the gifts are for the common good (1 Cor 12:7).

Paul summarizes the application of Gal 3:26–4:31 in Gal 5:1. This summary flows from the principle that barriers are overcome in Christ and applies it to practical issues in the church: "It is for freedom that Christ has set us free. Stand firm, then, and do not let yourselves be burdened again by a yoke of slavery." This freedom is then applied to circumcision and in 5:3 to the obligation "to obey the whole law." Since this summary of the application of the principle of Gal 3:28 is so focused on the practical life of the church, the principle it is applying must not have been divorced from the practical life of the church.

Paul's principle of freedom in Christ throughout Galatians applies to all believers. Paul makes no distinction between the freedom of Jews and Gentiles, slave and free, or male and female. Paul's principle of freedom in Christ specifically rejects the bondage of circumcision and the ritual requirements of the law. This frees Gentiles and women to full standing and participation in the life of the church. In light of the theme of freedom in Galatians, any interpretation of Gal 3:28 is dubious that explains it as though it were compatible with restrictions on the freedom of Gentiles, slaves, or women in the life and ministry of the church.

Galatians 5:6 highlights Paul's concern not just with the spiritual dimension of faith but its practical expression, "The only thing that counts

---

48. Johnson, "Galatians 3:28," *RBMW* 163.

is faith expressing itself through love." This continues in verse 7, "You were running a good race ... obeying the truth." Consequently, those who limit the reference of Gal 3:28 to faith viewed in isolation from the practical life of the church do not follow Paul's own understanding of faith in this part of Galatians.

Several other factors confirm that Gal 3:28 does not apply only to a person's standing before God. Such a restriction ignores the social implications of religious distinctions. In first-century Judaism, religious differences were the basis of social structure and dictated private and social practices. The absence in Christ of spiritual distinctions between Jew and Greek, slave and free, and male and female logically entailed in practice a corresponding removal of barriers in their social relationships.[49] All of these groups were baptized alike, and alike became full members of the covenant family in Christ. They all received the Spirit and all are gifted by Christ (Eph 4:4–7). There is no evidence that the church made any distinction between what gifts were appropriate to members of these different groups. The goal was that "all reach unity in the faith and ... become mature, attaining to the whole measure of the fullness of Christ" (Eph 4:13). This implies that Gentiles, slaves, and women shared the same worship responsibilities and privileges in the church as Jews, free persons, and men. Passages like Rom 16:1–16 confirm this.[50]

The absence in Christ of the distinction between Jew and Gentile is the foundation on which Paul denies the need for circumcision, the central practical issue of Galatians.[51] This implies that Paul did not intend the application of Gal 3:28 to be restricted to spiritual status. There is a sharp contrast between Judaism's focus on ancestral Israel as the people of God and Paul's insistence in Gal 6:15–16 that the Israel of God has nothing to do with circumcision but with the new creation in Christ. Within Judaism, kinship and racial purity were key issues in spiritual standing. Genealogies determined not just who could be a full Israelite, but also who could be a priest or Levite, and many believed that the merits of one's ancestors were inherited.[52] In Christ, however, Gentiles, slaves, and women have no dis-

49. This is acknowledged by Stephen B. Clark (*Man and Woman in Christ* [Ann Arbor, Mich.: Servant, 1980], 151).
50. Cf. above, pp. 61–68.
51. Cf. the references to circumcision in Gal 2:3, 7, 8, 9, 12; 5:2, 3, 6, 11; 6:12, 13, 15.
52. So, too, Clark, "even full proselytes could not achieve the status of the full Israelite" (*Man and Woman*, 152).

advantage. In Christ these divisions are abolished and all stand as one not just spiritually, but practically in church life.

Bifurcating spiritual equality and practical discrimination based on ethnic-religious background, economic status, or gender is in opposition to the Christian and Pauline principle that the test of spiritual standing is whether someone loves his or her neighbor (Rom 13:8–10; Gal 5:13–14). Love of God is inextricably linked with love of neighbor, and spirituality is demonstrated in love for one another. It is not loving to discriminate against people simply because of their background, status, or gender. God condemns partiality and favoritism based on external appearance, and human intuition and experience confirm this to be true. Throughout Scripture, both explicitly and in scores of narratives, God does not judge by outward appearance but by the heart.

For instance, God repeatedly overrode primogeniture in the founding of the nation of Israel.[53] Jesus repeatedly exalts people who are despised, as he does in the parable of the prodigal son, and he directly opposes discrimination based on external factors, as he does in the parable of the good Samaritan. To interpret Gal 3:28 as affirming spiritual equality but as irrelevant to discrimination based on ethnic-religious background, economic status, or gender is to divorce it from the moral core of Paul's message in Galatians and of the gospel of Christ.

The nature of spirituality in Galatians also excludes a dichotomy between spiritual equality and ethnic, economic, or gender discrimination in the church. A major theme of Galatians is the transformation of life in Christ.[54] For Paul, spirituality must result in practical expressions of love. "The fruit of the Spirit is love" (Gal 5:22). Consequently, Paul says, "Since we live by the Spirit, let us keep in step with the Spirit. Let us not become conceited, provoking and envying each another" (Gal 5:25–26). This statement presupposes that the barriers of Gal 3:28 are broken not only in the spiritual realm, but also in interpersonal relations in the church. Because believers from all these groups stand as equals

---

53. God chose the younger Abel over Cain (Gen 4), made his covenant with Isaac over Ishmael (Gen 17:19–21), blessed Jacob over Esau (Paul draws attention to this in Rom 9:10–13), Joseph over his brothers (Gen 48:21–49:28), Ephraim over Manasseh (Gen 48:11–20), Perez over Zerah in the line of Christ (Gen 38:27–30; Matt 1:3), Moses over Aaron (Exod 6:20), David over his seven elder brothers (1 Sam 16:1–13), and Solomon over Adonijah (1 Kgs 1–2).
54. Cf. below, pp. 102–4.

spiritually in Christ, in practice they must treat each other as equals, without self-conceit and envy.

The nature of the gospel is incompatible with assigning privileges and special treatment only to members of particular groups, whether ethnic, economic, or by gender. Thus, Paul in Gal 2:14 accused Peter of "not acting in line with the truth of the gospel." The nature of fellowship in Christ is one of mutual submission (Eph 5:21), enjoining even leaders to be servants after the model of Christ (e.g., Mark 10:44). Johnson grants "that the essence of the gospel's proclamation of oneness or equality in Christ demanded a walk in harmony with that position."[55] He then asks "if distinction of roles of believers within that equality necessarily violates that equality." If such distinctions of roles are based on the gifts and callings of individual believers, they would not violate that equality, but if every member of a group is automatically excluded from leadership or teaching in the church simply by virtue of their gender, yes, that would necessarily violate that equality.

For all of the reasons listed above, it is clear that Gal 3:28 carries important social and practical implications.[56] Ethnic-religious, socioeconomic, and gender barriers are overcome in Christ. Paul's repeated insistence on the practical implications of spirituality throughout Galatians necessitate that the equal standing that Christ has opened to Jews and Greeks, slaves and free, male and female not be divorced from a corresponding equality[57] of social standing in the practical life of the church. The scope of Paul's concern for freedom, oneness, and equality demonstrates that, as F. F. Bruce says, "the denial of discrimination which is sacramentally affirmed in baptism holds good for the new existence 'in Christ' in its entirety."[58]

BEING "ONE IN CHRIST" ENTAILS MORE THAN EQUALITY

Although entailing equality of standing, for Paul being "one in Christ" points beyond this to a whole new perspective on life modeled after Christ. Being "united with Christ" and "being one in spirit and purpose" entails a new ethical imperative: "Do nothing out of selfish ambition or vain con-

---

55. Johnson, "Galatians 3:28," *RBMW* 161.
56. Cf. also Clark, *Man and Woman*, 153.
57. Paul affirmed the principle of equality (ἰσότης) in master slave relations in Col 4:1, cf. above, pp. 90–92, and in 2 Cor 8:13–15 regarding charitable giving.
58. Bruce, *Galatians*, 190.

ceit, but in humility consider others better than yourselves. Each of you should look not only to your own interests, but also to the interests of others. Your attitude should be the same as that of Christ Jesus" (Phil 2:3–5). Thus, being "one in Christ" is more than avoiding discrimination against less socially powerful groups such as slaves and women; it is actively looking out for the welfare of others and even considering them better than oneself. It is adopting the servant attitude and life of Christ (Phil 2:7). The focus of life in Christ is not to defend my own rights, but actively to promote the welfare and dignity of others.

Some have doubted whether Paul's view of the new life in Christ could have such dramatic personal and social consequences that women could have equal standing and opportunity with men. James D. G. Dunn, however, shows that the cross created an "apocalyptic shift" replacing the old world with the new creation.[59] The following quotations from Galatians show how Paul progressively develops the theme of the radical newness of life in Christ lived through the Spirit. The equal standing of Jew and Greek, slave and free, and male and female fits perfectly into this theme and is not nearly as radical as some of Paul's other affirmations.

The opening of Galatians affirms the goal of Christ's work is "to rescue us from the present evil age" (1:4). Paul even says, "I have been crucified with Christ and I no longer live, but Christ lives in me. The life I live in the body, I live by faith in the Son of God, who loved me and gave himself for me" (2:19–20). He affirms that believers have received the Spirit who empowers this new life (3:2, 14). He argues, "After beginning with the Spirit, are you now trying to attain your goal by human effort?... Does God give you his Spirit and work miracles among you because you observe the law, or because you believe?" (3:3–5).

Paul insists that "Christ redeemed us from the curse of the law" (3:13). "Before this faith came, we were held prisoners by the law" (3:23; cf. 4:8–9, 22, 25–26). Formerly, "we were in slavery under the basic principles of the world" (4:3), but Christ came "to redeem those under law, that we might receive the full rights of sons. Because you are sons, God sent the Spirit of his Son into our hearts, the Spirit who calls out, 'Abba, Father.' So you are no longer a slave, but a son; and since you are a son, God has made you also an heir" (4:5–7). "Christ has set us free" (5:1). "You, my brothers,

---

59. Dunn, *The Theology of Galatians*, 50.

were called to be free" (5:13). "So I say, live by the Spirit, and you will not gratify the desires of the sinful nature ... if you are led by the Spirit, you are not under law" (5:16, 18). The Holy Spirit empowers the believer to avoid the deeds of the flesh (5:19–21) and instead produce the fruit of the Spirit (5:22–23). The transformation is so radical that "those who belong to Christ Jesus have crucified the sinful nature with its passions and desires. Since we live by the Spirit, let us keep in step with the Spirit" (5:25–26; cf. 6:3). The degree of Paul's own transformation is evident in his confession in 6:14 that through the cross, "the world has been crucified to me, and I to the world." Life in Christ is so radically changed that Paul calls it "a new creation" (6:15).

Central to this new creation is the new "Israel of God" (Gal 6:16) that gives no privileged status to Jews over Gentiles, to free persons over slaves, or to men over women. They are all one in Christ Jesus, redeemed from sin and the law by Christ and welcomed into the family of God. All now live in Christ, freed from control by the principles of the world and heirs of God's promises to Abraham. No one is a second-class citizen or excluded by ethnic-religious background, economic status, or gender from any position or privilege in the church.[60] The Spirit empowers each to put aside the prejudices of this world's point of view, to resist sinful temptations, and to adopt the servant attitude of Jesus Christ. The result is the fruit of the Spirit such as love, joy, and peace in the lives of people being transformed and learning to walk in tune with the Spirit. The Spirit gifts each believer for ministry in the church and in the world. The eschatological new creation in Christ overcomes the barriers that excluded Gentiles, slaves, and women and grants them acceptance and full participation in God's people.

The natural implication of the equality of male and female in Paul's teaching is that the gifts of women for ministry in the church should be recognized, welcomed, and exercised in all areas of church life, including teaching, pastoring, and church leadership. Dare we exclude women from offices of leadership and teaching to which God has gifted them and called them?

---

60. Cf. Gerhard Dautzenberg ("'Da ist nicht männlich und weiblich.' Zur Interpretation von Gal 3,28," *Kairós* 24, 3–4 [1982]: 181–206), who argues that Gal 3:28 reflects the experience in Paul's churches regarding status, collaboration, public activity, and proclamation.

5

1 CORINTHIANS 7 —
THE EQUAL RIGHTS OF
MAN AND WOMAN IN MARRIAGE

In 1 Cor 7, Paul specifies exactly the same conditions, opportunities, rights, and obligations for the woman as for the man regarding twelve distinct issues about marriage (vv. 2, 3, 4, 5, 10–11, 12–13, 14, 15, 16, 28, 32 and 34a, and 33 and 34b). In each he addresses men and women as equals. His wording is symmetrically balanced to reinforce this equality. What he affirms for man, he affirms equally for woman, often with exactly parallel expressions:

7:2: "Let each man have his own wife, and let each woman have her own husband."

7:3: "Let the husband fulfill his marital duty to his wife, and likewise the wife to her husband."

7:4: "The wife does not have authority over her own body, but her husband does. In the same way, the husband does not have authority over his own body, but his wife does."

7:5: "Do not deprive each other except by mutual consent."

7:10–11: "A wife must not separate[1] from her husband ... and a husband must not leave[2] his wife."[3]

7:12–13: "If any brother has a wife who is not a believer and she is willing to live with him, he must not leave her. And if a woman has a husband who is not a believer and he is willing to live with her, she must not leave him."

7:14: "For the unbelieving husband has been sanctified through his wife, and the unbelieving wife has been sanctified through her husband."

7:15: "But if the unbeliever separates ... the believing brother or sister is not bound."

7:16: "How do you know, wife, whether you will save your husband? Or how do you know, husband, whether you will save your wife?"

7:28: "But if you do marry, you have not sinned; and if a virgin marries, she has not sinned."

7:32, 34a: "An unmarried man is concerned about the Lord's affairs—how he can please the Lord.... An unmarried woman or virgin is concerned about the Lord's affairs: Her aim is to be devoted to the Lord in both body and spirit."

7:33, 34b: "But a married man is concerned about the affairs of this world—how he can please his wife—and his interests are divided.... But a married woman is concerned about the affairs of this world—how she can please her husband."

The strikingly egalitarian understanding of the dynamics of marital relations expressed in Paul's symmetry throughout this passage is without

---

1. This symmetry directly parallels Jesus' statements regarding divorce by a man or a woman recorded in Mark 10:9–12. 1 Cor 7:11 uses the same verb (χωρίζω) as Mark 10:9. This, and especially the contrasting "not the Lord" in v. 12, confirms that Paul is citing Jesus just as he does in his other explicit citations from Jesus, e.g., 1 Cor 9:14; 11:23–25; 1 Thess 4:15–17. Cf. Anthony C. Thiselton, *The First Epistle to the Corinthians* (NIGTC; Grand Rapids: Eerdmans, 2000), 521; D. C. Allison, "The Pauline Epistles and the Synoptic Gospels: The Pattern of the Parallels," *NTS* 28 (1982): 1–32; F. F. Bruce, "Paul and the Historical Jesus," *BJRL* 56 (1974): 317–35; D. Wenham, "Paul's Use of the Jesus Tradition: Three Samples," in *The Jesus Tradition outside the Gospels* (ed. D. Wenham; Gospel Perspectives 5; Sheffield: JSOT Press, 1985), 7–37.
2. Thiselton says that ἀφίημι means "*to divorce* in a legal context (as in Herodotus, 5.39).... '[Y]ou are to leave' constituted in Roman law all that was necessary for a husband to divorce his wife" (*First Corinthians*, 520). Also, BDAG 156.
3. Richard B. Hays (*First Corinthians* [IBC; Louisville, Ky.: John Knox, 1997], 120) notes on "to put asunder" and "to leave," that "there is no difference in the legal or practical effect of the action: the modern distinction between 'separation' and 'divorce' is not in view here, and Paul's formulation in verse 13 recognizes the woman's legal right to divorce her husband—though he is urging Christian women not to exercise it."

parallel in the literature of the ancient world.[4] It is all the more impressive because it is focused on the marriage relationship, a relationship that traditionalists regard as intrinsically hierarchical based on the "created order." Against a cultural backdrop where men were viewed as possessing their wives, Paul states in 7:2, "let each woman have her own husband." Against a cultural backdrop where women were viewed as owing sexual duty to their husbands, Paul states in 7:3, "Let the husband fulfill his marital duty to his wife."

It is hard to imagine how revolutionary[5] it was for Paul to write in 7:4, "the husband does not have authority over his own body, but his wife does." Paul's statement in 7:11 that "a husband must not leave his wife" and his insistence in 7:12 that this applies even if his wife does not share his faith stands in stark contrast to the ease with which a man could divorce his wife in Jewish and Hellenistic society. "Paul offers a paradigm-shattering vision of marriage as a relationship in which the partners are bonded together in submission to one another, each committed to meet the other's needs."[6] If, however, an unbelieving spouse should leave, Paul declares the believing husband or wife "not bound" (7:15).

The idea that the male, not the female, should be the spiritual leader of the home is challenged not only by Paul's affirmation in 7:14 that "the unbelieving husband has been sanctified through his wife," but also since this statement precedes its corresponding statement of the believing husband. Her spiritual influence is such that she may "save" her husband (7:16), presumably by sharing the gospel with him, which will save him if he accepts it. This, too, precedes its corresponding statement about the believing husband.

A woman's spiritual status does not, however, depend on being married. Indeed, Paul states in 7:34 that "an unmarried woman or virgin is concerned about the Lord's affairs: Her aim is to be devoted to the Lord in both body and spirit." Paul encouraged singleness for all those with that gift: "I wish that all of you [πάντας ἀνθρώπους] were as I am. But each

---

4. Cf. Marion L. Soards, *1 Corinthians* (NIBCNT; Peabody, Mass.: Hendrickson, 1999), 139.
5. Hays comments that this "must have struck many first-century hearers as extraordinary.... The marriage partners are neither placed in a hierarchical relation with one over the other nor set apart as autonomous units each doing what he or she pleases. Instead, the relationship of marriage is one of mutual submission, each partner having authority over the other" (*First Corinthians*, 116).
6. Ibid., 131.

[ἔκαστος] of you has your own gift from God" (1 Cor 7:7 TNIV). Paul used inclusive language, affirming that all believers, women as well as men, are gifted (cf. 1 Cor 12:4–11), unlike the NIV's "in all men … to each man" (12:6–7). By Greek convention, masculine grammatical forms and terms like ἄνθρωπος ("person"/"man") and ἀδελφοί ("brothers"/"brothers and sisters," BDAG 18) are commonly used when both men and women are in view. Thus, for example, in 1 Cor 7:24 "each" should not be translated "each man" (as the NIV does, corrected in the TNIV).

First Corinthians 7, then, presents a remarkable picture of Paul's vision of the equality of man and woman in marriage and in spiritual Christ-centered ministry, whether married or single.

6

1 CORINTHIANS 11:2 – 16:
INTRODUCTION

C. F. D. Moule wrote that the problems of 1 Cor 11:2 – 16 "still await a really convincing explanation."[1] G. B. Caird added, "It can hardly be said that the passage has yet surrendered its secret."[2] W. Meeks regarded it "one of the most obscure passages in the Pauline letters."[3] In light of the notorious difficulty of this passage, several scholars have concluded that it is an interpolation that was not originally in the text.[4] This, however, has been thoroughly refuted by several scholars who have shown that no solid textual evidence exists for interpolation, and the passage's language, syntax, and style are thoroughly Pauline.[5] Most interpretations, however, make lexically implausible translations of words and phrases throughout the passage, fitting facts to theories instead of letting the facts of the text constrain the interpretation.

---

1. C. F. D. Moule, *Worship in the New Testament* (London: Lutterworth, 1961), 65.
2. George B. Caird, "Paul and Women's Liberty," *BJRL* 54 (1972): 278.
3. Wayne A. Meeks, *The Writings of St. Paul* (New York: Norton/Scribners, 1972), 38.
4. E.g., W. O. Walker Jr., "1 Corinthians 11:2 – 16 and Paul's Views Regarding Women," *JBL* 94 (1975): 94 – 110; L. Cope, "1 Cor. 11:2 – 16: One Step Further," *JBL* 97 (1978): 435 – 36; G. W. Trompf, "On Attitudes toward Women in Paul and Paulinist Literature: 1 Corinthians 11:3 – 16 and its Context," *CBQ* 42 (1980): 196 – 215; W. Munro, *Authority in Paul and Peter: The Identification of a Pastoral Stratum in the Pauline Corpus and 1 Peter* (SNTSMS 45; Cambridge: Cambridge Univ. Press, 1983), 69 – 75; Christopher Mount, "1 Corinthians 11:3 – 16: Spirit Possession and Authority in a Non-Pauline Interpolation," *JBL* 124 (2005): 313 – 40.
5. Cf. Jerome Murphy-O'Connor ("The Non-Pauline Character of 1 Corinthians 11:2 – 16," *JBL* 95 [1976]: 615 – 21) and his response to Trompf in "Interpolations in 1 Corinthians," *CBQ* 48 (1986): 87 – 90; Gordon D. Fee, *The First Epistle to the Corinthians* (NICNT; Grand Rapids: Eerdmans, 1987), 492, esp. n. 3; John P. Meier, "On the Veiling of Hermeneutics (1 Cor 11:2 – 16)," *CBQ* 40 (1978): 212 – 26.

The key to letting the passage unfold is to take seriously its repeated identification of men's and women's "head coverings" as disgraceful, improper, and degrading (11:4, 5, 6, 13, 14) and morally what one "ought not" do (11:7, 10). Unfortunately, most interpretations continue to identify the "head covering" issue as something that substantial evidence from Hellenistic and Roman culture shows was not generally regarded as disgraceful and did not symbolize immorality.

Furthermore, most interpretations have not taken into account two crucially relevant cultural conventions regarding head coverings. First, it was generally regarded as disgraceful for men to wear long effeminate hair. Effeminate hair was commonly ridiculed as disgraceful because of its association with effeminate homosexual relations. Second, in Hellenistic, Roman, and Jewish cultures for centuries preceding and following the time of Paul, virtually all of the portraiture, sculpture, and other graphic evidence depicts respectable women's hair done up, not let down loose.[6] Most of the relatively few cases of hair let down loose depict disgraceful revelries. Recognizing these two cultural backgrounds is the key to understanding the various puzzling expressions in the passage.

This passage is of major concern to this book since 1 Cor 11:2–16 contains many statements that are central to understanding Paul's attitude toward women. The following analysis addresses each of the thorny problems that make this passage so apparently inscrutable. It proposes a coherent interpretation of this passage that presents Paul's argument as proceeding logically, that remains faithful to the vocabulary and structure of the passage and Paul's related teaching elsewhere, and that fits the cultural situation of Corinth in the first century.

OUTLINE OF 1 CORINTHIANS 11:2–16

11:2	Praise for upholding the traditions Paul had taught them
11:3	Theological introduction, establishing the basis for respect for one's source/head
11:4–6	Critique of hairstyles symbolizing sexual freedom in the Corinthian church
11:7–10	Theological basis for not adopting hairstyles symbolizing sexual freedom

6. E.g., Douglas R. Edwards, "Dress and Ornamentation," *ABD* 2:237.

11:11–12   Affirmation of the equal standing of woman and man in Christ

11:13–15   Argument from nature against adopting hairstyles symbolizing sexual freedom

11:16   The churches have no custom of displaying sexual freedom through wild hair.

7

1 Corinthians 11:2–3: Head/Source Relationships

The Disgraceful Head Coverings Were Novel (v. 2)

In verse 2, Paul praises the Corinthians for holding to the traditions he had "passed on" to them during his stay in Corinth. In light of Paul's use of the expression "the traditions" in Gal 1:14; Col 2:8; and 2 Thess 2:15 and 3:6, and particularly his specification of "just as I passed them on to you," "the traditions" probably carries its technical use in Judaism to refer to oral transmission of religious instruction.[1] The use of the plural with "traditions" indicates that this is an introduction to this whole section of the letter regarding worship traditions. He uses the same verb, "I passed on," later in the book to describe other traditions, such as the Lord's Supper (11:23) and the resurrection traditions (15:3). Since chapters 11–14 are about matters of worship, it is likely Paul had traditions about worship in mind in 11:2–16.

"In everything" modifies "you remember me" and does not necessarily also apply to "you hold to the traditions." This letter details a great many shortcomings in the Corinthians' implementation of Paul's teachings, but he praises them for what he can.

It would contradict Paul's commendation if the head covering issues he addresses next were a breach of traditions he had taught them. In light of

---

1.   Cf. Fee, *First Corinthians*, 499.

113

Paul's extensive ministry in Corinth[2] for at least a year and a half (Acts 18:1 – 18), surely these issues regarding head covering would have come up if all the churches followed such a custom. Thus, their head coverings must be something novel. This explains why 11:16 states, "the churches of God have no such custom."

Although some have regarded this praise as deliberate irony or sarcasm,[3] it is probably better understood as a generously phrased introduction to the practical matters of church worship addressed in chapters 11 – 14. The contrasting "I do not commend you" in 11:17 supports reading verse 2 as a real commendation. This letter addresses a series of issues the Corinthians had raised, indicating their desire to know Paul's teaching more fully. Paul's praise followed by verse 3, "But I want you to know …" is evidence that the Corinthians had not been defiantly rejecting Paul's previous teaching on this issue, but rather needed new instruction. Those who view Paul as speaking sarcastically here usually do so because they believe the Corinthians were knowingly breaking a universal church custom, but verse 16 states to the contrary, "we have no such custom."

"But I want you to know" in 1 Cor 11:3 implies Paul wants them to learn something,[4] as the same phrase does in Col 2:1 and as "I do not want you to be ignorant" does in 1 Cor 10:1 and 12:1. The δέ in 11:3 could either be continuing, translated "now," or contrasting, translated "but." Since the praise in 11:2 contrasts with Paul's following corrections of shameful head coverings, δέ in 11:3 is best understood as contrasting. Accordingly, almost all versions translate it "but."[5] This δέ implies that the praise of verse 2 was not a blanket approval, and certainly not of disgraceful head coverings by worship leaders. Since Paul does not use the introductory formula "now concerning" (περὶ δέ) that typically introduces his responses to their letter

---

2.   This occurred after the edict of Claudius in AD 49 that caused Aquila and Priscilla to move to Corinth (Acts 18:2). The Gallio inscription datings are listed in Hans Conzelmann, *A Commentary on the First Epistle to the Corinthians* (trans. J. W. Leitch et al.; Hermeneia; Philadelphia: Fortress, 1975), 12 – 13.

3.   E.g., J. C. Hurd Jr., *The Origin of 1 Corinthians* (New York: Seabury, 1965), 182 – 84, and J. Moffatt, *The First Epistle of Paul to the Corinthians* (MNTC; London: Hodder & Stoughton, 1943), 149.

4.   This is a crucial objection to Alan Padgett's argument in "Paul on Women in the Church: The Contradictions of Coiffure in 1 Corinthians 11.2 – 16," *JSNT* 20 (1984): 69 – 86 that 11:3 – 7b is all a quotation from Paul's opponents. In addition, nothing in the content of this passage specifies this, and this view is counter to the structure of the passage.

5.   "But": ASV, Berkeley, Geneva, GNB, Goodspeed, KJV, Moffatt, Montgomery, NASB, NEB, New Berkeley, NRSV, RSV, Williams. "However": JB, Weymouth. "Now": Fenton, NIV. "Well": Wey. δέ is left untranslated: NAB, Beck.

(7:1, 25; 8:1; 12:1; 16:1, 12), he more likely learned this information from Chloe's household (1 Cor 1:11).

A THEOLOGICAL CONTEXT FOR HEAD COVERINGS: RESPECT YOUR SOURCE

The function of 11:3 is to highlight the relationships affected by how men and women cover their heads. The "head" relationships in verse 3 lay a foundation for Paul's assertions, but they are not the topic of this passage. Paul does not explain these "head" relations or try to prove they exist. Since the issues he addresses are shameful ways some men and women were covering their literal heads, in 11:3 Paul introduces each of the three key foundational relationships that these actions affect, and in each one he uses the word "head" (κεφαλή) metaphorically.

Paul shows that he intends verse 3 to introduce his comments about head coverings by repeating key words from the first two clauses of verse 3 in verse 4. The first clause, "Christ is the head [κεφαλή] of every man [genitive of πᾶς ἀνήρ]," introduces the first practical problem in 11:4 regarding "every man" (πᾶς ἀνήρ) who disgraces his head (κεφαλή) by having something "down from" his literal head. The second clause, "the head [κεφαλή] of woman is the man," introduces the second practical problem in 11:5 – 6 regarding something that disgraces "the head" of every "woman" when her head is "uncovered." Paul uses the word κεφαλή ("head") nine times in 1 Cor 11:3 – 10 as the presiding image that ties the passage together. Verses 7 – 9 give theological reasons why a man should not cover his head (with effeminate hair) and verse 10 appeals to theological reasons why a woman should cover her head (with her hair done up).

The structure of the entire passage shows that Paul intends to alternate his focus back and forth between men and women. Paul states that both men (v. 4) and women (vv. 5 – 6) who display offensive head coverings "disgrace" (καταισχύνει) their heads, and he addresses both men (vv. 7 – 9) and women (v. 10) with parallel theological argumentation. Thereafter, he continues to alternate his focus: v. 11: woman – man, man – woman; v. 12: woman – man, man – woman; v. 13: woman; v. 14: man; and v. 15: woman. Paul addresses both man and woman in comparable detail and calls the behavior of both disgraceful. This implies that both men and woman were causing disgrace in the Corinthian church. The first class condition, one that is "real" or actually happening, confirms this regarding women in 11:6. The third class condition, expected from an existing general or concrete standpoint in the present combined with "does not even nature teach you," suggests this regarding the hair of men and women in 11:14–15.[6]

Although the people who regarded themselves as "spiritual" in Corinth may have defended their behavior on the basis of their individual freedom, Paul's introduction shifts the focus onto the relationships that the behavior affects and the responsibility Christians have to their Lord and to each other. The focus of verse 3 on personal relationships indicates that the foundational issue is not so much with literal head coverings as with the way they affect the relationships of man to woman and both to Christ and God.

Paul had a keen sense of relational theology, the importance of personal relationships as a foundation for theology. Salvation depends on the believer's relationship to Christ. Being "in Christ" is Paul's paradigm of the Christian community. Central to Paul's Christology is Christ's intimate relationship to God. Paul excelled at taking practical interpersonal problems and finding their solution in our relationship to Christ. Often he would broaden his perspective even further by showing Christ's relationship to God. For example, he introduces his discussion of schisms in the Corinthian church by affirming in 1:9, "God, who has called you into fellowship with his Son Jesus Christ our Lord, is faithful." Paul's appeal against schisms is intertwined throughout with affirmations of their relationship to Christ and God, and it concludes in 3:21–23, "So then, no more boasting about men! All things are yours, whether Paul or Apollos or Cephas or the world or life or death or the present or the future—all are yours, and you are of Christ, and Christ is of God." First Corinthians 3:23 has striking resemblance to the first and third clauses of 11:3 both in its terminology and the sequence of its terminology.

3:23 ὑμεῖς δὲ Χριστοῦ   Χριστὸς δὲ θεοῦ
11:3 παντὸς ἀνδρὸς ἡ κεφαλὴ ὁ Χριστός ἐστιν ... κεφαλὴ δὲ τοῦ
                                 Χριστοῦ ὁ θεός

In 1 Cor 3:23, as in 11:3, Paul chose to anchor a truth in the widest possible theological framework by adding the corresponding affirmation

---

6.   See below, pp. 141, 176, 200–201.

"Christ is of God." For Paul, a relationship to Christ is the necessary con-text for all spiritual life, and Christ is crucial because of his relationship to God. In the same way, the argument of 1 Cor 15:21–28, 57 proceeds from death in Adam to life in Christ and declares that the reigning Christ will hand the kingdom over to God the Father. In this case, because Paul is distinguishing between the persons of the Trinity, he specified "God even the Father" (τῷ θεῷ καὶ πατρί 15:24). In both of these cases Paul could have concluded his argument without appealing to Christ's relationship to God, but his appeal adds theological depth to his argument by show-ing its relationship to ultimate significance. Paul follows this same pattern in introducing his discussion of the practical problem of disgraceful head coverings for men and women. He lays a foundation in 11:3 by identify-ing the relationships affected by their head coverings. By adding the third clause, Paul shows that these relationships are ultimately rooted in Christ's relationship to God.

WHAT DOES "HEAD" (κεφαλή) MEAN?

The majority view in recent scholarship has shifted to understand "head" (κεφαλή) in this passage to mean "source"[7] rather than "authority,"

---

7. The translation "source" is advocated by scholars, such as the following in these works: R. W. Allison, "Let Women Be Silent in the Churches (1 Cor. 14:33b–36): What Did Paul Really Say, and What Did it Mean?" *JSNT* 32 (1988): 27–60, 33; Stephan Bedale, "The Meaning of κεφαλή in the Pauline Epistles," *JTS* NS 5 (1954): 211–15; Gilbert Bilezikian, *Beyond Sex Roles: What the Bible Says about a Woman's Place in Church and Family* (2nd ed.; Grand Rap-ids: Baker, 1985), 215–52; Colin Brown, "Head," in *NIDNTT* 2:160; Judy L. Brown, *Women Ministers according to Scripture* (Kearney, Nebr.: Morris, 1996), 213–15, 246; F. F. Bruce, *1 and 2 Corinthians* (NCBC; London: Marshall, Morgan & Scott, 1971), 103; Brendan Byrne, *Paul and the Christian Woman* (Homebush, NSW, Australia: St. Paul, 1988), 42; Raymond F. Col-lins, *First Corinthians* (SP; Collegeville, Minn.: Liturgical, 1999), 405; Terrence Alexander Crain, "The Linguistic Background to the Metaphoric Use of κεφαλή in the New Testament" (B.D. Honours Thesis, Murdoch University, 1990; probably the most thorough investigation); P. DeJong and D. R. Wilson, *Husband & Wife: The Sexes in Scripture and Society* (Grand Rapids: Zondervan, 1979), 148–53; Joël Delobel, "1 Cor 11:2–16: Towards a Coherent Explanation," in *L'apôtre Paul: Personnalité, style et conception du ministère* (ed. A. Vanhoye; BETL 73; Leuven: Leuven Univ./Peeters, 1986), 377–78; D. Ellul, "'Sois belle et tais-toi!' Est-ce vraiment ce que Paul a dit? A propos de I Co 11, 2–16," *FoiVie* 88 (1989): 52; Fee, *First Corinthians*, 502–5; Elisa-beth S. Fiorenza, *In Memory of Her: A Feminist Theological Reconstruction of Christian Origins* (New York: Crossroad, 1983), 229; J. Massyngberde Ford, "Biblical Material Relevant to the Ordination of Women," *JES* 10 (1973): 669–94, 680; Kevin Giles, *Women and Their Ministry: A Case for Equal Ministries in the Church Today* (East Malvern, Victoria, Australia: Dove, 1977), 38; David J. Hamilton, "I Commend to You Our Sister: An Inductive Study of the Difficult Passages Related to the Ministry of Women, 1 Corinthians 11:2–16, 1 Corinthians 14:26–40, and 1 Timothy 2:1–15" (M.A. thesis, University of the Nations, 1996), 186–96; Richard A. Horsley, *1 Corinthians* (Nashville: Abingdon, 1998), 153; E. M. Howe, *Women and Church Leadership* (Grand Rapids: Zondervan, 1982), 60; L. Ann Jervis, "'But I Want You To Know ...': Paul's Midrashic Intertextual Response to the Corinthian Worshipers (1 Cor 11:2–16),"

including many who argue that Paul believed men should have authority over women in social relationships.[8]

With the exception of many of the early patristic commentators, however, the vast majority of commentators before Barrett and Conzelmann interpreted κεφαλή in 11:3 as "authority," and a few versions specifically identify these as authority relationships (CEV, GWT, LB, TEV, TNT). One reason for the popularity of this interpretation is that in English, German, and Hebrew (and numerous other languages)[9] the most common metaphorical meaning of "head" is "leader." For example, "the heads of the tribes of Israel" are their leaders. Interpreters who in their native tongue associate metaphorical uses of "head" with "leader" naturally make this association when reading this passage. The translation "head" in English implies a hierarchical structure of authority and the corresponding obligation of the subordinate to submit to that authority. Readers assuming this meaning typically interpret the woman's head covering as a garment symbolizing subordination. Because this interpretation of κεφαλή to mean authority supports the subordination of women to men, a position that has enormous social consequences, it requires close examination.

Fifteen key reasons favor interpreting κεφαλή as "source" rather than "authority" here.

JBL 112 (1993): 240; Else Kähler, *Die Frau in den paulinischen Briefen unter besonderer Berucksichtigung des Begriffes der Unterordnung* (Zürich: Gotthelf, 1960): 52–53; Catherine C. Kroeger, "The Classical Concept of Head as 'Source'," appendix III of *Equal to Serve: Women and Men in the Church and Home*, by Gretchen G. Hull (Old Tappan, N.J.: Revell, 1987), 267–83; Meier, "Veiling of Hermeneutics," 217; Berkeley and Alvera Mickelsen, "The 'Head' of the Epistles," *CT* 25, no. 4 (February 20, 1981): 20–22 and "What Does *Kephalē* Mean in the New Testament?" in *Women, Authority and the Bible* (ed. Alvera Mickelsen; Downers Grove, Ill.: InterVarsity Press, 1986), 97–110; Mount, "Interpolation," 331; Jerome Murphy-O'Connor, "Sex and Logic in 1 Corinthians 11:2–16," *CBQ* 42 (1980): 490–92; idem, "1 Corinthians 11:2–16 Once Again," 269; idem, *1 Corinthians* (Wilmington, Del.: Michael Glazier, 1979), 108; P. B. Payne, "What Does *Kephalē* Mean in the New Testament? Response," in *Women, Authority*, 118–32; Ridderbos, *Paul*, 379–82; C. J. Roetzel, *The Letters of Paul: Conversations in Context* (Atlanta: John Knox, 1975), 2; Letha Scanzoni and Nancy Hardesty, *All We're Meant to Be: A Biblical Approach to Women's Liberation* (Waco, Tex.: Word, 1974), 30–31; Heinrich Schlier, "κεφαλή," *TDNT* 3:673–81; Robin Scroggs, "Eschatological Woman," 298–302; idem, "Paul and the Eschatological Woman: Revisited," *JAAR* 42 (1974): 534 n. 8; Spencer, *Beyond the Curse*, 104; C. Vander Stichele, "1 Kor 11,3: een sleutel tot de interpretatie van 1 Kor 11,2–16?" (S.T.L. diss., Leuven University, 1985), 145–62; Soards, *1 Corinthians*, 228–29; Nigel Watson, *The First Epistle to the Corinthians* (London: Epworth, 1992), 111–12; Don Williams, *The Apostle Paul and Women in the Church* (Ventura, Calif.: Regal, 1977), 64; J. J. Williams, "The Man/Woman Relationship in the NT," *Chm* 91 (1977): 41–42; Ben Witherington III, *Women in the Earliest Churches* (SNTSMS 59; Cambridge: Cambridge Univ. Press, 1988), 84–85; idem, *Women and the Genesis of Christianity* (Cambridge: Cambridge Univ. Press, 1990), 167–68.

8.   E.g., Ridderbos, *Paul*, 379–82; C. K. Barrett, *The First Epistle to the Corinthians* (HNTC; New York: Harper & Row, 1968), 249; S. Bedale, "Meaning of κεφαλή," 211–15.

9.   In Latin *caput* is used both for "the origin, source, spring" and for "a leader, chief, guide."

1. The Greek OT (LXX) shows that most of its translators did not regard "head" (κεφαλή) as an appropriate word to convey "leader." In order to translate the Hebrew metaphorical use of "head" (ראש) where it means "leader," this diverse group of OT translators naturally would want to choose a word that means "head" and can also be used metaphorically to mean "leader." The LXX translators overwhelmingly (in 226 of 239 instances) chose κεφαλή to translate literal instances of "head." Yet in only 6 of 171 instances where "head" (ראש) may convey "leader" did they translate it with the metaphor κεφαλή in a way that clearly means leader.[10] In contrast, the NASB, reflecting the natural metaphorical use of "head" to convey "leader" in English, translates 115 of these 171 instances "head."[11]

---

10. The six are: Judg 11:11; 2 Kgdms (2 Sam) 22:44; Ps 17:43(44) = MT 18:44; Isa 7:8a (Rahlfs lists it only as added by Origen to match the MT, but it is also in B 1009B, lines 11–12), 9b; Lam 1:5. In all but the Isa 7:8a, 9a cases, however, κεφαλή would not be metaphorical if εἰς in εἰς κεφαλήν means "As, expressing equivalence" (Dana and Mantey, *Grammar*, 103); cf. on the use of εἰς for "as": "εἰς (like normal Greek ὡς) may be added to this predicate: Mt 21:46 εἰς προφήτην (vl. ὡς)" (Nigel Turner, *A Grammar of New Testament Greek.* Vol. III *Syntax* [ed. James Hope Moulton; Edinburgh: T&T Clark, 1963], 247); "*as ... serve as someth*" (BDAG 290 4.d) and BAG 229 8.b. If any of these five are similes, then "head" could be understood literally rather than as a metaphor. Isa 7:8–9 also uses κεφαλή twice to mean "capital city." Payne ("*Kephalē*," 123 n. 35) was probably mistaken to include three others. Not only are they all "head-tail" idioms that require κεφαλή, in each case they are explained in the LXX to mean something other than "leader." The LXX explains the metaphor not in terms of leadership, but "above" (ἐπάνω, Deut 28:13) and "above above" (ἄνω ἄνω, Deut 28:43–44), namely as "top," cf. John Chadwick, *Lexicographica Graeca: Contributions to the Lexicography of Ancient Greek* (Oxford: Clarendon, 1996), 181, 178, possibly top as "the noblest part" (LSJ 945). Isa 9:13 LXX replaces the Hebrew, "palm branch and reed," with "great and small," thereby explaining "head" to mean "great" or "preeminent," not "leader." If it meant "leader," why in 9:14 LXX are "the old men and flatterers" included as the "head" but not "the lying prophets," who are identified, instead, as "the tail"? Isa 9:14 LXX does not translate the Hebrew ראש with "head" (κεφαλή), but with ἀρχή. Delling (TDNT 1:481) notes that in the LXX ἀρχή "usually denotes temporal beginning ... [and the] fairly automatic use of ἀρχή for ראש." Since the context is about God's judgment, they are the beginning of those the Lord takes away from Israel. Three variant readings of "head" meaning leader occur only in one manuscript (A): Judg 10:18; 11:8, 9, all in the space of ten verses. B has εἰς ἄρχοντα in each of these three verses, showing that its translator regarded ἄρχοντα a more appropriate translation than κεφαλή when "head" conveyed the sense of leader. The three A variants can reasonably be attributed to a single scribe who was unaware that this idiom was foreign to Greek and who was probably influenced by the Judg 11:11 translation of "head." These three are excluded since they are not in the older, more standard, LXX texts. Wayne Grudem ("The Meaning of *Kephalē* ['Head']: A Response to Recent Studies," *RBMW* 425–68, 441–42), appeals to one other occurrence, 3 Kgdms (1 Kgs) 8:1, included only in Origen's (d. ca. 254) text, but it means "top," not "leader": "Solomon assembled all the elders of Israel with all the tops (κεφαλάς) of the staffs of the fathers of the sons of Israel lifted up before king Solomon." The term for staffs refers to actual staffs even where the staff is a staff of office or scepter (LSJ 1562). Grudem appeals to BDB 641, but all of its other references to "tribe" use a different word, φυλή, in the LXX, and "tribes" would not make sense here: "with all the heads of the tribes of the fathers of the sons of Israel lifted up." The number 171 does not include instances where κεφαλή means "first" in sequence (1 Chr 12:9; 23:8, 11, 19, 20; 24:21; 26:10 twice, all translated "first" in the NASB) or "top" spacially (e.g., Judg 16:3 NASB).

11. It does not translate ראש "head" in "chief priest." The KJV translates "head" in some passages the NASB did not.

Wayne Grudem states, "the meaning [for 'head,' κεφαλή,] 'ruler, authority over' ... in Greek literature at the time of the New Testament ... was a well-established and recognizable meaning."[12] Cervin, however, analyzes every passage Grudem cites and concludes, "there are so far no clear and unambiguous instances in native Greek literature before the NT where κεφαλή (nor apparently κεφάλαιος ...) is so used. The use of κεφαλή as a personal metaphor for 'leader' first appears in the LXX, and ... this is best explained in terms of Hebrew influence."[13]

Grudem cites with effusive praise a letter from P. W. G. Glare, "κεφαλή is the word normally used to translate the Hebrew ראשׁ, and this does seem frequently to denote leader or chief ... and here it seems perverse to deny authority."[14] The LXX translators, however, almost always chose not to use κεφαλή when ראשׁ means "leader." They did this in spite of a strong tendency in the LXX for "Greek words to extend their range of meaning in an un-Greek way after the Hebrew word they render"[15] and their desire to convey the sacred text in Greek as closely as possible to the Hebrew.[16] This is compelling evidence that the vast majority of LXX

---

12. Wayne Grudem, "Does *Kephalē* ('head') Mean 'Source' or 'Authority' in Greek Literature? A Survey of 2,336 Examples," in *The Role Relationship of Men & Women: New Testament Teaching* (Wayne Grudem and George W. Knight III; Chicago: Moody, 1985), 49–80, 80.
13. Richard S. Cervin, "ΠΕΡΙ ΤΟΥ ΚΕΦΑΛΗ: A Rejoinder" (unpublished, 1991), 23, cf. 1–39, and also Cervin's "Does Κεφαλή mean 'Source' or 'Authority Over' in Greek Literature? A Rebuttal," *TJ* 10 NS (1989): 85–112. Cf. the similar assessment by Bilezikian ("A Critical Examination of Wayne Grudem's Treatment of *Kephalē*, in Ancient Greek Texts," in *Beyond Sex Roles* [2nd ed.; Grand Rapids: Baker, 1989], 215–52). Cervin also addresses passages raised by Joseph A. Fitzmyer in "Another Look at ΚΕΦΑΛΗ in 1 Corinthians 11.3," *NTS* 35 (1989): 503–11, and later in "*Kephalē* in I Corinthians 11:3," *Int* 47 (1993): 52–59. Wayne Grudem, "Over Fifty Examples of *Kephalē* ('Head') Meaning 'Authority Over/Ruler' in Ancient Literature," EF 544–51, 547, cites four passages from Aquila's second-century AD translation of the Hebrew Scriptures in support of "head" meaning "leader," but this is useless for establishing Greek usage since, as Alfred Rahlfs (*Septuaginta* [Stuttgart: Bibelanstalt, 1949], 1:xxiv) states, Aquila "rendered every detail of the sacred Text as precisely as possible into Greek, and he did not shrink from perpetrating the most appalling outrages to the whole essence of the Greek language" (cf. also xxv–xxvii). P. G. W. Glare also disagrees with many of the examples that Grudem says mean "leader": "Where I would agree with Cervin is that in many of the examples, and I think all the Plutarch ones, we are dealing with similes or comparisons and the word itself [κεφαλή] is used in a literal sense" (cited in Wayne Grudem, "The Meaning of κεφαλή ['Head']: An Evaluation of New Evidence, Real and Alleged," EF 552–99, 588). Grudem attempted to refute Cervin's "Κεφαλή" with his "Response to Recent Studies," RBMW 426–49. On May 1, 1991, Cervin submitted his "Rejoinder" to *Trinity Journal*, but its editor, Douglas J. Moo, refused to publish it even after devoting two articles totaling 111 pages to Grudem's view and only 34 pages to Cervin's. Cf. similar censorship above, p. 29 and below pp. 356 n. 47 and 411 n. 50.
14. Dated April 14, 1997. Varyingly cited with italics added by Grudem (EF 207, 551, 587).
15. Peter Walters, *The Text of the Septuagint: Its Corruptions and Their Emendations* (ed. D. W. Gooding; Cambridge: Cambridge Univ. Press, 1973), 143.
16. E.g., "This anomaly is due to the literal following of the Hebrew text" (F. C. Conybeare and St. George Stock, *Grammar of Septuagint Greek with Selected Readings, Vocabularies, and Updated*

This is compelling evidence that the vast majority of LXX translators did not regard κεφαλή as appropriate to convey the metaphorical meaning "leader."[17] Correspondingly, it would probably never occur to Paul's typical Greek readers that "head" (κεφαλή) might mean "leader" or "authority over." Murphy-O'Conner concludes, "There is simply no basis for the assumption that a Hellenized Jew would instinctively give *kephalē* the meaning 'one having authority over someone.'"[18]

2. "Authority" is not a well-established meaning of κεφαλή. Although the most exhaustive Greek lexicon, LSJ, lists forty-eight figurative translations for κεφαλή, neither it nor its supplement by Renehan,[19] nor the lexicons by Moulton and Milligan, Friedrich Preisigke, Pierre Chantraine, S. C. Woodhouse, or any of the thirteen additional lexicons cited by Cervin[20] give even one example of κεφαλή that implies authority. Schlier's article in the *TDNT* concludes that in secular usage this word "is not employed for the head of a society. This is first found in the sphere of the Gk. OT."[21] Four prominent specialists in early Greek literature, David Armstrong and Tom Palaima of the University of Texas at Austin and Michael Wigodsky and Mark Edwards of Stanford University, confirmed to this author that authority, leader, or any related meaning was not a standard meaning of κεφαλή.[22] Apart from a few NT lexicons, the vast majority of Greek lexicons list no such meaning.[23]

BAG (431) lists only one instance in secular Greek of κεφαλή used "in the case of living beings, to denote superior rank," that is, "Zosimus of

of the LXX is plainly not normal Greek in many places" (J. A. L. Lee, *A Lexical Study of the Septuagint Version of the Pentateuch* [Chico, Calif.: Scholars Press, 1983], 1).

17.   Cf. the same argument by Mickelsen ("*Kephalē*," 100–104), Bilezikian (*Beyond Sex Roles*, 239) and Cervin ("Κεφαλή," 95–96, 104), especially in Cervin's "Rejoinder," 9–13.

18.   Murphy-O'Connor, "Sex," 492.

19.   R. Renehan, *Greek Lexicographical Notes: A Critical Supplement to the Greek-English Lexicon of Liddell-Scott-Jones* (Hypomnemata 45; Göttingen: Vandenhoeck & Ruprecht, 1975), 120.

20.   Cervin, "Κεφαλή," 86–87.

21.   *TDNT* 3:674.

22.   Conversations at Stanford Univ., September 28, 1984; with Armstrong, correspondence with author, 1984; with Palaima, telephone conversation with author, September 19, 2008.

23.   Exceptions are Franz Passow, *Handwörterbuch der griechischen Sprache* (2 vols.; Leipzig: Vogel, 1831), 1:1270, listing *Hauptperson* but without any examples; H. van Herwerden, *Lexicon graecum suppletorium et dialecticum* (2 vols.; Leiden: Sijthoff, 1910), 797, "*dux*," which cites only the fourth century AD Libanius, *Orationes* 52.18; and Evangelinus Apostolides Sophocles, *Greek Lexicon of the Roman and Byzantine Periods (from B.C. 146 to AD 1100)* (New York: Frederick Ungar, 1887), 662, that gives only one example, from AD 952. D. Dhimitdrakou ([9 vols.; Athens: n.p., 1933–1950], 5:3880) lists the meaning "leader" as medieval. Liddell and Scott's seventh edition says the meaning "chief" is Byzantine. The ninth edition of LSJ excludes Byzantine literature (as noted on p. x).

Ashkelon [500 AD] hails Demosth. as his master: ὦ θεία κεφαλή." Besides Zosimus being far too late to confirm usage in Paul's day, Demosthenes (384–322 BC) could not have had a position of authority over Zosimus since Demosthenes had died over 800 years earlier. Furthermore, Mark Edwards notes that this salutation implies dignity, not authority.[24] BDAG (542) adds two more secular references, but neither of these denotes superior rank. Ps.-Aristotle (*De mundo* 6.4) does not even contain the word κεφαλή![25] Artemidorus (*Onir.* 4.24) states, "Furthermore, whatever signified one thing symbolizes reciprocally the very thing by which it is signified.... A man who dreamt that his father was sick got pains in his head. You already know from the first book that the head symbolizes the father."[26] This text explicitly states "that the head symbolizes the father." It states nothing about head symbolizing "superior rank" or "leader." Artemidorus's first book identifies the key resemblance between "head" and father, instead, as "source" since "the head [κεφαλή] is the source [αἴτιος] of life and light for the whole body" (1.2).

    C. K. Barrett concludes that the meaning "ruler ... was not a native meaning of the Greek word."[27] Unfortunately, some advocates of male authority have misrepresented the lexical evidence, making such blatantly false statements as, "All the lexical evidence suggests that the word head means authority,"[28] and, "All the recognized lexicons (dictionaries) for ancient Greek, or their editors, now give *kephalē* the meaning 'person in authority over' or something similar; but none give the meaning 'source.'"[29]

    Modern science regards the brain as the control center of the body and so reinforces the metaphorical use of head for leader, but this was not the consensus in ancient Greek thought. Although some medical writers argued that the brain is the seat of cognition, Plato "moved the command

24. Edwards stated this to this author at Stanford University, September 28, 1984. Similarly, LSJ 945 identifies a virtually identical salutation also from the fourth century as referring to "the noblest part." Cf. Payne, "*Kephalē*," 120.
25. E. A. Forster only uses "head" in his translation. See his *Aristotle (Ps.) De Mundo* (Oxford: Clarendon, 1914), 398a, 8.
26. Robert J. White, *The Interpretation of Dreams* (Park Ridge, N.J.: Noyes, 1975), 197, from *Onir.* 1.2. The standard Greek edition is Roger A. Pack, *Artemidori Daldiani Onirocriticon Libri V* (Leipzig: Teubner, 1963), 260.
27. Barrett, *First Corinthians*, 248.
28. Thomas R. Schreiner, "Head Coverings, Prophecies and the Trinity: I Corinthians 11:2–16," *RBMW* 124–39, 486 n. 9. He now, however, writes in "Women in Ministry," in *Two Views on Women in Ministry* (ed. James R. Beck and Craig L. Blomberg; Grand Rapids: Zondervan, 2001), 177–232, 228 n. 99, "Probably both 'authority over' and 'source' are involved" in 1 Cor 11:3.
29. Grudem, EF 206.

centre to the heart (*Tim.* 70a ff.), followed by Aristotle and Diocles (3) of Carystus. The debate continued until Galen reasserted the very early primacy of the liver in the 2nd cent. AD."[30] The ancient Greek world, exemplified by Paul's use of "heart,"[31] commonly believed that the heart, not the head, was the center of emotions and spirit, the "central governing place of the body."[32] Aristotle held that the heart was not only the seat of control but also the seat of intelligence.

Classicist Michael Wigodsky of Stanford is probably correct that many, even of the doctors with the most advanced anatomical understanding of the brain, did not really believe that the brain exerted more control over the body than the heart.[33] Such a notion seemed to contradict the nearly universal belief that, since the life is in the blood, the heart must be the center of life. In *De rerum natura* 3.138–145 Lucretius (ca. 97–54 BC) argues for the Epicurean distinction: "the rational power, which we call the mind and the intellect ... has its fixed place in the central area of the breast, because this is where fear and dread surge up, this is the vicinity in which joys caress us; here therefore is the mind and the intellect. The rest of the soul, distributed throughout the whole body, obeys, and moves at the mind's impulse and behest."[34] Thus, it is hardly surprising that the idea of authority was not normally associated with the word for "head" in Greek thought.

3. In contrast, "source" is an established meaning for κεφαλή listed from the earliest Greek lexicons to the present.[35] Galen (second century

---

30. J. T. Vallance, "Anatomy and Physiology," *OCD* (rev. 3rd ed.; 2003), 82–85, 83. E.g., Plato, "within the chest — or 'thorax,' as it is called — they fastened the mortal kind of soul ... between the midriff and the neck [comes] ... the word of command from the citadel of reason.... [70b] And the heart ... they appointed ... their best part to be the leader of them all" (*Tim.* 70a, b, 180–83 [LCL]).
31. Cf. below, pp. 128, 283–90.
32. Aristotle, *Mot. an.* 2.703a.35 (LCL). Aristotle wrote in *Part. an.* 3.4.665b and 3.10.672b.17 of the heart as the "primary or dominating part ... the centre wherein abides the sensory soul."
33. Wigodsky, conversations with the author at Stanford Univ., September 27 and October 4, 1984.
34. P. Michael Brown, trans., *Lucretius: De Rerum Natura III* (Warminster: Aris & Phillips, 1997), 28–29.
35. From the twelfth century Johannes Zonaras, *Lexicon,* ed. Johann August Henrich Tittmann (Leipzig: S. Siegfr. Lebr. Crusii, 1808); Henri Estienne, *Thesaurus graecae linguae,* 8 vols. (Geneva: Henr. Stephani Oliva, 1572; reprinted Paris: A. F. Didot, 1831–1865); Guillaume Budé, Jacobus Tusanus, Konrad Gesner, Hadrianus Junius, *Dictionarium Graecolatinum* (Basil: Henri C. Petrina, 1577); LSJ (first published 1843); Franz Passow, *Handwörterbuch der griechischen Sprache* (rev. ed.; Leipzig: Rost, Palm, and Kreussler, 1847); C. Schenkl, *Vocabolario Greco-Italiano* (Bologona: A. Mondadori, n.d.); Rudolf Bölting, *Dicionário Grego-Português* (Rio De Janeiro: Imprensa National, 1941); V. C. F. Rost, *Griechisch-Deutsches Wörterbuch* (Braunschweig: Westerman, 1959). Cf. also the affirmation of the meaning of "source" in C. Brown, "Head," in *NIDNTT* 2:160. *Pace* Grudem, "Real and Alleged," *EF* 590, writing that the

AD), in *On the Doctrines of Hippocrates and Plato* 6.3.21.4, identifies the "head" (in the singular) of a river as its "source":

> The greater is source of the smaller, just as the spring is greater than the channels into which it is divided. And yet some persons have reached such an extreme of absurdity that they suppose that what follows the source is greater than the source [τῆς ἀρχῆς]. They are misled by rivers, which are very small at their springs but increase as they advance, although this is not always necessarily the case. Some rivers grow larger, as we should expect, when tributaries flow into them, while some decrease in size as channels are separated off. No river that comes from a single spring is smaller at its head [τὴν κεφαλήν] than it is thereafter.[36]

Galen's *De locis affectis* 3.12 notes that whirlpools in a river might "rather arise when they are warmed by the sun or its source [singular τὴν κεφαλήν] is heated in some other way."[37] Herodotus, *History* 4.90, says regarding the Tearus river, "Its springs are thirty-eight in number, some cold and some hot, all flowing from the same rock," and 4.91 quotes Darius, "From the sources [κεφαλαί] of the river Tearus flows the best and fairest of all river waters."[38] "Heads" in conjunction with "springs" confirm that the term "heads" means "sources" here. *The Greek Anthology* also quotes this, "The sources [κεφαλαί] of the river Tearus supply the best water" (Epigrams 703 9:388–89 [LCL]). Hippocrates (fifth century BC) also uses κεφαλή metaphorically in *Coac.* 498 to identify the "origins" of muscle (τῶν μυῶν αἱ κεφαλαί).[39]

LSJ is "the only lexicon that mentioned the meaning 'source'" for κεφαλή. In contrast, see the detailed investigation of Catherine Clark Kroeger, "'Head' as 'Source,'" 267–83, and her "Toward an Understanding of Ancient Conceptions of 'Head,'" *Priscilla Papers* 20 no. 3 (Summer 2006): 4–8.

36. Phillip de Lacy, *Galen: On the Doctrines of Hippocrates and Plato: Edition, Translation and Commentary: Second Part: Books VI-IX* (Corpus Medicorum Graecorum vol. 5 pt. 4 sec. 1–2 no. 2; Berlin: Akademie-Verlag, 1980), 378–79: ποταμὸς δὲ οὐδεὶς ἐκ μιᾶς ὁρμώμενος πηγῆς ἐλάττονα τὴν κεφαλὴν ἔχει τῶν ἐφεξῆς.

37. C. G. Kühn, ed., *Claudii Galeni Opera Omnia* (Medicorum Graecorum Opera Quae Exstant 8; Hildesheim: Georg Olms, 1965), 202 lines 9–10, συμβαίνει δ' αὐτοῖς ταῦτα μᾶλλον, ὅταν ἡλιωθῶσιν, ἢ πως ἄλλως θερμανθῶσι τὴν κεφαλήν. Kroeger, "Classical Concept," 274, gives a similar translation and cites other examples.

38. Herodotus, 2:292–93 (A. D. Godley, LCL), W. R. Patton also translates κεφαλαί as "sources" in this famous epigram cited in the *The Greek Anthology* 9.703.2 (LCL).

39. LSJ Suppl. (1996), 175; É. Littré, *Oeuvres complètes D'Hippocrate* (Amsterdam: Adolf M. Hakkert, 1978), 5:698.

Metaphorical citations of "head" meaning "source" from Paul's time include Philo, "of all the members of the clan here described Esau is the progenitor, the head [κεφαλή] as it were of the whole creature" (*Prelim. Studies* 61).[40] Philo consistently uses the word "progenitor" (γενάρχης) to refer to the founder or first ancestor of a family,[41] as do other writers when referring to dead people who were the founder of a clan. This instance cannot mean "ruler of created beings" since this "sense invariably refers to a god"[42] and since Esau is dead and has no authority over the clan that continues. The core semantic value of "progenitor" is "the source from which something develops; originator,"[43] not merely that something is first, and certainly not "authority."

Philo in *Rewards* 125 identifies "the virtuous one, whether single man or people, will be the head [κεφαλή, explained by the editor as 'the source of spiritual life'] of the human race and all the others like the limbs of a body which draw their life from the forces in the head [κεφαλή]."[44] In both of these passages from Philo the person called "head" is not in authority over the group identified but is their source of life.[45]

Apoc. Mos. 19.3 calls "lust the head [κεφαλή] of every sin," with the obvious meaning "source/origin."[46] Similarly, *T. Reu.* 2.2 states, "For seven spirits are established against mankind, and they are the sources [lit., 'heads'] of the deeds of youth."[47]

When Artemidorus Daldiani, *Onir.* 1.35, writes, "If a man dreams that his head [κεφαλή] has been taken away (= beheaded),"[48] he is not

40. Philo, 4:488–89 (Colson, LCL). Grudem ("Response to Recent Studies," *RBMW* 454) erroneously calls this use of "head" a simile. Philo does not say "as a head," but that Esau is head "as it were of the whole creature."

41. Philo, *The Preliminary Studies* 133 (of Moses or Levi); *Who is the Heir* 279 (of Abraham); *On Dreams* 1.167 (of Abraham, Isaac, and Jacob).

42. Cervin, "ΚΕΦΑΛΗ," 28–29: of Zeus in Callimachus *Fragment* 36 and in Babrius 142.3; of Kronos in *Orphic Hymn* 13.8; of god in the *Corpus Hermeticum* 13:21. *Pace* Grudem, "Real and Alleged," *EF* 579, and "Response to Recent Studies," *RBMW* 454–55.

43. David B. Guralnik, ed., *Webster's New World Dictionary of the American Language: Second College Edition* (Cleveland: William Collins and World, 1974), 1135.

44. Philo, 8:389 (Colson; LCL). Grudem, in "2,336 Examples," although stating on p. 65 that he used the Loeb edition "where available; otherwise standard text and translations were used," on p. 74 did not give the Loeb translation "which draw their life from the forces in the head." Rather, he gave the translation "which are animated by the powers in the head." Grudem also omitted the Loeb "source" explanation.

45. *Pace* Grudem's allegation "that there is no instance of 'source' *apart from authority*" in "Response to Recent Studies," *RBMW* 464–65; cf. "Real and Alleged," *EF* 595–96

46. *APOT* 2:146. MSS A and B. MS C has "root and beginning/first cause." M. D. Johnson, who titles this work, *Life of Adam and Eve [Apocalypse of Moses]*, translates κεφαλή "origin" in *OTP* 2:279.

47. Charlesworth, *OTP* 1:782. *APOT* 2:297 notes MSS β–f g A ͣ S have "head" (singular).

48. Literal translation by the author; cf. White, *Dreams*, 34; Pack, *Artemidori*, 43.

speaking simply of a physical head.[49] He uses "head" to convey the met-aphorical meaning "source," namely, "a man dreams that his *source* [in this case, his parents] has been taken away." He makes it unmistakably clear that he intends this when he explains that this dream "is inauspi-cious both for a man with parents and a man with children. For the head [κεφαλή] resembles parents in that it is the cause [αἰτίαν] of one's living [τοῦ ζῆν]."[50] Artemidorus explicitly identifies the dreamer's parents as the "head" of the dreamer.[51]

This use of "head" fulfills the standard definition of metaphor since it "is applied to something to which it is not literally applicable [one's par-ents] in order to suggest a resemblance."[52] "Head" here conveys the estab-lished metaphorical meaning "source."[53] Artemidorus in *Onir.* 1.2 confirms this understanding: "Another man dreamt that he was beheaded. In real life, the father of this man, too, died; for just as the head [κεφαλή] is the source [αἴτιος] of life and light for the whole body, he was responsible for the dreamer's life and light.... the head [κεφαλή] indicates one's father."[54] Similarly, *Onir.* 3.66 states, "the head [κεφαλή] signifies the father of the dreamer.... Whenever, then, a poor man who has a rich father dreams that his own head [κεφαλή] has been removed by a lion and that he dies as a result, it is probable that his father will die.... For the head [κεφαλή] represents the father; the removal of the head, the death of the father."[55] Artemidorus explicitly identifies the dreamer's father as his own "head."[56]

Orphic fragment 168 records the widely quoted metaphor: "Zeus is the head, Zeus the middle, and from Zeus all things exist (Ζεὺς κεφαλή, Ζεὺς

---

49. *Pace* Grudem, "Artemidorus ... is simply speaking of a physical head" ("Response to Recent Studies," *RBMW* 456).
50. White, *Dreams*, 34; Pack, *Artemidori*, 43.
51. *Pace* Grudem, "no person is in these texts *called* 'head'" ("Response to Recent Studies," *RBMW* 455).
52. *Webster's Encyclopedic Unabridged Dictionary of the English Language* (New York: Random House, 1996), 1207.
53. This metaphor is easy to understand since the head is the source of nourishment for the body through the mouth and the source of sensations: of sight through eyes, sound through the ears, smell through the nose, taste through the tongue, and other sensations through what we now understand as the brain. Artemidorus confirms this understanding in *Onir.* 1.34, "the whole body depends upon the head," and in *Onir.* 1.35, "the head is, as it were, the house of the senses.... For the head, once it is separated from the body ... the rest of the body no longer feels pain." White, *Dreams*, 34–35.
54. White, *Dreams*, 16–17; Pack, *Artemidori*, 7.
55. White, *Dreams*, 175–76; Pack, *Artemidori*, 234.
56. *Pace* Grudem, "no person is in these texts *called* 'head'" ("Response to Recent Studies," *RBMW* 455).

μέσσα, Διὸς δ᾽ ἐκ πάντα τέτυκται)."⁵⁷ The final verb τέτυκται is from τεύχω, which LSJ 1784 defines, "*cause, bring to pass* ... of Zeus ... τέτυκται *there exists*," and so identifies Zeus as the maker from whom all things come into existence. Thus, for this saying to convey a symmetrical meaning, "head" must convey the meaning "source." The substitute final verb τελεῖται, the passive of τελέω, "are fulfilled" (cf. LSJ 1772), in *Orphic fragment* 21a⁵⁸ also favors that "head" means "source" to preserve the saying's symmetry. This line containing "head" is its primary context for meaning, and the myriad references to Zeus as the source through whom things come into existence reinforce this meaning.⁵⁹

Furthermore, there is a natural logical progression from Zeus being first in the previous statement to Zeus being the source. The fact that several manuscripts of this well-attested saying "have ἀρχή [source] instead of κεφαλή adds to its significance."⁶⁰ A scholion identifying it "as [the] producing cause" (ὡς ποιητικὸν αἴτιον)⁶¹ adds to its contextual evidence that κεφαλή here means source. Fitzmyer argues that each of the metaphors cited above mean "source" and concludes, "These examples show that *kephalē* could indeed be used in the sense of 'source.'"⁶²

Irenaeus (writing ca. AD 175 – 195) in *Haer.* 5.3, states "that the Demiurge imagined that he created all these things of himself, while in reality he made them in conjunction with the productive power of Achamoth. ..."

---

57. Otto Kern, *Orphicorum Fragmenta* (Berlin: Weidman, 1963), 2:201 and his citations on pp. 91–92, 201–2.
58. Kern, *Orphicorum Fragmenta* II, 91.
59. Barth, *Ephesians*, 1:185, documents an extensive tradition identifying the supreme god as the "head," namely, as the "originator and power source" of the universe. These include Orphic Fragments 167–88, Plato's *Timaeus* 30B–34B, Cleanthes' *Hymn to Zeus* 537, Stoic philosophers such as Cicero and Seneca, *Odes Sol.* 17.16–17, *Evangelium Veritatis*, Cod. Jung 18.29b–40a, the Magic Papyri such as Leiden Papyrus 5, the Naassene Sermon, and on through Mandaean literature. BAG 111 cites Ael. Aristides 43,9 K. = 1 p. 3 D, "ἀρχὴ ἁπάντων Ζεύς τε καὶ ἐκ Διὸς πάντα."
60. Barrett, *First Corinthians*, 248; Plutarch (ca. AD 46–120), *Def. orac.* 436D.8–9 (48.379.T.9): "Zeus the source (ἀρχή), Zeus the middle, Zeus through whom all things come into existence," substitutes πέλονται (LSJ 1338, "come into existence") for τέτυκται, confirming that ἀρχή means "source." Cf. Plutarch, *Comm. not.* 31.385; Achilles Tatius (third century AD), *fr.* 81.32–33 in Ernest Maass, *Commentariorum in Aratum reliquiae* (Berlin: Weidmann, 1898), 81; Proclus AD 410–485, *Theology* 6.8.363; *TDNT* 3:676. Cf. more citations of this saying with ἀρχή listed in Kroeger, "Classical Concept," 275 n. 45. Similarly, Josephus, *Ag. Ap.* 2.190, describes God as "ἀρχὴ καὶ μέσα καὶ τέλος" (source and middle and completion) of all, then identifies God as the creator. BDAG 138 ἀρχή 3 identifies the meaning of ἀρχή here as "the first cause."
61. In Eusebius, *Praep. ev.* 3.9.2.
62. Fitzmyer, *"Kephalē,"* 54, 58 and "ΚΕΦΑΛΗ," 509. Cervin, "Κεφαλή," 112, also accepts the meaning "source."

she desired to bring him forth possessed of such a character that he should be the head [κεφαλή] and source [ἀρχή] of his own essence, and the absolute ruler over every kind of operation."[63] This saying is quoted by the *Derveni Papyrus*, col. 13, line 12 (fourth century BC);[64] Ps.-Aristotle (*De mundo* 7, 401a.29–30; 3:406 [LCL]); Eusebius (ca. AD 265–339), *Praep. ev.* 3.9; Proclus (AD 410–485), *Commentary on Plato's Timaeus* 1.313.21;[65] and Stobaeus (fifth century AD), *Ecl.* 1.23.[66] Thus, this saying including "head" (κεφαλή) meaning "source" was one of the most widely quoted Greek metaphors spanning the time of Paul and the early church.

All these examples show that "source" is a well-established meaning of κεφαλή. In Paul's day, Philo (*Prelim. Studies* 120) also uses a related word for "head" to mean "sources": The Ten Commandments "are the general heads [κεφάλαια], embracing the vast multitude of particular laws, the roots [ῥίζαι], the sources [ἀρχαί], the perennial fountains [πηγαί] of ordinances" (518–19 [LCL]).

4. Paul refers repeatedly to Christ as κεφαλή in the sense of source of life or nourishment: e.g., Col 1:18, "he is the head [κεφαλή] of the body, the church, who is the ἀρχή," the "origin" (NEB) or "the source of the body's life" (TEV);[67] Col 2:19, "the Head, from[68] whom the whole body ... grows"; Eph 4:15–16, "the Head, that is, Christ. From him the whole body ... grows"[69]; and Eph 5:23, where κεφαλή is in apposition to "Savior," the source of life of the church.[70] Source makes good sense as the meaning of nine[71] of Paul's eleven metaphorical uses of κεφαλή, whereas not one instance can be conclusively demonstrated to mean "authority over."[72]

---

63. ANF 1:322–23 (PG 7:496). Interpreting "head" as "ruler" does not fit "of his own essence."
64. Guilelmus Quandt, *Orphei Hymni* (Zürich: Weidmann, 1973), 15.
65. E. Diehl, ed., Proclus, *Procli Diadochi In Platonis Timaeum commentarii* (3 vols.; Leipzig: Teubner, 1903–1906; repr., Amsterdam: Hakkert, 1965). Thomas Taylor, transl., *Proclus: Proclus' Commentary on the Timaeus of Plato* (Frome: Prometheus Trust, 1998, 1st ed. 1816).
66. TLG, Joannes Stobaeus Anthologus, Work 001, 1.1.23.2–6.
67. Cf. below, pp. 285–89.
68. Cf. BDAG 296–97, ἐκ 3, "denoting origin, cause, motive, reason ... source fr. which someth. flows or comes."
69. This passage is an original inspiration. Nowhere does the OT speak of Israel as "members of God's body." Thus, it cannot be properly argued that "head" here is an allusion to an OT image and so incorporates the Hebrew connotation of "leader". Cf. Marcus Barth, *Ephesians* (2 vols.; AB; Garden City, NY: Doubleday, 1974), 1:184; Gregory W. Dawes, *The Body in Question: Meaning and Metaphor in the Interpretation of Ephesians 5:21–33* (Leiden: Brill, 1998), 147, argues that "head" in 4:15 is a live metaphor for "source of the body's life and growth."
70. Cf. below, pp. 283–90.
71. 1 Cor 11:3 (3x), 4, 5; Eph 4:15; 5:23; Col 1:18; 2:19.
72. The meaning "top" or "crown" fits the remaining two: Eph 1:22 and Col 2:10; cf. Payne, "Kephalē," 118–32.

5. The items listed in 1 Cor 11:3 are not listed in a descending or ascending order of authority, but they are listed chronologically: man came from Christ's creative work, woman came from "the man," Christ came from God in the incarnation. When Paul wanted to make a hierarchical series elsewhere, he did so in a logical sequence, as in 1 Cor 12:28.

6. All attempts at interpreting each of these references to κεφαλή as "authority over" end up with three quite different authority relationships. Hodge admits, "this subordination is very different in its nature in the several cases mentioned. The subordination of the woman to the man is something entirely different from that of the man to Christ; and that again is at an infinite degree more complete than the subordination of Christ to God."[73] In contrast, "source" indicates that from which each came. The article[74] before κεφαλή only in the first clause highlights the special sense in which man came through Christ's creative work.[75]

7. "Source" fits better than "authority" as the meaning of κεφαλή in "the Christ is [ἔστιν] the κεφαλή of every man" (1 Cor 11:3). This statement should lay a foundation that can guide how people should cover their heads. If κεφαλή means authority, it implies that Christ is presently, as the present tense of ἔστιν in this context would then convey,[76] every man's authority. The prominent position of "*every man*" at the start of this statement emphasizes its universal scope.[77] "Authority" does not fit the context since many men in the present time do not acknowledge Christ as their authority, nor is Christ in fact their leader. Christ has not yet "put all his enemies under his feet" (1 Cor 15:25). The same theology is expressed elsewhere in the NT, e.g., Heb 2:8 – 9, "At present we do not see everything subject to him."

---

73. Charles Hodge, *Commentary on the First Epistle to the Corinthians* (Grand Rapids: Eerdmans, 1994; repr., 1969), 206; cf. R. C. H. Lenski, *The Interpretation of St. Paul's First and Second Epistle to the Corinthians* (Columbus: Lutheran Books, 1935), 439; Leon Morris, *The First Epistle of Paul to the Corinthians* (London: Tyndale, 1958), 151.
74. Since Greek has no indefinite article, even though the Greek article is most closely equivalent to the English definite article, this work uses the technical term "article" when referring to a definite article.
75. Cf. Turner, *Syntax*, 183, "the art. may be inserted if the predicate noun is supposed to be a unique or notable instance."
76. This is true whether one interprets ἔστιν here as timeless (always applying) or as describing the present time. Cf. BDF §318. The specialized uses of the present tense that might not apply to the present time do not fit this context if κεφαλή means "authority," cf. BDF §319 – 24; Robertson, *Grammar*, 864 – 70.
77. Cf. A. Robertson and A. Plummer, *First Epistle of St Paul to the Corinthians* (ICC; Edinburgh: Clark, 1914), 229; H. A. W. Meyer, *Epistles to the Corinthians* (New York: Funk & Wagnalls, 1884), 246.

Furthermore, Paul implies that Christ alone is "the" κεφαλή of every man by adding an article to it in contrast to the other two occurrences of κεφαλή in verse 3. Christ is not in the present, however, the only authority over men, but Christ as creator is uniquely the source of every man. Paul foreshadows this theme shortly before in 1 Cor 8:6 by writing about "Christ, through whom all things came." Not only does Paul return to the creation theme in 1 Cor 11:7, 8, and 12, this theme is foundational to his whole argument against hairstyles that repudiate marriage.

The "authority" interpretation fails to explain a distinctive sense in which Christ is the authority over every *male* person, as required by the Greek word usually translated "man" here, ἀνδρός. Why would Paul say that Christ is the authority of every male human being? Is there any sense in which Christ would be the authority over men but not over women? If so, that would undermine the universal lordship of Christ. The English translation "every man" conceals the awkwardness of the "authority" interpretation since, unlike ἀνδρός, "man" can refer to both sexes. The "source" interpretation does not have this problem because of Christ's role in first creating man,[78] then woman from the side of man. Unlike a difference in authority relationships, this temporal difference in creation does not undermine either the authority of Christ or the equality of man and woman as affirmed in 1 Cor 11:11–12.

8. "Source" fits better than "authority" as the meaning of κεφαλή in "the man [with an article] is κεφαλή of woman."[79] As with each of the three statements in verse 3, the second member is highlighted with an article: ὁ Χριστός, ὁ ἀνήρ, ὁ θεός. Since in each of the other cases an article identifies a specific entity (Christ, God) and since the most common use of an article is to specify, it is most natural to understand "the man," as in 11:12 as a reference to "the man," Adam, from whom woman came. This fits perfectly with the established meaning of κεφαλή (head) as

---

78. Since the source of all men goes back to the creation of Adam, it is appropriate to regard the temporal event of Adam's creation as the source of all men. This does not imply that Christ is not the source of woman. Verse 11:12 implies that God is also the source of every woman. This shift of subject from Christ to God shows Paul's high Christology.

79. *Pace* the CEV translation of the Greek article with "man" as an English indefinite article and adding "over" to suggest an authority relationship: "a man is the head over a woman." Phillips, "a man is the head of the woman," changes both the definite and the indefinite into the opposite! The NIV adds a definite article to "woman" and removes it from "the man": "the head of the woman is man." If husband and wife had been in view (as in the LB, NRSV, RSV, TEV), both should have an article, but here only "man" has an article.

source since Adam was the source from whom the woman was taken and since both verse 8 and verse 12 refer to this event.

The "authority" interpretation does not fit the creation accounts of Genesis, since they do not teach that God gave Adam authority over either Eve or women in general. The first statement of man ruling over woman is a description of one of the consequences of the fall in Gen 3:16. Even if "the man" is understood as generic for all men, the authority interpretation is still problematic. The Bible never states that all women are to be under the authority of all men or should submit to all men. At times a woman should not even submit to her own husband. God judged Sapphira for supporting her husband's lie (Acts 5:1–11). Paul probably knew about this since its author, Luke, was his fellow traveler. If κεφαλή means "authority" in 1 Cor 11:3, it could be concluded that women should *not* pray or prophesy in public, *contra* 11:5. Furthermore, verses 11–12's affirmation that man and woman are not separate seems to be incompatible with the "authority" interpretation.

Cyril of Alexandria's *De recta fide ad Pulcheriam et Eudociam* 5².131D states, "Because head [κεφαλή] means source [ἀρχή] ... man is the head [κεφαλή] of woman, for she was taken out of him."[80] Theodore of Mopsuestia's *Commentary on 1 Corinthians* explains the man as head of woman "since she had taken her being from him." Many other Greek fathers, such as those cited below in point 15, also explained κεφαλή here as "source."

9. "Source" fits better than "authority" as the meaning of κεφαλή in "God [with an article] is the κεφαλή of the Christ." Interpreting κεφαλή as authority here implies that Christ is at least presently subordinated to God, even after the resurrection and ascension. Hierarchical interpretations of κεφαλή, when applied to "God is the κεφαλή of Christ," typically embrace and logically imply subordinationist Christology.

Chrysostom, Theodoret, and Theophylact emphasize the misuse of 1 Cor 11:3 by Arians and others to subordinate the present, eternal, or ontological Christ to the Father.[81] Chrysostom's *Hom. in ep. 1 ad Cor.* 26.3 (PG 61:214) argues against heretics who read from this passage "that He

---

80. Kroeger, "*Head* as 'Source'," 268.
81. Meyer, *Corinthians*, 247; cf. Robertson and Plummer, *First Epistle of St Paul to the Corinthians*, 229.

[Christ] is under subjection." Chrysostom explains that the heretics interpret this passage as though it argues, "as the man governs the wife ... so also the Father, Christ." Chrysostom replies:

And who could ever admit this?[82] For if the superiority of the Son compared with us, be the measure of the Fathers' [sic] compared with the Son, consider to what meanness thou wilt bring Him. ... Therefore, if we choose to take the term, "head," in the like sense in all the clauses, the Son will be as far removed from the Father as we are from Him. Nay, and the woman will be as far removed from us as we are from the Word of God. And what the Son is to the Father, this both we are to the Son and the woman again to the man. And who will endure this?[83] ... had Paul meant to speak of rule and subjection, as thou sayest, he would not have brought forward the instance of a wife, but rather of a slave and a master. For what if the wife be under subjection to us? It is as a wife, as free, as equal in honor. And the Son also, though He did become obedient to the Father, it was as the Son of God, it was as God. ... His liberty is greater ... the Father ... begat such a son, not as a slave under command, but as free, yielding obedience and giving counsel. For the counsellor is no slave ... the Son hath the same honor with Him that begat Him. ... Wherefore, you see, she [Eve] was not subjected as soon as she was made; nor, when He brought her to the man, did either she hear any such thing from God, nor did the man say any such word to her: he said indeed that she was "bone of his bone, and

---

82. Fitzmyer ("*Kephalē*," 56–57) cites as Chrysostom's comments what is actually the heretics' interpretation that Chrysostom was emphatically opposing. He obscures this by replacing "And who could ever admit this?" with a mark of ellipsis.

83. Fitzmyer, "*Kephalē*," 57, states that Chrysostom "understood 'head' as meaning 'having authority over.'" The context, however, shows that Chrysostom was *refuting* the heretical interpretation that "head" means "having authority over" in Paul's statement, "God is the head of Christ." Chrysostom imported Paul's later image of Christ as head of his body, the church, into "Christ is the head of every man" and consequently restricted "all men" to Christian believers. In this homily he defines Christ as "head" of the church as a perfect union and "the first principle," which he explains as "the beginning." This implies that he understood "Christ is the head of every man" in the sense of "source." He also, however, refers to "head" as indicating a relationship of "superiority," of Christ over believers and man over woman, suggesting an inconsistency in how he interprets "head" in "Christ is the head of every man." Chrysostom never explicitly identifies what "head" means in "the head of woman is man." He writes that woman was subjected to man only after the fall, not in creation, and several times he identifies woman as "made out of" man, identifying a source relationship, but he also says that a woman's head covering is a symbol of subjection and inferiority to man, who is ordained to be ruler.

flesh of his flesh" (Gen. ii.23.); but of rule or subjection he no where made mention unto her.[84]

Chrysostom goes on to state that in the fall the woman became the ensnarer and subject to man, "But in God and in that undefiled Essence, one must not suppose any such thing."

Kevin Giles has sufficiently demonstrated that subordinationist Christology has been regarded as heresy since the early church creeds.[85] In addition to the consensus of orthodox theology, Paul's christological statements argue against subordination within the Trinity. Subordinationism conflicts with Paul's affirmations of Christ being now "over every power and authority" (e.g., Eph 1:20–22; Phil 3:21; Col 2:9–10), that God "has put everything under his feet" (1 Cor 15:27), and that Christ will turn over all authority to God the Father only in the future consummation (1 Cor 15:24–28). Revelation 7:17 even describes "the Lamb at the center of the throne." Revelation 22:3 depicts "the throne of God and of the Lamb" in the New Jerusalem, and Rev 3:21 and 12:5 depict Jesus Christ on the throne of God.[86]

Translating κεφαλή as "authority" entails a hierarchical authority of God over Christ. Those adopting this view typically regard the subordination of Christ as necessary and eternal, not simply voluntary submission. Subordinationism also conflicts with Christ's ontological equality with God the Father (e.g., Rom 9:5; Phil 2:6–11; Col 1:15–20; 2:9; Titus 2:13). Philippians 2:6–8 affirms that Christ relinquished "equality with God" and "made himself nothing ... humbled himself and became obedient to death — even death on a cross!" Christ's submission to incarnation and

---

84. Talbot W. Chambers, *The Homilies of Saint John Chrysostom on the Epistles of Paul to the Corinthians* (NPNF¹ 12:150–51).
85. Kevin Giles, *The Trinity and Subordinationism: The Doctrine of God & the Contemporary Gender Debate* (Downers Grove, Ill.: InterVarsity Press, 2002), and the even greater historical depth of idem, *Jesus and the Father: Modern Evangelicals Reinvent the Doctrine of the Trinity* (Grand Rapids: Zondervan, 2006). For the classic presentation of the same understanding of the Trinity that Giles presents, see Thomas F. Torrance, *The Christian Doctrine of God: One Being, Three Persons* (Edinburgh: T&T Clark, 1996), e.g., p. 189, "any implication of subordination (ὑποταγή) in the Trinity was completely ruled out by the Fathers of the Constantinopolitan Council ... rejecting any difference in Deity, Glory, Power and Being between the Father and the Son."
86. In contrast, Grudem, "Response to Recent Studies," *RBMW* 457, writes regarding Heb 1:3, "Jesus is at the right hand, but God the Father is still on the throne." Heb 1:3, however, unlike Heb 8:1 and 12:2, has no reference to the throne. Cf. Gilbert G. Bilezikian's critique of Grudem on this point in "Hermeneutical Bungee-Jumping: Subordination in the Godhead," *JETS* 30 (1997): 63.

death was the voluntary submission of an equal for the specific purpose of redemption. It was not the submission of a subordinate in a hierarchy of authority. "Although he was a son, he learned obedience from what he suffered" (Heb 5:8) implies that obedience was not inherent in his status as son but was a new experience to be "learned," specifically through his incarnate sufferings, not from some prior subordination.[87]

Those who interpret κεφαλή to mean "authority" typically assume that "the God" (ὁ θεός) in 1 Cor 11:3 means the Father and not the Godhead inclusively, namely, the Trinity. Even if "the God" in 11:3 were a reference specifically to the Father, it would still make good sense to understand κεφαλή to mean "source" referring to the incarnation. This is how Jesus himself expressed that he came from the Father in John 8:42; 16:27–28 and 17:8.

In light of the affirmations in 1 Cor 8:6 that it is the "Lord, Jesus Christ, through whom all things came," and 11:3 that Christ is the source of every man, in 11:12 "all this comes from the God (also ὁ θεός)," "the God" must include Christ. Consequently, "the God" in 11:12 should be understood as a reference to the Godhead, not exclusively to the Father. Paul's use of "the God" in 11:12 for the Godhead heightens the likelihood that "the God" in 11:3 is also a reference to the Godhead rather than restricted to the Father. In the one instance where Paul uses the distinct term for deity/the Godhead (Col 2:9), he includes the article (ὁ θεότης): "it is in Christ that the complete being of the Godhead dwells embodied" (NEB). "The God" may imply that there is no other, and Paul clearly did not exclude Christ from God.

Accordingly, 1 Cor 15:28, the primary text used to justify subordinationism, may be better translated "so that the Godhead (ὁ θεός) may be all in all." The shift from "God the Father" in verse 24 to "the God" in verse 28 makes sense as indicating a shift in reference from the Father to the Godhead. This is also suggested by what it affirms, namely, that God "may be all in all." This final statement, "that God may be all in all," is more appropriate as an affirmation of the oneness and encompassing authority of the Godhead than as a restricted reference to the Father.[88] Other state-

---

87. Cf. this same observation in Bilezikian, "Bungee-Jumping," 65; *pace* Robert Letham, "The Man-Woman Debate: Theological Comment," *WTJ* 52 (1990): 69.
88. *Pace* John V. Dahms, "The Subordination of the Son," *JETS* 37 (1994): 351–64. He gives no exegetical justification for his assertion on p. 352 that this passage implies that the subjection

ments by Paul show he did not believe that in the new age, God the Father would be everything to the exclusion of Christ. Romans 9:5 refers to Christ as "God over all, forever praised."[89] Ephesians 1:20–22 states that Christ is seated "at his right hand in the heavenly realms, far above all rule and authority, power and dominion, and every title that can be given, not only in the present age but also in the one to come." Consequently, "the God" in 1 Cor 15:28 makes best sense as referring to the Godhead and, therefore, does not entail subordinationist Christology.

Many who interpret κεφαλή as "authority" attempt to avoid the subordinationist heresy by saying that "the κεφαλή of Christ is God" refers to Christ's voluntary submission to the Father in his work of redemption. In so doing, however, they break Paul's κεφαλή analogy by interpreting the subordination of women to men as a contrasting hierarchical state established by God, not a voluntary submission corresponding to Christ's. Such a radical shift in the interpretation of κεφαλή in the same verse undermines the plausibility of this interpretation (see p. 129, point 6). If there is no permanent hierarchy of authority between God and Christ, then 11:3 is ill-suited to support such a hierarchy between man and woman.

In contrast to interpretations of κεφαλή as "authority over," the meaning "source" implies no inherent subordination of Christ. It simply affirms that Christ came from the Godhead in the incarnation. It does not imply that he was created or "eternally begotten" or was not preexistent. In addition to the Greek fathers' citations affirming the meaning source (see below, point 15), Cyril of Alexandria's *De recta fide ad Pulcheriam et*

---

of the Son to the Father "will be the condition forever thereafter." Dana and Mantey, *A Manual Grammar of the Greek New Testament*, §178, states that the future tense normally carries a punctiliar sense and when used in prediction identifies a future event. Robertson, *Grammar*, 871, states "that in the future passive we have with most verbs a purely punctiliar future." Ernest de Witt Burton, *Syntax of the Moods and Tenses in New Testament Greek* (Edinburgh: T&T Clark, 1898), 32, states, "any instance of the Predictive future not clearly progressive must be accounted as aoristic." Nor does Dahms deal with the evidence that Christ's subjection is part of a mutual putting-oneself-at-the-disposal-of-the-other that undermines a hierarchical view of the Trinity. None of the other passages he alleges to imply essential and eternal subordination, namely, John 17:24; Eph 3:21; and Phil 2:9–11, have any obvious correlation with the idea of eternal subordination. *Pace* his assertion on p. 354, the Son glorifying the Father no more makes the Son subordinate to the Father than the Father glorifying the Son (e.g., John 8:50; 13:31–32; 17:1, 5, 22, 24; Acts 3:13) makes the Father subordinate to the Son. Similarly, *pace* his assertion on p. 355, the fact that the purpose or result of something the Son does may be to glorify God, no more implies the subordination of the Son than John 11:4's "that God's Son may be glorified through it" implies the subordination of God to his Son.

89. Cf. *TDNT* 3:105, "Christ is not only called *Theos*, but He is also the subject of a sonorous benediction normally reserved in Judaism, and in Paul himself, for God alone."

Eudociam 5^2.131D states, "the Word was begotten of Him. Because head [κεφαλή] means source [ἀρχή]."[90]

10. Κεφαλή as "source" is perfectly suited to understand 1 Cor 11:3 as setting the theological stage for Paul's ensuing arguments. The man-woman relationship (v. 3b) is bracketed by Christ's role in creation (v. 3a) and the incarnation (v. 3c). Creation affirms marriage and provides the basis for respecting one's source. Christ's incarnation brings about a new reality "in the Lord," where woman is not set apart from man (11:11).

11. This passage discusses disgraceful head-covering practices in prayer and prophecy, not hierarchical roles.[91]

12. Verses 8 and 12 affirm woman's source from (ἐκ) man. Verse 12 also affirms man's source through (διά) woman and both from (ἐκ) God. First Corinthians 8:6 identifies the source of creation as from (ἐκ) God and through (διά) Christ, setting the stage to understand Christ as the source (κεφαλή) of every man in 11:3 and the three uses of these prepositions in 11:12 for source.

13. This passage says nothing about man's authority but rather affirms woman's authority. Paul recognizes her authority to pray and prophecy in 11:5, her authority over her own head in 11:10, and her equal standing with man in 11:11–12.

14. First Corinthians 11:11–12, which Paul introduces as his central concern, repudiates a hierarchy of man over woman, as chapter 11 of this book argues.

15. Much of the early Greek commentary on 1 Cor 11:3 specifically interprets κεφαλή to mean "source." Cyril of Alexandria's *De recta fide ad Arcadiam et Marinam* 5^2.63E states:

> The source [ἀρχή] of man is the Creator God [τὸν ποιήσαντα Θεόν]. Thus we say that "the head [κεφαλή] of every man is Christ," because he was made [πεποίηται] through him and brought forth to birth.... And the head [κεφαλή] of woman is man, because she was taken from his flesh and has him as her source [ἀρχή]. Likewise, the head [κεφαλή] of Christ is God, because He is from Him according to nature.[92]

---

90. Kroeger, "*Head* as 'Source'," 268.
91. Cf. Fee, *First Corinthians*, 516–17 n. 15; Harris, "Eve's Deception," 344.
92. Translation from Kroeger, "*Head* as 'Source'," 277.

Many other Greek fathers, including Theodore of Mopsuestia, Saint Basil, Athanasius, and Eusebius[93] also explain κεφαλή in 11:3 as "source." Photius (ninth century AD) sums up the work of earlier Greek fathers:

> For Christ is the head [κεφαλή] of us who believe ... being made by him. ... But the head [κεφαλή] of Christ is the Father, as procreator [γεννητής] and progenitor [προβολεύς] and of like substance with him. And the head [κεφαλή] of the woman is the man because he is her procreator [γεννητής] and progenitor [προβολεύς] and of like substance with her.[94]

Latin fathers like Ambrosiaster shared this view, "God is the head of Christ because he begat him; Christ is the head of the man because he created him, and the man is the head of the woman because she was taken from his side."[95]

Since the contextual support for κεφαλή meaning "source" is clear, any translation of this passage should convey this sense to the reader. In English, however "head" does not convey "source," but rather "authority over," so it is misleading merely to translate "head" here. The best solution is probably to translate κεφαλή as "source" and add a note, "literally, 'head.'"

IS PAUL WRITING ABOUT MAN AND WOMAN OR HUSBAND AND WIFE?

Some versions translate "man" and "woman" in 11:3 as "husband" and "wife," but there is no article or "his" before "wife," which could have supported this. A key reason they translate 11:3b "the husband is the head of his wife" is that they have read back into κεφαλή the metaphorical meaning it usually has in English (and some other languages, but not Greek), namely, "authority," and they have not felt comfortable with the idea that men in general have authority over women in general. This interpretation is expressed in *The New Translation*, "the authority over a woman is her husband," and the TEV, "the husband is supreme over his wife." Every

---

93. Kroeger, "*Head* as 'Source'," 271, 277 (Theodore of Mopsuestia), 276 (Saint Basil), 268, 276 (Athanasius), and 276 (Eusebius) cites the Greek texts and provides translations; cf. also Kroeger, "Ancient Conceptions," 6 – 8.

94. Kroeger, "*Head* as 'Source'," 278 – 79.

95. Ambrosiaster in CSEL 81.120 – 21. Translation from Gerald Bray, ed., *Ancient Christian Commentary on Scripture: New Testament VII 1 – 2 Corinthians* (Downers Grove, Ill.: InterVarsity, 1999), 104.

translation checked in this study that introduces "husband" in 11:3 reverts
to "man" and "woman" in every other occurrence of these words throughout this passage, even though the words "man" (ἀνήρ) and "woman" (γυνή)
are the same throughout.[96] This is because "woman" and "man" usually
become awkward or nonsensical if translated "husband" or "wife" in the
passage, as in the following list:

"Christ is the head of every husband." (v. 3)
"For a husband ... is the image and glory of God." (v. 7)
"For a husband was not made from a wife, but a wife from a husband."
(v. 8)
"For as the wife was made from the husband, so the husband is now
born through the wife...." (v. 12; cf. similarly vv. 4, 9, 11, 14, 15).

Obviously, "every man" includes husbands and "woman" includes wives,
and the creation of man and woman is also the creation of the first husband and wife, so appropriate application to husbands and wives should
be readily acknowledged. In the first "head" relationship in 11:3, however,
the undisputed use of ἀνήρ for "man," the lack of "his" or an article before
"woman" in the second "head" relationship in verse 3, which could have
suggested "his wife," the inclusion of the article with "man" in verses 3
and also in 12, where it clearly identifies Adam, the references to woman's
source being "from man" in verses 8 and 12, and the consistent use of ἀνήρ
for "man" and γυνή for "woman" throughout the rest of the passage strongly
oppose restricting the meaning of "man" to "husband" and "woman" to
"wife." Since verse 3 introduces this passage, surely the words that define
the subject matter of the entire passage should be translated in harmony
with their use throughout the rest of the passage. Accordingly, the context
clearly supports the translation: "and the man is the source of woman."

THE BRACKETING PILLARS OF CHRIST'S CREATION AND REDEMPTION

"God is the κεφαλή of Christ" anchors Paul's concerns in the Godhead. This most naturally refers to Christ's source as from God in the

---

96. Goodspeed, TNT, NAB, NRSV, RSV, Williams, Amplified (the one explanatory parenthesis,
"her husband," in v. 5 is inserted where the Greek has no corresponding word). The TEV adds
"husband" in 11:5 and 10 even though the Greek has no corresponding word in either verse.
Of these versions the only ones that translate woman in 11:3 "wife" are the NRSV, TEV, and
Williams.

incarnation,[97] as Paul expresses in Gal 4:4, "when the time had fully come, God sent forth his Son, born of a woman." This explains the order of these three κεφαλή (source) relationships as chronological: the creation of man, the creation of woman, and the incarnation. This argues against reference to "eternal generation."[98]

Murphy-O'Connor has drawn attention to a fascinating detail indicating that the order of the arrangement is intentional. The statement "the man is the κεφαλή [source] of woman," "is bracketed by two statements that mention Christ and that are so formulated that the name of Christ forms, as it were, an inner bracket"[99] around the creation of woman. Preceding the statement, "the man is the source of woman," is an affirmation of Christ's role in creation as the source of every man. Following it is an affirmation of Christ's role in redemption, since this is implied by the reference to God as the κεφαλή (source) of Christ in the incarnation. This bracketing suggests that Paul desired the Corinthians to view the relationship of man and woman in light of two pivotal events, creation and redemption. These two pivotal events are the keys to understanding natural and special revelation. The creation of humankind in the image of God and God's provision for redemption through his very Son provide the two pillars that uphold both the value of human life and the respect people should show to each other.

---

97. Alternatively it could be viewed as Christ, the hidden wisdom of God destined for our glory before time began (1 Cor 1:30; 2:7). This, however, could break the temporal sequence of the series and would not suggest the redemptive aspect of the incarnation as clearly.
98. As Fee, *First Corinthians*, 505, also argues.
99. Jerome Murphy-O'Connor, "1 Corinthians 11:1–16 Once Again," *CBQ* 50 (1988): 270. Christ is the last member of the preceding pair and the first member of the following pair. Thus, only the intervening words ἐστιν ("is") and κεφαλὴ δέ ("and head") separate the double reference to the Christ from "the man is κεφαλή of woman."

8

1 CORINTHIANS 11:4: THE DISGRACE OF A MAN "HAVING DOWN FROM THE HEAD"

Paul's extensive statements and serious argumentation regarding men throughout this passage (1 Cor 11:4, 7–9, 14) are earnest with no hint that they are merely a foil to introduce women's head coverings. In that culture built around shame and honor,[1] to identify something as disgraceful was no light thing. It is unlikely that Paul would identify a fictitious problem as disgraceful and give a theological defense for its prohibition.[2]

WHAT HANGING "DOWN FROM" A MAN'S HEAD CAUSES DISGRACE?

Something "down from" (κατά with the genitive, "lit. hanging down fr. the head," BDAG 511 A.1.a) or "over"[3] the head of men leading in worship was disgraceful. Paul does not in this verse identify what was down from the head, so any explanation, to be convincing, needs to cite evidence from this passage and its cultural context. What hanging down from a man's head would be disgraceful for men leading worship in Corinth, a Greek city and a Roman colony? Many assume it is a toga (*himation*).[4]

---

1. Cf. David A. deSilva, *Honor, Patronage, Kinship and Purity: Unlocking New Testament Culture* (Downers Grove, Ill.: InterVarsity Press, 2000), 23–93.
2. Cf. Murphy-O'Connor, "Once Again," 266; Thiselton, *First Corinthians*, 822–26; Richard E. Oster, "Use, Misuse and Neglect of Archaeological Evidence in Some Modern Works on 1 Corinthians (1 Cor 7:1–5; 8:10; 11:2–16; 12:14–26)," *ZNW* 83 (1992): 67–69.
3. LSJ 882 A.II.1 "*down upon or over*"; e.g., Plutarch, *Quaets. rom.* 267B "over her head" (κατὰ κεφαλῆς); *Mor.* 4:26–27 (Babbitt, LCL). This sense parallels the use of κατακαλύπτεσθαι regarding men in 11:7.
4. Plutarch specificies that the covering to which he refers is a *himation* in *Quaest. rom.* 200F (κατὰ τῆς κεφαλῆς ἔχων τὸ ἱμάτιον) and 267C, *Caes.* 56.6–7 (739D), *Pompeius* 40.5 (640C).

It was not, however, disgraceful in the cultural context of Corinth or in Jewish culture for a man to drape a garment over his head. The *capite velato*[5] custom of pulling a toga over one's head in Roman religious contexts symbolized devotion and piety, not disgrace. Jewish custom and the Hebrew Scriptures also approved head-covering garments for men leading in worship.[6]

Thus, to prohibit a garment head covering would have complicated Paul's relationships with synagogues and contradicted not only the Torah, but also Paul's missionary principle of becoming all things to all people and his principle of freedom in Christ. Thankfully, Paul identifies in verse 15 what "hanging down from the head" causes disgrace: "If a man has long hair, it is a disgrace to him."

LONG EFFEMINATE HAIR ON MEN CAUSED DISGRACE IN PAUL'S DAY

Greek, Roman, and Jewish literature of Paul's day frequently speaks of men wearing long effeminate hair as disgraceful, especially when done up like a woman's hair. "Effeminate," from Latin *effeminatus*, "made woman-ish" (*ex-* "out" + *femina*, "a woman"), entails a man presenting himself as a woman. Herter documents the moral indignation over effeminate hair-styles by men with over a hundred references to effeminate hair from clas-sical antiquity, the greatest number coming from around Paul's time.[7] For

---

5.   Richard Gordon, "The Veil of Power: Emperors, Sacrifices and Benefactors," in *Pagan Priests: Religion and Power in the Ancient World* (eds. Mary Beard and John North; London: Duckworth, 1990), 211. On p. 212 he cites about twenty statues of Augustus with his toga over his head as sacrificant. Cf. K. Vierneisel and P. Zanker, *Die Bildnisse des Augustus* (Munich: Glypotothek, 1979), 58–60; S. Walker and A. Burnett, *The Image of Ausustus* (London: British Museum, 1981), Maps 1–2; David W. J. Gill, "The Importance of Roman Portraiture for Head-Coverings in 1 Corinthians 11:2–16," *TynBul* 44, no. 2 (November 1993): 247; Cynthia L. Thompson, "Hairstyles, Head-Coverings, and St. Paul: Portraits from Roman Corinth," *BA* 51, no. 2 (June 1988): 101. While it is probably true in general that only leaders in the community would adopt this pose, since only they would be in a position of presiding over a sacrifice, the symbolism of the head covering was primarily one of piety and religious devotion, not status seeking. Such a posture of devotion, if adopted in Christian prayer, would logically imply devotion to Christ.
6.   E.g., Exod 28:4, 37, 39; 29:6; 39:28, 31; Lev 8:9; 16:4; Ezek 24:17; 44:18; Zech 3:5.
7.   H. Herter, "Effeminatus," *RAC* 2:620–50. Philip B. Payne, "Wild Hair and Gender Equality in 1 Corinthians 11:2–16," *Priscilla Papers* 20:3 (Summer 2006): 9 and 18 n. 15 cites many examples. This is available for free download at www.pbpayne.com. Cf. also James B. Hurley, "Man and Woman in 1 Corinthians: Some Exegetical Studies in Pauline Theology and Eth-ics" (Ph.D. diss., Cambridge, 1973), 54; idem, *Biblical Perspective*, 162–94, 254–71; idem, "Did Paul Require Veils or the Silence of Women? A Consideration of 1 Cor. 11:2–16 and 1 Cor. 14:33b–36," *WTJ* 35 (Winter 1973): 190–220; Jerome Murphy-O'Connor, "Sex," 485–87 and *Paul: A Critical Life* (Oxford: Oxford University Press, 1997), 279; Collins, *First Corinthians*, 396–99; Barrett, *First Corinthians*, 257; Scroggs, "Eschatological Woman," 297; G. Theissen, *Psychological Aspects of Pauline Theology* (Philadelphia: Fortress, 1987); S. Lösch, "Christliche Frauen in Korinth (I Cor. 11,2–16)," *TQ* 127 (1947): 251–58; Isaksson, *Marriage and Ministry,*

example, Pseudo-Phocylides (30 BC – AD 40) wrote, "Long hair is not fit for men ... because many rage for intercourse with a man."[8]

Many desiring homosexual liaisons advertised their sexual availability through display of effeminate hair, particularly in the Dionysiac cult that was influential in Corinth.[9] If any men in the church in Corinth attempted a theological justification for this, it may have been either "because man as male is the image and glory of God" (11:7) or the spiritualized eschatology Paul repeatedly argues against (e.g., 1 Cor 13:11; 15:12 – 58). In 1 Cor 6:9, Paul states his opposition to homosexual acts: "Make no mistake about it; neither ... catamites [μαλακοί][10] nor sodomites [ἀρσενοκοῖται][11] ... will inherit the Realm of God" (Moffatt), and 6:11 adds, "that is what some of you were," implying that some males in the church had engaged in passive or active homosexual acts prior to their conversion.

The extensive correspondence between statements in 1 Corinthians and Dionysiac practices[12] makes it probable that Paul was aware of Dionysiac influence in the Corinthian church and was deliberately addressing it in this letter. The evidence for Dionysiac influence in 1 Cor 11:2 – 16 is particularly compelling. Both male effeminacy and women letting their

165 – 86; W. J. Martin, "1 Corinthians 11.2 – 16: An Interpretation," in *Apostolic History and the Gospel: Biblical and Historical Essays Presented to F. F. Bruce* (ed. W. W. Gasque and R. P. Martin; Exeter: Paternoster, 1970), 233; Fiorenza, *In Memory of Her,* 227; Padgett, "Paul on Women," 69 – 86; Horsley, *1 Corinthians,* 154.

8.   P. W. van der Horst, *The Sentences of Pseudo-Phocylides with Introduction and Commentary* (SVTP 4; Leiden: Brill, 1978), 81 – 83.

9.   E.g., Pausanias, *Corinth* 7.5 – 6; Plutarch, *Mor.* 266C-E; Euripides, *Bacch.* 151, 353, 454 – 55, 695, 836, 852; Nonnus, *Dion.* 14.159 – 176; 45.47 – 48; Athenaeus, *Deipn.* 12.525; Lucian, *Syr. d.* 6; Livy 39.13.10 – 12; 39.15.9; 39.16.1; Aristophanes, *Frogs* 47 – 59; Philostratus, *Life of Apollonius* 4.21; *Imag.* 1.2; Aristides, *Oration* 41.4 – 5, 9; *Rhet.* 41.9; Apollodorus, *Bibliotheca* 3.4.3; Aeschylus, *fr.* 61; cf. David F. Greenberg, *The Construction of Homosexuality* (Chicago: Univ. of Chicago Press, 1988), 154.

10. Literally "soft ones," normally rendered "effeminates" or "catamites," implying receptive anal homosexual acts. Greenberg, *Homosexuality,* 212 – 13. Cf. Plato, *Phaedrus* 239C; Derrick Sherwin Bailey, *Homosexuality and the Western Christian Tradition* (London: Longmans, Green, 1955; repr., Hamden, Conn.: Archon Books, 1975), 38 – 39; Tom Horner, *Jonathan Loved David: Homosexuality in Biblical Times* (Philadelphia: Westminster, 1978), 97.

11. Cf. Greenberg, *Homosexuality,* 214. This term was apparently created to represent in one word either the Greek (ἄρσενος κοίτην) or the Hebrew construction of Lev 18:22 and 20:13. Cf. David F. Wright, "Homosexuals or Prostitutes? The Meaning of ΑΡΣΕΝΟΚΟΙΤΑΙ (1 Cor. 6:9; 1 Tim. 1:10)," *VC* 38 (1984): 125 – 53; Robin Scroggs, *The New Testament and Homosexuality* (Philadelphia: Fortress, 1983), 85 – 86.

12. E.g., 1 Cor 5:9 – 10; 6:9; 8:10; 10:8, 21; 11:21 – 22; cf. Athenaeus Soph., *Deipn.* 292 d., Plutarch, *Mor.* 56 F, 310 C, 362 B; Diodorus Siculus 4.3; Philostratus, *Imag.* 1.2; Euripides, *Bacch.* 814; 1 Cor 14:23, cf. Iamblichus, *de Mysteriis* 3.5; 1 Cor 14:26 – 33, cf. Philostratus, *Imag.* 1.19.4. In addition, standard Dionysiac cultic paraphernalia are reflected in the vocabulary of 1 Corinthians, including milk, sounding brass, tinkling cymbal, flute, harp, trumpet, and mirror. One citation for each in order follows: Euripides, *Bacch.* 143, 710; Nonnus, *Dion.* 24.152, 153; Aeschylus, *Fragment* 27 (57) line 7; Plutarch, *Mor.* 671E; ibid., 364F; Clement of Alexandria, *Protr.* 2.15.

hair down[13] were major characteristics of the Dionysiac cult. Men endorsing effeminism and women letting their hair down in ecstatic prophecy fit Paul's arguments in 1 Cor 11 perfectly, whereas all other attempts at interpreting this passage simply have not fit the data of the text.

FOURTEEN REASONS TO IDENTIFY MEN'S HEAD COVERING WITH EFFEMINATE HAIR

Fourteen key factors in this passage support identifying "hanging down from the head" as long, effeminate hair (or its homosexual symbolism) rather than a garment head covering.

1. It flows naturally from the affirmation in 1 Cor 11:3 that Christ is every man's source in creation. Men wearing effeminate hair present themselves as women and so shame Christ by not accepting how he created them. This symbolism undermines marriage as ordained by God and brings shame on the perpetrators and on Christ their head/source.

2. It is "disgraceful" (11:4). Men's long hair was disgraceful; a garment head covering was not.

3. Verses 4 (καταισχύνει) and 14 (ἡ φύσις αὐτή, ἀτιμία) repudiate this practice, using expressions that closely parallel Paul's denunciation of homosexual acts in Rom 1:26–27: "degrading" (ἀτιμίας), "against nature" (παρὰ φύσιν), and "shameful" (ἀσχημοσύνην). Two of these words are identical and the third shares the semantic domain, "shame."

4. This situation applies equally well to "every man" (11:4): Greek, Jewish, and Roman.

5. "Shaved" or "shorn" imply hair and occur four times in 1 Cor 11:5–6, but the only mention of a garment covering, in verse 15, says that hair is given as or instead of a garment wrap.

6. The offense is morally what one "ought not" do (11:7). This fits symbolizing homosexual relations far better than prohibition of a garment covering.

7. This background makes the best sense of "woman [not man] is the glory of man" (11:7).

---

13. Cf. women's impropriety in Plutarch, Vit. Alexander 2.5; Mor. 249 E-F; Cicero, Laws 2.15.38.

8. This interpretation avoids the implication that woman is not in the image of God.

9. Hair advertising for homosexual relations fits Paul's argumentation in verses 7–9, where he advocates sexual differentiation and woman as man's sexual partner, the one in whom he glories.

10. First Corinthians 11:14 states, "Does not the very nature of things teach you that if a man has long hair, it is degrading to him?" This concluding argument for Paul's prohibition explicitly denounces long hair and is irrelevant if he is prohibiting a garment head covering.

11. Effeminate hair fits this cultural setting, being well documented in the Dionysiac cult that was influential in Corinth, and Dionysiac practices are reflected throughout 1 Corinthians.

12. It does not require the assumption that Paul is reinterpreting standard iconography (of the *capite velato* or the *tallith*)[14] in an atypical fashion without explaining it.

13. It does not entail Paul contradicting the Torah, which would have undermined Paul's access to synagogues and his principle of becoming all things to all people to advance the gospel.

14. It does not undermine Paul's principle of freedom in Christ regarding morally neutral issues.

WHY DID PAUL USE THE VAGUE EXPRESSION "HAVING DOWN FROM THE HEAD"?

Paul probably used this vague expression in order to avoid speaking directly of such disgraceful things, as Eph 5:12 explains, "It is shameful even to mention what the disobedient do in secret." Even when Paul does identify men's long hair as disgraceful in 1 Cor 11:14, he avoids mentioning the shameful thing it symbolized, namely, effeminate homosexual relations. The Corinthians knew the homosexual associations of men wearing long effeminate hair and would understand Paul's euphemisms in 11:4 and 14, like those in 1 Cor 5:1 ("to *have* his father's wife" for sexual intercourse) and 7:1 ("to *touch* a woman" for sexual intercourse).[15] Anyone having seen

---

14. Fee, *First Corinthians*, 507 concludes, "The evidence for the use of the *tallith* in prayer is much too late to be helpful for Jewish customs in the time of Paul." Cf. similarly Robertson and Plummer, *First Corinthians*, 229.

15. E.g., Plutarch, *Pompey* 2.3; Aristotle, *Pol.* 7.14.12; Josephus, *Ant.* 1.163.

men in the Corinthian church pray or prophesy with effeminate hairstyles would immediately understand this euphemism.

Even if Paul had wanted to explain his reasoning explicitly, it would not have been easy to do concisely since, although Greek had lots of words for specific homosexual relations and roles, it did not have a generally recognized generic word for homosexual acts.[16] Verse 4's clever wordplay joins two senses of κατά with the genitive[17] and two senses of "head": "to pray or prophesy with [long effeminate hair] *down from* [your] *head*, is having [something] *against* [Christ your] *Head*. It disgraces both your *head* and your *Head*."

Several early church fathers explain Paul's concern regarding men in 1 Cor 11:2–16 as being about hair. John Chrysostom (ca. AD 344–407), *Hom. in ep. 1 ad Cor.* 26.4 (PG 61:219.3), states:

> But with regard to the man, it is no longer about covering but about wearing long hair, that he so forms his discourse ... signifying that even though he pray with the head bared, yet if he have long hair, he is like to one covered. "For the hair," said he, "is given for a covering." Similarly, Ambrose, a Latin father (ca. AD 339–397), commented on Paul's reference to men with long hair, "How unsightly it is for a man to act like a woman."[18]

Pelagius too recognized that Paul was talking about the hair of both men and woman being displayed erotically: "Paul was complaining because men were fussing about their hair and women were flaunting their locks in church. Not only was this dishonoring to them, but it was also an incitement to fornication."[19]

---

16. Cf. Greenberg, *Homosexuality*, 212–14. The idea of homosexuality as a sexual orientation was exceedingly rarely, if ever, expressed in Greek.
17. BDAG 511 senses A.1.a and A.2; cf. Matt 5:23; Mark 11:25; Herm. *Sim.* 9, 24, 2.
18. FC 26:436, translation from Bray, *1–2 Corinthians*, 109.
19. PL 30:749D, translation from Bray, *1–2 Corinthians*, 106.

9

I CORINTHIANS 11:5–6: THE DISGRACE OF A WOMAN'S HEAD "UNCOVERED"

The traditional garment-covering interpretation typically argues for a supposedly established universal church custom requiring women to wear a garment covering their heads in worship. This interpretation, however, is incompatible or incongruent with many statements in 11:2–16.

- It is incompatible with Paul's praise in 1 Cor 11:2, "you … maintain the traditions just as I handed them on to you" (NRSV). It does not make sense that Paul would praise them for maintaining the traditions in an introduction to a passage addressing a universal tradition they must have known, yet were breaking anyway.[1]
- "But I want you to understand" (NRSV) in 11:3 implies that Paul is addressing something new. It does not make sense that Paul would introduce a universal custom as something new to a church where he had ministered so long (Acts 18:1–11). Furthermore, Paul's introduction (1 Cor 11:3) lays a foundation for respecting one's source,[2] but abundant cultural evidence supports the conclusion that it was not disrespectful for women to pray without a head garment.[3]

---

1. Cf. above p. 114, which argues that sarcasm is unlikely in light of the contrasting rebuke in 11:17.
2. Cf. above pp. 115–17 and P. B. Payne, "What Does *Kephalē* Mean in the New Testament? Response," in *Women, Authority and the Bible* (ed. Alvera Mickelsen; Downers Grove, Ill.: InterVarsity Press, 1986), 118–32.
3. Cf. below, pp. 152–62.

- Paul addresses here an un-covering that disgraces "every woman" (11:5), but cultural evidence shows that lack of a garment head cover would not disgrace "every woman."[4]
- Paul says, "she is one and the same as the shaved woman" (11:5), but there is no convincing evidence that this was true of a woman not wearing a head-covering garment.
- "Judge for yourselves" in verse 13 shows Paul believed the Corinthian church would agree that it was disgraceful for a woman to pray "uncovered." The cultural evidence, however, strongly supports that they would not agree that lack of a head-covering garment is disgraceful.[5]
- If Paul's point were that a woman should cover her head with a garment, why would he state that hair is her "glory" (11:15)? Surely, this would encourage revealing it, not covering it.
- Paul's statement in 1 Cor 11:15, that a woman's "long hair is given to her as/instead of a covering" is incongruous as the conclusion of an argument that a woman must wear a garment head covering, whether ἀντί means "as" or "instead of."[6]
- If Paul's aim all along were to demand adherence to a veiling custom upheld by all the churches, it would be incongruous for him to conclude his argument in 11:16, "We, the churches of God,[7] have no such custom." Versions like the RSV that change "no such" custom to "no other" custom introduce a meaning for τοιαύτην that is the opposite of this word's meaning.[8]
- Interpreting the covering as a garment does not fit Paul's message of freedom in Christ from Jewish law, his usual strong opposition to legalism, or his principle of becoming all things to all people (10:33). It would be inconsistent for Paul to require women to follow a Jewish head-covering custom, but prohibit men from following a Jewish head-covering custom. Furthermore, there would be no need for Paul's and Peter's prohibition of women wearing braided

---

4.   Ibid.
5.   Cf. below, pp. 152–62.
6.   Cf. below, pp. 205–7.
7.   On this use of οὐδέ see below pp. 337–59 and especially 342.
8.   Cf. below, pp. 207–8.

hair interwoven with gold if church custom mandated that women wear a garment over their heads.[9]

PAUL HERE REGULATES PRAYER AND PROPHECY BY WOMEN IN PUBLIC WORSHIP

It is nearly universally acknowledged that prophesying presupposes a public church meeting.[10] No one questions that "praying and prophesying" by men in verse 4 implies a public house church setting, so the same naturally should also apply to the identical words regarding women in verse 5. Prophecy is a public act, and only public prophecy could be disgraceful or require regulated head adornment. Nor would such regulations make sense for private prayer. This context specifically refers to customs in the churches in verse 16 and the surrounding passages concern the Lord's Supper (10:16–22 and 11:17–33).

Paul encourages all believers to participate in public worship in varied vocal ministries (1 Cor 14:26), including prophecy (14:31). It is a striking affirmation of woman's equal standing with men in church leadership that Paul in verse 5 simply assumes that "every woman," like "every man," could pray and prophesy in public. Praying and prophesying by women leading in worship with appropriate head covering was an approved practice in meetings of the church.[11] Prophecy covers a range of messages believed to come from God, including messages with thoughtful preparation.[12]

Prophecy addresses community; it is horizontal. Prayer addresses God; it is vertical.[13] Thus, the terms "prayer" and "prophecy" suggest the entire

---

9. Cf. below, pp. 312–13.

10. A notable exception is Philipp Bachmann, *Der erste Brief des Paulus an die Korinther* (3rd ed.; Leipzig: A. Deichert, 1921), 350–51, whose argumentation is carefully refuted by Grosheide, *First Corinthians*, 252–53.

11. Cf. C. Holsten, *Das Evangelium des Paulus. II.1 Der brief an die gemeinden Galatiens und der erste brief an die gemeinde in Korinth* (Berlin: Reimer, 1880), 404–5; Fee, *First Corinthians*, 498; pace F. C. Synge, "Studies in Texts: 1 Cor. 11:2–16," *Theology* 56 (1953): 143; N. Weeks, "Of Silence and Head Covering," *WTJ* 35 (1972): 21–27. The weaknesses of Synge's and Weeks' views are examined by Isaksson, *Marriage and Ministry*, 153–57.

12. Cf. Thiselton, *First Corinthians*, 826, "Prophetic speech may include *applied theological teaching, encouragement, and exhortation to build the church*," cf. 956–63; Thomas W. Gillespie, *The First Theologians: A Study in Early Christian Prophecy* (Grand Rapids: Eerdmans, 1994), 23–28; Craig L. Blomberg, "Neither Hierarchicalist nor Egalitarian: Gender Roles in Paul," in *Two Views on Women in Ministry* (ed. James R. Beck and Craig L. Blomberg; Grand Rapids: Zondervan, 2001), 344–45; David H. Hill, *New Testament Prophecy* (London: Marshall, Morgan and Scott, 1979), 213.

13. Cf. Gordon D. Fee, "Praying and Prophesying in the Assemblies 1 Corinthians 11:2–16," in *Discovering Biblical Equality: Complementarity without Hierarchy* (ed. Ronald W. Pierce and Rebecca Merrill Groothuis; Downers Grove, Ill.: InterVarsity Press, 2004), 149.

scope of leadership in worship. Since Paul ranks prophets above teachers in 1 Cor 12:28, since he associates prophecy with revelation, knowledge, and instruction in 14:6, and since prayer and prophecy encompass both the vertical and horizontal dimensions of worship, Paul's approval of women prophesying should not be interpreted as excluding the related ministries of revelation, knowledge, and instruction.[14]

The crucial question is: What "uncovering" was disgraceful for every woman leading in worship? There are two basic alternatives. Most modern commentators have understood "with head uncovered" (ἀκατακαλύπτῳ τῇ κεφαλῇ) to refer to a woman not wearing a veil, shawl, or some other garment over her head (CEV). Many versions insert "veil" (ASV, Berkeley, Fenton, Goodspeed, JB, NAB, NEB, New Berkeley, NRSV, RSV, Way, Weymouth, Williams), even though it never occurs in this passage in Greek and seems to be repudiated by 11:15. The other alternative is that "uncovered" refers to hair let down loosely around the shoulders. "Covered" would then refer to a woman's hair done up over her head, whether wound around and held in by itself or held up with a clasp, hairnet, headband, ribbon, or some other utensil. The reference to hair is supported by the four references implying hair in 11:5–6 and the statement in 11:15 that long hair is a woman's glory "given to her as a covering."

Macarius Aegyptius (d. c. AD 390), *Homiliae spirituales* 12.18, explicitly identifies the covering: "Question: Why is it said, 'a woman praying with uncovered head?' Answer: Since in the present apostolic time they have been permitted hair instead of a covering."[15] He specifically interprets 1 Cor 11:5 as referring to hair, not to a veil. Ambrose (c. AD 339–397), *Duties of the Clergy* 1.46.232, writes, "Is it comely that a woman pray unto God uncovered; doth not nature itself teach you that 'If a woman have long hair, it is a glory unto her'? It is according to nature, since her hair

---

14. Cf. Fee, "Praying and Prophesying," 149; idem, *God's Empowering Presence: The Holy Spirit in the Letters of Paul* (Peabody, Mass.: Hendrickson, 1994), 272–81.

15. <'Ερώτησις:> τί ἐστι γυνὴ ἀκατακαλύπτῳ κεφαλῇ προσευχομένη; <'Απόκρισις:> ἐπειδὴ ἐν τῷ καιρῷ τῶν ἀποστόλων ἀφιεμένας εἶχον τὰς τρίχας ἀντὶ σκεπάσματος." See H. Dörries, E. Klostermann, and M. Kroeger, *Die 50 geistlichen Homilien des Makarius* (PTS 4; Berlin: DeGruyter, 1964). C. Peter Williams ("Macarius of Egypt," in *The New International Dictionary of the Christian Church*, 616) notes, "It is possible these writings were by an anonymous writer who was called 'blessed' (*makarios*)." *PGL* xxxiv, assigns this work to the fifth or sixth century. Luci Berkowitz and Karl A. Squitier, *Thesaurus Linguae Graecae Canon of Greek Authors and Works* (2nd ed.; New York: Oxford, 1986), 210, lists it as from the fourth century AD.

is given her for a veil, for it is a natural veil."[16] Likewise, Chrysostom (c. AD 354–407) quotes 1 Cor 11:6b followed by 11:14b–15,[17] and Clement of Alexandria, *Paed.* 3.11, writes, "It is enough for women to protect their locks, and bind up their hair simply along the neck with a plain hair-pin, nourishing chaste locks with simple care to true beauty."[18]

Some women in Corinthian worship services were doing something so widely recognized as shameful that it would cause shame to "every woman." Shame is an emotion caused when social conventions are broken. What about having one's head "uncovered" would cause shame to a woman leading in worship in the cultural setting of Corinth? The extensive evidence from portraiture, frescoes, sculptures, and vase paintings in Greek and Roman cities of Paul's day almost universally depicts respectable women with their hair done up.[19] Women in everyday public settings are not depicted with their hair hanging loose over their shoulders. Furthermore, they are only rarely depicted wearing a veil or other garment over their heads.

Consequently, the Corinthians would most certainly have agreed that it would be shameful for any woman to let her hair down while praying or prophesying, but there is insufficient evidence to be confident that Corinthians would have regarded lack of a veil or garment covering a woman's head as disgraceful, particularly in a house church setting among brothers and sisters in Christ. Since Corinth was a Greek-speaking, Roman colony, both Greek and Roman cultural influences need to be considered—Greek as primary and Roman as secondary. Jewish customs are also noted because of their possible influence among the minority Jewish members in the church.

---

16. H. de Romesin, *The Principal Works of St. Ambrose* (NPNF²; ed. Philip Schaff and Henry Wace; Grand Rapids: Eerdmans, 1955), 10:37.

17. Chrysostom, *Hom. in ep. 1 ad Cor. 1–44*), PG 61:219.3. He notes in *hom.* 26.4, "he said not, 'let her have long hair,' but, 'let her be covered,' ordaining both these to be one … he both affirms the covering and the hair to be one." Chrysostom also affirms a head-covering garment for women, as does Irenaeus, *Haer.* 1.8.2 (ANF 1:327); Tertullian, *De Corona* 14 (ANF 3:102); *On Prayer* 21–22 (ANF 3:687–688); *Marc.* 5.9 (ANF 3:446); *On the Apparel of Women* 2.7 (ANF 4:21–22); *On the Veiling of Virgins, passim*.

18. ANF 2:286, but he also advocates veiling in *Paed.* 3.11 (ANF 2:290). Augustine (*Letters*, 245 [NPNF² 6:292]) writes, "it is not becoming even in married women to uncover their hair, since the apostle commands women to keep their heads covered."

19. Exemplary hairstyles are illustrated in Rolf Hurschmann, "Hairstyle," in *Brill's New Pauly: Encyclopaedia of the Ancient World* (ed. Hubert Cancik and Helmuth Schneider; Leiden: Brill, 2005) 5:1099–103.

GREEK WOMEN DID NOT CUSTOMARILY WEAR A GARMENT OVER THEIR HEADS

Plutarch asked, "Why is it that when they [the Romans] worship the gods, they cover their heads?"[20] This implies that Greeks did not follow this custom of worshiping the gods with covered heads. Women appear to be prohibited from wearing a veil in the worship of the mystery religions according to an inscription from Andania.[21] Illustrations confirm that women at these religious ceremonies were not veiled.[22] This must have been a long-standing custom since the following regulations found in a temple in Despoina from the third century BC implied that women's hair could be seen, "Nor [let it be permissible to enter] for women with their hair braided, nor for men with their heads covered."[23]

The prohibition of "braided hair with gold" in 1 Tim 2:9 and 1 Pet 3:3 provides evidence that it was *not* NT church practice for women to be veiled or wear a garment over their heads in prayer. If church custom required women to cover their heads with a garment, this prohibition would have as little point as prohibiting certain types of similarly unseen undergarments. Consequently, if Paul in 1 Cor 11:5 were requiring a garment covering the head, he would have been advocating something that was not customary for Greek women,[24] nor was it customary in the Pauline or Petrine churches. Furthermore, Greek women, including women in prayer, were usually depicted without a garment covering the head. It does not make sense that Paul would assert something was disgraceful that in their culture was not considered disgraceful.

Concerning Greek customs A. Oepke observes:

> It used to be asserted by theologians that Paul was simply endorsing the unwritten law of Hellenic and Hellenistic feeling for what

---

20. Plutarch, *Quaest. rom.* 266C (*Mor.* 4:21) (Babbitt, LCL).
21. *Ditt. Syll.* 2:401–411 [no. 736]; cf. Oepke, "κατακαλύπτω," *TDNT* 3:562.
22. Johannes Leipoldt, *Die Religionen in der Umwelt des Urchristentums, Bilderatlas zur Religionsgeschichte* (ed. Hans Haas; Leipzig: Deichert, 1926), 9–11; nos. 105, 165, 168.
23. Horsely, *New Documents* 4 (1979 [1987]): 25 [108–9]; trans. of Maria Guarducci, *Epigrafica Greca*, 4 vols. (Rome: Istituto poligrafico dello Stato, Libreria dello Stato, 1967–78), 4:20; repr. of *IG* 5:2 (Berlin: 1913), 514. Cf. Ross Shepard Kraemer, *Her Share of the Blessings: Women's Religions among Pagans, Jews, and Christians in the Greco-Roman World* (New York: Oxford Univ. Press, 1992), 237 n. 74.
24. Cf. G. G. Findlay, "St. Paul's First Epistle to the Corinthians" (*The Expositor's Greek Testament*; London: Hodder & Stoughton, 1900), 2:872–3; Meyer, *1 Corinthians*, 248; Morris, *First Corinthians*, 152; Robertson and Plummer, *First Corinthians*, 229.

was proper. But this view is untenable.... It is quite wrong that Greek women were under some kind of compulsion to wear a veil in public.... Passages to the contrary are so numerous and unequivocal that they cannot be offset.... Empresses and goddesses, even those who maintain their dignity, like Hera and Demeter, are portrayed without veils.[25]

Hurschmann (over)states, "Greek and Roman women showed themselves outdoors only with headgear.... Otherwise, Greek women only gathered their hair with the *kekryphalos* [partial hairnet], the *sakkos* [hairnet], or ribbons."[26] Since most worship was indoors, hair done up would be expected.

Hurley notes further that "Grecian pottery provides abundant information concerning elegant hair styles and an absence of head-coverings among the Greeks from a very early period."[27] He concludes that "Graeco-Roman practice of the day, as evidenced by art and literature, did not include mandatory veiling of any sort.... Whether or not women pulled their garments [*palla*, Latin; *himation* or *peribolaion*, Greek] over their heads was a matter of indifference."[28] Jews referred to Gentile women as though they typically wore no veil.[29] DeVaux says that "feminine costume in Greek antiquity could include a veil on the head, but it seems to have been rarely worn."[30]

Galt's study of evidence for veiling demonstrates that some Greek women, particularly in the Hellenic period (late eighth century BC to 323 BC), are depicted as veiling their faces.[31] She has not, however, made a

---

25. *TDNT* 3:562.
26. Rolf Hurschmann, "Headgear," in *Brill's New Pauly* (2005): 6:19–20 with illustrations.
27. Hurley, "Man and Woman in 1 Corinthians," 44; cf. E. Pottier, M. Albert, and E. Saglio, "Coma," in *Dictionnaire des antiquités grecques et romaines* (ed. Ch. Daremburg and Edm. Saglio; Paris: Librairie Hachette et Cie, 1887): 1, 2:1367–71.
28. Hurley, *Biblical Perspective*, 269, cf. 67, 257.
29. *Num. Rab.* 9 on 5:18; Str-B 3:429; Oepke, "κατακαλύπτω," 3:562.
30. Roland de Vaux, "Sur le voile des femmes dans l'orient ancien," *RB* 44 (1935): 398, where he cites depictions of the *himation* draped over the back of a woman's head, but not the face, in Tanagra, Myrina, and Alexandria, probably with religious significance.
31. Caroline M. Galt, "Veiled Ladies," *AJA* 35 (1931): 373–93; *pace* Hurley's statement, *Biblical Perspective*, 269, "Facial veiling was unknown." Galt challenges the scholarly consensus by arguing the thesis that facial veiling by women in public, "now regarded as an 'oriental' custom, was the prevailing custom in Athens and possibly throughout Greece" (374). She acknowledges that "in no handbook, so far examined, does there seem to be the statement that when married women appeared in public their faces were veiled up to the eyes" (373–74). She cites major studies by Bieber (370) and Heuzey (380) that give no evidence for veiling and notes Pottier interprets the evidence differently (383).

solid case either that Greek society at large viewed it as shameful for a woman not to be veiled in public or that the predominant Greek custom for adult women in the Hellenistic age was to wear a head covering.[32] T. W. Davies concludes that "the ancient Egyptians were as much strangers to the face-veils as Europeans are, for on their paintings and sculptures such veils never appear. Nor were such veils worn by the ancient Ethiopians, Greeks, or the primitive inhabitants of Asia Minor."[33] Hays summarizes the crucial point:

> It was not the normal custom for women in Greek and Roman cultures to be veiled; thus, it is hard to see how their being unveiled in worship could be regarded as controversial or shameful. For women to have loose hair in public, however, *was* conventionally seen as shameful, a sign associated either with prostitutes or — perhaps worse from Paul's point of view — with women caught up in the ecstatic worship practices of the cults associated with Dionysius, Cybele, and Isis.[34]

Tertullian indicates that Jewesses stood out in the streets of North Africa because they wore veils,[35] implying that Gentile women ordinarily did not wear a veil. Written between AD 200 and 220,[36] Tertullian's *On the Veiling of Virgins* 1 insists that it is "not custom ... even ancient

---

32. Witherington (*Earliest Churches*, 81) misinterprets Galt's thesis and omits her more humble acknowledgments. Galt primarily addresses evidence hundreds of years before Paul, and her thesis is about facial veiling, not over-the-head coverings. Galt herself admits, "One looks in vain for confirmation of this theory in sculpture in the round" (377); "there are no sculptures in the round representing women with their faces partly covered" (380); "many stelae and other reliefs show ... a woman putting on or otherwise adjusting her mantle over her shoulders only" (386); "there are relatively few examples of veiling of the face to be found among published vases" (388). She also acknowledges that many or most of the examples of veiling she has found depict particular settings where veiling has long been regarded as an exceptional feature such as brides at their wedding (378, 388), the mantle dance where swaying draperies add an air of *coquetterie* (375–77), special religious acts (380), funerals (380, 387), and mourning (386). The vast majority of the evidence she does cite depicts women with their faces uncovered. For example, Galt's figure 10 (p. 385 of "Veiled Ladies"), depicting the Lansdowne Stele in the New York Metropolitan Museum of Art, shows a typical lady with hair done up modestly over her head with her entire face unobstructed. Galt's interpretation that women depicted with a raised hand were about to cover their faces to go out into public or had just uncovered their faces appears in many cases to be conjectural. She does not mention that a raised hand might have some other function such as a sign of modesty, common in most cultures, with no implication of a veil.
33. T. W. Davies, "Veil," in *A Dictionary of the Bible* 4:848.
34. Hays, *First Corinthians*, 185–86.
35. Tertullian (AD 160–240), *De Corona* 4; *De Oratione* 22.
36. Philip Schaff, *History of the Christian Church: Vol II. Ante-Nicene Christianity. A. D. 100–325* (7 vols.; 11th ed.; New York: Charles Scribner's Sons, 1914), 2:833.

custom" that is the basis for his argument for veiling virgins. He tries to defuse the obvious objection to veiling by arguing that the custom "is not 'strange' since it is not among 'strangers' that we find it but among ... the brotherhood."[37]

Women of the Hellenistic royal families (such as Arsinoe II, wife of Ptolemy II) are portrayed on coins with a *himation* draped over their heads, probably as a symbol of status or authority.[38] This parallels the Roman convention of draping a toga over one's head as a sign of social status, particularly while leading worship in the Roman cult. This is one of a limited number of settings where women are occasionally depicted wearing a garment draped over the head, notably match-making, the bride in her marriage ceremony,[39] funerals, mourning,[40] and the mantle dance.[41] Otherwise, depictions of women with a head-covering garment are rare.

ROMAN WOMEN WERE NOT REQUIRED TO WEAR A GARMENT OVER THEIR HEADS

A woman leader in Roman worship or sacrifice would, as customary practice, pull part of her *stola* or *palla* (the Greek *himation*) over her head just as men did in the Roman Empire.[42] Roman worship customs regarding a garment over the head made no distinction between the sexes.[43] Since in 1 Cor 11:2–16 Paul was specifically distinguishing between the sexes, he was not endorsing these Roman customs, at least not consistently. Furthermore, it is hard to believe that Paul, who was keen to suppress display of social standing in worship, should require that women display a sign of social status, namely, covering their heads in prayer and prophecy.

There is a general consensus within scholarship that Roman women were not required to wear any garment over their heads.[44] This does not

---

37. ANF 4:28.
38. Cf. R. R. R. Smith, *Hellenistic Royal Portraits* (Oxford: Oxford Univ. Press, 1985), pl. 75, 5–7; Gill, "Head-Coverings," 254.
39. Examples of a bride's complete facial veiling are Aeschylus, *Agamennon* 11.1178–1179, and Euripides *Iphigenia Taurica* 11.373.
40. Oepke, "κατακαλύπτω," 3:562.
41. Galt, "Veiled Ladies," 374–77.
42. Douglas R. Edwards, "Dress and Ornamentation" *ABD* 2:237; Thompson "Hairstyles," 112; R. MacMullen, "Women in Public in the Roman Empire," *Historia* 29 (1980): 208–18.
43. Oepke, "κατακαλύπτω," 3:562.
44. Cf. J. P. V. D. Balsdon, *Roman Women, their History and Habits* (London: Bodley Head, 1963), 252; Pottier, "Coma," 1355–71; Thompson, "Hairstyles," 112; L. Wilson, *The Clothing of the Ancient Romans* (Baltimore: Johns Hopkins Univ. Press, 1932).

mean, however, that veiling never occurred[45] or that it was rare for women to wear a garment over their heads. It does mean, however, that evidence is lacking that Roman culture at large regarded it as disgraceful for a woman not to wear a garment over her head. Some have argued, however, that it was shameful for a married woman to appear in public in Roman society without a hood over her head since it signaled sexual availability.

Thiselton adopts this view, citing Aline Rouselle as of "great importance for the issue of *head coverings*."[46] Rouselle's primary citation is Horace's *Sat.* 1.2.94 ("In a matron one can see only her face"), as though it implied that the head was covered, but the very next sentence identifies her "hairdressers" (1.2.98). Rouselle writes that "the satires were vague about a woman's social class,"[47] but the passage she cites (Horace, *Sat.* 1.2.70) identifies a woman of great rank and wealth, "the offspring of a great consul" "amidst snowy pearls and green emeralds" (1.2.80). This was not a typical woman, but one of great wealth from a powerful family keen to shield her from the public, as Horace explains. On the next page Rouselle notes that servants were unveiled. Since slaves made up a large proportion of Paul's churches and the nobility were a tiny minority (1 Cor 1:26), it is doubtful that Paul would call all women who prayed unveiled "disgraceful."

Rouselle next cites in support of this veiling custom a reference by Pliny, but each translation checked for this analysis, including Rouselle's, refers not to a veil but to a woman "sitting behind a curtain."[48] One does not "sit" behind a veil. Rouselle also cites Michna [sic.], *Ketubot* 7:6, as refer-

---

45. Dio Chrysostom, *Discourse* 33.15.9 (LCL), cites regarding Tarsus, which was heavily influenced by its oriental element: "Women should be so arrayed ... when in the street that nobody could see any part of them, neither of the face nor of the rest of the body." Cohoon and Crosby, *Dio Chrysostom*, 3:319 (LCL) note 2 states, "This prescription may have been due to the oriental element at Tarsus," indicating that this was an unusual custom.
46. Thiselton, *First Corinthians*, 801 and 829, both times citing pp. 296–337, even though only part of pp. 314–15 address this topic. Thiselton also cites D. B. Martin, *The Corinthian Body* (New Haven: Yale University Press, 1995), 229–49. Martin also cites evidence that loosened hair symbolized sexual availability on pp. 233, 237, n. 44. Because he assumes that "Paul cannot consider the female equal to the male" (249), he interprets the present tense future in Gal 3:28.
47. Aline Rouselle, "Body Politics in Ancient Rome," in *A History of Women in the West, I: From Ancient Goddesses to Christian Saints* (ed. G. Duby and M. Perot; Cambridge, Mass.: Harvard University Press, 1992), 314.
48. Rouselle ("Body Politics," 315) gives the impression of a veil by omitting the crucial verb "sit" and replacing it "with an eager ear hidden behind a curtain." Dr. Norman Lund, in an email to the author dated October 9, 2005, translates it literally, "she sits close at hand, separated [from us] by a curtain, and she listens to our praises with most greedy ears." Cf. the almost identical translations by W. Melmoth and W. M. L. Hutchinson, *Pliny Letters*, 2 vols. (LCL; Cambridge, Mass.: Harvard Univ. Press, 1961), 332–33, and Betty Radice, *The Letters of the Younger Pliny* (Harmondsworth, Middlesex: Penguin, 1963), 126.

ring to "head uncovered" when it actually says "with her hair unbound."[49] Witherington, who also adopts the garment headcovering view, acknowledges that "public portraits of women ... often show them bareheaded."[50] Conzelmann suggests that the rarity of illustrations or portraiture with veils "proves nothing" and cites three examples to try to prove something about the wearing of veils, but the first of the three has no veil, and the second is a standard empress Livia *capite velato* portrait.[51] He asserts, "It can be assumed that respectable Greek women wore a head covering in public. Ovid is of course no proof to the contrary."[52]

But why should Ovid's "impressively demonstrated"[53] variability of fashion and personal taste in hairstyles be so easily dismissed? Ovid (*Ars am.* 3:135–68) illustrates "that the different ways of dressing the hair in Rome were equal in number to the acorns of a many-branched oak, to the bees of the Hybla ... every new day adding to the number." Juvenal (*Sat.* 6.501–503) confirms, "So important is the business of beautifications; so numerous are the tiers and storeys piled one upon another on her head!" It does not make sense that art depicted respectable women with elaborate hairstyles in such a profusion of variations but that those women never showed their hair in public.

The absence of any comparable abundance of graphic evidence or such a variety of hairstyles in portraiture of women from societies that require veiling indicates that women's hair must have been commonly visible in the Greco-Roman world in the time of Paul. Baugh cites various evidence of the influence of elaborate Roman hairstyles in the Hellenistic world.[54] B. Winter writes, "Statue types displayed the simple hairstyles which epitomized the modest wife and were worn by members of the imperial family. These statues were replicated throughout the Empire and represented 'fashion icons' to be copied by modest married women."[55] S. E. Wood notes,

---

49. See below, pp. 162, 164–65, and 167.
50. Ben Witherington III, *Conflict & Community in Corinth: A Socio-Rhetorical Commentary on 1 and 2 Corinthians* (Grand Rapids: Eerdmans, 1995), 234.
51. Conzelmann, *1 Corinthians*, 185 n. 40, citing illustrations in J. B. Bury et al., *The Cambridge Ancient History* (12 vols.; Cambridge: University Press, 1923–39), plates on 4:167, 169, 171.
52. Conzelmann, *1 Corinthians*, 185 n. 40.
53. Acknowledged by Conzelmann, *1 Corinthians*, 185 n. 40.
54. S. M. Baugh, "A Foreign World: Ephesus in the First Century," WCA 35.
55. Bruce W. Winter, *Roman Wives, Roman Widows: The Appearance of New Women and the Pauline Communities* (Grand Rapids: Eerdmans, 2003), 104. For examples, see P. Scherrer, *Ephesus: The New Guide* (Turkey: Austrian Archaeological Institute, 2000), 199 fig. 2; A. T. Croom, *Roman Clothing and Fashion* (Stroud: Tempus, 2000), 98.

"Works of the visual arts would show her [a married woman] how they [imperial wives] dressed and how they wore their hair."[56] Juvenal (*Sat.* 6.617) confirms this influence, "What woman will not follow when an empress leads the way?"

In light of all of the typical depictions of women in the Roman world in social settings without a head covering, what is one to make of Plutarch's statement in *Roman Questions* 267A-B in response to the question "Why do sons cover their heads [συγκεκαλυμμένοι] when they escort their parents to the grave, while daughters go with uncovered [γυμναῖς] heads and hair unbound [κόμαις λελυμέναις]?" Regarding several possible answers, Plutarch raised the following question, "Or is it that the unusual is proper in mourning, and it is more usual for women to go forth in public with their heads covered [ἐγκεκαλυμμέναις] and men with their heads uncovered [ἀκαλύπτοις]?... But formerly women were not allowed to cover [ἐπικαλύπτεσθαι] the head at all.... Sulpicius Galus [divorced his wife] because he saw his wife pull her cloak [τὸ ἱμάτιον] over her head [κατὰ κεφαλῆς]."[57] Thompson notes, "This is the only significant literary evidence for a general custom of women's wearing head-coverings in Greece in the first century CE."[58] To be more precise, this saying is about Roman customs.

Several things should be noted about Plutarch's question before one concludes that it contradicts all of the portraiture evidence of dignified women without a garment covering their heads. Plutarch explicitly states that at a parent's funeral "daughters go bareheaded." So at least in this setting it was customary for daughters to be bareheaded in public. Plutarch also notes that "formerly women were not allowed to cover the head at all," implying such head covering to be a recent permission that was formerly prohibited. Since Plutarch lived from approximately AD 47–120, he wrote at least a generation after Paul. Furthermore, it is as part of his question, not as a separate assertion, that Plutarch asks if the reason might be that "it is *more usual* for women to go forth in public with their heads covered

---

56. S. E. Wood, *Imperial Women: A Study in Public Images, 40 BC–AD 69* (Leiden: Brill, 1999), 1.
57. Plutarch, *Mor.* 4:26–27 (Babbitt, LCL). Winter, *Roman Wives*, 82, notes that Valerius Maximus, writing in the time of Tiberius, in *Memorable Deeds and Sayings*, 6.3.10, "saw this as 'frightful marital severity' on the part of Sulpicius Gallus."
58. Thompson, "Hairstyles," 104.

and men with their heads uncovered?" Thompson stresses that this was a speculative suggestion.[59]

Plutarch's question addresses both the head covering of women and of men. Extensive evidence supports the second half of his explanation, that Roman men in public normally did not cover their heads. One reason Plutarch phrased this question tentatively may be that he was doubtful whether women covered their heads commonly enough to warrant this half of his generalization. In any event, Plutarch speaks only of what "is more usual," not of any requirement for women. Nor does he draw from this that it would be disgraceful for Roman women to go out in public without a head covering.

In Hellenistic and Roman cultures for centuries preceding and following the time of Paul, virtually all of the portraiture, sculpture, and other graphic evidence depicts respectable women's hair done up, not let down loose.[60] Not only formal portraits and busts, but also vase paintings and other depictions of daily life confirm this.

Roman customs for at least the socially prominent women's hairstyles in Corinth are exhibited in numerous marble busts and coins from Corinth. In these, the woman's hair is almost always done up neatly over her head, typically twisted or braided and tied up with a cord or hairnet and without any head-covering garment.[61] The famous portrait from the middle of the first century AD of a man and wife found in Pompeii in the part of a house used to display ancestral portraits depicts the wife without any head covering and holding a writing tablet.[62] A pair of bronze busts of a husband and his wife and another marble portrait of the same woman from Pompeii

---

59. Ibid.
60. E.g., Edwards, "Dress," 237. The one exception mentioned by Fee, *First Corinthians*, 510 n. 76, depicted in Goodenough, *Jewish Symbols*, XI, figure 99, is not really an exception because their hair is neatly curled over their entire head, so that even the ringlets that fall behind their necks are not "hanging loose." Furthermore, Sharon Kelley Heyob, *The Cult of Isis among Women in the Greco-Roman World* (Leiden: Brill, 1975), 60, and Fiorenza, *In Memory of Her*, 227, note that this was a distinctive hairstyle of devotees of Isis, "with a band around the forehead and curls falling on the shoulder."
61. Thompson, "Hairstyles," 106–11, gives sixteen photographs of portraits of women. Only two have any garment draped over the head. One of these is a coin, probably of Augustus's wife Livia wearing a crown with a veil covering the back half of the head but none of the face or frontal hair. Another coin depicting Livia has no veil. The only other figure with a head covering is flat-chested and appears to have a mustache and Arab-style chin beard but is described on p. 111 as follows, "The cap on the present figurine associates her with a conventional type of a female household servant or 'nurse.'" See also Johnson, *Sculpture*, 86–87, items 160–64.
62. See color plate 23 of J. Ward-Perkins and A. Claridge, *Pompeii AD 79* (London: Royal Academy of Arts, 1976), 20; cf. Gill, "Head-Coverings," 253.

have no head covering.[63] Similarly, most of the women in the frieze of the Ara Pacis Augustae in Rome, dating from 13 to 9 BC have no covering on their heads.[64] Since friezes, busts, and coins were made for public display of prominent persons, this probably implies that it was socially acceptable for women in Corinth to be in public without a head covering.

There is abundant evidence that it was customary for women to wear their long hair up neatly on their heads in Corinth as throughout the ancient Roman and Hellenistic world of that time.

- Professor E. A. Judge showed this author all of the huge collection of plaster cast copies of Greek and Roman portrait statuary in the Cambridge University Department of Classics.[65] Invariably, respectable women had their hair done up.[66] It only makes sense that the women being portrayed wanted their statues to depict them in a respectable light.

- Gill notes that such portraits suggest "it was socially acceptable in a Roman colony for women to be seen bare-headed in public.... It is this long hair [done up properly] that is seen as a head covering which is worn instead of a veil.... Long hair ... was a symbol in Roman society of a wife's relationship to her husband."[67]

- Thompson understood Paul to be suggesting "that women's long hair be a 'wrapping' ... that is, fastened up, as contrasted to being allowed to flow unimpeded around the shoulders."[68]

- Balsdon notes that "in the republic, younger women dressed their hair in simple style, drawing it to the back of the head to form a simple knot, which was thrust through with a pin,"[69] but that gradually they adopted more ornamentation. Older women, too, wore their hair up in standard conventions. Gradually "the simple strips of rough wool, emblem of chastity and symbol of the honour due to a married woman, which originally enclosed the mass of the

---

63. Ward-Perkins and Claridge, *Pompeii*, inv. 4992, no. 26 and inv. 120424.
64. Gill, "Head-Coverings," 252, 247.
65. In September, 1991.
66. The only exceptions were at specific occasions, notably for agonized mourning (unrelated to the Corinthian issue) and weddings (where the sexual implications of hair let down are blessed). Cf. Thompson, "Hairstyles," 112.
67. Gill, "Head-Coverings," 251, 258.
68. Thompson, "Hairstyles," 112.
69. Balsdon, *Roman Women*, 252.

tutulus [the mass of hair drawn together on the head], changed to linen or silk ribbons in bright colours."[70]

Tertullian (AD 160–240) confirms this convention in *On the Veiling of Virgins* 7: "Hair serves for a covering … for their very adornment properly consists in this, that, by being massed together upon the crown, it wholly covers the very citadel of the head with an encirclement of hair."[71] The typical way for a Roman, Greek, or Jewish woman to put up her hair was with a strip of cloth or a hairnet.[72] This widespread convention that women should wear their hair done up as a modest covering makes perfect sense of Paul's statement in 1 Cor 11:15 that long hair is given to women "as a covering." It also provides the perfect background for the kind of covering he required women to have on their heads while praying or prophesying in 11:5–6, 10, 13. Since having hair done up properly typically involved something to bind the hair up, such as a ribbon, hairnet, or cloth strip, references to a head covering may include the binding material as well as the woman's hair itself properly done up.

JEWISH CUSTOMS REGARDING GARMENT HEAD COVERINGS VARIED AND CHANGED OVER TIME

The OT does not indicate that the wearing of a garment or a veil over a woman's hair was a common practice or in any sense a requirement. It does, however, describe various head and hair ornaments that implied that a woman's head was not customarily covered with any garment: headbands, dangling earrings, headdresses, nose rings, and well-set hair (cf. Isa 3:18–24; cf. Gen 24:47; Ezek 16:12). Various OT passages depict women that could be clearly seen as beautiful, implying that their faces could not have been covered.[73]

The archaeological studies of Benzinger and Krauss emphasize that in NT times women faced no compulsion to be veiled, and Oepke adds that "Mary and other holy women are often depicted without veils."[74] A gradual shift to garment head coverings within Judaism in the centuries after Christ may possibly be reflected in the change recorded from the

70. Ibid., 255–56.
71. ANF 4:32.
72. Edwards, "Dress," 237.
73. Cf. this same conclusion by de Vaux, "Sur le voile des femmes," 408.
74. Oepke, "κατακαλύπτω," 3:563.

earlier Mishnaic rule that a woman may be divorced without receiving her Ketubah if "she goes out with her hair unbound" (*m. Ketub.* 7:6) to "if she goes out with uncovered head" (*b. Ketub.* 72a, b). The explanatory note at *b. Ketub.* 72a, "With hair loose or unbound," however, supports the original meaning, that an "uncovered head" is one not covered with hair modestly done up. This practice is still affirmed in *b. Giṭṭ.* 90b, "a wife go[ing] out with her hair unfastened."

Women followed Jesus almost everywhere. Paul spoke of the other disciples taking their wives with them in their travels, and the practice of the seclusion of women is incompatible with Paul's own associations with his women colleagues.[75] Since the NT shows that the seclusion of women extolled by certain Jewish authors was not widespread even in Palestine, one should not assume that the veiling that they similarly extol was all that widely practiced either. Although in the eyes of some Jewish leaders it was an ideal that should be fostered, it has not been demonstrated regarding even Palestine that veiling was a widely recognized social requirement for women or that the lack of a garment over the head was generally regarded as disgraceful.

DIONYSIAC DEBAUCHERY GAVE HAIR LET DOWN LOOSE DISGRACEFUL ASSOCIATIONS

In the Dionysiac cult, which had a prominent temple in Corinth, it was customary for women to let down their hair to "prophesy" and engage in all sorts of sexual debauchery. Many believed that in order for women to make prophetic utterances they had to let their hair hang loose.[76] Euripides (*Bacch.* 695) says, "They shook their long hair [κόμας] out over their shoulders."[77] Nonnus (*Dion.* 45.47–48) says, "Many a maiden driven crazy shook her hair loose."[78] Lucian (*Dionysus* 2) says, "They toss their hair in the wind."[79] Sayings like this are typical in the Dionysiac literature.[80] According to Livy 39.13.12, the matrons of the disreputable cult of Diony-

75. Cf. chapter 2 on Paul's women colleagues.
76. Cf. Lösch, "Christliche Frauen in Corinth," 236–46; Fiorenza, *In Memory of Her*, 227.
77. C.K. Williams, *The Baccae of Euripides* (New York: Farrar, Straus and Giroux, 1990), 45.
78. Nonnus, *Dion.* 3:322–23 (W. H. D. Rouse, LCL).
79. Lucian, 1:50–51 (A. M. Harmon, LCL).
80. E.g., Plutarch, *Mor.*, 249E-F. Cf. Dittenberger, *SIG* 2:401–11 (no. 736); Jan N. Bremmer, "Maenads," *OCD3* (1966), 908a.

sus (who discovered wine[81] — his Latin name is Bacchus) performed rites "with dishevelled hair." He describes the testimony of Hispana to the senate about their initiation rites:

> Men mingling with women and the freedom of darkness added, no form of crime, no sort of wrongdoing, was left untried.... If any of them were disinclined to endure abuse or reluctant to commit crime, they were sacrificed as victims. To consider nothing wrong, she continued, was the highest form of religious devotion among them.[82]

Diodorus 4.3 records that "Bacchic bands of women ... join in the frenzied revelry ... in this manner acting the part of the Maenads."[83] The Maenads, also known as Bacchae or Thyiades, were women who represented wild sexual freedom inspired by Dionysus. Depictions of lust-filled Maenads are common in sculptures and vase paintings, almost always with hair let down, hanging freely.[84] "More than any other figure of the Dionysiac worship they represent the complete liberation from conventions of daily life, the awakening of primeval instincts, and the union with nature achieved in the cult of Dionysus."[85]

Euripides (*Bacch.* 118) says that Dionysiac celebrations set women "free from shuttle and from loom." Women hailed Dionysus as the liberator. Pausanias 10.6.2 referred to "women who go mad in honor of Dionysos" and celebrate "mad revels" on Mount Parnassus near the Gulf of Corinth. Virgil's *Aeneid* 7.394–405 tells of Amata using a Dionysiac revel to incite anger against her husband for planning to marry their daughter to someone Amata despised. Mothers rallied to her: "Bare necks, hair to the winds ... doff the fillets from your hair, join the revels with me!" Stobaeus preserves a warning to husbands that "the best way to preserve their wives'

---

81. Diodorus Siculus 4.3.
82. Sage, *Livy* (LCL), 11:255.
83. *Diodorus of Sicily* 2:346–47 (C. H. Oldfather, LCL).
84. For illustrations of hair hanging loose in Dionysiac cultic celebrations, see Johannes Leipoldt, *Umwelt des Urchristentums*. III. *Bilder zum neutestamentlichen Zeitalter* (Berlin: Evangelische Verlagsanstalt, 1973), fig. 59 and 60; idem, *Bilderatlas zur Religionsgeschichte*, 9–11, fig. 105, 165, 168. Cf. Also the description in Gill, "Head-Coverings," 256; F. Matz, *ΔΙΟΝΥΣΙΑΚΗ ΤΕΛΕΤΗ: Archäologische Untersuchungen zum Dionysoskult in hellenistischer und römischer Zeit* (Abhandlungen der geistes-und sozial-wissenschaftlichen Klasse der Akademie der Wissenschaften und der Literatur in Mainz 15; Wiesbaden: Steiner, 1963), with plates 20–23 and pp. 15, 21 of veiled women about to be initiated.
85. George M. A. Hanfmann and John Richard Thornhill Pollard, "Maenads," *OCD* (2003), 636.

chastity was to keep them away from the worship of Dionysus and the Great Mother."[86]

Dionysiac practice reinforced the symbolism of hair let down loose: sexual looseness and repudiation of marital commitment to sexual fidelity.[87] Significantly, the very problems of disorder and too high an estimation of ecstatic experiences typified both the Dionysiac cult and the problems in the Corinthian church.[88] This background explains why women would let their hair down when prophesying in the Corinthian church, possibly to symbolize exultation in their freedom in Christ. Given the popularity of the Dionysiac cult, especially in Corinth, it is not surprising that Paul would write against women letting their hair down.[89]

IT WAS DISGRACEFUL FOR JEWISH WOMEN TO LET THEIR HAIR DOWN

Within Jewish culture, all respectable women wore their hair done up in public. "The head could be covered by a hairnet such as those found at Masada and the Cave of Letters which were similar to those in Roman society."[90] Str-B (3:428–29) lists evidence that a woman's dressed hair may meet Jewish requirements. Judith 10:3 and 16:8 describe Judith braiding her hair and fastening her hair with a tiara.

Judaism regarded it as shameful for a woman to have hair hanging down loose in public. Hair unbound was the sign of the accused adulteress. To "unbind her hair" (Num 5:18)[91] set her apart like a leper, but as morally unclean.[92] Rabbinic law forbade loosed hair, as in *m. Soṭah* 3:8, "How does a man differ from a woman? He may go with hair unbound and with garments rent, but she may not go with hair unbound and with garments rent."[93] It was so serious an offense that *m. Ketub.* 7:6 states, "These are they that are put away without their *Ketubah* [the contract that indicated the money that the bridegroom pledged himself to assign to the bride in

---

86.   Richard and Catherine Kroeger, "Evidence of Maenadism," *SBLSP* (1978): 2:333.

87.   Cf. the citations from the primary literature by Collins, *First Corinthians*, 397–401.

88.   Cf. above, pp. 143–44, 162–64 on allusions to Dionysiac religion in 1 Corinthians.

89.   So, Lösch, "Christliche Frauen in Korinth," 251–58; F. C. Grant, ed., *Hellenistic Religions: The Age of Syncretism* (LLA; Indianapolis: Bobbs-Merril, 1953), 26–27.

90.   Edwards, "Dress," 237.

91.   Cf. further on this passage below, pp. 171–73, 435.

92.   Cf. Lev 13:45: a leper must "let his hair hang loose"; Hurley, *Biblical Perspective*, 262.

93.   Danby, *Mishnah*, 298.

the event of his death or his divorcing her] … if she goes out with her hair unbound, or spins in the street, or speaks with any man."[94]

It was a crime to loose a woman's hair in the street, as *m. B. Qam.* 8:6 states: "If he … loosed a woman's hair in the street, he must pay 400 *zuz*. … It once happened that a man unloosed a woman's hair in the street and she came before R. Akiba [AD 120–140] and he condemned him to pay her 400 *zuz*."[95] This demonstrates that women wore their hair up in public, seems to imply that this particular woman was not wearing a garment over her hair, and shows how shameful it was regarded for a woman to let her hair down loose. Only in rare cases was a woman permitted to let her hair down in public, usually as a sign of extreme humbling and mourning.[96]

Consensus among Three Cultures: Loosed Hair Disgraces a Woman

There was in Paul's day an overwhelming consensus in Greek, Roman, and Jewish cultures that women should have their hair done up. It was a sign of her dignity and honor, and to let her hair down in public brought disgrace on a woman. "Women of all three societies put their hair up and decorated it in various, sometimes expensive, ways."[97] Virtually all portraiture from the Greco-Roman world of the first century, and for that matter for centuries surrounding the time of Paul, depicts respectable women with their hair done up. However, the Maenads in Dionysiac revelries and other female figures symbolizing promiscuous or illicit sexual relations are often portrayed with their hair let down. The iconography of hair let down loose was of "undisciplined sexuality."[98] Fee was simply mistaken to write "that

---

94. Ibid., 255; cf. Alfred Edersheim, *Sketches of Jewish Social Life in the Days of Christ* (London: Religious Tract Society, 1876), 157.

95. Danby, *Mishnah*, 343; 400 *zuz* was a large amount, the same fine that was given "if he tore his ear, plucked out his hair, spat and his spittle touched him, or pulled his cloak from off him." In contrast, this passage begins: "If a man cuffed his fellow he must pay him a *sela* [4 *zuz*]."

96. 2 Macc 3:19; 3 Macc 1:18; Add Esth 14:2; 2 Esd 9:38; Jos Asen. 10:14. *m. Ketub.* 2:1 cites as proof that a woman was married as a virgin, "if there are witnesses that she went forth [to the marriage] in a litter and with hair unbound (פָרוּעַ)" (Danby, *Mishnah*, 246). This implies that married women were expected to have their hair bound up. Edersheim, *Jewish Social Life*, 154, notes that a female proselyte had to have her hair unbound at her baptism; cf. W. C. van Unnik, "Les cheveux défaits des femmes baptisées: Un rite de baptême dans l'ardne ecclésiastique d'Hippolyte," VC 1 (1947): 87–89, 93.

97. Hurley, *Biblical Perspective*, 270–71; cf. 169, 257–59, 269; *m. Ketub.* 2:1; 7:6; *b. Ketub.* 72a, b; *b. Soṭah* 8b, 9a.

98. Cf. C. R. Hallpike, "Social Hair," *Man* NS 4 (1969): 256–64.

there is no sure first-century evidence that long [loosed] hair in public would have been a disgrace of some kind."[99]

In summary, there is abundant evidence that it would not have been disgraceful for women in Corinth in Paul's day to pray or prophesy without a garment covering their heads,[100] but there is abundant evidence that it would be disgraceful for a woman to lead worship in a public assembly with her hair let down loose.

FOURTEEN REASONS TO INTERPRET WOMEN'S "UNCOVERED HEAD" AS REFERRING TO HAIR LET DOWN

There are fourteen key reasons to interpret the "uncovered head" of women in this passage as referring to hair hanging loosely and the "covering" Paul requires as hair done up:

1. Paul identifies a woman's long hair as given to her to function "as a covering" in 11:15.[101]
2. Social convention in Corinth required women to wear their hair done up in public, but it was contrary to Hellenistic custom to pray in public with a garment over one's head. Loosed hair was disgraceful (11:5) and symbolized sexual looseness in Roman, Greek, and Jewish culture.
3. Loosed hair fits the cultural influence and specific practice of the Dionysiac cult, which was popular in Corinth and explains why women in Corinth might have let their hair down.
4. Women letting their hair down fits the warped Corinthian ideas about marriage and sex (cf. 1 Cor 5–7) and their overly realized eschatology.
5. Because wild hair was a peculiar and apparently new Corinthian church aberration,[102] it is compatible with Paul's praise in 11:2 and his implication of a new teaching in 11:3.

---

99. Fee, *First Corinthians*, 496.
100. Thiselton, *First Corinthians*, 801, 828–29, interprets the lack of a head covering garment as disgraceful since it symbolized sexual availability. If that is what Paul intended, it would still fit the following interpretation of the rest of this passage except that v. 15 would have to be reinterpreted as an analogy. Interpreting the woman's head covering as a garment would also lose the symmetry between vv. 4 and 5 both referring to hair just as vv. 14–15 do.
101. Cf. below, pp. 204–7.
102. Probably just reported by Chloe's people, cf. above, pp. 113–15.

6. Hair that was let down ties in more directly with Paul's introduction in 11:3 that lays a foundation for respect to one's source. Cultural evidence confirms that hair let down signaled disrespect.[103]

7. The only occurrence in the text Paul cited the most, the LXX, of "uncovered" (11:5; ἀκατακάλυπτος in Lev 13:45) translates פָּרוּעַ, from פרע, which Hebrew scholars agree means "to let the hair on the head hang loosely."[104] It is the earliest instance of the word "cover" (κατακαλύπτω) occurring with "head" in the *TLG* database.[105] Its phrase, "his head uncovered" (καὶ ἡ κεφαλὴ αὐτοῦ ἀκατακάλυπτος), parallels 1 Cor 11:5, "her head uncovered" (ἀκατακαλύπτῳ τῇ κεφαλῇ).

8. "Uncovered" (ἀκατακάλυπτος) is explained twice in verses 5–6, using "for" (γάρ). Both reasons explain the uncovering as equivalent to hair being clipped or shaved. This associates the covering as hair and fits most naturally if "uncovered" refers to a woman with her hair let down. In Greek literature, the word for "hair" was typically omitted in contexts involving the verb "shave" or "cut," and "head" often implied "hair."[106]

---

103. Cf. above pp. 142–44, 162–66.

104. *HALOT* 970; cf. KBL 779, "let the hair of the head go loose"; BDB 828 "let go, let loose, unbind head." פרע is regularly used to indicate long hair hanging down loose or disheveled, e.g., Lev 10:6; 13:45; 21:10; Num 5:18; 6:5; Ezek 44:20; *m. Ketub.* 2:1; 7:6, "with her hair unbound"; *b. Ta'an.* 17b. Preston T. Massey ("The Meaning of κατακαλύπτω and κατὰ κεφαλῆς ἔχων in 1 Corinthians 11.2–16," *NTS* 53 [2007]: 502–23, 523) alleges, in spite of the clear evidence of Lev 13:45 to the contrary, "when a text discussing the loosening or unbinding of hair is mentioned, the adjective ἀκατακάλυπτος is not used." He lists this as his second major conclusion even though he provides no support from any citation of Lev 13:45 that even hints it might refer to anything other than hair. He omits evidence of continuing use of this expression with hair let loose in Paul's time and dismisses the most natural reading of Paul's affirmation in v. 9 that woman is given hair "as a covering." Although he cites Callimachus's prohibition of women "with hair unbound" in *Hymn to Demeter* 6.5, he makes no mention of the relevance to the exegesis of 1 Cor 11:5–16 of the convention that respectable women wore their hair up and the wealth of evidence that women's hair let loose was shameful. His entire argument is structured to repudiate the straw man idea "that the verb κατακαλύπτω means 'to cover the head with long hair.'" For a detailed critique and refutation of each of Massey's conclusions, see www.pbpayne.com.

105. Next is Philo, *Spec. Laws*, III.60, referring to the custom described in Num 5:18, "the woman is to come forward with her head uncovered [ἀκατακαλύπτῳ τῇ κεφαλῇ]" (Philo 7:512–13 [Colson, LCL]). It is not clear whether this refers to hair, as does the Hebrew passage it is citing and was still practiced according to *m. Sotah* 1:5, or a garment covering. Philo's wording in 3.56 is entirely appropriate for describing the letting down of hair, which is the meaning of the passage Philo is describing, Num 5:18, and also its description in *m. Sotah* 1:5. Since a woman's hair done up symbolized marital faithfulness, when her hair is let down, she is stripped of her symbol of modesty.

106. For instance, using this same verb, Num 6:9 states (with omitted words in brackets), "But if a man dies very suddenly beside him and he defiles his dedicated head [of hair], then he shall shave his head [of hair] on the day when he becomes clean." In this case, it is clear that "head"

9. In Paul's day, an accused adulteress had her hair let down, and shaving was the penalty of a convicted adulteress.[107] This explains why an uncovered woman is the same as a woman with shorn hair (11:5). This explanation works only if "uncovered" refers to hair let down.

10. This interpretation consistently identifies the head covering for both men and women as referring to hair, as one would expect from their parallel terminology to convey opposites: women's heads should be covered (11:5–6), but men's should not (11:7).

11. It makes sense of verse 13, "Judge for yourselves." The Corinthians would agree; loosed hair is shameful.

12. It is perfectly consistent with Paul's statements that would be incongruous if he were enforcing a garment custom: a woman's long hair is her "glory" (v. 15), "long hair is given to her as a covering" (v. 15), and "We, the churches of God, have no such custom" (v. 16).

13. It avoids the inconsistency of Paul demanding that women follow a Jewish head-covering custom, but prohibiting men from following a Jewish head-covering custom.

14. It avoids making irrelevant both Paul's and Peter's prohibition of women wearing braided hair interwoven with gold, since hair would not be visible if covered by a garment.[108]

Not surprisingly, many scholars[109] advocate the hair interpretation over the dominant veil interpretation, and the NIV includes this alternate

---

substitutes for "hair" because it is followed by "shave his head." Numbers 6:18–19 states, "The Nazirite shall then shave his dedicated head [of hair] ... and shall take the dedicated hair of his head and put it on the fire ... after he has shaved his dedicated [hair]." Both the LXX and MT omit the word "hair" twice. "Hair" is also omitted as the object of the verb for "to cut" in LXX Jer 7:28–29, "This is the nation that has not obeyed the Lord its God or responded to correction. Truth has perished; it has vanished from their lips. Cut off [the hair of] your head and throw it away; take up a lament." MT Jer 7:29 has a feminine imperative and suffix, "cut off her hair." Callimachus, *Hymn. Cer.* 6.125 uses "head" to convey "hair": ὡς πόδας, ὡς κεφαλὰς παναπηρέας ("unsandaled with hair unbound").

107. Cf. below, pp. 171–73.
108. Cf. above, p. 152, and below, pp. 312–13.
109. Among the many advocates of this interpretation, detailed argumentation is given in Hurley, "Man and Woman in 1 Corinthians," 43–56; idem, "Veils," 190–220; and *Biblical Perspective*, 66–68, 168–71, 177–78, 254–71; Isaksson, *Marriage and Ministry*, 165–86; Martin, "1 Corinthians 11.2–16," 231–41; Murphy-O'Connor, "Sex," 488–500; E. Fiorenza, *In Memory of Her*, 227–30; David W. Odell-Scott, *A Post-Patriarchal Christology* (Altanta: Scholars Press, 1991), 178; Padgett, "ἀντί," *TynBul* 45 (1994): 181–87; Wolfgang Schrage, *Der erste Brief an die Korinther* (1 Kor 6,12–11,16) (EKKNT 7/2 1995; 4 vols.; Neukirchen-Vluyn: Neukirchener

reading. "Disgraces her head" entails the disgrace a woman brings on herself. It would probably have been embarrassing, if not an affront, to most men and women in the church. It would be particularly disgraceful to her husband, since it symbolized her repudiation of sexual fidelity to her husband.

WHY WOULD WOMEN LET THEIR HAIR DOWN IN THE CORINTHIAN CHURCH?

Women would let their hair down for the same reason it was popular in the Dionysiac cult. They enjoyed such revelry. Just as in the case of men displaying effeminate hair, social and personal reasons were probably far more influential for women letting their hair down than theological reasons. Given the extent of Dionysiac influence in Corinth, it is easy to imagine some women thinking, "Hey, let's have some fun and let our hair down in church!" Just as today many people see values in feminism, many people identified with positive aspects of the Dionysiac cult, such as Plutarch does in *Mor.* 367C, "the creative and fostering spirit is Dionysus." It is not surprising that some women who exulted in their freedom in Christ would express that freedom by letting their hair down just as the Dionysiacs did. This would not necessarily entail accepting the bad things associated with the Dionysiac cult.

The obvious objection to this—that Christianity does not permit such revelry—is blunted by the Corinthian acceptance of dualism that separated spirituality from actions of the body. It is also blunted by the tendency of the Corinthian church to take excessive liberties in several areas: divisiveness (ch. 3), immorality (5:1–5, 11; 6:15–18; 7:1; 10:8), lawsuits against one another (6:1–8), eating meats offered to idols (ch. 8; 10:14, 20–22), getting drunk at the Lord's Supper (11:21), and shameful and disorderly church gatherings (chs. 11; 12; 14). As a result, Paul writes,

---

Verlag, 1991–2001), 2:487–533, 492 n. 20; David E. Blattenberger III, *Rethinking 1 Corinthians 11:2–16 through Archaeological and Moral-Rhetorical Analysis* (Lewiston, NY: Mellen, 1997); Judith M. Gundry-Volf, "Gender and Creation in 1 Corinthians 11:2–16: A Study in Paul's Theological Method," in *Evangelium, Schriftauslegung, Kirche* (eds. J. Ådna, S. J. Hafemann, and O. Hofius; FS P. Stuhlmacher; Göttingen: Vandenhoeck & Ruprecht, 1997), 151–71; Horsley, *1 Corinthians*, 153–54; Marlis Gielen, "Beten und Prophezien mit unverhülltem Kopf?" *ZNW* 90 (1999): 220–49; Collins, *First Corinthians*, 401; Blomberg, "Neither Hierarchalist," 344; Jerome H. Neyrey, *Paul, in Other Words: A Cultural Reading of His Letters* (Louisville, Ky.: Westminster John Knox, 1990), 131; and M. Böhm, "Beobachtungen zur paulinischen Schriftrezeption und Schriftargumentation im 1. Korintherbrief," *ZNW* 97 (2006): 207–34.

"Come back to your senses as you ought, and stop sinning.... I say this to your shame" (15:34). Paul introduces this passage urging the Corinthians to "follow the example of Christ" (11:1), rather than (presumably) the example of pagan worship.

Apparently some people in the church felt that they were above the constraints of the marriage relationship. This explains why Paul writes, "A woman is bound to her husband as long as he lives" (1 Cor 7:39) and repeatedly warns against sexual immorality (e.g., 5:1 – 7; 6:12 – 19; 7:2 – 5; 10:8) and pagan revelry (10:7 – 11). First Corinthians 5 – 7 establishes that at least some in the Corinthian church had warped ideas about marriage and sexual relations. Paul had written them earlier as well "not to associate with sexually immoral people" (5:9) who claim to be believers. One man in the church even "has his father's wife. And you are proud!" (5:1 – 2).

Paul twice quotes what was apparently a slogan summing up the Corinthians' idea of freedom, "Everything is permissible for me," which Paul counters with two corrections, "but not everything is beneficial ... but I will not be mastered by anything" (6:12; 10:23). Similarly, "Food for the stomach and the stomach for food" (6:13) was apparently a Corinthian slogan implying permission to satisfy the body's appetites, including sexual appetites. Consequently Paul adds in 6:13 – 18, "but God will destroy them both. The body is not meant for sexual immorality." The saying in 1 Cor 7:1, "It is good for a man not to touch a woman," utilizes a standard Greek euphemism for sexual intercourse[110] and is almost certainly a Corinthian slogan that grew out of their overly realized eschatology according to which they were free from the sexual obligations of marriage. Paul in 7:2 – 5 opposes the withholding of sex within marriage.

The Corinthians' spiritualized[111] and overly realized eschatology[112] could also have made them want to symbolize a rejection of their marital obligations. Their attitudes toward marriage and their fascination with angels indicate a possible influence from the saying of Jesus in Luke 20:34 – 37

---

110. Cf. Fee, *First Corinthians*, 269 – 77.
111. 1 Corinthians contains fifteen of the twenty-four occurrences of πνευματικός in the entire Pauline corpus and two of the three occurrences of πνευματικῶς. Of special note are 1 Cor 2:13, 15; 3:1; 12:1; 14:1, 37; 15:44, 46.
112. See below, p. 302. The Corinthians expressed their overly realized eschatology using such terms as "wisdom" (16 of 26 Pauline occurrences, e.g., 1 Cor 2:5 – 6), "perfect" (3 of 8 Pauline occurrences, e.g., 2:6; 14:20), and "wise" (11 of 17 Pauline occurrences; e.g., 3:18).

(cf. Matt 22:30) that in the resurrection "they will neither marry nor be given in marriage, and they can no longer die; for they are like the angels," which could even have led to a subtle form of androgyny.[113] They had an extraordinarily exalted view of their current state (1 Cor 4:8–10). Given this mindset, it is easy to imagine women in Corinth thinking they were in the new age like the angels and could express their freedom in Christ by letting their hair down.

In sum, several factors converge that fit perfectly with the interpretation that a woman's "uncovered head" identified her hair being let down. It fits Paul's following arguments perfectly. It fits a well-known Corinthian Dionysiac custom expressing freedom from constraints. It fits the overly realized eschatology of the Corinthians, their dualistic separation of spirituality from actions of the body, their independent spirit, their tendency to express their freedom in inappropriate ways, and the evidence that some Corinthian women felt they were above the constraints of the marriage relationship. Any combination of these things may have contributed to explain why women in Corinth would let their hair down in church.

THE "SHORN WOMAN" SUGGESTS THE NUMBERS 5 "BITTER WATER" ORDEAL

Paul's explanation in 1 Cor 11:5b fits best with a shame related to hair. The conceptual contrast could hardly be stronger: long unbound hair and being shaved. How can these be one and the same? The article in "the shaved woman" may imply a recognized category of women.[114] This allusion perfectly fits the Num 5 "bitter water" ordeal, when a priest lets down the hair of an accused adulteress. An entire tractate, *Soṭah* ("The Suspected Adulteress"), of the Tosefta, Mishnah, Babylonian Talmud, and Jerusalem Talmud, is devoted to this issue.

---

113. Fee, "Praying and Prophesying," 159. Note 44 argues that in light of Luke's presence with Paul in much of his ministry, it is likely that Luke's expression of the gospel would be the best known in Paul's churches. In a broad sense this is probably true (cf. the partial parallels between Luke 22:19–20 and 1 Cor 11:24–25), but if Luke–Acts was written as a legal brief for Paul's defense before Caesar, it was written after 1 Corinthians.

114. Cf. Martin, "1 Corinthians 11:2–16," 234. His interpretation, however, that Paul is talking about a class of women in the church who were shorn and telling them to let their hair grow back makes vv. 5–6b grossly redundant, "Every woman who is shorn is one and the same with her that is shorn. If a woman is shorn, let her be shorn." Nowhere in this passage does Paul address "shorn" women, but rather argues that women who are uncovered are thereby associating themselves with the shameful state of being shorn.

The shorn adulteress is paralleled in non-Jewish customs.[115] Tacitus (AD 98), in *Germ.* 19, records the German custom regarding adultery: "Punishment is prompt and is the husband's prerogative: her hair close-cropped, stripped of her clothes, her husband drives her from his house in presence of his relatives and pursues her with blows through the length of the village."[116] Dio Chrysostom (AD 100) records in *Discourse* 64.2–3: "Demonassa, a woman gifted in both statesmanship and law-giving … gave the people of Cyprus" three laws, the first being, "A woman guilty of adultery shall have her hair cut off and be a harlot."[117] The woman who lets her hair down when praying or prophesying places on herself the accusation of adultery. In Paul's day, if a woman was convicted of adultery, the hair of her head was shamefully cut off as punishment.[118] This explains why an uncovered woman is "one and the same as the shaved woman" (1 Cor 11:5). By letting her hair down in public, a woman places on herself the accusation of adultery. This explanation works only if "uncovered" refers to hair let down. There is no such logical or moral relationship between the removal of a head-covering garment and being shorn.

Accordingly, 1 Cor 11:6 calls on such a woman to accept the punishment of a convicted adulteress. If she will not acknowledge her marital bond by doing her hair up, she should cut off her hair. The Greek first class condition Paul uses in 11:6 "*assumes* the condition to be a reality";[119] "the condition is considered a 'real case.'"[120] The following text, "then she should cut off her hair … [or] she should cover her head," confirms this is not just hypothetical. These imperatives are "stronger than a mere option, engaging the volition and placing a requirement on the individual."[121] This

---

115. John Lewis Burckhardt, *Notes on the Bedouins and Wahábys* (2 vols.; London: Henry Colburn and Richard Bentley, 1830), 1:271–72. For more examples see John Jacob Wettstein, *Novum Testamentum Graecum* (2 vols.; Amsterdam: Dommeriana, 1752/ Graz, Austria: Akademische Druck, 1962), 2:145–46; A. Büchler, "Das Schneiden des Haares als Strafe der Ekebrecker bei den Semiten," *WZKM* 19 (1905): 91–138; Hurley, "Man and Woman in 1 Corinthians," 50; Winter, *Roman Wives*, 82–83.
116. Tacitus, *Dialogus, Agricola, Germania*, 290–91 (William Peterson, LCL).
117. Tacitus (5:47 n. 5 [W. Peterson, LCL]) identifies Demonassa as "Daughter of Mithradates I and wife of Demetrius Nicator."
118. Hurley, *Biblical Perspective*, 169; "Man and Woman in 1 Corinthians," 50; cf. Büchler, "Das Schneiden des Haares," 91–138; Edersheim, *Sketches of Jewish Social Life*, 154.
119. Robertson, *Grammar*, 1007; cf. BDAG 277 εἰ 1.a "with the indicative—α. in all tenses, to express a condition thought of as real or to denote assumptions relating to what has already happened.... The negative in clauses where the reality of the condition is taken for granted is οὐ … 1 Cor 11:6."
120. BDF §371 (1), §372; cf. Robertson, *Grammar*, 1008, 1011; Martin, "1 Cor 11:2–16," 234.
121. Wallace, *Grammar*, 486 n. 97.

plus the construction shows that Paul believed this was actually happening in the Corinthian church. Paul wants any woman doing this to appreciate the shame she is causing to herself and her husband.

Paul concludes this verse, "but if it is disgraceful for a woman to have her hair cut off or to be shaved, she should cover her head [with her hair]." Corresponding to this, a woman found innocent of the bitter water ordeal had her hair done up again. Paul contrasts the two alternatives by using the aorist imperative "let her be shaved" in verse 6a, matching the punctiliar punishment of the woman found guilty of unfaithfulness, but the present imperative in verse 6b to state his ongoing command to cover her head (with her hair). The hair-let-down interpretation fits this custom perfectly and explains the word Paul chose in verses 5 and 13 for "uncovered." Philo cites Num 5:18 using the identical expression in 1 Cor 11:5 (ἀκατακαλύπτῳ τῇ κεφαλῇ;[122] Num 5:18 LXX uses ἀποκαλύψει τὴν κεφαλήν). It also fits the Dionysiac influence in Corinth, where women let their hair down or even shaved it.[123]

---

122. Philo, *Spec. Laws*, 3.60; see 7:512–13 (Colson, LCL).
123. Plutarch, *Mor.* 266C-E; Athenaeus, *Deipn.* 12.525; Lucian, *Syr. d.* 6; Euripides, *Bacch.* 695.

10

1 CORINTHIANS 11:7–10:
THEOLOGICAL REASONS
FOR HEAD-COVERING RULES

First Corinthians 11:7–10 recapitulates 11:4–6, adding theological justification for why men (vv. 7–9) and women (v. 10) ought not to wear hairstyles that repudiate marriage. "Ought" (ὀφείλει, vv. 7, 10) used in such contexts with an infinitive typically carries moral overtones and perfectly fits the understanding that Paul is referring to men who wear effeminate hairstyles and woman who let their hair down to symbolize rejection of Christian marital and sexual morality. After implying moral obligation, it is natural for Paul to explain the moral and theological basis for this, so he inserts a typical Pauline explanatory digression. The arguments from Gen 1–2 cited in 1 Cor 11:7–9 against effeminate hair for men are also applicable against women letting their hair down. To indicate this, Paul introduces his theological argument for women in verse 10, "On account of this …" instead of using the counterpart (δέ) to the (μέν) construction he had begun in 11:7.

Paul's first theological argument (1 Cor 11:7) focuses on abuse by men: "For[1] a man ought not to cover[2] his head, since[3] he is the image and glory of God."[4] Men wearing effeminate hair were deliberately making their hair look like a woman's hair, thus making themselves into the "image" or "likeness"[5] of a woman. Paul reminds these men that bearing the image of God obliges them to accept themselves as the men that God made them to be. This brings glory to God, whereas effeminate hair brings disgrace.

Paul introduces the "image of God" argument in order to place his argument in a broad theological framework, building on his theological introduction in 1 Cor 11:3. The normal associations of "the image of God" imply that man should not wear effeminate hair.[6] The image of God

---

1. This γάρ probably introduces theological reasons for the assertions of 11:4, as evidenced by the following participle conveying "since," though γάρ can simply "express continuation or connection," BDAG 189 γάρ 2, as in 1 Cor 10:1.

2. Cf. above, p. 141, for a reading of 11:4 that parallels this sense. More likely, however, the change in wording reflects the two aspects of shameful display of hair by men most prominent in the literature of Paul's day: wearing long hair (κομάω) and doing one's hair up like a woman. Because long hair is a prerequisite for effeminate hairstyles, it is not surprising that these two aspects are frequently mentioned together. Men displayed effeminate hair in order to attract attention, and the act of letting hair down and putting it up attracted special attention, as evident in Seneca's *Oedipus* 416–21 (ca. AD 60), "fling loose thy lawless-streaming locks, again to bind them in a knot close-drawn ... a pretended maiden with golden ringlets," and Juvenal's *Sat.* 2.93–96 (AD 116), which depicts "secret torchlight orgies" for "none but males: One ... drinks out of an obscenely shaped glass, and ties up his long locks in a gilded net." Pseudo-Phocylides 210–14 and Dio Chrysostom (AD 100) *Discourse* 33.52 ridicule males both with long hair and with hair done up. Such descriptions of men wearing long hair down and doing it up in the same context explain why Paul addresses both of the most common forms of this abuse in 1 Cor 11:4 (hanging down) and 11:7 (done up). The literary reason Paul uses κατακαλύπτω ("cover") for men in 11:7 is that he had just used the same word of women at the end of 11:6. This highlights the distinction between men, who "ought not cover their heads," and women, who ought to cover their heads.

3. If ὑπάρχων ("since he is") in 11:7 gives a reason "to cover," "man as male is the image and glory of God" would express a Corinthian slogan used to defend display of effeminate hair. This slogan fits perfectly with the exaltation of the male body that typifies homosexual display, the Corinthians' view of their own exalted status, their pride in their sexual freedom, their haughty spirit, and their overly realized eschatology. If Paul here quotes a Corinthian slogan, this explains why "man as male" (ἀνήρ) is used rather than the inclusive term "humankind" (ἄνθρωπος), as in Paul's other affirmations of the "image of God in man," why man is the image of God (elsewhere man is made in the image of God, whereas Christ alone is the image of God, 2 Cor 4:4; Col 1:15), and why man is the glory of God (difficult to reconcile with Rom 1:23; 3:23; 5:2). Cf. the slogans identified in the NIV by quotations marks in 1 Cor 1:11; 3:4; 6:12, 13; 7:1; 8:1 note; 10:23; 15:35. Just as every other time Paul uses ὀφείλω meaning "ought," he follows it with an explanation why, so here "but woman is the glory of man" explains why Paul repudiates a slogan defending homosexual display. But if this was not a slogan the Corinthians would recognize, they would more naturally read ὑπάρχων as introducing Paul's own theological argument as explained in the following text.

4. This confirms that v. 4 is not just a foil to introduce women. Men were subverting God's intention in creation.

5. Cf. BDAG 281–82, which defines εἰκών as "likeness," "living image," or "form, appearance."

6. Because Fee regarded Paul's references to men merely as a foil (*First Corinthians*, 513–17), he fails to explain the relationship between "image and glory" and men's head coverings. He inter-

entails moral responsibility (Gen 9:6; Col 3:8–10), but effeminate hair symbolizes rejection of God's moral standards. The image of God entails creativity, and procreation expresses that creativity (Gen 9:7). Effeminate hair undermines procreation by blurring the distinction between the sexes and by symbolizing homosexual relations. Paul (Rom 1:26–27; 1 Cor 6:9; 1 Tim 1:10) — and Judaism in general — viewed homosexual relations as an abomination and antithetical to God's intent in creation.[7] In Gen 1:26–27, being in God's image entails man *as male and female*. Consequently, Paul's "image of God" reference implies the distinction between man and woman made by God in creation. First Corinthians 11:8–9 proves that Paul intended to affirm the differentiation between man and woman, which is undermined by effeminate hair.

This differentiation between the sexes does not imply a difference in essential humanness. Genesis 1:26–27 and 5:1–2 teach that the image of God is in both man and woman and that dominion was given to man as male and female. Paul's agreement with this is implied by his arguments in 1 Cor 7:1–16; 11:11–12; and Gal 3:28 against a hierarchical distinction between man and woman. Paul's omission of "image and" regarding woman in 1 Cor 11:7c shows a conscious choice not to draw a distinction between man and woman regarding their standing in the image of God.[8] Further-more, there is no article with "image" in the phrase regarding men, which could have suggested exclusivity.[9] To the contrary, Col 3:10–11 explicitly affirms that all believers are "being renewed in the image of their Creator."

---

prets v. 7c as referring to woman's head covering even though man is the subject of v. 7 and woman's "ought to" clause is in v. 10.

7. John Boswell (*Christianity, Social Tolerance, and Homosexuality* [Chicago: Univ. of Chicago Press, 1980]) interpreted Rom 1:26–27 as referring only to homosexual acts committed by heterosexual persons. This has been shown to be anachronistic eisegesis. Some of the more important discussions demonstrating this are: Robert A. J. Gagnon, *The Bible and Homosexual Practice: Texts and Hermeneutics* (Nashville: Abingdon, 2001); Richard B. Hays, "Relations Natural and Unnatural: A Response to John Boswell's Exegesis of Romans 1," *JRE* 14 (1986): 184–215; idem, *The Moral Vision of the New Testament: Community, Cross, New Creation* (San Francisco: Harper San Francisco, 1996), 379–406 ("Paul on the Relationship between Men and Women"); David F. Wright, "ΑΡΣΕΝΟΚΟΙΤΑΙ," 125–53; idem, "Homosexuality: The Relevance of the Bible," *EvQ* 61 (1989): 291–300; Henry Mendell, "ΑΡΣΕΝΟΚΟΙΤΑΙ: Boswell on Paul," an unpublished detailed critique of Boswell's exegesis of Rom 1:26–27. Lev 20:13 condemned homosexual practices as punishable by death. The Mishnah and Talmud prescribe stoning for this in *m. Sanh.* 7:4; *b. Sanh.* 54a; cf. *m. Ker.* 1:2; 2:6; *b. Sanh.* 78a.

8. *Pace* Jouette M. Bassler, "1 Corinthians," in *The Women's Bible Commentary* (eds. Carol A. Newsom and Sharon H. Ringe; Louisville, Ky.: Westminster John Knox, 1992), 326–27.

9. Cf. BDF §273 "Predicate nouns as a rule are anarthrous. Nevertheless the article is inserted if the predicate noun … alone merits the designation," cf. Turner, *Syntax*, 183. Paul could have changed his word order. Apollonius' Canon construction permits articles before both the

Paul adds that man is the glory of God, for man is the "reflection of God" (BDAG 257 δόξα 1.d). Consequently, man should reflect the desire of the Creator. Effeminate hair, however, repudiates the purpose of the Creator and so brings disgrace on man and on God, his head, his source.

This passage, unless it cites a Corinthian slogan, "man as male is the image and glory of God,"[10] affirms an extraordinarily high anthropology. A hint of such an exalted view of believers, living in the Spirit, "being transformed into his likeness with ever-increasing glory, which comes from the Lord" occurs in 2 Cor 3:18. Similarly, 2 Cor 4:6 implies that believers participate to some degree in Christ's glory since God "made his light shine in our hearts to give us the light of the knowledge of the glory of God in the face of Christ." In the context of Christ's work in creation and in redemption, both being implied in 1 Cor 11:3, "man is the image and glory of God" heightens Christ's glory since he is the creator and redeemer of man.

Typical Jewish thought, exemplified by Apoc. Mos. 20:1–2; 21:6; 39:2[11] held that Adam and Eve lost "the glory of God" and that it would only be restored in the eschaton. The present verse, however, affirms that man is the glory of God. Unless it is a slogan Paul repudiates, this must be attributed to Paul's high view of Christ. Appropriately, then, this passage is immediately followed by Paul's discussion of the Lord's Supper (11:17–34), where the wonder of redemption in Christ confirms the value of man. In both passages this value demands treating others with respect (11:21–22, 33) and bringing glory to God, not shame.

It is striking that Paul approaches the Genesis narrative in a completely different way than Philo. Philo distinguishes between the earthly man and the separate incorporeal man made in God's image,[12] but here, the earthly man is God's image. Philo describes woman as intellectually inferior;[13] Paul

---

governing and the governed nouns. Cf. C. F. D. Moule, An Idiom-Book of New Testament Greek (2nd ed.; Cambridge: University Press, 1971), 114 and Turner, Syntax, 180.

10. Cf. above, p. 176 n. 3. Nothing in the context, however, identifies it as a slogan.
11. Also known as the Life of Adam and Eve [Apocalypse], as in OTP 2:281.
12. Ralph Marcus, trans., Philo Supplement I: Questions and Answers on Genesis (LCL, 1961): "Why does He place the moulded man in Paradise, but not the man who was made in His image?... the man made in His image is intelligible and invisible, and is in the class of incorporeal species ... the earth-formed man is a mixture, and consists of soul and body.... But he who was made in His image is in need of nothing, but is self-hearing and self-taught and self-instructed by nature" (QG 1.5).
13. Ibid., QG 1, 25.14–15: "Man is a symbol of mind.... The sense-perception of a very changeable reason is symbolized by woman.... Woman is half of man's body.... The moulding of the male is more perfect than, and double, that of the female."

does not. Philo assigns the public affairs to man and the affairs of home to woman;[14] Paul does not. Philo tries to explain the meaning of the Genesis account based on his perception that women are not equal to men in honor.[15] Paul cites the Genesis account as a guide for conduct that applies to both man and woman without assigning higher honor to man. Indeed, 1 Cor 11:11–12 explicitly argues against such a misapplication of Gen 1–2.

WOMAN IS THE GLORY OF MAN

First Corinthians 11:7c ("and[16] the woman is the glory of man")[17] affirms that woman, not another man, is the glory of man. The glory of someone is the person in whom he glories, as the man glories over the woman in Gen 2:23. Woman is depicted as the crowning glory of creation made specifically to be man's partner. Most men would agree that of all creation, woman is the most beautiful. The history of art typically exalts woman as the fairest of God's creation. Adam's "glorying" in the first woman is immediately followed by 2:24, "For this reason a man will leave his father and mother and be united to his wife, and they will become one flesh." When husbands treat their wives as their glory, marriage is beautiful.

---

14. Ibid., *QG* 1, 26.15: "For to man are entrusted the public affairs of state; while to a woman the affairs of the home are proper."
15. Ibid., *QG* 1, 27.16: "Woman is not equal in honour with man.... She is not equal in age, but younger."
16. Soards (*1 Corinthians*, 223) states what many assume should be added to this verse, "in verse 7 ... the woman's covering her head is explained in terms of her being the glory of man." Building on this assumption, Soards concludes on p. 224 that Paul's argument is a "morass of reasoning" and "bewilderingly difficult." But in fact, v. 7 states nothing about the woman covering her head. It explains the stated topic of the sentence, why *man* ought not to cover his head. Any attempt to interpret 11:7 as containing both halves of an "on the one hand ... on the other hand" adversative construction must postulate radical ellipsis unparalleled in Paul's μέν ... δέ expressions, and is structurally, exegetically, and theologically dubious. The contrasting statement that "woman ought to cover her head," which this construction would have required, is not mentioned in 11:7c (which instead has the verb "is"), but rather in 11:10, "woman ought to exercise authority over her head" (cf. Fee, *First Corinthians*, 514, and most expositors who address this question; particularly clear on this point is Jervis, "But I Want You To Know," 242–43). Consequently, v. 7 is not an adversative construction contrasting man, who ought not to cover his head since he is the image and glory of God, to woman, who ought to cover her head since she is not God's image or glory but the glory of man, *pace* the many commentaries that read into this verse the inferiority of women, e.g., Conzelmann, Robertson and Plummer, Meyer, J. Weiss, Lietzmann, Héring, Senft; J. Duncan Derrett, "Religious Hair," *Studies in the New Testament* 1 (Leiden: Brill, 1977), 172; Meier, "Veiling of Hermeneutics," 220. Delobel ("Coherent Explanation," 378) interprets this as teaching "women's proper secondary place, which does not necessarily involve her inferiority." He affirms the equal worth of woman (p. 381 n. 45) but undermines this by saying her place in the order of the cosmos is below man. The normal meaning of equality is corrupted when expressed like this.
17. If "man" were modified by "her" or an article, this would have supported translating, "The wife is the glory of her husband." Since it does not, "woman" and "man" are the more natural reading.

Paul's appeal to woman as the glory of man affirms woman as the proper sexual partner for man. This exposes the error of effeminate hair, for in symbolizing homosexual relations it repudiates woman as man's sexual mate. Probably the closest English expression to this sense of glory is "pride and joy," and an ideal translation that captures Paul's argument is "woman, *not another man*, is the pride and joy of man." She is the human splendor that catches man's eye (BDAG 257, δόξα 2). Seen in this light, it is clear that the exalting affirmation that woman is the glory of man does not imply or suggest that woman is any less the image of God or the glory of God than is man.[18] Indeed, it is precisely man as male and female that most fully images God and reflects his glory.

GOD CREATED WOMAN FROM MAN TO BE HIS SEXUAL PARTNER

"For [γάρ] man did not come from woman, but woman from man.[19] Neither [καὶ γάρ] was man created for the sake of woman,[20] but woman for the sake of man"[21] (1 Cor 11:8–9) gives reasons for the immediately preceding statement that woman is the glory of man in 11:7c.[22] The completely parallel sets of denial and affirmation in verses 8 and 9 reinforce Paul's stress on the differentiation of man and woman, his sexual mate, the very thing effeminate hair challenges.

Immediately prior to the man's "glorying" in woman is the narrative of God creating woman from man (Gen 2:21–22) to be his partner. First Corinthians 11:8 develops Paul's introduction in verse 3 that man was the source from which God made woman. Woman is the glory of man, for she came from him. It is because she corresponds to him, having come from

---

18. *Pace* Meyer, *Corinthians*, 251, "[Paul] refused to recognize the divine image in her ... in an *immediate* sense," and Hurley, *Biblical Perspective*, 177, "The woman is not called to image God or Christ *in the relation which she sustains to her husband*. ... In *this particular sense* of authority relationships, the main topic of 1 Corinthians 11, it is absolutely appropriate to say that the man images God and the woman does not." Surely, God's image ought to be evident and upheld at least in the most intimate and personal of all human relationships, that of husband and wife.

19. This is about source, not temporal priority. God repeatedly rejected primogeniture, cf. above p. 101.

20. Clearly, it would contradict the theology of Eph 5:25–33 to interpret this as meaning that a man should not act for the sake of his wife. Rather, it highlights God's purpose in creating woman as man's sexual complement. This clause is necessary for the structural parallelism with v. 8. Verses 8–9 explain why "woman is the glory of man."

21. To read subordination into "woman was made for man" introduces something foreign to both the Genesis account and to the context of 1 Cor 11:4–16, does not fit the problem of effeminate hair, and conflicts with 11:11–12.

22. God's purpose in sexual differentiation at creation also explains why men ought not to display effeminate hair (11:7a).

him, that she can complement him as his mate. God's central purpose in creating woman from man was to create an intimate and procreative partner for man (Gen 1:27–28; 2:20).

Paul proves that he had God's purpose in mind by his concluding affirmation that woman was created "for the sake of man," to fulfill man's need for an intimate sexual partner. Effeminate display, however, symbolizes a man presenting himself as a sexual mate for other men and so opposes God's creation of woman to be man's mate. The archetypal relationship of Adam to Eve is the antithesis of homosexual relationships. This affirmation by Paul strongly supports that the root of his disapproval of effeminate hair is its association with homosexual relations.

WHY A WOMAN OUGHT TO CONTROL HER HAIR

First Corinthians 11:10's "on account of this" (διὰ τοῦτο) alludes to the reasons from Gen 1–2 Paul had just stated and also anticipates "on account of the angels" at the end of this verse. The immediate context and Paul's typical usage, including both of Paul's other διὰ τοῦτο ... διά ...,[23] support this dual reference.[24] "On account of this" points back to Paul's preceding reasons why man should not wear effeminate hair in 11:7–9 and reapplies them to woman as reasons against letting her hair down in public worship. Each of these specific affirmations is a good reason for a wife to show respect to her husband: man is the image and glory of God (v. 7b), woman is the glory of man (v. 7c), woman's source was from man (v. 8), and woman was created to fulfill man (v. 9).

If 11:7–9 had been about *women's* head covering, as most commentators assume, contrary to the explicit subject ("men") of 11:7, "on account of this" would serve no purpose here. There would be no reason to reapply reasons for women to cover their heads if that was the topic in the first place. Paul's desire to reapply these arguments to women explains why he used "on account of this" instead of "on the other hand" (δέ), which would typically be paired with the μέν construction begun in verse 7.[25]

---

23. 2 Tim 2:8–10 and 1 Thess 3:6–7 (διά + genitive here functions similarly, e.g., NIV, TNIV "because of").
24. Cf. Fee, *First Corinthians*, 518 n. 21.
25. Thayer (*Greek-English Lexicon*, μέν II.3, 398) gives examples of when "the writer, in using μέν, perhaps had in mind a second member to be introduced by δέ, but was drawn away from his intention by explanatory additions relating to the first member." He lists Acts 3:13–15; Rom

"The woman ought" (ὀφείλει ἡ γυνή, 1 Cor 11:10) does not imply external compulsion but moral obligation, just as 11:7's "man ought" does. In light of this moral duty, it is probably best to translate "to have authority" as "to exercise authority" or "to have control over."

Many Bible versions and interpretations mistranslate ἐξουσίαν ἔχειν in 1 Cor 11:10, which means "to have control or to exercise authority" (as it does in Rev 11:6; 14:18; 20:6, also with the genitive) as though it meant, "sign or symbol of [man's] authority" (e.g., ESV, NEB, NIV, NRSV), "veil" (e.g., RSV), "covering," "subjection," or "submission." There is no lexical support, nor apparently any instance elsewhere, where "authority" means any of these things, and there is meager, if any, evidence that Hellenistic culture regarded a veil as a symbol of authority. It is probably an anachronism from Arabian culture to regard a veil as a symbol of subjection to authority. All 103 occurrences of ἐξουσία ("authority") in the NT refer to authority held in someone's own hand, whether inherent, assigned, or achieved. Likewise, all nine references to ἐξουσία in 1 Corinthians mean "to have power of one's own" or "to have under one's own power," whether inherent, assigned, or achieved.

Not only is woman (γυνή) the stated subject of "to have authority" in verse 10, woman must be its subject since woman (γυνή) continues as the subject of verse 11 in a way that guards against misuse of her authority: "Nevertheless, neither is woman separate from man." Several versions, including the KJV, LB, NEB, and Phillips, apparently assuming that verse 10 must affirm man's authority over woman, reverse Paul's order in verse 11 by first qualifying man's authority! In so doing they conceal verse 11's reinforcement that verse 10 is about woman's exercise of her authority. These translations go beyond eisegesis, reading into the text something that is not there. They actually change the text itself by altering the sequence and logic of Paul's argument.

"To have authority" in this context implies, as Paul's use of this expression normally does, "to have control over"[26] (e.g., 1 Cor 7:37, "having under

---

1:8; 3:2; 1 Cor 11:18. Cf. BDAG 630 μέν 2.b, gives examples from John 11:6–7; Rom 11:13–14; 7:12–25.

26. Cf. the same conclusion by Blomberg, "Neither Hierarchalist," 346; Collins, *First Corinthians*, 411; Jason D. BeDuhn, "'Because of the Angels': Unveiling Paul's Anthropology in 1 Corinthians 11" *JBL* 118 (1999): 302–3; Murphy-O'Connor, "Once Again," 271; Hays, *First Corinthians*, 188–89; Thiselton, *First Corinthians*, 839.

control"; 9:12, 18, "made use of this right"). The conceptual and verbal parallels between 11:7 ("man ought not cover his head") and 11:10 ("woman ought to exercise authority over her head") support the exercise of authority in verse 10. Although "to exercise control over" necessarily implies possession of authority, it is clear from the context that Paul's central point is that a woman ought to exercise control "over her head" (ἐπὶ τῆς κεφαλῆς) by wearing her hair up. Paul uses a set phrase meaning "to have/exercise authority over something." A straightforward reading of 11:10 makes perfect sense: "On account of this, the woman ought to exercise authority over her head [by putting her hair up]." Paul's use of the presiding image, "head," adds coherence to the passage.

"On account of the angels" (διὰ τοὺς ἀγγέλους) almost certainly refers to good angels, not human messengers or bad angels.[27] A few scholars interpret "angels" not as heavenly beings but rather as human messengers in the churches.[28] While this is lexically possible,[29] there is no other instance where Paul used ἄγγελος to mean "human messenger." Nor are there any clear cases where Paul writes about evil angels.[30] Paul's use of an article with "the angels" without any indication that a specifically bad group of angels is in view indicates that the group Paul usually refers to as angels, namely, the good angels, is in view here, too.[31]

There is hardly any similarity between 1 Cor 11:10 and the fallen Watchers described in *1 En.* 6–19 as seducing women.[32] Furthermore, the

---

27. Cf. the same conclusion by Barrett, *First Corinthians*, 254; Isaksson, *Marriage and Ministry*, 178; Robertson and Plummer, *First Corinthians*, 233.
28. Lightfoot, *Horae Hebraicae*, 4:238; Padgett, "Paul on Women," 17; Murphy-O'Connor, "Once Again," 271.
29. NT: Matt 11:10, Luke 7:24; 9:52; Jas 2:25; LXX: Gen 32:4, 7; Jdt 1:11; 3:1; 1 Macc 1:44; 7:10 Josephus, *Life* 17 §89; cf. Josephus, *Ant.* 14.15.11 §451. Barrett, *First Corinthians*, 254, calls patristic interpretations "bizarre" that identify the angels as bishops based on, e.g., Rev 2:1.
30. The statement in 2 Cor 11:14 that "Satan himself masquerades as an angel of light" does not refer specifically to evil angels, but rather to Satan posing as an angel. In Gal 1:8 Paul says that if an angel from heaven should preach a different gospel, he should be eternally condemned. This might imply the possibility of evil angels or it might simply be an emphatic way of saying, "Do not believe a different gospel no matter how reliable the source may seem to be." It is possible, though not necessary, that 1 Cor 6:4 envisages evil angels, "Do you not know that we will judge angels?" This could just as well refer to good angels who erred or even to judgment resulting in praise. Or it could refer to angels who fell with Satan but had nothing to do with what is mentioned in Gen 6:2–4. On evil angels, see Str-B 3:437–40.
31. As in every other instance in 1 Corinthians. Cf. Robertson and Plummer, *First Corinthians*, 233. De Vaux ("Sur le voile des femmes," 412) notes how minor the influence would have been of the "evil eye" proposal of Wellhausen.
32. Jewish and Christian tradition generally understood "sons of God" in Gen 6:2–4 not to refer to angels (e.g., John Skinner, *Genesis* [2nd ed.; ICC; Edinburgh: T&T Clark, 1930], 139–47). Targum Onkelos and Jonathan, the Greek translation of the OT by Symmachus, *Gen. Rab.*,

184 OR MAN AND WOMAN

Watchers myth has no reference to the head, face, hair, or a head covering of any sort, nor does it have any association with a worship setting,
prayer, or prophecy. Genesis 6 does not mention angels, nor is there any
mention of angels in Gen 1–15 that might support such an allusion. To
the contrary, Gen 6 gives several indications that it was man who sinned.
God's response was, "My Spirit will not contend with man forever" (Gen
6:3). God's judgment was on man, and the passage is immediately followed with, "The LORD saw how great man's wickedness on the earth had
become" (6:5). Nor is there any evidence that the Watchers myth was
ever taken literally around the time of Paul in the sense that angels might
actually violate women.[33] Paul is particularly unlikely to have taken the
Watcher myth literally in light of the prominence in the gospel tradition
that Jesus taught that angels neither marry nor are given in marriage
(Matt 22:30; Mark 12:25; Luke 20:34–35). For all of these reasons it is
virtually certain that Paul did not intend "angels" in 11:10 to refer to evil
angels.

Some who interpret the passage as promoting veils and male authority
also interpret the angels as guardians of the created order,[34] but evidence
for this idea is absent in Paul and unsubstantiated elsewhere.[35] Further-

---

and other early Jewish interpreters took "sons of god" as sons of aristocratic families. The traditional Christian interpretation, "pious sons of Seth," is defended by H. C. Leupold (*Exposition of
Genesis* [Columbus: Wartburg, 1942] 249–60); Meredith G. Kline argues that it refers to kings
("Divine Kingship and Genesis 6:1–4," *WTJ* 24 [1963]: 187–204). However, the extended discussion of the Watchers in all these works interpreted these "sons of God" as "angels": Josephus,
Ant. 1, 73; *T. Reub.* 5:3; *Jub.* 5:1; 1QapGen 2; and *1 En.* 6–19. "Sons of God" does refer to angels
in Job 1:6; 2:1; 38:7; and Dan 3:25, and the rescriptor of Codex Alexandrinus LXX Gen 6:2
used ἄγγελοι for "sons of God." Tertullian (*Virg.* 7) is the one who seems to have introduced
the seduction interpretation of 1 Cor 11:10.

33. An insight of Larry Hurtado during discussions in a conference held May 24–28, 1993, in
Cambridge, England. Jude 6 and 2 Pet 2:4 mention evil angels already bound, so they posed no
threat.

34. E.g., Charles H. Talbert, *Reading Corinthians: A Literary and Theological Commentary on 1
and 2 Corinthians* (New York: Crossroad, 1987), 69, states, "the context demands that they be
taken to mean the angelic beings entrusted by God to watch over the orders of creation." Yet
each of the examples he lists either does not mention angels (*1 En.* 82:3) or has nothing to do
with angels watching over human behavior (*1 En.* 60:12, 16–21; 61:10; 72:1; *Jub.* 2:2–3; 1QH
9.10–11).

35. Lenski (*Corinthians*, 452) calls it "only an invention to find some explanation for Paul's phrase."
Barrett (*First Corinthians*, 254) cites 1 Cor 4:9 as referring to "angels as watchers of the created order," but this passage says nothing about the created order, let alone any implication of
a creation ordinance giving men authority over women. The following articles list abundant
evidence that angels were present in the assembly and could be offended by improprieties, but
none of the evidence refers to angels as guardians of "the creation order": Morna D. Hooker,
"Authority on Her Head: An Examination of 1 Cor XI.10," *NTS* 10 (1963–64): 410–16; J. A.
Fitzmyer, "Features of Qumran Angelology and the Angels of 1 Cor. XI.10," *NTS* 4 (1957–58):
48–58; Bruce J. Waltke "1 Corinthians 11:2–16: An Interpretation," *BSac* 135 (1978): 53.

more, as "ought to have control" implies, Paul is focusing here not to some external compulsion angels might give but to the exercise of a right that the woman herself has. The idea that the angels are like cosmic policemen enforcing veiling customs or the subordination of women does not fit this context.

Something about angels explains why a woman ought to exercise authority over her head, something the Corinthians could recognize simply from "on account of the angels." The context is church worship.[36] The presence of angels in worship is a recurring theme in Paul's writings and the rest of the NT.[37] Paul refers to angels more in 1 Corinthians than in any of his other epistles. It is hardly surprising that angels would be present where people speak with "tongues of angels" (1 Cor 13:1). First Corinthians 4:9 states, "God has put us apostles on display at the end of the procession, like men condemned to die in the arena. We have been made a spectacle to the whole universe, to angels as well as to men." When Paul writes in 1 Tim 5:21, "I charge you in the sight of God and Christ Jesus and the elect angels," he is implying the angels' ongoing observation of the church. Hebrews 1:14 asks, "Are not all angels ministering spirits sent to serve those who will inherit salvation?" The seven letters of Revelation are addressed to "the angels of the seven churches,"[38] implying their presence in the churches. Consequently, liturgy includes phrases like, "with angels and archangels and all the company of heaven."

The presence of angels in worship is rooted in the OT. Psalm 138:1 (LXX 137:1) says, "I will sing psalms to you before the angels [ἀγγέλων]." Similarly, 1QSa 2:8–9; 4QD^e 10:11; 1QM 7.6; and 4QM^a refer to angels as present in the assembly. Judaism regarded angels as guardians of good manners (b. Šabb. 119b) and propriety (b. Ber. 60b).[39] Not only is the presence of angels in worship Paul's most prominent theme regarding angels, it perfectly fits as a reason why women should restrain themselves from

---

36. As noted in Soards, *1 Corinthians*, 226.
37. Cf. Thompson, "Hairstyles," 112; Hooker, "Authority on Her Head," 410–16; Foerster, "ἔξεστιν," *TDNT* 2:560–75; Fitzmyer, "Qumran Angelology," 48–58; Kenneth T. Wilson, "Should Women Wear Headcoverings?" *BSac* 148 (1991): 454–56.
38. Rev 1:20; 2:1, 8, 12, 18; 3:1, 7, 14.
39. Gerhard Kittel, "ἄγγελος, ἀρχάγγελος, ἰσάγγελος," *TDNT* 1:86. Scroggs, "Eschatological Woman," 300, also notes *Gen. Rab.* 8.3–5; 17.4; b. Šabb. 88b; b. Sanh. 28c; *Tanḥ. Bub. Behukkotai,* 56b; *Mishpatim,* 11 *Pesikta,* ed. Bub., 176a; *Pirqe R. El.* 19, and the commentary by Moore, 1:535.

impropriety in worship. It ought to be embarrassing enough for a woman to be seen by others in the church with her hair let down, but knowing she is being observed by God's holy angels should be reason enough for even the most foolhardy woman to restrain her urge to let her hair down. Consequently, Paul writes that a woman ought to have control over her head on account of the angels' presence in worship.[40]

Jesus' saying that "angels in heaven always see the face of my Father in heaven" (Matt 18:10) reinforces this reason. Philo (*Dreams* 1.140–41) says that angels are "the eyes and ears of the Great King, they watch and hear all" and so are called "'angels' or messengers."[41] *Jubilees* 4:6 says that angels "announce when we come before the Lord our God all the sin which is committed in heaven and on earth, and in light and in darkness and everywhere."[42] *First Enoch* 99:3 states that "angels ... place the sin of the sinners for a memorial before the Most High."[43] Thus, if it were not sufficient embarrassment for angels to witness women letting their hair down in church, the belief that angels have audience with God and report what they see would be a decisive reason for any woman to avoid a hairstyle that symbolized infidelity to her husband.

The NT theme that Christian worship reflects the worship by angels before the throne of God[44] may well reinforce the message Paul intended by "on account of the angels." This would explain his shift in focus in 11:11–12, which affirms the equality of women and men. In worship, the new age breaks into the present age (e.g., 1 Cor 14:25), the structures of privilege of this world are overcome in a oneness in Christ where all believers are leveled at the foot of the cross and are united in the body of Christ (e.g., 1 Cor 11:17–34). Jew and Gentile, slave and free, and male and female (Gal 3:28) all join in equally without division after the pattern of heavenly worship. The model of worship by angels who do not marry

---

40. Cf. also Collins, *First Corinthians*, 412.
41. Philo, 5:373 (Colson, LCL).
42. APOT 2:18.
43. APOT 2:270.
44. This same concept of the human worship as a reflection of and participation in the heavenly worship of angels has been demonstrated in the Qumran material and Judaism through the time of Paul (see, e.g., the *Sabbath Shirot* 12.1.2; 12.3.3 comparing worship on earth with the heavenly angelic worship; 1QSb 4.24–26; 13.8.2; 8.3.2; cf. S. F. Noll, "Angelology in the Qumran Texts" (Ph.D. Diss., Manchester, 1979); Michael Mach, *Entwicklungsstadien des jüdischen Engelglaubens in vorrabbinischer Zeit* (Tübingen: Mohr, 1992), 114–278; Maxwell J. Davidson, *Angels at Qumran: A Comparative Study of 1 Enoch 1–36, 72–108 and Sectarian Writings from Qumran* (JSPSup 11; Sheffield: Academic, 1992), 315–19.

(Matt 22:30; Mark 12:25) implies that women should have authority to pray and prophesy. With that authority comes the obligation to exercise it responsibly, so Corinthian women had a moral obligation to exercise control over their heads by not letting their hair down, since that symbolized sexual looseness.

11

1 Corinthians 11:11 – 12:
The Equal Standing of
Woman and Man in Christ

According to BDAG (see πλήν, 826 [1.c]), the first word of 1 Cor 11:11, "However" (πλήν), "break[s] off a discussion and emphasiz[es] what is important." Similarly, BDF §449 states that Paul uses πλήν "to conclude a discussion and emphasize what is essential." Echoing this, A. T. Robertson wrote, "Paul uses it at the end of an argument to single out the main point ... [e.g.] 1 Corinthians 11:11."[1] In every occurrence in Paul's letters, πλήν points to the matter of his central concern, and in each case it indicates a change in perspective from what went before.[2] Consequently, verses 11 – 12 should not be regarded merely as an aside, as the parentheses in the RSV may seem to imply.[3] Rather, they point to the heart of Paul's concern.

"However" in 1 Cor 11:11 relates Paul's conclusion to his earlier comments but does so by introducing a new perspective, emphasizing something essential that is established in Christ: "neither is woman set apart from man, nor is man set apart from woman in the Lord" (οὔτε γυνὴ χωρὶς ἀνδρὸς οὔτε ἀνὴρ χωρὶς γυναικὸς ἐν κυρίῳ). Unfortunately, unlike

---

1. Robertson, *Grammar*, 1187. Ironically, Fee, although emphasizing the need to respect the grammatical markers of the text, describes vv. 11 – 12, Paul's main point, in these words: "The latter part of this argument seems to go astray a bit" (*First Corinthians*, 495).
2. In addition to this passage, see Eph 5:33 (church/marriage); Phil 1:18 (even in pretense); 3:16 (live it); 4:14 (concern/sharing).
3. Or Murphy-O'Connor, "1 Corinthians 11:2 – 16 Once Again," 271 – 72, 274, although, to his credit, he views this parenthesis as an important statement of Paul's conviction.

the above literal translation, "no single modern English VS translates the Greek exactly as it stands without addition or modification."[4]

The absence of articles is better suited to men and women in general than husband and wife. None of the five brief clauses in 11:11–12 has a verb, but the standard ellipsis "is" perfectly fits both clauses in verse 11. Each clause in verses 11–12 is so pithy, simple, and memorable that they sound like a liturgical formula, possibly a baptismal formula.

THE CENTRAL QUESTION FOR 1 CORINTHIANS 11:11

The central question about the meaning of verse 11 regards the word χωρίς ("set apart from"), and its context sets specific constraints on its meaning. The "however" introducing verse 11 implies that χωρίς gives a new perspective from what preceded about the relationship of woman and man, something that Paul regards as essential. The end stress given to "in the Lord" requires that it should affirm something that is established in Christ, hence presumably something that was not already established in society apart from Christ. Finally, since the completion of this sentence in verse 12 begins with "for just as" and parallels the wording of verse 11,[5] what verse 12 affirms should give supporting evidence for the affirmation of verse 11.

The most common translations of χωρίς in its sixteen occurrences in Paul's letters are "separated from," "apart from," and "without." "Without" does not make sense unless the usual elliptical verb "is" is changed to "exists" or "is in existence," as Moffatt and Phillips translate it. Their translation teaches that neither woman nor man exists without the other, namely, that they need each other to reproduce biologically. Although the translation "[exists] without" closely reflects verse 12, it is improbable for four reasons:

1. It does not do justice to the distinctively Christian sense called for by "in the Lord."
2. It makes verses 11 and 12 redundant.
3. Consequently, it does not provide an adequate basis for the logical relationship normally expressed by "for" (γάρ), which introduces verse 12.

---

4.   Thiselton, *First Corinthians*, 841.
5.   Both affirm something about woman in relation to man followed by its reverse, man in relation to woman. Verse 12 concludes with "all this [is] from God," paralleling "in Christ" in v. 11.

4. In elliptical constructions when "is" makes sense (as it does here), it is more likely that this was understood than a more complex idea such as "exists."

Many English versions translate χωρίς in 1 Cor 11:11 "independent" (e.g., HCSB, ESV, NAB, NASB, NIV, NRSV, RSV, TEV, TNT, Amplified, Goodspeed, New Berkeley, Weymouth, Williams). This meaning for χωρίς, however, is not listed regarding persons in either LSJ[6] or BAG.[7] Thiselton notes that "is not independent of" "adds a nuance which goes beyond the adverb χωρίς."[8] This translation presupposes that after "without" something like *dependence upon* should be supplied by the reader, which would then be conceptually equivalent to "independent." Normally, however, when Paul intends a particular meaning that might not be understood by his readers, he uses words that express it so that his meaning is not left up to the readers' imagination. In light of verse 12, the translation "independent" points to the biological interdependence of the sexes for procreation. Yet nothing in the new standing of believers in Christ has changed the biological interdependence of the sexes for procreation, so this translation does not do justice to the distinctively Christian sense called for by "in the Lord."

The translation, "However, woman is not independent of man," implies that something in verse 10 might lead women to feel justified in asserting their independence. On subordinationist interpretations of ἐξουσία ("authority") in verse 10 as the husband's authority, there is no such thing in the preceding context. On these interpretations one would expect Paul to begin, "However, *man* is not independent of woman," since they regard everything preceding verse 11 as affirming man's authority over woman. The translation, "However, woman is not independent of man ...," suggests that by itself verse 10 entails the independence of woman, which is only possible if verse 10 is an affirmation of the authority of woman. The context of 11:10, however, indicates that it is focusing not on the authority

---

6. LSJ 2016 II.3, "independently of, without reckoning," refers to the accomplishment of something without reference to something else, not "being independent" of another person.
7. BDAG 1095 does include 2: "*independent(ly of)*," but in the sense of "pertaining to the absence or lack of something," which does not fit 11:11, and 2.b.δ: "*without relation to* or *connection with something, independent(ly) of something*," as in "*without regard to the observance of the law* Ro 3:28." This sense does not fit 1 Cor 11:11 well.
8. Thiselton, *First Corinthians*, 841.

of woman per se, but rather on her obligation to exercise her authority. Thus, both lexically and contextually, the translation "independent" is problematic.

Kürzinger also concluded that there is little evidence for interpreting χωρίς as "independent" and showed that a common use of the word is to communicate the idea expressed in words like, "different from," "unlike," "otherwise," "heterogeneous," or "of another kind." He and others like Murphy-O'Connor, Fiorenza, and Collins conclude that the proper understanding of 1 Cor 11:11 teaches equality: "As Christians (in the Lord), woman is not different from man, and man is not different from woman."[9] LSJ 2016 identifies the metaphorical use of χωρίς as "of different nature, kind, or quality."[10] If this is applied to 1 Cor 11:11, it gives this translation: "Neither is woman of different nature than man, nor is man of different nature than woman in the Lord." A slightly different nuance to essentially this same meaning is given in LSJ 2016, "distinguish."[11] Following this nuance produces the translation, "neither is woman distinct from man, nor is man distinct from woman in the Lord." Each of these translations gives an adequate translation conveying the sense of equality. The one drawback to them is that they could be misinterpreted as implying a denial of the very sexual distinctions Paul is arguing for in verses 3–10. Although Christ overcomes the hierarchical privileges that society assigns by gender, there are still biological differences between men and women that enhance and complement their relationships to one another in Christ.

This same idea of the overcoming of barriers can be expressed using the common translation of χωρίς as "separated from someone."[12] Fenton translates it, "However, woman is not separate from man, nor man separate

---

9. Josef Kürzinger, "Frau und Mann nach 1 Kor 11,11f.," BZ 22 (1978): 270–75; Murphy-O'Connor, "Once Again," 273; Fiorenza, In Memory of Her, 229; Collins, First Corinthians, 412; Neyrey, Paul, in Other Words, 134.
10. Cf. Euripides, Alcestis 528 states, "Diverse (χωρίς) are these—to be and not to be" (Euripides, 4:450–51 [Arthus S. Way, LCL]). In Sophocles, Oed. col. 808, χωρίς clearly differentiates: "Tis one thing to speak much, another well" (Sophocles, 1:222–23 [F. Storr, LCL]).
11. E.g., Plato, Laches 195A, "Why, surely wisdom is distinct [χωρίς] from courage." Plato, Prot. 336B speaks of a joint discussion and a harangue as "two distinct [χωρίς] things" (Plato, II Laches Protagoras Meno Euthydemus [W. R. M. Lamb, LCL], 2:176–77). Cf. also Semonides, Iambographa 7.1; Isocrates 12.160; 15.68; Timocles 27.6; Euripides, Hec. 860.
12. BDAG 1095 in 1 Cor 11:11; cf. this use of χωρίς to mean "separated from" in 2 Cor 12:3; Eph 2:12; Heb 11:40; 2:9 (some mss.); Ignatius, Trall. 9:1 and 2. Isaksson, Marriage and Ministry, 182, translates χωρίς "separate from" but interprets it in a way that is awkward in English: "In any case the wife is not separate from her husband (i.e., exempt from paying any regard to him) nor is the husband separate from his wife in the Lord." The idea of "paying regard to" is not mentioned in this context, so it is hard to see how the Corinthians could have determined that

from woman in the Lord." This same use of χωρίς to indicate set apart as regards privilege is used by Paul shortly before this passage in 1 Cor 4:8, "set apart from us you have already become kings." Following this we have the translation, "However, neither is woman set apart from man, nor man set apart from woman in the Lord." This translation highlights that woman and man are one in Christ with equal standing and that the barriers of privilege separating woman from man are overcome in the Lord.[13]

Translations like the above (*different, distinct, separated, set apart from*) fit all but four[14] of Paul's sixteen uses of χωρίς.[15] Consequently, translating 1 Cor 11:11 "However, in the Lord neither is woman set apart from man, nor man set apart from woman" fits well with Paul's use of χωρίς and fits the context admirably. This affirms that, in spite of the created differences between man and woman (which should be upheld in this life), Paul's key point is that the barriers between man and woman have been overcome in Christ.[16] There is no gender-based, special privilege in Christ. Neither sex has inherently greater authority. "Any competitiveness about 'authority' becomes obsolete in the new order."[17] Man and woman have equal rights and standing in Christ. All believers enjoy his blessings without distinction.

Verse 11 expresses the theological basis for Paul's judgment in 11:5 that women as well as men may pray and prophesy in the public ministry of the church.[18] This interpretation of verse 11 affirms the oneness of man and woman in Christ in a distinctively Christian sense paralleling Gal 3:28. The new creation theme undergirds both verses. Galatians 3:28's "male and female" cites Gen 1:27 and 5:2 LXX. The "image of God" in 1 Cor 11:7 refers to Gen 1:26–27, and 1 Cor 11:8–9 refers to the account of the creation of woman in Gen 2:18–25. Verse 11 picks up 11:3's references both

---

Paul meant this, and an article or possessive pronoun would have been expected if "husband" and "wife" were meant.

13. Cf. Murphy-O'Connor, "Sex," 497–98, who also concludes from this verse, "there is no difference in the social status of man and woman in Christ."
14. And even these four, which are better translated "without," can be expressed meaningfully using "set apart from": Phil 2:14: "Do all things set apart from [χωρίς] complaining or arguing"; 1 Tim 2:8: "lift up holy hands in prayer, set apart from [χωρίς] anger or disputing"; 1 Tim 5:21: "Keep these instructions set apart from [χωρίς] partiality"; Phlm 14: "I did not want to do anything set apart from [χωρίς] your consent."
15. The others (meaning *different, distinct, separated, set apart from*) are Rom 3:21, 28; 4:6; 7:8–9; 10:14; 1 Cor 4:8; 2 Cor 11:28; 12:3; Eph 2:12.
16. Gundry-Volf, "Gender and Creation," 152, who also sees here women's new social equality in Christ without denying their differences.
17. Thiselton, *First Corinthians*, 822.
18. Cf. the association of prophecy and ministry in 1 Cor 12:5 and Eph 4:11–12.

to Christ's work in creation as the source of man and as the redeemer coming from God. Christ established the new creation that replaces man's rule over women resulting from the fall (Gen 3:16) with oneness in the church. The next chapter reinforces the unity of woman and man in Christ by teaching the oneness of the body where there should be no division (1 Cor 12:13, 25–27).

Significantly, both hair display issues addressed in this passage symbolize men or women setting themselves apart from each other: man presenting himself as woman (implying that man does not need woman), and woman wearing her hair down (symbolizing sexual freedom from her husband). Hence, it is most appropriate that Paul should highlight as his central concern in this passage that, in Christ, man and woman are no longer set apart from one other.

To summarize, the normal meaning of χωρίς virtually demands that this statement be understood as an affirmation that in Christ there is no separation between woman and man. The introductory "however" shows that this is a new perspective, one that Paul regards as essential. "In the Lord" shows that it is something established in Christ, not something that was already established in society apart from Christ. Consequently, verse 11 must mean something other than the biological interdependence of man and woman stated in verse 12. Verse 12's introductory "for" implies that verse 12 does not simply repeat the meaning of verse 11 but rather provides reasoning that supports Paul's affirmation of the equality of woman and man in the Lord. It does this by pointing out that every man's source in woman balances woman's source in Adam and by asserting that all this comes from God. Thus, the equal standing of woman and man in Christ is rooted in creation and biology and has its source in God. These factors confirm that 11:11 is not about biological interdependence but rather about the equal standing of woman and man in the Lord. Paul clearly does not want his specific instructions regarding the "head covering" issues raised by the Corinthian church to support any subordination of woman to man in Christ.

Sadly, most interpreters of 1 Cor 11:11 ignore the concluding words "in the Lord," in spite of its end stress position. "In the Lord" (ἐν κυρίῳ) is a set expression meaning "in the *experience* of faith in Christ." It is not just about theoretical standing but points to the new community established in

Christ.[19] Unless Paul intended something distinctively Christian about his statement in verse 11, he would not have concluded it with "in the Lord."

Being "in the Lord" transforms relationships such that "we regard no one from a worldly point of view" (2 Cor 5:16). Being "in Christ" is the basis of Paul's theology of the new creation (5:17) and applies to all believers, not just males. In 1 Cor 7, Paul expresses the equal rights of men and women in Christ in twelve distinct issues, including sex, divorce, and the spiritual life.[20] In 1 Cor 11 as well, the equal standing of man and woman in Christ is the basis of women as well as men having authority to lead in prayer and to prophesy (11:5, 13). Scholars who give the weight to "in the Lord" that its end stress deserves are far more likely to acknowledge 11:11's affirmation of the equal standing of man and woman in Christ. For example, Lenski notes, "as far as being 'in the Lord' is concerned both are altogether equal."[21]

FIRST CORINTHIANS 11:12 UNDERMINES HIERARCHICAL VIEWS OF MAN AND WOMAN

Paul immediately defends his affirmation of the equality of the sexes, "For *just as* woman came from [ἐκ] man, so man comes through woman." This unmistakably refers back to 11:8, "For man was not made from [ἐκ] woman, but woman from [ἐκ] man." First Corinthians 11:12 uses the identical phrase that occurs in the LXX of Gen 2:23, ἐκ τοῦ ἀνδρός, to describe woman coming "from the man." In order to make it clear that his point is not that man as the source of woman has priority over woman, Paul highlights that in giving birth, woman is man's source. Paul is intentionally counterbalancing his earlier statement that man is the source of woman. As Adam was the instrumental source of the first woman, so woman is the instrumental source in the order of nature of all subsequent men (including Jesus, Matt 1:16; Gal 4:4).

Paul is the first writer known to derive theological significance from the fact that every man is born through [διά] woman.[22] In 11:12 Paul uses

---

19. E.g., Rom 16:12, 13, 22; 1 Cor 4:17; 7:22, 39; 9:1, 2; 15:58; 16:19; Phil 4:2; cf. Murphy-O'Connor, "Once Again," 273; Rudolph Bultmann, *Theology of the New Testament* (2 vols.; London: SCM, 1965), 1:329, notes that "in the Lord" points to a particularly Christian understanding.
20. Cf. above, pp. 105–8.
21. Lenski, *Corinthians*, 453. Cf. Robertson and Plummer, *First Corinthians*, 234, "There can be no separation between man and woman where both are members of Christ."
22. In *Gen. Rab.* 8:9; 22:2 "neither man without woman nor woman without man" is about the procreation of children, not theological standing; cf. Str-B 3:440; Murphy-O'Connor, "Once Again," 273.

the same two prepositions in the same order to highlight the source of women from (ἐκ) man and of man through (διά) woman that he did in 8:6 to identify the source of all things as being from (ἐκ) God and through (διά) Christ. Paul sets the conceptual stage in 8:6 that he develops in his use of "head" for source in 11:3 and particularly that Christ is the head of every man.

Just as verse 12a unmistakably refers back to verse 8, verse 12b is borrowed word for word from verse 9, using the same preposition but now with the genitive instead of the accusative:

11:9   ἀνὴρ διὰ τὴν γυναῖκα ("neither was man created for woman")

11:12b ἀνὴρ διὰ τῆς γυναικός ("so also man is born through woman")

Verse 12, then, recapitulates in the same order key terminology from 11:8–9 to show that the temporal priority of man in creation and his being the instrumental source of woman is balanced by the order of nature (natural birth) where woman is temporally prior and is the instrumental source of all subsequent men. Consequently, both men and women should show respect to the other as their source. Paul's own unmistakable counterbalancing in 11:12 of his former comments about man's temporal priority excludes a subordinationist interpretation of 11:8–9.

"But all this comes from God (τὰ δὲ πάντα ἐκ τοῦ θεοῦ)" in 11:12b further confirms the importance of source relations in this passage. Paul is arguing from creation, looking back beyond Adam as the instrumental source of Eve to God, the primary and determinative source of both. Paul's point is that ultimately, even in creation, the source of man and woman is the same. Both the context about man and woman and the article in τὰ πάντα indicate that the "all these" Paul has in view are specifically all men and all women, probably not everything God had created.[23] The identical phrase, τὰ δὲ πάντα ἐκ τοῦ θεοῦ, occurs in 2 Cor 5:18, where it also means, "All this is from God" (ESV, NIV, TNIV, NRSV, RSV).

Similarly, "all" with an article has specifically identified referents in 2 Cor 4:15 ("all this"); 1 Cor 12:6, 19; 2 Cor 12:19 ("all of these"); and

---

23. Lenski, *Corinthians*, 453–54; Meyer, *Corinthians*, 254; BDAG 784 πᾶς 4.d.β "As a summation of what precedes *all this*."

1 Cor 9:22; 2 Cor 5:14; Gal 3:22; Phil 2:21 ("all people"). When Paul uses "all" with general reference, not just to modify another word, he typically omits the article.[24] Paul's specification of God as the ultimate and decisive source of both man and woman clearly limits what implications can properly be drawn from his earlier statements about the man as the source of woman in 11:3 and the reasons in 11:7–9 for a man not to do his hair up like a woman's.[25] Fee correctly notes, "This seems clearly designed to keep the earlier argument from being read in a subordinationist way."[26]

First Corinthians 11:12c emphasizes that God has ordained the equality of man and woman. It is ultimately God who repudiates a hierarchy of man over woman based on source. Verses 11–12 undermine at five crucial points any argument for a hierarchy of man over woman:

1. There is such a fundamental unity between man and woman that "in the Lord" man and woman are "not separate" from each other (v. 11). Neither has special privileges in Christ.

2. Man as the source of woman (vv. 3 and 8) is merely the instrumental source. God, the ultimate and determinative source of both (v. 12), equalizes their standing in Christ. Man is not in any sense a cause or an active source in woman's origin.

3. As Lenski observed about the structure of verse 12, "'Even as ... so also' makes plain this equality ... neither sex has an advantage."[27]

4. The birth of every man through woman (v. 12) balances Adam's creation prior to Eve.

5. Paul implies in 11:12 the *need* man has for woman and vice versa. By referring to childbirth he shows that the need is for a partner in procreation. The verbal parallels between verse 12 and verse 9 indicates that Paul was referring in verse 9 to man's need for a sexual partner, not for a subordinate being. He had plenty of them

---

24. The occurrences in 1 Corinthians are 1:5; 2:10, 15; 3:21, 22; 6:12 (3x); 9:12, 22, 23, 25; 10:23 (4x), 31, 33; 11:2; 13:7 (4x); 14:26, 40; 15:27 (2x), 28; 16:14. In comparison there are only a few cases where the article is included for general reference in 1 Cor, and even these have various mitigating factors: in 2:15 (a variant reading); 8:6 (twice in a citation from Mal 2:10, where the context identifies all Malachi's readers as created by God); and 15:27–28 (four times pointing back to what was originally identified twice by $\pi\tilde{\alpha}\varsigma$ without an article in 15:27).

25. This cautions against adopting interpretations that impugn the integrity of Paul's thought, e.g., Conzelmann, *1 Corinthians*, 190, "The contradiction between v 8 and v 12 seems particularly crass."

26. Fee, *First Corinthians*, 524.

27. Lenski, *Corinthians*, 453.

already, and they did not bring him fulfillment. But the woman did bring fulfillment. The interdependence of man and woman highlighted in 11:12 proves that Paul's statement in verse 9 that man was *not* made for woman did not imply either the independence of man from woman or that man should not fulfill woman. Paul is clarifying that woman was specifically made *for* man in the Genesis sense of a partner in procreation corresponding to him.

This analysis concludes that Paul is *not* attempting to derive a hierarchy of authority of men over women from his "head" statements in verse 3, either as meaning authority directly or as somehow implying the man's authority over woman from the idea that man was the source of woman. After all, if that were Paul's intention in verse 3, why does he undermine it so drastically in verses 11 – 12? Paul specifically undermines the argument used to support a hierarchy of authority of men over women at the five key points listed above.

These same arguments also undermine any interpretation of 11:7 that infers that women are not in "the image of God" or are only so in a secondary or derived sense. If Paul is taking back in 11:11 – 12 what he argues for strongly in 11:3 – 10, it would be rhetorically counterproductive, inept, and quite out of character with his rhetorical skills throughout 1 Corinthians.[28] Paul's return in 11:13 – 16 to the issue of wild hair with no contrasting conjunction implies that he intends his comments about the equality of man and woman to relate to and be consistent with his restrictions on wild hair.

---

28. Cf. Also Witherington, *Conflict*, 235.

12

1 Corinthians 11:13 – 16: Shameful Head Coverings Explained as Hair

Paul's Requirement Fits the Corinthians' Cultural Expectations

Paul's imperative, "Judge within yourselves [ἐν ὑμῖν αὐτοῖς κρίνατε]" in 11:13 shows that he is confident the Corinthian church will agree that for a woman to pray "uncovered" is shameful. Paul emphasizes their own judgment by placing "in you yourselves" at the beginning of the sentence and by adding αὐτοῖς to ὑμῖν.[1] "In yourselves" implies an internal judgment,[2] not something imposed on them. Paul's earlier repudiation of idolatry followed by his invitation in 10:15 "to sensible people, judge for yourselves" parallels this new invitation to judge after making clear his own assessment. In both passages, Paul follows up with a series of questions to help them make the right judgment.

"Is it proper for a woman to pray to God with her head uncovered?"[3] shows that Paul trusts the Corinthians to agree with his assessment in 11:5 – 6. "To pray to God" in this verse substitutes for "praying or prophesying" in 11:4 and 5. This suggests that "praying or prophesying" may also

---

1. Morris, *First Corinthians*, 155.
2. Cf. 4:5; 5:3; 6:2 – 3; 7:37; 10:15, 29; 11:31, 32.
3. Padgett ("Paul on Women," 81) and Katherine C. Bushnell (*God's Word to Women: One Hundred Bible Studies on Woman's Place in the Divine Economy* [Oakland, Cal.: Katherine C. Bushnell, 1923], §249) take this as a statement. This entails treating vv. 5 – 9 as an interpolation or a quote from Paul's opponents without textual support.

represent any kind of leading in ministry. Surely Paul would have objected to any kind of leadership in church worship done with a hairstyle that undermined sexual distinctions or symbolized rejection of fidelity in marriage. "To God" suggests that the offense was not just social but an offense to God. This fits what a woman symbolized by letting her hair down: the repudiation of her marriage vows.

It would not make sense for Paul to make this invitation to judgment if he did not expect most of the Corinthians to agree with his own stated opinion in 11:5–6. Consequently, we can be confident that the custom Paul described as disgraceful in 11:5 was, in fact, regarded as disgraceful in Greek society. This fits perfectly if Paul is referring to a woman who lets her hair down loose since that did in fact expose her to social indignity. It does not, however, fit for a veil or some other head-covering garment, since an abundance of evidence indicates that Hellenistic women did not normally wear a garment over their heads.

LONG HAIR IS DEGRADING TO A MAN

"Does not even [οὐδέ[4]] the very nature of things teach you" (1 Cor 11:14a) introduces Paul's final argument against men and women displaying wild hair. Each of the ten occurrences of this conjunction (οὐδέ) meaning "not even" in Paul's letters (Rom 3:10; 1 Cor 4:3; 5:1; 11:14; 14:21; 15:13, 16; Gal 2:3, 5; 6:13) ties into what precedes in the text. Even where it does not carry the sense of "not even," this conjunction typically ties into the prior context. Consequently, this conjunction naturally associates 11:14–15 with Paul's prior argument, and with 11:13 in particular.

"If a man has long hair, it is degrading to him" (1 Cor 11:14b) uses the "if" + the present subjunctive grammatical construction of a third class condition, one that "denotes that which under certain circumstances is expected from an existing general or concrete standpoint in the present."[5] This identical construction is used regarding man in verse 14, then regarding woman in verse 15. In the case of woman, there is no question that most women in Corinth, as everywhere else in the Greco-Roman world, had long hair and that it was their glory. Consequently, from either

4. Since early manuscripts had no spaces between words, it is possible to read it οὐ δέ; cf. Orr and Walther, *I Corinthians*, 261; Fee, *First Corinthians*, 526.
5. BDF §371 (4), 188; cf. Robertson, *Grammar*, 1016 (γ).

the general standpoint of his culture or the concrete standpoint of the Corinthian church, Paul expected that women in the Corinthian church would have long hair and that it would be their glory if it was done up appropriately.

Paul's use of the identical construction for man show that for man, too, he is basing this condition on an existing general or concrete standpoint in the present. Appropriately, BDAG (κομάω 557) notes, "Perhaps Paul refers to the effeminate manner in which some males coiffured their long hair." Thus, the use of the third class condition combined with "Does not even nature teach you," its use in the parallel statement of reality regarding women, and Paul's argumentation against effeminate hair (11:7 – 9) give evidence that Paul believed that some man (or men) there had long hair that was self-degrading.

Almost all exegetes have correctly understood verses 14 – 15 as a two-part rhetorical question, not two statements. Mark 12:10 and Luke 23:40 also use οὐδέ to introduce a rhetorical question. The perfectly parallel μέν ... δέ construction requires that verses 14 and 15a be treated as a grammatical pair. Long hair on men *was* considered degrading, so 11:14 would not have been read as a statement denying this. Similarly, since verse 15b confirms the positive value of long hair on women, verse 15a would not have been read as a statement denying this.[6] The assumed answer to both of these rhetorical questions is, "Yes."

The cultural background is summarized in Plutarch's *Roman Questions* 267B, "In Greece ... men cut their hair short; women let it grow [κομᾶν]."[7] This custom accentuates the natural differentiation between man and woman. Men who wore long effeminate hair blurred the natural differentiation between man and woman. Pseudo-Phocylides, writing about the beginning of the first century, stated, "Long hair is not fit for men."[8] The same cultural expectation was prevalent in Roman society, where men's hair in general was cut even shorter than in Greece.[9] According to Pliny,[10]

---

6. Only if v. 14 were a statement (which would defy typical social judgment) and if Paul had added "hanging loose" to v. 15a (which he did not) to modify women's long hair would one be justified in taking v. 15 as a statement. The assumption of "hanging loose," however, is incompatible with the article, since it identifies the long hair in v. 15b used as a covering with the hair just referred to in v. 15a.
7. Plutarch, *Mor.* 4:26 – 27 (Babbitt, LCL).
8. Van der Horst, *Pseudo-Phocylides*, 81 – 83; citation from v. 213.
9. Murphy-O'Connor, "Once Again," 268; "Sex," 486; cf. also Hurley, *Biblical Perspective*, 257.
10. Pliny, *Nat.* 7, 59.

Roman men adopted shaving and wearing short hair about 300 BC. Since the time of Alexander the Great (c. 350 BC) up to the second century AD, short hair was fashionable for men.[11]

It is generally agreed that Greek[12] and Roman[13] custom at the time of Paul was for men to have short hair. Spartan soldiers centuries before Paul wore long hair, but this was a matter of curiosity, not current custom. Dio Chrysostom (*Discourse* 35.11) criticizes philosophers for associating their long hair with moral superiority, pointing out that barbarians and farmers also have long hair, as do some people for religious reasons. Dio Chrysostom's criticism of long-haired philosophers represents the conventional judgment that long hair is a disgrace to a man.

There is evidence for this in Jewish culture as well. Ezekiel 44:20 mandates that priests "must not shave their heads or let their hair grow long, but they are to keep the hair of their heads trimmed." Leviticus 10:6 commands priests, "do not let your hair become unkempt." Leviticus 21:10 says the high priest "must not let his hair become unkempt." *B. Ta'an.* 17b states, "The following [priests] incur the penalty of death, those who are intoxicated with wine and those whose hair has grown long."[14]

Paul probably knew that some male animals (e.g., lions, monkeys, and peacocks) have more hair or plumage than females. In light of the Jewish Nazarite vow to "let the hair of his head grow long" (Num 6:5), Paul certainly knew that men's hair will grow if left to nature, just as a woman's will. This suggests that Paul is not speaking in a purely biological sense of nature. Nor is it likely that Paul is invoking Mother Nature as a personification of a deity in light of 1 Cor 8:4–6, "there is no God but one." Paul's only use in this passage of the noun "nature" (φύσις) most naturally, then, carries the meaning that BDAG 1070 (3) gives for 1 Cor 11:14, "the regular or established order of things."

This meaning was common from the Stoic idea that Nature is the origin and guarantor of culture.[15] Panaetius, for example, states, "We try

---

11. Thompson, "Hairstyles," 104; Rolf Hurschmann, "Hairstyle," *Brill's New Pauly* (2004), 5:1102.
12. Cf. Walther Bremer, "Haartracht und Haarschmuck," PW 7:2112; Pottier, "Coma," 1355–60; *Bulletin de correspondence hellénique* 2 (1878): 626–32, pl. iv, vi.
13. Thompson, "Hairstyles," 99–111.
14. J. Rabbinowitz, *Hebrew-English Edition of the Babylonian Talmud: Ta'anit* (I. Epstein, ed.; London: Soncino, 1984), 17b.
15. David Jobling, "'And Have Dominion …' The Interpretation of Genesis 1, 28 in Philo Judaeus," *JSJ* 8,1 (1977): 79. cf. Gill, "Head-Coverings," 257; Conzelmann, *1 Corinthians*, 190, nn. 96, 97; Fiorenza, *In Memory of Her*, 229.

with our own hands to create within nature as it were a second nature."[16] Stoics believed that the highest good was to live in tune with nature, in accordance with the natural order of things. Nature expressed itself in the finest fruits of culture. Hence Marcus Aurelius Antoninus (AD 121 – 180), philosopher and emperor of Rome, wrote, "O Nature (ὦ φύσις), All things come from thee, subsist in thee, go back to thee."[17] Paul uses a strikingly parallel series of phrases in Rom 11:36, "For from him and through him and to him are all things," indicating the prevalent usage of this expression at that time and Paul's familiarity with Stoic literature.[18] Marcus Aurelius continued, "There is one who says *Dear City of Cecrops!* Wilt thou not say *O dear City of Zeus?*"[19] Nature is depicted as a dear city, a possibility only where culture is seen as a vehicle of nature. The Stoic philosopher Epictetus (AD 55 – 135) appeals to nature to dissuade a man from dressing his hair like a woman since it would "confuse the sexes."[20]

It is precisely this understanding of nature as natural expectation within the culture that fits perfectly with all the words Paul uses here. Nature teaches what is "degrading" to a man and what is "glory" to a woman. "Degradation" and "glory" are terms describing cultural perception that could not be deduced solely from the natural world, just like his earlier terms "disgrace" (11:4, 5, 6) and "proper" (11:13). This is not an appeal to natural law per se,[21] but rather what is perceived in their cultural setting as natural because it upholds rather than undermines the actual distinction of the sexes in nature. The NIV translates this well, "Does not the very nature of things teach you...?" Appropriately, Fee describes this as an appeal to "the way things are," to the "natural feeling" shared in their contemporary culture.[22] Nature here is not some law of "the created order" ordained by

---

16. Max Pohlenz, *Die Stoa: Geschichte einer geistigen Bewegung* (2 vols.; Göttingen: Vandenhoeck & Ruprecht, 1948 and 1949), 1:197.
17. *Marcus Aurelius* 4.23, cited from C. R. Haines, trans., *The Communings with Himself of Marcus Aurelius Antoninus Emperor of Rome* (LCL), 80 – 81.
18. Cranfield, *Romans*, 2:591, cites Stoic uses of this expression.
19. *Marcus Aurelius* 4.23 (LCL), 80 – 81.
20. Epictetus 3.1 and in 3.22.10 – 11; cf. 1.16.9 – 14.
21. In contrast, Rom 1:26 – 27 uses "nature" to refer to biology in describing homosexual acts: "even their females changed the natural [τὴν φυσικήν] use into the [use] against nature [παρὰ φύσιν]."
22. Fee, *First Corinthians*, 527. This understanding is also supported by Yeo Khiok-Khing, "Differentiation and Mutuality of Male-Female Relations in 1 Corinthians 11:2 – 16," *BR* 43 (1998): 20; Blomberg, "Neither Hierarchalist," 347; Thiselton, *First Corinthians*, 844 – 46; Schrage, *Korinther*, 2:521 – 22; John Calvin, *The First Epistle of Paul to the Corinthians* (trans. J. W. Fraser; Calvin's New Testament Commentaries; ed. David and Thomas Torrance; 9th ed.; Grand Rapids: Eerdmans, 1960), 252.

God that must be followed.[23] Otherwise, things like the Nazarite vow, rules that God commanded for both men and women, would contradict "the created order" here described. The Nazarite vow, being exceptional in nature, demonstrated that it was "normal" for men to wear hair short.

LONG HAIR IS THE GLORY OF A WOMAN WHEN SHE USES IT AS A COVERING

Long hair is disgraceful to a man, but long hair is a woman's glory if she uses it "as a covering" (11:15b). When is a woman's hair her glory? When it is done up respectably. BDAG 557 states regarding κόμη, "Well-bred women would wear their tresses gathered up on their heads." Paul's concern throughout this passage has been the public display of hair.[24] Achilles Tatius records about the shaving of Leucippe, "She has been robbed of the crowning glory of her hair [τῆς κεφαλῆς τὸ κάλλος],"[25] literally, "the beauty of her head." As in 1 Cor 11:4–6, "head" implies "hair." Thompson states that almost all the Roman portraiture from Corinth shows women with long hair, noting only one with short hair, a young girl with bangs.[26] Jewish women, too, regarded long hair as beautiful (Song 4:1; 6:5).[27]

Verse 15b explains, "For [ὅτι] her long hair is given to her as [ἀντί] a covering." As Paul commonly uses it, ὅτι here is a loose causal conjunction best translated "for."[28] The word for "a covering" (περιβόλαιον) here is a compound word joining "to throw" and "around." BDAG 800 describes this word as "an article of apparel that covers much of the body, *covering, wrap, cloak, robe*." LSJ 1369 describes it as "*that which is thrown round, covering . . . corpse-clothes . . .* woman's *head-gear, 1 Ep.Cor. 11.15 . . . warm wrap*." MM 505 notes that it was used "in the wider sense of 'covering,' 'clothing,' rather than 'veil' in 1 Cor 11:15." This is the first occurrence in this passage of any word identifying any kind of garment.

---

23. *Pace* the unsupported allegation of Hurley, "Veils," 215.
24. Remarkably, in spite of Paul's use of "disgrace" and "glory" in the context of rules for public worship, Fee (*First Corinthians*, 528) writes, "Although he may be thinking of hair as it is done up in public, more likely he is not thinking of the public appearance of women but of the more 'natural' phenomenon of the hair itself ... not how people appear, but how they are by the nature of things."
25. Achilles Tatius 8.5 (S. Gaselee, LCL), 2:398–99.
26. Thompson, "Hairstyles," 112.
27. Cf. T. K. Cheyne, "Hair," in *Encyclopædia Biblica* (4 vols.; London: Adam and Charles Black, 1901), 2:1940–41.
28. As also in 1 Cor 1:25; 4:9 and 10:17; cf. BDF §456; BDAG 732 4b; Robertson, *Grammar*, 962–63.

Ἀντί can mean "instead of" (indicating replacement)[29] or "as" (indicating equivalence). There are no other occurrences of ἀντί to mean "instead of" in the Pauline corpus, and it is rare in the NT (Matt 2:22 and Luke 11:11). Apart from two formulaic uses,[30] both of Paul's other uses of ἀντί indicate equivalence (Rom 12:17; 1 Thess 5:15), so based on Paul's usage elsewhere, "as" is the more natural reading.[31] Virtually all Bible versions translate ἀντί "as" or "for." This equivalence meaning of ἀντί entails "as a substitute for" or "to function as" or "that one thing is equivalent to another."[32] BDAG 88 (2) translates the equivalence usage *"for, as, in place of,"* but gives no meaning, "in addition to."

In thirty-six years studying this passage this author cannot recall any passage adduced where ἀντί conveys "in addition to." If ἀντί here conveys equivalence, this verse teaches that a woman's hair is equivalent to a wrap-around and so implies that her hair functions as a wrap-around. Thus, the recognized range of meaning of ἀντί does not include the possibility that this sentence argues that women need an additional covering as well as their hair. This is not an appropriate way to express the idea that a further veil is needed besides the one provided by nature. Scroggs recognized this, but since he interpreted 11:5 as referring to a garment, he concluded that "Paul is actually self-contradictory."[33]

---

29. BDAG 87 – 88. JND translates this, "the long hair is given [to her] in lieu of a veil." This interpretation is adopted by Hurley, *Biblical Perspective*, 168, cf. 179; idem, "Man and Woman in 1 Corinthians," 70; idem, "Veils," 215; Gill, "Head-coverings," 258; Fiorenza, *In Memory of Her*, 227; Isaksson, *Marriage and Ministry*, 185; Martin, "1 Corinthians 11.2 – 16," 233; Padgett, "Paul on Women," 82 – 83. Isaksson *Marriage and Ministry*, 186, proposes that long hair is given "instead of a prophet's cloak," but neither the context (note *prayer and prophecy*, summarized as simply "prayer" in 11:13) nor the word περιβόλαιον supports such a narrow meaning. Hurley's suggestion in *Biblical Perspective*, 179, that Paul is opposing a very conservative group that sought to impose veiling on women is culturally improbable, as he acknowledges. It is also unlikely that Paul would raise a new issue in passing at the conclusion of his arguments for women wearing their hair up. Furthermore, if Paul had been aware when he wrote that there were problems both with hair let down and demands for a garment over the head, he should have specified either hair or garment coverings in 11:5 – 6 and 13 so that the Corinthians would understand which one he was addressing. The fact that he did not specify this earlier indicates that there was probably not a separate garment-imposing contingent.
30. ἀνθ' ὧν = "because" in 2 Thess 2:10; ἀντὶ τούτου = "for this reason" in Eph 5:31.
31. *Pace* Hurley, *Biblical Perspective*, 168, cf. 179; "Lifted out of this chapter, this verse would be universally rendered as teaching that long hair is given *instead of* or *to take the place of* a veil"; cf. also his "Man and Woman in 1 Corinthians," 70; idem, "Veils," 215.
32. LSJ 153 §A.III.2; Murphy-O'Connor, "Sex," 489 n. 32. The point is not, as Massey, "κατακαλύπτω," 516 n. 52, ridicules, that "περιβόλαιον means hair wrapped around the head" but that hair is given to function as a περιβόλαιον (covering/wrap around).
33. Scroggs, "Eschatological Woman," 298 n. 40.

Whether ἀντί means "as" or "instead of," it views long hair as the covering. This implies that Paul did not require women to wear any item of clothing on top of their modestly-done-up hair. After all, why would Paul end his argument by stating that a woman has been given long hair as a covering if his point all along was to require a garment head covering?[34] The only way to make it clear that this statement is compatible with a demand for a garment head covering would be to interpret the word ἀντί to mean "as well as." This, however, is not a legitimate translation. Standard Greek lexicons do not include "as well as" as a possible meaning of ἀντί.

Fee appeals to the use of ἀντί for equivalence as a basis for treating this as an argument "by analogy that since women have by 'nature' been given long hair as a covering, that in itself points to their need to be 'covered' when praying and prophesying."[35] Nothing in verses 14–15, however, hints that hair is "an analogy" pointing to the need of an additional covering. Instead, the equivalence interpretation identifies a woman's hair as her covering. Ironically, although Fee argues that a woman's long hair "is equivalent to" a "wraparound,"[36] he states one page earlier that the "natural meaning of these words is that her long hair, let down, functions for her as a natural covering." Nothing in the passage, however, says that long hair "let down" is a woman's glory. To the contrary, a woman's hair let down in public symbolized her sexual looseness that was widely regarded as shameful. Yet Fee asks the right question, "The question is whether the preceding rhetorical question (vv. 14–15) was intended to deal with hair specifically, thus implying that this had been the issue right along."[37] The answer is, "Yes"; 1 Cor 11:14–15 deals specifically with hair, unambiguously repudiating long hair on men as disgraceful and affirming that a woman's long hair done up as a covering is her glory.

If verses 14–15 had stated instead, "Does not even the very nature of things teach you that if a man covers his head with a garment it is

---

34. Mount, "Interpolation," *JBL* 124 (2005): 333, regards vv. 4–5 to be about garment head coverings and so concludes, "If περιβόλαιον is translated 'covering' (the usual translation), then 11:15 seems to contradict 11:4–5. Is a woman's hair her covering, or does a woman's hair need to be covered?"

35. Fee, *First Corinthians*, 529. Fee acknowledges that his "argument is not tight for some modern tastes." The same unsupported extension of the normal meaning of ἀντί is made by Meier, "Veiling of Hermeneutics," 222.

36. Fee, *First Corinthians*, 529.

37. Ibid., 528.

degrading to him, but if a woman covers her head with a garment it is her glory? For a garment is given to her as a covering," then these verses would appropriately be accepted as establishing beyond doubt what the previously unidentified coverings were. For exactly the same reasoning, the words of these verses ought to be accepted as establishing that the covering Paul is speaking about is hair. In addition, Paul's express statement in verse 15 that women have been given long hair "as a covering" specifically identifies the function of long hair as a covering, and so links this statement to the topic Paul has been addressing, shameful head coverings. The Corinthians did not need this explanation since they had direct experience of seeing these shameful head coverings in their worship services, but for readers lacking this experience, Paul's explanation is essential to confirm what he meant.

The Churches Have No Such Custom

Paul introduces his conclusion by referring to the novel and contentious display of wild hair in the Corinthian church: "But if anyone wants to be contentious" (1 Cor 11:16a). "If anyone seems to be [εἴ τις δοκεῖ]" is a recurring phrase in 1 Corinthians, each time listing a key word describing a major problem in the Corinthian congregation. "If anyone thinks he is wise" (3:18) exposes their exaltation of human wisdom. "If anyone thinks he knows something" (8:2) exposes their exaltation of knowledge. "If anyone thinks he is a prophet or spiritual" (14:37) exposes their exaltation of manifestations of spirituality. Here in 11:16, "If anyone wants to be[38] contentious" identifies these particular troublemakers' contentious spirit and indicates that their wild hair has led to contention in the church. Since every other instance of "if anyone seems to be" identifies actual people causing a problem in the church, Paul's references to shameful head coverings in 11:4–16 should not be viewed as hypothetical. Men, by displaying effeminate hair, and women, by letting their hair down, gave evidence of their contentious spirit.

Paul concludes, "we have no such [τοιαύτην] custom." "We" must always be identified by its context. In 1 Cor 4:8–10 and 15:11 it refers to Paul and the apostles. In 2 Cor 1:18–19 it refers to Paul, Silvanus, and Timothy. Here "we" is associated with "the churches of God" and regards customs they do not hold. Both "the churches of God" and "custom" presuppose

---

38.   BDAG 254, "is disposed to be."

organized social groups. Οὐδέ could join two separate groups of churches, such as the Pauline churches and other churches.[39] More likely, however, this is an example of Paul's typical use of οὐδέ to join two elements to convey a single idea.[40] Accordingly, Paul's meaning is, "We, the churches of God, have no such custom."

This alleviates the problem of separating Paul's churches from another group ("the churches of God"), a title that assuredly Paul would want to characterize the churches he had founded. This fits Paul's association of himself with "the churches" in 4:17, "my way of life in Christ Jesus, which agrees with what I teach in every church," and 7:17 "this is the law that I lay down in all the churches." Unless this is the one exception, Paul nowhere separates himself from any reference to the churches or to generic references to the whole church throughout 1 Corinthians.[41]

Τοιοῦτος means "such a kind" and with the negative is properly translated "no such custom" in most versions.[42] Versions that change "no such custom" to "no other custom" (e.g., HCSB, NIV, NASB, NAB, RSV, TNIV, TEV, LB, Amplified, Goodspeed, Phillips, Williams) introduce a meaning for τοιοῦτος that not only has no support in any standard Greek lexicon such as BDAG or LSJ; it is the opposite of this Greek word's meaning.

The closest possible referent for "no such custom" is "to be contentious," and in fact many older commentators identified contentiousness as the custom, understood as "habit."[43] They probably did this because they realized that if "no such custom" referred to a custom that women should be veiled, this verse would imply that the churches had no such custom. These commentators refused to identify this reference to "custom" with the veiling of women since they had interpreted this whole passage as a vigorous defense of this custom. Contentiousness, however, is a temperament or bad habit,

---

39.   E.g., Fee, *First Corinthians*, 530.
40.   Cf. below, pp. 337–59, especially 342.
41.   Cf. 1:2, which though not using the word "churches" shows Paul's association of himself with "all those everywhere who call on the name of the Lord Jesus," as does 14:33, "as in all the congregations of the saints," and 10:32; 11:22; 12:28; 14:19, 34–35 (probably an interpolation); 15:9; 16:1, 19.
42.   E.g., Beck, Berkeley, New Berkeley, ESV, Fenton, JND, KJV, NRSV, Philadelphia Bible Society (1823), REB, TNT, Weymouth, and the old Geneva Bible, or in equivalent terms by ASV, NEB, and JB. Cf. Fee, *First Corinthians*, 530 n. 28, "there is no evidence of any kind that it means 'other.'"
43.   This is endorsed by T. Engberg-Pedersen, "1 Corinthians 11:16 and the Character of Pauline Exhortations," *JBL* 110 (1991): 684; Collins, *First Corinthians*, 414.

not a custom.[44] Even though "habit" is a legitimate possible meaning of the word συνήθειαν, it is unlikely that it should be interpreted as "habit" for several reasons:

1. This entire passage has been about customs, not habits.
2. Parallel passages referring to "all the churches" (e.g., 1 Cor 7:17; 14:33) clearly refer to church customs.
3. Individuals have habits, but churches have customs, not habits, so "the churches of God have no such habit" is logically odd.
4. If "custom" refers to "contentiousness," it fails to conclude the passage since it neither summarizes the passage nor even refers specifically to either of the two major head-covering customs the passage addresses throughout.

The nearest custom-like antecedent is the reference to women letting their hair down, the issue Paul has just addressed in verse 15 and also the topic of verses 5–6, 10, and 13. Secondarily, it probably is also reapplying to women the arguments of verses 7–9 that were originally directed to men's effeminate hair. Most interpreters identify the custom of verse 16 to refer to woman's head covering.[45] Paul's use of the singular noun "custom," not "customs," may support particular focus on this custom. If this is correct, Paul concluded that the churches of God have no such custom of women letting their hair down in worship.

Alternatively, Paul may have intended "no such custom" to refer to the advocacy of either of the misguided head coverings addressed throughout this passage. The statement that the churches have no such custom (singular) does not require that Paul referred to only one custom, but only that the churches had "no such custom." This applies just as naturally to no such custom as permitting men to wear effeminate hair or women to let their hair down loose. The close correlations between these two customs enhance the likelihood that Paul had them both in mind, not just one. In both cases, wild hair symbolized rejection of God's desire that marriage be

---

44. Cf. also Witherington, *Earliest Churches*, 90.
45. E.g., the commentaries on 1 Corinthians by Barrett, 258; Morris, 156; Bruce, 108; Frederic Louis Godet, *Commentary on First Corinthians* (Edinburgh: T&T Clark, 1889), 559–60; Findlay, 876; Robertson and Plummer, *First Corinthians*, 235–36. David E. Garland, *1 Corinthians* (Grand Rapids: Baker, 2003), 532, affirms that a garment cover is "the universal practice in other churches," but he does not even address Paul's statement that the churches have "no such custom," just as he avoids addressing the meaning of ἀντί in v. 15.

an intimate, faithful relationship between a man and a woman. Both customs symbolized rebellion against God's will. Both symbolized sexual freedom. This interpretation has the advantage that it summarizes the whole passage, from verses 2 to 16. The fact that the churches had no such custom implies that some in Corinth were practicing novel customs, not breaches of established church rules.

Verse 16 contradicts any interpretation that this passage requires women to wear a garment over the head to conform to church custom. Why would Paul conclude, "we, the churches of God, have no such custom" if the churches had just such a head covering custom?[46]

---

46. *Pace* Schreiner, "Women in Ministry," 229, who asserts, "in verse 16 he reminds the Corinthians that all the other churches practice the custom that the Corinthians are resisting."

13

1 CORINTHIANS 11:2–16:
CONCLUSION AND APPLICATION

Once the "head coverings" are understood as wild hair, the structural logic of 1 Cor 11:2–16 makes perfect sense and all its vocabulary can be understood within its normal range of meaning. Men's effeminate hair attracted homosexual liaisons, and women's hair let down loose symbolized sexual freedom in the Dionysiac cult, which was influential in Corinth. Both were disgraceful and undermined marriage. Consequently, Paul prohibits those leading in worship from either practice. Men ought to respect Christ, their source in creation, by not displaying effeminate hair. Women ought to exercise control over their heads by wearing their hair up in public worship to symbolize fidelity in marriage and respect to man, their source in creation.

The climax of the passage affirms that in Christ women and men are not set apart from each other. This entails their equal standing and privileges. Consequently, both men and women may pray and prophesy in church but should do so in a way that does not undermine marriage or the sexual differentiation God created. Understood in the light of these backgrounds, all the vocabulary of the passage takes its normal meaning, including "authority" (not "veil") in 11:10, χωρίς as "set apart from" (not "independent") in 11:11, long hair is given her "as" (not "as well as") a covering in 11:15, and "no such" (not "no other") custom in 11:16.

The structural logic of the passage develops as follows: 1 Cor 11:2–3 introduces a new topic that Paul had not formerly addressed, that is, hairstyles in worship that symbolized sexual freedom: men's effeminate hair and women's hair let down loosely over their shoulders. Paul lays a foundation of source relationships implying the respect man owes to Christ as his source and women owes to man as her source. Paul addresses first the disgrace of men's effeminate hair (11:4), then the disgrace of women's hair let down (11:5–6). He then gives theological grounding, first against men's effeminate hair (11:7–9), then against women's hair let down (11:10, which reapplies to women the argumentation from creation in 11:7–9).

In 11:11–12, Paul focuses on the matter of prime importance, that "in the Lord" nothing sets woman apart from man. Having their source in one another and ultimately in God are reasons 11:12 gives for their equal standing in Christ. Paul then in 11:13 invites the Corinthians to judge for themselves whether women should pray with their hair let down. The very nature of things shows both that man should not have long effeminate hair (11:14) and that woman should not let her hair down (11:15) in public. The churches have no such custom as permitting either kind of wild hair (11:16).

The flow of Paul's argument in 1 Cor 11:2–16 can be clearly seen in the following translation of the Greek meaning with brief explanatory comments in parentheses:

> [2]I praise you for remembering me regularly in everything and for holding to the traditions as I delivered them to you. [3]But I want you to know that the source [lit. *head*] of every man is Christ, and the source [lit. *head*] of woman is Adam [lit. *the man*], and the source [lit. *head*] of Christ is the Godhead. [4]Every man who prays or prophesies with effeminate hair hanging down from his head disgraces himself [lit. *his head*]. [5]And every woman who prays or prophesies with her hair hanging down loose [lit. *head uncovered*, the sign of a suspected adulteress] disgraces herself [lit. *her head*], for she is one and the same with her who is shaved [the punishment of a convicted adulteress]. [6]For if a woman does not do her hair up [lit. *cover her head*], let her have her hair cut off; but if it is disgraceful for a woman to have her hair cut off or shaved, let her do her hair up [lit. *cover her head*]. [7]For a man ought not to display effeminate hair [lit. *cover his head*], since he is the image and glory of God [and so should live in

a way that upholds God's design in creation and brings God glory]. The woman [not another man] is the pride and joy of man. [8]For man did not come from woman, but woman from man [to be his sexual partner]; [9]neither was man created for woman, but woman for man [to be his sexual partner]. [10]On account of this,[1] the woman ought to have control over her hair [lit. *head*] by doing it up modestly, on account of the angels [who observe worship and report to God].

[11]However, the crucial thing is that woman is not set apart from man, nor is man set apart from woman in the Lord [in the experience of community in Christ there is no gender barrier; woman and man have equal rights]. [12]For as woman came from man, so also man is born of woman [counterbalancing any basis man might have for special standing or privilege]. But all this [man and woman] is from God. [13]Judge within yourselves: Is it proper for a woman to pray to God with her hair let down [lit. *head uncovered*]? [14]Does not the very nature of things teach you that if a man has long hair, it is a disgrace to him,[15] but if a woman has long hair, it is her glory? This is because long hair is given her as a covering. [16]If anyone wants to be contentious [by displaying hairstyles that symbolize sexual freedom], we, the churches of God, have no such custom [of men displaying effeminate hair or women letting their hair down].

First Corinthians 11:11 affirms the equality of women and men in the Lord in ways that parallel Gal 3:28. In contrast to the barriers separating man and woman as a result of the fall, "man and woman are not set apart in the Lord." In verse 12, Paul specifically counterbalances woman's creation from man (formed from Adam's rib) with the fact that every man is born through woman and that both come from God. In light of Paul's "just as ... so also" argument in this verse for the equality of woman and man, it is not surprising that verse 5 assumes without argument that women may pray and prophesy in church worship. This analysis shows Paul's theological depth and coherence throughout. It shows that he was not focusing

---

1.   Since woman is from and for man, she ought to show due respect to man (and married women to their husbands) by not letting her hair hang down loose since this symbolized unrestrained sexuality, and hence infidelity.

on superficialities, but was applying central theological principles to stop displays of sexual freedom that were subverting the sanctity of marriage in Corinth.

How do we apply this passage today? The reason Paul objects to men in church leadership wearing effeminate hairstyles is its association with homosexual relations and its repudiation of the biblical distinction between man and woman. Manly long hairstyles today do not carry that association and message, so this passage should not be used to object to manly long hair today. Similarly, the majority of women today wear their hair down—and this is not associated with repudiation of sexual fidelity in marriage—so it would be a misuse of this passage to object to women wearing their hair down today.

This passage may be properly applied today, however, against leaders in worship who adopt hairstyles, dress, or demeanor that symbolizes homosexual relations or that undermines fidelity in marriage by being sexually suggestive. For instance, in any culture that regards men wearing their hair like a woman's as advertising for homosexual liaisons, Paul's restriction would still apply. The transcultural message is, "Don't use your freedom in Christ as an excuse to dress in a way that is sexually suggestive or subversive. Keep it clean!" Paul's words apply specifically to activities of leaders in church worship.

It would be wrong, however, for the church to close its doors to sinners who need to hear the gospel. Paul's rules should not be used to exclude people from church simply because they have hairstyles that symbolize some form of sexual immorality. Paul's argumentation challenges each church to use its collective judgment to exclude only what in its culture is disgraceful and symbolizes a repudiation of Christian sexual morality and marriage. In contrast to the comparatively uniform cultural conventions of the Greco-Roman world, in western cultures today there is great cultural diversity. Rarely does a particular dress or hairstyle convey a uniform symbolism. Since conventions can change quickly, any such rules should be provisional, culturally sensitive, and restricted to unambiguous issues symbolizing immorality.

The most important application of this passage today is what Paul stresses in the climax of the passage, that men and women should show respect to each other, honoring the opposite sex as their source. As Paul stresses in the climax of this passage, believers must affirm the equal rights and privileges of women and men in the Lord. Women as well as men may lead in public Christian worship. Since in the Lord woman and man are not separate, women who are gifted and called by God ought to be welcomed into ministry, just as men are.

14

1 CORINTHIANS 14:34–35: DID PAUL FORBID WOMEN TO SPEAK IN CHURCH?

This passage, commanding women to be silent in the churches, lacks any difficult vocabulary or syntax, but its widely varying interpretations face three key issues: textual, exegetical, and systematic. The central textual issue is whether these verses are an interpolation not in the original text. This chapter addresses this issue in detail after summarizing the exegetical and systematic issues as well as the weaknesses of other proposed interpretations.

The central exegetical question is whether Paul's first-century Hellenistic audience would accept the obvious meaning of these words or would demand some qualification. These verses make the same unqualified statement in three different ways: "women must be silent [imperative] in the churches, for they are not permitted to speak ... it is a disgrace for a woman to speak in church." Lest there be any question of exceptions, verse 34 explains that if women, out of a desire to learn something, have questions, "they must ask [imperative] their husbands at home."

Today this sounds extreme, but in a Greek public meeting (an ἐκκλησία, the same word used in 1 Cor 14:34 for church), the normal convention was that women were not allowed to speak.[1] For instance, Plutarch (ca. AD 46–120) states in *Advice to the Bride and Groom* 31:

---

1. See *OCD* 376. D. A. Carson ("'Silent in the Churches': On the Role of Women in 1 Corinthians 14:33b–36," *RBMW* 153) states, "in a Greek *ekklēsia* ... women were not allowed to speak at all."

Not only the arm of the virtuous woman, but her speech as well, ought to be not for the public, and she ought to be modest and guarded about saying anything in the hearing of outsiders, since it is an exposure of herself.... For a woman ought to do her talking either to her husband or through her husband ...; if they [women] subordinate themselves to their husbands, they are commended, but if they want to have control, they cut a sorrier figure than the subjects of their control.[2]

The depiction of women taking over Athen's assembly (ἐκκλησία) in Aristophanes's comedy *Ecclesiazusae* was funny because it was so incongruous. Aristotle (*Pol.* 1260.a.31) quotes Sophocles (*Ajax* 293), "Silence [σιγή, the root of the first imperative in 1 Cor 14:34] adorns a woman." Democritus (a.k.a. Democrates) *Saying* 110 states, "Let a woman not practise speech; for that is terrible."[3] Aelius Aristides 41D (*In Defense of Oratory* 129), writing between AD 145 and 147, states, "Let the man, he says, talk much, but let the wife be pleased with whatever she hears."[4] Similarly, synagogues in practice as well as principle generally forbade women from speaking in public.[5] First Corinthians 11:5, 11–12, and Gal 3:28 challenge cultural conventions, but 1 Cor 14:34–35 does not. Women's public prophecy must have upset many people, who would welcome the demands of 14:34–35. Consequently, this passage's thrice-repeated command that women not speak in the churches would not invite any qualification based on its cultural context.

Furthermore, the reiteration of the prohibition three times maximizes its demand. Delling (*TDNT* 4:216) explains that in the Greek and Hellenistic Roman world, "threefold utterance of a word, expression, or sentence gives it full validity and power ... three is characterized by fullness and solidity." Threefold repetition commonly reinforces NT messages.[6] Consequently, the threefold repetition calling for the silence of women without qualification in 1 Cor 14:34–35 must be given its full validity and power, namely,

---

2. Plutarch, *Mor.* 142D (2:308–9, 310–11, 320–23 in Babbitt, LCL).
3. Taylor, *Democritus*, 238; cf. pp. 44–45, fragments 137 (4.22.199), "A woman is much more impetuous in foolish speech than a man," and 138, "Having little to say is an ornament for a woman."
4. Aristides 1:354–55 (LCL).
5. Str-B 3:467; cf. above, pp. 39–40 .
6. E.g., John 21:15–17; Acts 5:36–39; Rom 4:7–8; Phil 2:3–5; 1 John 5:11c–12.

that in the churches women must not speak, period. This absolute meaning would be obvious to readers throughout antiquity. Chrysostom (*Hom. in ep. ad. 1 Cor.* 37.1) states that here Paul "sews up their mouths ... and if this be so in respect of husbands, much more in respect of teachers, and fathers, and the general assembly of the Church.... Now if they ought not to ask questions, much more is their speaking at pleasure contrary to law."[7] Modern attempts to limit 14:34–35's threefold prohibition are so anachronistic they would strike first-century readers as obvious distortions of the writer's clear intent.

The central systematic issue is how to reconcile this triple demand for women to be silent in church with: (1) Paul's approval of women praying and prophesying in church when their heads are "covered" (1 Cor 11:4–13); (2) "each has a hymn, a word of instruction, a revelation, a tongue or an interpretation" (14:26); (3) "you can all prophesy" (14:24, 31); (4) "all speak in tongues" (14:5, 18, 23, cf. 27); (5) the "Amen" custom (14:16);[8] and (6) "be eager to prophesy and do not forbid speaking in tongues" (14:39).

Scholars adopt four kinds of solutions to reconcile this apparent contradiction:

1. Paul required silence of all women in all assemblies of the church.
2. Paul required women to be silent in some qualified sense.
3. These verses cite a false prophecy by a self-proclaimed Corinthian prophet.
4. These verses are an interpolation.

Proposal 1: Paul Required Silence of All Women in All Church Assemblies

Origen shows awareness of the tension with Paul's various statements that "all" may prophesy[9] but concludes, "even if she speaks marvelous and holy things, 'it is shameful for a woman to speak in church' simply because it comes from the mouth of a woman. For a woman to speak forth in church brings her under shame and the condemnation of the whole church."[10] This

---

7. Chambers, *Chrysostom, Corinthians, NPNF¹*, 12:222.
8. Robertson and Plummer (*First Corinthians*, 324) recognize this to conflict with absolute silence.
9. See below, p. 264.
10. Claude Jenkins, "Origen on 1 Corinthians IV," *JTS* 10 (1909): 40, line 37.

is the natural way to read 1 Cor 14:34–35,[11] as Jewett[12] does, arguing that 1 Cor 14:34–35 contradicts 11:5. Jewett, unfortunately, attributes 14:34–35 to Paul as a hangover from his Jewish upbringing that directly conflicted with his new view of freedom in Christ. Psychologically, however, it is improbable that Paul contradicted himself this radically and in such close proximity.[13]

Some insist that silence for women is the norm, but grant occasional exceptions. "*Every* woman praying or prophesying" (1 Cor 11:5), however, suggests a widespread practice. Some describe 11:5's permission as a concession granted with extreme reluctance to those who would not submit to 14:34–35,[14] but 1 Cor 11:5 and 13 are not written as concessions. The fulfillment of Joel 2:28–29's prophecy is a gift for the edification of the church, not a reluctant concession. Luke, Paul's associate for years, records this in Acts 2:16–18, so presumably Paul knew about it. Alternatively, some such as T. C. Edwards say that upon mature reflection Paul withdrew his earlier permission.[15] Such a hermeneutical principle invites abuse. It insults Paul's coherence to suppose that his thought matured to such a radical degree from chapter 11 to 14, and, indeed, from 14:23–26 and 31 to its withdrawal in 14:34–35, then reaffirmation in 14:39.

Tertullian (ca. AD 160–230), *Marc.* 5.8.11, interprets Paul as "enjoining on women silence in the church, that they speak not for the mere sake of learning (although that even they have the right of prophesying, he has already shown when he covers the woman that prophesies with a veil)."[16] Yet if "no speaking in public gatherings of the church" is the rule, the exception for prophesying (11:5, 13) makes the rule vacuous.

Proposal 2: Paul Required Women to be Silent in Some Qualified Sense

Although most interpretations suggest some qualified sense of silence, none of the proliferation of suggestions commands wide acceptance.

11. Nicholas Wolterstorff, "The Bible and Women: Another Look at the 'Conservative' Position," *The Reformed Journal* 26.6 (June 1979): 23; Godet, *1 Corinthians*, 741; Lenski, *1 Corinthians*, 628.
12. P. K. Jewett, *Man as Male and Female*, 115. So also Jack W. MacGorman, *The Gifts of the Spirit: An Exposition of 1 Corinthians 12–14* (Nashville: Broadman, 1974), 113, and John Koenig, *Charismata: God's Gifts for God's People* (Philadelphia: Westminster, 1978), 174.
13. Cf. Ridderbos, *Paul*, 461.
14. Robert L. Thomas, *Understanding Spiritual Gifts: The Christian's Special Gifts in the Light of 1 Corinthians 12–14* (Chicago: Moody Press, 1978), 230–31.
15. Thomas C. Edwards, *The First Epistle to the Corinthians* (London: Hodder & Stoughton, 1885), 382.
16. ANF 3:446.

Some limit it to a specific type of meeting, such as "the official teaching assembly"[17] or "assemblies open to non-Christians"[18] and propose that 1 Cor 11 applies to a different meeting. Barrett appropriately describes this as "special pleading."[19] Such a distinction is not indicated in 1 Cor 11[20] or 14, both of which describe informal worship where everyone can contribute, or any other early Christian document. Furthermore, 1 Cor 11 regulates women's prophesying in the context of the Lord's Supper in "your meetings" (11:17), "when you come together as a church" (v. 18), and in "the church of God" (v. 22). Women even prophesied at Pentecost (Acts 2:4, 17–18), the most public evangelistic and teaching event described in the NT, to which 1 Cor 12:13 appears to appeal.

Some say that silence is required only of a limited group of women, such as women who are false teachers, uneducated women, or women who are not prophesying or otherwise vocally contributing to worship. There is, however, no hint in the context that the command for silence applies only to a restricted group of women.[21] To the contrary, all three calls for silence sound as if they apply to all women. The proposed specifications do not, in any event, remove the tension with Paul's statement about "every woman" prophesying with appropriate head covering (11:5) or with Paul's encouragements in chapter 14 for "all" to participate vocally in worship.

Many say Paul prohibits only a specific type of speech, but nothing in 14:34–35 limits the kind of speech. Instead, it expresses this rule three times without qualification.

The view that only disruptive chatter is prohibited finds some plausibility from Classical Greek use of λαλεῖν to mean "chatter,"[22] but each of the

---

17. Ridderbos, *Paul*, 462; Grosheide, *First Corinthians*, 341.
18. E.g., Russell C. Prohl, *Woman in the Church: A Restudy of Woman's Place in Building the Kingdom* (Grand Rapids: Eerdmans, 1957), 35.
19. Barrett, *First Corinthians*, 331; cf. below, p. 326.
20. Head coverings and prophecy presuppose a public meeting.
21. Verse 35a gives one example that cannot be exhaustive. Silence would be far more necessary "if anyone did *not* want to learn." Any woman with an unbelieving husband could not expect such answers. Even believing husbands might miss church or otherwise be unable to answer questions. "If anyone wants to learn …" is open-ended and the conclusion to 14:35 appears to include all women, "for it is disgraceful for a woman [not 'their women,' which might have implied only married women] to speak in church." Verse 35a answers the anticipated objection, "If women can't speak, how can they learn answers to their questions?" It would be assumed *a fortiori* that if married women must be silent, then, of course, younger women must also be silent in church. Similarly, the example suggests that any woman, whether married or not, should ask a man in her own home if she has questions about a church service. Wives constituted the majority of adult women in Greek culture, so it is natural that this example mentions wives.
22. BDAG 582; LSJ 1025–26.

twenty-two other occurrences of λαλεῖν in this passage describe inspired speech.[23] Elsewhere in this chapter, any specific sense of "to speak" (e.g., "in tongues") is always specified.

Probably the most widely held view understands λαλεῖν to refer only to asking questions during a worship service.[24] Barrett, however, argues that such a reading is not "worthy of serious consideration."[25] It ignores the obvious meaning of "be silent." Specific prohibitions require specific modifers. Not only does verse 35a not limit "speak" to this one example or even substitute a more specific verb like "inquire" (*pace* NIV), logically it has to entail other examples.[26] Verse 35's concluding prohibition of the original encompassing "to speak" shows that the writer did not intend to narrow the prohibition from "speaking" to "asking questions."

W. Klein was apparently the first to suggest that the questioning of prophecy is prohibited.[27] Yet several proponents of a hierarchical view of man over woman, recognizing that all other attempts to restrict the meaning of "to speak" had failed, have recently embraced it.[28] Only four words in verse 29b refer to this: καὶ οἱ ἄλλοι διακρινέτωσαν, "and the others should weigh carefully [what the prophets say]." On this view, verse 29a is elaborated in verses 30–33, and verse 29b is elaborated in verses 34–35. Verses 30–33, however, must not elaborate 14:29a, since verse 31's "all may prophesy" contradicts verse 29a's limitation to two or three prophets speaking. This indicates, instead, that verses 30–32 introduce something other

---

23. Cf. Barrett (*First Corinthians*, 332) and Thiselton (*1 Corinthians*, 1157), who argue this interpretation is "unlikely." Not even the description of uninterpreted speaking in tongues as unintelligible "speaking into the air" (14:9) or uncomprehended speech in 14:11 and 21 can mean "to chatter."

24. E.g., Bruce, *1 & 2 Corinthians*, 135–36; G. Osborne, "Hermeneutics and Women in the Church," *JETS* 20 (1977): 344; Krister Stendahl, *The Bible and the Role of Women: A Case Study in Hermeneutics* (FBBS 15; Philadelphia: Fortress, 1966), 29.

25. Barrett, *First Corinthians*, 332. Cf. also Fee, *First Corinthians*, 703–4; Ralph P. Martin, *The Spirit and the Congregation: Studies in 1 Corinthians 12–15* (Grand Rapids: Eerdmans, 1984), 86.

26. Cf. above, p. 221 n. 21.

27. W. Klein, "The Church and the Prophets," *ATR* 44 (1962): 8. This was adopted, e.g., by Margaret E. Thrall (*I and II Corinthians* [CBC; Cambridge: Cambridge Univ. Press, 1965], 102); Ben Witherington III (*Women in the Earliest Churches* [SNTSMS 51; Cambridge: Univ. Press, 1988], 102–4); Thiselton (*First Corinthians*, 1158).

28. Hurley, *Biblical Perspective*, 185–94, and "Veils," 217–19; W. J. Dumbrell, "The Role of Women—A Reconsideration of the Biblical Evidence," *Interchange* 21 (1977): 20–21; Wayne Grudem, *The Gift of Prophecy in 1 Corinthians* (Washington, D. C.: University Press of America, 1982), 245–55; Carson, "Silent," *RBMW* 145–53. Carson's rebuttal of the arguments of Fee, *First Corinthians*, 699–708, gives unsatisfying responses to two of Fee's seven objections and does not even mention the other five. James Greenbury, "1 Corinthians 14:34–35: Evaluation of Prophecy Revisited," *JETS* 51 (2008): 721–31, exposes weakness of 14:34–35 meaning "weigh prophecy."

than what verse 29 addresses. Furthermore, the four words about judging prophecies are not only too far from 14:34–35 for this association to be apparent, they are in separate paragraphs since verse 33 concludes the preceding section. Verses 34–35 are a unit in all of the earliest manuscripts, and in every Western text-type manuscript they follow verse 40.

The one specific application in 14:35 of women being silent mentions nothing about judging prophecy, but is rather about women asking questions of their husbands out of a desire to learn. "Learning" implies a position of sitting under, not standing over and so is an inappropriate word to express "evaluating." Furthermore, no lexicon or Pauline usage supports "to speak" meaning "to evaluate," and its reiteration with the similarly unqualified expressions "remain silent" and "it is disgraceful for a woman to speak in the church" show why for 1,900 years this interpretation never occurred to anyone.[29] Furthermore, since prophecies can conflict (implied in v. 29), the prophesying permitted to women in 1 Cor 11:5 entails at least as much authority as that exercised by those evaluating the prophecies. Since women are permitted to prophesy, it is natural that they should be included in "the others" who weigh prophecies in 14:29, especially since the gifts are for all according to 12:7, 11 (*pace* the NIV's addition of "each man" in 12:11).

Others say only tongues is prohibited to women,[30] but that would require the fuller expression λαλεῖν γλώσσαις as in 14:2, 4, 5, 6, 9, 11, 13, 18, 21, 23, 27, 39 to distinguish it from prophecy (14:3, 6, 29, cf. 9, 11, 19, 21) or other speech. Nor does speaking in tongues fit the specific example regarding questions out of a desire to learn in 14:35.

Might Paul have intended 14:33b to modify "be silent" and so to restrict its meaning, namely, "as [is customary] in all the churches of the saints," to a ban on disorderly speech (14:33, 40) or asking questions of husbands? The external and internal evidence is against this. Every early manuscript, including 𝔓[46] B* Origen,[31] ℵ A D[P] 33 223 876 1175 1739 1780

---

29. Ironically, Piper and Grudem ("Charity, Clarity, and Hope," *RBMW* 84) assert their confidence in their view since, "We test our conclusions by the history of exegesis," and Grudem (*Gift of Prophecy*, 60) states regarding ἄλλοι in 14:29, "if Paul had meant to restrict his instructions ... he would not have used such a general term ... without further specification. Such a restricted meaning would not have been clear to his readers." Grudem should have applied these fine principles to "to speak" in v. 35.

30. Martin, *The Spirit and the Congregation*, 87.

31. Origen's *1 Corinthians*, 71 and 74 in Jenkins, "Origen on 1 Corinthians," 40, lines 6–8, and 41, lines 24–27.

and 1881, shows a break both before 14:34 and after 14:35. Early commentary associated 14:33a with 33b (e.g., Chrysostom's *Hom. in ep. 1 ad Cor.* 36 and 37).[32] Attaching verse 33b to verse 34 is redundancy and "utmost clumsiness,"[33] but "God is not a God of disorder but of peace, as [he is] in all the churches" makes a fitting conclusion to verse 33. How would "just as the law says" support a ban of an unspecified custom for silence? No OT law requires women to ask questions of husbands at home. In any event, it seems too great a stretch to try to apply such a qualification to all three prohibitions.

Proposal 3: 14:34–35 Cites a False Prophecy by a Self-Proclaimed Corinthian Prophet

Many scholars have argued that 1 Cor 14:34–35 expresses the view of a group in Corinth who opposed Paul.[34] The content of 14:34–35 seems un-Pauline.[35] Paul introduces both rhetorical questions in 14:36 with ἤ, as he did twelve times in 1 Corinthians to argue against a Corinthian viewpoint or deed. In each case except 9:10, "you" (plural) or "I" highlight the contrast between Paul's position and the Corinthians' position. ἤ follows *immediately* after a description of a Corinthian deed five times.[36] Everything in 14:36–38 works well to refute a Corinthian prophecy.

The weaknesses of this interpretation are:

---

32. Fee, *First Corinthians*, 697, "The idea that v. 33b goes with v. 34 seems to be a modern phenomenon altogether."
33. Eduard Schweizer, "The Service of Worship: An Exposition of I Corinthians 14," *Int* 13 (1959): 400–408 (402 n. 12).
34. E.g., Gottfried Fitzer, *Das Weib schweige in der Gemeinde: über den unpaulinischen Charakter der mulier-taceat-Verse in 1. Korinther 14* in *Theologische Existenz Heute*, Neue Folge 110 (Munich: Christian Kaiser, 1963); Walter C. Kaiser Jr., "Paul, Women, and the Church," *Worldwide Challenge* 3 (1976): 9–12; Neal M. Flanagan and Edwina Hunter Snyder, "Did Paul Put Down Women in 1 Cor. 14:34–36?" *BTB* 11 (1981): 10–12; D. W. Odell-Scott, "Editorial Dilemma: The Interpretation of 1 Cor 14:34–35 in the Western Manuscripts of D, G, and 88," *BTB* 30 (2000): 68–74; idem, "In Defense of an Egalitarian Interpretation of 1 Cor 14:34–36. A Reply to Murphy-O'Connor's Critique," *BTB* 17 (1987): 100–103; idem, "Let the Women Speak in Church: An Egalitarian Interpretation of 1 Cor. 14:33b–36," *BTB* 13 (1983): 90–3; Chris Ukachukwu Manus, "The Subordination of the Women in the Church: 1 Cor 14:33b–36 Reconsidered," *NRTh* 106 (1984): 23–58; Bilezikian, *Beyond Sex Roles*, 144–153; Murphy-O'Connor, "Interpolations," 90–92; Allison, "Let Women be Silent," 27–60; Talbert, *Reading Corinthians*, 91–95; Collins, *First Corinthians*, 517, 522; Michel Gourgues, "Who Is Misogynist: Paul or Certain Corinthians? Note on 1 Corinthians 14:33b–36," in *Woman Also Journeyed with Him: Feminist Perspectives on the Bible* (ed. Gérald Caron et al.; Collegeville, Minn.: Liturgical Press, 2000), 117–24; Soards, *1 Corinthians*, 304, calls this view "sensible and attractive."
35. Cf. below, pp. 253–54, 256–63.
36. 1 Cor 6:2, 9, 19; 10:22; 11:22; + 11:13 variant reading' (+14:36?). The others are: 1 Cor 1:13; 6:16 (a textual variant); 9:6, 8, 10; 14:36.

1. Verses 14:34–35 are not introduced as a false prophecy.
2. None of the other Corinthian quotations Paul refutes are nearly this long.
3. Nothing in verses 36–38 requires that it refutes verses 34–35.
4. It does not explain why every Western text-type manuscript puts verses 34–35 at the end of the chapter.
5. Verses 34–35 interrupt the flow of Paul's argument.

Only if verses 34–35 were written in the margin of the text to identify the false prophecy referred to in verses 36–38 could this view adequately answer objections 4–5, but without verses 34–35 in the text, it is doubtful verses 36–38 would suggest a particular false prophecy. If verses 34–35 were in the margin, this is the most credible of the many attempted interpretations of 14:34–35 viewed as part of Paul's original letter delivered to the Corinthians, yet still speculative since nothing in the text identifies it as a quotation.

Proposal 4: 1 Corinthians 14:34–35 Is an Interpolation

Understanding 1 Cor 14:34–35 as an interpolation, namely, a passage that was not originally in the text but was inserted later (here from the margin), makes perfect sense of the entire passage and resolves all the problems of the above three proposals. Only interpolation solves the contextual problem that these verses disrupt the flow of Paul's argument; everything else in chapter 14 is about tongues and prophecy. Only interpolation adequately explains why all Western text-type manuscripts have verses 34–35 after verse 40. Interpolation also provides the most satisfying answer to the systematic problem, and it does so on a factual, not speculative, basis.

Many who study the NT are unaware that the oldest surviving NT manuscripts differ, sometimes significantly, and various passages do not appear in the most reliable texts at all, which has led virtually all biblical scholars to conclude that some passages are interpolations.[37] If this marginal note was not in the original letter, it is not authoritative for anyone who assigns authority to the original text.[38] Discerning whether verses

---

37. Including R. A. Torrey, *Difficulties and Alleged Errors and Contradictions in the Bible* (Chicago: Bible Institute Colportage Association, 1907), 17–18.
38. "The Chicago Statement on Biblical Inerrancy," Article X, 291, states that "inspiration, strictly speaking, applies only to the autographic text of Scripture, which in the providence of God can be ascertained from available manuscripts with great accuracy."

34–35 are an interpolation can transform one's understanding of what Paul taught about women.

Most scholars who have published their analyses of the text-critical aspects of this passage have argued that it is an interpolation.[39] However,

---

39.   E.g., Allison, "Let Women Be Silent," 27–60, esp. 44–48; Barrett, *First Corinthians*, 331–33; S. C. Barton, "Paul's Sense of Place: An Anthropological Approach to Community Formation in Corinth," *NTS* 32 (1986): 229–30, suggests the marginal gloss is Paul's; Jouette M. Bassler, "1 Corinthians," in *Women's Bible Commentary, Expanded Edition* (ed. Carol A. Newsom and Sharon H. Ringe; Louisville: Westminster John Knox, 1998), 418–19; W. A. Beardslee, *First Corinthians: A Commentary for Today* (St. Louis: Chalice, 1994), 140; Arnold Bittlinger, *Gifts and Graces: A Commentary on I Corinthians 12–14* (trans. Herbert Klassen; London: Hodder and Stoughton, 1967), 110–11; Wilhelm Bousset, *Die Schriften des Neuen Testaments neu übersetzt und für die Gegenwart erklärt* (2 vols.; Göttingen: Vandenhoeck & Ruprecht, 1917–1920), 2:120; F. X. Cleary, "Women in the New Testament: St. Paul and the Early Pauline Tradition," *BTB* 10 (1980): 78–82; Conzelmann, *1 Corinthians*, 246, who includes 33b and 36; Clarence Tucker Craig, "The First Epistle to the Corinthians" (*IB*; New York: Abingdon, 1953), 212–13; Gerhard Dautzenberg, *Urchristliche Prophetie: ihre Erforschung, ihre Voraussetzungen im Judentum und ihre Struktur im ersten Korintherbrief* (BWANT 104; Stuttgart: Kohlhammer, 1975), 257–73; D. J. Doughty, "Women and Liberation in the Churches of Paul and the Pauline Tradition," *Drew Gateway* 50 (1979): 1–21; Peter W. Dunn, "The Influence of 1 Corinthians on the Acts of Paul," *SBL Seminar Papers, 1996* (Atlanta: Scholars Press, 1996), 438–54 (452–53); E. Earle Ellis, "The Silenced Wives of Corinth (I Cor. 14:34–5)," in *New Testament Textual Criticism, Its Significance for Exegesis: Essays in Honour of Bruce M. Metzger* (ed. Eldon Jay Epp and Gordon D. Fee; Oxford: Clarendon, 1981), 213–20, proposes it is a marginal gloss from Paul; Eldon J. Epp, *Junia: The First Woman Apostle* (Minneapolis: Fortress, 2005), 15–20; Fee, *First Corinthians*, 699–709; Fitzer, "*Das Weib schweig*"; J. Massyngberde Ford, "Women Leaders in the New Testament," in *Women Priests: A Catholic Commentary on the Vatican Declaration* (ed. Arlene and Leonard Swidler; New York: Paulist, 1977), 133–34; Paul Gallay, *Des Femmes Prêtres?* (Paris: Bordas, 1973), 59–60; Jean Galot, *Mission et ministère de la femme* (Paris: Lethielleux, 1973), 51–52, 139–41; Roy A. Harrisville, *1 Corinthians* (ACNT; Minneapolis: Augsburg, 1987), 242–44; Hays, *First Corinthians*, 244–48; Karl Heim, *Die Gemeinde des Auferstandenen: Tübinger Vorlesungen über den Ersten Korintherbrief* (ed. Friso Melzer; Giessen: Brunnen, 1987), 204–5; Holsten, *Evangelium des Paulus. II, 1*, 404–5; David G. Horrell, *The Social Ethos of the Corinthian Correspondence: Interests and Ideology from 1 Corinthians to 1 Clement: Studies of the New Testament and its World* (Edinburgh: T&T Clark, 1996), 184–95; Horsley, *1 Corinthians*, 188–89; Hans-Josef Klauck, *1. Korintherbrief* (NEchtB 7; Würzburg: Echter, 1984), 104–6; idem, *Ancient Letters and the New Testament: A Guide to Context and Exegesis* (Waco, Tex.: Baylor Univ. Press, 2006), 307–8; Leipoldt, *Die Frau*, 123–26, 190–91; A. Lindemann, *Der erste Korintherbrief* (HNT 9/1; Tübingen: Mohr, 2000), 317–21; P. F. Lockwood, "Does 1 Corinthians 14:34–35 Exclude Women from the Pastoral Office?" *Lutheran Theological Journal* 30:1 (1996): 30–38; Meeks, "Androgyne," 200–208 tentative; Moffatt, *First Corinthians*, 233–34; Munro, *Authority*, 67–69; Murphy-O'Connor, "Interpolations," 90–92; idem, *1 Corinthians* (NTM; Wilmington, Del.: Michael Glazier, 1979), 133; Oepke, "γυνή," 1:787; C. Osiek and D. L. Balch, *Families in the New Testament World: Household and House Churches* (Louisville: Westminster/John Knox, 1997), 117; Jacobus H. Petzer, "Reconsidering the Silent Women of Corinth: A Note on 1 Corinthians 14:34–35," *ThEv* 26 (1993): 132–38; John S. Ruef, *Paul's First Letter to Corinth* (Pelican; Baltimore: Penguin, 1971), 154–55; P. W. Schmiedel, *Die Briefe an die Thessalonischer und an die Korinther* (Tübingen: Mohr, 1892), 2:181–82; Schrage, *Korinther*, 3:481–87; Schweizer, "Service of Worship," 402–3; Charles A. Anderson Scott, *Christianity according to St Paul* (Cambridge: Cambridge Univ. Press, 1927), 227–28; Scroggs, "Eschatological Woman," 294–96; G. Sellin, "Hauptprobleme des ersten Korintherbriefes," *ANRW* 25.4: 2984–85; Christophe Senft, *La Première Épître de Saint-Paul aux Corinthiens* (Neuchâtel: Delachaux & Niestlé, 1979), 182–83; G. F. Snyder, *First Corinthians: A Faith Community Commentary* (Atlanta: Mercer, 1992), 184–85; August Strobel, *Der erste Brief an die Korinther* (Zürich: Theologischer Verlag, 1989), 222–25; Andrie du Toit, "Die swyggebod van 1 Korintiërs 14:34–35 weer eens onder die loep," *HvTSt* 57 (2001): 172–86; Trompf, "Attitudes toward Women," 196–215; Wat-

several reputable scholars put up stiff resistance to the possibility of this interpolation. On a personal note, for over ten years I defended variations on proposals 2 and 3 above until I concluded that they would be exceedingly unlikely to occur to a first-century reader. Only then did I seriously examine the text-critical data. I now firmly believe that anyone looking at the data with an open mind will acknowledge considerable evidence for interpolation. Furthermore, much of the crucial evidence that 14:34–35 is an interpolation is unique to this passage and so does not undermine the reliability of any other passage. Viewing verses 34–35 as an interpolation in fact bolsters the authority of Scripture, in that it resolves what would otherwise contradict other teachings by Paul as well as other affirmations of women's ministry throughout Scripture.

EXTERNAL EVIDENCE FOR 1 CORINTHIANS 14:34–35 AS AN INTERPOLATION

Although it is often alleged that manuscript "evidence favoring omission ... [is] entirely lacking in this instance,"[40] there is significant textual evidence that 1 Cor 14:34–35 was not originally in the text, including early manuscripts that support the omission.

1. Transcriptional Probability Argues That 1 Corinthians 14:34–35 Is an Interpolation

Transcriptional probability is the analysis of what a copyist is most likely to have done. It seeks to explain the known variations in surviving manuscripts. Bengel's first principle is the most important criterion for determining the original form of a text: the form of the text that best explains the emergence of all other forms is most likely the original. Fee convincingly argues that the only adequate explanation why every Western text-type manuscript has 14:34–35 at the end of the chapter is that

---

son, *First Corinthians*, 153–54; Walker, "1 Corinthians 11:2–16," 95; idem, "The 'Theology of Women's Place' and the 'Paulist' Tradition," *Semeia* 28 (1983): 101–12; Heinrich Weinel, *St. Paul: The Man and his Work* (London: Williams & Norgate, 1906); Johannes Weiss, *Der erste Korintherbrief: Kritisch-exegetischer Kommentar über das Neue Testament* (ed. H. A. W. Meyer; 9th ed.; Göttingen: Vandenhoeck & Ruprecht, 1910), 342; Günther Zuntz, *The Text of the Epistles: A Disquisition upon the Corpus Paulinum* (London: The British Academy, Oxford Univ. Press, 1953), 17.

40. Carson, "Silent," *RBMW* 144; Grudem, *EF* 236, "not one [manuscript] has ever omitted these verses."

these verses were not in the original text,[41] but are an interpolation.[42] Fee clarifies his view "contrary to the suggestion of some (e.g., Grudem, 241, '[this view] depends on the conviction that they seriously conflicted with 11.5 …').… The transcription question comes first, and has always been the primary reason for thinking it an interpolation."[43] Nevertheless, Grudem continues to allege, "the most decisive factor for Fee's conclusion is not the evidence from ancient manuscripts but rather that he thinks that these verses … are impossible to reconcile with 1 Corinthians 11."[44] This egregiously misrepresents Fee's view and fails to identify or rebut Fee's central arguments. It is not just that interpolation is plausible; it is the only adequate explanation of the position of 14:34–35 in the entire Western text-type tradition.

Fee argues that every Western witness has 1 Cor 14:34–35 after verse 40: D E F G a b it[ar], d, e, f, g Ambrosiaster Sedulius-Scotus.[45] By comparing the Western witnesses with the Greek text used by Hippolytus (d. 234) it is clear that the text represented by the Western witnesses was established by his time. Most text critics date the beginnings of the Western text in the first half of the second century AD.[46] Presumably, then,

---

41. The "original" text of each of Paul's letters is simply the text he sent to churches or friends. Using Epp's words more broadly than he did, the original delivery of these letters is "when they were 'published' or were circulated (in some official sense)." Eldon Jay Epp, "It's All about Variants: A Variant-Conscious Approach to New Testament Textual Criticism," *HTR* 100 (2007): 275–308, 284. Without any original texts, there is no historical explanation for the existence of any of the Pauline manuscripts from which the "earliest attainable" (ibid., 282) texts are derived. A key (but not only) goal of the textual criticism of Paul's letters is to ascertain as far as possible the wording of the original texts Paul sent. It is precisely because textual criticism elucidates the content of the original text of Paul's letters that Epp can attribute things to Paul, e.g., "it is clear that Andronicus and Junia, in Paul's description, were 'outstanding apostles,'" *Junia*, 78, and "Cor 14:34–35 is likely a non-Pauline interpolation into Paul's letter," *Junia*, 81.

42. Fee, *First Corinthians*, 699–710, addresses both transcriptional and intrinsic probability. Carson ("Silent," *RBMW* 141–45) tries to undermine, with meager success, Fee's masterful study.

43. Fee, *First Corinthians*, 701 n. 12, citing Grudem's, *Gift of Prophecy*, 241.

44. Grudem, *EF* 237; cf. 236 ("11:5 … is his primary argument against their authenticity").

45. D[P], Claromontanus, 6th c.; E, Sangermanesis, 9th c. copy of Claromontanus of no independent value; F, codex Augiensis, 9th c.; G, Boernerianus, 9th c. Albert Bengel, *Novum Testamentum Graecum* (Tübingen: Georgii Cottae, 1734), 673, writes that Hilary (d. 367) also identifies 14:34–35 after v. 40. Curt Niccum, "The Voice of the Manuscripts on the Silence of Women: The External Evidence for 1 Cor 14.34–5," *NTS* 43 (1997): 247 and 254, rather than using the standard text-type definition of "Western text," treats Fee's statement as though it were a merely geographic statement extending far beyond the time period Fee identifies: "The attestation is hardly so balanced as Fee maintains" and "the external evidence precludes viewing the attestation of the two known readings as equal." Fee never claims that the group of manuscripts designated as "Western" is balanced or equal in number or distribution with later Vulgate texts.

46. E.g., Carlo M. Martini, "La tradition textuelle des Actes des Apôtres et les tendences de l'Église ancienne," in *Les Actes des Apôtres: traditions, rédaction, théologie* (ed. J. Kremer; Louvain: Louvain Univ. Press, 1979), 34; James Hardy Ropes, "Part I: The Acts of the Apostles," in *The Text of Acts* (vol. 3 of *The Beginnings of Christianity*, ed. F. J. Foakes Jackson and K. Lake; London:

the position of verses 34–35 after verse 40 was established throughout the Western church at least by the time of Hippolytus. Apart from the eighth century Vulgate MS Reginensis (R) and the thirteenth century MS 915,[47] whose scribes apparently copied this reading of 1 Cor 14:34–35 from a Western text, no non-Western manuscript supports the reading of verses 34–35 after verse 40. How could the Western church unanimously accept verses 34–35 after verse 40 for at least three hundred years[48] while the rest of the church put them after verse 33?

There are three possibilities: that verses 34–35 originally followed verse 33, but were moved to follow verse 40; that they originally followed verse 40, but were moved to follow verse 33; or that they were originally not in the text, but were later added at two different places. If verses 34–35 were written in the margin, following standard scribal practice, one scribe could easily insert it after verse 33 and another scribe after verse 40.

It is virtually inconceivable that a scribe would take verses 34–35 out of an original position after verse 33 and place them after verse 40. Fee correctly observes, "The transpositions in the Gospels (Matt 5:4–5; Luke 4:5–10), where immediately joining verses are transposed for obvious harmonistic reasons, are of a completely different kind."[49] Scribes copied texts word for word, line for line. They might make what they believed to be spelling or style corrections, but they did not transpose such large blocks of text to other places to improve the logic of a passage without obvious reason. Unless this is the only occurrence, no scribe of any extant manuscript of the Pauline letters ever moved this large a block of text this far to improve its logic for no clear reason. It would have been totally out of character and convention for a scribe to do this. Fee stated, "I am now 99% sure that 1 Corinthians 14:34–35 is an interpolation. It is virtually impossible that a scribe, let alone several scribes independently, would transpose verses

Macmillan, 1926), ccxxiii–ccxxiv; R. P. C. Hanson, "The Provenance of the Interpolator in the 'Western' Text of Acts and of Acts Itself," *NTS* 12 (1965–66): 211–20; R. I. Pervo, "Social and Religious Aspects of the 'Western' Text," in *The Living Text: Essays in Honor of Ernest W. Saunders* (ed. D. E. Groh and R. Jewett; New York: Univ. Press of America, 1985), 240.

47. The margin of the Vulg. text Fuldensis (AD 546) could be interpreted as also belonging to this category, but as is argued below, pp. 246–48, Bishop Victor had Fuldensis rewritten without vv. 34–35. As explained below, pp. 249–50, MS 88* signals that vv. 34–35 should not follow v. 40, but v. 33, and so does not support the Western reading.

48. Fee, *First Corinthians*, 700.

49. Ibid., 700 and note 9.

34–35 from after verse 33 to after verse 40. There is not one comparable instance in any New Testament manuscript."[50]

Similarly, it is virtually inconceivable that a scribe would take these verses out of an original position after verse 40 and place them after verse 33. Thus, neither of the two positions of verses 34–35 could reasonably have given rise to the other. But if they did not, what caused this divergence between the entire Western text tradition and other MS traditions?

There is only one reasonable explanation. Early in the text transmission, someone, probably influenced by the vocabulary of 1 Tim 2:8–15,[51] added this text in the margin. Scribes who copied the manuscript containing this marginal text would assume that their exemplar's scribe omitted this text inadvertently and someone wrote it in the only remaining space, the margin. Then, as was customary, the scribe copying this exemplar entered the text into the body of the letter, just like any secretary retyping an edited letter today will move marginal text into the body of a letter.

In this case, however, the gloss is so long that it is not obvious where it should be entered into the text. Verses 34–35 in a side margin would have extended along the margin from approximately verse 36 to verse 40. One scribe, noticing the commands requiring silence (σιγάτω) in verses 28 and 30, inserted the gloss at the first point where a new command for silence could fit, namely, after verse 33. Another scribe, perhaps recognizing that the reason for the demand for silence in verses 34–35 is not based on any contextual circumstances (unlike the other two restrictions), but simply on gender, inserted it at the end of Paul's section, namely, after verse 40.

Several factors could have motivated insertion at this point. Verse 40 is a logical break in the text. To place the gloss after verse 33 interrupts the natural flow from verses 33b and 36. The mention of "properly" (εὐσχημόνως) in verse 40 could be seen as a natural introduction to the content of this gloss. Placing these verses after the conclusion to the sec-

---

50. Fee, conversation with the author in his office at Gordon-Conwell Theological Seminary, S. Hamilton, Massachusetts, May 15, 1986. Perhaps the closest example, though not Pauline, is when the scribe of codex Bezae (D) moved Luke 6:5 to follow Luke 6:10. This change, however, was caused by the scribe's insertion after Luke 6:4 of an extended interpolation (which is cited below on p. 265), so it is not comparable to 1 Cor 14:34–35 being moved. Metzger (*Textual Commentary*[2], 476) notes that the transposition of the Rom 16:20b benediction to follow 16:24 prevents the greetings of vv. 21–23 from appearing to be an afterthought. This and even briefer stylistic transpositions are not comparable to the change in Paul's argument required by the alleged transposition of 14:34–35.
51. Cf. below, pp. 262–63.

tion on order in the church, however, leaves them as isolated commands without connection either to the flow of Paul's argument or the Corinthian situation. Thus, although it explains this insertion point, once verses 34–35 became situated after verse 33, it is not an adequate reason to cause a scribe to move them to follow verse 40.

Thus, two separate texts emerged very early, the Western text with the gloss entered after verse 40, and the remaining text traditions with the gloss entered after verse 33. These two texts existed for centuries until the influence of the Latin Vulgate "vulgatized" the Western text, standardizing the position of verses 34–35 after verse 33.

The suggestion of Metzger, that "such scribal alterations represent attempts to find a more appropriate location in the context for Paul's directive concerning women,"[52] is contrary to what is known of scribal practice. The evidence of the entire history of Pauline texts shows that scribes simply did not move so much text so far. Specifically regarding this passage, it appears that no scribe ever changed the position of verses 34–35 without manuscript evidence. The Western reading apparently affected MS 915 and Reginensis (R), and both the reading in the margin of Fuldensis and 88* were apparently copied from a manuscript that omitted these verses. It is unwarranted to suppose that Western scribes had the audacity to change the order of Paul's argument to this extent, especially since they never did a comparable change anywhere else in Paul's letters. "It is simply a modern invention that someone in the early church would have been troubled by the placement of these words in the text, since all who comment on it find the arrangement very logical."[53] Furthermore, moving the verses makes no appreciable improvement to the flow of the passage. Consequently, it probably would not have occurred to any scribe at that time to "help Paul out"[54] by transposing verses 34–35 to a new position after verse 40.

The most valiant attempt yet to defend the inadvertent or deliberate change of 1 Cor 14:34–35's location, by Wire, fails miserably. Even she admits, "there is no single, obvious explanation why such an inversion of

52. Metzger, *Textual Commentary*[2], 499; cf. Carson, "Silent," *RBMW* 142–43; and Hurley, *Biblical Perspective*, 185 n. 12. Hurley includes 14:33b in the "transposition" even though no text transposes it.

53. Fee, *First Corinthians*, 700. E.g., Chrysostom, *Hom. in ep. 1 ad Cor.* 36 and 37, Theodoret, Ps-Oecumenius, and John of Damascus. See, however, below, pp. 254–56. These verses do interrupt the context.

54. Cf. Fee, *First Corinthians*, 700.

sentences or omission and reinsertion took place."[55] She fails to produce a single comparable scribal change. She proposes that the corrector assumed "perhaps, in light of later household codes, that what was said to women concerned household rather than church order."[56] Would a scribe regard verses 34–35 as about household codes rather than church order in spite of it being preceded by "in the churches," beginning "in the churches," and concluding "in the church"? Verses 34–35 specifically contrast their ruling regarding church with what is permitted at home.

Aware of the weakness of this explanation, Wire then suggests the alternate explanation "that the passage is displaced due to the corrector's ideological point of view,"[57] but without explaining either the ideological motivation or how the displacement would advance it. Wire fails to provide a reasonable explanation for the displacement. She properly acknowledges, "Most New Testament copyists were conservative, and changing the text's meaning, or even clarifying it, were not common scribal practices."[58]

2. Codex Vaticanus's Distigme[59] at the End of 14:33 Points to Interpolation

Codex Vaticanus has a mark of a textual variant, two horizontally aligned dots in the margin at mid-character height, by the last line of

---

55. Antoinette Clark Wire, The Corinthian Women Prophets: A Reconstruction through Paul's Rhetoric (Minneapolis: Fortress, 1990), 151. Her suggestion on p. 150 for how this might have happened from accidental scribal haplography entails many improbable assumptions about the particular manuscript being copied, including the following six: (1) It had the variant "churches" in the plural. This variant is so rare that it is not noted in either the Nestle-Aland or the UBS NT text. (2) The word "churches" in both v. 33 and 35 was the last word in its line. (3) Even though the skipped text was one contiguous unit, the corrector split it into two parts, putting "of the saints" in the right hand margin after "churches" in v. 33 but vv. 34–35 in the lower margin. (4) "Of the saints" was put in the right margin at the end of v. 33 so that it obscured the sign marking where vv. 34–35 should be inserted. No scribe is likely to obscure his own insertion sign. (5) First Corinthians 14:34–35 is put in the lower margin without any mark to alert future copyists that it is out of place. (6) The last line on the page coincided with the end of the chapter, namely, the end of v. 40.

56. Ibid., 151.

57. Ibid., 152.

58. Ibid.

59. New Testament textual critics David Parker, Hugh Houghton, Tommy Wasserman, Philip Payne, Michael Holmes, Paul Canart, Timothy Brown, and classicist Adrian Kelly, with advice from Bart Ehrman and codicologist Patrick Andrist, agreed to designate distigme (pl. distigmai) as the official name for these pairs of dots. This term is an ideal name since di is the standard Greek prefix meaning two, and the feminine noun stigme (pl. stigmai) is the standard Greek word for dots in manuscripts. The final "e" of distigme is pronounced "ei" since it represents a Greek eta. Traditionally words like distigme and distigmai are not italicized, capitalized (unless beginning a sentence), or put in quotes, and the final "e" of distigme should not have a macron or accent. This writer formerly called these pairs of dots "umlauts" because of their shape, but their function is unrelated to umlauts. Stigme and stigmai were used as text-critical signs in

1 Cor 14:33, in the proper position to note an interpolation immediately following verse 33.[60] The omission of verses 34–35 is the most obvious candidate for a textual variant here. NA[27] lists no variants here other than the Western text transposition of 14:34–35 and Straatman's conjecture that originally 14:34–35 was not in the text. The only other variant that has been proposed, the addition of "is taught" to verse 33, occurs only in Western manuscripts that also position verses 34–35 after verse 40. If the scribe of Vaticanus were noting a variant from any such text, by far the most obvious variant here is the absence of verses 34–35 after 33. If this distigme had signified the Western text reading that puts 14:34–35 after 14:40, however, there should have been a second distigme at the end of verse 40 to identify the equally great difference in the text there. Since there is no distigme by verse 40, it is far more likely the distigme marks a text without verses 34–35, like the text of 1 Cor 14 in Fuldensis[Victor mg.] (examined next), than the Western dislocation of these verses.[61]

The text many scholars regard as an interpolation here (14:34–35), like the interpolations following John 7:52 (7:53–8:11) and Luke 14:24 ("for many are called but few are chosen"), both of which Vaticanus omits, begins *immediately* after the line adjacent to the distigme, with no text intervening. Thus, the distigme by the last line of 14:33 is positioned appropriately to mark the absence of verses 34–35.[62]

---

the Homeric tradition, in MSS, in the *scholia vetera* and the *scholia recentiora*, by Origen, and also in modern treatments of Homeric textual criticism. For example, Wilhelm Dindorf (*Scholia Graeca in Homeri Iliadem ex Codicibus aucta et emendata* [Oxford, Clarendon, 1875], xlvi) notes that Codex Harleianus 5693 includes a text-critical sign list written in a sixteenth-century hand citing two horizontally aligned dots named "duo stigmai" (δύο στιγμαί) and the explanation: "The antisigma and the duo stigmai [are used] in this order when the same thought is written twice. The antisigma is put on the former, and the duo [Friedrich Gotthilf Osann added this third instance of "duo"] stigmai on the latter." Adrian Kelly (*A Referential Commentary and Lexicon to Iliad VIII* [Oxford: Oxford Univ. Press, 2007], 400–401) identifies "critical signs in the margins of MS A (antisigma to 535–7, and stigmai to 538–40) … Aristarkhos considered 535–37 a doublet to 538–40 and preferred the latter … almost every editor considers that something should be excised or bracketed." Stigme is part of the ancient name of various symbols that identify textual variants containing dots, including diplē periestigmenē, obelos periestigmenos, and antisigma periestigmenon.

60. On this pattern of distigme by the line immediately preceding long interpolations that begin or would begin at the start of the next line cf. Philip B. Payne, "Fuldensis, Sigla for Variants in Vaticanus, and 1 Cor 14.34–5," *NTS* 41 (1995): 259 and below, pp. 237–40.

61. This also applies to the "is taught" variant since it occurs only with this dislocation.

62. Philip B. Payne, "Vaticanus Distigme-Obelos Symbols Marking Added Text, including 1 Corinthains 14.34-5," *NTS* 63 (forthcoming, July 2017) documents with photographs that the distinctive symbol introducing 1 Cor 14:34-35 in all eight of its occurrences in Vaticanus marks the location of later added text.

Articles by this author and Paul Canart,[62] the senior paleographer at the Vatican Library, and a book by Eldon Jay Epp[63] argue that the distigme at the end of 1 Cor 14:33 in Codex Vaticanus B is the earliest surviving evidence in an actual NT manuscript that 1 Cor 14:34–35 is an interpolation. This author and Canart argue that B's distigmai were written at the time of its original production and so mark readings in manuscripts written before B. The only surviving manuscript of 1 Cor 14:34–35 older than B is 𝔓[46]. The manuscript cited by this distigme, though not extant, is the oldest manuscript of this passage cited in an actual NT manuscript. Thus, of the two oldest surviving or critically cited manuscripts containing 1 Cor 14, one apparently omitted verses 34–35.

There are significant parallels between 1 Cor 14:34–35 and John 7:53–8:11, which is almost universally recognized as a later interpolation:[64]

1. In both, the doubtful verses occur at different locations in the text.
2. Manuscripts of both display a high concentration of textual variations.[65]
3. Both contain word usage atypical of the book's author.[66]
4. In both, the doubtful verses disrupt the narrative or topic of the passage.[67]
5. In both, marginal symbols or notes indicate scribal awareness of a textual problem. In particular, Vaticanus has a distigme at the beginning of both passages.

---

62. Payne ("Fuldensis," 240–62) first demonstrates the text-critical function of distigmai, with photographs on p. 262 of the distigmai at the end of 1 Cor 14:33 and John 7:52; Philip B. Payne and Paul Canart, "The Originality of Text-Critical Symbols in Codex Vaticanus," *NovT* 42 (2000): 105–13, give details of their examinations at the Vatican Library confirming that eleven distigmai match the original ink of Codex Vaticanus (both are online at www.pbpayne. com); Philip B. Payne, "The Text-Critical Function of the Umlauts in Vaticanus, with Special Attention to 1 Corinthians 14.34–35: A Response to J. Edward Miller," *JSNT* 27 (2004): 105–12, answers objections raised by Miller (available online at www.user.uni-bremen.de/~wie/ Vaticanus/Payne-2004.pdf); Philip B. Payne and Paul Canart, "Distigmai Matching the Original Ink of Codex Vaticanus: Do They Mark the Location of Textual Variants?" in *Le manuscrit B de la Bible (Vaticanus graecus 1209): Introduction au fac-similé, Actes du Colloque de Genève (11 juin 2001), Contributions supplémentaires* (ed. Patrick Andrist; Lausanne, Switzerland: Éditions du Zèbre, forthcoming 2009), 199–226 identifies fifty-one original ink distigmai, explains the significance of mirror impression distigmai and provides chi-square probability test results confirming the text-critical function of distigmai.
63. Epp, *Junia*, 14–20, confirms the findings of Payne.
64. Metzger, *Textual Commentary*[1], 219–22; *Textual Commentary*[2], 187–89.
65. Cf. below, pp. 252–53.
66. Cf. below, pp. 256–61.
67. Cf. below, pp. 254–56.

Carson notes that "those [manuscripts] that do include it [John 7:53 – 8:11] display a rather high frequency of textual variants.... The diversity of placement confirms the inauthenticity of the verses."[68] Other generally recognized glosses display most of these characteristics.[69] These parallels highlight the standard criteria for identifying an interpolation and show that 1 Cor 14:34 – 35 exemplifies them. Although Vaticanus does not include John 7:53 – 8:11, its distigme is the earliest evidence for this text after John 7:52. Similarly, although Vaticanus does include 14:34 – 35, its distigme here is the earliest manuscript evidence for a text that omitted these verses.

Curt Niccum, however, dismissed these conclusions as "untenable."[70] His central assertion is that "these [distigmai] postdate the fourteenth century, probably belonging to the sixteenth" since "these [distigmai] continue into this [fifteenth century] minuscule text [from Heb 9.14] through Heb 10:1" where "no other original markings ... occur.... Evidence suggests Sepulveda introduced these [distigmai].... Sepulveda must have shared ... the reading καυδα at Acts 27.16 ... attested only in Vaticanus and Sinaiticus[corr]."[71] However, Canart's research identifying fifty-one distigmai matching B's original ink color disproves Niccum's allegation that all Vaticanus distigmai are late.[72]

Niccum's argument contains many false or exaggerated statements[73] and conjecture,[74] all of which are stated as fact. Features at the beginning of the minuscule text show that T. C. Skeat, to whom Niccum appeals,[75] is probably correct that the minuscule leaves appended to Vaticanus replaced damaged uncial leaves.[76] On the first page of the minuscule text there is only one distigme by its first column (1519A 12 from Heb 9:18 – 19), two

---

68. D. A. Carson, *The Gospel according to John* (PNTC; Grand Rapids: Eerdmans, 1991), 333. Carson, however, inconsistently calls Fee's application of these same principles to 1 Cor 14:34 – 35, "weak and speculative" in "Silent," *RBMW* 142.
69. Mark 16:9 – 20 shares 2, 3, 4, 5; John 5:3c – 4 shares 2, 3, 5; Acts 8:37 shares 2, 3, 5; 1 John 5:7b – 8 shares 2, 4, 5.
70. Niccum, "Voice," 243.
71. Niccum, "Voice," 245 n. 20. Yet this reading is also in 𝔓[74], 1174, it, etc., cf. UBS[4]. This error is pivotal since Niccum argues from this reading's rarity that distigmai "originated with Sepulveda."
72. Payne and Canart, "Distigmai," 202 – 14; cf. Payne and Canart, "Originality," 105 – 13.
73. Niccum, "Voice," 245 n. 17, "Nearly 400 [distigmai] occur in the Gospels alone." There are 276 unambiguous distigmai in the Gospels. Cf. below, pp. 236 – 37, 248 n. 129 and above, p. 228.
74. E.g., Niccum, "Voice," 254, "Its [the Western reading of 1 Cor 14:34 – 35 following v. 40] origin in a remote region only makes it more difficult."
75. Niccum, "Voice," 245 n. 18.
76. T. C. Skeat, "The Codex Vaticanus in the Fifteenth Century," *JTS* 35 (1984): 454 – 65.

much smaller, non-horizontal, raised dots of undetermined purpose by its second column (1519B 12 from Heb 10:1) and also a chapter break symbol shaped like a square root sign at the beginning of Heb 10:1 (1519B 8). Both the distigme and chapter symbol (e.g., 1518B, 1517A and C, and 1516B) mimic the form of these symbols in the preceding uncial text of Vaticanus, and both occur only here in the minuscule text.

The simplest explanation for this is that, in order to preserve these markings, a scribe copied both of these symbols from the damaged uncial leaf into their corresponding positions in the first minuscule page that replaced it. Niccum objects that if a scribe had copied these symbols from a torn leaf, he also would have copied other original markings such as paragraph bars.[77] He assumes that paragraph bars were on whatever then remained of the damaged uncial page. This is a precarious assumption since there is only one such bar in the previous complete uncial page, and the distinctive features all occur in a one-inch-by-four-inch portion of that page (4 of the 110 square inches of a full page).

Furthermore, the text where the only distigme occurs in the minuscule text was the standard reading at the time it was written and so would probably not have been marked as a variant reading then. Nor is it likely that a fifteenth- or sixteenth-century scribe would mark so many other Vaticanus readings as textual variants that were standard in his day. Nor does Niccum's conjecture explain the distigmai that occur where no known manuscript has a variant. Such occurrences are natural, however, if the original scribe was noting variants in the fourth century. Niccum gives no evidence that distigmai were conventionally used to note textual variants in the fifteen or sixteen centuries, nor does he explain why anyone would undergo such painstaking collation in an ancient manuscript that was falling apart, or what manuscript source at that time would account for the diversity of textual variants represented by the distigmai in B.

It is also doubtful that someone like Sepulveda, with the scholarly care and observant eye necessary to document textual variants, would not only mark up this very ancient manuscript but would continue to note textual variants even after the change from uncial to the obviously different and later minuscule text. Niccum acknowledged to this author by phone that Sepulveda mentions nothing about adding distigmai, and he admitted that

---

77. Niccum, "Voice," 245.

he does not think it likely that Sepulveda introduced these distigmai. Nevertheless, Niccum writes, "One can only conclude that some scholar after 1400 compared Vaticanus with another text, noting places of variation and/or agreement in the margin."[78] This is not the only possible conclusion, and it has the distinct disadvantage, besides those listed above, of having to explain why fifty-one distigmai match the original ink color of Vaticanus where it was not traced over and why the remaining distigmai match the ink used to trace over the text of B, for which the overwhelming consensus is that this was done in the Middle Ages, many centuries before AD 1400.

Niccum also states, "Payne … confused two separate markings [bars and distigmai]."[79] The current author's *NTS* 1985 article did, however, note that traditionally, horizontal bars extending into the margin of Vaticanus have been regarded as paragraph markers (*paragraphoi*),[80] and when they occur without a distigme, they in general do indicate paragraph divisions. Only nine of twenty-eight bars adjacent to a distigme, however, overlap or abut the beginning of a paragraph in the UBS[4] rev, and only eleven of them overlap or abut the beginning of a NA[27] paragraph.[81] Although many of the rest of the bars could be regarded as overlapping a paragraph break, others are unlikely places for one. For instance, this would put the vocative "Adulterous people" in James 4:4 in a separate paragraph from the rest of the direct address, "Adulterous people, don't you know that…?"[82] Consequently, one should not assume that all bars in Vaticanus are paragraphoi. Furthermore, composite symbols that independently have separate meanings are common: colons, exclamation marks, and question marks are periods with added significance, and semicolons are commas with added significance.

The original scribe of Vaticanus may have added a bar to some distigmai in order to highlight them as particularly significant variants, such as interpolations. This explains their use by some of the passages most widely

---

78. Ibid.
79. Ibid., 244 and 244 n. 15.
80. Payne, "Fuldensis," 255 and n. 61. There are enough bars and distigmai in Vaticanus that some bars next to a distigme probably just mark a paragraph break.
81. The nine are: Matt 13:50–51; Luke 14:24; 21:19; John 7:39–40; 9:41–10:1; Acts 2:47–3:1; 14:18; Phil 2:24; Col 2:15–16. Matthew 18:10, 12 and 2 John 8–9 also have paragraph breaks in this line in the NA[27]. Payne, "Fuldensis," 263 missed Luke 14:24 due to the inferior color facsimile available then.
82. Cf. also these odd places for paragraph divisions: Matt 24:6–7; Acts 13:16–17.

regarded as interpolations: John 7:53 – 8:11, "for the Son of Man has come to seek and to save the lost" after Matt 18:11, "blessed are you among women" at the end of Luke 1:28, "many are called but few are chosen" at the end of Luke 14:24, "in the church. In those days" after Acts 2:47, and 1 Cor 14:34 – 35. It also explains why bars just below distigmai that mark some especially important textual variants extend noticeably farther into the margin (and hence closer to the adjacent distigme) than typical paragraphoi, arguably to associate them with the adjacent distigme. Each of the five passages cited above where the bar extends toward a distigme extends approximately 3 mm or more into the margin.[83] Virtually all such long bars that extend toward adjacent distigmai occur by widely recognized interpolations.[84]

In contrast, the seventy-five other bars in 1 Corinthians extend, on average, 2.0 mm into the margin beyond the left edge of the character it underlines, and only one other extends 3.0 mm into the margin (1475B 29).[85] Distigmai next to bars contain the highest percentage of NA[27] variants of any group of distigmai yet analyzed.[86] Furthermore, in ten of the twenty-eight distigme + bar lines in Vaticanus, the original scribe of Vaticanus left an open space in the middle of a line at the exact location of a known textual variant.[87]

External support for a distinction between distigmai and at least some distigmai + bars includes the use of horizontal lines or lines plus dots in other Greek literature to indicate spurious passages or textual variants.

---

83. The distigme at the end of John 7:52 is in its right margin, but the bar is in its left margin, so this distigme does not attract the bar farther left.

84. A possible exception is Mark 5:40, but other MSS insert "but Jesus" in the middle of this Vaticanus line. Rom 16:5, has a shorter bar, and other MSS replace "Asia" with "Achaia" here.

85. Excluding the bar at 1470B 2 since it does not match the surrounding text's ink color, its shape is irregular, and, unlike every other bar in 1 Corinthians, it does not underscore the first letter of its line.

86. The NA, which aims to list all significant variants, lists a variant in all but four of them, over 85 percent, supporting this signification. Cf. evidence cited in Payne, "Response to J. Edward Miller," 107 – 12.

87. Matt 13:50 – 51; 18:10, 12; Mark 5:40; 14:70 – 71; Luke 1:28 – 29; John 7:39 – 40; Acts 2:47 – 3:1; 14:13 – 14; 1 Cor 10:24 – 25; and Phil 2:24. Gaps also occur at precisely the point in the text where a variant occurs in some of the lines adjacent to a distigme where there is no bar, as in 1253B, 1292C, 1300C, 1428A, 1438A, 1438B, 1446A, 1452A, 1470A, 1478A, 1480A, 1483C, 1491A. Most of these gaps occur at the end or beginning of a sentence, so they could simply indicate a sentence break, but in 1253B 39, 1446A 22, and 1480A 36 the gap occurs in the middle of a sentence. This is evidence that the original scribe may have noted variants during the copying of the manuscript, and not just after the codex was bound. One apparent use of a gap to indicate the location of a variant follows Mark 16:8, where one and a third columns (1303B-C) are left blank, by far the longest text gap in the codex, just where longer endings of Mark occur.

LSJ 1196 identifies ὀβελός: *"horizontal line,* — (representation of an arrow acc. to Isid. *Etym.* 1.21.3), used as a critical mark to point out that a passage was spurious... [including one that has] one point below and one above, ÷, ὁ περιεστιγμένος, in texts of Plato, denoted τὰς εἰκαίους ἀθετήσεις, D.L. 3.66." Origen's Hexapla uses the obelos (÷) for Septuagint sections absent from the Hebrew text.[88] Brock notes that Origen "quite frequently speaks of the current LXX text as being corrupt."[89] Bishop Victor in Codex Fuldensis uses bars and dots as sigla to mark textual variants.[90] Jewish scribes also identified doubtful passages of Scripture with "dots or strokes."[91] Notation of textual variants should not be surprising since this practice was well established even in Sumerian and Akkadian texts.[92]

When bars extend significantly farther into the margin than usual toward an immediately preceding distigme in a passage where manuscript evidence exists for an interpolation, the hypothesis that best explains all the data is that this is a distigme-obelus marking the location of an interpolation. This occurs in Matt 18:10; Luke 1:28; and Acts 2:47 for an interpolation in a gap in the middle of the Vaticanus line, so its distigme-obelos precedes and underscores that line, like a paragraphos underscores the line when a paragraph break occurs in the middle of a line. A distigme + extended obelos also occurs at the end of Luke 14:24 and 1 Cor 14:33, marking widely recognized interpolations that begin immediately after the end of that Vaticanus line, like a paragraphos underscores the preceding line when a paragraph break occurs at the beginning of the next line.

Just as the paragraphos in these cases marks the interface between two paragraphs, the distigme-obelos marks the interface between the original text and the interpolation. Each of the eight obeloi extend farther into the margin than usual, making them distinguishable from most paragraphoi, and in each case but Acts 6:10 a gap in the text marks the exact location of

---

88. Cf. Ernst Würthwein, *The Text of the Old Testament: An Introduction to the Biblia Hebraica* (Grand Rapids: Eerdmans, 1995), 56; C. E. Cox, *Hexaplaric Materials Preserved in the Armenian Version* (SBLSCS 21; Atlanta: Scholars, 1986), 2.

89. S. P. Brock, "Origen's Aims as a Textual Critic of the Old Testament," StPtr 10/1 (TU 107; Berlin: Akademie, 1970), 218; cf. B. M. Metzger, "Explicit References in the Works of Origen to Variant Readings in NT Manuscripts," in *Historical and Literary Studies: Pagan, Jewish, and Christian* (NTTS 8; Leiden: Brill, 1968), 88–103; F. G. Kenyon, *Our Bible and the Ancient Manuscripts* (rev. ed. A. W. Adams; London: Eyre & Spottiswoode, 1958), 75–76.

90. Ranke, *Codex Fuldensis* 465 and 573, a photo of a page containing many bar plus dot sigla.

91. Kenyon, *Our Bible and the Ancient Manuscripts*, 75–76.

92. J. Krecher, "Glossen," *Reallexikon der Assyriologie und vorderasiatischen Archäologie* (ed. E. Ebeling et al.; New York: de Gruyter, 1971), 3:435–36; cf. Payne, "Fuldensis," 258.

a widely recognized, significant interpolation. The distigme-obelos at the end of 1 Cor 14:33 fits this pattern, and so it is best understood as marking 1 Cor 14:34–35 as an interpolation.

There are 765 unambiguous distigmai in the Vaticanus NT. Since most lines of Vaticanus contain only fifteen to eighteen letters of text, its distigmai locate variants quite precisely. A scribe in the Middle Ages[93] traced over every letter of Codex Vaticanus unless it appeared to be incorrect, apparently to reinforce its fading ink.[94] Thus, unreinforced letters reveal the original apricot color ink of the codex. The most obvious examples are where the original scribe inadvertently duplicated a word,[95] phrase[96] or clause.[97] In these cases the reinforcer traced over only one of the duplicates, usually the second, so the other reveals the original ink of the codex. In addition, he or she[98] did not trace over letters that did not conform to current spelling conventions, such as the final nu (ν) of verbs when the next word begins with a consonant. Surprisingly, the NA[27] does not note several significant variants in the original unreinforced text of Vaticanus.[99]

Paul Canart, whose analysis of Codex Vaticanus as professor of paleography at the Vatican has spanned over four decades, confirmed that fifty-one[100] distigmai match the apricot color of the original ink of Vaticanus

---

93. Critical consensus dates this between the ninth and eleventh century, cf. Skeat, "Fifteenth Century," 461; Ropes, Text of Acts, xl; Frederick G. Kenyon, Handbook to the Textual Criticism of the New Testament (London: MacMillan, 1926), 80; William Henry Paine Hatch, The Principal Uncial Manuscripts of the New Testament (Chicago: Univ. of Chicago Press, 1939), pl. XIV.

94. Metzger, Text, 47; Hammond, Outlines of Textual Criticism, 49; Ropes, Text of Acts, xli; Paul Canart and Carlo M. Martini, The Holy Bible: The Vatican Greek Codex 1209 (Codex B) Facsimile Reproduction by order of his Holiness Paul VI. The New Testament. Introduction (Vatican City: Vatican, 1965), 8. Examples include 1257C 36, 1267A 34, 1271A 31, 1286B 30, 1375C 19–20, 1409A 23–24, 1409B 31, 1424A 27, 1474A 41, and 1515B 42. A corrector substituted another word for a word still displaying the original apricot color ink of Vaticanus in 1248C 12, 1253B 15, 1253C 31, 1256B 30, 1257A 21–22, 1265A 19, and 1330B 37.

95. 1258A 26, 1266A 23, 1291A 32, 1325C 33, 1363B 30, and 1413C 7.

96. 1262C 28–29 from Matt 21:4, 1305B 13–14 from Luke 1:37, and 1488B 5–6 from Gal 1:11.

97. 1273B 22–23 from Matt 26:57, 1370C 33–35 from John 13:14, 1375C 29–30 from John 17:18, 1448B 16–20 from Rom 4:4–5 (a high resolution image is at www.linguistsoftware.com/codexvat.htm), 1454A 30 from Rom 9:18, and 1479B 33–36 from 2 Cor 3:15–16.

98. Eusebius, Hist. eccl. 6.23.2, records employment of "girls trained in penmanship" in Origen's scriptorium at Caesarea. For more evidence of female scribes, cf. Kim Haines-Eitzen, Guardians of Letters: Literacy, Power, and the Transmission of Early Christian Literature (New York: Oxford Univ. Press, 2000), 41–51.

99. Notable are the presence in Vaticanus of ἐπεί instead of ὅτι in Matt 14:5 (1253C 31), the second occurrence of μου in Matt 17:15 (1258 A 26), the omission of ἐκ τοῦ κόσμου ἀλλ' ἵνα τηρήσῃς αὐτούς from John 17:15 (1375C 19–20), the omission of John 17:15b (which is inserted in its margin), the omission of the article before ἀληθείᾳ in John 17:17 (1375C 23), and the original passive reading ἐνεφανίσθησαν in Acts 25:15 (1420A 34).

100. These are tabulated with their location, verse reference, type of variant in NA, and the location of unreinforced text on that page in Payne and Canart, "Distigmai," 204–7. The fifty-one by

through examination with the naked eye, a magnifying glass, and finally with different types of loupes, including a high-powered, internally lighted one.[101] This author examined the original manuscript with Canart to identify the first eleven, then discovered most of the last forty based on their apricot color in the magnificent new facsimile of Codex Vaticanus.[102] Canart confirmed each one. Twenty of the fifty-one original ink color distigmai are in passages that occur in no early papyri[103] and so open up a window onto the earliest history of the text.

The appropriate statistical test to determine the probability of a relationship between distigmai and textual variants is the chi-square test.[104] It shows the odds that distigmai by bars (like the one at the end of 1 Cor 14:33) are independent of textual variants are far less than one in 10,000. This gives extraordinarily high confirmation that there is a co-occurring relationship between distigmai by bars and textual variants. This strongly supports the conclusion that distigmai mark the location of textual variants.

Applying the chi-square statistical test to the fifty-one distigmai that match the original apricot color ink of Vaticanus also shows the odds that original ink color distigmai are independent of textual variants are far less than one in 10,000.[105] The odds against getting such results by chance in

---

page, column, and line of Codex Vaticanus are: 1243B 21, 1261A 21, 1264C 29, 1276C 31, 1277C 19, 1279B 1, 1279C 41, 1285C 14, 1287C 29, 1288B 26, 1296A 14, 1300A 37, 1300A 39, 1308B 27, 1309A 23, 1332B 10, 1332B 15, 1332C 20, 1336A 22, 1339A 42, 1339C 42, 1339C 42, 1342C 41, 1345B 11, 1346B 40, 1349B 19, 1350B 18, 1351A 6, 1352A 40, 1355B 40, 1356B 24, 1357C 1, 1368C 15, 1370A 32, 1380A 26 or 1381C 26 (mirror impressions), 1382C 39, 1383A 4, 1396B 26, 1401C 41, 1419B 36, 1457B 24, 1459B 32, 1459C 41, 1466A 25, 1466B 6, 1468B 3, 1471A 38, 1473A 6, 1475B 11, 1499C 42, 1501A 32.

101. Loupe model: Peak light scale Lupe 7X. Cf. Payne and Canart, "Originality," 107–8.
102. *Bibliorum sacrorum graecorum* (fac-similé de B; vol. 1 of *Codex Vaticanus B: Bibliothecae Apostolicae Vaticanae Codex Vaticanus Graecus 1209;* Rome: Istituto Poligrafico e Zecca dello Stato, 1999). The remaining copies are available at www.linguistsoftware.com/codexvat.htm.
103. Based on the index of NT passages in papyri in Comfort and Barrett, *The Text,* 5–10.
104. It reveals the statistical probability that the null hypothesis may be rejected. In this case, the null hypothesis is that occurrences of distigmai and textual variants are independent. The chi-square value comparing how many of the twenty-seven distigme + bar lines listed in Payne, "Fuldensis," 253, contain NA variants to how many of the twenty lines following them (540 total lines) contain NA variants is $\chi2 = 25.081$, a chi-square value so high it goes off standard chi-square charts. Cf. the Chi-square Distribution table in E. Hatch and A. Lazareton, *The Research Manual: Design and Statistics for Applied Linguistics* (Boston: Heinle & Heinle, 1991). $p < 0.001$ *d.f.* = 1; *d.f.* stands for "degrees of freedom." This calculation includes Yate's correction for continuity. This chi-square value permits confident rejection of the null hypothesis. Including the Luke 14:24 original ink distigme + bar further enhances this probability.
105. It also rejects the null hypothesis at an extraordinarily high level of probability, $p < 0.001$ [$\chi2 = 24.431$, *d.f.* = 1]. Cf. Hatch and Lazareton, *The Research Manual,* 603. Only one of the mirror-image distigmai at 1380A 26 and 1381C 26 originally marked a textual variant, so only one is included in this test.

back-to-back tests are astronomically high unless distigmai mark textual variants. Since the fifty-one distigmai in this second group all match the original ink color of Vaticanus, this result strongly supports the conclusion that distigmai marking textual variants date to the original production of Vaticanus.

Apricot color mirror-image distigmai show that these Vaticanus distigmai were added after the binding of the codex. At least five original ink color mirror-image distigmai are at identical points on facing pages.[106] This indicates that before the ink of these distigmai was thoroughly dry, their pages were pressed together, causing the mirror-image distigmai. The apricot color distigme at 1345 B 11 left a mirror impression in the identical position of the adjacent and facing quire, proving that the codex had been at least provisionally bound when this distigme was penned. In numerous cases, other distigmai follow on the same page or on its facing page that did not leave a mirror impression.[107] This shows that the distigmai were not all penned in a single continuous progression through the manuscript since, in that case, the later-penned distigmai should have also left mirror impressions. The distigmai on the same page that did not leave a mirror impression were almost certainly penned either in an earlier or in a later collation of Vaticanus and mark the location of variant readings in different manuscripts.

The known variants where distigmai occur come from such diverse manuscript traditions that the distigmai must note the location of variants in multiple manuscripts. Multiple manuscript comparisons also explain

---

106. 1345B 11 leaves a slight impression on the right side of 1344B between lines 10 and 11. 1346B 40 appears to leave an impression on the left side of 1347C 41. 1349B 19 leaves an impression on the right side of 1348B 19. 1380A 26 mirrors 1381C 26, but it is not clear which distigme caused the mirror impression. 1457B 24 leaves an impression on the right side of 1456B 24. 1501A 32 leaves an impression on the right side of 1500C 32. 1409B 25 leaves an impression on the right side of 1408 B 25, but is not included in our statistics since Canart identified it as "probable" but not certain to match the original ink. It is possible that a seventh (or eighth) does this as well: 1276A 18 may be a mirror impression of 1277C 19, a mirror impression that was later reinforced, or 1277C 19 may be a mirror impression of 1276A 18.

107. The apricot color distigme at 1346B 40 appears to have caused a mirror impression, but a distigme follows it at 1347B 8 that did not leave a mirror impression. The apricot color distigme at 1457B 24 caused a mirror impression, but on the same page, four other distigmai follow it that did not leave mirror impressions: 1457B 36 and 1457C 4, 11, and 25. The apricot color distigme at 1501A 32 caused a mirror impression but the distigme at 1501B 42 did not. If the apricot color distigme at 1380A 26 is the original that caused its mirror image at 1381C 26, this is a fourth example since it is followed by distigmai at 1380B 7 and 1381B 28 that did not leave a mirror impression. A possible fifth example is 1409B 25, which Canart classifies as "probable" but not certain to match the original ink. The distigme at 1409B 25 caused a mirror impression but the distigmai at 1409C 8 and 10 did not.

why some portions of Vaticanus have far more distigmai than others. Early papyrus manuscripts, after all, contained only parts of the NT text. Presumably the scribe who penned the distigmai compared the text of Vaticanus to other manuscripts at that location, which is generally thought to be the scriptorium of Alexandria or Caesarea. Both would have had many NT manuscripts.

Since surviving manuscripts preserve textual variants in the vast majority of the apricot color distigme locations, these distigmai provide a statistical basis for concluding that most of the variants available to the scribe of Vaticanus have survived in extant manuscripts. This provides a new basis for confidence in the reliability of the transmission of the NT text from the ancient manuscripts[108] available to the scribe of Vaticanus until today. Thus, even though the distigmai in Codex Vaticanus may either add credibility to the originality of a passage, as in the case of John 7:53–8:11, or cast doubt on the originality of a passage, as in the case of 1 Cor 14:34–35, their overall impact is to affirm the reliability of the transmission of the NT text.

Various factors support regarding the chocolate brown distigmai as part of the original text of Vaticanus that was traced over in the Middle Ages. The fifty-one original apricot color distigmai are not limited to a specific section, but are scattered throughout the Vaticanus NT. The vast majority of them are either so faded[109] that they would be far more likely than most distigmai to be overlooked by the reinforcer of the manuscript, or else are sufficiently dark[110] that they would not stand out as needing reinforcement. Five apricot-color distigmai are the only distigme on their page,[111] making them easy to overlook. Furthermore, distigmai at the very end of the sixth

---

108. The close correlation between Vaticanus and $\mathfrak{P}^{75}$ shows that MSS available to its scribe contained texts that go back at least to AD 200, cf. S. Pisano, "The Text of the New Testament," *Bibliorum Sacrorum*, 2:34–41. Those MSS must have included many times more pages of NT text than all extant papyri written before Vaticanus, so it multiplies the basis for confidence, cf. above, p. 241.

109. 1243B 21, 1264C 29, 1277C 19, 1279B 1, 1279C 41 (also at the end of the far right column of the open codex), 1345B 11, 1350B 18 (also on the right side of its column), 1380A 26, 1381C 26, 1457B 24, 1466A 25, 1499C 42, 1501A 32, cf. Payne and Canart, "Originality," 110.

110. 1261A 21, 1276C 31, 1285C 14, 1287C 29, 1288B 26, 1300A 37, 1300A 39, 1308B 27, 1309A 23, 1332B 10, 1332B 15, 1332C 20, 1339A 42, 1346B 40, 1349B 19, 1351A 6, 1355B 40, 1356B 24, 1357C 1, 1370A 32, 1383A 4, 1401C 41, 1419B 36, 1459B 32, 1459C 41, 1466B 6, 1468B 3, 1471A 38, 1473A 6, 1475B 11, cf. Payne and Canart, "Originality," 110–11. Presumably these were even less faded in the Middle Ages.

111. 1296A 14, 1345B 11 (also faded), 1350B 18 (also in an unusual position on the right side of the column and so would be less likely to be noticed), 1356B 24, and 1370A 32.

column of the open codex were immediately lost from sight when a page was turned. In contrast, the reinforcer might notice and trace over earlier overlooked distigmai at any time until completing the collation of all six columns of the open codex. This explains why so many (six)[112] of the fifty-one apricot color distigmai occur at the very end of the sixth column even though these last two lines constitute only 1/126th of the open codex's number of visible lines.

Together, these four categories account for all but six[113] of these fifty-one distigmai and support the view that their lack of reinforcement was inadvertent. One striking indication of inadvertent nonreinforcement is the distigme at 1409B 25 (Acts 18:16), where the left dot appears to be reinforced but the right dot is not reinforced and still displays what Canart classifies as "probable" to be the original ink of the codex. In addition, Canart discerned traces of the original ink color of the codex protruding from the distigme at 1469A 3 (1 Cor 9:22), which is also clearly visible in the new facsimile, and from the distigme at 1501B 42 (Phil 3:16–17).[114] The NA[27] notes early variants in all three of these distigme locations. If these three were included with the original ink color distigmai, they would provide even weightier statistical evidence that distigmai mark the location of textual variants. More importantly, they prove that distigmai (at least these) were traced over just like the text of Vaticanus was. These observations support the view that the scribe in the Middle Ages who reinforced the text of Vaticanus probably also reinforced original ink distigmai with the same dark chocolate color ink.

It never became a scribal convention after the writing of Vaticanus in the fourth century to use distigmai to mark textual variants. Thus, it is unlikely that a later corrector would originate these distigmai to represent variants. While Codex Vaticanus was in the scriptorium where it was written, manuscripts there to which it was compared could easily be checked to confirm the purpose of the distigmai. As soon as it was separated from those manuscripts, however, the likelihood that the purpose of the Vati-

---

112. 1279C 41, 1339C 42 (two), 1401C 41, 1459C 41, 1499C 42.

113. 1336A 22, 1342C 41, 1352A 40, 1368C 15, 1382C 39, 1396B 26.

114. However, in reexamining each distigme, Canart was unable to confirm his earlier observation by the last line of 1 Cor 14:33, of a small protrusion to the left of its first dot more like the apricot color of the original text than the chocolate brown of the reinforcement, cf. Payne and Canart, "Originality," 110.

canus distigmai would be recognized drops sharply.[115] Consequently, the more time elapsed from the writing of Codex Vaticanus, the less likely becomes the addition of new distigmai, especially since no other NT Greek manuscript has ever been identified using distigmai in its margins to mark textual variants.[116] Thus, unless there is evidence to the contrary, the presumption is that the dark chocolate brown distigmai trace over apricot color distigmai that date to the original writing of Codex Vaticanus, or at least to the early period when it was in the scriptorium with manuscripts whose variants they note.[117]

The most likely candidate for the person who originally penned the distigmai is the original scribe of the Vaticanus NT since there is scholarly consensus that a single scribe wrote almost all of the NT of Vaticanus,[118] the distigmai's ink matches that of the original text, and there is remarkable consistency in the positioning of the distigmai (indicating their insertion by a skilled calligrapher, such as the original scribe of the NT of Vaticanus).[119] No variant reading accompanies any Vaticanus distigme. It is understandable that the original scribe, familiar with the revered exem-

---

115. There is evidence that the reinforcer associated distigmai, instead, with spelling corrections. There is a reinforced distigme in front of five lines where the reinforcer corrected spelling over an unreinforced letter: 1361C 1, 1468A 26, 1479A 12, 1481C 21, 1501B 42. It seems likely that the reinforcer in a sixth such instance regarded his change of H into EI in 1262A 2 also as a spelling correction. The best evidences of the reinforcing scribe's association of distigmai with spelling corrections are two instances where corrected spelling is marked in the margin by a symbol that is similar to a distigme but is shaped and positioned differently. In both cases the marks are positioned lower than typical distigmai and are not two dots but rather two short slanted strokes somewhat like grave accents: 1409A 23–24 (pointed out by P. Andrist) and 1423A 14. The first of these distinctive marks is halfway between two lines, unlike any original distigme, since "TITIOΥ" begins on line 23 and wraps onto line 24. "TITIOΥ" is unreinforced, which effectively changes the spelling of the name from "TITIOΥ IOΥΣTOΥ" to "IOΥΣTOΥ" alone. Their distinctive shape and location indicate that the reinforcing scribe did not trace over original distigmai in these two instances but created these two marks. Since these marks originally inserted by this scribe are recognizably different than distigmai, the expectation is that dark chocolate brown distigmai that do match the shape and positioning of original distigmai are reinforcements of original apricot color ink distigmai.
116. James Snapp notes a pair of dots in the margin (though not aligned with any line of the text) of page 174 of the Latin Codex Sangallensis 50 (AD 800s) next to annotations, and a corresponding pair of dots above the text in Mark 2:1 to which the annotation pertains, photo at www.e-codices.unifr.ch/en/csg/0050/174/large (confirmed May 2009).
117. Cf. Payne and Canart, "Distigmai," 213–15, for more evidence that distigmai were reinforced.
118. E.g., Canart and Martini, *The Vatican Greek Codex 1209*, 8. Cf. C. R. Gregory, *Canon and Text of the NT* (Edinburgh: T&T Clark, 1907), 345. Ropes (*Text of Acts*, xxxviii) reckons another scribe wrote Ps 77:72–Matt 9:5.
119. Thus, the distigme text-critical siglum should be included with "the marks of quotation (>), a small line interposed at the beginning of a section, the apostrophus ('), and a punctuation as from the original scribe who wrote Vaticanus, not a later hand" (Hammond, *Outlines of Textual Criticism*, 49). Marks that resemble distigmai but are not in their standard position or are irregular in shape are the most likely to have come from a different hand than the original scribe, possibly from a less-skilled contemporary.

plars Vaticanus copied, would be reluctant to attach variants, since they could distract from or challenge its text. If later scribes introduced these 700+ chocolate color distigmai, however, it is surprising that none of them ever decided any variant was sufficiently worthy to cite.

To summarize, chi-square tests confirm that the Vaticanus distigmai mark the location of textual variants. They probably date to the original production of Vaticanus. The distigme-obelos at the interface between 1 Cor 14:33 and 14:34–35, with the bar extending farther left than typical paragrophoi, is the symbol particularly associated with interpolations. Its most obvious significance is to mark 14:34–35 as an interpolation.

3. Codex Fuldensis's Text Corrected by Bishop Victor Omits 1 Corinthians 14:34–35

St. Victor, Bishop of Capua, ordered the text of 1 Cor 14:34–40 rewritten and corrected in the bottom margin of Codex Fuldensis with verses 34–35 omitted.[120] Victor, who commissioned the writing of this codex between AD 541 and 544,[121] read Codex Fuldensis twice, making corrections both times and noting that he completed these on May 2, AD 546, and April 12, AD 547.[122] As a result of Victor's oversight and corrections, its text is "very good,"[123] "one of the oldest and most valuable manuscripts of the Vulgate."[124]

Victor was a remarkable scholar, citing four works of Origen that would otherwise be unknown. A testimony to his acute text-critical perception is the omission in Fuldensis of "the Father, the Son, and the Holy Spirit" interpolation at 1 John 5:7–8, even though a preface purporting to be St. Jerome's is included that accuses the Latin translators of omitting this testimonium.[125] His astute judgments, combined with his keen interest in ancient manuscripts and his privileged access to them as a bishop, gives special credibility to his corrections in Codex Fuldensis.

---

120. For the most complete analysis of this, with a photograph of the manuscript see Payne, "Fuldensis," 240–62.
121. E. A. Lowe, Codices Latini Antiquiores: A Paleographical Guide to Latin Manuscripts Prior to the Ninth Century. Part VIII Germany: Altenburg—Leipzig (Oxford: Clarendon, 1959), 49.
122. F. H. Blackburne Daniell, "Victor, Bishop of Capua," in A Dictionary of Christian Biography (ed. W. Smith and H. Wace; 4 vols.; London: John Murray, 1877–1887), 1:1126.
123. Metzger, Text, 77.
124. Eberhard Nestle, Introduction to the Textual Criticism of the Greek New Testament (trans. William Edie and Allan Menzies; 2nd ed.; London: Williams and Norgate, 1901), 122.
125. Daniell, "Victor," 1126, who lists many other examples of Victor's scholarship.

When this author showed a facsimile of Fuldensis to Bruce M. Metzger, he agreed that Victor almost certainly ordered the original scribe of Fuldensis to rewrite the text in the margin, since a scribe would require authorization to rewrite that much text. He also agreed that the most natural explanation is that Victor ordered the rewriting of 1 Cor 14:36–40 to replace all of verses 34–40 in the text above and that this implies that Victor believed verses 34–35 are an interpolation.[126]

Victor left the reader a simple trail to follow. The symbol h͞s at the end of verse 33 shows where to begin reading the text in the bottom margin, just as it always does in its eight other occurrences in Fuldensis.[127] The symbol h͞s at the end of the replacement text in the margin tells the reader to continue reading above. The point to continue reading is clearly marked with a large Roman numeral in the margin at the beginning of chapter 15. Readers know they are in the right spot because the words just read in the margin coincide with the last words in chapter 14, immediately before the large Roman numeral.

It would be much harder to follow the text if one read the replacement text as an insertion that did not replace verses 34–40. In that case the reader would have to go first to the bottom margin to read the text, then back to the original siglum, and then continue reading until recognizing the text that was duplicated in the margin. The reader would have to compare the text in the bottom margin to find both where the overlap began and where it ended. This would make it difficult for the reader to follow the flow of the text and, all in all, seems like an unnatural way to read it.

It is perfectly natural that the original text of Fuldensis reproduces the traditional position of 1 Cor 14:34–35 since of the over eight thousand extant Vulgate texts,[128] every other one containing this passage reproduces this position except one, the mid-eighth century Codex Reginensis (R). Consequently, there was no reason for Victor to correct this passage in

126. Based on discussions at the AAR-SBL Meeting in late November, 1991, in Kansas City, and November 1992, in San Francisco, when he read a draft of this study. Payne, "Fuldensis," 243–45, gives six reasons why it is more natural to read this gloss as a replacement of vv. 34–40 rather than only vv. 36–40.
127. Only in 1 Pet 3:14 is h͞s in the text directing the reader *supra* to a gloss in the top margin.
128. Metzger, *Text*, 76.

248 CR MAN AND WOMAN

Fuldensis based on the manuscript from which it was copied or from any other standard Vulgate text.[129]

Because of Victor's stature and text-critical interests, his text in the margin omitting 1 Cor 14:34–35 is far more important for textual criticism than his scribe's inclusion of verses 34–35 in the body of the text above. Since all of Victor's other textual decisions reflect known textual variants, and since the omission of 14:34–35 is contrary to his normal tendency to edit in favor of standard Vulgate readings, the most natural explanation is that he ordered his scribe to rewrite the text after seeing a manuscript that did not contain 14:34–35. Fuldensis[Victor mg.] thus fulfills the criterion C. K. Barrett posed, "If any significant MS omitted the verses altogether it would probably be right to follow [the view that] ... verses 34f ... were added later as a marginal note."[130]

---

129. Kurt Aland and Barbara Aland, *The Text of the New Testament: An Introduction to the Critical Editions and to the Theory and Practice of Modern Textual Criticism* (trans. Erroll F. Rhodes; Grand Rapids: Eerdmans; Leiden: Brill, 1987), 188, note that Pelagius and his followers in the early fifth century, over a century before Fuldensis, quote the Vulgate text of Paul's epistles, so the Vulgate text was well-established by Victor's time. Niccum, "Voice," 246, incorrectly states, "Codex Fuldensis is the oldest extant Vg MS." Metzger, *Text*, 76–78, lists older ones, two of which, Sangallensis and Mediolanensis, Niccum's survey, surprisingly, does not mention. In light of Niccum's many other false statements (e.g., "Payne himself admits ..." [p. 246 n. 26]—Payne did not; "Victor ... copied vv. 36–40 in the margin" [p. 246]—it does not match Victor's handwriting; cf. above pp. 246 and 247) one ought to question his speculative assertions: "For the Pauline epistles Victor of Capua employed two MSS. At first he primarily relied upon a text strongly mixed with OL readings. By the time he finished 2 Corinthians he realized that the other MS, from northern Italy, preserved a superior Vg text. He therefore finished copying the epistles with greater reliance upon the second exemplar. Victor then went back through Romans and 2 Corinthians making corrections." No one possesses the manuscripts that Victor used or can be sure how many he used or their provenance. If Victor relied primarily on the second exemplar after 2 Cor, one would expect the corrections to be predominantly in the earlier material, but there are just as many marginal corrections marked with hᷓ and hᷓ following 2 Cor (Col 1:2; 2 Thess 3:10; 2 Tim 2:20; 1 Pet 3:14) as there are in Rom through 2 Cor (Rom 9:25; 1 Cor 7:35; 9:4–5; 14:36–40). Six of these eight glosses bring Fuldensis into greater conformity with the standard Vulgate readings, so Victor was undoubtedly influenced by Vulgate texts. It far exceeds the evidence, however, to suggest that all the changes came from a single MS and to assert that MS to be a Vorlage of the *only* other Vulgate text with the Western order of the end of 1 Cor 14, Reginensis, written in the eighth century. Scholars do not even know if the distinctive reading of 1 Cor 14 in Reginensis came from a Vulgate Vorlage. The only extant Vulgate text that could have been a Vorlage to Reginensis's positioning of 1 Cor 14:36–40 is Fuldensis, and it differs from Reginensis twice in 1 Cor 14:34 alone, so it does not adequately explain Reginensis's text. A Latin or Greek Western text seems more likely than Fuldensis to be Reginensis's source here. Whether there is a genetic relationship between Fuldensis and Reginensis, and if so, which text or its Vorlage affected the other, is a complicated issue highly dependent on a conjectural Vorlage. If there was influence, the antiquity of Fuldensis makes it more likely that its text of 1 Cor 14 influenced Reginensis than vice versa. Niccum's suggestion (pp. 246–47) that a Vorlage of Reginensis was the source of Victor's marginal reading of 14:36–40 faces the further obstacle that Victor's marginal text does not include vv. 34–35, but Reginensis's text does. If, however, Fuldensis influenced Reginensis, one would still expect Reginensis to add vv. 34–35 in spite of the omission in Fuldensis[mg], both to avoid conflicting with all other Vulgate texts and because vv. 34–35 still stand in Fuldensis's body text.

130. Barrett, *First Corinthians*, 332.

4. The Most Reasonable Explanation of MS 88's Treatment of 14:34–35 Is That MS 88 Was Copied from a Manuscript That Omitted These Verses

In MS 88, verse 36 follows immediately after verse 33.[132] The scribe of 88 realized that verses 34–35 were missing before starting to write chapter 15 and inserted them at the first logical break in the text, separating them from the last word of verse 40 by two slashes on the baseline. Similar slashes are at the baseline level in the margin after verse 33 and over the last letter of verse 33, not on the baseline, since there is no room on the baseline. This makes it clear that the scribe intended the reader to insert verses 34–35 after verse 33. Therefore, verses 34–35 must not have followed verse 33 in the exemplar of 88. Since 88 is not a Western text-type manuscript, there are only two plausible possibilities: derivation from a non-Western manuscript with verses 34–35 displaced, or derivation from a non-Western manuscript without verses 34–35.

NA[27] does not list any non-Western Greek manuscript with 14:34–35 displaced. Wire writes, "a review of the ms. 88 text of 1 Corinthians shows that it seldom parallels 'Western' readings except where they also appear in the eighth-to-ninth-century manuscript Ψ and go on to become the majority reading."[133] Verses 34–35, however, do not follow verse 40 in the text stream from which MS 88 arose, represented by the closely related MS Ψ, nor does this become the majority reading. Quite the opposite, no non-Western Greek manuscript prior to MS 88 has verses 34–35 after verse 40.[134] The last Western texts, F and G, were written in the ninth century, three hundred years before MS 88.[135] Consequently, MS 88's text stream does not support the explanation that it was copied from a manuscript with verses 34–35 following verse 40.[136]

---

132. Philip B. Payne's detailed analysis, "MS. 88 as Evidence for a Text without 1 Cor 14.34–35," *NTS* 44 (1998): 152–58, includes a full page photograph of this passage in MS 88 and a close-up photograph showing its details.
133. Wire, *Corinthian Women Prophets*, 151. MS 88 follows Ψ and is followed by 𝔐 in its reading of υποτασσεσθαι in 1 Cor 14:34 but does not follow Ψ or 𝔐's επιτετραπται.
134. The only subsequent Greek text that has vv. 34–35 following v. 40 is the thirteenth-century MS 915.
135. UBS[4], 10*.
136. Furthermore, if the scribe of MS 88 were copying a manuscript with vv. 34–35 following v. 40, that scribe probably would have copied it exactly as it was in the exemplar. But instead, he inserted a double slash on the baseline at the end of v. 40. If he had been copying a non-Western text that for whatever reason had vv. 34–35 after v. 40 and if he had intended to note that this reading is contrary to the standard reading, one would expect him to use corresponding

The inconsistent positions of the double slashes, however, fit perfectly if they were copied from a manuscript that omitted verses 34–35. The explanation that MS 88 was copied from a manuscript without verses 34–35 does not depend on its scribe having access either to a Western manuscript or a non-Western manuscript with a reading totally out of keeping with its textual tradition. On this explanation, the source from which the scribe of MS 88 copied verses 34–35 presents no difficulty, since the scribe could have copied just these two verses (vv. 34–35) from any other manuscript in the scriptorium. This evidence that MS 88 was copied from a text of 1 Cor 14 without verses 34–35 provides additional external support for the thesis that verses 34–35 were not in the original text. The most natural implication of Codex Fuldensis and MS 88 is that a manuscript that omitted 1 Cor 14:34–35 not only influenced Victor's editing of Fuldensis in AD 546–547 but was a Vorlage of MS 88 in the twelfth century.

5. Clement of Alexandria Reflects a Text of 1 Corinthians without 14:34–35

Clement of Alexandria discusses the behavior of women in church in *Paed.* 3:11, where he states, "Woman and man are to go to church decently attired, with natural step, embracing silence ... fit to pray to God.... For this is the wish of the Word, since it is becoming for her to pray veiled.... Such ought those who are consecrated to Christ appear, and frame themselves in their whole life, as they fashion themselves in the church for the sake of gravity."[136] "Pray veiled" is clearly an allusion to 1 Cor 11:5, 13 and shows that Clement is concerned with women's behavior, including behavior in church,[137] and "woman ... embracing silence" would normally be regarded as an allusion of 1 Cor 14:34–35. Clement cites elsewhere from

---

notation both after v. 33 and v. 40. Either both sets of slashes should have been between the lines or both should have been on the baseline. The fact that the double slash is between the lines after v. 33 but on the base line after v. 40 indicates that the scribe deliberately inserted vv. 34–35 after v. 40 in order to correct an error in the text he was copying, not that he was replicating his exemplar's reading and accompanying it with consistent notation of the standard reading. Thus, the inconsistent positions of the double slashes do not fit well with the explanation that they were copied from a MS that included vv. 34–35 after v. 40. For these reasons, it is implausible that the scribe of MS 88 was copying a non-Western Greek manuscript with vv. 34–35 after v. 40.

136. A. Roberts and J. Donaldson, *Ante-Nicene Fathers* (9 vols.; repr., Edinburgh: T&T Clark, 1989), 2:290.

137. *Pace* Niccum ("Voice," 244 n. 11), who defines "going to church" as exclusive from women's behavior in church. It is not mere lack of a citation but the presence of an incongruity with vv. 34–35 that is evidence of its omission from Clement's New Testament text.

1 Cor 14:6, 9, 10, 11, 13, 20; 15:32, 33, 34, 41, 50, 55 but never any part of 14:34–35. If Clement's text of 1 Cor had included 14:34–35, one would expect some mention of its restrictions when his discussion of the behavior of women specifically mentions "embracing silence." Instead, however, he writes of both "woman and man ... embracing silence," which seems incongruent with a text including verses 34–35. All this is best explained if his text did not include 14:34–35.

A further indication of this is *Strom.* 4.19, where Clement affirms, "The sister of Moses ... was the prophet's associate in commanding the host, being superior to all the women among the Hebrews who were in repute for their wisdom.... It is not then possible that man or woman can be conversant with anything whatever, without the advantage of education, and application, and training."[138] These statements show that Clement accepted women "in repute for their wisdom" for prophetic roles and endorsed education and training for both men and women. This combined with his call to both men and women without distinction to silence in church are evidence indicating that 14:34–35 was not in the text of 1 Corinthians he was using about AD 190–202.[139]

6. The Apostolic Fathers Give No Sign of Awareness of 1 Corinthians 14:34–35

Interpolation explains why, in spite of this prohibition's enormous practical implications, and even though 1 Corinthians was the most quoted epistle by Christian writers in the second century,[140] none of the Apostolic Fathers cite 1 Cor 14:34–35. Nor did any of the following quote 14:34–35: Justin Martyr (d. ca. AD 165),[141] Athenagoras (d. ca. 177) even though he cites both 14:32 and 14:37, Irenaeus (d. ca. AD 202), *The Shepherd of Hermas* (second century), Tatian (d. post AD 172), Clement of Alexandria (d. pre-AD 215), Caius (d. AD 217), Hippolytus (d. AD 235), Novatian, Gregory Thaumaturgus, Dionysius of Alexandria, Julius Africanus, Anatolius, Archelaus, Alexander of Lycopolis, Peter of Alexandria, Alexander of Alexandria, Methodius, Arnobius, Lactantius, Venantius, Asterius

---

138. ANF 2:431–32.
139. G. L Carey, "Clement of Alexandria," in *NIDCC*, 234.
140. Walter Bauer, *Orthodoxy and Heresy in Earliest Christianity* (trans. by a team from the Philadelphia Seminar on Christian Origins; ed. Robert A. Kraft and Gerhard Krodel; Philadelphia: Fortress, 1971), 219.
141. This and the following dates of death are from *PGL*.

Urbanus, Victorinus, Dionysius of Rome, Theodotus, the *Apostolical Teach-ings, Canons, Testaments of the Twelve Patriarchs, Two Epistles concerning Virginity,* Clementine Recognitions, Clementine Homilies, Apocrypha of the New Testament, Decretals, ancient Syriac documents, the *Testament of Abraham, Acts of Xanthippe and Polyxena, Narrative of Zosimus,* epistles of Clement, *Apology* of Aristides, *Passion of the Scillitan Martyrs,* and the apocalypses of Peter, Visio Pauli, Maria Virgo, and Sedrach.

In particular, the *Acts of Paul* 41 reports that Paul told Thecla: "Go and teach the word of God!" and sec. 43 speaks of her "enlightening many with the word of God."[142] Peter W. Dunn argues that the author of the *Acts of Paul* "could not have had 1 Cor 14:34–35 in his copy, for he depicts a woman prophesying in the assembly, when otherwise he seems quite determined to show that the practice of the Corinthians follows Paul's teachings to the letter."[143] Dunn also states that "Irenaeus apparently interprets 1 Cor 11:4–5 to mean that a woman may prophesy in church (*Haer.* 3.11.9). This combined with his silence about 1 Cor 14:34–35 in his extant corpus suggests that his copy of the epistle also lacked these verses."[144]

The earliest extant citation of 1 Cor 14:34–35 appears to be by Ter-tullian, writing about AD 200. His knowledge of these verses produces remarks in sharp contrast to Clement's, cited above: "For how credible would it seem, that he who has not permitted a woman even to learn with overboldness, should give a female the power of teaching and of baptizing! 'Let them be silent,' he says, 'and at home consult their own husbands.'"[145]

7. There Is a High Incidence of Textual Variants in 1 Corinthians 14:34–35

These two verses contain an unusually large number of textual varia-tions, which is typical of interpolations (e.g., John 7:53–8:11). Wire notes that "14:34–35 shows about twice as many word reversals and other small

142. Edgar Hennecke and Wilhelm Schneemelcher, *New Testament Apocrypha II: Writings Relating to the Apostles, Apocalypses and Related Subjects* (trans. R. McL. Wilson; Louisville, Ky.: West-minster John Knox, 1991), 2:246. *The Acts of Paul and Thecla* 11:15 calls her an "apostle of God."
143. Dunn, "Acts of Paul," 452. Kent Sparks independently reported the same conclusion in 2007.
144. Dunn, "Acts of Paul," 453.
145. *Bapt.* 15.17, cited from *ANF* 3:677. Dating by D. F. Wright, "Tertullian" in *NIDCC*, 961. Cf. above pp. 154–55, 220 and below, p. 264.

variants as other verses in the context."[147] The NA[27] lists twelve sets of variant readings in 14:34–35. For example, "your" (ὑμῶν) is added after "women" in 14:34 in D F G 𝔐 a b sy; Cyprian, Ambrosiaster, and "to their husbands" (τοῖς ἀνδράσιν), as in Col 3:18, is added in A after "must be in submission." Both indicate apparent attempts to make the command less problematic by restricting it to wives.

Tischendorf notes five more variants just in Codex Claromontanus.[148] The present author examined two unpublished manuscripts of 1 Corinthians at the VanKampen Scriptorium, which each contain a textual variant not noted above. VK0908, now officially MS 2892, substitutes ἐστι γυναιξίν for ἐστιν γυναικί. VK0902, now MS 909, substitutes ἐστι γυναιξὶν ἐν ἐκκλησίαι λαλεῖν for ἐστιν γυναικὶ λαλεῖν ἐν ἐκκλησίᾳ.

INTERNAL EVIDENCE

Nine important internal evidences argue that 1 Cor 14:34–35 is an interpolation.

1. Verses 34–35 Contradict Paul's Encouraging Women to Speak in Church

Prayer and prophecy by women as well as men is permitted in 11:5 and 13 as long as they have a proper head covering.[149] This, and the church setting of both chapters 11 and 14,[150] make it natural that references to "all" people in the church engaging in verbal ministry, like prophesying, should include women.[151] The thrice-repeated prohibition of 14:34–35, however, contradicts this.

It was precisely because these statements in 11:5, 13, and throughout chapter 14 effectively encourage women to prophesy that someone desiring to safeguard male privilege might have added 14:34–35 as a gloss.[152]

---

147. Wire, *Corinthian Women Prophets*, 150, citing various examples, cf. 284 n. 16. Three variants here in MS 88 are not noted in NA[27]. Cf. also Metzger, *Textual Commentary*[1], 219–22; *Textual Commentary*[2], 187–89.
148. Tischendorf, *Codex Claromontanus*, 558. Cf. the variant from *ordine* to *ordinem* in Fuldensis.
149. Cf. above, pp. 147–215.
150. Cf. above, p. 149–51, 221.
151. Cf. above, pp. 219–20, and below, pp. 326, 331–33.
152. *Pace* Carson ("Silent," RBMW 142), who ridicules the idea of a glossator as "Biblically informed enough to worry about harmonization with 1 Timothy 2 but who is so thick he cannot see that he is introducing a clash between 1 Corinthians 14 and 1 Corinthians 11." It is perfectly natural that someone sensing a clash between 1 Corinthians 11–14 and his understanding of male privilege would want to "interpret" the passage using Paul's vocabulary.

Anyone understanding 1 Tim 2:12 to prohibit women from teaching or having authority over men could feel justified that a gloss is necessary to correct possible "misinterpretation" of 1 Cor 11–14. Taken at face value, however, 11:5, 13 and 14:34–35 are incompatible.

2. Verses 34–35 Interrupt the Flow of Paul's Argument

Verses 1–25 form a sustained argument that prophecy is more edifying than tongues unless tongues are interpreted (14:1, 2–3, 4, 5, 6, 22, 23–25). Each subsection of 14:1–25 concludes similarly: "that the church may be edified" (v. 5); to "build up the church" (v. 12); to be "edified" (v. 17); to "instruct others" (v. 19); and to "worship God" (v. 25).

Verses 26–40 is a coherent structural unit that builds on verses 1–25 by enumerating a series of instructions for tongues and prophecy to enhance edification. The unifying principle behind all these rules is the need for order, not confusion, in Christian assemblies for worship. The literary structure of verses 26–40 is chiastic.[153]

A. Order everything to strengthen the church (v. 26).

   B. Tongues: two or at most three, one at a time, someone must interpret (v. 27).

   Be silent if there is no interpreter (v. 28).

      C. Prophets: two or three, others weigh it carefully (v. 29).

      Be silent if someone else has a prophecy (v. 30).

      Prophesy in turn (v. 31).

      Prophets are not out of control (v. 32).

         D. God is a God of order in all the churches (v. 33).

      C´. Prophets: Did God's word originate with you or reach only you? (v. 36).

      Acknowledge what I write is the Lord's command (v. 37).

      If he ignores this, he himself will be ignored (v. 38).

      Be eager to prophesy (v. 39a).

   B´. Tongues: do not forbid speaking in tongues (v. 39b).

A´. Everything should be done in a fitting and orderly way (v. 40).

---

natural that someone sensing a clash between 1 Corinthians 11–14 and his understanding of male privilege would want to "interpret" the passage using Paul's vocabulary.

153. Lynn Fox, a Bible teacher at Peninsula Bible Church in Palo Alto, California, pointed this out to the present author in the fall of 1995, although the following analysis is an independent development of that idea.

As is standard in chiasm, the climax is at the center,[153] "For God is not a God of disorder, but of peace, as in all the congregations of the saints."[154] The theme of the climax is order. The theme is closely related both to the beginning and the end of the literary structure. The symmetry of the structure is broken, however, if verses 34 – 35 are inserted. This introduction of unqualified silence for women in 14:34 – 35 is extraneous to the literary structure, introducing a new element after the climax instead of recapitulating the prior issue of prophecy, which 14:36 – 39a does so nicely. Verses 34 – 35 are not a climax and do not mention any issues that tie in with the introduction or conclusion of the literary structure (prophecy, tongues, interpretation, other spiritual gifts, edification, order),[155] nor does it have any corresponding text within this passage's chiastic structure. Thus, not only are verses 34 – 35 out of place in the logical development of this pas-sage, they break its otherwise consistent literary structure.

Instead of listing particular instances when silence is required to enhance edification, as in each of the passage's other calls for silence, 14:34 – 35 demands unqualified silence in church of all women without any explanation of how this will enhance the edification of the church. Fur-thermore, unlike the references to women in chapters 7 and 11, 14:34 – 35 has no corresponding reference to men. Thus, 14:34 – 35 is an awkwardly placed, intruding comment that interrupts the structure of Paul's argument and does not advance the argument of 14:26 – 40 or of chapters 12 – 14.

Carson objects that "most glosses of substantial size, like this one . . . do not introduce major problems of flow into the text."[156] This, however, does not give glosses that are more awkward any greater claim to authenticity. Surely, just the opposite is true. Accordingly, Metzger includes breaks in the flow of text as part of his evidence that a gloss has occurred in various passages, such as Mark 16:9 – 20 and 1 John 5:7b – 8.[157]

---

153. E.g., Kenneth E. Bailey, *Poet and Peasant and through Peasant Eyes: A Literary-Cultural Approach to the Parables of Luke* (Grand Rapids: Eerdmans, 1983), 50.

154. Cf. above, pp. 223 – 24, and below, p. 256, on the appropriateness of associating 33b with 33a.

155. When Paul uses the word "church" referring to a church custom in 1 Corinthians, he typically follows it immediately with a criticism of the Corinthians' rejection of customary church practice, as in 1 Cor 4:17 – 18; 6:4; 11:16 – 17, 18, 22; 14:19 – 20, 23, so the prohibition of disorder "in all the churches of the saints" leads directly to his rebuke of the Corinthians in 14:36 – 38. Paul's use of ἤ to introduce his rebuke fits his unbroken pattern of using ἤ to introduce rhetorical questions in 1 Corinthians. Cf. above, p. 224 on ἤ.

156. Carson, "Silent," *RBMW* 142.

157. Metzger, *Textual Commentary2*, 104 – 5, 649.

Some try to connect 1 Cor 14:34–35 to its context by treating 14:36 as an appeal to women who dared to speak in church, "Did the word of God originate with you? Or are you the only people it has reached?" Grammatically, however, this is impossible since the adjective "only" modifying the pronoun "you" (ὑμᾶς μόνους) is masculine plural. If Paul were addressing women only he should have used a feminine (ὑμᾶς μόνας) rather than a masculine form (cf. Luke 10:40 μόνην με, referring to Martha). The masculine form implies that at least some men were included in the group he was addressing.

Similarly, in 1 Cor 14:37, "If anyone thinks he is a prophet (masculine singular) or spiritual (masculine singular)," cannot be directed exclusively to women.[158] Thus, the verses immediately following verses 34–35 give no grammatical hint that they were intended by Paul to address women or that they originally followed a passage specifically regarding women.

3. Verses 34–35 Make Alien Use of Vocabulary from the Chapter

These verses appropriate words and phrases from the context, but use them in ways that are alien to its context.[159] In 14:35, ἐν ἐκκλησίᾳ is identical in form to 14:19 and 28, but there Paul's purpose is instruction in church, not the delay of learning until after church. "In the churches" (ἐν ταῖς ἐκκλησίαις in 14:34) repeats almost verbatim "in all the churches" (ἐν πάσαις ταῖς ἐκκλησίαις) at the end of verse 33. This, however, introduces an awkward redundancy if verse 33b is joined with verse 34.

The command for silence (σιγάτωσαν) in verse 34 is third person plural, present active imperative, similar to the third person singular, present active imperative of the same verb in 14:28 and 30. These others, however, command silence for a practice normally approved, but specifically restricted in order to enhance worship and learning. Only 14:34 demands unqualified silence, and only 14:34 demands it of only a specific social group.

"To speak" (λαλεῖν, v. 34) occurs twenty-four times in chapter 14, including this identical infinitive in verses 5 and 39. All the other uses, however,

---

158. Cf. the similar observation by Robert A. Bryant on p. 3 of his review of Robert L. Thomas, *Understanding Spiritual Gifts: A Verse-by-Verse Study of 1 Corinthians 12–14* (rev. 2nd ed.; Grand Rapids: Kregel, 1999) in *Review of Biblical Literature* n.p. 2000. Online: www.bookreviews.org/Reviews/0825438292.html.

159. This is argued, e.g., by Allison, "Let Women Be Silent," 37–38; Meeks, "Andryogyne," 203–4.

identify the nature or content of the speech, such as speaking in tongues or in prophecy.[160] Verse 34, however, prohibits all speech in church by women.

"As the law says" (καὶ ὁ νόμος λέγει) picks up the reference to the law in 14:21 (cf. these identical words in 9:8). Nowhere else, however, does Paul appeal to the law without a corresponding OT reference, and nowhere else does he appeal to a precept of the law to establish an ethical requirement for Christian behavior or Christian worship.[161]

The verb "to learn" (μαθεῖν, v. 35) also occurs in 14:31, "you can all prophesy in turn so that everyone may learn," which affirms that everyone can prophesy and learn in church, but verses 34–35 instead tell women if they want to learn, they may not ask questions in church, but must do so at home.

Although house (οἴκῳ, v. 35) has a superficial resemblance to upbuilding (οἰκοδομή) in 14:3, 5, 12, 26, in context it cuts women off from their participation in the upbuilding.

"Disgraceful for a woman" (αἰσχρὸν ... γυναικί, v. 35) follows this exact form of these words from 11:6, where it establishes that women may pray and prophesy when properly covered, but 14:35 prohibits women from speaking in church. Thus, the extensive borrowing of terminology from the context of 1 Cor 14 is done in ways foreign to that context. Interpolation best explains this.

4. Verses 34–35 Conflict with the Goal of Instruction in Church

According to verse 35, if women want to learn, they are to ask questions at home. The central thrust of this chapter, summarized in 14:26 and 31, however, is that in church "everyone may be instructed." For Paul, the church is "the locus of God's Spirit's most powerful presence and action."[162] It is unreasonable to assume that a woman's husband would be better prepared to answer questions than the church as a whole, especially not unbelieving husbands. Furthermore, Paul states in 14:29 that others in the group should provide a check against prophecies that might be misleading, a check lacking at home.

---

160. Cf. speaking in tongues in 14:2 (2x), 4, 5 (2x), 6, 9 (2x), 11, 13, 18, 19, 23, 27, 28, 39; speaking mysteries in 14:2; speak revelation, knowledge, or prophecy in 14:3, 6, 29; speak with my mind in 14:19; I will speak through strange tongues and the lips of foreigners in 14:21.
161. For detailed argument of this point cf. pp. 258–60, and Fee, *First Corinthians*, 707.
162. Soards, *1 Corinthians*, 306–7.

5. This Use of "just as[163] the Law says" Does Not Fit Paul's Theology or His Style of Expression

In all other instances when Paul appeals to the law, the passage cited is clearly recognizable as an OT passage. Yet none of the immediately preceding statements in 1 Cor 14:34, "Let the women be silent in the churches, for they are not permitted to speak, but let them be in submission," is even close to a quotation of any OT passage. Most commentators suggest a possible vague allusion to the statement in Gen 3:16 about the consequences of the fall, "he [your husband] will rule over you," but that is a statement of what the husband will do, not what he should do, and it says nothing about what the wife should do. Some say this is a summary of what the OT says about the submission of wives to husbands, but no such principle is stated in the OT.[164] Both the silence and submission of women, however, are required by Jewish oral law,[165] but all of Paul's references to the law clearly refer to OT passages.

Of Paul's 115 uses of "law" (νόμος), some form of the expression "the law says" occurs elsewhere only three times. Romans 3:10, "just as it is written," introduces a series of OT quotations that continue up to 3:19, "We know that whatever the law says...." Romans 7:7–8 identifies "the law said, 'Do not covet'" as "the commandment." In 1 Cor 9:8, "the law says" precedes "For it is written in the Law of Moses," introducing a quotation from Deut 25:4. The next closest reference is Gal 4:21–22, where "hear-

---

163. In each of the twenty-three other occurrences καθὼς καί means simply "just as": Rom 1:13; 15:7; 1 Cor 10:33; 11:1; 13:12; 2 Cor 1:14; 11:12; Eph 4:4, 17, 32; 5:2, 25, 29; Col 1:6 (2x); 3:13; 1 Thess 2:14; 3:4; 4:1, 6, 13; 5:11; 2 Thess 3:1. Paul's use of the parallel expression καθὼς γέγραπται always means simply, "just as it is written." Accordingly, most English versions translate καθὼς καί "as": CEV, JB, NAB, NEB, NIV, REB, TEV, Beck, Berkeley, New Berkeley, Fenton, Moffatt, Phillips, TNT; or "just as": Goodspeed, Way, Williams. W. Gutbrod ("νόμος," TDNT 4:1077 and n. 245), however, interprets it as "confirmation of what is already known to be right on other grounds." Of his two examples, 1 Cor 9:8 does not use the expression καθὼς καί, and in 1 Cor 14:34 this is the first reason listed and so could not mean "as also" unless v. 33b is linked with v. 34, against the punctuation in all the early manuscripts, cf. above, pp. 223–24. "As also": ASV, KJV, NRSV, Weymouth; "just as also": Amplified, NASB; and "as even": RSV, also go against typical Pauline usage.
164. Carson ("Silent," RBMW 152) suggests Gen 2:20b–24, but it says nothing about submission or silence. Rather it is full of expressions that in all other OT occurrences imply equality, not submission: "a power corresponding to him," "bone of my bones, flesh of my flesh," and "they shall become one flesh." Cf. above, pp. 44–45, 52–53.
165. M. Ketub. 7:6 says it is a transgression of Jewish custom for a woman to "speak with any man." Cf. above, pp. 38–40, 164–65, for more examples. Josephus (Ag. Ap. 2.200–201 1:373 [LCL]) says, "The woman, says the Law, is in all things inferior to the man. Let her accordingly be submissive." This is a nearly exact parallel not just to the command that women be submissive but also to its basis in what the law "says." Thus, although 1 Cor 14:34 is out of harmony with Paul's use of "the law," it fits Jewish appeals to oral law perfectly.

ing" the law is immediately followed by "for it is written," which introduces a reference to Gen 16:15 and 21:2, 9–10. Thus, not only does "as the law says" never occur anywhere in Paul's letters except 1 Cor 14:34, this is the only instance where "it is written" or "the commandment" does not accompany a reference to what the law "says."

Paul's sixteen "just as it is written" (καθὼς γέγραπται or καθάπερ γέγραπται) all introduce an OT quotation, but not one introduces a regulation of the law. Furthermore, Paul never uses the OT citations introduced by it to make a rule for church practice. Instead, these citations of the law reinforce the centrality of faith (Rom 1:17; 4:17; 8:36; 9:33), humanity's unrighteousness (2:24; 3:10), God's election apart from works (9:13), preaching (10:15; 15:21), salvation (11:26; 1 Cor 1:31; 2:9), Christ's suffering (Rom 15:3), mercy (15:9), the principle of equality (2 Cor 8:15), and God's provision (9:9).

Furthermore, the appeal to "the law" in 1 Cor 14:34 to establish a rule for Christian worship appears to contradict one of Paul's dominant themes. Although he affirms the law in various ways,[166] he repeatedly insists that believers stand in a new relationship to the law, in sharp contrast to the focus on Torah within Judaism. "Christ redeemed us from the curse of the law" (Gal 3:13), "by abolishing in his flesh the law with its commandments and regulations" (Eph 2:15). "Christ is the end of law" (Rom 10:4). Consequently, "you are not under law" (Rom 6:14–15; 1 Cor 9:20–21; Gal 3:23–25; 5:18); "you died to the law [and] ... have been released from the law" (Rom 7:4–6; Gal 2:19). For Paul, Christ supplanted the Torah as the center of faith and life. He makes it unmistakably clear that Christ's covenant of grace has superseded the covenant of Torah. Consequently, Paul's ethics are fundamentally grounded in Christ, not the law. Christ frees his people to live in love through the power of the Spirit.[167]

It is hardly surprising in light of Paul's theme of the believer's freedom from the law that, unless 1 Cor 14:34 is the one exception, he never uses the Greek word ὁ νόμος ("the law") to establish an ethical requirement for

---

166. Paul's positive statements about the law make it clear that he believed that God gave the law and that it reveals God's standards and judgments: Rom 2:20; 3:20; 7:12, 14, 22; 8:4; cf. 1 Tim 1:8–9. Paul regards the precepts listed in Rom 13:8–10 as summed up in Jesus' law of love. Although love is far more than not committing adultery, murdering, stealing, and coveting, these are things that must be avoided because doing them does not express love.

167. Cf. F. F. Bruce, *Paul: Apostle of the Heart Set Free* (Exeter: Paternoster, 1977), 192.

Christian behavior or worship.[168] Paul does illustrate or explain points by reference to events in Scripture.[169] On two occasions Paul reinforces his argument for how Christians should live by appeals to a precept where he cites "the law," but in both passages he is either using the precept as a metaphorically applied example, not as a new Christian law (1 Cor 9:8), or he uses it only as correlative support for what he establishes foundationally based on Christ (Rom 13:8–10).[170] In Rom 13:8–10, Paul lists several precepts of the law, but he does so not to establish them as rules Christians must follow, but to show that they are all summed up in Christ's command, "Love your neighbor as yourself."[171] The love of neighbor command is not identified in the OT as a summary of the law, so Paul's use of it as a summary of the law is almost certainly drawn from Jesus (Matt 22:39–40).[172] Rather than defining sin on the basis of the law, Paul defines sin in Rom 14:23 as "whatever is not of faith."

Again and again, especially in 1 Corinthians, even when the citation of a precept from the Mosaic law would have made a perfect defense of

---

168. Paul occasionally, without using the word "law," applies various parts of the OT to support principles for Christian behavior. Rom 12:19–20 cites Deut 32:35 (which is not a precept but is a statement of God's authority) and quotes from Prov 25:21–22, adopting a wisdom saying that obviously reflects Jesus' teachings on love for one's enemy. Rom 14:10–11 cites a prediction from Isa 45:23; 2 Cor 6:14–18 cites a prophecy from Isa 52:11 LXX to bolster the arguments from Christ that believers should not be yoked together with unbelievers. In none of these cases are OT precepts being treated as binding law. Cf. Gutbrod, "νόμος," TDNT 4:1077.

169. 1 Tim 2:13–14's reference to the creation narrative of Genesis 2 is not a reference to a precept of the law, but rather to an event described in Scripture.

170. Rom 7:7 does not fit this category since Paul does not apply "do not covet" as a rule for Christian behavior, but simply uses it as an example to explain the function of the law in awakening awareness of sin and stimulating sin. 1 Cor 14:21's citation of Isa 28:11–12 and Deut 28:49 is not a citation of a precept, but of a prophecy applied metaphorically to the situation in Corinth. 1 Cor 9:8 applies, "Do not muzzle an ox while it is treading out the grain" (Deut 25:4) to missionary support. This metaphorical application of a specific law adds to Paul's arguments from apostolic practice (9:5, 12), common sense (9:7–8, 11, 13), and "the Lord has commanded that those who preach the gospel should receive their living from the gospel." But even given this right, Paul chose not to exercise it (9:12, 15–18). Thus, Paul must not have intended it to establish Deut 25:4 as an ethical requirement for Christian behavior.

171. Paul also does this in Gal 5:14, "The entire law is summed up in a single command: 'Love your neighbor as yourself.'" In both cases, Paul follows the heightened significance that Jesus gives to the love of neighbor rule from Lev 19:18 and 34, making it foundational to and fulfilling the entire law.

172. Paul's fundamental contrast of law and grace is anticipated in John 1:17; cf. Matt 5:17–19; 26:28; Mark 7:14–23; 13:31; Luke 16:16; 22:20. When Jesus called people to "take my yoke upon you" in Matt 11:29–30, he probably intended to contrast his gentle yoke and light burden (φορτίον) to the yoke of the law, as seen in the following passage on the Sabbath laws (12:1–14) and the heavy burdens (φορτία) imposed by the scribes in Matt 23:4. 2 Bar. 41:3, "I see many of Thy people who have withdrawn from Thy covenant, and cast from them the yoke of Thy law" (APOT 1:501; cf. Sir 51:26; Pss. Sol. 7:8; Pirqe Aboth 3:8). Jesus affirms the heart of the law, but applies it flexibly (Matt 8:21–22; 23:23; Luke 12:52–53), not legalistically (Luke 10:29–37; John 10:34–35).

Paul's position, he does not establish principles for ethical behavior or church life by citing precepts of the law. Whether it be sexual immorality (1 Cor 5:1–7; 6:12–20), problems related to marriage (ch. 7), to food offered to idols (ch. 8), or to idolatry (ch. 10),[173] he appeals to the believers' standing in Christ. Perhaps because Paul's previous Pharisaic legalism led him to persecute Christians, he carefully avoids expressions that could encourage legalism.

In other words, the rule that women must be silent in church and must be in submission "just as the law says" (1 Cor 14:34) stands in sharp contrast to Paul's repeated theme that believers are no longer under the law. This theological tension between 14:34–35 and Paul's teaching about freedom from the law, along with the absence of appeals to a precept of the law to establish rules for Christian worship elsewhere in Paul's letters, and the absence of any OT statement that matches what 14:34 commands, are irrefutable evidence that 1 Cor 14:34 is out of harmony with what Paul teaches about the law and how he expresses it elsewhere.

6. Contrary to Paul Championing the Downtrodden, Verses 34–35 Subordinate a Weak Social Group

In 1 Corinthians, Paul consistently champions the cause of the downtrodden, as he did for the poor who went hungry at the Lord's Supper in 11:21–22, 33–34. He decries practices that offend the weak in 8:7–13 and 10:31. He attacks the use of lawsuits in 6:1–8, a means of establishing social status.[174] In chapter 11 he supports women praying and prophesying, and in chapters 12 and 14 he repeatedly encourages all to participate in ministry in the church.[175] He emphasizes the oneness of the body, especially defending the parts that seem to be weaker in 10:16–17 and 12:12–31. Chapter 16 appeals for a collection for the poor in Jerusalem. Horrell notes that "the only place in 1 Corinthians where

---

173. The closest Paul comes is the quotation in 1 Cor 10:7 from Exod 32:5–6, when Aaron announced "a festival to the LORD" and "the people sat down to eat and drink and got up to indulge in pagan revelry," but this is not a precept.
174. Cf. David W. J. Gill, "In Search of the Social Elite in the Corinthian Church." *TynBul* 41.2 (1990): 330–31; Andrew D. Clarke, "Secular and Christian Leadership in Corinth," *TynBul* 43.2 (1992): 397–98.
175. Cf. above, pp. 219–20.

the subordination of a social group is demanded is 14:34–35."[176] Thus, its suppression of a weak social group is further evidence that 14:34–35 is an interpolation.

7. The Vocabulary of Verses 34–35 Appear to Mimic that of 1 Timothy 2:11–15

The crucial vocabulary of 14:34–35 reflects 1 Tim 2:12 and its surrounding verses, but restricts women's activities more than 1 Timothy does.[177] The only close NT parallel to "it is not permitted" (ἐπιτρέπεται) in 1 Cor 14:34 is "I am not permitting" (ἐπιτρέπω) in 1 Tim 2:12.[178] In both cases "permit" governs more than one verb, the last introduced by "but" (ἀλλά). Remarkably, both 1 Tim 2:12 and MSS D F G Ψ 0243 1739 1881 𝔐 lat(t) sy of 1 Cor 14:34, reading ὑποτάσσεσθαι, exhibit zeugma, since "permit" fits only the first verb ("to speak"/"to teach"), not the last verb ("to submit"/"to be in quietness").[179] The call for women to be silent and the prohibition of women from speaking in 14:34–35 reflects the double call to women's quietness and a restriction on their teaching in 1 Tim 2:11–12.

Similarly, the command that women be in submission reflects the call for women to "be in all submission" in 1 Tim 2:11. The reference to the law reflects 1 Tim 2:13–14's references to the accounts of creation and fall in Genesis. Μαθεῖν is the infinitive of the identical verb "to learn" in 1 Tim 2:11. Αἰσχρὸν γυναικί ("shame for a woman," 14:35) reflects the repeated concern in 1 Tim 2:9–15 for women to avoid shameful things (2:9, 12) and to do what is fitting for women of propriety (2:10, 15). Both are set in the context of rules for church worship.[180] The parallels are graphically laid out below with lexically related words in bold and words that function as synonyms are underlined:

---

176. D. Horrell argued this in a paper read to the Cambridge NT Seminar on February 2, 1993.
177. See chs. 18–20 on 1 Tim 2:12.
178. Only these are present indicative. Paul's only other occurrence, 1 Cor 16:7, is aorist subjunctive. Cf. Conzelmann, *1 Corinthians*, 246, who cites Weiss regarding 1 Cor 14:34, "The passive points back to an already valid regulation."
179. Cf. BDF §479 (2); Andrew C. Perriman, "What Eve Did, What Women Shouldn't Do: The Meaning of ΑΥΘΕΝΤΕΩ in 1 Timothy 2:12," *TynBul* 44 (1993): 129–30; idem, *Speaking of Women: Interpreting Paul* (Leicester: Apollos, 1998), 157 n. 47. The second infinitive requires, e.g., "I urge" or "I desire." Cf. above, p. 394.
180. Cf. 2:8 ἐν παντὶ τόπῳ, referring to places of church worship; 1 Tim 3:5 and 15 use the word ἐκκλησία.

1 Cor 14:34 αἱ **γυναῖκες ἐν** ταῖς <u>ἐκκλησίαις</u> <u>σιγάτωσαν·</u> **οὐ** γὰρ **ἐπιτρέπεται** αὐταῖς <u>λαλεῖν,</u>

1 Tim 2:12   **γυναικί** 2:8 **ἐν** <u>παντὶ τόπῳ</u> 2:12 <u>διδάσκειν</u> **οὐκ ἐπιτρέπω** ... ἀλλ' <u>εἶναι ἐν ἡσυχίᾳ</u>

1 Cor 14:34–35a ἀλλὰ **ὑποτασσέσθωσαν,** <u>καθὼς καὶ ὁ νόμος λέγει.</u> εἰ δέ τι **μαθεῖν** θέλουσιν,

1 Tim 2:11 ἐν πάσῃ **ὑποταγῇ** (<u>2:13–14 cites the law</u>) 2:11 **μανθανέτω**

1 Cor 14:35b ἐν οἴκῳ τοὺς ἰδίους ἄνδρας ἐπερωτάτωσαν· <u>αἰσχρὸν</u> γάρ ἐστιν   **γυναικί** <u>λαλεῖν</u> **ἐν** <u>ἐκκλησίᾳ.</u>

1 Tim 2:15 <u>τεκνογονίας</u>[181] 2:15 <u>σωφροσύνης</u>[182] 2:10 ὁ <u>πρέπει</u> **γυναιξίν** 2:12 **γυναικί** 2:11 <u>ἐν ἡσυχίᾳ μανθανέτω</u> 2:8 **ἐν** <u>παντὶ τόπῳ</u>

Many scholars view this extensive verbal correspondence as evidence that 1 Tim 2:12 affected the wording of this interpolation.[183] This degree of verbal similarity is evidence that 1 Cor 14:34–35 was interpolated sometime after the writing of 1 Timothy.

8. The Command in Verse 34 Addresses Women "in the churches"

No other command in 1 or 2 Corinthians addresses[184] a category of people "in the churches." This wording more naturally fits a later time when the letter was distributed throughout the churches, not its original audience.[185]

9. The Content of Verses 34–35 Fits an Obvious Motive for Interpolation

The content of 1 Cor 14:34–35 implies an obvious motive, namely, to silence women in church. The dominant social perspective throughout Hellenistic, Roman, and Jewish culture wanted to keep women in their

---

181. "Husbands" and "at home" in 1 Cor 14:35 reflects "childbirth" in 1 Tim 2:15.
182. Asking questions at home in 14:35 reflects the call for propriety (σωφροσύνης) in 1 Tim 2:15.
183. E.g., Richard I. Pervo, "Social and Religious Aspects of the 'Western' Text," pp. 229–41 in *The Living Text: Essays in Honor of Ernest W. Saunders* (ed. Dennis E. Groh and Robert Jewett; New York: Univ. Press of America, 1985), 239; Conzelmann, *1 Corinthians*, 246 and n. 55.
184. Mentioning commands to other churches in 1 Cor 7:17 and 16:1 is entirely different.
185. Hays, *First Corinthians*, 246, argues this.

place.[186] It is not at all surprising that a scribe copying 1 Cor 14 would want to clarify the text, lest its various statements about "all" prophesying, teaching, and otherwise ministering verbally in church be interpreted to include women. Male chauvinist editorial patterns evident in the Western text[187] demonstrate that these attitudes pervaded the church as well as society in general.

The apparent borrowing of terminology from 1 Tim 2:11–15 indicates that the interpolator probably felt justified in this "clarification" of Paul's message. The prominence of women in Christian circles affected by early forms of Gnosticism may have motivated this interpolation. In response to incipient Gnosticism, a polemic soon developed against women taking leadership positions in the church. This eventually resulted in the barring of women from offices over men in the church. It is precisely against the prominence of women in circles influenced by Marcion that Tertullian appealed to 1 Cor 14:34–35.[188] Every manuscript containing 1 Cor 14:34–35, or an allusion to it, comes from after the period of the church's reaction against women in leadership in Gnostic circles.

The earliest references to 1 Cor 14:34–35 acknowledge its seeming tension with other statements in chapter 14 and 11:5. Tertullian treats prophecy as an exception to 14:34–35's prohibition of women speaking in church.[189] Origen resolves the tension by using verses 34–35 as a basis for excluding women from prophesying in church. He states:

> "For you may all prophesy one by one." There would have been an abundance of those speaking and giving instruction. Therefore the apostle permits all to speak in church; he all but goes on to permit women to speak, except he goes on to say, "Let women keep silent in the churches ... [citing 14:34–35 in full]." For as all were speaking and were empowered to speak if revelation is given to them, it states, "Let women be silent in the churches."[190]

Thus, the interpolator was successful in causing subsequent readers to interpret Paul's many references in 1 Cor 14 to "all" in the church par-

---

186. Cf. above, pp. 32–35, 37–40.
187. E.g., Ben Witherington III, "The Anti-Feminist Tendencies of the 'Western' Text in Acts," *JBL* 103 (1984): 82–84; Pervo, "Social and Religious Aspects," 235–41.
188. *Marc.* 5.8.
189. *Marc.* 5.8.11 (cf. above, pp. 220, 252).
190. Jenkins, "Origen on 1 Corinthians," 40–42.

ticipating in vocal ministry narrowly, namely, to exclude women. Consequently, 1 Cor 14:34–35 matches the typical function of interpolations of this size, namely, to clarify the meaning of the text.[191]

The combination of all this internal evidence with the external evidence makes a powerful case that 1 Cor 14:34–35 is an interpolation.

OBJECTIONS TO REGARDING 1 CORINTHIANS 14:34–35 AS AN INTERPOLATION

Three objections have been raised against regarding 1 Cor 14:34–35 as an interpolation. The first is the erroneous view, answered above, that there is no manuscript evidence favoring omission. The second objection is that 14:34–35 is too long to be an interpolation. Finally, based on the assumed validity of the first objection, it is alleged that the interpolation must have been extraordinarily early to be in all surviving texts.

1. Could an Interpolation Be This Long?

Some object that 14:34–35's thirty-six words is too long to be an interpolation. Many interpolations, however, including the most famous ones, make 14:34–35 short by comparison. Almost all textual scholars identify the much longer pericope of the woman taken in adultery in John 7:53–8:11 and the even longer ending of Mark as interpolations. Codex Bezae and Φ insert a sixty-word long interpolation after Matt 20:28. It is a freely reworked version Luke 14:8–10 in much the same way that 1 Cor 14:34–35 is similar to 1 Tim 2:11–15. Codex Bezae adds after Luke 6:4, "On the same day he saw a man working on the Sabbath and said to him, 'Man, if you know what you are doing, you are blessed; but if you do not know, you are accursed and a transgressor of the law.'"[192] Similarly, both Marcion and Ephraem insert Eph 1:21 after ἥτις ἐστίν in Gal 4:26.[193] Romans 3:13–18 was probably interpolated after Ps 14:2. This interpolation likely was made first as a note in the margin but then included in the text of some editions of the LXX,

---

191. Carson ("Silent," *RBMW* 142) notes that "most glosses of substantial size, like this one, seek to explain the text, or clarify the text, or elucidate the text (e.g., John 5:4; Acts 8:37; 1 John 5:7b–8)."

192. Metzger, *Text* (1994), 117.

193. Cf. John James Clabeaux, *A Lost Edition of the Letters of Paul: A Reassessment of the Text of the Pauline Corpus Attested by Marcion* (CBQMS 21; Washington, D.C.: Catholic Biblical Association of America, 1989), 118.

several versions in other languages, and the Hebrew MS De-Rossi, IV, 7 (cod. Kenn. 649).[194]

2. When Would This Interpolation Have Been Added?

Carson alleges that if 14:34–35 was not originally in 1 Corinthians, "the gloss must have been extraordinarily early ... no manuscript that has come down to us attests the omission."[195] Manuscripts, do, however, attest to the omission, including the distigme-obelos in Vaticanus, Fuldensis[Victor mg.], MS 88, and Clement of Alexandria.

The verbal parallels between 1 Cor 14:34–35 and 1 Tim 2:11–15 favor an interpolation date after the writing of 1 Timothy. It is unlikely, however, to have been made after the collected letters of Paul were being distributed in codex form since that should have resulted in more MSS without 14:34–35. *First Clement*, probably written in the last decade of the first century,[196] alludes to Matthew, Mark, Luke, John, Acts, Romans, 1 and 2 Corinthians, Ephesians, 1 Timothy, Titus, Hebrews, James, 1 and 2 Peter, and Revelation.[197] Such extensive allusions are most easily explained if codices of the NT or of Paul's letters were in circulation by then.

The gloss could have been entered into the margin of any manuscript that became the exemplar (or Vorlage of the exemplar) of the first copy of Paul's collected letters as a codex. The gloss could even have been written into the very first codex collecting Paul's letters sometime late in the first century. Since it was common for scribes to write text in the margin that they had omitted by mistake, subsequent scribes would insert 1 Cor 14:34–35 from the margin into the body text.[198]

From that manuscript with 1 Cor 14:34–35 in the margin, at least two copies must have been made, one or more with these two sentences interpolated into the body text after verse 40 and one or more with these two sentences interpolated into the body text after verse 33. The manuscript(s) with 14:34–35 after verse 40 became the exemplar(s) of the Western text-type tradition. Manuscript(s) with 14:34–35 after verse 33 became the

---

194. Cf. C. A. and E. G. Briggs, *A Commentary on the Book of Psalms* (2 vols.; ICC; New York: Charles Scribners' Sons, 1906, 1909), 1:104; P. C. Craigie, *Psalms 1–50* (WBC 19; Waco, Tex.: Word, 1983), 146–47.
195. Carson, "Silent," RBMW 142; cf. Wire, *Corinthian Women Prophets*, 149.
196. Lake, *The Apostolic Fathers*, 1:5 (LCL).
197. Ibid., 8–121.
198. Cf. above, pp. 230–31.

exemplar(s) from which all the non-Western text families descended. This hypothesis makes sense of the entire manuscript tradition and fulfills Bengel's first principle of transcriptional probability. It also explains why 14:34–35 disrupts the flow of Paul's argument in chapter 14 and all the conflicts that 14:34–35 has with other statements in 1 Cor 11–14 and elsewhere in Paul's letters.

The thesis that 1 Cor 14:34–35 is an interpolation fits the external and the internal evidence far better than any other thesis. If 1 Cor 14:34–35 is a non-Pauline interpolation, it does not carry apostolic authority and should not be used as such to restrict the speaking ministries of women, nor should it influence the exegesis of other NT passages.

PART TWO

15

EPHESIANS 5:21–33 AND COLOSSIANS 3:18–19: HUSBAND-WIFE RELATIONSHIPS

In Eph 5:21–33 and Col 3:18–19, the apostle Paul addresses the husband–wife relationship as part of a series of statements about fundamental social relationships in first-century households. These key relationships also include children and parents (Eph 6:1–4; Col 3:20–21) and slaves and masters (Eph 6:5–9; Col 3:22–4:1). Secular "household tables" directly address only the duties of the party in authority (not the subordinate wife, children, or slaves)[1] and serve only the interests of the patriarch.[2] In contrast, Paul addresses all members of the body of Christ, and his goal is the nurture and Christlikeness of each member of the household. Secular "household tables" focus on the patriarch controlling his wife, children, and slaves,[3] but Paul says nothing about husbands controlling their wives, parents their children, or masters their slaves. In contrast to the secular goal of a well-ordered society, Paul's goal is the actualization of the "new humanity,"[4] where all members are filled with the Spirit and nurtured in Christ (Eph 5:18).

The two verses introducing these passages (Eph 5:19–20; Col 3:16–17) share each of the following expressions in Greek: "one another in psalms ...

---

1. Howard Marshall, "Mutual Love and Submission in Marriage: Colossians 3:18–19 and Ephesians 5:21–33," in *Discovering Biblical Equality*, 186 n. 1.
2. E.g., Aristotle, *Nichomachean Ethics* 8.1160b–1161a, "the master's interest is aimed at."
3. Timothy G. Gombis, "A Radically New Humanity: The Function of the *Haustafel* in Ephesians,"*JETS* 48 (2005): 325.
4. Ibid., 323.

hymns ... spiritual songs ... singing ... in your hearts to the ... giving thanks ... everything ... in the name ... of Lord ... Jesus ... Christ ... to the God ... Father." The extensive overlap between these two passages[5] indicates that they deal with the same issues and so can shed light on each other. Since Col 3:18–19 is essentially a subset of Paul's teaching in Eph 5:21–33, this analysis will focus on the more comprehensive passage.

In both passages, Paul guides believers in how they should live in obedience to Christ within these fundamental social structures. He writes against behaviors that would bring discredit to Christ and the gospel and advocates behavior that will advance the testimony and freedom of believers living within those social structures. One of the motivations for encouraging slaves to respect their masters is "so that God's name and our teaching may not be slandered" (1 Tim 6:1) and to make the gospel "attractive" (Titus 2:9–10). In both Ephesians and Colossians, the first half (Eph 1–3; Col 1–2) lays the theological foundation for the practical injunctions for the conduct of believers that will be addressed in the second half of each book (Eph 4–6; Col 3–4), where these "house tables" appear.

Applying these statements to social situations far different from Paul's day requires understanding the principles of the gospel that underlie Paul's statements, the social situation Paul was addressing, and our own social situation. To begin with, patriarchal marriage and family life in Paul's day was markedly different than contemporary Western marriages, both in the dominant position of the husband over his wife, who in many cases was far younger and far less educated, and in the longer period of subservience of children. As well, the socioeconomic structure of slavery is now outlawed and replaced with a system including trade unions and judicial oversight over employer–employee relations. While Paul's wording was framed in order to speak to people in his own social structure, one must not assume that he intended to make those social structures normative for all societies. If Paul were writing today, he would probably give different commands to uphold the same principles.

Advocates of a hierarchical structure in marriage of wives to their husbands in effect endorse the patriarchal structure of marriage that was pervasive in Paul's day. If they were consistent, they probably would also advocate the corresponding dictates of the patriarchal structure (as many

---

5. See the further parallels listed below, pp. 275, 285–87.

used to do) that children, even much older children, ought to be subordinate to their parents, and that slaves ought to be subordinate to their masters. People in contemporary Western culture, however, generally recognize that slavery is dehumanizing, since it puts one human under the absolute command of another and removes the slave's freedom to act according to his or her convictions. Similarly, Western culture affirms that when children reach a certain age or have a full-time job, they should be free to pursue their dreams and marry whom they wish.

Those who affirm a hierarchy of authority of husband over wife, but not between parents and adult children or between slaves and masters, say that creation ordinances demand this only of husbands and wives.[6] Ephesians 5:21–33 and Col 3:18–19, however, say nothing about creation,[7] and the passages that do mention creation, both in the OT and the NT, do not teach a hierarchy of authority based on them.[8] The risk in interpreting "the husband is the head of the wife" as establishing an authority structure in the context of these other "house codes" is that one thereby embraces "a very odd understanding of what marriage is: a relationship in which a wife is basically a person controlled by her husband in every respect in the same way as children and slaves."[9]

PAUL'S TREATMENT OF SLAVERY DETRACTS FROM HIERARCHICAL STRUCTURES

Paul's statements about slavery in Eph 6:5–9 and Col 3:22–4:1 illuminate whether his "house tables" simply endorse hierarchical structures. I. Howard Marshall, in an otherwise insightful article, writes that Paul accepted slavery and did not recognize "that his own teaching contained the seeds of its [slavery's] inevitable abolition."[10] As examined above under Gal 3:28, however, Paul's statements do not endorse this hierarchical structure; rather, they effectively undermine slavery, showing that he did understand the implications of his teachings. His theology of the image of God

---

6. E.g., Peter T. O'Brien, *Colossians* (WBC; Waco, Tex.: Word, 1982), 222–23.
7. *Pace* George W. Knight III, "Husbands and Wives as Analogues of Christ and the Church: Ephesians 5:21–33 and Colossians 3:18–19," *RBMW* 165–78, 177.
8. Cf. above, pp. 41–54, and below, pp. 176–81, 195–98, 399–415.
9. Marshall, "Mutual Love," 193. Those who reject reciprocity do not take the reciprocal pronoun at face value, e.g., Perriman, *Speaking of Women*, 52–53; Gombis, "Radically New Humanity," 323.
10. Marshall, "Mutual Love," 194.

in humankind and of the family of believers who are one in Christ is fundamentally incompatible with slavery. Considering his general command to slaves to gain freedom if possible and his command to the slave-owner Philemon to free his slave Onesimus, Paul's practical advice to slaves should not be equated with acceptance of slavery in the sense of its approval. Paul in 1 Tim 1:10 states that slave-dealing (ἀνδραποδιστής; BDAG 76; LSJ 127–28) is contrary to sound doctrine.[11]

DID PAUL'S VISION OF MARRIAGE DEVELOP AS FAR AS MUTUAL CONSENSUS AND LOVE?

As M. Barth summarizes, from the time Tiberius was emperor of Rome (AD 14–37) both sacral marriage and patriarchal contractual marriage were being supplanted by a third type of marriage, where "a mutual consensus guaranteed the rights of both partners."[12] Marshall asserts that although Paul "moved to love-patriarchalism, and the road is open to mutual love between brothers and sisters in Christ, this final step was not taken by Paul."[13] Marshall insightfully argues, however, that egalitarian relationships in marriage are the logical implication of Paul's teaching and that fidelity to Paul's principles requires this. While it is certainly true that Paul advised how people should respond within their social structures, one should not assume that Paul simply accepted hierarchical marriage as inevitable, particularly since he was not married and urged others with the gift of celibacy to adopt the single life (1 Cor 7:7, 32–35).

It is precisely by analyzing Paul's word choices and how he defines his terms in this and related passages that one can understand Paul's distinctive and creative vision of marriage in Christ. In order to avoid an anachronistic reading of this passage, one ought to consider the evidence for reading this passage without reading back into Paul's words the association of "head" as "leader" that fits English, but is dubious for Greek.[14]

Before addressing husbands and wives, the content of the letter to the Ephesians highlights the importance of mutuality and love:

---

11. Exod 21:16 stipulates the death penalty for "anyone who kidnaps another and either sells him or still has him when he is caught." Cf. God's wrath in Amos 1:6; Joel 3:6; cf. also Lev 25:39–43; 26:13, "Israelites ... must not be sold as slaves."
12. Barth, *Ephesians*, 2:656, cf. above p. 34.
13. Marshall, "Mutual Love," 194.
14. Cf. above, pp. 113–39.

- "Be completely humble and gentle; be patient, bearing with one another in love" (Eph 4:2).
- "We are all members of one body" (4:25).
- "Be kind and compassionate to one another, forgiving each other" (4:32).
- "Live a life of love, just as Christ loved us and gave himself up for us" (5:1).
- "Submit to one another out of reverence for Christ" (5:21).

The Colossians parallel passage states similarly:

- "Clothe yourselves with compassion, kindness, humility" (Col 3:12).
- "Bear with one another" (3:13).
- "Over all these virtues put on love" (3:14).
- "Teach and admonish one another" (3:16).

Paul continues his stress on love in his statements about marriage (Eph 5:25–29, 33; Col 3:19). This contrasts sharply with how rarely the concept of "love" is mentioned in the non-Christian writings about marriage of that time,[15] even within Judaism. "How many rabbis had ever said that a man should love his wife as Yahweh loved Israel?"[16] If husbands love their wives, it transforms the relationship. True love for one's wife is not compatible with a husband completely controlling her life, just as true love is not compatible with a master completely controlling his slave's life or for a parent completely controlling his mature child's life.

Does this absence of absolute control contradict Eph 5:24: "as the church submits to Christ, so also wives [should submit] to their husbands in everything"? And what about the commands in Col 3:20 to children to obey their parents and in 3:22 for slaves to obey their masters "in every respect"? In light of Paul's focus on love, not even these should be interpreted as endorsements of a hierarchy of complete control. Paul's use of the reciprocal pronoun in 5:21, "submitting one to another," indicates that he is not endorsing hierarchical social structures.[17] The reasons he gives

---

15. Cf. Marshall, "Mutual Love," 187 n. 4.
16. Paul K. Jewett, *Man as Male and Female: A Study in Sexual Relationships from a Theological Point of View* (Grand Rapids: Eerdmans, 1975), 145.
17. E.g., Andrew T. Lincoln, *Ephesians* (WBC; Dallas: Word, 1990), 365; Knight, "Husbands and Wives," *RBMW* 166–67; Keener, *Paul, Women,* 157–72; Martin Kitchen, *Ephesians* (New

276 MAN AND WOMAN

for wives to submit are reverence for Christ (Eph 5:21), Christ's command to love, and a desire to follow his example (Eph 5:1–2; Phil 2:3–8), not to uphold a hierarchical structure. Another reason Paul gives for wives to submit to their husbands in Titus 2:5 is "so that no one will malign the word of God."

Likewise, the reason Peter calls wives to submit to their husbands is not to uphold a hierarchical social structure, but "so that [their husbands] will be won over" (1 Pet 3:1–2) by purity, reverence, gentleness, submission, and courageous good deeds (3:3–6). Peter's affirmation that wives and husbands are "heirs with you of the gracious gift of life" implies their equal standing in Christ, not their subordination.

Reinforcing the newness of Paul's vision of marriage is the grand distinctive that marriage is *Christ*-centered. Paul weaves Christ throughout his vision of marriage in Eph 5: "in the fear of Christ" (Eph 5:21), "as to the Lord"[18] (v. 22), "as also Christ" (v. 23), "as to Christ" (v. 24), "as also Christ loved" (vv. 25–27), "just as also Christ" (v. 29), and "in the Lord" (Col 3:18). In Eph 6, Paul continues to focus on Christ, who transforms each household relationship. Children should obey their parents "in the Lord" (v. 1), fathers should bring up their children in the "admonition of the Lord" (v. 4), and slaves should obey their masters "as you would obey Christ" (v. 5), "like slaves of Christ" (v. 6), as "serving the Lord" (v. 7), "the Lord will reward ... slave or free" (v. 8), for "their Master and yours ... [shows] no favoritism" (v. 9).

The context surrounding both Eph 5 and Col 3 highlights the newness of Paul's vision of marriage. Both of these passages depict the life in Christ as radically new. Ephesians 4:17 states, "No longer live as the Gentiles do," and 4:22–24 adds, "put off your old self ... be made new in the attitude of your minds, and put on the new self." Similarly, Col 3:9–10 affirms, "you have taken off your old self with its practices and

---

Testament Readings; London: Routledge, 1994), 99–100; Russ Dudrey, "'Submit Yourselves to One Another': A Socio-Historical Look at the Household Code of Ephesians 5:15–6:9," *ResQ* (1999): 40; Thomas R. Yoder Neufeld, *Ephesians* (Scottdale, Pa.: Herald, 2002), 243–44; John Muddiman, *The Epistle to the Ephesians* (BNTC; Peabody, Mass.: Hendrickson, 2004), 256–57; Marshall, "Mutual Love," 197.

18. Unlike "savior," which Paul uses only once (Phil 3:20) prior to Ephesians, "Lord" occurs approximately 266 times as a title for Christ in the Pauline corpus. Especially with the article, as here, it functions as a name identifying Christ and need carry no special implication of authority into the surrounding vocabulary.

have put on the new self, which is being renewed in knowledge in the image of its Creator."[19]

Finally, Paul's stress in these passages on the unity of the body of Christ reinforces his vision of marriage as mutual love. The body of Christ imagery permeates Ephesians and Colossians.[20] Paul applies this same image of the unity of the body to husband and wife, to such a degree that he says, "he who loves his wife loves himself. After all, no one ever hated his own body, but he feeds and cares for it, just as Christ does the church" (Eph 5:28–29).

PAUL'S VISION OF MARRIAGE IN EPHESIANS 5:21–33

In Eph 5, Paul compares the relationship between husband and wife[21] to the relationship between Christ and the church. This passage, often read at weddings, is famous for its call for wives to submit to their husbands and for husbands to love their wives. Some people say that Paul's commands to husbands and wives are irreversible, that wives are to submit to husbands, not vice versa, and that Paul calls only husbands to love their wives, not vice versa. Yet Eph 5:2 commands all believers to "live a life of love, just as Christ loved us." Thus, Paul taught that wives, too, should mirror Christ. Titus 2:4 specifically calls wives "to love their husbands." Consequently, Paul calls both husbands and wives to love each other. Furthermore, the dependence of verse 22 for its verb on verse 21's reciprocal "submit to one another," shows that Paul expects husbands to submit to their wives, too.

Why, then, does Paul call women to "submit" and men to "love"? Paul highlights for women and men what each tends to need to hear most. Women tend to need a call to submit, men to love. Cultural issues add to the importance of both commands. Graeco-Roman and Jewish social conventions called for the subordination of wives to their husbands.[22] Titus 2:5 explains that women are to submit to their husbands "so that no one will malign the word of God." Paul opposes cultural denigration of relations with women by telling husbands, "love your wives."

---

19. The section on 1 Corinthians 7 discussed above shows how thoroughly Paul describes the rights and privileges of wives and husbands as equal and reciprocal.

20. Eph 1:23; 2:16; 4:1–16; 5:23, 30 (cf. 2:19–22 substituting "building/temple"); Col 1:18, 24; 2:19; 3:15.

21. "To their own husbands" in v. 22, "to their husbands" in v. 24, and the articles specifying "the wives" in 5:22, 24 and "the wife" in 5:23 show that Paul intends to refer to "wives," not "women."

22. Cf. Marshall, "Mutual Love," 186, 188, 192; Witherington, *Earliest Churches*, 8, 17.

There are two crucial issues that qualify and define Paul's vision of marriage in Eph 5:21–33; one is syntactical, linking verse 22 to verse 21; the other is grammatical—that "savior" is in apposition to "head." The syntactical issue concerns the structure of Paul's argument. Paul embeds his call to wives in a single long sentence that includes everything in Eph 5:18–24. The sentence includes two primary verbs, contrasting present imperatives: "Do not get drunk on wine … but be filled with the Spirit." A series of participles then illustrate life filled with the Spirit. The final participle provides the context and verb for Paul's appeal to wives (lit.): "submitting to one another out of reverence for Christ [v. 21], wives to your own husbands as to the Lord [v. 22], for the husband is the head of the wife as Christ is the head of the church [v. 23], he the savior of the body [v. 24]; but as the church submits to Christ, so also ought wives to their husbands in everything." Even the complementarians George W. Knight III and James Bassett Hurley agree with this author that this sentence links the submission of wives to husbands in verse 22 to the principle of mutual submission, giving one instance of it.[23]

Virtually all critical editions of the Greek NT, including the NA[27], UBS[4], Nestle, Westcott and Hort, Tasker, Souter, Alford, Tischendorf, and Goodrich and Lukaszewski (2003) follow $\mathfrak{P}^{46}$ B Cl[1/2] Origen Greek mss[acc. to Jerome] in having no verb in Eph 5:22. Verse 21 expresses the verb "submit" that must be supplied for verse 22. Later manuscripts add the imperative "submit" to Eph 5:22 either as a second or third person plural after either "women" or "men." Metzger explains that the shorter reading "accords with the succinct style of the author's admonitions, and explain[s] the other readings as expansions introduced for the sake of clarity, the main verb being required especially when the words αἱ γυναῖκες stood at the beginning of a scripture lesson."[24] Scribes by the mid-fourth century apparently split the original paragraph after verse 21 to make Paul's statements about marriage a distinct unit.

The unanimity of the inclusion of some form of "submit" somewhere in every surviving manuscript of Eph 5:22 written after AD 350, but its omission in each surviving manuscript prior to AD 350, shows two things.

---

23. Knight, "Husbands and Wives," RBMW 165–67 and 492 n. 1; contrast the editors' n. 6, pp. 493–94. Hurley, Biblical Perspective, 139–41.
24. Textual Commentary[2], 541.

First, it shows that, once included, no scribe would remove "submit" from 5:22. The manuscripts and early patristic evidence thus confirm that the absence of "submit" was not caused by its removal, but indeed represents the original text of 5:22. Second, it shows how important the inclusion of "submit" is in order for 5:22 to stand as the beginning of a paragraph on marriage.

These two together provide irrefutable evidence that the original text did link verse 22 with verse 21, just as both the NA[27] and the UBS[4] do. The NA[25] treats Eph 5:15–6:9 as a single paragraph, respecting the integrity of Paul's sentence. All this evidence links the submission of wives to their own husbands to the principle that Christians should submit to one another out of reverence for Christ. This dependence of verse 22 on verse 21 is hidden from readers of English translations of this passage that begin a new paragraph at verse 22,[25] thereby separating the submission of wives to husbands from Paul's command to submit to one another.

One of the most socially revolutionary and linguistically creative[26] teachings of Paul is his command, "submit to one another out of reverence for Christ." The combination of "to place oneself under" with the reciprocal pronoun defies social stratification, but it fits perfectly with Paul's view of mutuality in the body of Christ in Ephesians: "bear with one another in love" (4:2), "you are all members of one another" (4:25), and "be kind and compassionate to one another, forgiving each other as in Christ God forgave you" (4:32).[27] Every occurrence of ἀλλήλων in Paul's letters fits its identification in BDAG 46 as "the reciprocal pronoun" with the English equivalents, "each other, one another, mutually."[28] A reciprocal pronoun by definition is one "expressing mutual action or relation."[29] Neither LSJ nor BDAG lists any meaning that escapes the idea of reciprocity. Writers choose it only for

---

25. E.g., ASV, HCSB, ESV, NAB, NEB, NIV, TNIV, NRSV, REB, TEV, JND, Fenton, Goodspeed, Phillips, Weymouth, Williams. Beck, Berkeley, New Berkeley, JB, LB, REV, RSV, and TNT correctly link v. 21 to 22.

26. Aristotle, *Politics*, I 1259B, which comes closest, states only, "In most constitutional states the citizens rule and are ruled by turns." Nigel Turner, *Christian Words* (Edinburgh: T&T Clark, 1980), xiii, notes particular creativity in Christian words concerning life within the fellowship of the Christian Church.

27. Cf. the obvious reciprocal uses of "one another" in the other Pauline letters: Rom 1:12, 27; 2:15; 12:5, 10 (twice), 16; 13:8; 14:13, 19; 15:5, 7, 14; 16:16; 1 Cor 7:5; 11:33; 12:25; 16:20; 2 Cor 13:12; Gal 5:13, 15 (twice), 17, 26 (twice); Eph 4:2, 25, 32; Phil 2:3; Col 3:9, 13; 1 Thess 3:12; 4:9, 18; 5:11, 15; 2 Thess 1:3; Titus 3:3.

28. As argued by Harris, "Eve's Deception," 340; and his "The Buck Stops Where? Authority in the Early Church and Current Debate on Women's Ministry," *Interchange* 41 (1987): 31.

29. *Webster's New World Dictionary*, 1184.

situations where there is mutuality or reciprocity. Even George W. Knight III accepts mutual submission here, as he also does in 1 Pet 5:4–5, and he argues that Eph 6:5–9 "implies reciprocity between masters and slaves."[30]

Grudem, however, proposes an extreme view of reciprocity in order to create the unwarranted impression that ἀλλήλων does not always go both ways. He writes, "The reason that the mutual submission interpretation is so common is that interpreters *assume* that the Greek pronoun *allēlous* ('one another') must be completely reciprocal (that it must mean 'everyone to everyone')."[31] But the straw man idea he proposes of "everyone to everyone" is not commonly, if ever, assumed. Grudem alleges that ἀλλήλων means merely "some to others"[32] in Matt 24:10, "many will betray and hate each other"; Luke 2:15, "the shepherds said to one another"; 12:1, "they were trampling on one another"; 24:32, "they asked each other"; 1 Cor 11:33, "when you come together to eat, wait for each other"; Gal 6:2, "carry each other's burdens"; and Rev 6:4, "men slay one another."

Each, however, does refer to a reciprocal situation involving the group(s) identified. Matthew 24:10 does not state that everyone will betray everyone else, but it does state that many will betray and hate each other. If there were no mutuality or reciprocity, the text would not have used the reciprocal pronoun in "hate each other," "betray each other," "said to one another" or "asked each other." Grudem alleges of Rev 6:4, "It simply means that *some* killed *others*." If, however, John had simply envisaged men slaying others but never being slain, he would not have used the reciprocal pronoun in "men slay one another." If Paul had intended "bear one another's burdens" (Gal 6:2) to be always one way, the same people always bearing the burdens of others but their burdens never being borne by others, he would not have used the reciprocal pronoun.

Second Corinthians 8:13–15 proves Paul's reciprocal intent. The nature of the mutuality or reciprocity must be determined by the context, but wherever there is a reciprocal pronoun there is reciprocity. Consequently, when Grudem states "submitting to one another" in Eph 5:21 means merely "some be subject to others"[33] and denies mutuality, he is violating the heart of the meaning of the reciprocal pronoun. By claiming

---

30. Knight, "Husbands and Wives," *RBMW* 166.
31. Grudem, *RBMW* 493 n. 6; cf. also idem, *EF* 196–98.
32. Grudem, *EF* 197.
33. Ibid.

that his interpretation "has a 'reciprocal' meaning,"[34] he is stripping "reciprocal" of its universal core of meaning, for he denies any sense of reciprocal submission and makes it "a one-directional activity": "Be subject to others in the church who are in positions of authority over you."[35]

Paul's vision of mutual submission within the body of Christ permeates his writings, such as: "in humility consider others better than yourselves. Each of you should look not only to your own interests, but also to the interests of others," which is modeled on Christ's voluntary subordination of his own interests (Phil 2:3–8). It is the attitude of serving one another after the pattern of Christ, who takes the role of a slave in washing the feet of the disciples as a model for them to follow. This is contrary to the pattern of the world, but it is perfectly in keeping with Paul's picture of how the members of the body of Christ should interrelate.

BDAG (1042) defines ὑποτάσσω here, "Of submission in the sense of voluntary yielding in love, **1 Cor 16:16; Eph 5:21; 1 Pt 5:5b v.l.;** **1 Cl 38:1.**" Probably the earliest noncanonical Christian letter, *1 Clem.* 37:5–38:1, explains the view of the church of Rome that submission to one's neighbor in the body is incumbent upon each member of the church:

> Let us take our body; the head is nothing without the feet, likewise the feet are nothing without the head; the smallest members of our body are necessary and valuable to the whole body, but all work together and are united in a common subjection [ὑποταγῇ] to preserve the whole body. Let, therefore, our whole body be preserved in Christ Jesus, and let each be subject [ὑποτασσέθω] to his neighbour, according to the position granted to him.[36]

Clement's affirmation that all "are united in a common subjection … let each be subject to his neighbor," contradicts Grudem's contention that submission in the body of Christ is one-directional.[37]

None of the italicized meanings given for ὑποτάσσω in BDAG 1042 or LSJ 1897 include in their definition: "to someone else's authority"[38] or

---

34. Ibid.
35. Ibid., 198, 197, following the view of Hurley, *Biblical Perspective*, 142–43. Cf. the same criticism of Grudem by Linda L. Belleville, "Women in Ministry," in *Two Views on Women in Ministry* (ed. James R. Beck and Craig L. Blomberg; Grand Rapids: Zondervan, 2001), 75–154, 132.
36. Kirsopp Lake, *The Apostolic Fathers* 1:72–73 (LCL).
37. Grudem, *EF* 198.
38. *Pace* Grudem, *EF* 193, cf. 198.

anything else specifying "authority." Nor is authority apparent in "the creation was subjected to frustration" (Rom 8:20, BDAG 621). The question is: "Can one submit to an equal or subordinate?" The following five instances show the answer is "yes":

1. "The spirits of the prophets are subject to [ὑποτάσσω] the control of the prophets" (1 Cor 14:32).

2. First Corinthians 16:15–16 urges the "brothers" in Corinth to "submit" (ὑποτάσσω) to the household of Stephanas, who devoted (τάσσω) themselves to the service of their fellow Christians. It is to those who have so submitted themselves for service that Paul calls the Corinthians to "submit." It is virtually inconceivable that no one in the church had higher authority than anyone in the household of Stephanas. There must have been at least one woman,[39] slave, or other person in the household of Stephanas in a lower position of authority than some other church member.

3. First Peter 2:18–3:1 presents Jesus as an "example" of "submitting" (ὑποτάσσω) even to unjust treatment. Jesus submitted himself by washing his disciples' feet (John 13:1–17) and by serving (Matt 20:25–28; Luke 22:25–27).

4. Luke 2:51 shows that Jesus at age twelve voluntarily submitted (ὑποτάσσω) himself to Joseph and Mary.

5. Eph 5:21: "Submit [ὑποτάσσω] to one another." Each of Paul's "one anothers" addressed to the entire church and applies to all believers, never to selected segments only.[40]

Grudem asserts "the plain sense" of subordination by wives, children, and slaves[41] as though it is a single unvarying concept. Aristotle, however, in *Nichomachean Ethics* 8.1160B–1161A, rejects the autocratic subordination of wife to husband: "When the husband controls everything, he transforms the relationship into an oligarchy, for he governs in violation of fitness, and not in virtue of superiority. And sometimes when the wife

---

39. The reference to Priscilla in v. 19 shows that Paul's thinking did not exclude women while writing this passage.

40. Rom 1:12; 12:5, 10 (2x), 16; 13:8; 14:13, 19; 15:5, 7, 14; 16:16; 1 Cor 11:33; 12:25; 16:20; 2 Cor 13:12; Gal 5:13, 15 (2x), 26 (2x); 6:2; Eph 4:2, 25, 32; 5:21; Phil 2:3; Col 3:9, 13; 1 Thess 3:12; 4:9, 18; 5:11, 15; 2 Thess 1:3; Titus 3:3.

41. Grudem, EF 189–190.

is an heiress, it is she who rules. In these cases authority goes not by virtue but by wealth and power, as in an oligarchy."

Tertullian, too, in his book to his wife describes the husband–wife union as deeply mutual, each instructing, exhorting, and supporting the other: "What a union of two believers — one hope, one vow, one discipline, and one worship! They are brother and sister, two fellow-servants, one spirit and one flesh.... They pray together, fast together, instruct, exhort, and support each other."[42]

Since "submitting to one another" in Eph 5:21 is "voluntary yielding in love," and since the verb of 5:22 is borrowed from 5:21, the wife's submission naturally carries the same sense of "voluntary yielding in love." Since subjection to another's authority is not voluntary, mutual submission does not require but is in tension with subjection to another's authority.

The second crucial issue is the grammatical apposition in Eph 5:23 that defines Christ "head of the church" as "savior of the body." Robertson's *Grammar* 399 identifies this in Eph 5:23 as "emphatic apposition." J. Armitage Robinson explains:

> This last clause is added to interpret the special sense in which Christ is here called "the head of the church".... "Christ is the head of the church, as being Himself the saviour of the body." It is the function of the head to plan the safety of the body, to secure it from danger and to provide for its welfare. In the highest sense this function is fulfilled by Christ for the Church: in a lower sense it is fulfilled by the husband for the wife.... The Apostle interpreted the headship of Christ by the insertion of the clause "being Himself the saviour of the body."[43]

Apposition is "the placing of a word or expression beside another so that the second explains and has the same grammatical construction as the first."[44] In this case, apposition is abundantly clear since the grammatical construction of the parallel expressions exactly match: subject, descriptor, genitive article, descriptor's object in the genitive:

42. Tertullian, *Ad Uxorem*, 1.II.c.8, translation from Schaff, *Christian Church*, 2:364–65.
43. J. Armitage Robinson, *St. Paul's Epistle to the Ephesians* (2nd ed.; London: James Clarke, 1904), 124–25. Knight, "Husbands and Wives," *RBMW* 494 n. 12, cites this function of "head" with approval.
44. *Webster's New World Dictionary*, s.v. "apposition."

Christ	head	of the church	ὁ Χριστὸς	κεφαλὴ	τῆς ἐκκλησίας
He	savior[45]	of the body	αὐτός	σωτὴρ	τοῦ σώματος

There is no question that "he" (αὐτός) is Christ and that "the church" is "the body." Paul places "savior" in apposition to "head," showing that he intends "head" to be understood as equivalent in meaning to "savior." Recognizing this apposition is crucial in interpreting "head" since, apart from this explanation, Paul's intention would not be clear. The appositional structure is evident, for example, in the ASV: "Christ also is head of the church, *being* himself the savior of the body"; in the NASB: "Christ also is the head of the church, He Himself *being* the Savior of the body"; in Weymouth: "Christ also is head of the church, Himself the Saviour of the body"; and in the Amplified: "Christ is the Head of the Church, Himself the Savior of [His] body."

If Paul had intended to convey "head" in the sense of authority, he should have used an appositional phrase like, "he the authority of the body," but instead, he explained it with "savior." His subsequent description of Christ's relationship to his body, the church, states nothing about Christ's authority either, but says that Christ loved and gave himself for the church (Eph 5:25), to make her holy, cleansed without stain, and blameless (5:26–27), feeding and caring for her (5:29). These are his actions as savior, the source of life and nourishment of his body, the church. Paul calls the husband to imitate Christ's actions in relations with his wife (5:28–31, 33), not to assume authority over her.

Unlike Greek,[46] the most common figurative meaning of "head" in English is "leader/ruler/chief/director/headmaster/manager/boss," so it is the way most English readers understand the English translation "head" in Eph 5:23. Furthermore, most versions[47] conceal Paul's use of apposition to

---

45. This and Phil 3:20 are Paul's only uses of "savior" (σωτήρ) prior to the Pastoral Epistles, and neither has a definite article. Consequently, "savior" is clearly descriptive, not a title, so it should not be capitalized.
46. Cf. above pp. 121–23; also Payne, "*Kephalē*," 118–32.
47. E.g., the NIV's, "Christ is the head of the church, his body, of which he is the Savior." By adding "of which" and the verb "is" the NIV changes the appositional phrase from explaining "head" as "savior" into a new clause that modifies "body" and makes "savior" grammatically unrelated to

define "head." Describing these passages as about "headship" exacerbates the lexical anachronism since "headship" has only one meaning in English: "the position of authority of a chief or leader; leadership; command."[48] The word "headship" never even occurs in the NT. Furthermore, the absence of references to "brain" or "nerves" in Paul's letters and his use of "heart" fifty-two times for functions now attributed to the brain (e.g., "no heart has conceived God's plans," 1 Cor 2:9) make it doubtful that Paul regarded the head as the "command center" of the body.[49] Even if "leader" had been a common metaphorical meaning of "head" (κεφαλή) in Paul's day, his use of "savior" in apposition to "head" shows that he did not intend "leader" here, since "savior" is semantically unrelated to "leader."

The parallel use of "head" in Col 1:18 confirms that Paul could use this image to convey "source." Colossians 1:15–20 is a poem about the person and work of Christ. It begins in verse 15 with the fundamental assertion of his nature, "He is the image of the invisible God, the firstborn of[50] all creation," namely, first in honor.[51] Verses 16–18 give reasons why Christ is first in honor: in him all things were created, all things were created through and for him, he is before all things, and in him all things hold together, "and he is the head of his body, the church; he is the source of the body's life; he is the firstborn Son who was raised from death" (TEV).[52]

"He is the head of the body" combines a memorable anatomical pair (head/body), but it begs for explanation, which Paul provides with a pair of appositional phrases. First, he defines body by apposition, "the body, the church [τοῦ σώματος, τῆς ἐκκλησίας]." Then he explains "head" with the immediately following appositional phrase in verse 18, "who is the source [ὅς ἐστιν ἡ[53] ἀρχή]," which exactly matches the grammatical construction of "he is the head [αὐτός ἐστιν ἡ κεφαλή]." The word for "source," ἀρχή,

---

"head." In addition, the NIV's insertion of definite articles and capitalization of "Savior" turns it into a title, further concealing Paul's explanation of "head."

48. *Webster's New World Dictionary*, s.v. "headship."
49. Payne, *"Kephalē,"* 119–21; above, pp. 122–23.
50. The NIV adds "over all creation" but no Greek manuscript adds a preposition suggesting a relationship of authority.
51. PGL 1202 notes that this word used of Christ as eternal Son, "denotes primacy of honour, not temporal priority."
52. Cf. "He is, moreover, the head of the body, the church. He is its origin, the first to return from the dead" (NEB).
53. Both of the earliest MSS of Colossians, 𝔓[46] and B, include ἡ ἀρχή with no punctuation separating this appositional phrase from what precedes. 075 0278 6 104 1175 1739 1881 *pc* also include ἡ ἀρχή.

commonly refers to originating power, source, or origin,[54] and this sense fits the context perfectly. Christ is the source of the church, the one who gives it life and sustains its life.

This understanding of "head" is immediately confirmed by the following reference to Christ's resurrection in verse 18, by Paul's explanation of Christ's goal in verse 20 ("to reconcile to himself all things ... by making peace through his blood, shed on the cross"), and the theme in verses 21–23 of reconciliation "by Christ's physical body through death to present you holy in his sight." This all reinforces that Christ is the source of the church as he is the source of creation, "in him all things were created ... all things were created through him" (v. 16).

The reference to Christ as the head of the body follows a series of other affirmations of Christ as the source of all things as Creator (Col 1:15–17). The meaning of κεφαλή ("head") in this context is that Christ is the source of the church through his redemptive death and resurrection. Because of who Christ is, the creator of all things and of the church, he is rightly first[55] in everything (Col 1:18). The parallels with Eph 5:23 and its goal in verse 27 are striking:

Eph 5:23	Christ	head	of the church	ὁ Χριστὸς	κεφαλή	τῆς ἐκκλησίας
	he	savior	of the body	αὐτὸς	σωτήρ	τοῦ σώματος
Col 1:18	He is	the head	of the body,	αὐτός ἐστιν	ἡ κεφαλὴ	τοῦ σώματος
	who is	the source	the church	ὅς ἐστιν	ἡ ἀρχή	τῆς ἐκκλησίας
Eph 5:27	the goal:	present	holy and blameless	παραστήσῃ	ἁγία καὶ ἄμωμος	
Col 1:22	the goal:	present	holy and blameless	παραστῆσαι	ἁγίους καὶ ἀμώμους	

54. Cf. LSJ 252, "beginning, origin ... source"; BDAG 138 ἀρχή 1.b *"beginning, origin* in the absolute sense"; 2. "one with whom a process begins, *beginning*" Col 1:18 3. "the first cause, *the beginning.*"
55. The NIV changes the verb from "be" (γένηται) to "have" and translates the closing participle, "being first," with a noun that is not listed in BDAG 892, "the supremacy." It thereby focuses on the idea of authority where the Greek instead affirms that Christ is first/preeminent in everything.

The almost identical wording favors understanding κεφαλή similarly in both: Christ as κεφαλή is the source of the church (Col 1:18), the source of its life and nourishment as savior (Eph 5:23).

The key to understanding this metaphor in Eph 5:23 is to recognize its originality, as affirmed by Markus Barth:

> Jewish and medical sources ... never associate "headship" with "saviorship."[56] ... [Furthermore,] no evidence has yet been produced from literary or other sources that anybody near or far from Paul's environment held the opinion ... "The husband is the head of the wife" [so it] must be understood as original with the author of Ephesians. In consequence, it has to be explained by the context of Ephesians in which it is found.[57]

Since none of the forty-eight English metaphorical equivalents LSJ lists for "head" means "savior" ("source" is the closest), this image of Christ as "head-savior" of his "body," modeling how husbands should be "head" to their wives is not a dead metaphor with a simple established meaning, but is an original living metaphor. Paul's explanation of "head" by apposition implies his awareness that the meaning of "head" of the church would not be self-evident to his readers.

The apposition, "he savior of the body," helps identify the message of the metaphor in two ways. First, it identifies the concept Paul intends to convey by the metaphor "head," namely, "savior." Second, it identifies that Paul has in mind the relationship between "head" and "body." By his apposition Paul invites his readers to think about what a head does for a body and to apply this both to Christ's saving relationship to the church and to a husband's relationship to his wife. Paul's following statements about Christ and husbands identify a series of ways they function as "head": providing love (5:25, 28, 33), cleansing through the word (5:26–27), nourishing (ἐκτρέφει), and literally "keeping it warm," namely, cherishing it, caring for it, and protecting it, especially from cold (5:29).

---

56. There are, however, military texts that associate "head" and "savior," e.g., Herodotus, 7.148, "Guarding thy head [κεφαλή] from the blow; and the head shall shelter [σαώσει from σώζω] the body"; see A. D. Godley, *Herodotus* 3:456–457 (LCL). Plutarch's Lives, *Pelopidas* 2.1–2, "the general [is] like [ἐοίκασιν] the head [κεφαλῇ] ... inasmuch as their safety [σωτηρία] depends on him, and their destruction too.... His first duty is to save [σώζειν] the one who saves [σώζοντα] everything else"; see Bernadette Perrin, *Plutarch's Lives* 5:342–45 (LCL).

57. Barth, *Ephesians*, 2:617–18.

    Paul's "head" metaphor reflects common ideas about the head. Hippocrates describes the head as "the source of supply for the members of the body.... From the head, the veins reach to every part of the body and give nourishment [ἡ τροφή] and provide [διαδίδωμι] what the body needs (*Nat. Hom.* 19.11).[58]

    Paul's metaphor invites his readers to consider how a head does these sorts of things for its body. This metaphor can trigger new ways of perceiving these head–body relationships. For instance, through its mouth the head provides nourishment to keep it warm and water to cleanse the body, washing out items that corrupt. Through its eyes, ears, nose, and tongue, it alerts the body to danger and protects it. Through its lips, it expresses words of love and exhortation that purifies. The head is the source of all these things for the body. Paul's metaphor effectively resonates with his readers, inviting these associations, because "source" was an established meaning of "head,"[59] as LSJ 945 states, "generally, *source, origin.*"

    Consequently, "head" encourages readers to consider how a head is a source for the body. Paul prepares his readers for this understanding in Eph 4:16, which teaches that Christ the head provides for the body.[60] As Fee and Marshall have argued from Paul's cultural context, "the husband is the person on whom the wife depends just as the church depends on Christ, and therefore submission is appropriate. The statement that Christ is the Savior of the body favors such an understanding of the husband as essentially the provider, the one who cares for his wife."[61] Wives depended on their husbands as the source of food, clothing, shelter, the physical source of her children, and her emotional source of love.

    Lest there be any ambiguity of the sense in which Christ is savior, in Eph 5:25 Paul presents Christ's self-giving as a pattern for husbands to follow, "Husbands, love your wives, just as Christ loved the church

---

58. Clinton E. Arnold, "Jesus Christ: 'Head' of the Church (Colossians and Ephesians)," in *Jesus of Nazareth: Lord and Christ: Essays on the Historical Jesus and New Testament Christology* (ed. Joel B. Green and Max Turner; Grand Rapids: Eerdmans, 1994), 352; W. H. S. Jones, *Hippocrates* 4:30–33 (LCL).
59. Cf. above, pp. 123–28 on the "source" meaning in Greek and Pauline literature.
60. Cf. Barth, *Ephesians*, 1:186; cf. also Col 2:19, where Christ the "head" causes the church to grow.
61. Marshall, "Mutual Love," 198. Cf. Gordon D. Fee, "The Cultural Context of Ephesians 5:18–6:9," *Priscilla Papers* 16, no. 1 (2002): 3–8; Gordon D. Fee, "Praying and Prophesying," 153 n. 33, 154.

and gave himself up for her." For husbands, as for Christ, the goal is the purity of the bride (vv. 26–27). Verses 28–29 continue the analogy, "In this same way, husbands ought to love their wives as their own bodies ... just as Christ does the church." When a husband is the "head" of his wife in this sense, his wife has good reason to submit to him (5:23 "because," ὅτι), and submission to loving nourishment becomes a joyous response. Meditation on this increases appreciation for what Christ the head provides for the church's ongoing life, evoking willing submission. Christ's love, nourishment, and protection give believers the security that enables them to submit to one another (v. 21). Appropriately, Robertson's *Grammar* (1206) identifies Paul's use of "body" in Ephesians as "the greatest metaphor in the NT."

The grammatical construction of Eph 5:23 makes it clear that the sense in which "the husband is the head of the wife" is "as [ὡς] Christ is head of the church, he savior of the body." Ephesians 5:24 confirms that it is "as [ὡς] the church submits to Christ that so also [οὕτως καί] wives [are to submit] to their husbands in everything." Since Christ never asks the church to do anything wrong and since it is as the church submits to Christ that wives are to submit to their husbands, this command does not require submission that would entail doing anything wrong.[62] If a husband asks his wife to do something wrong, as Ananias asked Sapphira to join in his deception, she should not submit to that, as her punishment by death in Acts 5:7–11 proves. The principle of Acts 5:29 also applies to wives, "We must obey God rather than men!"

How should Bible versions translate "head" for readers who because of English usage miss its better-established Greek meaning "source" as well as Paul's explanation of his meaning by apposition? First, in order to preserve the "head" and "body" interrelated imagery and to encourage readers to think about this richly instructive living metaphor, "head" should be in the translation. Second, the translation should clearly reflect Paul's appositional structure. Third, a note should be added to both passages explaining how Paul's apposition clarifies that by "head" he means "source," an established Greek meaning for "head." The note for Col 1:18 could be as simple as, "Paul explains that 'head' means

---

62. Cf. F. F. Bruce, *The Epistle to the Colossians, to Philemon and to the Ephesians* (Grand Rapids: Eerdmans, 1984), 386 n. 89.

'source' here." The note for Eph 5:23 could be, "Paul explains that 'head' means 'savior' here, for Christ is the source of life, love, and nourishment for the church as husbands should be for their wives. 'Source' is better established as a meaning for 'head' in Hellenistic Greek than 'leader' or 'authority.'"

16

1 TIMOTHY 2:8–15: INTRODUCTION: THE EPHESIAN CHURCH SITUATION ADDRESSED IN 1 TIMOTHY

The most crucial verse regarding women in church leadership is 1 Tim 2:12, often translated, "I do not permit a woman to teach or to have authority over a man." Since this is the only verse in Scripture that, at least according to this translation, prohibits women from teaching or being in positions of authority over men, and since the meaning of the word sometimes translated "have authority over" (αὐθεντεῖν) is debated and occurs nowhere else in Scripture, it demands careful examination.

First Timothy is a letter. Raymond F. Collins correctly notes, "Of all literary genres it is the epistolary genre that is most conditioned by the coordinates of time and space, historical and relational circumstances.... They are ad hoc compositions whose essential import relates immediately and directly only to the situation that dictated their composition."[1] It is crucial, therefore, to understand the problem that led to this restriction on women teaching.

IS 1 TIMOTHY A LETTER FROM PAUL?

To lay a foundation for the analysis of 1 Tim 2:12, the context and overall aims of the letter must be examined. If Paul wrote these verses in 1 Timothy, one ought to interpret it from the framework of Paul's teachings about

---

1. Raymond F. Collins, *1 & 2 Timothy and Titus: A Commentary* (NTL; Louisville: Westminster John Knox, 2002), 75.

women elsewhere. Many scholars believe that 1 Timothy and the other Pastoral Epistles teach some doctrines that are inconsistent with Paul's theology.[2] Consequently, they deny its authority and appeal elsewhere (a canon within the canon) for authoritative teaching about women.

There are too many issues regarding the question of the authorship of 1 and 2 Timothy and Titus, both about their content (e.g., vocabulary) and their historical situation, to address them thoroughly here. Nevertheless, the issue is unavoidable for hermeneutics and authority. Judgments regarding authorial intent depend on who the author is. Apostolic authority also depends on authorship. If the letter's claim to be from Paul is false, then the letter is not inerrant and the authority of its other statements becomes suspect. The primary objection to Paul's authorship (variations in style and vocabulary) may result from his giving his secretaries some freedom of expression.

Perhaps because of his "thorn in the flesh" (2 Cor 12:7) — probably poor eyesight (Gal 4:15) evidenced by his large distinctive handwriting (Gal 6:11; 2 Thess 3:17) — Paul typically used a secretary (Rom 16:22; 1 Cor 16:21; Gal 6:11; Col 4:18; 2 Thess 3:17). Amanuenses, or secretaries, of epistle writers had varying degrees of freedom, even regarding word choice and content. In general, the more trusted the secretary, the more freedom he or she had in composition. C. F. D. Moule and others argue that Luke was Paul's amanuensis for the Pastorals.[3] Luke was a frequent companion of Paul as is evident in the "we" passages of Acts. Luke was with Paul in his first Roman imprisonment; note Paul's greetings from "our dear friend Luke" in Col 4:14 and from Luke "my fellow worker" in Phlm 24. If Luke was Paul's secretary, as is implied by "only Luke is with me" in 2 Tim 4:11, he presumably would have had relatively broad freedom in composition.

The many similarities in style between Luke – Acts and the Pastoral Epistles also give evidence that Luke was indeed Paul's secretary.[4] Marshall notes that out of 554 words the Pastorals have in common with Luke – Acts, 34 occur nowhere else in the NT. Although Luke – Acts is 37 percent longer than the other ten Pauline epistles, the Pastorals share even more words

---

2.   E.g., Robin Scroggs, "Paul and the Eschatological Woman," *JAAR* 40 (1972): 283 – 303.
3.   C. F. D. Moule, "The Problem of the Pastoral Epistles: A Reappraisal," *BJRL* 47 (1965): 430 – 52; August Strobel, "Schreiben des Lukas? Zum sprachlichen Problem der Pastoralbriefe," *NTS* 15 (1968 – 69): 191 – 210; George W. Knight III, *The Pastoral Epistles: A Commentary on the Greek Text* (NIGTC; Grand Rapids: Eerdmans, 1992), 4 – 52.
4.   See the concise summary of the data and earlier analyses in Knight, *Pastoral Epistles*, 48 – 49.

with the other Pauline epistles (574 words), and 55 of these occur nowhere else in the NT.[5] This indicates that although there is a strong Lukan influence, there is an even stronger Pauline influence on the vocabulary of the Pastorals. This result fits perfectly with the thesis that the Pastorals were authored by Paul but penned by Luke, entrusted with a significant degree of freedom in composition. This explains why some of the vocabulary and syntax is not typical of Paul but sits side by side with many expressions that are characteristic of Paul.

Regarding the historical situation, if Paul's first Roman imprisonment ended any time between AD 61 and 63, there would be time for the events mentioned in the Pastoral Epistles to occur and for Paul to have been reimprisoned in Rome and executed under Nero during his persecutions from AD 64–68. Paul expected release from imprisonment in Rome (Phil 1:19, 24–26) and further ministry in the East (Phil 1:26; 2:24; Phlm 22).[6] Late in the first century, *1 Clem* 5:6–7 states of Paul that "seven times he was in bonds ... and when he had reached the limits of the West he gave his testimony before the rulers, and thus passed from the world." Clement's association of Paul's martyrdom with Peter's (*1 Clem* 5:1–7) and that of "a great multitude" (*1 Clem* 6:1) fits perfectly with Nero's persecution of Christians. Eusebius (*Hist. eccl.* 2.25.5–8; 3:1) confirms Paul's martyrdom under Nero with citations from the late second-century Gaius of Rome, and Dionysius, bishop of Corinth.

It seems unlikely that someone would write three letters with so much overlapping content if his intent was to give his own ideas credibility by claiming they were from Paul. Also, as Fee and even some proponents of pseudepigraphy have argued, "it seems highly unlikely that a pseudepigrapher, writing thirty to forty years later, would have tried to palm off such traditions as Paul's evangelizing Crete, the near capitulation to heresy of the Ephesian church, or a release and second imprisonment of Paul if in

---

5. I. H. Marshall, "Review of *Luke and the Pastoral Epistles* by Stephen G. Wilson," *JSNT* 10 (1981): 72. Cf. S. G. Wilson, *Luke and the Pastoral Epistles* (London: SPCK, 1979), 6–9, notes another 37 words, various stylistic traits, and parallels in the use of verbs by both Luke–Acts and the Pastorals that are rare in the rest of the NT. Four of these stylistic traits and ten verb uses are not found in the other ten Pauline epistles. Armin D. Baum, "Semantic Variation within the Corpus Paulinum: Linguistic Considerations concerning the Richer Vocabulary of the Pastoral Epistles," *TynBul* 59 (2008): 271–92, lists extensive similarities/synonyms between Paul's vocabulary and that of the Pastorals.
6. On Philemon living in Colosse, cf. Col 4:9 and J. B. Lightfoot, *Saint Paul's Epistles to the Colossians and to Philemon* (London: Macmillan, 1882), 303–14.

294 ᘒ MAN AND WOMAN

fact they had never happened."[7] Specific details ring true, such as the naming of false teachers in 1 Tim 1:20 and 2 Tim 2:17 and the personal appeals in 2 Tim 4:9–21, including, "bring the cloak that I left with Carpus at Troas, and my scrolls, especially the parchments.... Do your best to get here before winter" (4:13, 21).

It is sometimes alleged that pseudepigraphy was sufficiently widespread in the ancient world that it was perfectly natural and in no sense unethical for a pious person to write in Paul's name. This view that pseudonymity would be acceptable in the church faces two major objections. First, it was not common in the period of the Apostolic Fathers (which began at the close of the NT era). Second, where it was discovered, it was condemned. The correspondence between Paul and Seneca is from the fourth century and does not have a form like the NT letters. The Muratorian Canon says that the letter to the Laodiceans and a lost letter to the Alexandrians were "both forged in Paul's name ... [and] cannot be received into the Catholic Church; for it is not fitting that gall be mixed with honey."[8]

The *Acts of Paul*, written about AD 160, contains a "3 Corinthians" letter that was briefly included in the Syrian and Armenian canon. Tertullian records its spurious creation and the punishment of its author in *De baptismo* 17.5: "In Asia the presbyter who compiled that document, thinking to add of his own to Paul's reputation, was found out, and though he professed he had done it for love of Paul, was deposed from his position."[9] In the final analysis, it is a close reading of the Pastoral Epistles themselves that fits better with the thesis of Paul's authorship through a trusted secretary than some later writer, as is shown throughout Fee's commentary. Throughout this study, references to Paul's letters include all the letters attributed to Paul in the canon even though apart from his customary greeting (1 Cor 16:21; Gal 6:11; Col 4:18; 2 Thess 3:17; Phlm 19) he probably penned none of them with his own hand.

Paul's primary purpose in writing this first letter was to advise Timothy how to overcome false teaching. This explains the lack of an overriding

---

7. Gordon D. Fee, *1 and 2 Timothy, Titus* (NIBCNT; Peabody, Mass.: Hendrickson, 1988), xviii. Proponents of pseudepigraphy have argued similarly, e.g., A. T. Hanson, *The Pastoral Epistles* (NCBC; Grand Rapids: Eerdmans, 1982), 22–23, regarding the mission to Crete, and J. D. Quinn, "Paul's Last Captivity," in *Studia Biblica 1978 III. Papers on Paul and Other New Testament Authors* (JSNTSup 3; ed. E. A. Livingstone; Sheffield: JSOT Press, 1980), 289–99.
8. J. Stevenson, *A New Eusebius* (London: SPCK, 1963), 146.
9. Ernest Evans, *Tertullian's Homily on Baptism* (London: SPCK, 1964), 37.

theological theme throughout the book but rather snippets of Paul's theology (e.g., 1 Tim 1:2, 15, 17; 2:3–6; 3:13; 4:4, 9; 6:10, 14–16), personal reminiscences (1:11–16; 2:7), and personal appeals (1:18–19; 3:14–15; 4:6–8, 11–16; 5:1–3, 7, 11, 21–23; 6:11–14, 17–18, 20–21). This perfectly fits a letter by Paul. It does not fit a pseudepigraphical manual of church order.

THE EPHESUS CHURCH SITUATION THAT 1 TIMOTHY ADDRESSES

Acts 18:19–20:1 describes the beginning of the church in Ephesus. After it split from the synagogue, it soon became a mixed Jewish and Gentile fellowship. Gentiles "openly confessed their evil deeds" (19:18). There were enough sorcerers among them to denounce and burn fifty thousand days' wages worth of scrolls about the magic arts. By the time Paul wrote Ephesians, it was a predominately Gentile congregation (Eph 3:1, "you Gentiles"; cf. 2:11; 3:8; 4:17) that Paul warns against libertarian influences (4:17–5:18, "no longer live as the Gentiles do"). A continuing Jewish influence is evident in Paul's reference to "those who call themselves 'the circumcision'" in 2:11 and in his assurances that the Gentiles are heirs together with Israel in 2:11–3:12.

The description of false teachers who "want to be teachers of the law" in 1 Tim 1:7 probably indicates Jewish influence, though it may simply reflect the use of the OT throughout the Christian churches. Paul cautions against misuse of the law in 1:8–11. Several other recurring issues are addressed that suggest Jewish influence: abstaining from certain foods (4:3; 6:17); promoting controversies and arguments that result in envy, quarreling, malicious talk, evil suspicions, and constant friction (1:4; 6:4–5); arrogance (6:4, 17), devotion to endless genealogies (1:4; cf. Titus 3:9, "foolish controversies and genealogies and arguments and quarrels about the law"), and myths (1 Tim 1:4; 4:7; cf. Titus 1:14, "Jewish myths").

Paul continues to address this same cluster of problems in 2 Tim 2:14, 23; 3:2–7; 4:4. The heart of the problem was prophesied by Paul as recorded in Acts 20:29–30, "I know that after I leave, savage wolves will come in among you and will not spare the flock. Even from your own number men [ἄνδρες] will arise and distort the truth in order to draw away disciples after them."

THE CENTRAL PROBLEM: FALSE TEACHERS

First Timothy begins with a paragraph that outlines its central and overriding concern: the havoc wrought by false teaching. This concern dominates the entire letter through its conclusion in 6:20 – 21 and is also explicitly developed in 1:18 – 20; 4:1 – 8; 5:11 – 15; 6:9 – 10. Paul's goal is to guide Timothy in ways to help him stop the false teaching. The false teaching is of such central concern to Paul that nearly every verse in this letter relates to it, as Gordon Fee's commentary on the Pastorals has demonstrated in detail. First Timothy 1:3 – 11 identifies five aspects of the false teaching: myths and endless genealogies, controversies, causing people to leave the faith, meaningless talk, and inappropriate application of the law.

This leads smoothly[10] into Paul's confession of his own persecution of believers and God's mercy on him because he acted in ignorance. One would not expect a pious forger to call Paul a "blasphemer," "a violent insolent man," and "the worst of sinners" (1 Tim 1:13 – 16). Paul's reference to his own ignorance reflects those who through the influence of the false teachers "wandered away from [a sincere faith] and turned to meaningless talk. They want to be teachers of the law, but they do not know what they are talking about or what they so confidently affirm" (1:6 – 7). Paul apparently gave this confession to encourage misled Ephesian Christians to receive God's mercy and turn from their foolishness.[11]

The "charge" (τῆς παραγγελίας) of 1 Tim 1:5 (cf. v. 3) concerning false teachers is reiterated as "this charge" (ταύτην τὴν παραγγελίαν) in verse 18 to Timothy to fight the good fight for the faith against the false teachers, as Paul had done (vv. 19 – 20). Paul builds on this in 2:1, using the conjunction he typically uses when he wants to drive home exhortations based on what he had just written, "therefore" (οὖν).[12] This logically connects chapter 2 to the problem of the false teachers. The link to false teaching is also required by the "first of all" in 2:1 that identifies the first thing to do in order to address the contentiousness caused by the false

---

10.   E. H. Askwith, "On Two Points in 1 Tim 1," *The Expositor* 8th ser., 7 (1914): 377 – 78; cf. C. D. Osburn, "ΑΥΘΕΝΤΕΩ," *ResQ* 25 (1992): 9.
11.   Cf. Osburn, "ΑΥΘΕΝΤΕΩ," 10.
12.   E.g., Rom 12:1; 1 Cor 4:16; Eph 4:1; cf. Gordon D. Fee, "Issues in Evangelical Hermeneutics, Part III: The Great Watershed—Intentionality and Particularity/Eternality: 1 Timothy 2:8 – 15 as a Test Case," *Crux* 26 (1990): 37.

teaching.[13] The stress on God's desire that all be saved (2:3–6) undermines false teaching either from proto-Gnostic elitism based on "knowledge" or from Jewish exclusiveness.

The theme of chapter 2 is Paul's desire for quietness and peace (e.g., 1 Tim 2:2, 8, 11, 12, 15).[14] This peace is a peace in contrast to the contentiousness of the false teachers (e.g., 1:4), who are clearly still on Paul's mind as is evidenced by 2:3, "knowledge of the truth," and 2:7, "I was appointed a herald and an apostle — I am telling the truth, I am not lying — and a teacher of the true faith to the Gentiles." Paul's first letter to Timothy continues to emphasize the truth and the true faith (3:15; 4:3; 6:5; cf. "the faith" implying its content in 3:9; 4:1, 6; 6:12, 21) in contrast to false teaching.

False teaching is almost certainly the reason for Paul's reference to Eve's deception by Satan in 1 Tim 2:14 as a basis for restricting teaching by women (cf. 5:15, "Some younger widows have in fact already turned away to follow after Satan"). Peace is the context where true teaching can flourish. This chapter focuses on what Timothy should do to suppress further false teaching by the people who were apparently most influenced by it: women.

Chapter 3 identifies overseer and deacon qualifications that are well-suited to exclude the quarrelsome (1 Tim 1:4–5; 6:4, 20), money-loving (6:5, 9–10), and morally dubious (1:5–6; 5:22; cf. 3:6–8) false teachers. Even 3:15, the one verse that has been interpreted as identifying the letter as a manual for church order, identifies the basis of Paul's concern as with "the truth," which in context is opposed to the false teaching. The false teachers "have been robbed of the truth" (6:5), "have wandered away from the truth" (2 Tim 2:18), "oppose the truth" (2 Tim 3:8), and "turn their ears away from the truth" (2 Tim 4:4). The church is the "bulwark of the truth" (1 Tim 3:15) standing against false teaching.

First Timothy 4:1–5 describes the false teaching as "doctrines of demons." They forbid marriage and enjoin abstinence from foods. This explains why Paul is so keen in this letter to affirm marriage. The rest of chapter 4 gives Timothy instructions in light of the false teachers. He is to

---

13. This is argued by Harris, "Eve's Deception," 339.
14. Ibid., 340; Leland E. Wilshire, "1 Timothy 2:12 Revisited: A Reply to Paul W. Barnett and Timothy J. Harris," *EvQ* 65 (1993): 49.

have nothing to do with "myths characteristic of old women" (4:7). The elitism of the false teachers is again undermined by the affirmation that God "is the Savior of all people" (4:10).

Chapter 5 deals with the two key problem groups affected by the false teaching: some younger widows (5:3–16), "who have already turned away to follow Satan" (v. 16), and their "captors," the straying elders whom Timothy is to "rebuke publicly" (5:20; cf. 2 Tim 3:6–7).

First Timothy 6:3–10 further describes the false teachers and urges Timothy to guard against them. Paul concludes the letter in 6:20–21, "Timothy, guard what has been entrusted to your care. Turn away from godless chatter and opposing ideas of what is falsely called knowledge, which some have professed and in so doing have wandered from the faith." "Guard what has been entrusted" refers to guarding it from false teaching. The description of the false teaching as "falsely called knowledge [γνῶσις]" indicates that teachers of an early form of Gnosticism or proto-Gnosticism had infiltrated the Ephesian church.

This indication seems to be confirmed since each of the five problems listed in the first paragraph of 1 Timothy typified later Gnostic thinking: false teaching, controversies, causing people to leave the faith, meaningless talk, and misuse of the law. The Gnostic ascetic attitude toward marriage and a low view of the material world also fits the description of the false teaching in 1 Tim 4:3–4. The prominent teaching role of women in Gnostic circles helps explain Paul's restriction on women teaching in this situation. This "falsely called knowledge" probably entailed Greek dualism's disparagement of the material world, hence the forbidding of marriage (4:3) and spiritualizing the resurrection, teaching that it had already taken place (2 Tim 2:18). Because of their low view of the body, dualists regarded what one did with one's body as of little importance. This allowed them to excuse libertarian behavior. The libertarian tendency is opposed in statements throughout 1 Timothy that urge holiness, propriety, modesty, and the avoidance of arguments.

False teachers were still an acute problem when Paul wrote 2 Timothy. Second Timothy 2:16–17 states: "Avoid godless chatter, because those who indulge in it will become more and more ungodly. Their teaching will spread like gangrene. Among them are Hymenaeus and Philetus, who have wandered away from the truth. They say that the resurrection has already taken place, and they destroy the faith of some." This passage shows that the ringleader specified in 1 Tim 1:20, Hymenaeus, was still a key instigator, though presumably working from outside the church.

Paul repeatedly refers to false teachers using terms that usually encompass men and women, such as "any one/someone" (τὶς, 1:3, 6, 8, 19; 4:1; 5:24; 6:3, 10, 21) and "person" (ἄνθρωπος, 5:24; 6:5, 9). Unfortunately, many versions, like the NIV,[15] substitute "men" (1:3; 5:24; 6:5, 9) or "man" (1:8) or insert "he" (6:4 twice), thereby concealing the usual inclusiveness of these Greek terms. They exclude the most natural reading of the text, namely, one that identifies the false teachers with terms that are appropriate for including both men and women.

WOMEN'S INVOLVEMENT IN THE FALSE TEACHING

Marshall argues that there are "strong indications that women were involved in the heresy (and therefore teaching falsely),"[16] but Douglas Moo alleges, "there is no evidence in the pastoral epistles that the women were teaching these false doctrines."[17] In fact, however, Paul repeatedly describes women using identical or similar expressions he uses to describe the false teachers. Some younger widows "turned aside after Satan" and gave the enemy "opportunity for slander" (1 Tim 5:12–15). Similarly, the false teachers Hymenaeus and Alexander were "delivered to Satan in order that they might not blaspheme" (1:20). Just as some younger widows "turned aside [ἐξετράπησαν] after Satan" (5:15), so false teachers "turned aside [ἐξετράπησαν] to meaningless talk" (1:6). The sensual desires of some women overcame their dedication to Christ, incurring judgment because they set aside their first faith (5:11–12, cf. 15; 2:15). Similarly, false teachers "abandon the faith and follow deceiving spirits and doctrines of demons, speaking lies in hypocrisy" (4:1–2; cf. 1:4–6, 19; 6:10, 21; 2 Tim 2:18; 3:8).

Paul urged Timothy to instruct gently those caught in "the trap of the devil, who took them captive to do his will" (2 Tim 2:25–26). This appears to be directed at those (predominantly women) deceived by the false teachers. This gentle instruction contrasts with Paul's harshness to Hymenaeus and Alexander (1 Tim 1:20). Paul summarizes the false teaching as "myths characteristic of old women" (1 Tim 4:7, BDAG 660; cf. 1:4; 2 Tim 4:4;

---

15. The TNIV and CEV, however, are faithful to the Greek in each of these instances.
16. Marshall, *Pastoral Epistles*, 466.
17. Douglas Moo, "What Does It Mean Not to Teach or Have Authority Over Men? 1 Timothy 2:11–15," in RBMW 179–93, 495–99, 190.

Titus 1:14, all with μῦθοι) and devoid of real significance (βέβηλος, BDAG 173 applied to false teachings in 1 Tim 1:9; 6:20; 2 Tim 2:16).

No other book of the Bible has a higher proportion of verses focused specifically on problems regarding women: 21 out of 113 verses (1 Tim 2:9–15; 4:7; 5:3–7, 9–16). The following table lays out many close parallels between Paul's description of the false teachers and of women in the Ephesian church.

The false teacher's description	Similar statements concerning women
1:3: "certain persons (τισὶν) teach false doctrines"	2:12: "I am not permitting a woman to teach" 5:14: giving the enemy opportunity for slander
1:4: "myths" (μύθοις)	4:7: "myths" (μύθους) characteristic of old women
1:4: "promote controversies"	3:11: "women must ... not be malicious talkers"
1:7: "some persons [τινες] want to be teachers of the law but they do not know what they are talking about or what they so confidently affirm."	5:13: "talk nonsense, saying things they ought not" 2:11: "let a woman quietly receive instruction with entire submissiveness ... in quietness." 5:13: "going about from house to house ... talk nonsense, saying things they ought not ..." 2:14: "the woman being thoroughly deceived"
4:1: "some persons [τινες] will follow deceiving spirits of things taught by demons"	5:15: "already some [younger widows] have turned away to follow Satan."
4:2: "hypocritical liars whose consciences have been seared as with a hot iron"	3:11: "women must ... not be malicious talkers [but be] ... trustworthy in everything."
6:20: "opposing arguments of what is falsely called knowledge"	5:13: "nonsense, saying things they ought not"
6:21: "which some have professed [ἐπαγγελλόμενοι] and in so doing have wandered from the faith."	2:10: "women who profess [ἐπαγγελλομέναις] godliness" 5:11: "they have set aside their first faith." 5:15: "already some [younger widows] have turned away to follow Satan."

Parallel Descriptions of False Teachers and Women in 1 Timothy

The description of women in 5:13 includes φλύαροι, meaning "silly talk, foolery, nonsense, tattler, babbler."[18] This word is commonly used to identify teachings or philosophies that are opposed to the truth. For example, 4 Macc 5:10–11 uses it to describe "preposterous [φλυάρου] philosophy."[19] Josephus gives various examples of this: *Ag. Ap.* 2.22 describes an astonishing etymology as "nonsense," φλυαρίας; *Ag. Ap.* 2.116 describes a dubious historical narrative as a "ridiculous story," φλυαρήμασι;[20] and *Life* 150 states, "I ridiculed the nonsense [φλύαρον] of any arguments about charms."[21]

Fee states that, contrary to many English translations, "there is no known instance in Greek where the word *phlyaroi* means 'gossips.'"[22] This is important because it indicates that these young widows were not merely gossiping but were probably conveying rubbish philosophy, for nonsense is what the term normally describes. It is difficult to imagine Paul saying that these women had "already turned aside to follow Satan" (1 Tim 5:15) if φλύαροι meant merely gossips and had nothing to do with false teaching. Elsewhere Paul only refers to Satan where a specific act of Satan[23] or false teaching or practice is in view.[24]

The obvious reason why Paul bases his argument for limiting teaching by women on Eve's deception (1 Tim 2:14) is that false teaching had deceived women in Ephesus. Eve's deception epitomizes serious theological deception. Since Ephesian believers probably met in house churches, the reference to younger widows going "house to house ... saying things they ought not" in 5:13 may refer to house churches. This "rubbish" propounded by women had a serious effect on the church, which is implied

---

18. LSJ 1946.
19. APOT 2:672.
20. H. St. J. Thackeray, LCL 1:300–301, 338–39. Karl Heinrich Rengstorf, *A Complete Concordance to Flavius Josephus* (4 vols.; Leiden: Brill, 1983), 4:311, translates these "balderdash, raving, babble."
21. Steve Mason, *Life of Josephus: Translation and Commentary* (vol. 9 of *Flavius Josephus: Translation and Commentary*; ed. Steve Mason; Leiden: Brill, 2001), 86; cf. "absurdity" (H. St. J. Thackeray; LCL, 1:59).
22. Gordon Fee, "Great Watershed," 37, cites BAGD's reference, "Josephus," *Vita* 150, "*gossipy*" as an error. Neither occurrence of this word in Josephus, both cited above, can mean gossip. BDAG 1060 also appeals to Plutarch, *Mor.* 39a, but it means "foolish talk," not gossipy; 169e, but it means "foolish," not gossipy; and 701a, but it means "nonsense," not gossipy. Nor does LSJ list the meaning "gossip."
23. 1 Cor 7:5; 2 Cor 2:11; 12:7; 1 Thess 2:18.
24. Rom 16:20; cf. 17–18; 1 Cor 5:5 (by sinful example); 2 Cor 11:13–14; 2 Thess 2:9–10; 1 Tim 1:20; 5:15. Cf. 1 Tim 4:1, "deceiving spirits and things taught by demons"; 2 Tim 2:23–26.

by Paul's increasingly critical descriptions of their error from "idle" to "talk nonsense" to "saying things they ought not" to "some have in fact already turned away to follow Satan" (TNIV). The descriptions of the false teaching as rubbish (1:4–7, "myths, meaningless talk"; 6:20, "falsely called knowledge"; 2 Tim 2:23, "foolish and stupid arguments") supports understanding φλύαροι as referring to women conveying the false teachers' rubbish, not merely gossiping.

What about the false teachers' message had such an appeal to women, especially widows? Three characteristics of their message stand out that would have little appeal to men, and each has parallels in 1 Corinthians, proving that these issues were well-known to Paul:

1. 1 Tim 4:3: "They forbid people to marry" (cf. 1 Cor 7:1–5).
2. 1 Tim 4:3: "They order people to abstain from certain foods" (cf. 1 Cor 10:23–31).
3. 2 Tim 2:17–18: "They say that the resurrection has already taken place" (cf. the denial of the resurrection of the body in 1 Cor 4:8; 15:12, 22, 29, 35; 2 Thess 2:2).

Forbidding marriage, saying that the resurrection has taken place, and abstaining from certain foods express overly realized eschatology. Presumably these people argued, based on Jesus' statement, "At the resurrection people will neither marry nor be given in marriage" (Matt 22:30), that since the resurrection has already taken place, they should forbid marriage now. Similarly, since things of this world are of no spiritual value, they denied the goodness of God's created world and advocated abstinence from sex and food. These false teachings would appeal particularly to women in Ephesus, especially widows, since having no husband, they were social outsiders relegated to the fringes of power in their society.

This false teaching affirmed their dignity. Indeed, it affirmed that they were already in the ideal (eschatological) state of being single before Christ. It proclaimed an exalted status for women and a freedom from the obligations of marriage. It is no wonder that this new teaching attracted women. It is likely that it attracted few men besides the original false teachers. After all, it implied that the married state of most men was not ideal and so might have encouraged rejection by their wives. This explains why the false teaching is summarized in 1 Tim 4:7 as "myths characteristic of old women." The false teachings' special appeal to women at Ephesus probably explains why Paul specifically restricts teaching by women.

The false teachers' greed (1 Tim 6:5–10) suggests that they targeted women who could afford to pay tutors. Although they forbade marriage, the way Paul describes the false teachers suggests that they had illicit sexual relations with women caught up in their teaching. Just before stating, "They forbid people to marry" (4:2), Paul writes, "Such teaching comes through hypocritical liars, whose consciences have been seared as with a hot iron." They "thrust away good conscience" (1:19) and "follow deceiving spirits" (4:1). Timothy is to "flee youthful lusts" (2 Tim 2:22) in contrast to false teachers, whom "Satan has taken captive to do his will" (2:26). Second Timothy 3:4–6 warns Timothy to have nothing to do with such "lovers of pleasure.... They are the kind who worm their way into homes and gain control over weak-willed women, who are loaded down with sins and are swayed by all kinds of evil desires."

This explains why Paul tells women "to dress modestly, with decency and propriety" (1 Tim 2:9), "to continue in holiness with propriety" (2:15), and to be "worthy of respect" (3:11), and this is why he refers to widows "who live for pleasure" (5:6), whose "sensual desires overcome their dedication to Christ" (5:11), and who "have in fact already turned away to follow Satan" (5:14). It also explains the stress Paul gives to sexual fidelity (1:10; 3:2, 12; 5:9), purity (1:5; 3:7; 4:12; 5:2, 22), and holiness (2:8; 4:16). The false teachers could maintain a "form of godliness" (2 Tim 3:5) while using the philosophy of dualism to justify illicit sex as irrelevant to their spiritual life. Dualism held that the body is spiritually unimportant, and consequently, it does not matter what one does with one's body. In response to this same error in Corinth, Paul tells Christian men they must not go to prostitutes (1 Cor 6:15–18), since "your body is the temple of the Holy Spirit." He also argues against abstinence from sex within marriage, a practice that may have exacerbated their use of prostitutes (7:1–5).

In the face of women dressing indecently (1 Tim 2:9) and involved in false teaching, it would be only natural for the Jewish elements of the church to be tempted to return to the synagogue custom of excluding women from assemblies where the law was taught and for socially conservative Gentiles in the church to want to restrict women's place in the assemblies. To counteract such thinking and the problem of ignorance highlighted in 1:7,

Paul commands, "Let women learn" (2:11); and to counteract the women's excesses he adds "in all quietness" ("tranquility of spirit," not necessarily "silence") and then restricts women's teaching (2:12).

Several factors in the situation in the Ephesian church evidently called for this restriction from Paul. Most prominent seems to have been the deception of women by false teachers since this is the focus of the historical example of Eve's deception and the fall mentioned in 1 Tim 2:14. Women in Ephesus were being deceived by false teaching and "saying things they ought not" (5:13–15). This parallels the description of the false teachers in Titus 1:11, "teaching things they ought not." Women may have been the originators of some of the false teaching as is suggested by Paul's warning against "myths characteristic of old women" in 4:7. This, combined with the ingrained Jewish tradition of not allowing women to teach in the synagogues, would have led to deep concerns on the part of the Jewish pillars of the Ephesian church and a fighting spirit on the part of the Judaizers. In Paul's desire to bring peace, the compromise evident in 2:11–12 is a most practical solution: let them learn but not assume for themselves authority to teach a man.

First Timothy's many statements regarding problems caused by women depict a situation where women had become central to the false teaching that was dividing the church. The evidence for this is so strong that it has led three of the most prominent advocates that 1 Tim 2:12 forever prohibits women from teaching or having authority over men to acknowledge, respectively: "The false teachers had persuaded many women to follow them in their doctrines (1 Timothy 5:15; 2 Timothy 3:6–7)";[25] the text "explicitly pictures only women as being influenced by the heresy";[26] and "it is likely that the prohibition [1 Tim 2:12] is given because some women were teaching men."[27] The occasion that elicited the particular statements in 1 Tim 2:11–15 is important for understanding both what Paul was prohibiting and the reasoning he gives for it.

---

25. Moo, "What Does It Mean," RBMW 181.
26. William D. Mounce, Pastoral Epistles (WBC; Nashville: Nelson, 2000), 120, though some men evidently instigated the false teachings (1 Tim 1:20; 2 Tim 2:17; 4:14). Cf. above, pp. 299–304, on the influence of false teaching on women.
27. Thomas R. Schreiner, "An Interpretation of 1 Timothy 2:9–15: A Dialogue with Scholarship," WCFA, 141. Changed in the second edition, WCA 112, to "it is certainly possible that...." Unless otherwise noted, the second edition of this article is cited hereafter.

DOES 1 TIMOTHY 3:15 TEACH THAT 1 TIMOTHY IS A MANUAL FOR CHURCH ORDER?

Many critical scholars argue that 1 Tim 3:15 reveals the "plot"[28] of the pseudepigrapher of the Pastoral Epistles, to create a manual for church order after Paul's death. Those who appeal to this verse for vindication that this epistle is a manual for church order must assume that this verse introduces, albeit elliptically, a new subject other than the stated subject of the verse, identified by the two singular pronouns "you" in verse 14 and second person singular verb "you may know" in verse 15, referring to Timothy: "in order that you might know how it is necessary to conduct yourself in the church of living God." Most commentators and versions interpose a new subject by elliptically inserting, as is grammatically possible: "it is necessary for [one] to conduct [one]self." According to this view, Paul simply wanted Timothy to know how people in general should conduct themselves in the church, not how Timothy should conduct himself in meeting this crisis with false teaching, even though Paul demands specific conduct of Timothy in 1:3, 18–19; 4:6–8, 11–16; 5:1, 3, 7, 11, 19, 20, 22–23; 6:2, 11–12, 17, and 20.

Many factors support retention of the focus on Timothy rather than a change of subject. Paul never elsewhere uses this verb of general conduct in church, but he does use "conduct" (ἀναστρέφω) to refer to his and Timothy's conduct "especially in our relations with you [the Corinthian church]" in 2 Cor 1:12 (cf. v. 1, "Paul and Timothy"). Therefore, there is no question that it is a verb that Paul could use, and did use elsewhere, to describe Timothy's relationship to a church. Timothy has to know what the church needs in order to guide it. Understanding this verse as directed specifically to Timothy does not deny that what Paul is saying also illuminates indirectly how people in general in the church should act. Of course it would, and Paul wants Timothy to do whatever he can to cause believers in Ephesus to adopt Christlike behavior. The following additional eight reasons show that it is more likely that Paul intended 1 Tim 3:15 as a charge to Timothy than to the church at large (as a manual of rules for church order).

---

28. E.g., C. K. Barrett, *The Pastoral Epistles* (Oxford: Clarendon, 1963), 63. So, also, E. F. Scott, *The Pastoral Epistles* (MNTC; London: Hodder & Stoughton, 1936), 38–39.

1. More Than Rules for Worship

The concerns of the letter are far wider than merely a series of "rules for worship."[29] The letter is not structured as a manual of church order, but as a series of instructions for Timothy to counter false teachings. Paul supports his instructions with personal encouragement and theological underpinnings that expose the errors of the false teachings.

2. Grammatical Concern

In every other case where Paul uses "it is necessary" (δεῖ) without stating a personal subject for its infinitive, but where he does identify in the context a personal subject that could be associated with δεῖ, that personal subject should be associated with δεῖ:

Rom 12:3: "do not think of yourselves more highly than [you] ought to think."

1 Cor 8:2: "he does not yet know as [he] ought to know."

2 Cor 11:30: "I ... I ... If [I] must boast."

2 Cor 12:1: "I ... I ... [I] must go on boasting."

2 Thess 3:7: "you know how [you] ought to imitate us."

1 Tim 3:7: "The overseer ... must have a good reputation."

Titus 1:11: "They are ruining whole households by teaching what [they] ought not."

Consequently, unless this is the one Pauline exception, 1 Tim 3:15 should read, "in order that you [singular, referring to Timothy] might know how [you] should conduct [your]self in the church of the living God." Accordingly, BDF §405 (cf. 407) notes:

> Classical Greek has only a few exceptions to the rule that the subject of the infinitive, if it is identical with the subject of the governing verb, is not expressed, but supplied ... from the governing verb ... the insertion of δεῖ ... causes no change in the rule. ... In the majority of cases in the NT too, a subject already given in or with the main verb is not repeated with the infinitive.

---

29. Cf. Gordon Fee, *The Pastoral Epistles*, 30–38; Fee, "Great Watershed," 32–37. Cf. Osburn, "ΑΥΘΕΝΤΕΩ," 10–11. E.g., Timothy is to turn believers from anger, disputing, and immodest dress to decency, propriety, and good works.

In this case where the personal subject of the governing verb fits the action introduced by δεῖ, the only way Paul could make it clear that he intended a different subject would be to identify it (e.g., ἄνθρωπον). Since he did not identify a new subject, it is natural to understand "you" (Timothy) as the continuing subject. Paul and Luke both use δεῖ elsewhere to identify the continuation of the subject "you" (Luke 12:12; Rom 12:3; 2 Thess 3:7).

The grammatical expectation that Timothy is the subject of the infinitive is heightened in this case by two additional factors. First, just eight verses earlier, the unstated subject of the infinitive and δεῖ must be the same subject, the overseer, as that of the prior main verb. Thus, not only is this a uniform pattern in Pauline usage, it is also the pattern used in this very context. Second, when the personal subject of the infinitive is stated, it takes the accusative case,[30] and "you" (σέ) identifying Timothy occurs in the accusative case in this same sentence (1 Tim 3:14–15).

3. Proper Conduct for Timothy

First Timothy 3:15 is introduced by 3:14: "I write these things to you [singular], hoping to come to you [singular] quickly." Timothy's knowledge of these things is presented as essential "in order that" the proper conduct may ensue. If the proper conduct is Timothy's own rather than people in general in the church, the logical connection is more direct, and the urgency necessitating this letter—even though Paul may come soon—is more apparent.

First Timothy has eight statements about "these things" (ταῦτα): 3:14; 4:6, 11, 15; 5:7, 21; 6:2, 11. In every case ταῦτα refers to things that Paul is giving Timothy to do. Since 3:15 is a further explication of 3:14, this supports understanding 3:15 as also directed specifically to Timothy. The use of the present tense, "I write" or "I am writing," combined with Paul's concern that he might be delayed in coming, indicates that "these things" probably has in view the entire letter Paul is writing. In fact, the whole letter gives Timothy instructions on how to conduct himself in his leadership position among God's people in Ephesus, particularly in view of the false teaching he is charged with counteracting. Not only does Paul refer throughout the letter to Timothy's official conduct, he also specifically highlights his concern with Timothy's personal conduct in the church in 4:12, 16; 6:11.

---

30. Paul states the subject of the infinitive of δεῖ using the accusative in 1 Cor 15:25, 53; 2 Cor 2:3; 5:10; Eph 6:20; Col 4:4, 6; 1 Thess 4:1; 1 Tim 3:2; 2 Tim 2:6, 24; Titus 1:7, 11.

4. The Second Person Singular

The entire letter is directed specifically to Timothy. The extent of the personal appeals to Timothy throughout this letter is missed since in English "you" can be either singular or plural. There are thirty second person singular imperative verb forms in 1 Timothy specifically addressed to Timothy[31] and nine more verbs that do not have this form but carry the imperative sense of a command specifically to Timothy.[32] In addition, there are eight other second person singular verbs stating things about Timothy[33] and eighteen singular "you" pronouns identifying Timothy in this letter.[34]

In 1 Tim 1:3, 18–19, Paul explicitly charges Timothy to conduct himself in the church in specific ways. Furthermore, chapters 2 and 3 contain specific guidance that Timothy is to implement, such as 3:10, "let deacons first be tested, and then if there is nothing against them, let them serve as deacons."[35] It is implausible to assume that Timothy had no influence in the fulfillment of this command for deacons. Just before a parallel list of qualifications for overseers in Titus 1:8, Paul writes (1:5): "The reason I left you in Crete was that you might straighten out what was left unfinished and appoint elders in every town, as I directed you." Even in the more established church in Ephesus, Paul has clearly assigned Timothy to "clean house."[36] Thus, it fits the letter (in general) and the qualifications for leaders (in particular) to understand 1 Tim 3:15, "so that you will know how you ought to conduct yourself in God's household," as a personal exhortation to Timothy.

5. No General Address to the Ephesians

Nowhere does this letter address the members of the Ephesian church, let alone all churches or all Christians. All of the imperative verbs that are not directed specifically at Timothy are framed in such a way that

---

31. 1 Tim 4:7, 7, 11, 11, 12, 13, 14, 15, 15, 16, 16; 5:1, 3, 7, 11, 19, 20, 22, 22, 22, 23, 23; 6:2, 2, 11, 11, 12, 12, 17, 20.
32. 1 Tim 1:3, 18, 19; 4:6, 12; 5:1, 21, 21; 6:20.
33. 1 Tim 3:15; 4:6, 6, 6, 16, 16; 6:12, 12.
34. 1 Tim 1:3, 18, 18; 3:14, 14; 4:7, 12, 14, 14, 15, 16, 16, 16; 5:22, 23; 6:11, [13], 14.
35. Cf. Paul's use of the third person imperative with personal application in Rom 6:12.
36. Verlyn D. Verbrugge, "Paul as Pastor: Can You Serve as a Pastor from a Distance?" paper presented at the ETS Annual Meeting in Washington, D.C. (2006), analyzes Paul's attempts to influence the church at Corinth while being stationed in Ephesus and concludes that Paul was most successful in dealing with problem churches not through painful letters directed at them, but through a personal emissary. Consequently, it fits Paul's experience that he would direct a letter like 1 Timothy to his emissary rather than to the problem church.

they urge Timothy to implement them.[37] Throughout chapter 3, Paul gives Timothy guidance about qualifications for overseers and deacons. He does not address these qualifications to the church or command Timothy to address them to the church, as he did to Titus.[38] Nor is chapter 3 a list of job descriptions or duties of overseers or deacons. No responsibilities are listed for overseers or deacons except implicitly in the statement that overseers should be "apt to teach."

6. Paul's Purpose

Understanding "you" as the continuing subject avoids interpreting Paul as though he is giving two competing purposes for the letter. Instead, it reaffirms the purpose already stated in 1 Tim 1:3 of guiding Timothy's conduct to counteract false teaching.

7. The Future of the Church in Ephesus

The future of the church in Ephesus depended on Timothy more than anyone else,[39] so it makes sense that Paul would address Timothy's own actions. The verb "to conduct yourself" fits the exercise of official duties.[40] In fact, Paul uses this verb in 2 Cor 1:12 to describe himself and his close associates who suffered persecution with him: "We have conducted ourselves in the world, and especially in our relations with you, in the holiness and sincerity that are from God." This is precisely the kind of conduct that Paul wanted from Timothy.[41]

8. Text-Critical Issues

Some texts add a second singular "you" (σε) to 1 Tim 3:15, requiring the understanding that this specifically addresses Timothy, including some Greek manuscripts, the Latin Vulgate, Armenian, and the church fathers Origen, Hilary, and Ambrosiaster,[42] as well as translations like the

---

37. 1 Tim 3:10; cf. also 2:11, 3:12; 5:4, 9, 16, 16, 17; 6:1; 2, 2.
38. In Titus 2:1–6, where Paul does this, his imperatives are still directed at Titus, who is to teach and encourage these rules (Titus 2:1, 6).
39. Cf. J. N. D. Kelly, *A Commentary on the Pastoral Epistles: I Timothy II Timothy Titus* (HNTC; New York: Harper & Row, 1963), 87.
40. Cf. Donald Guthrie, *The Pastoral Epistles: An Introduction and Commentary* (Grand Rapids: Eerdmans, 1957), 87–88.
41. Note BDAG 72, which describes the verb ἀναστρέφω this way: "to conduct oneself in terms of certain principles."
42. Tischendorf, *Novum Testamentum Graece*[8], 2:849.

KJV and Luther. Most other careful commentators acknowledge the grammatical and factual appropriateness of this understanding,[43] not just those commentators who advocate this interpretation.[44] Many who interpret a change of subject here generally do so on the assumption that the letter is "a semi-public"[45] document, but unlike the book of Philemon, which is addressed to Philemon "and the church that meets in your house," 1 Timothy is addressed only to Timothy and includes no general charges addressed to the church.

In light of the evidence that 1 Timothy is not a manual of church order but is rather a letter from Paul giving Timothy specific instructions for dealing with false teaching in Ephesus, 1 Tim 2:12, "I am not permitting a woman to teach and assume authority over a man," fits the specific problem 1:6–7 describes: "They want to be teachers of the law, but they do not know what they are talking about or what they so confidently affirm." Paul's solution may be paraphrased: "Let them learn so that eventually they may fulfill their teaching aspirations, but this privilege requires responsible study first." Philo (*The Sacrifices of Abel and Cain* 48) addresses a similar contrast: "Ignorance is an involuntary state, a light matter, and its treatment through teaching is not hopeless."[46] Paul's goal is to establish women in the true faith so they will not teach the church error.

---

43. E.g., Walter Lock, *The Pastoral Epistles* (ICC; Edinburgh: T&T Clark, 1924), 43; Joh. Ed. Huther, *Critical and Exegetical Hand-book to the Epistles to Timothy and Titus* (Meyer's 6th ed.; Edinburgh: T&T Clark, 1883), 128 n. 1. Huther criticizes Hoffman for arbitrarily introducing a new subject, "one who has to govern a house of God." The same criticism could be applied to any changing of the subject from "you."

44. E.g., William Hendriksen, *Commentary on I & II Timothy and Titus* (London: Banner of Truth, 1959), 136; H. Alford, *The Greek Testament* (4 vols.; London: Rivingtons, 1871), 3:330, refutes objections to understanding the subject as unchanged from "you"; Guthrie, *Pastoral Epistles*, 87–88.

45. Knight, *Pastoral Epistles*, 179.

46. Philo, 2:131 (Colson and Whitaker, LCL).

17

1 TIMOTHY 2:8–11:
"LET A WOMAN LEARN IN QUIETNESS AND IN ALL SUBMISSION"

First Timothy 2 advocates peace without self-assertiveness in response to controversies caused by false teachings. Verses 1–7 pray for peace and affirm the truth of Paul's teachings. Verse 8 calls on men throughout the house churches ("in every place") to lift up holy hands in prayer without the anger and disputing that characterized the controversies (1:4) sparked by false teachers. Presumably Paul wrote 1 Tim 2:8 because men in the Ephesian church had become angry and were disputing. The explicit references to controversies in 1:4 and 6:4–5 support this presumption.

Paul also applies this desire to women, as implied by the word "similarly" (ὡσαύτως, 2:9). This is clear from verse 9, which is grammatically dependent on the reader supplying its main verb from verse 8. Conzelmann is probably correct that "I wish them to pray" should be supplied from verse 8,[1] since this lets "similarly" retain its normal meaning and clarifies the association of the following prepositional phrases. Accordingly, verse 9 calls on "women similarly to pray in modest deportment, to adorn themselves with decency and propriety." The NIV imports "I want" from verse 8, due to the grammatical dependence of verse 9 on verse 8, but unfortunately, the NIV obscures this dependence by translating "similarly"

---

1. Martin Dibelius, rev. Hans Conzelmann, *The Pastoral Epistles* (4th ed.; Hermeneia; Philadelphia: Fortress, 1972), 45. Only if learning in quietness in v. 11 demands total silence in the churches would v. 11 conflict with women praying in church.

as "also," a meaning not supported by LSJ or BDAG 1106, which identifies ὡσαύτως as "a marker of similarity that approximates identity, *(in) the same (way), similarly, likewise.*" The corresponding call for women to decency or self-control (σωφροσύνη) parallels the restriction on prayer given to men, and both counter the effects of false teaching.

Paul objects to immodesty and to the flaunting of wealth for both spiritual and practical reasons (1 Tim 5:6, 11–14; Titus 2:5). Immodesty posed a risk because Gentile Christian communities, unlike synagogues, lacked the protection of legal associations ratified by the emperor and the Roman senate, so they were vulnerable to private prosecution for criminal action if they were seditious or promiscuous.[2] Contemporary standards also affirmed modesty and decried ostentation.[3] Judging by portraiture, the entwining or braiding of hair was a relatively common hairstyle that would not by itself have implied wealth. In light of this, it is probably significant that Paul used the conjunctive "and" (καί BDF §442) to join "braided hair and gold,"[4] rather than the disjunctive "or" (ἤ BDF §446) that separates the other members of the list.

Proof that this distinction was noticed and was felt inappropriate for expressing a simple series comes from variations in the textual tradition that changed this "and" to "or" (ἤ in D² H Ψ 𝔐 lat syʰ; Cl) to make each member of the series separate and parallel. The normal conjunctive use of καί implies that Paul is viewing the conjunction of "plaited hair and gold" as the problem, namely, the sort of ostentatious hairstyle described by Tucker, "it might be plaited over the head and fastened by ... a net of

---

2. Cf. Winter, *Roman Wives*, 122; Bruce W. Winter, "Roman Law and Society in Romans 12–15," in *Rome in the Bible and the Early Church* (ed. P. Oakes; Grand Rapids: Baker, 2002), 69–75.

3. For similar statements from Plutarch, Phintys, Perictione, Seneca, Musonius Rufus, Juvenal, and Jewish writers, see David Scholer, "Women's Adornment: Some Historical and Hermeneutical Observations on the New Testament Passages," *Daughters of Sarah* 6 (1980): 5.

4. Hurley (*Biblical Perspective*, 199) states that Paul "is not, in fact, speaking against all braids, gold wedding-rings and pearl ear-rings" but "he probably meant braided hair decorated with gold or with pearls." While this is possible, three factors make it seem unlikely. First, it distinguishes between the function of the two "or's." It links pearls specifically to hair but treats expensive clothing as a separate issue, even though both "or's" make perfectly good sense understood in their normal use to separate elements in a series. It is unlikely that the Corinthians would have interpreted Paul's disjunctive "or" as associating pearls with "plaiting of hair and gold." Second, unlike gold, which literature contemporary with Paul specifically identifies as a hair ornament, this author has not found evidence that pearls were commonly used as hair ornamentation. Third, Hurley's suggestion seems motivated to avoid an interpretation that is critical of the sorts of gold and pearl jewelry that are in common use in churches today. It is unlikely, however, that Paul would have objected to pearls in hair but not pearls in jewelry.

gold thread."[5] This is confirmed by the almost identical distinction in use of καί and ἤ in 1 Pet 3:3, where "and" (καί) again associates braided hair with gold and "or" (ἤ) separates it from fine clothing: "braided hair and [καί] the putting round [περιθέσεως] of gold ornaments (plural) or [ἤ] fine clothing."

The word for "putting round" (περιθέσεως) is particularly appropriate for gold ornaments put around the hair. The combination of "putting around" and gold in the plural would be an inappropriate expression, however, to identify an individual piece of gold jewelry or to jewelry that was simply attached, such as an earring, nose ring, or broach, which are not "put around." Pearls at that time were extremely valuable. Unlike today when cultured pearls are relatively inexpensive and fake pearls are cheap, the only pearls available then were natural ones. They were of such value that they were put on kings' crowns and made the appropriate focus of Jesus' parable of the pearl of great price.

First Timothy 2:10 addresses women who were "professing [ἐπαγγελλομέναις] godliness [θεοσέβειαν]." BDAG 356 defines the first word to mean "to claim to be well-accomplished in someth., *profess, lay claim to, give oneself out as an expert in someth[ing]* ... **1 Tim 2:10.**" Consequently, this word identifies women engaged in vocal profession of godliness. Paul uses the same verb in 6:21 to describe the profession of false teachings: "the opposing ideas of what is falsely called knowledge, which some have professed [ἐπαγγελλόμενοι] and in so doing have wandered from the faith." Second Timothy 3:5–6 refers to those having "a form of godliness [εὐσεβείας]" who "worm their way into homes and gain control over weak-willed women, who are loaded down with sins and are swayed by all kinds of evil desires." Since "professing" falsely called knowledge in 6:21 is an activity of the false teachers, and since the false teachers were professing godliness, this expression in 1 Tim 2:10 is particularly appropriate if Paul wrote this with women in mind who were "professing godliness" in accordance with false teachings. The use of the unexpected preposition "through, by means of" (διά + gen.)[6] may imply that good works, not public profession, is what expresses godliness.

---

5.   T. G. Tucker, *Life in the Roman World of Nero and St. Paul* (London: MacMillan, 1910), 311; cf. Pliny, *Nat.*, 9.
6.   Instead of "adorn *with*" (μετά) as in v. 9, as most versions translate διά, e.g., KJV, NEB, NIV, NRSV.

The use of these terms associated with false teaching prepares for Paul's immediately following command that women learn in quietness (v. 11) and not assume for themselves authority to teach men (v. 12, which would be in public worship), and the explanation citing the deception of Eve (vv. 13–14). Paul's concern for "good deeds" and "self-control" in contrast to immodest dress and ostentatious display parallels his critique of the widow who "lives for pleasure" (5:6) and "sensuous desires" (5:11). Consequently, he urges the church to support only those widows "well known for good deeds" and devoted to "all kinds of good deeds" (5:10).

The one grammatical imperative in this passage is "let a woman[7] learn in quietness and in all submission." This command for women to learn contrasts with the absence of women from any list of students in Ephesian schools of that time.[8] It also contrasts with the Jewish tradition that women are not obliged to study the law, but they are to encourage their sons and husbands to study it (e.g., *b. Ber.* 17a).[9] R. Eliezer (ca. AD 90), a staunch upholder of the old tradition, even said, "If any man gives his daughter a knowledge of the Law it is as though he taught her lechery" (*m. Soṭah* 3:4; cf. *b. Soṭah* 21b), and according to *y. Soṭah* 3.4 (VII.D) he said, "Better to burn the Torah than to teach it to women."[10]

The importance to Paul of women learning is rooted in the gospel, as he expresses just prior in 1 Tim 2:3–6, "For this is good, and pleases God our Savior, who wants all people to be saved and to come to a knowledge of the truth." To come to knowledge of the truth, they must be taught. Moo appropriately notes that "almost certainly it [quietness] is necessary because at least some women were not learning 'in quietness.' These women had probably picked up the disputatious habits of the false teachers."[11]

The meaning of ἡσυχία ("quietness") in the context of this passage's consistent desire for peace without trouble (e.g., 2:2, 8, 11, 12, 15) is not

---

7. The generic singular applies the command to women in general. Cf. Marshall, *Pastoral Epistles*, 452.
8. E.g., Baugh, "Foreign World," WCA 34, 193–94 n. 136.
9. Women were excluded from certain parts of the temple, Josephus, *Ant.* 15.418f. The teaching portion of the synagogues was called the "man's part." Women would have been taught aspects of the law relating to women.
10. But *y. Soṭah* 3.4 (F) and *m. Soṭah* 3.4 state: "Ben Azzai says: A man ought to give his daughter a knowledge of the Law so that if she must drink [the bitter water] she may know that the merit [she had acquired] will hold her punishment in suspense."
11. Moo, "What Does It Mean," RBMW 183.

silence but quietness-peace, the opposite of discord and disruption.[12] ʿΗσυχία indicates a manner of learning that was culturally regarded as being the appropriate attitude and deportment of a well-bred serious student. Paul here commands that women be permitted to learn as proper students, with a quiet and teachable spirit.

Moo alleges: "ἡσυχία is the only word in his [Paul's] known vocabulary which could clearly denote silence."[13] Σιγή, however, occurs in Acts 21:40, a passage referring to Paul and written by his friend and traveling companion, Luke, and its verb form, σιγάω, occurs four times in Paul's letters, Rom 16:25; 1 Cor 14:28, 30, and 34, and six times in Luke – Acts. Σιγή was the most specific term in Greek meaning "the absence of all noise, whether made by speaking or by anything else, *silence, quiet*."[14] It much more clearly denoted silence than ἡσυχία. It is amazing that Moo would suggest that Paul might not know a noun whose related verb he repeatedly uses. Even if the noun form σιγή were so rare (it was not) that Paul might not have known it, he could have used its verb σιγάω or φιμόω ("silence," "muzzle," or its noun form φιμός) if he had wished to specify "silence."[15] Paul's choice of ἡσυχία instead of σιγή favors "quietness" as a more appropriate translation than "silence." "Silence" would also contradict Paul's approval of women prophesying in 1 Cor 11:5 – 13. ʿΗσυχία's pairing with submission in 1 Tim 2:11 further supports "quietness" since "quietness" is a more natural pair with submission than "silence."

Paul concludes his command that women learn "in all submission" (1 Tim 2:11). It is sometimes assumed that this implies a marriage context and refers to submission to one's husband, but 1 Tim 1 – 2 says nothing about marriage. Treggiari argues that "subordination of the wife ... was not essential or important by the time of Cicero [106 – 43 BC]."[16] Bruce Winter, too, affirms "the demise of the image of the subordination of wives by the end of the Roman Republic."[17] Instead, the submission here enjoined specifically modifies "to learn." Consequently, it is natural to understand the

---

12. Harris, "Eve's Deception," 340; Paul W. Barnett, "Wives and Women's Ministry (1 Tim 2:11–15)," *EvQ* 61 (1989): 229; A. Padgett, "Wealthy Women at Ephesus: 1 Timothy 2:8–15 in Social Context," *Interpretation* 41 (1987): 22–24; Collins, *1 & 2 Timothy and Titus*, 68–69.
13. Douglas J. Moo, "The Interpretation of 1 Timothy 2:11–15: A Rejoinder," *TJ* 2 NS (1981): 199.
14. BDAG 922.
15. Wilshire, "1 Tim 2:12 Revisited," 48.
16. S. Treggiari, *Roman Marriage: Iusti Coniuges from the Time of Cicero to the Time of Ulpian* (Oxford: Clarendon, 1991), 261.
17. Winter, *Roman Wives*, 113.

submission to be submission to the truths that they are learning, "not to a wife's submissiveness to her husband."[18]

There are several interesting parallels with 1 Tim 2:14, where Paul gives the key reason or explanation for this command. Woman learning (v. 11) is the opposite of woman being deceived (v. 14). Learning "in all submission" (ἐν πάσῃ ὑποταγῇ) is the opposite of falling "in transgression" (ἐν παραβάσει). Since transgression was disobedience to God's command, submission in contrast is best understood as obedience to God's commands, specifically by welcoming the truth and letting it become a protective shield against the temptations of the false teachers and their enticing teaching of overly realized eschatology. This supports the view that verse 11 is about submission to Christian doctrine.

Similarly, in verse 14, the woman was thoroughly deceived about God's command. The Genesis account of the woman's deception deals entirely with the serpent's distortion of God's word, not the man's authority.[19] Nothing in the serpent's deception states anything about man's authority. The following analysis of the word αὐθεντέω will show that properly granted authority is a later development of this word with no established instances before or near the time of Paul. Furthermore, Paul always uses παράβασις ("transgression") to refer explicitly to transgression of God's law, never against male authority, and the same is true of the entire NT.[20]

Does submission describe the manner in which women are to learn, hence paralleling "in quietness," namely, receptive hearing with the intent to obey? Or does it describe their response to the learning, namely, that women are to learn and to obey?[21] The former seems preferable for two key reasons. First, the parallel form of ἐν ἡσυχίᾳ and ἐν πάσῃ ὑποταγῇ suggests that the two are parallel descriptions of the manner in which women should learn. Second, for Paul to indicate submission as a response to learning, it would then parallel learning and so would more naturally be conveyed by a grammatical structure parallel to "learn" (e.g., "let women learn and obey God's Word") rather than an adverbial phrase modifying

---

18. Ibid.
19. Cf. Padgett, "Wealthy Women," 24; Perriman, "What Eve Did," 131; Barnett, "Wives and Women's Ministry (1 Tim 2:11–5)," 230; cf. above, pp. 47–49, 53–54, 316, 406–13.
20. Rom 2:23; 4:15; 5:14; Gal 3:19; Heb 2:2; 9:15; cf. Perriman, "What Eve Did," 131.
21. E.g., Perriman, "What Eve Did," 131.

"learn." Although addressed here specifically to women, submission should characterize men, too (e.g., 1 Cor 16:16; Eph 5:21).

To counteract the influence of false teachers on women, Paul calls them to modesty and good works (1 Tim 2:9–10) and commands, "Let women learn in quietness and full submission" to the true faith (1 Tim 2:11).

18

1 Timothy 2:12: Part I: "I Am Not Permitting a Woman to Teach"

The only verse in the Bible alleged to explicitly prohibit women from teaching or having authority over men is 1 Tim 2:12. It is the basis for Moo's position that women are prohibited from "preaching ... and the teaching of Bible and doctrine in the church, in colleges, and in seminaries."[1] Thomas Schreiner calls 1 Tim 2:12's prohibition "universal" and states, "Women are prohibited from teaching or exercising authority because of the creation order."[2]

There is a powerful symmetry to the argument in verses 11 and 12. These verses are framed in the inclusio of an introducing and concluding call for a quiet spirit (ἐν ἡσυχία). Within this inclusio is a command for women to "learn in all submission" and a restriction on their teaching. This is explained in verses 13–14 by an appeal to the primal events of human history, showing that woman owes respect to man since he was formed prior to woman,[3] and warning that the deception of women in the church in Ephesus risked its fall just as Eve's deception led to the original fall.

---

1. Moo, "What Does It Mean," *RBMW* 186.
2. Schreiner, "Dialogue," *WCA* 101, 120.
3. Paul makes a similar argument in 1 Cor 11:8, 12, cf. above, pp. 181, 196.

DOES THE GRAMMATICAL FORM "I AM NOT PERMITTING" FAVOR A PRESENT OR UNIVERSAL PROHIBITION?

The English translation of ἐπιτρέπω in 1 Tim 2:12, "I do not permit," conveys an ongoing universal prohibition, but this Greek verb and its grammatical form are better suited for a presently ongoing prohibition. Paul often chose the first person singular ("I") present active indicative ("am not permitting") to indicate his own personal advice or position for a situation that is not universal.[4] Four times in 1 Cor 7:7, 26, 32, 40 and again in Phil 4:2 Paul uses the identical grammatical construction: first person singular present active indicative verb form (θέλω, νομίζω, θέλω, δοκῶ, παρακαλῶ) associated with one or more present active infinitives (εἶναι, ὑπάρχειν, εἶναι, εἶναι, ἔχειν, φρονεῖν) to express his current desire or conviction, not a universal demand.[5] Moo justifiably states, "Paul's use of the present indicative in exhortations and commands is also relatively rare.... Advice for a current situation was being given [to Timothy]."[6] Paul frequently, however, uses imperatives to make universally applicable exhortations.[7]

Every occurrence of ἐπιτρέπω in the Greek OT refers to a specific situation, never to a universally applicable permission. Similarly, the vast majority of the NT occurrences of ἐπιτρέπω clearly refers to a specific time or for a short or limited time duration only.[8] There are only two cases where ἐπιτρέπω seems to refer to a permission with continuing effect. The third person singular form in 1 Cor 14:34 may be a rabbinic formula[9] and may not have been in the original text.[10] In response to Mark 10:4 and Matt 19:8 ("Moses permitted [ἐπέτρεψεν] you to divorce your wives"),

---

4. E.g., 1 Cor 7:6, 7, 8, 25 (2x), 26, 28, 29, 32, 35, 40. Similarly, the vast majority of Paul's uses of this form of the verb λέγω ("I say") are limited, not universal.
5. As Paul does with this identical construction but with a different infinitive form in Rom 15:30.
6. Moo, "A Rejoinder," 200. Nevertheless, he writes on p. 199, "the prohibitions are universal."
7. Daniel B. Wallace, *Greek Grammar beyond the Basics: An Exegetical Syntax of the New Testament* (Grand Rapids: Zondervan, 1996), 525 n. 30, lists 56 verses to argue that 1 Tim 2:12's prohibition is "a general precept that has gnomic [= "timeless" 523] implications." However, these 56 verses contain 74 imperatives and four participles that elaborate an imperative. Not one of the commands he lists is in the indicative like 1 Tim 2:12.
8. Matt 8:21; Mark 5:13; Luke 8:32; 9:59, 61; John 19:38; Acts 21:39, 40; 27:3; 28:16; 1 Cor 16:7; in Heb 6:3 ("If God should permit") is clearly contingent, and leaving behind the elementary teaching about Christ is clearly not universal, *pace* Marshall, *Pastoral Epistles*, 455 n. 144 citing Ign. *Eph.* 10.3, which does not even use this verb.
9. S. Aalen, "A Rabbinic Formula in 1 Corinthians 14:34" (SE II; Berlin: Akademie, 1964), 513–25; Ben Witherington III, *Women in the Earliest Churches* (SNTSMS 59; Cambridge: Cambridge Univ. Press, 1988), 122; Marshall, *Pastoral Epistles*, 455.
10. Cf. above, pp. 225–67.

Jesus replied, "because your hearts were hard. But it was not that way from the beginning" (Matt 19:8; cf. Mark 10:5–12) and "what God has joined together, let man not separate.... Anyone who divorces his wife and marries another woman commits adultery against her" (Mark 10:9; cf. Matt 19:9, adding an exception for illicit sex). Jesus' reply shows that ἐπιτρέπω does not refer to a universal or permanent permission.

Furthermore, neither case is parallel in verbal form to 1 Tim 2:12. "They are not permitted" in 1 Cor 14:34 is third person present passive, and "Moses permitted" in Mark 10:4 and Matt 19:8 are third person aorist active forms. Both are more appropriate to introduce an ongoing permission than the first person present active indicative of 1 Tim 2:12. Even the two occurrences of this verb in the present tense with God as subject ("if God permits"), 1 Cor 16:7 and Heb 6:3, refer to specific situations and not to a universal permission.

Another confirmation that ἐπιτρέπω carried a different semantic and connotative range of meaning than the English "I (do not) permit" is that practically all English versions of Acts 26:1 translate ἐπιτρέπεται (third person present passive, lit., "it is permitted") as though it were in the second person, "You have permission to speak." This is because in English, unlike Greek, "it is permitted" almost invariably implies a continuing state. Moo correctly states, "It must be admitted that the verb ἐπιτρέπω is not often used in Scripture of universally applicable commandments."[11] All of these factors give evidence that this verb, especially in the first person singular present active indicative, is not well-suited to identify a universal prohibition.[12] The English translation "I do not permit," however, implies a universality that runs counter to the normal connotations of this verb.[13] An English translation more faithful to its usage in the Greek Bible is "I am not permitting," indicating a new, case-specific injunction in response to a problem in Ephesus that does not carry the weight of church tradition.[14]

---

11. Moo, "Rejoinder," 199. On p. 193, however, he writes, "the restrictions imposed by Paul in 1 Timothy 2:12 are valid for Christians in all places and all times."
12. So, too, Perriman, "What Eve Did," 130, and Richard Clark Kroeger and Catherine Clark Kroeger, *I Suffer Not a Woman: Rethinking 1 Timothy 2:11–15 in Light of Ancient Evidence* (Grand Rapids: Baker, 1992), 82–83.
13. Only by confusing "evidence" with "proof" can Moo ("Rejoinder," 200) allege that "the first person present of ἐπιτρέπω ... does not constitute clear evidence for" a present, not universal, sense, especially in the indicative.
14. Marshall, *Pastoral Epistles*, 454–55; Witherington, *Earliest Churches*, 120.

Paul, who more than any other NT writer distinguished his personal advice for a particular situation from permanent instructions, did not give 1 Tim 2:12's restrictions on women in the Ephesian church any universalizing qualifier. Nor did he claim that these restrictions on women were from the Lord or that they should apply in all the churches. In most of the few cases where Paul did use the first person singular in the present tense with a continuing future sense, he included some sort of universalizing phrase, as in Rom 12:3 ("to every one of you"), 1 Cor 4:16–17 ("everywhere in every church"), Gal 5:3 ("to every man"), 1 Tim 2:1 ("for all men"), and 1 Tim 2:8 ("in every place"). There is no such universalizing phrase in 1 Tim 2:12.

Moo, however, alleges, "of the twelve examples I have found in which Paul uses the first singular indicative to give what looks like universal advice, only two (1 Tim 2:1 and 8) have a 'universalizing qualifier.'"[15] Yet four of Moo's twelve examples are not singular at all, but plural—2 Cor 5:20; 1 Thess 4:1; 5:14; and 2 Thess 3:6—which suggests a wider authority than Paul's. Of the remaining eight, seven *do* have universalizing qualifiers, namely, words such as "all" or "every" in the context that show that Paul has a universal application in mind:

1. Rom 12:3: "To every [παντί] one of you," confirms its universality.
2. Rom 12:1: γάρ in verse 3 logically connects "every one" in this verse to the single Greek sentence, 12:1–2.
3. 1 Cor 4:16: "Imitate me" is explained in verse 17, "my way of life in Christ Jesus, which agrees with what I teach everywhere [πανταχοῦ] in every [πάσῃ] church."[16]
4. Gal 5:2: Gal 5:3's "*Again* I declare to every [παντί] man" requires that this also applies to 5:2.
5. 1 Tim 2:1: specifies "for all [πάντων] persons."
6. 1 Tim 2:8: specifies "in every [παντί] place."

In spite of their "universalizing qualifiers," not all of these are universal. Most Christians do not regard Gal 5:2–3 (or 1 Tim 2:8) as binding today: "Mark my words! I, Paul, tell you that if you let yourselves be circumcised, Christ will be of no value to you at all. Again I declare to every man

---

15. Moo, "Rejoinder," 200.
16. 1 Cor 4:16, however, is specifically addressed to people Paul had "fathered in the gospel" through initial evangelism and bringing them to faith. Its content, "I urge you to imitate me," presupposes a direct personal relationship that is not universal to all Christians.

who lets himself be circumcised that he is obligated to obey the whole law." Paul's circumcision of Timothy "because of the Jews that lived in that area" (Acts 16:3) proves that Paul himself did not treat this as a universal prohibition of circumcision. Thus, of Moo's twelve examples, the only one without a universalizing qualifier is Eph 4:1, and by its content it could be nothing other than universal: "I urge you to live a life worthy of the calling you have received." In contrast, Paul uses eleven first person singular indicative verbs in a single chapter (listed above, p. 320 n. 4) that give advice that is not universal.

If ἐπιτρέπω in 1 Tim 2:12 is temporally limited, as it usually is in the LXX and NT, then its prohibition is not universal. Unless there is something in the context that universalizes it, Paul's verb choice favors a limited, not universal, prohibition. One cannot simply assume it to be universal any more than one can assume that the prohibition of braided hair, gold, pearls, and wearing expensive clothing (2:9) is universal or that men everywhere must raise their hands when they pray (2:8). Now that Moo has wisely repudiated his earlier view that Eve's deception was causative of the nature of women in general,[17] his universal interpretation lacks adequate textual support. Nor can he legitimately import a universal prohibition of women teaching or having authority from the qualifications for overseers in 3:1–7 since its subject is "anyone" (3:1, 5).[18]

In contrast to the lack of evidence that 1 Tim 2:12's prohibition is universal, there are eight exegetical indicators that Paul did *not* intend a universal prohibition on women teaching:

1. The overall purpose of 1 Timothy is to silence false teachers, and there is ample evidence, elaborated above in ch. 16, that Ephesian women at that time were especially influenced by and participated in the false teaching.

2. Paul's only grammatical imperative in this section, "let women learn," implies that the prohibition of teaching is not universal based on the principle that learning ought to result in teaching. Thus, *b. Qidd.* 29a–b states, "whoever is commanded to study

---

17. Moo, "Rejoinder," 204; idem, "What Does It Mean," *RBMW* 190, repudiating Douglas J. Moo, "1 Timothy 2:11–15: Meaning and Significance," *TJ* 1 NS (1980): 70, which adds, "this susceptibility to deception bars them from engaging in public teaching"; cf. below, pp. 411, 412.
18. Cf. below, p. 448.

is commanded to teach," and Heb 5:12 states, "by this time you ought to be teachers [διδάσκαλοι]."

3. The positive connotations of ἡσυχία indicate serious learning that eventually would enable women to teach. Aída Spencer quotes many rabbinic and early church citations of well-bred learning expressed in quietness.[19] Paul's use of the adversative δέ in 2:12 shows he was conscious of the tension between his command to learn and his present prohibition of teaching.

4. ἐπιτρέπω is a verb that is rarely used for universal permission or prohibition, and never elsewhere to this author's knowledge in the first person present active indicative.

5. Paul states in 3:1, "Anyone who desires the ministry of being an overseer desires a noble task." This is surely an encouragement to all who would hear these words, including women, to aspire to be an overseer.[20] Would Paul encourage desire for forbidden fruit?

6. Paul's life and writings elsewhere did not follow this rule as universal. Rather, he mentions many women among his fellow workers in the gospel and involved in teaching.[21] No other Pauline passage prohibits women from teaching.[22]

7. Timothy himself was taught by his mother and grandmother (2 Tim 1:5; 3:14–16).

8. Titus 2:3 commands older women to be "teachers of what is good." Since Paul wrote this passage about this same time, he must not have intended a universal ban on women teaching.

Moo's affirmation that "the words are still the words of the Apostle Paul, writing inspired Scripture"[23] evades the issue. The question is whether the Holy Spirit gave this text in order to meet the particular needs at Ephesus, needs that may or may not be pertinent in other places and times, or whether he gave it as a universally binding prohibition. It is a question of exegesis and hermeneutics, not a question of inspiration or authority. Paul frequently wrote advice or instructions for particular situations,

---

19. Spencer, *Beyond the Curse*, 74–80.
20. Cf. below, p. 448.
21. Cf. above, pp. 61–68, and below, pp. 328–34.
22. Cf. above, pp. 225–67, on 1 Cor 14:34–35 as an interpolation. Those who accept it as Pauline typically do not interpret it as referring to teaching, anyway.
23. Moo, "Rejoinder," 199.

instructions that were never intended to be universal commands. Understanding his epistles as letters to particular situations can be vital to their proper interpretation. Principles, some of them universally valid principles, lie behind most of what Paul said and guided his actions and advice, as they should guide action today. Careful study can often detect the presence of such principles underlying his statements. But this does not mean that most of Paul's statements are "universally valid principles."[24]

Moo further alleges, "The point to be made here is that ἐπιτρέπω is never used of a permission or prohibition which *could* be universal but is restricted."[25] His statement is false as shown by Mark 10:4 and Matt 19:8–9, "Moses permitted you to divorce your wives." Not only could this permission be treated as universal, it was so treated by the school of Hillel and by Akiba and Josephus. But this permission of divorce was specifically restricted by the school of Shammai and also by the NT. All these factors, combined with Paul's use of this present active indicative verb, strongly favor a translation such as the JB, "I am not giving permission."

"To Teach" Identifies an Action, Not an Office

The prominent position of "to teach" at the beginning of verse 12 indicates this is Paul's key concern in this verse. The contrast between the command to learn in verse 11 and the prohibition involving teaching in verse 12 indicates that Paul intends the most common use of δέ in verse 12, adversative: "Learn but do not teach." This parallels the adversative δέ in both verse 14 and verse 15.

Paul chose active verbs entailing performance of activities (to teach, to assume authority) to express his prohibition, not nouns specifying an office in the church such as pastor-teacher, overseer, or elder.[26] Paul's use of "teacher" in 1 Tim 2:7 and "the office of overseer" in the next chapter prove that he had the words at his disposal to express offices if he had wanted to exclude women from particular offices in the church. The verbs he chose, however, do not specify an office. In other words, the text of 1 Tim 2:12 simply does not restrict women from holding a specific position[27] such as

---

24. *Pace* Moo, "Rejoinder," 199. If by "usually giving" Moo refers not to Paul's statements per se, but to principles that may underly them, he is evading the objection.
25. Moo, "Rejoinder," 199.
26. *Pace* Blomberg, "Neither Hierarchalist," 364.
27. *Pace* Schreiner, "Dialogue," WCA 101–2: "women are proscribed from functioning as elders/ overseers ... they are prohibited from the function of public and authoritative teaching of man

overseer, pastor-teacher, or elder. Rather, it prohibits an activity. The crucial question, then, is: What activity is prohibited?

IS TEACHING LIMITED TO PUBLIC AUTHORITATIVE DISCOURSE?

Schreiner writes regarding 1 Tim 2:12 that "teaching here involves the authoritative and public transmission of tradition about Christ and the Scriptures."[28] Moo even writes, "In the Pastoral Epistles, teaching always has this restricted sense of authoritative doctrinal instruction."[29] Such a precise definition appears to be anachronistic, designed to make the restriction applicable in modern churches where women engage in various forms of teaching, including Sunday school and Bible studies. While they are probably correct in suggesting that the context of the verse refers to a public worship setting, in Paul's day public worship consisted primarily of relatively unstructured home meetings. This is evident from Paul's descriptions of participation by "all" in worship in 1 Cor 14 as well as the many references to churches meeting in homes. Typical worship services, then, probably resembled more closely the kinds of gatherings they wish to exclude from Paul's prohibition than modern "church worship services."

Furthermore, their precise definitions of "to teach" are not at all apparent in this context or anywhere else in Paul's writings. Indeed, it is implausible that Paul intended such a narrow definition of "to teach" that his prohibition would permit women who had adopted false teachings to teach anything as long as it did not mention Christ and the Scriptures. The examples Schreiner and Moo cite do not restrict teaching to "public transmission about Christ and the Scriptures." The question is not whether the word "teach" can apply to specific content or venues, but whether Paul so restricts its use in 1 Tim 2:12. Some of Paul's references to "teaching" include public teaching, at least in part.[30] But other passages Schreiner and Moo cite, such as 2 Tim 2:2, describe personal discipleship with no reference to public transmission. Paul calls older widows to be "teachers of what is excellent" (Titus 2:3). Ironically, according to Moo's definition of

---

by this verse as well."

28. Schreiner, "Dialogue," WCA 101.
29. Moo, "What Does It Mean," RBMW 185.
30. Public teaching is often entailed when the person teaching is a church leader, such as Timothy, but Paul probably intended even 1 Tim 4:2, "Command and teach these things," also to apply in nonpublic settings (e.g., 1 Tim 1:3). The teaching in 1 Tim 6:2 specifically addresses slaves, so it probably included or was primarily private teaching.

"teach" in the Pastorals, Paul calls these older widows to give "authoritative doctrinal instruction," the very thing Moo's view prohibits.

The Pastoral Epistles frequently contrast sound doctrine to false teaching (1 Tim 1:3, 10; 4:1, 6–7; 6:3; 2 Tim 4:2–3; Titus 1:9–2:4), which by definition is not authoritative. "They are ruining whole households by teaching things they ought not to teach" (Titus 1:11) proves that teaching is not always authoritative instruction in the Pastoral Epistles and suggests that teaching can occur in households as well as broader gatherings of the church. None of these passages imply that only overseers and teachers "teach." Whether teaching has authority depends on who teaches and what they teach.

Others try to restrict the locus of teaching to something like "the official teaching assembly." Yet this presupposes a distinct "official teaching assembly,"[31] for which Paul's letters give no evidence. Furthermore, 1 Cor 14:26; Col 3:16; and 2 Tim 2:2 describe teaching as an activity enjoined on believers in general. These passages conflict with an unqualified prohibition against women teaching, even if there was an "official teaching assembly."

In Greek, as in English, "to teach" "is the basic, inclusive word for the imparting of knowledge or skills and usually connotes some individual attention to the learner."[32] Paul uses this verb not only of teaching others (Rom 2:21; Gal 1:12; Col 1:28) but of teaching oneself (Rom 2:21). He uses it of the gift of teaching (Rom 12:7) and of his own teaching in the churches (1 Cor 4:17), but he also encourages all believers to "teach and admonish one another" (Col 3:16). Paul refers to teaching by word of mouth or by letter (2 Thess 2:15). Paul even uses this same word to say that nature "teaches" that long hair disgraces a man but is the glory of a woman (1 Cor 11:14–15). In the Pastoral Epistles, Paul teaches (1 Tim 2:7; 6:1; 2 Tim 1:11; 3:10), Timothy teaches (1 Tim 4:11, 13, 16; 6:2), Titus teaches (2:7), overseers should be able to teach (1 Tim 3:2; 5:17; Titus 1:9), and Paul urges Timothy to disciple people who will be able to teach others (2 Tim 2:2). Their teaching contrasts with teaching by rebellious deceivers.

---

31. Cf. above, p. 221.
32. *Webster's New World Dictionary*, s.v. "teach."

Paul, then, uses the verb "to teach" broadly of anyone teaching either good or bad content in public or private to groups or individuals. It is precisely because "to teach" covers so much, including things that Paul approves for women in other passages,[33] that one properly looks to the content of 1 Tim 2:12 for qualification.

DOES TEACHING HAVE AUTHORITY, BUT NOT PROPHECY?

Some contend that teaching has authority but that prophecy does not and that teaching is an official ministry of the church but prophecy is not.[34] Such a bifurcation of authority between charismatic and official ministries is not a NT distinction.[35] Insofar as there are "official" ministries in the NT at all, they include both prophets and teachers. In 1 Cor 12:25–27, Paul describes the unity of members in the body and the importance of each part working together so there is "no division." Within this unity, verses 28–31 give special priority to certain gifts, "And in the church God has appointed first of all apostles, second prophets, third teachers.... Are all apostles? Are all prophets? Are all teachers?... Eagerly desire the greater gifts."

In Eph 4:11–12, the focus is on persons who are gifted, but the sequence of priority is maintained, "It was he who gave some to be apostles, some to be prophets, some to be evangelists, and some to be pastors and teachers." Teaching and prophecy are both gifts from God. Both have authority only to the degree that their message is from God, so both are subject to judgment based on Scripture. Thus, according to Paul, prophecy has at least as much authority as teaching, if not more.

IN OTHER PASSAGES, PAUL AFFIRMED WOMEN TEACHING

Elsewhere Paul repeatedly encourages women to teach, in contrast to Moo's assertions that in the NT "teaching is restricted to particular individuals ['the elder-overseer' in the Pastorals] and that the NT nowhere depicts women as teachers of men."[36] Affirmations of women teaching are particularly prominent in the Pastoral Epistles. In a letter written about the same

---

33. Cf. below, pp. 328–34.
34. E.g., Barnett, "Wives and Women's Ministry," 233.
35. James D.G. Dunn, *Jesus and the Spirit* (Philadelphia: Westminster, 1975), 280ff.; Harris, "Eve's Deception," 344; Kevin Giles, *Patterns of Ministry among the First Christians* (Melbourne: Collins Dove, 1989), 14–19, 146–47.
36. Moo, "Rejoinder," 200. Pp. 326–28 above show that "teaching" in the NT is not restricted to particular individuals.

time as 1 Timothy, Paul commanded Titus to "speak things fitting sound doctrine [διδασκαλίᾳ] .... [teaching] older women ... to be teachers of what is excellent [καλοδιδασκάλους]" (Titus 2:1–3). The things that Titus is to teach older men and older women in verses 2–3 are remarkably similar to the things that the older women are to teach younger women in verses 4–5. Both are to teach others to be self-controlled (σώφρονας) and loving.

It is arbitrary and goes beyond what this text says to assert, as many have, that "the word cannot refer to public teaching ... but must refer to ministry in the home,"[37] or that "no formal instruction is implied, and perhaps no instruction put into words,"[38] or that what is referred to is "teaching by example."[39] An examination of all the words Paul uses with the root "teach" shows that in every other instance teaching had verbalized content, and in this case the content is enumerated for older women just as it is for Titus. Thus, those who would interpret Titus 2:3 as teaching solely by example do so in opposition to Paul's universal use of this word in any form (noun, verb, participle, compound, root derivative) in this and every other context. They strip "teacher" in 2:3 of its basic meaning (one who verbally imparts knowledge or skills) in only this one instance simply because women are the teachers.

It cannot be validly argued that the teaching root had some other connotation in "teachers of what is excellent" simply because this particular derivative of the root "teach" is not attested elsewhere. The component parts of this compound seem to indicate a particularly sound and well-thought-out message: "a teacher of what is excellent" (Titus 2:3).[40] If it is true, as is frequently stated, that this compound word was a linguistic innovation[41] by Paul, then he intentionally created this impressive noun for a teacher of what is excellent specifically to apply to women. There is no sufficient reason to reject the normal meaning of "teacher" in Titus 2:3: one ministering "not so much by example as by exhortation and teaching."[42]

---

37. Guthrie, *Pastoral Epistles*, 193; cf. J. H. Bernard, *The Pastoral Epistles* (Cambridge: Cambridge Univ. Press, 1899), 166; Kelly, *Pastoral Epistles*, 240; Homer A. Kent Jr., *The Pastoral Epistles* (Chicago: Moody, 1982), 222.
38. Scott, *Pastoral Epistles*, 164.
39. Hendriksen, *I & II Timothy and Titus*, 364; cf. Hanson, *Pastoral Epistles*, 180.
40. Cf. Lock, *Pastoral Epistles*, 140; Hendricksen, *I & II Timothy and Titus*, 364.
41. A search of the Duke Papyri and the TLG CD-ROM disk C on the Ibycus computer uncovered no other occurrence of καλοδιδάσκαλος apart from church fathers, who were clearly dependent on Paul.
42. Huther, *Timothy and Titus*, 296; cf. John Calvin, *Commentaries on the Epistles to Timothy, Titus, and Philemon* (trans. William Pringle; Grand Rapids: Eerdmans, 1949), 312; Barrett, *Pastoral Epistles*, 134.

Indeed, this normal meaning seems to be required by what Paul delineates in Titus 2:4–5 as a result of the elder women being "teachers of what is good." Paul chose "a classical verb for indoctrinating ... and ... of schooling someone in a needed lesson,"[43] "so that they can train the younger women." It is sometimes mistakenly asserted that "the teaching activity of these women is explicitly restricted to the younger women (2:4–5)."[44] Purpose clauses are rarely exhaustive. Only if Paul stated that these women were to be teachers in some restricted sense, e.g., "*only* in order to train younger women," could one know that their teaching was restricted to younger women. No such restriction is stated in Titus 2:3–5. The text does enumerate some of the results when older women are "teachers of what is excellent," but it does not restrict their teaching either in scope or audience. An important, but not exclusive, result is that they will train the younger women. Paul's praise for Timothy's grandmother Lois and mother Eunice for teaching him the Holy Scriptures shows that younger women were not the only group older women should teach what is excellent. It also shows that the scope of their teaching includes Holy Scripture.

The classic verse encapsulating personal discipleship is 2 Tim 2:2: "The things you have heard me say in the presence of many witnesses entrust to faithful persons [ἄνθρωποι], who will be able to teach [διδάξαι] others also." Although many translations have "faithful men," Paul chose the generic term ἄνθρωποι that includes all human beings, women as well as men (cf. its use of women in 1 Pet 3:4), as expressed in the JB, NRSV, and TNIV.

This pattern is beautifully exemplified in this very letter by Timothy's own mother and grandmother: "I have been reminded of your sincere faith, which first lived in your grandmother Lois and in your mother Eunice and, I am persuaded, now lives in you also (2 Tim 1:5)." "Continue in what you have learned and have become convinced of, because you know those from whom you learned it, and how from infancy you have known the Holy Scriptures.... All Scripture is God-breathed and is useful for teaching, reproof, correcting, and training in righteousness ..." (3:14–16). Paul praised these two women for their part in making the sacred writings known to Timothy "from infancy," a phrase expressing when their teaching

---

43. E. K. Simpson, *The Pastoral Epistles* (London: Tyndale, 1954), 104.
44. Moo, "Rejoinder," 201; idem, "What Does It Mean," *RBMW* 497 n. 17.

began but giving no indication that it stopped at any point in Timothy's life. The implication is natural that these women, who had made known the Holy Scriptures to Timothy, used them for "teaching" (3:16) as well as for "rebuking, correcting and training in righteousness." The association of "teaching" with these other functions that typically occur outside of formal settings implies that teaching, too, in Paul's usage is not restricted to formal settings.

Priscilla[45] and Aquila accompanied Paul to Ephesus (Acts 18:18), and he left them there (18:19) to carry on the ministry. There they "explained the way of God more accurately" (Acts 18:26b NASB) to the eloquent teacher Apollos. Paul writes from Ephesus in 1 Cor 16:19, "Aquila and Prisca greet you heartily in the Lord, with the church that is in their house." In 2 Tim 4:19, Paul again greets Prisca and Aquila, who are apparently back in Ephesus.[46] In light of these three women (Lois, Eunice, Prisca) specifically identified by name in 2 Timothy, all of whom taught effectively in personal discipleship, it is surely mistaken to think that women are excluded from the "faithful persons who will be able to teach others also" in 2 Tim 2:2.

In 1 Cor 14:26, Paul writes, "whenever you come together, each one [ἕκαστος encompasses men and women] has a psalm, a teaching [διδαχή], a revelation, a tongue or an interpretation." First Corinthians 11:5 and Acts 21:9 (Philip's four daughters, who had the gift of prophecy) show that it would be contrary to Paul's intent to exclude women from the "each of you" who has a revelation. It is generally agreed that women, just as well as men, may share a psalm, a tongue, or an interpretation. "Teaching" has the same grammatical subject as each of these others. "Each of you" is an inclusive subject. It is qualified only by the goal of edification.

Normally, not everyone will do everything in the same service, as verse 27 implies. Nevertheless, "each of you" naturally encourages women as well as men to share a teaching. Two verses earlier in 1 Cor 14:24 Paul writes approvingly of a situation where "all prophesy." Five verses later in 14:31 he writes, "For you can all prophesy one by one so that all may learn and all may

---

45. Cf. above, pp. 64, 282.
46. In Rom 16:3 Paul greets Prisca and Aquila, showing that they were then in Rome. 1 Tim 1:3 addresses Timothy in Ephesus. Evidence that 2 Timothy was also written to Ephesus includes: 2 Tim 4:12—Paul sent Tychicus to Ephesus (presumably to replace Timothy), 1:18—Timothy knows of Onesiphorus's work in Ephesus, and Hymenaeus (2:17) and Alexander (4:14) are still a threat (cf. 1 Tim 1:20). Cf. Acts 18:19; 1 Cor 16:19; Conzelmann, *1 Corinthians*, 299; Knight, *Pastoral Epistles*, 9.

be encouraged," using the same word for "all" three times. Since the "all" who may learn and the "all" who may be encouraged are inclusive of all believers in the church, including women, so, too, the "all" who may prophesy logically should include women. These "all's" must include women since three chapters earlier, in 1 Cor 11:5, Paul regulates the head covering women should have when they lead worship in prayer and prophesy. Since this is true of the higher gift of prophecy,[47] "each one" who has a teaching just five verses earlier must not exclude women either. Since this passage does not restrict any member of the congregation from participating in any of these ministries, but rather uses inclusive language ("each," ἕκαστος), it is arbitrary and counter to the context for Moo to exclude all women from teaching.

Similarly in Col 3:16, Paul commanded the whole church, including women, "Let the word of Christ dwell in you richly as you [plural, addressing the whole church, including women] teach and counsel one another with all wisdom, and as you sing psalms, hymns and spiritual songs with gratitude in your hearts to God." The "all" of verse 11 of this chapter (see its parallel in Gal 3:28) and their identification in verse 12 as "God's chosen people" require the inclusion of women. Furthermore, both sentences immediately following Col 3:16–17 specifically mention women. Paul uses "one another" three verses earlier in the command, "forgive one another," addressing the entire congregation. Just as it would be wrong to exclude any particular group from those who may forgive one another or sing psalms, so it is wrong to exclude women as a group from those who may "teach and counsel."

Eduard Lohse appropriately comments, "The functions of 'teaching' [διδάσκειν] and 'admonishing' [νουθετεῖν] ... are not bound to a distinct office, but were exercised by members of the community because of the gifts of the Spirit bestowed upon them (1 Cor 12:28; 14:26)."[48] Some churches today allow only a few to teach, and the teaching is virtually all one way, teacher to learner, without any reciprocal element. This, however, is not what Paul advocates in 1 Cor 14:26 and Col 3:16, as even Schreiner admits, "women can teach men publicly and officially ... the mutual instruction that occurs among all the members of the body. Unfortunately,

---

47. Cf. 1 Cor 12:28–29; 14:1–5, 24; Eph 4:11.
48. Eduard Lohse, *Colossians and Philemon* (Hermeneia; Philadelphia: Fortress, 1971), 150–51. Cf. Rom 15:14.

some churches ban women from doing even this, although it is plainly in accord with Scripture."[49] While this verse does not teach that all believers have the *gift* of teaching or require that every member minister in each of the ways here listed, it does teach a widely shared teaching ministry, not one restricted to particular individuals.

The seven men the apostles originally appointed to serve (διακονεῖν) tables, whom Eusebius (*Hist. eccl.* 2d) says were "ordained to the diaconate," were "full of the Spirit and wisdom" (Acts 6:3). Of these Philip taught the Scriptures to the Ethiopian eunuch (Acts 8:26–40), and Stephen (6:5) taught forcefully to the Sanhedrin in 7:2–53. Saul was present at Stephen's stoning (8:1), so he was familiar with his teaching. Thus, Paul's inclusion of women in his qualifications for deacons (1 Tim 3:11) and his praise of Phoebe, "deacon of the church in Cenchrea" in Rom 16:2, suggest support for women teaching, as does his affirmation of women prophesying (e.g., 1 Cor 11:5–13; 14:5, 24, 31, 39; cf. Acts 21:9), since prophecy often entails teaching. Even regarding overseers, 1 Tim 3:1–2 affirms, "whoever [τὶς encompasses men and women] desires the office of overseer desires a good thing … [overseers must be] able to teach [διδακτικός]."[50]

Clearly, then, Paul encouraged women to teach, and in his word usage "teaching" was not an activity restricted solely to particular individuals. Repeatedly, Paul implies that women are to be involved in the teaching ministry of the church—a ministry open to all believers. Paul also teaches that particular individuals are specifically gifted by the Holy Spirit as teachers. He often stresses the importance of the office of teacher. There is no convincing evidence that Paul excluded all women either from the gift or the office of teacher. The Spirit is free to bestow the gift of teaching on whomever he pleases and to appoint whomever he wills (1 Cor 12:11).

Paul's use of words like "teach" and "teacher" in contexts applying to both men and women shows not simply that women as well as men are exhorted to "teach one another" in the body of believers but also shows that men may be included in the scope of those taught by women. Consequently, to interpret 1 Tim 2:12 as a universal prohibition of women teaching men[51] causes this passage to conflict with Paul's teaching elsewhere.

---

49. Schreiner, "Dialogue," *WCA* 101.
50. Cf. below, p. 448.
51. E.g., Moo, "What Does It Mean," *RBMW* 189, "it was Paul's position in every church that women should not teach or have authority over men."

Rather, one should expect that Paul is here prohibiting women from teaching in some qualified sense.

WHY DID PAUL SPECIFICALLY RESTRICT TEACHING BY WOMEN?

Moo states, "If Paul were here concerned with the problem of false teaching *per se*, surely he would have prohibited all false teachers from addressing the church, not just the women."[52] Paul, however, had already done that, as he states in 1:3, "As I urged you when I went into Macedonia, stay there in Ephesus so that you may command certain people [τις] not to teach false doctrines any longer." Hymenaeus and Alexander had already rejected the faith (1:19–20), and Paul had already turned them over to Satan. The implication is that they were no longer under the discipline of the church nor were they teaching within it,[53] though Hymenaeus's influence continued.

Second Timothy 2:17–18 refers to Hymenaeus and Philetus as outsiders, "who have wandered away from the truth. They say that the resurrection has already taken place, and they destroy the faith of some." Paul's letters do not tell Timothy to confront the original false teachers. Rather, 2 Tim 2:16 says regarding Hymenaeus and Philetus's teaching, "Avoid godless chatter." Similarly, 2:23 commands, "Don't have anything to do with foolish and stupid arguments." In 2:24–26, Paul instructs Timothy when there is opposition in the church to "gently instruct, in the hope that God will grant them repentance"; but in describing the false teachers in 3:1–9 he commands, "Have nothing to do with them."

Paul's primary concern in 1 Timothy is not the original false teachers, but with the impact they have made, especially on women. Paul wants Timothy to address a second round of false teaching particularly by women in the Ephesian church.[54] Thus, although Paul's letters affirm many women in church leadership, here in Ephesus false teaching by women was a big enough threat that Paul restricts teaching by women.

The most likely reason Paul commands women to learn in quietness, restricts their teaching and argues for it, based on Eve's deception, is that there was a significant problem with women who had been deceived and

---

52. Moo, "Rejoinder," 203.
53. Cf. Moo, "Rejoinder," 217.
54. Cf. above on the influence of the false teachers on women, pp. 299–304.

were spreading this destructive teaching. One ought to try to understand this restriction within the occasion for the letter stated in 1:3 – 11, namely, false teaching. Similarly, at about the same time, Paul silences the teaching of the circumcision group in Crete "because they are ruining whole households by teaching things they ought not to teach" (Titus 1:11). Both prohibitions address the most problematic group confronting Paul's colleague.

A probable contributing factor to Paul's restriction was that most women in Ephesus from either a Jewish or Gentile background would have had little knowledge of the Scriptures and the Christian message. Paul's most complete description of the false teachers concludes, "They want to be teachers of the law, but they do not know what they are talking about or what they so confidently affirm" (1:7). This description fits women in the Ephesian church who, because of inadequate Christian education, were deceived by the false teaching. Particularly significant in this statement is the implication that their error was not in desiring to be teachers of the law, but rather in teaching without adequate knowledge. Until they are properly taught, they should not make blundering attempts at teaching, but rather learn, just as 2:11 – 12 requires.

19

1 Timothy 2:12: Part II:
Does Οὐδέ Separate Two
Prohibitions or Conjoin Them?

Two crucial questions must be answered in order to understand 1 Tim 2:12. The next chapter examines the crucial question of the meaning of the second infinitive of this prohibition (αὐθεντεῖν). Since the lexical and contextual evidence favors the meaning BDAG 150 gives for αὐθεντεῖν, "to assume a stance of independent authority," this chapter translates this verb "to assume authority." The other crucial question, rarely asked, is whether Paul intends the conjunction οὐδέ to separate two different prohibitions — (1) to teach and (2) to assume authority over a man — or to merge these into a single prohibition.[1]

Surprisingly, although various scholars have argued that the οὐδέ construction in 1 Tim 2:12 gives a single prohibition,[2] the first thorough analysis of the use of οὐδέ in the Pauline corpus was not presented publicly until 1986.[3] This chapter shows that the overwhelming majority of

---

1. This may be called hendiadys, ἓν διὰ δυοῖν, "one by means of two," whereby a conjunction connects two expressions to convey a single idea. Some, however, define hendiadys more narrowly, so this book avoids this term.
2. E.g., Hurley, *Biblical Perspective*, 201; Spencer, *Beyond the Curse*, 88; Robert L. Saucy, "Women's Prohibition to Teach Men: An Investigation into Its Meaning and Contemporary Application," *JETS* 37 (1994): 90; U. Wagener, *Die Ordnung des «Hauses Gottes»: Der Ort von Frauen in der Ekklesiologie und Ethik der Pastoralbriefe* (WUNT 2.65; Tübingen: J. C. B. Mohr [Paul Siebeck], 1994) 75–76; Belleville, "Teaching and Usurping," 217–19; Marshall, *Pastoral Epistles*, 460.
3. Philip B. Payne, "οὐδέ in 1 Timothy 2:12," presented at the Evangelical Theological Society Annual Meeting in Atlanta, Ga., Nov. 21, 1986; revised and published as: "1 Tim 2.12 and the Use of οὐδέ to Combine Two Elements to Express a Single Idea," *NTS* 54 (2008): 235–53.

the uses of οὐδέ[4] and of the οὐκ + οὐδέ + ἀλλά syntactical construction in the undisputed letters of Paul combine two elements to express a single idea. It argues that this is the most natural way to interpret 1 Tim 2:12 within its context. The conclusion to be reached, therefore, is that this verse does not prohibit women such as Priscilla from teaching men, as long as their authority is properly recognized, not self-assumed. It simply prohibits women from assuming for themselves authority to teach men.

Thirty-one uses of οὐδέ occur in Paul's undisputed letters, thirty-two including the second οὐδέ in many early manuscripts of Gal 1:12. Eight of these οὐδέ are not coordinating conjunctions and so are not analogous to 1 Tim 2:12; seven of these eight express the idiom "not even": 1 Cor 11:14; 14:21; 15:13, 16; Gal 2:3, 5; 6:13. Each of these, along with the eighth (Rom 4:15), introduces an idea that is meaningful by itself. This study argues that, excluding the ambiguous case of 1 Thess 2:3, seventeen of the twenty-one uses of οὐδέ as a coordinating conjunction in the universally accepted letters of Paul make best sense conveying a single idea. The four exceptions each convey naturally paired ideas that focus on the same verb.

The Use of Οὐδέ in the Undisputed Letters of Paul

Paul typically uses οὐδέ to join together expressions that reinforce or make more specific a single idea.[5] Appropriately, BDF §445 calls οὐδέ a "correlative" and a "connective," indicating "correlation" of members and contrasts its use with "independent continuation." When "not" (οὐ or οὐκ) occurs in the first expression, this negation encompasses the entire single idea. The οὐ in οὐδέ underscores the continuing negation.

Paul's uses of οὐδέ as a coordinating conjunction fit into four categories:

1. those joining two equivalent expressions to convey a single idea
2. those joining naturally paired expressions to convey a single idea

---

4. Μηδέ is not included here since Paul tends to use it differently, to list separate items.
5. Non-Pauline examples of οὐδέ joining two infinitives in order to convey a single idea include the LXX of Isa 42:24b; Polybius, *Histories* 30.5.8.4–6; 30.24.2.3–4; 31.12.5–6; Diodorus Siculus 3.37.9.1–4; Josephus, *Ant.* 6.20.3–5; 7.127.1–3; Plutarch, *Def. orac.* 426.B.1; *Tranq. an.* 474.A.12; 475.D.3; A. J. Köstenberger, "A Complex Sentence: The Syntax of 1 Timothy 2:12," *WCA* 53–84, 63–71, cites these but does not reveal that they convey a single idea.

3. those joining conceptually different expressions to convey a single idea

4. those joining naturally paired ideas focusing on the same verb

1. Οὐδέ *Joins Equivalent Expressions to Convey a Single Idea*

In seven instances (eight including the textual variant in Gal 1:12), οὐδέ joins two expressions that are equivalent in meaning. In each of these cases οὐδέ joins expressions to convey a single idea. This chapter italicizes all English translations of οὐδέ.

1. Rom 2:28: "For the true Jew is not the man who is outwardly a Jew, *and* true circumcision is *not* that which is outward and bodily" (Weymouth; cf. Goodspeed, Williams, also translating οὐδέ "*and . . . not*"). The TEV clearly conveys the equivalence in meaning: "After all, who is a real Jew, truly circumcised? Not the man who is a Jew on the outside, *whose* circumcision is a physical thing."

2. Rom 9:6–7: "For not all Israelites truly belong to Israel, *and not* all of Abraham's children are his true descendants" (NRSV, RSV).

3. 1 Cor 15:50: "Flesh and blood cannot inherit the kingdom of God: *and* the perishable can*not* inherit what lasts for ever" (JB; cf. Goodspeed, NAB, TEV).

4. Gal 1:1: "Paul an apostle—not from men *nor* through man" (RSV). The equivalence in meaning is conveyed by Phillips: "Paul, who am appointed *and* commissioned a messenger not by man but by Jesus Christ."

5. Gal 1:11b–12: "The gospel I preached is not of human origin. [οὐδέ] I did *not* receive it from any human source" (TNIV, cf. JB). Οὔτε (οὐδέ in ‭א‬ A D*·c F G P Ψ 0278 33 81 104 365 1175 1241ˢ 1739 1881 2464 *al*) emphasizes this with a third equivalent expression, "*nor* was I taught it" (NRSV, NIV, TNIV).

6. Gal 4:14: "What must have tried you in my physical condition, you did not scorn *and* despise, but you welcomed me like an angel of God" (Goodspeed).

7. Phil 2:16: "I had not run in the race *and* exhausted myself for nothing" (JB).

In all seven (or eight), οὐδέ joins two expressions having equivalent meanings. The second expression in each case reinforces the single idea and introduces no separate idea.

2. Οὐδέ Joins Naturally Paired Expressions to Convey a Single Idea

In four instances οὐδέ joins naturally paired expressions, couplets that by their very nature are closely associated with each other, to convey a single idea:

1. Rom 11:21: "For if God did not spare the natural branches, he will *not* spare you [engrafted branches] *either.*" Verse 24 confirms the "how much more" logic of this single, internally cohering idea.

2. & 3. Gal 3:28: "There is no such thing as Jew *and* Greek, slave *and* freeman, male and (καί)[6] female" (NEB; cf. Fenton, Goodspeed, JB, TEV, Way, Weymouth, also translating οὐδέ *"and"*). Here οὐδέ parallels καί ("and"), and in the same couplets in Col 3:11 and Rom 10:12, καί replaces οὐδέ. These must not be separate statements, "there is no Jew in Christ" and "there is no Greek in Christ," since both statements are obviously false. The context of discrimination against Greeks confirms that Paul means there is no "Jew–Greek" dichotomy in Christ.[7] The antagonistic barrier represented by each pair is overcome in Christ. Each pair functions together to convey a single coherent idea: there is no "Jew–Greek," or "slave–free," or "male–female" dichotomy in Christ.

4. 1 Thess 5:5: "We have nothing to do with night *and* darkness" (Beck; cf. LB). Οὐδέ joins night with darkness to specify the single internally cohering idea of night viewed as darkness, a metaphor for evil as separation from the light of God.

In all four, οὐδέ joins naturally paired expressions to convey a single idea. In each case, the second expression specifies the meaning and is essential to convey this single idea.

---

6. R. J. Swanson, *New Testament Greek Manuscripts: Galatians* (Carol Stream, Ill.: Tyndale, 1999), 44–45, notes MS 88 has the variant reading καί οὐδέ and D* substitutes ἤ for οὐδέ in "slave or free."
7. Gal 2:11–3:14 and 3:23–25 identify discrimination against Greeks. Cf. above, pp. 79–85, 89–92.

3. Οὐδέ *Joins Conceptually Different Expressions to Convey a Single Idea*

In six passages in the undisputed letters of Paul, οὐδέ joins conceptually different expressions to convey a single internally cohering idea. Each passage makes better sense if it conveys one idea rather than two.

1. Rom 3:10: "There is no one who is righteous, *not even* one" (NIV, NRSV). "Not even one" gives an emphatic clarification that "no one" is without exception. The two elements are intrinsically intertwined and should not be interpreted as two separate ideas.

2. Rom 9:16: "It does not, therefore, depend on human desire *and* effort, but on God's mercy." Grammatically this could convey two separate ideas, namely, that mercy does not depend on desire, nor does it depend on effort. The context, however, shows that Paul objects to mercy being dependent on the combination of desire and effort, continuing the concern of verse 12, "not by works" (cf. v. 11). "Desire and effort" in verse 16 conceptually parallels "pursued by works" in verses 31–32: "the people of Israel, who pursued the law as the way of righteousness, have not attained their goal. Why not? Because they pursued it not by faith but as if it were by works" (TNIV). Since Paul affirms pursuit by faith but opposes pursuit by works, he must not oppose desire for righteousness itself, but instead, desire for righteousness achieved by works. Therefore, the single idea "desire *combined with* effort" in 9:16 fits the context better than "desire or effort" understood separately.

3. 1 Cor 2:6: "wisdom not of this age, *and specifically* not of the rulers of this age" (cf. JB). Paul's use of "wisdom" and "the wise" interchangeably (1:19–20; 3:19–20), and the continuing focus in 2:8 on the misunderstanding of "the rulers of this age" (τῶν ἀρχόντων τοῦ αἰῶνος τούτου, repeated exactly from 2:6) support understanding 2:6's οὐδέ construction as focusing specifically on the rulers of this age.

4. 1 Cor 5:1: "There is sexual immorality among you, and of a kind that is *not* [found] *even* (ἥτις οὐδέ) among pagans; for a man is living with his father's wife" (NRSV). The relative pronominal adjective ἥτις ("which") makes it explicit that οὐδέ introduces a

qualifying description. MS 2147 omits ἥτις,[8] showing that, with
or without ἥτις, οὐδέ introduces this qualifying description. The
text following οὐδέ narrows down what sort of illicit sex Paul has
in mind, just as the text following οὐδέ in 1 Tim 2:12 may identify
what teaching is prohibited, "teaching *combined with* assuming
authority over a man."

5. 1 Cor 11:16: "We *and* the churches of God" (Phillips; cf. LB) "have
no such custom" (ASV, KJV). Since the custom in view regards
head covering in church, "we" most naturally refers to churches.
Paul consistently identifies with the churches elsewhere, e.g.,
1 Cor 4:17; 7:17, and stresses the unity of the one body, e.g., Rom
12:4–5; 1 Cor 10:17; 12:12–25; Eph 4:4–6. Paul's letters never
separate himself from the churches, but this separation is required
if οὐδέ distinguishes "we" from "the churches of God."[9] Paul's
meaning, then, is "we, the churches of God, have no such custom."
The two elements joined by οὐδέ ("we ... the churches of God"),
as in 1 Tim 2:12 ("to teach ... to assume authority over a man"),
are at opposite ends of their clause separated in the same order
by (1) the complement of the main verb (τοιαύτην συνήθειαν/
γυναικί), (2) οὐκ, (3) the main verb (ἔχομεν/ἐπιτρέπω), and
(4) οὐδέ. In both, the main verb ("have/permit") is a first person,
present active indicative. These structural parallels support understanding οὐδέ in 1 Tim 2:12 as also conveying a single idea.

6. Gal 1:16–17: "I did not consult human authority,[10] *specifically* I
did *not* go up to Jerusalem to see those who were apostles before
me, I went off at once to Arabia." Paul's testimony described in
Acts 22:12–16 affirms Ananias's consultation with Paul specifically regarding Paul's mission. According to Luke, Paul met with
Ananias and the disciples in Damascus for several days after his

---

8. R. J. Swanson, *New Testament Greek Manuscripts: 1 Corinthians* (Carol Stream, Ill.: Tyndale, 2003), 58, also notes that MSS 6 104 460 1241[S] 1243 1874* 1891* omit "and of a kind" (καὶ τοιαύτη). This shows that even without καὶ τοιαύτη, οὐδέ still introduces this qualifying description.
9. If Paul had intended to distinguish his churches from the other churches, he could easily have said, as he does in 2 Cor 11:8, ἄλλας ἐκκλησίας ("*other* churches"). Cf. the discussion of 1 Cor 11:16 above, pp. 207–8.
10. Lit., "flesh and blood." "To reveal" (1:16) implies divine authority in contrast to human author-ity, as Paul emphasizes in 1:1: "nor from human authorities" (NRSV), cf. 6–9, 10, 11, 12: "not from man, but through revelation."

divine commission to the Gentiles (9:15–19; cf. 26:12–20). This testimony from Paul's "fellow worker" (Phlm 24), who was surely familiar with the most formative event in Paul's life, affirms that Paul did consult at least with Ananias. If Gal 1:16 denies any human consultation, it contradicts Paul's consultation with Ananias. There is no contradiction, however, if οὐδέ combines elements to specify the apostles in Jerusalem. This and Paul's typical use of οὐδέ support its specifying function here.

In every case in this third category, οὐδέ conjoins conceptually different expressions to convey a single idea. In each case, adding the second expression specifies the meaning: case 1 intensifies; cases 2, 3, 4, 5, and 6 combine elements to focus on a particular meaning. Similarly, each case in the second category (joining naturally paired expressions to convey a single idea) also specifies the meaning. Thus, within Paul's dominant use of οὐδέ to convey a single idea, his most common use of οὐδέ is to specify meaning.[11] The fundamental function of οὐδέ in these cases is not to subordinate one expression to another, but simply to merge them together to convey a single more specific idea. In each case, the context and the expressions conjoined adequately elucidate the nature of their interrelationship.

4. Οὐδέ *Joins Naturally Paired Ideas Focusing on the Same Verb*

Four occurrences of οὐδέ in Paul's undisputed letters join naturally paired but clearly distinguishable ideas focusing on the same verb:

1. Rom 8:7: "The flesh ... does not submit to God's Law — *indeed* it cannot" (NRSV).
2. 1 Cor 3:2: "I gave you milk, not solid food, for you were not yet ready for it. Indeed, you are *still not* ready."
3. 1 Cor 4:3: "I care very little if I am judged by you or by any human court; indeed, I do *not even* judge myself" (cf. NRSV).
4. 2 Cor 7:12: "So although I wrote to you, it was not on account of the one who did the wrong *nor* on account of the one who was wronged, but in order that your zeal for us might be made known to you before God" (NRSV).

---

11. Ten out of seventeen occurrences in the undisputed letters of Paul specify meaning. In Titus 2:13 also, hendiadys specifies meaning: "our blessed hope, (καί) the appearing of the glory of our great God and Savior Jesus Christ" (RSV; cf. BDF §442 16.).

In all four of these cases, οὐδέ joins statements that together form a natural pair focusing on the same verb: does not submit/cannot submit,[12] you were not yet ready/you are still not ready, judged by you/judge myself, and the one who did wrong/the one who was wronged. None of these parallels 1 Tim 2:12, since "to teach" and "to assume authority" (and every other proposed meaning for αὐθεντέω) are unrelated verbs and are not a natural pair.

The one remaining verse containing οὐδέ in the undisputed letters of Paul (1 Thess 2:3) is hard to classify: "For our appeal does not spring from deceit or impure motives or trickery" (NRSV). Both the first (πλάνη) and third (δόλος) nouns οὐδέ joins commonly mean "deceit" (BDAG 822, 256), which fits this context perfectly. The second (ἀκαθαρσία) identifies impure motives (BDAG 34), so each of the three points to impure intent. It is ambiguous whether they are closely interrelated, equivalent expressions (category 1), conceptually different expressions that convey a single, internally cohering idea (category 3), or three distinct ideas.

To summarize, Paul's overwhelmingly dominant use of οὐδέ to combine two elements is to express a single idea. Paul's seventeen uses of οὐδέ to conjoin expressions that together convey a single idea fit into three categories:

1. Seven join equivalent expressions.
2. Four join naturally paired expressions.
3. Six join conceptually different expressions.

Paul uses οὐδέ unambiguously to convey separate ideas in only four cases, and in each case οὐδέ joins a natural pair focusing on the same verb. Strikingly, there is not a single unambiguous case where Paul joins two conceptually distinct expressions with οὐδέ to convey two separate ideas.

An English Expression Equivalent to Paul's Use of Οὐδέ

The closest English equivalent to Paul's use of οὐδέ to join together two expressions to convey a single idea is the use of " 'n," as in "hit 'n run," "nice 'n easy," and "spick 'n span." In almost every case, 'n joins two words to convey a single idea. "Don't eat 'n run!" prohibits leaving immediately after eating. It does not prohibit either eating or running by itself. "Don't

---

12. The word immediately prior to οὐδέ, "submit," is the necessary complement of "cannot," cf. BDAG 262.

hit 'n run" prohibits the *combination* of hitting someone with a vehicle, then fleeing the scene of the accident. Similarly, 1 Tim 2:12a viewed as a single idea does not prohibit teaching in itself, nor does it prohibit taking authority into one's own hands, though, like "hitting" in "hit 'n run," taking authority into one's own hands is negative in most public situations, whether by a woman or a man. Instead, it prohibits women from teaching combined with assuming authority over a man.

In both the οὐδέ construction in 1 Tim 2:12 and in "eat 'n run," one part of the expression viewed independently is positive (teach/eat) and the other negative (assume authority over a man/run [in the sense of breaking social convention by leaving prematurely]). Paul's use of οὐδέ further parallels the English idiom 'n since both often join naturally paired expressions, e.g., "night 'n day" and "black 'n white," and can connect one word with predominantly positive overtones to another with predominantly negative overtones. Furthermore, Paul's use of οὐδέ functions to join various kinds of grammatical forms, including verbs, nouns, and adjectives in order to convey a single concept, just as 'n does in English.

PAUL'S AND LUKE'S USE OF Οὐδέ CONTRASTED

The occurrences of οὐδέ in Luke–Acts exhibit a significantly different pattern of uses than those in the undisputed letters of Paul. Eight of Paul's thirty-one uses of οὐδέ are not coordinating conjunctions, but introduce an idea that is meaningful by itself. A higher proportion (14 of 33) of Luke's uses of οὐδέ are not coordinating conjunctions. Roughly three-fourths (17 or 19[13]) of Paul's 23 uses of οὐδέ to conjoin two elements express a single idea. In contrast, roughly half (10 of 19) of Luke's uses of οὐδέ to conjoin two elements express a single idea, and in all but three of these, οὐδέ conjoins equivalent expressions. Paul's undisputed letters contain six instances where οὐδέ joins two conceptually distinct expressions that are not a natural pair to convey one idea, but Luke–Acts contains only one. Paul uses οὐδέ four times to focus on the same verb; Luke never does this. There is not even one unambiguous case where Paul uses οὐδέ to join conceptually distinct concepts to convey two separate ideas, but Luke uses οὐδέ nine times to do this.[14] The following table itemizes these differences.

---

13.   Including two ambiguous uses in 1 Thess 2:3.
14.   Luke 12:27, 33; 18:4; 23:15; Acts 9:9; 16:21; 17:25; 24:13, 18.

Categories of Οὐδέ in the Undisputed Letters of Paul and in Luke-Acts

	Not joining	Joining separate expressions together					
		to express one idea joining:			to express two ideas that:		
		equivalents	natural pairs	two[15]	focus on same verb	are separate	Total
Paul	8	7	4	6	4	0	31[16]
Luke	14[17]	7[18]	2[19]	1[20]	0	9[21]	33

THE USE OF Οὐδέ IN THE DISPUTED LETTERS OF PAUL

Each of the four instances of οὐδέ in the disputed Pauline epistles fits one of the patterns identified above in the undisputed letters of Paul. Three of these make best sense understood as joining conceptually different expressions to convey a single idea. The first is 2 Thess 3:7–8: "we were not idle when we were with you, *and* we did not eat anyone's bread without paying for it; but with toil and labor we worked night and day, so that we might not burden any of you" (NRSV). At first glance this may appear to be a denial of two separate issues, idleness and eating free food. The conclusion of the sentence, however, that Paul and his companions worked hard for their food, clearly stands in opposition to the combination of both elements joined by οὐδέ.

This idea is reiterated in 2 Thess 3:10–12, which explicitly prohibits freeloading, the combination of idleness and taking free meals from others.

---

15. Cases where οὐδέ joins two conceptually different expressions together to convey a single idea.
16. The two ambiguous instances in 1 Thess 2:3 are in the total but are not assigned to a category.
17. Luke 6:3; 7:7, 9; 12:26, 27b; 16:31; 18:13; 20:8, 36; 23:40; Acts 4:12, 32, 34; 19:2.
18. Luke 6:44; 8:17; 11:33; 12:24b; 17:21; Acts 2:27; 8:21.
19. Luke 6:43; 12:24a.
20. Acts 7:5.
21. Luke 12:27: work/spin; 12:33: thief comes near/moth destroys; 18:4: fear God/care about men; 23:15: I (Pilate)/Herod; Acts 9:9: ate/drank; 16:21: accept/do; 17:25: does not live in hand-made temples/is not served by human hands; 24:13: they did not find me arguing or stirring up a crowd/they cannot prove these charges; 24:18: crowd/disturbance.

To eat food given as a gift (δωρεάν) has positive connotations unless it is joined with the negative idea of idleness. Cultural convention supports that Paul received meals without financially reimbursing each host. Furthermore, 1 Cor 9:3–14 argues that Paul should have this right, 1 Cor 10:27 commands acceptance of hospitality, Rom 12:13 commands hospitality, Phil 4:16–19 praises the Philippians for sending him aid, and 1 Tim 3:2 and Titus 1:8 identify hospitality as a necessary quality of overseers and elders. Thus, the interpretation that Paul never accepted free meals stands in tension with the explication of verses 7–8a in verses 8b–12, with cultural conventions, and with Paul's teachings. All this supports interpreting οὐδέ in 2 Thess 3:7–8 as merging a negative concept and a positive concept to specify the single idea, freeloading.

The second such use of οὐδέ is 1 Tim 2:12. This chapter argues that its οὐδέ conveys a single prohibition: the combination of a woman teaching and assuming authority over a man.

The third is 1 Tim 6:16: "whom no man has seen *and* no man is able to see" (JB). Every line of this poem praises God's nature: his authority, lordship, immortality, light-filled life, and invisibility. "No man has seen God," however, conveys only human experience, not God's nature, unless οὐδέ joins it to "no man is able to see" to specify God's invisibility. First Timothy 1:17 supports this specific sense by affirming that God is invisible (ἀόρατος). In both 1 Tim 2:12 and 6:16, οὐδέ immediately precedes an infinitive, and in both verses the verbs οὐδέ joins are about as far removed from each other in their clauses as possible. Thus, the distance between the two infinitives in 1 Tim 2:12 does not militate against its οὐδέ forming a single internally cohering idea.

Each of these three, like the six instances of category 3 of οὐδέ usage in the undisputed letters of Paul, makes best sense understood as conjoining two elements to express a single, more specific idea.

The one remaining occurrence of οὐδέ in a disputed letter in the Pauline corpus is 1 Tim 6:7: "we have brought nothing into [εἰσφέρω] the world, *and* we can bring nothing out [ἐκφέρω] of it." This highlights two derivatives of the same verb, φέρω ("bring"), that form a natural pair: "bring in" and "bring out." Like the four instances of category 4 of οὐδέ usage in the undisputed letters of Paul, its conjoined elements focus on the same verb and express a natural pair.

Thus, each instance of οὐδέ in the disputed Pauline epistles fits one of the distinctive categories in Paul's undisputed letters, a category that occurs only once (category 3) or is absent (category 4) in Luke–Acts. Furthermore, each is either attributed in the first person to Paul (1 Tim 2:12: "I am not permitting a woman to teach"; and 2 Thess 3:7–8: "we were not idle when we were with you, *and* we did *not* eat anyone's bread without paying for it") or is a memorable aphorism (1 Tim 6:16: "[God,] whom no one has seen *or* can see"; and 6:7: "we brought nothing into the world, *and* we can take *nothing* out of it"). These exemplify statements that even a secretary with considerable freedom would be most likely to reproduce in Paul's wording.

Οὐδέ IN 1 TIMOTHY 2:12

Paul's typical use of οὐδέ elsewhere to convey a single idea shows that οὐδέ is the perfect conjunction to combine "to teach" and "to assume authority" into a single prohibition. To interpret οὐδέ in 1 Tim 2:12 as separating two different prohibitions for women, however, one against teaching and the other against having authority over a man, does not conform to Paul's customary use of οὐδέ. It does not even have a single close parallel in the entire Pauline corpus.

The closest parallels to 1 Tim 2:12's distinctive οὐδέ syntactical structure both convey a single idea, not two separate ideas. Of the passages listed in Köstenberger's Ibycus search of ancient Greek literature, only one other passage perfectly replicates 1 Tim 2:12's syntactical structure: (1) a negated finite verb + (2) infinitive + (3) οὐδέ + (4) infinitive + (5) ἀλλά + (6) infinitive.[22] This passage is in Polybius (ca. 202–120 BC), *History* 30.5.8.4–6, who states, "As they wished none of the kings and princes to despair of gaining their help and alliance, (1) they did not desire (2) to run in harness with Rome (3) and (4) engage themselves by oaths and treaties, (5) but preferred to remain unembarrassed and able (6) to reap profit from any quarter."[23] The content after οὐδέ clarifies that "to run in harness" is to "engage themselves by oaths and treaties [to Rome]." Together these express the one idea of alliance with Rome. This one idea stands in

---

22.   Köstenberger, "Complex Sentence," *WCA* 55, 63–71. Polybius, *History* 5.11.5 has a different syntactical structure: Not A, but B, nor C, but D. Dionysius Halicarnassensis, *De Thucydide* 7.13–15 has no verb in (6).

23.   The following classical translations are from the LCL.

contrast to the statement following ἀλλά, which affirms their openness to other alliances. This parallels the statement preceding the οὐδέ construction, which also affirms other alliances. Thus, an inclusio of parallel bracketing statements surrounds this οὐδέ construction.

Similarly, in 1 Tim 2:12, the contrasting statement introduced by ἀλλά, "but to be in quietness (ἐν ἡσυχίᾳ)," parallels and reiterates the statement immediately preceding its οὐδέ construction, "Let women learn in quietness [ἐν ἡσυχίᾳ] in all subjection." Just as in the Polybius example, this inclusio construction brackets the two infinitives joined by οὐδέ. Thus, Polybius's syntax is completely parallel to 1 Tim 2:11–12's, including the inclusio + (1) negated finite verb + (2) infinitive + (3) οὐδέ + (4) infinitive + (5) ἀλλά + (6) infinitive reiterating the inclusio. Since Polybius's two infinitives joined by οὐδέ convey a single idea, this structural parallel to 1 Tim 2:12 favors interpreting its οὐδέ construction as conveying a single idea, too.

The next closest parallel to 1 Tim 2:12's six-part structure also uses οὐδέ to join two infinitives to convey a single idea that stands in opposition to the statement introduced by ἀλλά. This passage is in Josephus (ca. AD 37–100), *Ant.* 7.127.1–3, "This defeat (1) did not persuade the Ammanites (2) to remain quiet (3) or (4) to keep the peace in the knowledge that their enemy was superior. (5) Instead they (6) sent [a participle, not an infinitive] to Chalamas." The second infinitive phrase, "to keep the peace in the knowledge that their enemy was superior," reiterates the first, "to remain quiet." This is yet another example where two infinitives joined by οὐδέ express a single idea, not two separate ideas. This single idea contrasts with the ἀλλά phrase: "Instead they sent to Chalamas." Thus, the second closest structural parallel to 1 Tim 2:12 favors interpreting the διδασκεῖν οὐδέ αὐθεντεῖν construction of 1 Tim 2:12 as conveying a single concept. Consequently, both of the closest structural parallels to 1 Tim 2:12 support interpreting its οὐδέ construction as communicating a single idea.

The οὐκ + οὐδέ + ἀλλά syntactical construction contrasts the content of both the οὐκ statement and the οὐδέ statement to the following ἀλλά statement. The central core of this complex construction is a contrast between two ideas: "not this, but that" (οὐκ ..., ἀλλά ...). In nine[24] of

---

24. Eleven if 1 Thess 2:3–4 is included. On any reckoning, its elements are closely interrelated, not independent ideas, and are in direct contrast to the immediately following ἀλλά statement. See above, p. 344.

the instances analyzed above, Paul uses οὐδέ to combine two elements in order to specify a single idea, then uses ἀλλά to introduce an idea in sharp contrast to this single idea: Rom 2:28–29; 9:6–7, 16; 1 Cor 2:6–7; Gal 1:1, 11–12, 16–17; 4:14; Phil 2:16–17. There is only one clear instance in Paul's letters where an οὐδέ construction conveys two separate ideas that contrast with the following ἀλλά statement, 2 Cor 7:12. Yet even its two ideas form a single natural pair that united together contrasts with the ἀλλά clause: "I wrote not for the sake of the one who did the wrong or the one wronged, but to manifest your zeal."

There is only one[25] occurrence in the entire rest of the NT outside the Pauline letters of this οὐκ + οὐδέ + ἀλλά construction: John 1:13. Here, οὐκ + οὐδέ + οὐδέ join three elements that all express human birth, and ἀλλά contrasts all of these virtually equivalent expressions to divine spiritual birth. In light of its rareness elsewhere in the NT, it is striking that this characteristically Pauline οὐκ + οὐδέ + ἀλλά syntactical construction occurs twice in letters whose Pauline authorship is disputed: 2 Thess 3:7–8 and 1 Tim 2:12. The statements joined by οὐδέ in both these passages make best sense understood as together conveying a single idea. The contrasting "but" increases the probability that the οὐκ + οὐδέ portion of the construction conveys a single idea, since "not this, but that" most naturally applies to two contrasting ideas. To summarize, both Paul's and the NT's overwhelmingly dominant use in οὐκ + οὐδέ + ἀλλά syntactical constructions for the οὐκ + οὐδέ statements to convey a single idea that stands in sharp contrast to the following ἀλλά statement, supports this same understanding of 1 Tim 2:12.

In what Baldwin says "may be the earliest commentary on 1 Tim 2:12,"[26] Origen (ca. AD 185–254) explains this οὐδέ construction as a single prohibition. After quoting 2:12, Origen explains it as "concerning woman not becoming a ruler over man in speaking" (περὶ τοῦ μὴ τὴν γυναῖκα ἡγεμόνα γίνεσθαι τῷ λόγῳ τοῦ ἀνδρός).[27] This unambiguously expresses "to teach" and "to assume authority over a man" as a single prohibition. Origen's use of the infinitive "to become" (γίνεσθαι) implies entry

---

25. Luke 11:33 uses οὐδείς instead of οὐκ, and its οὐδέ phrase is a textual variant. In Matt 5:14–15 and 9:16–17 (which also uses οὐδείς instead of οὐκ) the ἀλλά statement does not respond to the οὐκ statement, only to the οὐδέ statement.
26. H. S. Baldwin, "An Important Word: αὐθεντέω in 1 Timothy 2:12," WCA 39–51, 199 n. 30.
27. Jenkins, "Origen on 1 Corinthians. IV," 42.

into a position of authority over man. This may suggest a woman assuming this authority for herself, especially since Origen in this context affirms Priscilla, Maximilla, the four daughters of Philip, Deborah, Miriam, Hulda, and Anna.

Blomberg interprets the οὐδέ construction in 1 Tim 2:12 in light of "Paul's more informal pattern throughout 1 Timothy 2 of using pairs of partly synonymous words or expressions to make his main points,"[28] citing verses 1, 2a, 2b, 3, 4, 5, 7a, 7b, 8, 9a, and 9b. He concludes, "in every instance they are closely related and together help to define one single concept. This makes it overwhelmingly likely that in 1 Tim 2:12 Paul is referring to one specific kind of ... teaching rather than two ... activities."[29] Other scholars also argue that οὐδέ in 1 Tim 2:12 joins two expressions to convey a single more focused prohibition.[30]

Interpreting 1 Tim 2:12 as a single prohibition of women teaching combined with assuming authority over men fits its context perfectly. This prohibition fits the central concern of 1 Timothy, namely, false teaching. Teaching combined with assuming authority is by definition not authorized. This is exactly what false teachers were doing in Ephesus. This single prohibition is particularly appropriate to the theme of this chapter, peace without self-assertiveness. Calls to quietness bracket this prohibition and counteract the aggressiveness inherent in unauthorized women (or men) assuming authority over men. The immediately following twofold explanation fits this interpretation well. "Adam was formed first, then Eve" (2:13) implies that woman should respect man as her source, just as the parallels in 1 Cor 11:8 and 12 do. For women to assume authority for themselves over men disrespects men. Furthermore, 2:14 specifically states that Eve was deceived. Eve's deception is relevant only if women's deception is a reason for verse 12's prohibition.

The false teaching described in 1 Tim 4:7 as "myths characteristic of old women" deceived women in particular (cf. 2 Tim 3:6–7).[31] To prevent

---

28. Blomberg, "Neither Hierarchalist," 363.
29. Ibid., omitting "independent" before "activities" to avoid excluding legitimate conceptual overlap. It is Paul's typical use of οὐδέ and the context that make a single point overwhelmingly likely.
30. E.g., Kroeger and Kroeger, I Suffer Not, 83–84, 189; Clarence Boomsma, Male and Female, One in Christ: New Testament Teaching on Women in Office (Grand Rapids: Baker, 1993), 72–73; Steve Motyer, "Expounding 1 Timothy 2:8–15," VE 24 (1994): 96.
31. Cf. above, pp. 299–304.

further deception and the potential fall of the church, 1 Tim 2:11–12 addresses both the reception and the teaching of the error. To prevent the reception of false teaching by more "Eves in Ephesus," 2:11 commands women to learn in quietness and full submission to authorized church doctrine.[32] Healthy doctrine will inoculate or cure these women from false teachings. Paul had earlier instructed Timothy to command the instigators "not to teach any false doctrine" (1 Tim 1:3). Now, to prevent the group Paul specifically identifies as influenced by the false teaching from advocating it to the assembled church, 2:12 prohibits women from teaching combined with assuming authority for themselves over a man.

The specification "man" is best understood as generic, encompassing any and all men, and so prohibits women from assuming authority to teach one or more men. This would apply at least to the assembled church, where such unauthorized teaching posed the greatest risk of spreading the false teaching and causing contention. The specification "man" is essential, since without this limitation, 2:12 would also prohibit women from assuming authority to teach other women or children, contrary to Titus 2:3–5; 2 Tim 1:5; and 3:14–17. The specification "man" also has the practical advantage that it avoids ambiguity. It is obvious when a man is being taught, but if 1 Tim 2:12 had read not "man," but "in the assemblies," there might be disagreement as to which assemblies should exclude women teaching with self-assumed authority. The specification "man" focuses on the primary threat of unauthorized women teaching men, without in any way undermining women's freedom to assume authority to teach other women and children.[33]

Even if "man" is not understood as generic, since it is impossible to teach men without teaching a man, this prohibition must apply to groups of men as well as individual men. It is a denial of the obvious implication of the singular noun "a man," however, to say, as Schreiner does, that this view prohibits only the teaching of men (plural) in groups while permitting teaching of individual men. In order to keep his interpretation from opposing the "private teaching of Apollos by Priscilla," Schreiner says "the word is used generically."[34] Generic use, however, means that "the whole class is in view."[35] Since individual men are part of the class, they must be in view too.

---

32. Cf. above, pp. 315–17.
33. "Man" contrasts both with "woman" and "child/boy," e.g., 1 Cor 13:11; Eph 4:13; BDAG 79.
34. Schreiner, "Dialogue," WCA 101 and 206 n. 115; cf. Knight, *Pastoral Epistles*, 142.
35. Wallace, *Grammar*, 734.

Furthermore, since Paul describes women in Ephesus as deceived by false teaching[36] and uses Eve's deception to explain this prohibition, he clearly intends to restrict false teaching by women. It would undermine achievement of this goal to permit women to teach individual men, especially if Grudem is correct that "God gave men in general, a disposition that is better suited to teaching and governing in the church, a disposition that inclines more to rational, logical analysis of doctrine and a desire to protect the doctrinal purity of the church, and God [made women] ... less inclined to oppose the deceptive serpent."[37] Even Schreiner, who formerly advocated this view, now wisely argues that it calls "into question ... the goodness of God's creative work" and "strays from the text."[38]

If 1 Tim 2:12a is an unqualified prohibition of women teaching, it prohibits what Paul's letters and the Pastoral Epistles in particular repeatedly affirm.[39] If, however, this οὐδέ construction conveys the single idea of women assuming authority to teach men, it perfectly fits the theological context of the Pastoral Epistles and the Pauline corpus.

The positive counterpart to this prohibition "but to be in quietness" (2:12), which 2:11 associates with "to be in full submission," is the opposite of assuming authority for oneself. It is possible and desirable to teach "in quietness," namely, with a calm spirit, but it is not possible for a woman "in quietness" to teach while assuming for herself authority over a man. Therefore, "but to be in quietness" makes a better literary contrast with the single idea combining "to teach and to assume authority over a man" than it does with "to teach" and "to exercise authority over a man" understood as two separate prohibitions. Thus, understanding 1 Tim 2:12's οὐδέ construction as conveying the single prohibition of a woman assuming authority to teach a man fits its literary context perfectly.

IS IT NATURAL TO TAKE 2:12A AS A SEPARATE PROHIBITION AGAINST WOMEN TEACHING MEN?

Some attempt to reconcile 1 Tim 2:12 with women teaching other women by proposing that οὐδέ in 1 Tim 2:12 separates two conceptually

---

36. Cf. above, pp. 299–304.
37. Grudem, *EF* 70–72; similarly, Schreiner, "Dialogue," *WCFA* 145–46; Daniel Doriani, "Appendix 1: History of the Interpretation of 1 Timothy 2," *WCFA* 213–68, esp. 263–65.
38. Schreiner, "Dialogue," *WCA* 225 n. 210, with a bibliography of arguments against this view.
39. Cf. above, pp. 328–34.

different prohibitions and that the first prohibition is not of women teaching, but rather of women teaching men.[40] They assert that the final word of the second prohibition, "man," in isolation from the phrase where it occurs, limits the first prohibition as well. Moo argues for this since "in Greek, objects and qualifiers of words which occur only with the second in a series must often be taken with the first also (cf. Acts 8:21)."[41] Acts 8:21, however, uses οὐδέ to join synonyms to make one point, not two: "You have no part or [οὐδέ] share in this ministry." This verse does not transfer only the qualifier but merges the two elements to convey one idea. Moo, however, alleges that 1 Tim 2:12 expresses two separate prohibitions. This removes the syntactical justification for requiring that their verbs have the same object.

Acts 8:21's use of οὐδέ to join two elements to express one idea parallels 1 Tim 2:12, and thus supports understanding 1 Tim 2:12's οὐδέ construction as a single prohibition. Unless 1 Tim 2:12 is the one exception, none of Paul's οὐδέ constructions selectively transfers to the first element only a qualifier extracted from the second. Whenever Paul does use the text following οὐδέ to qualify the element before οὐδέ, the entire construction expresses this by combining the two elements into one idea. Furthermore, Acts 8:21 and 1 Tim 2:12 differ in five ways that highlight crucial evidence against treating "man" in isolation from its phrase as the object of "to teach":

1. "You have no part" in Acts 8:21 requires the additional "in this ministry" to make sense. "I am not permitting a woman to teach" in 1 Tim 2:12, however, makes sense without any addition and, indeed, corresponds with conventional wisdom at that time. So a typical reader would feel no need to look for a personal object for "to teach."[42] Furthermore, nowhere else in 1 Timothy does "to

40. E.g., Schreiner, "Dialogue," WCFA 128 and n. 98; Knight, *Pastoral Epistles*, 142.
41. Moo, "Rejoinder," 202.
42. Moo, "Rejoinder," 202 n. 5 appeals to H. W. Smyth, *A Greek Grammar for Colleges* (New York: American Book, 1920), 364–65, §1634–35, but in all Smyth's examples, in order for the first statement to make sense, the object of the second verb *must* also apply to the first verb, unlike 1 Tim 2:12. Within first-century culture, it was commonplace to prohibit women from teaching and even from being educated. Baugh, "Foreign World," WCA 34 and n. 136, writes that "women do not appear as the sophists, rhetors, teachers, philosophers, doctors, and their disciples in ancient sources from Ephesus.... Women teachers were not integral to Ephesian society." Consequently, "I am not permitting a woman to teach" in its cultural milieu does not invite the addition of any qualifier, such as "a man."

teach" (4:11; 6:2) or "to teach a different doctrine" (6:3) have a personal object. Consequently, neither cultural convention nor the use of "to teach" elsewhere in 1 Timothy supports importing "man" in isolation as its personal object here.

2. It is only because "part" and "share" in Acts 8:21 are synonyms that the object of "share" must also apply to "part." Since 1 Tim 2:12's infinitives are not synonyms, they do not need to share the same object, unless they together convey one idea.

3. In Acts 8:21 the qualifier "in this ministry" is as close as possible to both synonyms, "part or share in this ministry," but "to teach" and "man" in 1 Tim 2:12 are at opposite ends of their clause in Greek word order, literally: "*To teach*, however, by a woman I am not permitting οὐδέ to assume authority over *a man*." This reduces the likelihood of this conceptual transfer.

4. The grammatical form of the transferred element in Acts 8:21 perfectly fits the first element, but "a man" is genitive, the wrong case for "to teach."[43] A. T. Robertson states, "We have no right to assume in the N.T. that one case is used for another. That is to say, that you have a genitive, but it is to be understood as an accusative."[44] This is exactly the incongruity in case if ἀνδρός is interpreted to be the object of "to teach."

5. The transference in Acts 8:21 does not teach anything in conflict with other NT statements, but to say a woman must not teach a man conflicts with Priscilla's instruction of Apollos and Paul's affirmations of women teaching.[45]

All these differences between Acts 8:21 and 1 Tim 2:12 are crucial evidence that "a man" extracted from its phrase does not modify "to teach" as an object. Paul could hardly have chosen a wording less conducive to express that "a man" in isolation should modify "to teach." If Paul had wished to make it clear that he was prohibiting "to teach a man," he could have added the single word "man" (ἄνδρα, accusative singular) to the first

43. "To teach" can take either accusative (cf. Rom 2:21; 1 Cor 11:14; Col 1:28; 3:16) or dative (Rev 2:14).
44. Robertson, *Grammar*, 454 (b). R. Y. K. Fung, "Ministry in the New Testament," *The Church in the Bible and the World* (ed. D. A. Carson; Grand Rapids: Baker, 1987), 154–212, 198–99, argues that "man" does not modify "to teach."
45. Acts 18:26; cf. above, pp. 328–34.

prohibition, but he did not. Furthermore, if 1 Tim 2:12a were a universal prohibition of a woman teaching a man, it would prohibit any woman from teaching any man, even Priscilla teaching Apollos. In short, the evidence is overwhelming against interpreting 1 Tim 2:12a as a separate prohibition of a woman teaching a man.

Οὐδέ CAN CONNECT A POSITIVE CONCEPT WITH A NEGATIVE CONCEPT

Οὐδέ can join positive and negative concepts, as in Gal 3:28's "slave *and* free." Paul's ensuing description proves that he regards slavery as negative but freedom as positive (Gal 4:7–9; 5:1). Of course, when οὐδέ joins two synonymous expressions, it is natural that both will be either positive or negative. There is, however, no grammatical or syntactical rule that keeps οὐδέ from conjoining a positive activity with a negative activity. BDF §445 states that the use of οὐδέ in the "correlation of negative and positive members is, of course, admissible."[46]

Köstenberger, however, alleges that "the construction negated finite verb + infinitive + οὐδέ + infinitive ... in *every instance* yield[s] the pattern positive/positive or negative/negative ... I found *no evidence* [against this.... This] should now be considered as an *assured result* of biblical scholarship" [emphases added].[47] Although many of the passages Köstenberger quotes contradict his thesis that οὐδέ cannot join a positive activity and a negative activity, a few scholars have accepted this thesis.[48] In the following seven passages Köstenberger cites,[49] five joining two infinitives, οὐδέ joins a verb with positive connotations to a verb with negative connotations.

    1. 2 Cor 7:12: "It was not on account of the one who did the wrong *nor* (οὐδέ) on account of the one who was wronged" (NRSV). One of

---

46.   BDF §445 continues, "though it is not common in the NT. E.g., Jn 4:11 ... (οὐδέ D sys, which seems to be better Greek)." The passage BDF cites, "You have nothing to draw with and the well is deep," is a rare case of negated and nonnegated correlatives used together. If "negative and positive" refers, instead, to expressions with negative or positive connotations, as this study does, examples are much more common.

47.   Köstenberger, "Complex Sentence," WCA 78, 77, 84. On pp. 55–56 he repeatedly misrepresents my paper, then as editor of *JETS* he kept my study, though earlier accepted by *JETS*, from being published. It was published in revised form as "1 Tim 2.12 and the Use of οὐδέ to Combine Two Elements to Express a Single Idea," *NTS* 54 (2008): 235–53.

48.   E.g., Mounce, *Pastoral Epistles*, 129–30; Blomberg, "Neither Hierarchalist," 363.

49.   Köstenberger, "Complex Sentence," WCA 59, 63–71. Payne, "Use of οὐδέ," 251–52, identifies more such passages.

the participles οὐδέ joins elicits sympathy (the innocent, "wronged" party), the other antipathy ("the one who did the wrong").

2. 2 Thess 3:7–8: "We were not idle when we were with you, *and* we did not eat anyone's bread without paying for it" (NRSV, this passage is analyzed above, pp. 346–47).

3. LXX Sir 18:6: "Who can fully recount God's mercies? It is not possible to diminish *or* (οὐδέ) increase them." To diminish God's mercies in any way is negative. Scripture, however, encourages prayer to increase God's mercies, e.g., Ps 40:11; 51:1; 79:8; 119:77, so their increase is positive, even though people cannot control or fully recount them.

4. Diodorus Siculus 3.30.2.8–9: "Nor is there any occasion to be surprised at this statement *or* (οὐδέ) to distrust it, since we have learned through trustworthy history of many things more astonishing than this which have taken place throughout all the inhabited world." "Surprise" is normally positive, and is so here, as the immediately following statement identifies "astonishing things" as "trustworthy history." "Distrust," however, is negative.

5. Plutarch, *Sayings of Kings and Commanders* 185.A.1, depicts Themistocles as saying, "the trophy of Miltiades does not allow me to sleep *or* to be indolent."[50] The positive description of dreams in Plutarch, *Them.* 26.2–3, evidences Themistocles' positive view of sleep as does the normal positive connotation of sleep. Indolence, however, is negative.

6. Plutarch, *Quaest. rom.* 269.D.8–9: "We must not follow out [διώκειν 'to pursue, seek,' normally a positive verb] the most exact calculation of the number of days *nor* [οὐδέ] cast aspersions [συκοφαντεῖν,[51] a negative verb] on approximate reckoning; since even now, when astronomy has made so much progress, the irregularity of the moon's movements is still beyond the skill of mathematicians, and continues to elude their calculations." Plutarch's explanation praising the progress of astronomy shows that he regards the pursuit of exact calculations positively. He opposes

---

50. Plutarch, *Mor.* 3:89 (Babbitt, LCL); Köstenberger ("Complex Sentence," WCA 69) incorrectly identifies this as 185.A.2.
51. All the meanings LSJ 1671 lists are decidedly negative.

exact calculation here only because it is *in combination with* casting aspersions on approximate reckoning, which may be necessary.

7. Plutarch, *Brut. an.* 990.A.11: "Our sense of smell ... admits what is proper, rejects what is alien, and will not let it touch[52] or (οὐδέ) give pain[53] to the taste, but informs on and denounces what is bad before any harm is done." Smell prevents harm by warning against touching what is alien and thereby experiencing pain. Οὐδέ does not convey two alternatives: touch or give pain. It combines positive and negative verbs to convey the single idea that smell prevents touch that would cause pain.

These seven examples show that οὐδέ can connect two verbs, one conveying a positive concept, the other a negative concept. If the expressions joined by οὐδέ describe the abuse of an activity normally regarded as positive (like teaching), it is perfectly natural that the positive concept will be associated with a negative concept. What 1 Tim 2:12 prohibits, it must regard as negative. Paul usually refers to teaching as positive, but here he associates it with self-assumed authority, which is exactly what the false teachers were doing. Consequently, it is natural to understand 1 Tim 2:12 as prohibiting this combination.

In conclusion, Paul typically uses οὐδέ to convey a single idea, as do the two closest syntactical parallels to 1 Tim 2:12. In the overwhelming majority of Paul's and the NT's οὐκ + οὐδέ + ἀλλά syntactical constructions, οὐδέ joins two expressions to convey a single idea in sharp contrast to the statement following ἀλλά. Furthermore, the earliest known commentary on 1 Tim 2:12 (Origen's) treats it as a single prohibition. Blomberg supports this by identifying eleven other instances in this chapter where pairs of complementary expressions convey a single idea. Understood as a single prohibition, 1 Tim 2:12 conveys, "I am not permitting a woman to teach and [in combination with this] to assume authority over a man." The only established category of οὐδέ usage in the entire Pauline corpus that makes sense of this passage joins conceptually different expressions to convey a single idea.[54]

---

52. Θιγεῖν is almost always positive, LSJ 801. The one hostile sense, *attack*, does not fit this context as well.

53. Every meaning for λυπεῖν in LSJ 1065 is decidedly negative.

54. The expressions οὐδέ joins in 1 Tim 2:12 are not equivalent in meaning (category 1) or a natural pair (category 2), nor do they convey naturally paired ideas focusing on the same verb (category 4), cf. above, pp. 338–44.

The function of οὐδέ in these cases is not to subordinate one expression to another, but to merge them together to convey a single more specific idea. There is no unambiguous case where Paul joins two conceptually distinct verbs with οὐδέ to convey two separate ideas, so there is no clear support in Paul's letters for treating 1 Tim 2:12 as two separate prohibitions, of women teaching (or of women teaching men) and of women having authority over men. Consequently, this οὐδέ construction makes best sense as a single prohibition of women teaching with self-assumed authority over a man.[55]

This understanding fits the text and its context lexically, syntactically, grammatically, stylistically, and theologically. This single specific restriction perfectly fits the danger of false teaching by women in Ephesus. It does not contradict Paul's and the Pastoral Epistles' affirmations of women teaching nor does it prohibit women such as Priscilla, who was evidently in Ephesus at this time,[56] from teaching men, as long as their authority is properly recognized, not self-assumed. Addressing a church situation where women were deceived and spreading false teaching, 1 Tim 2:12 prohibits women from assuming for themselves authority to teach men.

---

55. Frederic Schroeder, Professor Emeritus of Classics, Queen's University, Kingston, Canada, emailed this author on April 12, 2008, "I think you are right to construe 1 Tim 2:12 as you do, taking the two clauses together."
56. See above, pp. 331 n. 46.

1 TIMOTHY 2:12: PART III: DOES Αὐθεντέω MEAN "ASSUME AUTHORITY"?

The most crucial question about 1 Tim 2:12 is the meaning of αὐθεντεῖν. It is a transitive verb that takes the genitive[1] for its object, "man." Consequently, this analysis does not discuss possible intransitive meanings such as "to act independently" and "to exercise one's own jurisdiction" since they do not fit this context. Similarly, it does not discuss meanings that do not fit the context, including "murder," nor the meanings that, as Baldwin notes,[2] do not fit with the object "a man": "to rule,"[3] "to reign sovereignly," "to grant authorization," "to instigate," and the rare middle voice use meaning "to be in effect, to have legal standing."

Besides 1 Tim 2:12, there are only two established and uncontested occurrences of the verb αὐθεντέω through the end of the first century AD: BGU 1208, and the first-century BC–first-century AD[4] grammarian Aristonicus Alexandrinus in *De signis Iliadis* 9.694, where it simply combines the meanings of αὐτός and ἀνύω,[5] "the one self-accomplishing

---

1. Cf. Robertson, *Grammar*, 506; BDF §177 (for other verbs that take a genitive, see, e.g., Mark 10:42; Rom 6:9; 15:12; 1 Cor 7:4).
2. Henry Scott Baldwin, "A Difficult Word: αὐθεντέω in 1 Timothy 2:12," *WCFA* 78–80; and its 2005 second edition, "Important Word," *WCA* 51.
3. The first instance of this usage appears to be ca. AD 325 Eusebius, *On Ecclesiastical Theology* 3.5.21.1, which refers to God the Father as "ruling" (αὐθεντοῦντος).
4. Luci Berkowitz and Karl A. Squitier, *Thesaurus Linguae Graecae: Canon of Greek Authors and Works* (3rd ed.; New York: Oxford Univ. Press, 1990), 61–62. Al Wolters, "A Semantic Study of Αὐθέντης and Its Derivatives," *Journal of Greco-Roman Christianity and Judaism* 1 (2000): 149, dates it to the late first c. BC.
5. Ludwig Friedländer, ed., *Aristonici περὶ σημείων Ἰλιάδος reliquiae emendatiores* (Göttingen: Dieterich, 1853; repr., Amsterdam: Hakkert, 1965), note on line 694. This same scholium on

[ὁ αὐθεντῶν] the speech had set forth something astounding."[6] Wolters notes that this passage contrasts Achilles, who does the actual speaking, with Odysseus, who reports what was spoken.[7] Another possible instance is a papyrus fragment of the *Rhetorica* of Philodemus. The following detailed analysis of this and BGU 1208 corrects fallacious assertions about them and establishes as far as possible the meaning of αὐθεντέω in them.

A fourth possible instance of αὐθεντεῖν is a copy of a scholarly note on Aeschylus' *Eumenides* 42a that many scholars believe to be derived from Didymus (80–10 BC). If this attribution to Didymus is correct, "to murder" was a meaning of αὐθεντέω in Paul's day.[8] Unless there was some metaphorical sense of "murder" that the church in Ephesus would understand,[9] however, this meaning does not fit 1 Tim 2:12. Consequently, this abbreviated summary does not pursue this meaning further. Because 1 Tim 2:12 is one of the first occurrences of this verb, its etymology is particularly important in investigating how it was originally understood. The paucity of

---

Homer's *Iliad* is cited in a tenth-century AD work, Hartmut Erbse, ed., *Scholia Graeca in Homeri Iliadem (scholia vetera)* (Berlin: de Gruyter, 1971), 2:543, book 10, entry 694b.

6.   Baldwin, "Important Word," WCA 203, translates it "the one doing the speech had set forth something astounding." Wolters, "Semantic," 149, translates it "speaker." Both are equivalent to "the one self-accomplishing the speech."

7.   Wolters, "Semantic," n. 70.

8.   LSJ 275, and most other commentators cite this passage for the meaning "commit a murder." There is some doubt about the date of this occurrence, however, since this scholium on line 42 is documented in the tenth c. AD Medicean MS M and a similar but expanded scholium on line 40 occurs in MS T from ca. AD 1325 and in MS E from the 15th century AD. David Huttar ("ΑΥΘΕΝΤΕΙΝ in the Aeschylus Scholium," *JETS* 44 [2001]: 615–25) proposes that αὐθεντέω in MS M means "initiated." Although scholia are supposed to explain obscure references, his translation does not explain what the obscure "dripping" refers to, whereas "murder" does. The quotations in the Philodemus fragment suggest that in it, too, αὐθεντέω may have meant "murder." A. Adler, ed., *Svidae Lexicon* (Part 1; Stuttgart: Teubner, 1928–1938; repr., Stuttgart: Teubner, 1971), 412, A4426 (10th c. AD) cites αὐθέντης to mean "murderer" and states regarding the verb, "Αὐθεντήσοντα itself does not require that one wear the sword himself. For Mithridates ... ordered them to kill." This implies that αὐθεντέω can mean murder whether with one's own hand or at one's command. The incident cited is from ca. 87 BC. This, which H. Scott Baldwin, "αὐθεντέω in Ancient Greek Literature," WCFA 303–4, cites, confirms αὐθεντέω meaning "to murder," *pace* Baldwin, "Important Word," WCA 48; Huttar, "ΑΥΘΕΝΤΕΙΝ," 625.

9.   Cf. Kroeger and Kroeger (*I Suffer Not*, 87–104, 185–88), who suggest various possibilities: "to teach in a way that figuratively or symbolically murders men," "to teach men ritual or sham murder," "to teach a man in such a way that virtues are destroyed," as well as "to proclaim herself author of man" (p. 103). Cf. Catherine C. Kroeger, "Ancient Heresies and a Strange Greek Verb," *The Reformed Journal* 29.3 (March 1979): 12–15, 14. For rebuttals see A. J. Panning, "ΑΥΘΕΝΤΕΙΝ—A Word Study," *Wisconsin Lutheran Quarterly* 78 (1981): 185–91; Carroll D. Osburn, "ΑΥΘΕΝΤΕΩ (1 Timothy 2:12)," *ResQ* 25 (1982): 1–12. Leland E. Wilshire, "I Timothy 2:12 Revisited: A Reply to Paul W. Barnett and Timothy J. Harris," *EvQ* 65 (1993): 48, suggests "instigating violence," but he cites no other examples with this translation, must assume a narrowly defined meaning of "to teach," and does not integrate vv. 13–15 with this translation.

early occurrences of this verb makes it more important than usual to consider the meanings of other forms of the word to help establish its meaning.

The Origin or Etymology of Αὐθεντέω

The etymology of most, if not all, αὐθεντ- root words is agreed upon by Pierre Chantraine, Paul Kretschmer,[10] LSJ 275, MM 91, and nearly every other Greek lexicographer to be "self-achieving," a combination of αὐτός and ἕντης, derived from ἀνύω. Chantraine writes: "Etymology: The sense of the word, the existence in Sophocles of the form of this word written αὐτοέντης, and the gloss by Hesychius Lexicographicus συνέντης / συνεργός lead us to recognize a compound of αὐτός signifying 'by one's self, of one's own initiative' and a second term *ἕντης 'who finishes, achieves,' from the root of ἀνύω."[11] The etymology stresses the activity of the self first of all in its use of αὐτός, but also in the nuance that ἀνύω could carry of "accomplish for one's own advantage ... make one's way, win ... get, obtain."[12]

Thus, it is not surprising that many of the uses of the αὐθεντ- root refer to self-initiated activities and, consequently, usually up through Paul's day carry a negative nuance. As Chantraine noted, the αὐθεντ- root words are typically strong and emotionally-laden words with negative or dominating overtones such as: murderer,[13] domestic murderer, perpetrator, or autocrat. Etymology provides no basis for isolating the αὐθεντ- verbs from its cognate forms in studying its range of meanings. Αὐθεντέω is a denominative verb formed from the noun αὐθέντης.[14] Consequently, George W. Knight III and Henry Scott Baldwin err procedurally in ignoring meanings of the noun as evidence for the meaning of the related verb.[15] Knight unduly

---

10. Paul Kretschmer, "Griechisches: 6. αὐθέντης," *Glotta, Zeitschrift für griechische und lateinische Sprache* 3 (1912): 289–93. *Webster's New World Dictionary*, s.v. "authentic," correctly identifies its Greek etymology, "one who does things himself" from "self + to prepare, achieve."

11. Chantraine, *Dictionnaire étymologique*, 1:138–9, translation by P. B. Payne. Wilshire praises Chantraine's "reasoned conclusion" in his article "The TLG Computer and Further Reference to ΑΥΘΕΝΤΕΩ in I Timothy 2:12," *NTS* 34 (1988): 129.

12. LSJ 168.

13. Wolters, "Semantic," 145–75, lists twenty-seven instances of αὐθέντης meaning "murderer" in Classical Greek, four in the first century AD and eight in the second century AD.

14. Robertson (*Grammar*, 147–48) who also notes that most -έω verbs are compound; Wolters, "Semantic," 149–50.

15. George W. Knight III, "ΑΥΘΕΝΤΕΩ in Reference to Women in 1 Timothy 2:12," *NTS* 30 (1984): 153, apparently does this to support the meaning, "authority, in the objective and positive sense"; Baldwin ("Important Word," *WCA* 49) sweeps away substantial evidence to the contrary, alleging, "What we can say with certainty is that we have no instances of a pejorative use of the verb before the fourth century AD."

restricts evidence only to verbal forms on the basis of an improbable etymology that "two quite different words have by similar pronunciation and spelling come to have an identical form."[16]

The verbal root of ἕντης, ἀνύω, accepted by Chantraine and most other lexicographers, had two meanings: "effect, accomplish" and "make an end of, destroy, kill."[17] Consequently, this one simple origin explains both the sense of "perpetrator" and the sense of "perpetrator of a murder." The meanings of the noun αὐθέντης include murderer, suicide, perpetrator, author, doer, and master. At about AD 180, Phrynichus wrote, "Never use 'αὐθέντης' for 'master' as [do] the orators in connection with the law courts, but for murderer."[18] Paul may have known of the noun's use in LXX Wis 12:6, "murderers of their own helpless babes." Common to these meanings is that the αὐθέντης is one who takes authority into one's own hand to do something. What is done is generally regarded as reprehensible, an act of unlawfully assumed authority.

Since achievement tends to lead to power, it is not surprising that the αὐθέντ- root gradually began to be used for power and authority, sometimes with repressive overtones such as: dominate, domineer, absolute master, autocrat, or absolute sway. Particularly in the patristic writings, the meaning "authority" came to predominate, usually in a positive sense. The dictionary of modern Greek by Σταματάκου gives as synonyms for αὐθεντέω and αὐθέντης terms both of authority (e.g., ἡγεμονεύω, ἄρχω, βασιλεύω, κύριος, ἄρχων) and of dominating (δεσπόζω = dominate, τυραννεύω = tyrannize, and δεσπότης = despot, τύραννος = tyrant).[19]

The meanings of other αὐθέντ- root words are clearly derived from their component elements: self + achieve: αὐθεντία *with his own hand*[20] or *absolute sway, authority*. The verbal form αὐθεντίζω meant *take in hand*.[21]

16. Knight, "ΑΥΘΕΝΤΕΩ," 154. Robertson's (*Grammar*, 148) proposal regarding ἕντεα is also improbable.
17. LSJ 168; cf. Pindar, *Pythian* 12.11, for the meaning "murder" from the fifth century BC.
18. Phrynichus I.20: αὐθέντης μηδέποτε χρήσῃ ἐπὶ τοῦ δεσπότης ὡς οἱ περὶ τὰ δικαστήρια ῥήτορες ἀλλ᾿ αὐτόχειρος ἐπὶ τοῦ φονέως. Quoted in Chr. Augustus Lobeck, *Ρηματικον sive Verborum Graecorum et Nominum Verbalium Technologia* (Regimontii: Borntraeger, 1846), 121. Quotation translated by Caroline Bammel (August 26, 1991), slightly modified.
19. Ιωννου Δρ. Σταματάκου, *Λεξικον της νεας Ελληνικης Γλωσσης* (3 vols.; Athens: Εκδοτικος, 1971), 1:680. English equivalents are from George A. Maqazis, *Langenscheidt's Standard Greek Dictionary* (Berlin: Langenscheidt, 1990). For extensive references to αὐθεντέω, αὐθέντης, etc. from AD 1100–1669 see Εμμανουηλ Κριαρα, *Λεξιχο της Μεσαιωνικης Ελληνικης Δημωδους Γραμματειας* (3 vols.; Thessalonika: Σφακιανάκη, 1968–1973), 3:333–38.
20. E.g., the second/third century AD Dio Cassius, *Fragment* 102.12.
21. E.g., BGU 103.3.

The adjective form αὐθεντικός meant *with one's own hand, principal, warranted, original, authentic.*[22] English's *authentic,* Latin *authenticus,* and the German *authentisch,* are derived from αὐθεντικός. The adverb form αὐθεντικῶς meant *with perfect clarity*[23] or *authoritatively.*[24] The comparative form αὐθεντικώτερον meant *with higher authority* in the second century. Each of these nuances derive from the root idea of "self + achieve."

Αὐθεντέω IN BGU 1208.38

Probably the single most important document illuminating the use of αὐθεντέω in 1 Tim 2:12 is the papyrus BGU 1208, since it is the closest in time to Paul, it establishes a clear context that limits its meaning, and its meaning fits 2:12. Knight also identifies this as the most important passage for understanding the meaning of αὐθεντέω in 1 Tim 2:12.[25] BGU 1208 gives the text of a papyrus dated 27/26 BC by Schubart, who entitled it, "A Letter from Tryphon (?) to Asklepiades (?)" concerning the matter of ferrying and related payments.[26] It relates an incident when a slave of Asklepiades refused to pay the boatman Calatytis his boat fare. Tryphon writes an apology to the slave's owner, explaining that when he intervened, acting with self-assumed authority (αὐθεντηκότος) over the slave, he consented to pay within the hour.

John R. Werner[27] translated BGU 1208 lines 37–42 for Knight in this way: "I called him to account [αὐθεντηκότος], and he consented to provide for Calatytis the Boatman on terms of the full fare, within the hour." Knight, however, falsely attributes to Werner's letter of March 18, 1980, the following translation of BGU 1208: "I exercised authority over him."[28]

---

22. Kretschmer, "αὐθέντης," 290; E. A. Sophocles, *A Glossary of Later and Byzantine Greek: Memoirs of the American Academy of Arts and Sciences* (New Series; Cambridge & Boston: Welch, Bigelow, 1860), 7:215. LSJ 275 adds "authoritative" for the adjective, but the example it cites from Ptolemy, *Tetrabiblos* 182, is translated "independent" by F. E. Robbins (*Ptolemy Tetrabiblos,* 390–91, LCL).

23. BAG 120 and BDAG 150, citing two occurrences in Cicero's *Epistulae ad Atticum* 9.14.2, and 10.9.1 and its use in contrast with enigmas and parables later in *Preaching of Peter* 4.

24. The earliest recorded by *PGL* is Origen (d. AD 254), *Fragmenta in Lam.* 116, 4:20 (GCS 3, p. 277.7; M 13.660B). Cf. LSJ 275.

25. Knight, "ΑΥΘΕΝΤΕΩ," 154, cf. 145.

26. *Aegyptische Urkunden aus den koeniglichen Museen zu Berlin: Griechische Urkunden* (Berlin: Weidmann, 1912), 4:351.

27. John R. Werner authorized this author to quote from his letters to Knight.

28. Knight, "ΑΥΘΕΝΤΕΩ," 145, 150, and 155 n. 13 states, "Dr. John R. Werner ... provided this and several other translations.... This particular translation [of BGU 1208] was provided in a letter dated March 18, 1980." It is a matter of public record that this attribution is false. Werner made carbon copies of this letter to Knight for the 1 Timothy files of the Wycliffe Bible Translators

Werner's letter to Knight on April 8, 1980, clarifies, "I've come out with neither 'have authority' nor 'domineer,' but 'assume authority to oneself,' i.e., without that authority having been delegated to oneself or to anyone else." To this Werner adds on p. 3, "Note that Carney has preceded me in seeing 'of its own initiative' as an important component of *authenteo*."

Werner explains, "In the next sentence the author reports how Calatytis returned to him with a report of the insolent failure of the debtor to execute that agreement."[29] Werner adds, "I am reminded of the situation in Exodus 2:13 – 14 when Moses tried to break up a fight between two Hebrews by asking the one in the wrong, 'Why are you hitting your fellow Hebrew?' and his attempt to *authentein* was rebuffed by the latter's, 'Who made you ruler and judge over us?'" Werner's letter to Knight of April 8, 1980, confirms that Werner had not changed his opinion:

> The more evidence you send me, the more I'm convinced that the kind of authority denoted by *authenteō* is … authority that is assumed by the person exercising it…. A King of Thieves is not exercising an authority that has been delegated to him by a higher authority (*exousia*)…. He simply has taken it upon himself to give orders to the other thieves … apparently 1 Timothy 2:12 does not prevent a higher authority from delegating to a woman, equally as to a man, an authority to direct activities and/or to settle disputes

---

Translation Department and for himself, and provided copies of it and later correspondence with Knight to this author, who provided a copy of Werner's letter to editor Lieu of *NTS*.

29. March 18, 1980 letter from Werner to Knight, p. 2. BGU 1208 lines 42 – 47 states, "But Calatytis, having been summoned by you, explained (ἐξηγήσατο) to me in full the subsequent insolence." Baldwin, "αὐθεντέω in Ancient Greek," WCFA 74, writes instead, "In BGU 1208 the influence the writer exercises on the boatman is viewed as achieving positive results and even the boatman gets his 'full fare.'" On p. 276 n. 5 Baldwin quotes from the current author's unpublished 1986 study on οὐδέ, "Of Payne's arguments the last is the most important." The quoted paragraph also states, "the person who was called into account, did not in fact pay the boatman." Baldwin's assertion to the contrary is partly explained by his email to Payne on February 5, 2006, explaining that he had not seen BGU 1208 but drew the text of BGU 1208 from the Duke website, which misrepresents BGU 1208's "you" (σοῦ) as ὤου. Baldwin, as explained in "Important Word," WCA 203 n. 50 emended the Duke text, which had only one letter wrong at this point, by deleting two letters and replacing them with three different letters, thereby changing BGU 1208's "you" (σοῦ) to "me" (ἐμοῦ). This changes the context from Calatytis reporting to the writer the insolent failure of the debtor, to the writer summoning Calatytis, whom Baldwin then interprets as showing insolence to the writer. Baldwin also changes "in the hour" to "at that time," thereby obscuring why it was only later the author learned of the debtor's failure to pay. Baldwin's translation also fails to convey that ἐξηγήσατο means "explained," as in John 1:18. Werner emailed Payne on June 22, 2006, after assessing Baldwin's contention, "it still looks to me as if the passenger reneged on his promise to pay [C]alatytis the boatman." He concluded that even if Baldwin's conjectural emendation and interpretation were accepted, in this context αὐθεντέω would still mean "having assumed authority."

involving men. When she exercises that authority, she will not be *authenteōing*: she will be exercising *exousia*.

Knight's article states, "No attempt has been made to select a translation favourable or unfavourable to a particular rendering or meaning and no alternative translation has been excluded."[30] Knight, however, not only excluded Werner's translation of BGU 1208, he also excluded Werner's translation of αὐθεντέω twice in BGU 103, "accept jurisdiction," instead alleging "assume authority" as the translation "provided in Werner's letter dated March 18, 1980."[31] Although Knight in these cases substitutes his own translation of αὐθεντέω, he writes, "the linguistic evidence provided by a translator or lexicographer will always be that of someone other than the author of this article. This will help ensure impartiality and objectivity."[32]

Werner, upon further investigation, confirmed to the present writer his conclusion that "*authentia* is authority that is taken upon oneself."[33] He writes that it is better to translate αὐθεντηκότος in BGU 1208 "assumed authority" or "took authority" than "exercised authority." "The stranger certainly did not have *exousia* over another man's slave. That is why he says he 'assumed authority,' admitting that his command was not a command based on pre-existing authority."[34] Werner states, "The very reason the letter was written was that the patrician who exercised *authentia* did not have *exousia* over the slave. Just as Americans normally refrain from disciplining other people's children, so Romans ordinarily refrained from commanding other people's slaves. That is why the author feels a need to send the slave's owner an *apologia*, an explanation of the circumstance."[35]

Knight's misquotation of Werner has been repeated in numerous subsequent studies. For instance, Baldwin states, "G. W. Knight, 145, gives Werner's translation here":[36] "exercised authority over." In the footnote citing this translation, Baldwin also cites extensively from the very paragraph where P. B. Payne identifies "the actual translation sent by

---

30. Knight, "ΑΥΘΕΝΤΕΩ," 155 n. 3.
31. Ibid., 147 (the citation) and 156 n. 22 (the attribution).
32. Ibid., 144, cf. 149.
33. July 21, 1993, letter from John R. Werner to Philip B. Payne, page 2.
34. Ibid., page 3.
35. Ibid., page 2.
36. Baldwin, "αὐθεντέω in Ancient Greek," WCFA 276 n. 5.

John Werner to Knight, 'I called him to account.'"[37] Yet Baldwin does not provide Werner's actual translation, nor does he give any hint that Knight had misquoted Werner. Since Payne's essay was unpublished, readers could not discover this. This is just one of several instances where Knight and/or Baldwin cite erroneous data to give the false impression that αὐθεντέω consistently conveyed positive authority in Paul's day. In particular, Knight's staunch rejection of negative meanings of αὐθεντέω, such as "dominate" and in BGU 1208 "to assume authority," has dissuaded interpreters from considering these historically better-supported solutions to its meaning in 1 Tim 2:12.[38]

Knight identifies αὐθεντέω in BGU 1208 as being "in the category of authority, in the objective and positive sense,"[39] thus implying objectively sanctioned rather than self-assumed authority. Six factors in the content of BGU 1208 make Knight's proposed translation doubtful:[40]

1. Nothing in the narrative shows that the person who forced the slave to agree to pay had any recognized authority over that slave. His letter of apology to the slave's owner confirms that he had no such authority. Unless he had a position of authority over the slave, the translation "exercised authority" is inappropriate.

2. BGU 1208.39–42 states, "He consented [ἐπιχωρέω] to provide for Calatytis the boatman on terms of the full fare, within the hour." Normally, only someone who has a choice "consents" to provide something. The person who consents to provide can also set terms and a timetable for that provision just as the nonpaying rider did. These expressions are more appropriate from a man agreeing to accept a responsibility than from a man obeying a command from someone in a recognized position of authority over him.

---

37. Payne, "Use of οὐδέ," 10.
38. E.g., Wilshire, "The TLG Computer," 130 and n. 7; Baldwin, "Difficult Word," WCFA 67, 74, 276; Moo, "What Does It Mean," RBMW 186 and 497 n. 18; Wolters, "Semantic," 151–53; and Perriman, "What Eve Did," 132, and Speaking of Women, 144 n. 22, who cites Knight to reject meanings related to "misuse of authority by women. Such a nuance, however, is barely, if at all, warranted by the lexicological evidence."
39. Knight, "ΑΥΘΕΝΤΕΩ," 153.
40. These six reasons also weigh against the LSJ 275 erroneous listing of αὐθεντέω in BGU 1208.37 (it is actually 1208.38) as "to have full power or authority over someone." The eighth edition of LSJ had more properly noted this meaning as "Byzantine." If he had full authority over the debtor, it is unlikely that the debtor would have acted insolently in not paying the fare. These reasons similarly show the inadequacy of the unexplained translation "came to have authority," in Wilshire, "Revisited," 46.

3. The debtor did not pay the boatman after all. If the writer had recognized authority over him, it would be foolhardy for him to so blatantly lie to that person and disobey him.

4. If the person assuming authority over the slave had recognized authority over him, it would have been more typical in this sort of context to use a word such as "commanded" or "told" or "ordered" rather than "exercised authority over," even if that were a meaning of αὐθεντέω at that time.

5. Since no instances of αὐθεντέω meaning "exercised authority" have been established prior to or near Paul's time, it is doubtful that it would have been understood in this way among Paul's audience.

6. αὐθεντηκότος is followed by πρός with the accusative to denote a "relationship (hostile or friendly), *against, for* — **a**. hostile *against, with* after verbs of disputing, etc."[41] This passage is about a hostile relationship; the debtor's action is called "insolence." None of the other uses of πρός in the over three columns devoted to it in BDAG seem to fit this context. Werner wrote, "I'm sure the slave, at least, regarded the stranger's action as hostile to him!"[42]

Paul D. Peterson's translation of αὐθεντηκότος in BGU 1208 "when I had prevailed upon him to provide ..." implies a person taking authority unto himself to resolve the dispute,[43] just as does Werner's translation, "I called him to account." Osburn pushes the negative nuance much further by translating αὐθεντηκότος in BGU 1208 "domineer."[44] John Werner gives a decisive objection to the translation "domineer": "I can hardly imagine anyone saying 'I domineered,' as would thus be the translation of BGU 1208.38 lines 37–38."[45] Since it is unlikely that the author would have described himself with this word if he thought it would have been understood to have as strong a pejorative sense as "I domineered him," this provides evidence that "domineer" was not the primary meaning of the word at that time.

---

41. BDAG 874; cf. LSJ 1497.
42. July 21, 1993 letter from Werner to Payne, page 3.
43. Translation provided for the author in Hamilton, Massachusetts, in 1986.
44. Osburn, "ΑΥΘΕΝΤΕΩ," 5.
45. August 27, 1984 letter from John R. Werner to Philip Barton Payne.

Friedrich Preisigke expresses the meaning of αὐθεντηκότος in BGU 1208 as "fest auftreten."[46] Ernst Bammel assured the current author that "fest auftreten" is appropriate to convey the sense of "to force one's way."[47] Although more plausible than "I domineered him," one would not expect the author of this sort of letter to write, "I forced my way on him" or "I dominated him." Thus, even though the sense of "dominate" is conceptually congruent with this passage, it is psychologically improbable that the author would describe his own act in this way. The translation, "I took the matter with him into my own hands [lit., 'I assumed authority against him'] and he consented to provide for Calatytis the Boatman on terms of the full fare, within the hour," however, fits in the context of this particular letter of apology and explanation perfectly. It acknowledges what is indisputable, that he took authority into his own hands that only rightfully belonged to the slave's master, without implying that his manner was oppressive.

Thus, the grammatical construction and content of BGU 1208 imply that the bystander took authority into his own hands over the debtor. Its date and verbal form make it especially important for establishing the meaning of this verb at the time Paul wrote. The continuing use of αὐθεντέω, documented below, further supports as current in Paul's day the meaning "assume authority over" in the sense of taking authority unto oneself that had not been generally recognized.

Αὐθεντέω IN THE RHETORICA OF PHILODEMUS

A papyrus fragment of the Rhetorica of Philodemus, who lived between ca. 110 and 40/35 BC,[48] is tantalizing because of its date. The interspersed lacunae throughout the text include both the letters after αὐθέντ, which are essential to be sure that it is a verbal form,[49] and all but αν of the word that may be its object. If the proper reconstruction is the noun αὐθένταισιν, it means "with lords [who are] murderers," in keeping with

---

46. Friedrich Preisigke, Wörterbuch der griechischen Papyruskunden (vol. 1; Berlin: Selbstverlag der Erben, 1925), 235–36.

47. On September 16, 1991, in the Cambridge University Library, commenting on the judgment of the meaning of this occurrence of αὐθεντέω by Preisigke in Wörterbuch der griechischen Papyruskunden, 235–36.

48. Piero Treves, "Philodemus," OCD, 818–19.

49. Kroeger and Kroeger, I Suffer Not, 96. Wolters, "Semantic," n. 60, and Baldwin, "αὐθεντέω in Ancient Greek," WCFA 275, note that αὐθένταισιν is the Old Attic dative plural of αὐθέντης, as in Aeschylus, Agamemnon 1573. It also occurs in the 256–246 BC papyrus PCairo Zenon 4.59.532,15.

the closest parallel to this quotation from Euripides, who is cited earlier in this sentence, and the usual meaning of the noun αὐθέντης prior to Paul's day. If the proper reconstruction is αὐθεντοῦσιν, it is a verbal form and of more relevance to 1 Tim 2:12. Since there are over 148 columns of entries in LSJ beginning with αν (all that is left of the object of this verb), reconstruction of the text is of necessity conjecture. Sudhaus reconstructs the Greek text as follows, lacunae indicated by square brackets:

Ἀλλ' εἰ δε[ῖ τὰ-	But if one is to
ληθῆ κα[ὶ γι]νόμενα [λέ-	speak the truth
γειν, οἱ ῥ[ήτ]ορες καὶ μ[εγά-	the rhetoricians do greatly
λα βλάπτ[ουσι] πολλοὺς [καὶ	harm many [and]
μεγάλους καὶ περὶ τῶν ["δει-	great men, and concerning those things (ambitions)
νοῖς ἔρωσι το[ξ]ευομέ-	which are "aimed at with strong desires"
νων" πρὸς τοὺς ἐπιφαν[εσ-	against distinguished personages—
τάτους ἑκάστοτε διαμά-	on each occasion they contend earnestly
χονται καὶ "σὺν αὐθεντ[οῦ-	and "with dominating
σιν ἄν[αξιν]" ὑπὲρ τῶν ὁμοί-	masters,"—to similar
ων ὡσ[αύτως.⁵⁰	ends.

Jay Shaynor translates this: "But if one is to speak the truth the rhetoricians do greatly harm many (and) great men, and they do contend earnestly both with distinguished personages—concerning those things (ambitions) which are 'aimed at with strong desires'—and also 'with

---

50. Siegfried Sudhaus, ed., *Philodemi: Volumina Rhetorica* (3 vols.; Leipzig: Teubner, 1896; repr., Amsterdam: Hakkert, 1964), 2:133 lines 6–16. Line 14 contains αὐθεντ.

authorized rulers'—to similar ends."[51] Osburn renders διαμάχονται καὶ "σὺν αὐθεντ[οῦ]σιν ἄν[αξιν]," "fight even with dominating masters,"[52] which is more in keeping with the other early occurrences of αὐθεντέω.

Proper interpretation, and for that matter proper reconstruction, depends on identifying what is being quoted in the two phrases Sudhaus has put into quotation marks. Werner notes, "The quoted phrase, *sun authentousin anaxin*, employs the poetic word *anax* and scans as the latter half of a line of dactylic-hexameter poetry. Since Philodemus writes in prose, I would suspect that the half-line is quoted from some earlier source than himself, perhaps as early as the Epic Cycle of poems."[53]

The first quotation in this sentence, "aimed at with strong desires" ([δει]νοῖς ἔρωσι το[ξ]ευομένων) has remarkable similarity to fragment 850 from the works of Euripides, "τοξεύεται δεινοῖς ἔρωσιν"[54] and is properly recognized as a quotation by Sudhaus. Wilshire states that the second phrase quoted in this sentence, "σὺν αὐθεντ[οῦ]σιν ἄν[αξιν]" also finds its closest parallel in the entire *TLG* database to Euripides fragment number 645, which reads "sharing the house with murdered children," ἢ παισὶν αὐθένταισι κοινωνῇ δόμων.[55] In light of these apparent citations, Wilshire properly questions Sudhaus' reconstruction of αὐθεντ[οῦ]σιν ἄν[αξιν] and especially a translation of it as "authorized rulers."[56] Since eight out of nine of Euripides' known uses of αὐθεντ- mean "murderer," an interpretation in line with this would seem to be preferable. A quotation including the idea of murder would be appropriate at this point given the context at the beginning of this sentence, "the rhetoricians do greatly harm many (and) great men," and also the prior quotation, "aimed at with strong desires."

Unfortunately, the lack of certainty of what Philodemus's σὺν αὐθεντ__ σιν ἄν____ was quoting makes it impossible to be confident what he meant by αὐθεντ_σιν. The closest known parallels to the quotations in this passage suggest that Philodemus meant "murderers" (αὐθέντ[αι]σιν) or "those who murder" (αὐθεντ[οῦ]σιν). Thus, the only meaning of αὐθεντέω that

---

51. Wilshire, "The TLG Computer," 134.
52. Osburn, "ΑΥΘΕΝΤΕΩ," 5, cf. p. 6, "the present participle of αὐθεντέω, used here in its normal sense of 'domineer.'" Cf. above, pp. 380–85.
53. April 8, 1980 letter from Werner to Knight, p. 3.
54. August Nauck, *Tragicorum Graecorum Fragmenta* (Leipzig: Teubner, 1889), 637.
55. Nauck, *Tragicorum Graecorum Fragmenta*, 562.
56. Wilshire, "The TLG Computer," 134. On the same basis Wilshire appropriately questions the paraphrase "those in authority" cited by Knight from Harry M. Hubbell, "The Rhetorica of Philodemus," *Transactions of the Connecticut Academy of Arts and Sciences* 23 (1920): 306.

fits in 1 Tim 2:12 and is also established prior to Paul's day is "assume authority." "To dominate" appears in literature shortly after Paul's time, but "to have authority" or "to exercise authority" are meanings that can be confirmed only much later in ecclesiastical writings.

Knight writes that "Hubbell as a translator gives the phrase 'those in authority' "[57] for Philodemus's αὐθεντ[οῦ]σιν. Belleville identifies this as a misidentification by Knight since "Hubbell actually renders *authent[ou] sin* rightly as an adjective meaning 'powerful' and modifying the noun *lords:*[58] 'they [rhetors] fight with powerful lords [διαμάχονται καὶ 'σὺν αὐθεντ[οῦ]σιν ἄν[αξιν].'" Werner's April 8, 1980, letter to Knight states, "Hubbell's 'powerful' paraphrases *megalous, epiphanestatous* and *authentousin* all together."[59] He thereby alerted Knight prior to publication that he had mischaracterized Hubbell's paraphrase as a translation and also that he had misidentified "those in authority" as Hubbell's translation of αὐθεντ[οῦ]σιν.

DOES Αὐθεντεῖν IN 1 TIMOTHY 2:12 MEAN "TO HAVE AUTHORITY OVER"?

Not even one instance of the later ecclesiastical use of αὐθεντέω with the meaning "to have authority over" or "to exercise authority" has been established before or near the time of Paul. Nevertheless, because this is how many Bible versions translate 1 Tim 2:12,[60] this analysis examines it in some detail. In both editions of the most detailed volume trying to prove that 1 Tim 2:12 prohibits women from having authority over men, Baldwin's study of αὐθεντέω "narrows down the range of meaning that might be appropriate in 1 Tim 2:12" to four possible meanings: to dominate, to compel, to assume authority over, and to flout the authority of.[61] Baldwin says Schreiner will identify which best fits 1 Tim 2:12.[62] Schreiner, however, adopts none of these, but rather "exercise authority over."[63]

Although there are no established instances with this meaning until centuries after Paul, the interpretation "to teach and have authority over

---

57. Knight, "ΑΥΘΕΝΤΕΩ," 154, cf. 145.
58. Belleville, "Usurping Authority," 215.
59. April 8, 1980 letter from Werner to Knight.
60. E.g., "to have authority": HCSB, Beck, RSV, NRSV, NIV, NAB, TEV, Weymouth; "exercise authority": ESV, NASB; "put them in authority": Phillips; "have dominion": RV, ASV.
61. Baldwin, "A Difficult Word," WCFA 78–80; "Important Word," WCA 45–51.
62. Baldwin, "A Difficult Word," WCFA 80; "Important Word," WCA 51.
63. Schreiner, "Dialogue,"WCA 97, 101, 102, 104.

374   MAN AND WOMAN

a man," namely, to teach a man authoritatively, solves several problems for people who feel that a hierarchy of man over woman is compatible with Paul's teaching. Unlike unqualified separate prohibitions of a woman teaching and of a woman having authority over a man, which contradict so much of Paul's teaching and practice, it prohibits only authoritative teaching of a man by a woman. Nor does it restrict in any way women teaching women. It appeals to a symmetry of permitting women to learn in submission but not to teach men authoritatively. If "in quietness" is translated "silence,"[64] this, too, contrasts with teaching. The following γάρ clause in verse 13, if interpreted as implying a hierarchy based on temporal priority in creation,[65] gives a theological basis for not permitting a woman to teach a man authoritatively. The reference to the deception of Eve, if interpreted as establishing that women tend to be deceived in a way that men are not,[66] gives a further reason for prohibiting a woman from teaching a man authoritatively. The final affirmation of woman's role in salvation through the birth of Christ gives consolation in spite of woman's subordinate position and inherent susceptibility to deception. Under this view, the final condition for salvation, "with self-control," reminds women to stay in their restricted role. This interpretation, how-ever, in addition to all its exegetical weaknesses, faces major problems both lexically and theologically.

Lexically, as demonstrated above, no other passage prior to or near the time of Paul clearly supports the meaning, "have authority over."[67] There is support for this meaning considerably after Paul's day. The first instance of αὐθεντέω[68] confirmed to mean "exercise authority" is ca. AD 370 in Saint Basil, *The Letters* 69, line 45: "he [the bishop of Rome] may himself exercise full authority [αὐθεντῆσαι] in this matter, selecting men capable

---

64. Cf., however, above, pp. 314–15.
65. Cf., however, above, pp. 43–44, and below, pp. 399–404.
66. Cf., however, above, p. 47, and below, pp. 410–15.
67. Despite Knight's assertions to the contrary, Knight, "ΑΥΘΕΝΤΕΩ," 152, as shown above, pp. 362–72.
68. It is unclear whether αὐθεντέω describing "inhumane despots" in Pseudo-Hippolytus (of unknown date, possibly late fourth century). *On the End of the World* 7.5, means "lord it over" (e.g., Roberts, ANF 5:243), "dominate," "assume authority over," or "have legal authority over." Baldwin, "αὐθεντέω in Ancient Greek," WCFA 278, notes that Codex B of Hippolytus omits αὐθεντέω here, so the "text may be corrupt." Since this, like all other statements in this pas-sage, exemplifies "all shall walk after their own desire," since all of the parallel verbs are nega-tive ("lay hands upon," "hand over to death," "hand over to judgment," "assume an unruly disposition"), and since the subject of αὐθεντέω is inhumane or savage masters, "lord it over" or "dominate" (in the sense of "domineer") fits the context best.

of enduring the hardships of a journey."[69] The Lexicon of Hesychius of Alexandria (fifth century AD), which survives only in a fifteenth-century manuscript known to have been redacted in many places,[70] states: αὐθεντεῖν = ἐξουσιάζειν,[71] which means "to exercise authority."

Lampe has established the patristic use of αὐθεντέω predominantly to convey various nuances of assuming, having, or exercising authority. Although there is a significant difference between "to exercise authority" and the root meaning of αὐθεντέω, "self-achieving," the original meaning of αὐθεντέω could have shifted first to "self-achieving through assuming authority," then "assuming authority" and eventually to "exercising authority." This shift, however, is not at all self-evident from the root meaning of αὐθεντέω and so should not be assumed to have occurred much before its first confirmed occurrence in AD 370 and certainly not in Paul's day over three centuries earlier.

Paul does refer to exercise of authority in many passages, but nowhere else does he use this word, and many scholars question that Paul would have chosen such an unusual verb to convey the simple idea of positive authority, especially since the αὐθεντ- root normally through the time of Paul carried negative connotations. If Paul wanted to convey the meaning "to have authority" without any negative nuances, it would have been natural for him to use a term such as he did in verse 2 of this chapter ἐν ὑπεροχῇ εἶναι or ἐξουσίαν ἔχειν[72] or ἐξουσιάζειν[73] or one of the many other expressions Paul uses for having, using, or sharing authority.[74] Wilshire states that "everywhere [else] in the NT where teaching and authority are mentioned together ... it is always the word ἐξουσία that is the word used for 'authority.'"[75]

---

69. Roy J. Deferrari, trans., *Saint Basil* 2:40–43 (LCL).

70. Baldwin, "Important Word," *WCA* 197 n. 19. John Chadwick (*Lexicographica Graeca: Contributions to the Lexicography of Ancient Greek* [Oxford: Clarendon, 1996], 13) cautions that one must not "believe everything Hesychius tells us. Some entries are plainly wrong, or partially wrong, as when he gives a series of synonyms, only one of which appears to be correct. And the text is often too corrupt for any emendation to carry conviction."

71. Kurt Latte, ed., *Hesychii Alexandrini Lexicon* (2 vols.; Copenhagen: Einar Munksgaard, 1953, 1966), 1:279, entry A8259. Cf. entry H49, ἡγεῖτο [the imperfect of ἡγέομαι, "I lead, guide, think, consider, regard"] = ηὐθέντει, ἦρχεν [from αὐθεντέω and ἄρχω].

72. Rom 9:21; 1 Cor 7:37; 9:4, 5, 6, 12 (μετέχω); 11:10; 2 Thess 3:9.

73. 1 Cor 6:12; 7:4 (twice); cf. "to submit to authorities" (ἐξουσίαις ὑποτάσσεσθαι) in Titus 3:1.

74. E.g., "to use authority" in 1 Cor 9:12; "to make full use of authority" in 9:18; "have a share of authority" in 9:12; "to be given authority" in 2 Cor 10:8. See further in Walter L. Liefeld, "Women and the Nature of Ministry," *JETS* 30 (1987): 52.

75. Wilshire, "The TLG Computer," 131.

Moo objects that "Paul's three other uses of that verb hardly put it in the category of his standard vocabulary, and the vocabulary of the pastorals is well known to be distinct from Paul's vocabulary elsewhere."[76] Moo's statement is misleading since Paul also uses "to have authority" (ἐξουσίαν ἔχειν) seven times.[77] These combined with the four other verbal composite forms using ἐξουσία (1 Cor 9:12, 18; 2 Cor 13:10; Titus 3:1) and his fifteen other uses of ἐξουσία as a noun,[78] not in a verbal construction, firmly establish ἐξουσία as Paul's standard vocabulary for authority. The occurrence of ἐξουσία in Titus 3:1 confirms its use in the Pastoral Epistles. Luke, the most likely amanuensis for 1 Timothy,[79] uses ἐξουσία twenty-two times in Luke–Acts, the majority in verbal composite constructions, and Luke 22:25 also uses the verb ἐξουσιάζω, so these are confirmed vocabulary for him as well.

Theologically, this interpretation of αὐθεντέω prohibits the sort of authoritative teaching of a man that Paul approves for women elsewhere, including Priscilla, along with Aquila, instructing Apollos.[80] It also conflicts with Paul's theological principles implying the equal standing of men and women in Christ.[81] Some affirming a hierarchy of men over women have tried to explain Priscilla's teaching as an exception[82] and may well grant other exceptions when they believe men would benefit from the teaching of a woman. To be consistent, however, they cannot also affirm 1 Tim 2:12 is a *universal* restriction against women teaching and/or having authority over a man. Nor can they also affirm that woman being formed after man or Eve being deceived demands this as a *universal* restriction.

Understanding αὐθεντέω in 1 Tim 2:12 as a present prohibition[83] for the specific situation in Ephesus, where many women were deceived by false teachers, resolves these theological tensions. Interpreting this verb "to exercise authority," however, still must face the objection, "Why would all women be restricted from authoritatively teaching men if they were not all deceived by the false teachers?" Would this apply to Priscilla, whom Paul

---

76. Moo, "Rejoinder," 186.
77. Rom 9:21; 1 Cor 7:37; 9:4, 5, 6; 11:10; 2 Thess 3:9, and 1 Cor 9:12 has ἐξουσίας μετέχουσιν.
78. Rom 13:1, 1, 2, 3; 1 Cor 8:9; 15:24; 2 Cor 10:8; Eph 1:21; 2:2; 3:10; 6:12; Col 1:13, 16; 2:10, 15.
79. Cf. above, pp. 292–93.
80. Cf. above, pp. 64, 328–34.
81. Cf. above, pp. 69–76.
82. Cf. Calvin, *Timothy, Titus, and Philemon*, 67 and above, pp. 66, 219.
83. Cf. above, pp. 319–25.

greets in 2 Tim 4:19? In contrast, if Paul's prohibition is against "assuming [undelegated] authority over men," it places no restriction on women with properly delegated authority.

Knight states: "The 'authority' in view in the documents is understood to be a positive concept and is in no way regarded as having any overtone of misuse of position or power, i.e., to 'domineer.' "[84] His statement and the evidence he presents for it are misleading:

1. None of the translators or lexicographers he cites implies that αὐθεντέω conveys "a positive concept ... in no way regarded as having any overtone of misuse of position or power.' "

2. BAG 120 specifically defined αὐθεντέω as *"have authority, domineer over someone."* In Knight's chart of "Meaning Given by Lexicographer" he omits this definition of BAG in every case but one, and in this one he deletes "domineer" from his quotation! It is only later on page 153 that he acknowledges BAG's use of "domineer."

3. Knight acknowledges that in *PGL* 262, under "assume authority, act on one's own authority," there "is a more negative usage proposed in two homilies," but he does not give the meanings there cited: "play the despot, act arbitrarily."[85] Beyond these two, Lampe also lists the negative meaning "presume on one's own authority."[86]

4. Knight acknowledges that Sophocles' *Lexicon* lists the meaning "compel," a meaning that is appropriate to misuse of power.[87]

5. A classic argument from misunderstanding German comes in this statement: "The 1957 English translation and edition of the 1952 4th ed. of Bauer by Arndt and Gingrich faithfully renders this German word by the English equivalent 'have authority ... τινός over someone' as does the newest English edition by Gingrich and Danker (1979). The riddle appears with the insertion of the word 'domineer' between 'authority' and 'τινός'

---

84. Knight, "ΑΥΘΕΝΤΕΩ," 150–51. Cf. Baldwin, "Important Word," WCA 200, "The most basic sense is the positive exercise of authority."
85. Cf. below, pp. 380–85.
86. G. W. H. Lampe, ed., *A Patristic Greek Lexicon* (Oxford: Clarendoon, 1961), 262.
87. Knight, "ΑΥΘΕΝΤΕΩ," 157, in footnote 50, as does Baldwin similarly, "αὐθεντέω in Ancient Greek Literature," WCFA 66.

in both the 1957 and 1979 English editions."[88] Apparently
Knight overlooked the fact that the German words *"herrschen"*
and *"beherrschen"* have a semantic range including both "have
authority" and "domineer," as a check of virtually any standard
German-English dictionary shows.[89]

6. Ptolemy describes the planets' "dominating" as "injurious to the
subjects."[90] Knight does not cite this description but instead writes,
"The following parallel clause speaks of such an αὐθεντέω and
rule as a position of dignity."[91] The following clause, however, is
not explaining αὐθεντέω. It is merely stating that if Saturn has a
dignified position with reference to the universe and the angles,
various traits result, including: "dictatorial, ready to punish, lovers
of property, avaricious, violent, amassing treasure, and jealous."

7. The preponderance of examples of forms of αὐθεντ- up to Paul's
time have negative connotations. This forms part of the background from which people understood early occurrences of
αὐθεντέω. If Paul had wanted to select a neutral term for positive
authority, αὐθεντέω was a bad choice. There are many ways he
could easily have done so without inviting the negative associations the αὐθεντ- word group carried at that time.

8. It is also surprising, if Paul intended to exclude women from
authority positions over men, that he specifically refers to women
in his description of the requirements for deacons, listing their
requirements for this office in 1 Tim 3:11. Furthermore, he introduces the requirements for an overseer by saying that *anyone* desiring the office of overseer desires a noble task, and nowhere in the
requirements does he use a masculine pronoun.[92]

---

88. Knight, "ΑΥΘΕΝΤΕΩ," 153.
89. E.g., Cassell's dictionary lists for *herrschen* both "rule" and "domineer," and translates some of
its compounds as "despot, autocrat, lust of power, despotism, tyrannical, tyranny." Harrap's
dictionary lists for *beherrschen*: "to rule (country/people/the known world/the universe), to
dominate (a person, one's children, etc.); to hold someone in one's power, in one's grip; to have
dominion over someone … to be dominated, ridden by fear." Note that *beherrschen* when used
with persons as objects tends to be negative but when used of nations tends to refer to executive
authority. Similarly, Langenscheidt: Muret Sanders lists for *beherrschen*: "to rule over (ein Volk)
… bad sense: 'to domineer over' (of a person 'to boss it over')."
90. Cf. Robbins' translation cited below, p. 381.
91. Knight, "ΑΥΘΕΝΤΕΩ," 146. Baldwin ("Important Word," WCA 199 n. 28) alleges similarly,
"Robbins clearly does not mean anything pejorative like 'domineer' here."
92. Cf. further on this below, p. 448.

Knight alleges, "there is the passage in the historian Diodorus of Sicily (I BC) which utilizes the word κυριεύειν, rather than αὐθεντεῖν as in 1 Tim 2:12, but with a nearly identical form both as to construction and content. The statement says the Egyptians have made a law 'contrary to the general custom of mankind' ... with the result that κυριεύειν τὴν γυναῖκα τἀνδρός."[93] Knight confuses two different laws. Diodorus writes, "The Egyptians also made a law, they say, contrary to the general custom of mankind, permitting men to marry their sisters."[94] By omitting, "permitting men to marry their sisters," Knight gives the false impression that Diodorus identifed women ruling men to be "contrary to the general custom of mankind." To the contrary, Diodorus stated that the rule of Isis gave

> greater blessings to all men than any other. It is for these reasons, in fact, that it was ordained that the queen should have greater power and honour than the king and that among private persons the wife should enjoy authority over her husband [κυριεύειν τὴν γυναῖκα τἀνδρός], the husbands agreeing in marriage contract that they will be obedient in all things to their wives.[95]

This passage shows not only a high regard for women in authority, but also that the idea of a woman having authority over a man could be expressed quite naturally with the common word κυριεύω, which Paul used six times, including 1 Tim 6:15, and could have used here if he had intended to convey this meaning.

Either "to assume authority" or "to dominate" makes a better contrast with "quietness" in 1 Tim 2:12 than "to exercise authority" or "to have authority." Furthermore, either "to assume authority" or "to dominate" makes a better contrast with "to be in full submission." Dibelius and Conzelmann state, "'to be domineering' (αὐθεντεῖν) would be the opposite [of ὑποταγή]."[96]

---

93. Knight, "ΑΥΘΕΝΤΕΩ," 149.
94. Oldfather, *Diodorus of Sicily*, Book I, §27, 1:84–85.
95. *Diodorus of Sicily*, 1:84–87 §27 (trans. C. H. Oldfather, LCL). Cf. Sophocles' *Oed. col.* 337–41.
96. Dibelius and Conzelmann, *Pastoral Epistles*, 47. Baldwin ("Important Word," WCA 199 n. 28), in attempting to exclude "domineer" as a possible meaning of αὐθεντέω in 1 Tim 2:12, incorrectly describes "dominate" as a transitive verb in contrast to "domineer," which he states "is defined as an intransitive verb." Either can be transitive or intransitive: e.g., *Webster's New World Dictionary*, 417; *Webster's Encyclopedic Dictionary*, 582.

In the wider context as well, either "to assume authority" or "to dominate" fits better than "to have authority." It fits Paul's mention of the temporal priority of Adam in creation. Since man was formed before woman and since woman was formed from man, she should respect[97] man, not assume authority over him or dominate him. In Paul's day the need to respect one's source was reinforced by a strong tradition of respect for one's ancestors. There is no necessary or logical link, however, between temporal priority in creation and authority. In the Genesis account man and woman are equally given the creation mandate. Nowhere else does the Bible state that man's temporal priority in creation grants man authority over woman.[98]

DOES Αὐθεντεῖν IN 1 TIMOTHY 2:12 MEAN "TO DOMINATE"?

Although some scholars have argued that αὐθεντέω in BGU 1208 means "dominate," the above study agrees with Werner that this meaning is unlikely in BGU 1208. The meaning "dominate," however, is attested in many other passages. The closely related noun αὐθεντία means *domination* in 3 Macc 2:29, written about 100 BC. Ptolemy decreed

> that all Jews should be degraded to the rank of natives and the condition of serfs, and that those who spoke against it should be taken by force and put to death; and that those who were registered should even be branded on their bodies with an ivy-leaf, the emblem of Dionysus, and be reduced to their former *domination* [εἰς τὴν προσυνεσταλμένην αὐθεντίαν].... But if any of them prefer to join those who are initiated into the mysteries, they shall have equal rights with the citizens of Alexandria.[99]

The sense of "domination" is required by the contrast between "degraded to the rank of natives and the condition of serfs" and its contrast to "equal rights with the citizens."

---

97. Respect for the earth, plants, and animals created prior to humankind is implied in God's call in Gen 2 to "take care of" the garden. This provides a theological basis for ecological respect for nonhuman life forms and the earth itself.

98. Cf. above on 1 Cor 11:2–16, the one passage sometimes alleged to do so (pp. 130–31, 181).

99. *APOT*, 1:165–66, with the exception that Charles has "limited status" in place of "domination." "Domination" fits the established range of meanings of αὐθεντία and the context better than any other suggestion, such as "restriction," "rights," or "limited rights" in Wilshire, "The TLG Computer," 124; idem, "I Timothy 2:12 Revisited," 46. Cf. LSJ 1529 on προσυστέλλομαι.

Nägeli argued that the verb αὐθεντέω was introduced into common Greek as an equivalent to κρατεῖν τινος, "to dominate someone."[100] This is seen in Ptolemy, *Tetrabiblos* 3.13.10 (127–148 AD),[101] the first confirmed use of the verb αὐθεντέω meaning "dominate."

> The powers, however, of the nature of the planets that dominate [ἐπικρατησάντων] or overcome [καθυπερτερησάντων] them are vigorous and injurious to the subjects.... If Saturn alone is ruler of the soul and dominates [αὐθεντήσας] Mercury and the moon, if he has a dignified position with reference to the universe and the angles, he makes his subjects lovers of the body, strong-minded, deep thinkers, austere, of a single purpose, laborious, dictatorial, ready to punish, lovers of property, avaricious, violent, amassing treasure, and jealous; but if his position is the opposite and without dignity, he makes them sordid, petty, mean-spirited, indifferent, mean-minded, malignant, cowardly, diffident, evil-speakers, solitary, tearful, shameless, superstitious, fond of toil, unfeeling, devisers of plots against their friends, gloomy, taking no care of the body.[102]

These characteristics are particularly negative and "injurious to the subjects." The verbs that parallel αὐθεντέω, "dominate" and "overcome," reinforce that αὐθεντέω conveys a negative sense in this passage. Moo, however, citing Knight, alleges, "the occurrences of this word—the verb—that are closest in time and nature to 1 Timothy mean 'have authority over' or 'dominate' (in the neutral sense of 'have dominion over,' not in the negative sense 'lord it over')."[103]

Chrysostom (d. AD 407) writes in *Hom. in ep. ad Col.* 10.1 (11.396C), "Do not, therefore, because thy wife is subject to thee, act the despot"[104]

100. Theodor Nägeli, *Der Wortschatz des Apostels Paulus* (Göttingen: Vandenhoeck & Ruprecht, 1905), 49–50.

101. G. J. Toomer, "Ptolemy (4)" *OCD* 897–88.

102. Robbins, *Ptolemy*, 338–41. Note 1 explains that "dignified positions with reference to the angles" refers to particular angles of the horoscope, especially mid-heaven angles. Baldwin, "αὐθεντέω in Ancient Greek," *WCFA* 275, repeats Knight's error of misreading "angles" as "angels": "ΑΥΘΕΝΤΕΩ," 146. The critical edition is Franz Boll and Æ. Boer, eds., Ptolemy, *Apotelesmatika* (vol. 3.1 of *Claudii Ptolemaei Opera quae exstant omnia*; ed. Franz Boll and Æ. Boer; Leipzig: Teubner, 1940; repr., 1957), 158.

103. Moo, "What Does It Mean," *RBMW* 186 and n. 18; Knight, "ΑΥΘΕΝΤΕΩ," 146.

104. *NPNF¹* 13:304; PG 62:366. Pace Wilshire, "The TLG Computer," 132, who states that "the word is used in regard to a wife, respecting the authority of her husband." Baldwin ("Important Word," *WCA* 51) acknowledges that αὐθεντέω means "domineer" here, but alleges without evidence or contextual warrant that this is "a clear use of hyperbole."

(Μὴ τοίνυν, ἐπειδὴ ὑποτέτακται ἡ γυνή, αὐθέντει).[105] *PGL* 262 translates this, "play the despot, act arbitrarily." As in 1 Tim 2:12, "being subject" contrasts with αὐθέντει, except here it is men who are not to αὐθέντει. If it means "to have authority," then, Chrysostom wrote, "do not have authority over your wife"!

PGL 263 gives three fourth- to fifth-century AD examples of this noun meaning "high-handedness; tyranny." The fifth- to sixth-century AD Christian grammarian and philosopher Joannes Philoponus wrote "ignorance dominates," using the verb form αὐθεντεῖ ἄγνοια in *Commentaria in Aristotelem Graeca* 15.487.12. Papyrus 9239,8 from AD 548 describes a woman who was dominated, cast aside, and suffered a life-threatening blow as "αὐθεντίᾳ κ(αὶ) τυραννικ(ῷ)."[106] In the sixth century AD,[107] Johannes Malalas' *Chronographia*[108] uses αὐθεντήσαντες τὸν ἡγεμόνα to mean "put pressure on."[109] Clearly, then, there are many instances where the verb αὐθεντέω means "dominate." Depending on the context, appropriate translation could use an equivalent expression such as "domineer, compel, force, prevail upon, put pressure on, prevail over, or call to account." Harris even went as far as to say, "in all of the occurrences of the verb close to the NT period, there is one indispensable element: that to exercise *authentein* was 'to hold sway or use power, to be dominant.'"[110] Many Bible versions translate αὐθεντεῖν with some equivalent of "dominate":

"dominate": Fenton, TNT
"domineer": Berkeley, New Berkeley, Goodspeed, NEB, Williams[111]
"exercise dominion": Reina-Valera 1960, 1995 (*ejercer dominio*)

---

105. F. Field, *Joannis Chrysostomi interpretatio omnium epistularum Paulinarum* (vols 1–7; Oxford: J. H. Parker, 1845–1862); *Homilias in Epistolae ad Philippenses, Colossenses et Thessalonicenses* (1855), 5:276 line 5.
106. Emil Kiessling, *Sammelbuch Griechischer Urkunden aus Ägypten* (Wiesbaden: Otto Harrassowitz, 1963), 6:139.
107. LSJ xxxii.
108. Ludwig Dindorf, *Ioannis Malalae Chronographia* (Bonn: Weber, 1831).
109. As translated by Elizabeth Jeffreys, Michael Jeffreys, and Roger Scott, *The Chronicle of John Malalas: A Translation* (Melbourne: Australian Association for Byzantine Studies, 1986), 136. Baldwin ("Important Word," *WCA* 46) concludes "that 'compel' is the intended meaning, if not something stronger."
110. Harris, "Eve's Deception," 342. This does not, however, apply to Aristonicus Alexandrinus, *De signis Iliadis*, 9.694, cf. above, pp. 361–62.
111. Cf. also Dibelius and Conzelmann, *Pastoral Epistles*, 47 ("to be domineering"); Marshall, *Pastoral Epistles*, 456–60; Osburn, "ΑΥΘΕΝΤΕΩ," 4–12.

"lord it over": LB, Way[112]

"to tell a man what to do": CEV, JB, *The Message*

"dictate to men": Moffatt, REB

"lay down the law": JBCerf (*faire la loi*)

Several NT Greek lexicons include "domineer" as a meaning for αὐθεντέω in 1 Tim 2:12.[113] Similarly, Marshall concludes, "Ideas such as autocratic or domineering abuses of power and authority appear to be more naturally linked with the verb in view of the meanings of the cognate nouns αὐθέντης and αὐθεντία."[114]

Furthermore, almost everything in the logical development of the passage makes sense with "to teach and dominate a man." Just as submission should characterize a woman's learning (1 Tim 2:11), domination should not characterize a woman's teaching a man (2:12). Domination is the opposite of submission and so makes an excellent contrast. Dominating teaching is the opposite of tranquil learning (2:11). Verse 12 contrasts αὐθεντέω with, "but to be in quietness" (ἀλλ᾽ εἶναι ἐν ἡσυχίᾳ) and the same phrase from the prior verse, "let a woman learn with a quiet spirit (ἐν ἡσυχίᾳ)." "To dominate a man" implies forceful imposition of one's will that is the opposite of a quiet spirit.[115] "To dominate" fits the context better than "to have authority," since it is diametrically opposed to "quietness," as required by "but" (ἀλλ᾽, 2:12).

Wilshire properly observes, "Calmness is the opposite of violence, not of authority or power."[116] Calmness and authority are compatible, not contrasting concepts.[117] Although no verse in 1 Timothy explicitly states that women in the Ephesian church were dominating men, "women must ... not be malicious talkers" (3:11) may allude to some form of domination. Moreover, 1 Tim 6:4–5 may imply a dominating spirit on the part of "anyone [who]

---

112. Cf. J. H. Bernard, *The Pastoral Epistles* (Cambridge: Cambridge Univ. Press, 1899), 48 ("to lord it over").

113. BAG 120; L&N, 1:474 §37.21; John Groves, *A Greek and English Dictionary* (5th ed.; London: George Cowie, 1833), 100; Barclay M. Newman, Jr., *A Concise Greek-English Dictionary of the New Testament* (New York: United Bible Societies, 1971), 28; Souter, *Pocket Lexicon*, 42; and Parkhurst, *Lexicon*, 79.

114. Marshall, *Pastoral Epistles*, 457.

115. Since ἐν ἡσυχίᾳ structurally parallels ἐν πάσῃ ὑποταγῇ at the end of v. 11, the structure contrasts αὐθεντέω with "in full submission." "To dominate" is the opposite of "to be in full submission." "To have authority" would also contrast with "to be in full submission," but the contrast is greater with "dominate" or "to assume authority."

116. Wilshire, "1 Tim 2:12 Revisited," 48.

117. Cf. Harris, "Eve's Deception," 343. *Pace* Barnett, "Wives and Women's Ministry," 232.

384 MAN AND WOMAN

teaches false doctrines ... controversies and arguments that result in envy, quarreling, malicious talk, evil suspicions and constant friction between men [ἀνθρώπων may include women] of corrupt mind" (cf. 1:4, 7; 4:3).

The "for" clause in 1 Tim 2:13 indirectly supports the "dominate" interpretation since dominating teaching is the opposite of the respect a woman owes to man as prior in creation and the one from whom she was formed. The translation "to dominate" also contrasts well with Paul's final word in verse 15, his insistence that women exercise "self-control" (σωφροσύνης). Furthermore, for women to dominate men in teaching would be particularly offensive and reflect poorly on the gospel. It fits the contentiousness of the false teachers in Ephesus and provides guidance on how "you ought to behave" in the church of the living God (1 Tim 3:14–15). Yet unlike the "have authority" interpretation, it does not conflict with any other Pauline passage. Consequently, there is sufficient lexical and contextual evidence to give serious consideration to translating αὐθεντεῖν in 1 Tim 2:12, "to dominate."

If Paul intends this as a separate prohibition from "to teach," then in light of the false teaching he is not permitting a woman "to teach" or "to dominate a man." The goal of this double prohibition would be to stop the major source of the false teaching and to shield the church from a major source of conflict and from a bad reputation due to women dominating men.

In light of Paul's usual use of οὐδέ, however, it is more likely that Paul is conveying a single idea that merges "to teach" and "to dominate a man": "I am not permitting a woman to teach and dominate a man, but she should have a quiet spirit." One weakness of the "dominate" interpretation is that it is not clear what "to teach and dominate a man" would have meant.

Dominating teaching could refer to bombastic or threatening teaching or teaching that forces a man to change his belief or behavior. There is evidence that most women lacked the training in Scripture available to men and that women were particularly susceptible to the false teaching.[118] Since their message would not be welcome, it would cause the kinds of controversies troubling Ephesus and would be more likely to be perceived as dominating. Any teaching aims to influence, and some people in a male-dominated culture such as Paul's might have considered women teaching men to be dominating under any circumstance.

---

118. Cf. above, pp. 299–304.

The major weakness of the "teach and dominate a man" interpretation is that the appeal to Eve's deception does not directly support it. If Paul is specifically prohibiting teaching that dominates a man, one would expect his supporting illustration to exemplify dominating teaching. Nothing in Gen 3:6 or its context, however, gives any hint that the first woman dominated Adam. Paul's stress on the deception of the woman that led to the fall seems designed instead to support a prohibition focused on stopping women in Ephesus who were deceived by the false teaching from assuming authority for themselves to teach men, which could lead to a corresponding fall of the church there.

DOES Αὐθεντεῖν IN 1 TIMOTHY 2:12 MEAN "TO ASSUME AUTHORITY [TO ONESELF]"?

Several key factors make "to assume authority" the best-supported meaning of αὐθεντέω in 1 Tim 2:12. Of only two cases of αὐθεντέω unambiguously documented up to Paul's time, the meaning of only one fits 1 Tim 2:12, BGU 1208, "to assume authority [to oneself]." Like the only other case,[119] it is closely associated with the word's etymology: "self-achieving." BDAG 150 defines αὐθεντέω, "to assume a stance of independent authority." This precisely identifies the meaning argued here for 1 Tim 2:12.

Perriman also correctly identifies the focus in the use of αὐθεντέω in Paul's time as the "assumption" of authority and "the active wielding of influence (with respect to a person)."[120] Werner identifies the "assumption of authority" as the core meaning of αὐθεντέω.[121] Baldwin correctly notes that "assume authority over" is an appropriate translation of αὐθεντέω in 1 Tim 2:12.[122] He also states that αὐθεντέω

> occurs several times in negative contexts, where it refers to a condition that results when one has taken to himself or herself the judgments or authority belonging to another. Thus, the word is used

---

119. Cf. above, pp. 361–62.

120. Perriman, "What Eve Did," 136, 138; cf. Andrew Perriman, *Speaking of Woman: Interpreting Paul* (Leicester: Apollos, 1998), 151–57.

121. Cf. above, pp. 365–69 and below, 386–87, 390–91. *Pace* Wolters, "Semantic," n. 82.

122. Baldwin, "Difficult Word," WCFA 75, 79, 80, but he incorrectly states on p. 75 and in "Important Word," WCA 47, that it is "a positive term" even though his "Important Word," WCA 201 n. 32 states, "Submission to authority, not independence, was one of the driving values of the early church. So several of the examples given are in a context where the author undoubtedly intends the context to have negative connotations."

three times to speak of an underlord who carries out an execution that ought to have been sanctioned by the king. It is used of other officials who release prisoners, lighten tribute, or convene assemblies without full authorization. In this it is like "usurp."[123]

Various lexicons[124] and Bible versions reflect the taking of authority that has not been properly delegated: "usurp authority": Bishops (1589), Geneva (1560), KJV; "take authority": Segond (1910) and A. Crampton, La Sainte Bible (1864, 1938) ("*prendre autorité*"), Casiodoro de Reina (1569) ("*tomar autoridad*"). The meaning "to assume authority" is well-documented in occurrences of αὐθεντέω after Paul's time as well.

Werner argues that αὐθεντέω means "assume authority" in a fifteenth-century astrological papyrus believed to reproduce a third-century text attributed to Hermes.[125] Walter Scott states, "Most of [the extant *Hermetica*], if not all, were written in the third century after Christ...Probably none [were written] so early as the first century."[126] Just as one properly identifies later NT manuscripts as identifying first-century text, Osburn may not be far off in identifying this text as second-century AD,[127] but a third-century date fits better with most of the *Hermetica*. In this passage, "A king of thieves gets his authority by assuming it (and then defending it against rivals, like Robin Hood dousing Little John), not by having it delegated to him by a higher official or recognized as his by cultural custom."[128]

---

123. Baldwin, "Important Word," WCA 47. Baldwin, "Αὐθεντέω in Ancient Greek," WCFA 276, 291, 301, 304, includes in this category the second-century AD Moeris's *Attic Lexicon*, the ca. AD 450 Olympiodorus 456.3, the ninth-century AD Photius *Bibliothèque* 80.59a.11; 80.62b.31; and 238.317b.7; and the thirteenth- to fourteenth-century AD Thomas Magister's *Attic Sayings* 18.9. Baldwin distinguishes uses of αὐθεντέω from "usurp" by saying they do not refer to actions but to states, but his own translations of Olympiodorus and Photius in "Αὐθεντέω in Ancient Greek," WCFA 291, 301, prove this to be false.
124. E.g., Groves, *Greek and English*, 100 ("to usurp power").
125. Franciscus Cumont, *Codicum Parisinorum* in *Catalogus Codicum Astrologorum Graecorum*, VIII (vol. 1; Brussels: A. M. Lamertin, 1929), 177.7–8. Cumont (*Codicum*, 20, 32, 172–175) entitles the work "Hermetis Trismegisti methodus mystica" and identifies three manuscripts of it. Cumont (*Codicum*, 172) identifies this passage as possibly being "from the book of mysteries in the *Catalogo Apomasaris* column 799 that is attributed to Hermes. Its attribution to Hermes indicates that it cites a far earlier Hermetic tradition."
126. Walter Scott, ed., *Hermetica Part 1: The Ancient Greek and Latin Writings Which Contain Religious or Philosophic Teachings Ascribed to Hermes Trismegistus* (Introduction, Texts and Translation; 4 vols.; Oxford: Clarendon, 1924–1936), 1:10. His work does not analyze or date the astrological texts attributed to Hermes.
127. Osburn, "ΑΥΘΕΝΤΕΩ," 6. Scott, *Hermetica* 1:76 states, "The earliest evidence for the writings of similar character to our religious and philosophic Hermetica is that of Athenogoras, AD 177–80."
128. July 21, 1993 letter from Werner to Payne, page 3, confirmed in a January 27, 2006 email to Payne. A letter from Werner to Knight dated April 8, 1980 translated it "exercises authority"

John Chrysostom, *In Joannen* (PG 59), writes ca. AD 386–407 about Greeks asking to see Jesus, "But neither does he [Philip] at once *assume authority* (αὐθεντεῖ); for he heard, 'Go not in the way of the Gentiles.' Therefore, having communicated with the disciple [Andrew] he brings it up to the Teacher [Christ]" (John 12:21). Chrysostom *Hom. in ep. ad. Col.* 11.2 (11.406E) uses αὐθεντεῖν similarly, "Do not then wish *to assume authority for yourselves,* but redeem the time. And he said not simply, 'buy,' but 'redeem,' making it your own after another manner."[129]

Hesychius of Alexandria, the fifth-century AD lexicographer, who reportedly based his work on earlier lexicons, states: αὐτοδικεῖ = αὐθεντεῖ ὅταν αὐτος λέγῃ[130] "he takes independent jurisdiction = he assumes authority when he speaks for himself."

Council of Chalcedon[131] 2,1,3.48.12, AD 451, states, "While this reckless deed was being done, *they assumed authority* [ηὐθέντησαν] and broke into my room and seized me."[132] Council of Chalcedon 2,1,3.131.26, states, "During these acts, hunting down the notably pious as dangerous criminals, *he seized authority* [ηὐθέντησεν] and broke into the prisons in order to put in his power the facility to release those subject to trial, that is to say, to offend the guiltless."[133]

Lampe's *PGL* 262 cites many fifth-century AD passages where αὐθεντέω meant "assume authority; act on one's own authority," including Ammonius Alexandrius, *Fragmenta in Acta apostolorum* 10:18 (PG 85:1537B): "It is not necessary for one *to assume authority*[134] [αὐθεντεῖν] to oneself and to introduce innovations into the faith." Eusebius of Alexandria, *Sermones* V (PG 86:348D), "So the deacon ought to practice based on discernment of the elder['s intention] ... not *to assume authority* [αὐθεντεῖν] over the

---

but explained, "He has simply taken it [authority] upon himself." Knight, "ΑΥΘΕΝΤΕΩ," 148, quotes Werner's translation but omits his key explanation.

129. *NPNF¹* 13:309, but *NPNF* translates αὐθεντεῖν with the equivalent "to have your own way."

130. Latte, *Hesychii,* 2:A8049.

131. E. Schwartz, ed., *Concilium universale Chalcedonese anno 451* (vol. 3; Berlin: deGruyter, 1935; repr., 1965).

132. The translation of ηὐθέντησαν is by the present author. The rest of the passage is cited from Baldwin ("αὐθεντέω in Ancient Greek," *WCFA* 292–93), who translates ηὐθέντησαν as "they *exercised their own initiative.*"

133. The translation of ηὐθέντησεν is by the present author. The rest of the passage is cited from Baldwin ("αὐθεντέω in Ancient Greek," *WCFA* 293), who translates ηὐθέντησεν as "he *assumed his own jurisdiction.*"

134. Baldwin ("αὐθεντέω in Ancient Greek," *WCFA* 293) translates it, "*to act independently.*"

people, but to do everything by the command of the elder. When the elder
is present, neither does he have authority to banish or to do other things."
Victor Antiochenus, *Catena in Marcum* 2:25 – 26,[135] says: "For if a prophet
assumes his own authority against the law ... should you be vexed and judge
the law?"[136]

Αὐθεντέω occurs again with the sense of assumed authority in "an
arbitration in a family dispute concerning an inheritance" in P. Lond.
1708, line 38, written in AD 567 or 568. Bell, in the following summary
of the paragraph containing αὐθεντέω, translates the words αυθεντῆσαι
ἐκμισθώσαντα, "took to his own uses":

> Apollos died after Heraïs leaving to the children all his own and his
> wife's property, but Psates, being the eldest brother, deprived and defrauded
> us of the inheritance, and took to his own uses [αὐθεντῆσαι] all the rent
> ... of the houses; this although he had promised me when I married his
> sister that immediately after the solemnization of the marriage he would
> hand over all her share of household utensils inherited from her parents
> and also my share, in right of my wife, of the house-property to live in ...
> but up to the present he has given us nothing of all this, though we have
> grown weary first of demand and then of reproaches.[137]

The award given by the arbitrator confirms that Psates unfairly com-
mandeered the inheritance: "Psates is to hand over whatever he has
received from his parents for the general division. The houses too are to be
divided equally and also whatever may be left from the rent after the payment of the cost of building.... Psates is ... not to make further claims on
them."[138] Clearly, αὐθεντέω in this case does not mean a neutral or warranted authority, but rather an unauthorized seizing of assets. This is further
confirmed by the two verbs with which it stands in parallel in this sentence, "deprived us [of the inheritance]" and "defrauded us." Consequently,
note 38 (5:119), which gives two alternative reconstructions of the word
following αὐθεντέω, was not intended to translate αὐθεντέω as a posi-

---

135. John A. Cramer, ed., *Catenae in Evangelia S. Matthaei et S. Marci ad fidem Codd. MSS.* (Catenae Graecorum Patrum in Novum Testamentum 1; Oxford: Oxford Univ. Press, 1840; repr.,
Hildesheim: Olms, 1967), 292.29.
136. Translation by Baldwin, "αὐθεντέω in Ancient Greek," WCFA 297.
137. F. G. Kenyon and H. I. Bell, *Greek Papyri in the British Museum: Catalogue, with Texts* (5 vols.;
London: Trustees of the British Museum, 1893 – 1917), 5:114 – 15.
138. Kenyon and Bell, *Greek Papyri*, 5:117.

tive activity at all,[139] but rather to show that this phrase taken together explains how Psates took control of income from the houses: "αυθεντησαι εκμισθωσαντα: 'seized authority and leased.'"

Werner wrote regarding this passage to Knight, "It seems to me that this one works against you. The words reported are those of the plaintiffs, and from their point of view the defendant was acting wrongly when he assumed authority over their parents' buildings, i.e., he 'usurped' that authority."[140] This case, like many others, demonstrates that Baldwin is incorrect to allege, "Not a single example can be evidenced from anywhere that αὐθεντέω is ever used of anything other than the exercise of authority."[141] Psates never had authority to do what he did. He did not abuse authority. He wrongly seized authority.

The meaning "to assume authority" continues in the sixth-century AD Evagrius Scholasticus, *Historia ecclesiastica* 2.18 (PG 86:2564C), which states, "For this fellow took upon himself the communion ... having been legally deposed by his own bishop—the one we among the saints think of as our father, even the archbishop Flavian—*assuming his own jurisdiction* [= *taking authority upon himself*] without regulation in order to receive communion before sitting in council in Ephesus with the God-loving bishops."[142] Leontius Hierosolymitanus, *Contra Nestorianos* 4.49 (PG 86:1720D), writes, "*We will not assume authority* (αὐθεντήσομεν) to call the Mother of Jesus, 'Theotokos,' since the Holy Scriptures nowhere address her thus, nor any of the Fathers."[143]

Also in the sixth century AD (*PGL* xxxii) Johannes Malalas' *Chronographia*[144] repeatedly used αὐθεντέω to identify the assumption or seizing of authority:

- "The army ... proclaimed Albinus emperor, *assuming authority over the senate*" (*Chron.* 291.12).

---

139. *Pace* Knight, "ΑΥΘΕΝΤΕΩ," 147, 155, "a negative nuance which is not found in any of the documents."
140. *Pace* Knight, "ΑΥΘΕΝΤΕΩ," 155, "the now evidently erroneous usage of the K.J.V. 'to usurp authority'"; repeated by Baldwin, "Difficult Word," WCFA 67–68. Cf. above, pp. 385–86.
141. Baldwin, "Important Word,"WCA 201 n. 31.
142. Translation by Baldwin, "αὐθεντέω in Ancient Greek," WCFA 295. PGL 262 cites this to mean "assume authority; act on one's own authority."
143. Baldwin ("αὐθεντέω in Ancient Greek," WCFA 296) translates αὐθεντήσομεν as "*act on our own authority.*" PGL 262 cites it to mean "presume on one's own authority."
144. Translations of αὐθεντέω are in each case by this author. The rest of each translation is from Jeffreys, *John Malalas*, whose translations of αὐθεντέω are respectively: "overruling" (155), "flouting the authority of" (185), "seized" (196), "on his own authority" (235–6), and "on his own initiative" (270). Each implies the assuming of authority.

- "The army made a man named Eugenios emperor, *assuming authority over* the senate. He reigned twenty-two days and was immediately assassinated" (*Chron.* 341.15).

- "At that time the Alexandrians, given free rein by their bishop, *seized authority* and burnt on a pyre of brushwood Hypatia the famous philosopher, who had a great reputation and who was an old woman" (*Chron.* 359.13).

- "Theodotos, *assuming authority*, put him [Theodosios, who held the rank of illustris] to death without reporting this to the emperor. This met with the emperor's anger and he was dismissed from office, deprived of his rank and ordered into exile in the East" (*Chron.* 416.14).

- "Belisarios was angry with Sounikas because he had attacked the Persian army, *assuming authority on his own*" (*Chron.* 462.12).

The sixth- to seventh-century AD BGU 103.3 twice uses the related word αὐθεντίζω meaning "assume authority."[145] In this papyrus, a "lower church official [village headman, Abraam] lets the higher official decide whether he will assume authority over the case of the heirs, or refuse to assume authority by referring the case back to the judicial authority of the minor official."[146]

> Since the brothers of the blessed Enoch have come to us saying, "We want to go to law with his wife," please be so good, Your [pl.] Godhelp, if you will assume authority [αὐθεντίσεις] over the matter and receive them in the city, and they will come to terms with each other; but if not, please be so good as to have both sides come here and we shall have them come to terms in accordance with justice.... But do not defer, Your [pl.] Piety-to-the-Father, because of a deposit, to send them forth; but if, again, you assume authority [αὐθεντῖς] and receive them in the city, fine.[147]

---

145. *Berlin: Griechische Urkunden*, 1:122. Cf. Ulrich Wilcken, ed., *Grundzüge und Chrestomathie der Papyruskunde* [Leipzig: Teubner, 1912], 1: ii. p. 160), who translates αὐθεντίσεις τῷ πρᾶγμα, "die Sache selbst in die Hand nehmen" ("take in hand"); cf. LSJ 275; MM, 91. Knight properly renders these "assume authority" in "ΑΥΘΕΝΤΕΩ," 147. Nägeli (*Wortschatz des Apostels Paulus*, 49–50), without warrant, cites it as an example of the meaning κρατεῖν τινος ("to dominate someone").

146. July 21, 1993 letter from Werner to Payne, p. 3.

147. Werner provided the translations, "assume authority" in a letter to Payne dated July 21, 1993, p. 3. The rest of the translation is from Werner's March 18, 1980 letter to Knight, where he rendered the verbs, "accept jurisdiction."

The ninth-century AD Photius, *Library* 80.62b.31[148] states that when the emperor died, "a certain Joannes *assumed authority* [αὐθεντήσας] and ruled tyrannically."[149] The tenth-century AD Emperor Constantine VII Porphyrogenitus, *About Strategy* 159.33[150] quotes, "the army made him emperor, *assuming authority over* [αὐθεντήσας] the senate,"[151] and his *About Virtues and Vices* 1.160.18[152] quotes, "He [Emperor Decius] published his godless decree so that the ones finding those called Christians *assumed authority* [αὐθετοῦντας] and murdered them and seized all their goods with impunity."[153]

In each of these uses of αὐθεντέυ, the authority that is assumed is an authority that had not been properly granted, so it usually carries a negative connotation. Werner concludes, "The common element ... is the taking of authority upon oneself, deciding to act authoritatively, and doing so, whether or not one has the legitimate authority (*exousia*) to do so."[154] Werner goes so far as to say that "initiative, lack of delegation from above, is a common component in all the examples, contradicted only by Hesychius' *exousiazein*."[155] He notes that "3 of the 4 Patristic definitions involve undelegated authority."[156] Similarly, the noun αὐθεντία has the meaning "arbitrarily, on one's own responsibility, unauthorized" in various passages cited by *PGL* 263, including Basil (d. AD 379).

This understanding of αὐθεντέω reflects Paul's central concern in 1 Timothy: to counteract false teachings. On this interpretation, Paul is not permitting a woman to assume authority that she had not been properly delegated. "Assume authority" fits naturally with the following reference to Eve's deception and fall. Eve took it on herself to eat the forbidden fruit and to offer it to Adam. John Chrysostom (d. AD 407) explains Paul's

---

148. R. Henry, ed., *Photius: Bibliothèque* (8 vols.; Paris: Les Belles Lettres, 1959–1977).

149. The translation of αὐθεντήσας is by the present author. The rest of the passage is cited from Baldwin ("αὐθεντέω in Ancient Greek," *WCFA* 301), who translates αὐθεντήσας "took charge."

150. C. de Boor, *Exerpta historica iussu imp. Constantini Porphyrogeniti confecta, vol. 3: excerpta de insidiis* (Berlin: Weidmann, 1905).

151. The translation is by the present author.

152. T. Büttner-Wobst and A. G. Roos, *Exerpta historica iussu imp. Constantini Porphyrogeniti confecta, vol. 2: excerpta de virtutibus et vitiis* (vol. 2, pt. 1; Berlin: Weidmann, 1906).

153. The translation of αὐθετοῦντας is by the present author. The rest of the passage is cited from Baldwin ("αὐθεντέω in Ancient Greek," *WCFA* 303), who in n. 27 suggests "took justice into their own hands" to translate αὐθετοῦντας.

154. July 21, 1993 letter from Werner to Payne, page 4, referring to BGU 1208, BGU 103, and fragment 21 of Codex Paris gr 2419.

155. April 8, 1980 letter from John R. Werner to George W. Knight III, p. 4.

156. Ibid.

statement, "'I am not permitting a woman to teach.' Why? She taught [Ἐδίδαξε] Adam once wickedly. 'Nor to assume authority over a man.' Just why? She assumed authority [ηὐθέντησεν] once wickedly."[157] Here αὐθεντέω cannot mean "exercised authority"[158] since she had no authority to eat the fruit; God had forbidden it. The narrative makes it clear that she assumed authority but says nothing about her dominating Adam. "Assumption of authority" perfectly fits Paul's contrasting statements, "but [ἀλλ'] to be in quietness [ἐν ἡσυχίᾳ]" in 2:12b and its structural parallel "in full submission" (ἐν πάσῃ ὑποταγῇ) in 2:11, which together bracket 2:12a. Taking authority is aggressive. Being "in quietness" is the opposite of being aggressive. Accordingly, the Peshitta's Syriac translation of αὐθεντέω in 1 Tim 2:12 is the Aphel infinitive of mrh, meaning "to venture, dare, be rash, hasty, headstrong, presumptuous,"[159] or "to be assuming."[160]

The component parts of αὐθεντέω, "self-achieving," make the meaning "to assume authority" easy to understand. The earlier one gets to the coining of words, the more important etymology becomes for identifying that word's meaning. Based on the number of words that occur first in Paul's letters, he was fond of coining expressions. In these cases one can almost always identify the meaning from the word's component parts. This is obviously the case in such Pauline words as "teachers of what is excellent" (καλοδιδάσκαλος) in Titus 2:3;[161] "regions beyond" (ὑπερέκεινα) in 2 Cor 10:16; "super abundantly/most earnestly" (ὑπερεκπερισσοῦ) in Eph 3:20 and 1 Thess 3:10 and 5:13; "super intercedes" (ὑπερεντυγχάνω) in Rom 8:26; and "over abounded" (ὑπερπερισσεύω) in Rom 5:20 and 2 Cor 7:4.

The assuming of authority for oneself is directly confronted by 1 Tim 2:14 and its reference to the fall. The original sin of the woman in the garden was not her teaching with authority but her taking authority unto herself to take the fruit in spite of God's prohibition. Grasping for authority was also part of the temptation "to be like God" (Gen 3:5). It is this grasping of authority for oneself that Paul prohibits. It led to the fall in the garden and it threatened the fall of the church in Ephesus. Bruce Winter

---

157. Chrysostom, In Genesim (Sermons) ser. 1–9, PG 54:595.1.
158. Pace Baldwin, "Important Word," WCA 46.
159. J. Payne Margoliouth, A Compendious Syriac Dictionary (Oxford: Clarendon, 1903), 300.
160. James Murdock, The New Testament: A Literal Translation from the Syriac Peshitto Version (New York: Robert Carter & Brothers, 1851), 381.
161. Cf. above, pp. 329–30.

highlights just such a seizing of authority on the part of "new women" who had "a desire to dominate in the Forum and the courts" to conclude "that here [in 1 Tim 2:12] the term carries not only the connotation of authority but also an inappropriate misuse of it."[162] Part of women's justification for assuming for themselves authority to teach men may have been their overly realized eschatology.[163]

If Paul intends this as a separate prohibition from "to teach," then, because of the false teaching he "is not permitting" a woman "to teach" or "to assume authority over a man." The goal of this double prohibition would be to stop women, the major source of the false teaching, both from teaching and from assuming authority over a man. This view has three key weaknesses. First, it does not fit the normal pattern of Paul's use of οὐδέ to convey a single idea. Second, it results in an overly broad and difficult-to-apply prohibition of women teaching that conflicts with Paul's principles and practice. Arbitrarily importing the qualifier "man" from the second prohibition does not resolve this conflict.[164] Third, a separate prohibition of women assuming authority over a man does not relate to any known problem this letter addresses and appears unmotivated.

In light of Paul's usual use of the conjunction οὐδέ, it seems more likely that Paul is conveying a single idea that merges "to teach" and "to assume authority over a man." What Paul says is this: "I am not permitting a woman to teach and assume authority over a man," namely, to take for herself authority to teach a man without authorization from the church. Practically, this excluded women in Ephesus from assuming to themselves authority to teach men in the church. It would not, however, prohibit women with recognized authority from teaching men (e.g., Priscilla).

This restriction of women assuming authority for themselves to teach men is a change from Paul's earlier descriptions of teaching in the church as open to all believers. Formerly, Paul had appealed to all members of the body of Christ to teach one another.[165] The crisis of the false teachers' influence over women exposed a danger in the open approach to worship Paul had advocated earlier. It is because of this crisis that Paul describes the

---

162. Winter, *Roman Wives*, 119.
163. As argued by Marshall, *Pastoral Epistles*, 458–59; cf. 2 Tim 2:18.
164. Cf. above, pp. 353–56.
165. Cf. above, pp. 331–33, e.g., 1 Cor 14:26; Col 3:16. Paul viewed this as fully compatible with individuals' gifts such as wisdom (1 Cor 12:8) and God appointing teachers (12:28).

taking of authority with a verb that had negative associations in his day. The one imperative mode verb in this passage is "let women learn" in full submission. Paul's goal is that as they learn in submission to the church's teaching, they will repudiate the false teaching. Paul's use of the present indicative "I am not permitting"[166] gives evidence that he hopes that the danger of the false teaching will subside enough that once again the Ephesian believers can practice a more open form of worship.

In contrast to taking authority to teach men, Paul desires that women be tranquil. The meaning of ἡσυχία in the context of this passage's consistent desire for peace without self-assertiveness (e.g., 2:2, 8, 11, 12, 15) is not silence but quietness-peace.[167] This fits the pattern of word usage in 1 Thess 4:11; 2 Thess 3:12; and 1 Tim 2:2. "I am not permitting" is an inappropriate main verb for introducing "to be quiet" or "to be silent." Either the main verb in 1 Tim 2:8, "I desire" (βούλομαι), or in 1 Tim 2:1, "I urge" (παρακαλῶ) would be a proper fit.[168] This lack of smooth connection with the main verb of 2:12, known as zeugma, implies that "but to be in quietness" was an afterthought. In spite of its grammatical incongruity, it directly addresses the central problem of chapter 2—the need to bring peace, not more trouble, in the wake of the contentions raised by the false teachers. Thus, it should probably not be regarded as a parenthesis.[169]

WHY PROHIBIT WOMEN FROM ASSUMING AUTHORITY OVER MEN?

Paul's restriction focuses on the most critical problem for the advance of false teaching in Ephesus, namely any woman under the sway of false teaching assuming for herself authority to teach a man. In the worship context implied by prayer (1 Tim 2:8), learning (2:11), and teaching (2:12), this most obviously applies to teaching in public assemblies of the church, where men would be present. Not only was this the place where the most people would be influenced, it is also the public face of the church. This restriction was necessary in order to keep the false teaching from being associated with church teaching. Paul does not establish a rule that would be impossible for Timothy to monitor, namely, teaching by women when no men were present.

---

166. Cf. above, pp. 320–25.
167. Cf. above, pp. 314–15.
168. Cf. Perriman, "What Eve Did," 129–30, and above, p. 262.
169. *Pace* Perriman, "What Eve Did," 129–31; idem, *Speaking of Women*, 157–61.

In addition to Paul's concern about the spread of false teaching, a theme of 1 Timothy is the image of the church before the watching world. Chapter 2 is concerned throughout with propriety since impropriety detracts from the appeal of the gospel. Propriety is also the central theme of the requirements for church leaders in chapter 3. In 5:14, Paul counsels young widows "to give the enemy no opportunity for slander." For women to assume to themselves authority to teach, if it had never affected men, would not have caused particular social notoriety in Paul's day. But in Paul's day, for women to teach with self-assumed authority over men could bring shame to the church, especially if they teach the nonsense associated with false teaching.

CONCLUSION: THE MEANING OF 1 TIMOTHY 2:12

In order to limit the teaching of false doctrine that threatens the life of the church in Ephesus, in 1 Tim 2:12 Paul restricts the group most affected, "I am not permitting a woman to assume authority to teach a man." With only one exception, 1 Cor 14:34, which is widely regarded as an interpolation,[170] the verb "to permit" (ἐπιτρέπω) never refers to a universal or permanent situation in any of its uses in the LXX or NT. Especially its use in the first person singular present indicative makes it unlikely that Paul intended 1 Tim 2:12 as a universal or permanent prohibition. It is therefore best translated "I am not permitting." Since Paul typically uses οὐδέ to join together elements that reinforce or make more specific a single coherent idea, he probably intends 1 Tim 2:12 to convey a single prohibition: "to teach and [in combination with this] αὐθεντεῖν a man."

This study has analyzed the three major interpretations of αὐθεντέω in 1 Tim 2:12: "exercise authority," "dominate," and "assume authority." BGU 1208, a papyrus dated at 27/26 BC, uses αὐθεντέω to mean "assume authority." Its first confirmed use to mean "dominate," is from 127–148 AD, Ptolemy, *Tetrabiblos* 3.13.10, and its first confirmed use to mean "exercise authority" is ca. AD 370 Saint Basil, *The Letters* 69, line 45. "To dominate" fits the immediate context better than "to exercise authority," but it is not obvious what would or would not be dominating teaching, nothing in the narrative of Gen 3:6 implies that Eve dominated Adam, and it is unrelated to women's deception in either Eden or Ephesus. The third alternative, "to

---

170. Cf. above, pp. 225–67.

assume authority to teach a man" has the best lexical support and also fits the context best.

To teach with self-assumed authority is the opposite of the tranquility of being "in quietness" (2:11 – 12). It is what Eve did in leading Adam astray (1 Tim 2:14). It is something that would be particularly offensive in that culture. It is also the best fit in relation to the central problem of false teaching in Ephesus. The false teachers were teaching their own unauthorized doctrines with self-assumed, not delegated, authority. "Self-assumed authority" is based on readily recognized root meanings of the word αὐθεντέω, so Paul's readers could understand it. Furthermore, it fits Paul's theology best, and unlike "to teach and exercise authority over a man," it does not contradict Paul's principles and practice expressed elsewhere. Therefore, lexically, contextually, and theologically by far the most natural reading of 1 Tim 2:12's prohibition is: "I am not permitting a woman to teach and [in combination with this] to assume authority over a man."

Since false teaching is the occasion of this letter (1 Tim 1:3 – 11), and since false teaching influenced the women in Ephesus particularly, Paul first commands that women learn in quietness and full submission in order to turn deceived women away from the false teaching and to encourage them to embrace the true gospel. Combined with this, he institutes a present prohibition against any woman seizing authority for herself to teach a man. Paul's goal is to exclude any unauthorized woman from teaching men in the church. This prohibition does not, however, restrict teaching by authorized women, such as Priscilla (2 Tim 4:19), since just such teaching might be critical in influencing deceived women to reject error and embrace the truth.

Paul's prohibition of women with self-assumed authority teaching men does not imply that he approves men teaching with self-assumed authority, particularly if they also promote false teaching. Indeed, he had already commanded certain men not to teach false doctrine (1 Tim 1:3, 20). Paul's letters address current problems and their primary promulgators.[171] He gives appropriate corrections to the groups who need them most. Because men were disputing and expressing anger, Paul commands men to "lift up holy hands in prayer, without anger or disputing." This does not imply that women are permitted to dispute and express anger. It is in light of

---

171. Cf. above, p. 291.

the particular influence the false teaching had on women in Ephesus that Paul temporarily prohibits them from assuming authority to teach men. Although one might properly apply this prohibition in analogous situations of deception and improper assumption of teaching authority by women, it is not worded as a universal rule and should not be treated as though it is one. Once the threat of false teaching has waned, Paul's preferred more open style of mutual instruction can again prevail.

1 Timothy 2:13 – 14: The Need for Respect, the Danger of Deception

Paul immediately explains his restriction on women teaching in 2:12 by citing events from the creation narrative in Gen 2 – 3.[1] He begins his explanation, "For [γάρ] Adam was formed first, then Eve." An examination of Paul's usage shows γάρ to be an extremely common conjunction, even more common than "but" (ἀλλά). Γάρ is used commonly in a variety of senses. Often γάρ is better left untranslated in English. In Rom 8:18 – 24, Paul begins every sentence with γάρ, but only two are given any English equivalent ("for") in the NIV. Verlyn Verbrugge's analysis of Paul's 139 uses of γάρ in Romans concludes "that only 35 percent could be considered directly causal; another 40 percent are indirectly causal (used to move Paul's argument along or occurring in a γάρ-cluster)."[2]

Γάρ often has an illative use (giving a reason), and it is frequently explanatory ("for, you see," "for example," "for instance," "now"). A. T. Robertson writes, "It is best in fact, to note the explanatory use first. Thayer wrongly calls the illative use the primary one."[3] Grammarians agree that the NT use of γάρ conforms to classical use, and the explanatory use of

---

1. Baldwin ("Important Word," WCA 200 n. 31) incorrectly identifies these historical statements as "theological principles." Historical statements can convey theological principles, but in themselves they are not theological principles. Whether they convey theological principles must be argued, not merely asserted, as Baldwin does.
2. Verlyn D. Verbrugge, "Driving Your γάρ with Caution," paper presented at the Midwest Regional SBL Conference, Grand Rapids, 2001.
3. Robertson, *Grammar*, 1190.

γάρ is common both in Homer and the NT.[4] Explanations often imply a reason or show the reasonableness of something, and reasons are often expressed through explanations. Either the explanatory or the illative use of γάρ, or a mixture of the two, can make good sense in the context of 1 Tim 2:13.

Moo objects to the suggestion that γάρ in 2:13 may be explanatory on the basis that "the usage is rare, BAG cites only twelve examples of the explanatory force of γάρ in the NT, in agreement with Dana and Mantey; Thayer likewise gives a small number of such examples and Zerwick cites only fourteen instances in Paul where the conjunction does *not* have its usual causal force."[5] Moo's statement implies that Dana and Mantey's examples agree with BAG's and that Thayer and Zerwick do not add significantly to this number. In fact, these scholars cite the following references, only three of which (each in bold-italic) occur in more than one list:

- BAG: explanatory "for, you see": 12 examples: Matt 12:40, 50; 23:3; 24:38; Mark 7:3; Luke 9:14; John 3:16; 4:8, 9; Rom 7:2; Heb 3:4; 2 Pet 2:8.
- Dana and Mantey: "for instance, now": 13 examples (only 3 overlap): Matt 9:5; Luke **14:27–28**; John 4:8, 44; Acts 13:36; 18:3; 19:37; 20:16; 1 Cor **10:1**; 11:6, 7 (2x), 19; 2 Cor **1:12**.
- Thayer: "explain, make clear, illustrate" a preceding thought: 12 examples (none overlap): Matt 1:18; 4:18; 19:12; Mark 1:16; 2:15; 5:42; 16:4; Luke 11:30; 18:32; Rom 7:1; 8:18; 1 Cor 16:5.
- Zerwick §473: "same sense as δέ ... especially in Paul ... [&] Luke": 24 examples (only 3 overlap): Luke 1:15; 12:58; **14:28**; Acts 2:34; 4:34a; 8:39; 13:27; 15:28; 16:37; 23:11; Rom 1:18; 2:25; 4:3, 9; 5:7; 12:3; 14:5; 1 Cor **10:1**; 2 Cor **1:12**; 10:12; 11:5; Gal 1:11; 5:13; 1 Tim 2:5.

Thus, the works selected by Moo to show the infrequency of the explanatory use of γάρ list fifty-eight separate instances, and only three verses occur in more than one list! The presence of slight overlapping shows that these lists were not written simply as supplements to the others and suggests that there are many more occurrences of explanatory

4. Ibid.
5. Moo, "Rejoinder," 202.

γάρ beyond these. BDAG γάρ 2 (189 – 90) lists 39 NT instances of γάρ as a "marker of clarification, *for, you see*," many of which are not in any of these lists. Moo misleadingly concludes, "Payne is attempting to establish a meaning for γάρ which is relatively rare."[6] As the evidence cited above shows, the explanatory use of γάρ is not rare, nor was the current author "attempting to establish such a meaning," but merely showing that such a meaning, which has long been established, makes good sense of this passage.

Moo does make a valuable point, however, about γάρ usually implying a reason when used after a command in the Pastoral Epistles. It is appropriate to look for a reason when a command is followed by a γάρ clause.[7]

What precisely, however, is the command for which Paul gives a reason or explanation? Paul gives one grammatical imperative in verse 11: "Let women learn." It is modified by "in quietness and all submission." Then Paul adds, "However, I am not permitting a woman to teach and assume authority over a man, but rather to be in quietness." Is what Paul introduces with γάρ the reason for letting them learn, for their being quiet, for their being submissive, for their not teaching, for their not seizing authority over a man, or for a combination of these?

Furthermore, how much of what follows the γάρ is the reason or explanation? The sequence in which Adam then Eve were formed by God? That Adam was not deceived? That Eve was thoroughly deceived? And/or that Eve became a transgressor? These are the sorts of questions that grammar alone cannot answer definitively. Zerwick notes "that sometimes the real reason is expressed in the second place only, preceded by something not alleged as a reason but merely conceded parenthetically as well known."[8] Only by comparing the various parts of Paul's commands with the content of what he says regarding Adam and Eve can one identify possible options and try to determine what reason or explanation fits best.

If Paul intended the γάρ as explanatory, he cites the example of Eve to explain his prohibition. Significantly, he does not deduce from this

---

6. Ibid., 203. Moo states, "Thayer and BAG introduce the causal meaning first." In fact, Thayer lists cause second, not first. Ironically, on pp. 198 – 99 Moo argues against identifying the first meaning of a word in a lexicon as its most common usage.
7. Yet Moo overstates his case. Of the twenty-one instances he adduces in "Rejoinder," 203, three are clearly not causal: 1 Tim 3:13; 2 Tim 3:6; Titus 3:3; and the NIV does not translate 1 Tim 5:15 as causal either..
8. Maximilian Zerwick, *Biblical Greek Illustrated by Examples* (Rome: Iura, 1963), 159 §474.

example that women should be subordinate to men[9] or that women in general are more prone to deception than men. Neither does he deduce from it any other hierarchical or anthropological principle. Yet just such a deduction is needed to establish that the γάρ clause expresses a reason for the prohibition(s).

Those who interpret the γάρ in 1 Tim 2:13 as illative (giving a reason) must not forget Robertson's caution that even in purely illative uses of γάρ the "force of the ground or reason naturally varies greatly.... The precise relation between clauses or sentences is not set forth by γάρ. That must be gathered from the context if possible."[10] The vast majority of Paul's reasons have nothing to do with anthropological norms. Any identification of a reason in 2:13–14 should be based on the statements of this text. If the statements of the text provide a good explanation for Paul's prior commands, there is no need to read into them an anthropological norm.

If Paul's restriction in 2:12 is rooted in creation and verses 13–14 imply a principle of creation, what is that principle? Paul gives us no explanation here of what significance he draws from Adam being formed first. In the one other passage where Paul refers to Adam being created first (1 Cor 11:8–12), he affirms in verse 11 the equal standing of woman and man, "woman is not separate from man, nor is man separate from woman" and in verse 12 he affirms that woman is also the source of man, apparently to keep readers from interpreting his affirmation that woman came from man as a basis for subordinating women to men.[11] Yet many interpreters assume that Paul's statement of the creation of man prior to woman in 1 Tim 2:13 implies a principle of subordination of woman to man[12] even though Paul argued against this in the parallel passage.

Grudem interprets 1 Tim 2:13 as teaching that "women should not teach or have authority over men in the congregation of God's people.... Because God gave Adam a leadership role when He created him first and Eve second ... Paul ... prohibits *all women* from teaching and governing the

---

9.   1 Tim 2:11 probably refers to submission to church teaching, not submission to man, cf. above, pp. 315–17.
10.   Robertson, *Grammar*, 1191.
11.   Cf. above, pp. 195–98.
12.   E.g., Moo, "Meaning and Significance," 70, "In vv 13–14, then, Paul substantiates his teaching in vv 11–12 by arguing that the created order establishes a relationship of subordination of woman to man, which order, if bypassed, leads to disaster, and by suggesting that there are some activities for which women are by nature not suited." Witherington (*Earliest Churches*, 122) argues against this view and against taking γάρ as illative.

assembled congregation."[13] Genesis, however, is not restricted to religious or domestic matters, so if it assigns leadership to men, then logically this should apply in society, business, and government as well as church and home. Grudem affirms to the contrary that women may exercise authority over men in politics and business but not in the church or home.[14] This is a remarkably narrow interpretation of what Grudem claims to be a creation order of male leadership and authority,[15] especially since there is no assembled congregation in the creation narratives that could suggest this restriction. To rephrase John Ball's repudiation of such logic in 1381, "When Adam delved and Eve span, who was then the preacherman?"[16]

The best basis for understanding 1 Tim 2:13 is Paul's argument that woman comes from man in 1 Cor 11:8 and 12. Paul argues that woman should respect man since he is the source from which God made woman (1 Cor 11:3 – 12).[17] Similarly, in 1 Tim 2:13 man being "formed" first, then woman, implies woman being "formed" out of man and so points to the respect woman owes man as her source.[18] Philo's QG 1.27 also argues that since woman was formed from the side of man, woman should "honor man."

Does this give a valid reason for any of the immediately prior statements? Yes! Immediately prior to this "for" clause Paul wrote that woman is to be "in quietness," repeating these words from verse 11. A woman's quiet teachable spirit in submitting (v. 11b) to the teaching she receives shows proper respect to her Christian teachers such as Timothy. Furthermore, woman's obligation to respect man is an excellent reason for Paul to state, "I am not permitting a woman to teach and assume authority[19] over a man." The disrespect of a woman seizing authority over a man was compounded by the content of the false teaching they were foisting on men, such as: "They forbid people to marry and order them to abstain from certain foods that God created to be received with thanksgiving" (1 Tim 4:3).

---

13. Grudem, EF 72 – 73.
14. Grudem stated this in a public lecture at Wheaton College's Blanchard Hall, April 13, 2005. He went so far as to say he would be "fine" with having a woman as president of the USA.
15. Grudem, EF 29 – 42 (on "male leadership," 35 – 36; on "authority," 40).
16. Suggested by Brendan Payne in Edmonds, WA, June 10, 2009. Ball, a Lollard and follower of Wycliffe, ended this famous retort affirming social equality with the word "gentleman."
17. Cf. above, pp. 113 – 39, 180 – 81, 194 – 98, 211 – 12.
18. Cf. A. T. Hanson, *The Pastoral Letters* (Cambridge: Cambridge Univ. Press, 1966), 37, "The author probably means that Adam was Eve's source, as she was created from his body."
19. Cf. above, pp. 361 – 97.

Therefore, understanding verse 13 as a call for woman to respect man, the source from whom woman was formed, provides appropriate support for every part of 1 Tim 2:11–12. Paul's argument in 1 Cor 11:12, "just as woman came from man, so also every man is born through woman," implies that this obligation to respect the other sex is mutual. Similarly, 1 Tim 2:15 points to a reason for man to respect woman: the Savior came through woman. Correspondingly, 1 Pet 2:17 also calls believers to "show proper respect to everyone."

All of the various things Paul has just commanded woman—learn in quietness and full submission, do not teach and assume authority over a man, but be quiet—are predicated on respect for man.[20] Woman should respect man since man was created before woman and since woman was formed out of man. The sequence of God forming Adam first, then Eve, highlights that Adam is the source of Eve and through her of all women. Out of respect for man as her source, a woman should not assume authority over man (or possibly, dominate a man).

The Judaizers may well have used the saying, "Adam was formed [ἐπλάσθη] first" (2:13) to indicate male superiority. Their basis for this would be that the OT specifically states that God formed (LXX: πλάσσω) Adam (Gen 2:7, 8, 15; Job 38:14; cf. also 1 Clem. 33:4; Sib. Or. 3:24; Philo, Creation 137), but it never uses this verb of God "forming" Eve or any other woman.[21] The LXX, however, identifies many men as "formed" (πλάσσω) by God: Job (Job 10:8, 9), David (LXX Ps 138:5, 16), Jacob/Israel (Isa 43:1, 7; 44:2, 21, 24), Isaiah (Isa 49:5), the Servant (Isa 53:11), the writer of Ps 119:73, Habakkuk (Hab 1:12), and even an idol maker (Wis 15:11). Paul's addition of "then Eve" is the first-documented occurrence that Eve as well as Adam was "formed" by God. By including Eve as also "formed" by God, Paul affirmed the essential equality of men and women.

Thus, if Paul here alludes to an argument for the superiority of male over female since Adam was formed by God, his addition of "then Eve" undermines the argument by affirming that woman, too, was formed by

---

20. Cf. Marshall, Pastoral Epistles, 467: "v. 13 merely calls for … respect for their first-created male counterparts."
21. Gen 2:22 says, instead, God "built [οἰκοδομέω] the rib, which he took from Adam, into woman."

God.[22] Verses 14–15 also counterbalance the role of woman in the fall with her role in giving birth to the Savior. Similarly, the other passage citing the sequence of the creation of man, then woman, 1 Cor 11:8–9, counterbalances this in 11:11–12.[23]

R. C. and C. C. Kroeger have elucidated the Gnostic and proto-Gnostic teachings that Eve preceded Adam, gave him life, and was not deceived but wisely ate the fruit that imparted knowledge.[24] In light of Paul's reference to "falsely called *gnosis*" in 1 Tim 6:20 and other parallels between Gnostic teaching and the false teaching described in 1 and 2 Timothy, especially the references to "myths and endless genealogies" (1:4), it is possible that Paul intended 1 Tim 2:13–14 to refute false teaching about the relationship of Adam and Eve. If the false teachers had taught any of these myths exalting Eve, it would explain part of the special appeal their message had to women. It would further explain Paul's specification that Adam was formed first, especially if it contributed to women's unauthorized or domineering teaching.[25]

FIRST TIMOTHY 2:14

"And" (καί) links verse 14 to verse 13 and establishes verse 14 as a continuation of the γάρ clause beginning in verse 13. Eve's deception in verse 14 fits perfectly as a reason for or explanation of Paul's restriction on women teaching in verse 12. Since the theme of the entire letter is false teaching and since the letter repeatedly identifies women as deceived by the false teaching,[26] it is natural to regard the deception of women as a reason for Paul to restrict teaching by women.[27] The link between false

---

22. Marshall (*Pastoral Epistles*, 461) does not note this and so concludes, "'then' established Eve's secondary status."

23. Cf. above, pp. 195–98. These equalizing affirmations contradict the statements in Marshall, *Pastoral Epistles*, 462, "the first is best," and Guthrie, *Pastoral Epistles*, 77, "the priority of man's creation places him in a position of superiority over woman, the assumption being that the original creation, with the Creator's own imprimatur upon it, must set a precedent for determining the true order of the sexes." For contrasting arguments that the later is superior, see *Gen. Rab.* 19.12d, Str-B 3:249, and W. Nauck, "Die Herkunft des Verfassers der Pastoralbriefe: Ein Beiträg zur Frage der Auslegung der Pastoralbriefe" (unpublished diss., Göttingen, 1950), 95–97.

24. Kroeger and Kroeger, *I Suffer Not*, 117–25; cf. Hans Jonas, *The Gnostic Religion: The Message of the Alien God and the Beginning of Christianity* (2nd ed.; Boston: Beacon, 1963), 93. Moo "Rejoinder," 204 n. 10, writes, "it may be that this tradition was partially responsible for the statement."

25. Cf. Harris, "Eve's Deception," 345.

26. Cf. above, pp. 299–304.

27. So, too, Marshall, *Pastoral Epistles*, 461.

teaching and the deception of women is made in 2 Tim 3:6–13, "deceiving and being deceived."[28] The reference to "falsely called knowledge" in 1 Tim 6:20 also implies deception.

The problems caused by women in the Ephesian church are reminiscent of Eve in Eden. The false teachers' lies, like the serpent's lies, came from Satan. Both were persuasive and turned women from the truth to transgression. Eves in Ephesus were causing havoc, even bringing spiritual death to themselves and others. Paul draws on the example of Eve's deception and fall to explain how disastrous the consequences can be when a woman is deceived and conveys her deception to a man. Paul's wording stresses Eve's deception in several ways:

1. He uses emphatic heightening to say that Eve was not merely deceived ($\dot{\eta}\pi\alpha\tau\dot{\eta}\vartheta\eta$) but was "thoroughly deceived" ($\dot{\epsilon}\xi\alpha\pi\alpha\tau\eta\vartheta\epsilon\hat{\iota}\sigma\alpha$).[29]
2. He contrasts Adam's not being deceived to Eve's being deceived.
3. The sentence builds up to the woman's deception.
4. End stress highlights the consequence of her deception: she became a transgressor.

The example of Eve's deception in verse 14 demonstrates with the greatest possible force how tragic the outcome can be when a woman is deceived and conveys her deception to a man. Her experience epitomizes why women should learn in quietness and full submission to recognized church teaching,[30] namely, to overcome their deception. It also epitomizes why they should not "teach and assume authority over a man." Otherwise women who had not been authorized might teach their deception to the church. This explanation fits whether the $\gamma\dot{\alpha}\rho$ is understood as giving a reason for the prohibition(s), as explanatory, or as a combination of both.

In spite of the pervasiveness throughout 1 Timothy of Paul's concern with false teachers, Moo formerly insisted, "The problem of the false teachers is foreign to the context [of 2:14]."[31] If so, why the emphasis on deception as a key reason for the prohibition? Why the restriction specifically

---

28. This is obscured by the NIV's translation "men" in 3:8 (2x) and 3:13 for $\dot{\alpha}\nu\vartheta\rho\omega\pi\sigma\iota$, which includes women.
29. Unless it is just a stylistic variation, a possibility noted in *EDNT* 1:117.
30. Cf. above, pp. 315–17.
31. Moo, "Rejoinder," 203–4.

regarding teaching? As Gordon Fee has so clearly demonstrated throughout his commentary on the Pastoral Epistles, the problem of false teachers underlies everything. To deny this entails not taking 1 Timothy seriously as a letter from Paul to Timothy with the purpose laid out in 1 Tim 1:3 – 7, to meet the issues raised by false teachers. Moo rightly now acknowledges, "In fact, it is likely that the false teaching does give rise to Paul's instruction in 2:9 – 15.... Eve stands ... as a type of Ephesian women who were *being deceived by* false doctrine."[32] Baldwin, too, acknowledges the parallel between 2:12's "prohibition and Eve's deception."[33]

HOW BROADLY SHOULD ONE INTERPRET "ADAM WAS NOT DECEIVED"?

"Adam was not deceived" uses the same verb as Gen 3:13 (3:14 LXX), "The serpent deceived me [the woman] and I ate." Is the serpent also the implied subject of "Adam was not deceived," or is this a general statement that Adam was in fact not deceived, whether by the serpent, the woman, himself, or anything else? Various passages are difficult to reconcile with a general statement that Adam was not deceived when he ate the forbidden fruit. Paul appears to identify with Adam: "sin deceived me and through the commandment put me to death" (Rom 7:11). If Paul does identify with Adam here, then he did believe that sin deceived Adam. Genesis 3:1 – 5 describes the conversation between the serpent and the woman in detail, but says nothing about Adam conversing with the serpent. Furthermore, God says to Adam in Gen 3:17, "you listened to your wife and ate from the tree about which I commanded you, 'You must not eat of it.'" God, therefore, identifies his wife's words, not the serpent's, as decisive in influencing Adam.

Paul elsewhere clearly regards Adam as culpable for the fall (Rom 5:12 – 19; 1 Cor 15:21 – 22), describing his "transgression," "trespass," and "sin." Therefore, Adam knew he was eating in disobedience. If someone or something had not deceived him, why would he disobey God? After the expulsion from the garden and facing his own mortality, Adam would almost certainly acknowledge that he had been deceived. Knight explains 1 Tim

---

32. Moo, "What Does It Mean," *RBMW* 189.
33. Baldwin, "Important Word," *WCA* 201 n. 31.

2:14, "he sinned willfully, not as a result of deception,"[34] but as Schreiner has argued, "An appeal to Adam sinning willfully and Eve sinning mistakenly (being deceived) would seem to argue against men teaching women, for at least the woman wanted to obey God, while Adam sinned deliberately."[35]

Various solutions have been proposed to reconcile the evidence that Adam was deceived and 1 Tim 3:14. John Calvin wrote, "By these words Paul does not mean that Adam was not entangled by the same deceitfulness of the devil, but that the cause or source of the transgression proceeded from Eve."[36] Fee writes, "To say that it was not Adam who was deceived simply means that Adam was not deceived by the 'snake.'"[37]

Verse 14's focus on deception may provide the most satisfying solution to what Paul meant by "Adam was not deceived." Both "deceived" verbs in verse 14 are passive. Who was the deceiver in the Garden of Eden? It was "the serpent," always with an article in the MT and LXX in the narrative of the fall and probably understood by Paul as Satan, as evidenced by Rom 16:20, "The God of peace will soon crush Satan under your feet," alluding to Gen 3:15. The passive implies the role of Satan just as a divine passive implies God's action. One could call it a "satanic passive."[38] These passives support the view that Satan was the tempter in the narrative of the temptation and fall. Paul probably would have made "Satan" the subject of verse 14 if the word "Satan" had occurred in the Genesis fall narrative. Paul probably chose the passive instead of the active voice with "the serpent" as subject since "the serpent" would not apply seamlessly to women in Ephesus.

Some women in Ephesus had already turned aside after Satan (1 Tim 5:15). It was Satan's deception that concerned Paul in Ephesus, and by using the passive he conveyed this without mentioning "the serpent." Similarly, he chose "the woman" (as in the Genesis narrative) rather than "Eve" in verse 14b in order to facilitate the application to women in Ephesus. "Adam was not deceived" is another way of saying, "the serpent did not deceive Adam." This passive need not mean anything more than this. This faithfully reflects Gen 3:1–5, where Satan did not target Adam for this deception but rather the woman. Like Eve, women in Ephesus were the

---

34. Knight, *Pastoral Epistles*, 215; cf. Moo, "Rejoinder," 204; Guthrie, *Pastoral Epistles*, 77.
35. Schreiner, "Dialogue," WCA 113–14; cf. Fung, "Ministry in the New Testament," 201–2.
36. Cf. Calvin, *Timothy, Titus, and Philemon*, 70.
37. Fee, *1 and 2 Timothy, Titus*, 37; cf. Schreiner, "Dialogue," WCA 115.
38. This term was suggested to the author by Robert L. Brawley of McCormick Theological Seminary.

target of false teachers, "who worm their way into homes and gain control over weak-willed women" (2 Tim 3:6–9). The only other case of ἀπατάω ("deceive") in Paul's letters, Eph 5:6, also warns against a deceiver, "Don't let anybody deceive you with empty words."[39]

To What Does Eve's Deception Refer?

The concluding statement of 1 Tim 2:14, that the woman being thoroughly deceived "became a transgressor," unmistakably refers to the fall. The perfect tense of the verb "became" highlights "a condition or state as the result of a past action."[40] Paul uses end stress to highlight the consequence of the woman's deception, selecting the same word for transgression (παράβασις) that he used of Adam's breaking God's command in Rom 5:14.[41] Paul understood transgression with its standard denotation: disobedience of a command or law. Romans 4:15 demands this meaning, "where there is no law there is no transgression (παράβασις)." In every Pauline usage, "transgression" refers to the breaking of a commandment of God. In this case both the woman and Adam transgressed God's command by eating the forbidden fruit. This must be the transgression Paul intended since this was the only prohibition God gave prior to the fall and since "I ate" in Gen 3:13 identifies the woman's transgression as disobedience of this command. Furthermore, since Paul identifies the deception as causing the transgression, the deception must refer to the serpent's deception described in Gen 3:1–7, 13. This deception led the woman to doubt God's warning and to desire both the knowledge of good and evil and to be like God.

Moo, to the contrary, states, "Eve was deceived by the serpent in the Garden (Gen 3:13) precisely in taking the initiative over the man."[42] The content of the serpent's deception, however, had nothing to do with her taking initiative over the man and everything to do with questioning God's word (Gen 3:1, 4–5). Similarly, Eve's description of this deception in Gen 3:13 is not, "The serpent deceived me and I took the initiative," but rather, "The serpent deceived me and I ate." Nothing in Genesis or Paul's letters says that

---

39.   BDAG 98 gives the meaning of the passive of ἀπατάω as "be led astray" in 1 Tim 2:14 and Jos. *Ant.* 12.20.
40.   BDF §318 (4), p. 166.
41.   Sir 25:24, "The beginning of sin was by the woman, and through her we all die," attributes to the woman what Paul in Rom 5:12–19 attributes to Adam. 1 Tim 2:14, however, does not mention death through Eve, but includes woman's role in the fall, expanding on Rom 5:12–19.
42.   Moo, "What Does It Mean," *RBMW* 190.

Eve was deceived to take initiative over Adam or that God had prohibited Eve from taking initiative in her relations with Adam. Since initiative was not prohibited, her "transgression" cannot be this. Moo is so keen to identify the problem in Ephesus as women "seeking roles that have been given to men in the church"[43] that he substitutes woman "taking the initiative over the man" for the real transgression actually identified in the verse he cites.

DOES EVE'S DECEPTION IMPLY THAT WOMEN ARE MORE SUBJECT TO DECEPTION THAN MEN?

Many complementarians argue from verse 14 that women are more susceptible to deception than men and so should not teach men but should be subordinate to men.[44] Paul does note the significance of Eve's deception, namely, her fall into transgression, but he does not draw from this any anthropological principle regarding women in general being more prone to deception than men. Nor does the account of creation in Gen 1–2 express any such principle. This passage does not warrant generalizing about the gullibility of women.

If Paul had argued that all women are by nature easily deceived and therefore not reliable teachers and that men are not so deceived, it would be an argument for prohibiting women from teaching at all, whether that teaching be to men or women, with or without a position of authority in the home, church, or society. Few today, however, take this interpretation to its logical conclusion. In any event, Paul's affirmation of women as teachers elsewhere, including the Pastoral Epistles,[45] undermines such a generalization. Furthermore, if Paul believed women were more vulnerable to deception by Satan than men, why would he affirm women prophesying in 1 Cor 11:2–16?

Neither the Genesis narrative nor Paul draws any anthropological generalization from Eve's deception. Neither says that "the serpent subverted the pattern of male leadership" by addressing the woman.[46] Neither says that Eve or women in general are more gullible than men,[47] "that all

---

43. Ibid.
44. E.g., Grudem, EF 72, "the nature of women ... made Eve less inclined to oppose the deceptive serpent."
45. Cf. above, pp. 328–34; Marshall, *Pastoral Epistles*, 465.
46. As does Schreiner, "Dialogue," WCA 115.
47. As does J. N. D. Kelly, *The Pastoral Epistles* (London: A&C Black, 1963), 68–69: "Eve was so gullible a victim of the serpent's wiles, she clearly cannot be trusted to teach.... [Paul] regards

women as a result are 'deceived' "[48] or more susceptible to deception,[49] or, as Moo formerly did, that women's "susceptibility to deception bars them from engaging in public teaching ... there are some activities for which women are by nature not suited."[50] In response to the present author's critique,[51] Moo now admits the real difficulties of "viewing v. 14 as a statement about the nature of women."[52] He now agrees that "there is nothing in the Genesis accounts or in Scripture elsewhere to suggest that Eve's deception is representative of women in general ... this interpretation does not mesh with the context."[53] The only other reference to Eve's deception in the NT (2 Cor 11:3, a close parallel to 1 Tim 2:14) is not used by Paul to draw any generalizations about women, but rather as an example to everyone in the church: "But I am afraid that just as Eve was deceived by the serpent's cunning, your minds may somehow be led astray from your sincere and pure devotion to Christ."

Paul's abundance of citations about the susceptibility of men as well as women to deception significantly reduces the plausibility that he intends an anthropological generalization that women are more prone to deception than men in 1 Tim 2:13–14. In the Pastoral Epistles, 2 Tim 3:13 states that "evil men [ἄνθρωποι, generic for men and women] and impostors will proceed from bad to worse, deceiving and being deceived," and Titus 3:3 acknowledges, "we also once were foolish ourselves, disobedient, deceived."

Adam and Eve as ... archetypes of the human race. Their characters and propensities were transmitted to their descendants ... 'he shall rule over you' [applies] to the entire female sex."

48. E.g., Stanley E. Porter, "What Does it Mean to be 'Saved by Childbirth' (1 Timothy 2.15)?" *JSNT* 49 (1993): 93.

49. As does Stephen B. Clark, *Man and Woman in Christ: An Examination of the Roles of Men and Women in Light of Scripture and the Social Sciences* (Ann Arbor: Servant Books, 1980), 203: "women are more easily deceived than men"; and implied by Grudem, *EF* 70. Schreiner, "Dialogue," *WCA* 114, says that most who contrast Adam's deliberate sin to Eve's deception "are reluctant to draw this ... conclusion."

50. Moo, "Meaning and Significance," 70, cf. 82, "to teach men ... she is not suited"; Robert Culver, "A Traditional View: Let Your Women Keep Silence," in *Women in Ministry* (ed. B. Clouse & R. G. Clouse; Downers Grove, Ill.: InterVarsity Press, 1989), 36; Hendrickson, *I & II Timothy and Titus*, 110: "Let none assume the role that was not intended for her. Let not the daughter of Eve teach, rule, lead, when the congregation gathers for worship." Moo's article is rebutted by Philip B. Payne, "Libertarian Women in Ephesus: A Response to Douglas J. Moo's Article, 'First Tim. 2:11–15: Meaning and Significance,'" *TJ* NS 2 (Fall 1981): 169–97.; idem, "The Interpretation of I Timothy 2:11–15: A Surrejoinder," in *What Does The Scripture Teach about the Ordination of Women? Differing Views by Three New Testament Scholars* (A study commissioned by the Committee on Ministerial Standing; Minneapolis, Minn.: The Evangelical Free Church of America, 1986), 2:96–115. The editor of *Trinity Journal*, D. A. Carson, published Moo's rejoinder but notified Payne he would not consider his surrejoinder.

51. Payne, "Libertarian Women," 169–97.

52. Moo, "Rejoinder," 204.

53. Moo, "What Does It Mean," *RBMW* 190.

Throughout his letters, Paul clearly regarded the tendency to deceive and to be deceived to affect men as well as women.[54] Paul's call at about this time for women to be "teachers of what is excellent" in Titus 2:3 shows that he does *not* agree that women are so prone to deception that they should not teach.

Since Moo acknowledges that the normal sense of the verb that covers all of 1 Tim 2:12 is *not* universal[55] and repudiates that "Eve's deception is representative of women in general,"[56] what is left that would make verse 12's prohibition universal? Moo exposes the extent of his assumptions about the created nature of man and woman: "[In] the pre-fall situation ... the man bears responsibility for religious teaching."[57] It is unclear how Moo reads this into Gen 1–2, but OT scholars such as Claus Westermann and J. Barton Payne have not found this or any other teaching of separate roles for men and women or of a hierarchy of men over women in the early chapters of Genesis.[58]

As Timothy J. Harris has clearly shown,[59] verse 14 is a crucial verse that shipwrecks views that interpret it as a universal based on "the created order." If verse 14 expresses an anthropological norm declaring the nature of men and women as God created them, this verse provides a reason for prohibiting women from teaching or having authority over men. But it also entails much more than its advocates are prepared to admit, including the following:[60]

1. If verse 14 expresses an anthropological norm, women by their created nature are prone to deception but men are not. This contradicts human experience that men, too, are prone to deception.

2. Logically, such deception should also exclude women from teaching women or children. Paul, however, explicitly permits women teaching women in Titus 2:3.

---

54. Cf. Rom 1:29; 3:13; 7:11; 16:18; 1 Cor 3:18; 6:9; 15:33; 2 Cor 11:13; 12:16; Gal 6:3, 7; Eph 4:14, 22; 5:6; Col 2:8; 1 Thess 2:3; 2 Thess 2:3, 10; 1 Tim 4:1; Titus 1:10.

55. Moo, "Rejoinder," 199; cf. above, pp. 320–25.

56. Moo, "What Does It Mean," *RBMW* 190. Moo, "Rejoinder," 204, now states, "I am now inclined to see the reference as a means of suggesting the *difference* between Adam and Eve in the Fall—he sinned openly; she was deceived."

57. Moo, "Rejoinder," 204.

58. Cf. above, pp. 41–54.

59. Harris, "Eve's Deception," 345–50.

60. Cf. Nicholas Wolterstorff, "The Bible and Women: Another Look at the 'Conservative' Position," *The Reformed Journal* 29,6 (1979): 25.

3. Logically, such deception should exclude women from teaching and leading in society as well as the church and home. This fosters a condescending view of women in general.[61]

James Hurley holds that Eve was not at fault but merely deceived, whereas Adam "was not deceived but, deliberately and with understanding, chose to sin."[62] Hurley says that Adam had the unique privilege not shared by Eve of being "prepared by God to discern the serpent's lies."[63] Consequently, he asserts that in 1 Tim 2:14, "the divine assignment of headship in religious affairs to the husband is the point in view."[64] None of these assertions are made or implied by the text of Genesis or of 1 Tim 2:13–14. Hurley says, "Eve was *not* at fault,"[65] but Paul states, "she became a transgressor." To become a transgressor entails breaking God's command, and according to Gen 3:3 Eve knew she was breaking God's command, so she was at fault. God's statements to Eve in Gen 3:13, 16 also imply that she was at fault. Satan deceived her about being able to avoid the consequences of her disobedience, but Eve knew what she wanted and was willing to disobey God to get it. Hurley states that Adam "became responsible for their falling into sin."[66] But for Adam to be responsible for Eve's transgression is contrary to the ethical principle that everyone is responsible for his or her own sin (Jer 31:30; cf. Acts 5:1–11).

Hurley also makes the dubious assumption that God did not communicate directly with the woman but only with Adam, and that the woman was not "prepared by God to discern the serpent's lies."[67] Genesis does not say that God did not communicate directly with the woman or that God talked to her only through Adam. It would be strange indeed if God brought forth the climax of creation, so that it was at last "very good," but

---

61. This probably explains why Wayne Grudem avoids direct statements such as "women are more prone to deception than men" in explaining 1 Tim 2:14, but writes circuitously (EF 70–72), "Paul is saying something about the nature of men and women as God created them.... Men have some strengths that are generally lacking in women.... God gave men, in general, a disposition that is better suited to teaching and governing in the church, a disposition that inclines more to rational, logical analysis of doctrine and a desire to protect the doctrinal purity of the church.... Paul understands the kinder, gentler, more relational nature of women as something that made Eve less inclined to oppose the deceptive serpent." Grudem's description is foreign to Paul's own descriptions of woman and obscures the sharp contrast of 1 Tim 3:14.
62. Hurley, *Biblical Perspective*, 215.
63. Ibid., 216.
64. Ibid. This view is also reflected in Clark, *Man and Woman*, 23–28, 128–30.
65. Hurley, *Biblical Perspective*, 215.
66. Ibid., 216.
67. Ibid.

did not bother even once to tell Eve about this mortal danger at hand. God created woman as the man's equal: "bone of my bones and flesh of my flesh," "taken out of man," and made "in God's image," which entails at a bare minimum the ability to communicate.

In fact, Gen 3:3 seems to imply that God did speak to the woman, for Eve attributed directly to God, "God did say ..." not, "Adam said that God said...."[68] The seven verbs of God's statements to "you" in the plural in both the MT and LXX in Gen 3:1–5 also imply that God gave the commandment to them both. God spoke directly to the woman in Gen 3:13 and 16. The fact that both of them hid when they heard the sound of the Lord God walking in the garden in the cool of the day (3:8) seems to imply that God was in the habit of talking to both of them. The priesthood of all believers in Christ in the NT and in Pauline theology especially opposes the view that only males, not females, can approach God directly. Adam and the first woman had the special privilege of receiving God's word firsthand.

Hurley asks regarding his own interpretation, "Could it be that his point in v. 14 is that Adam was the one appointed by God to exercise religious headship, and that he was the one prepared by God to do so?"[69] If that were Paul's point, Paul's words fail to express it. Nothing in 1 Tim 2:14 implies divine assignment of headship in religious affairs to the husband. The context of 1 Tim 2:14 is about disruption of harmony in the gathering of believers, not husband–wife relations. Hurley's view flies in the face of women in both the OT (e.g., Deborah and Huldah) and the NT (e.g., Priscilla, Phoebe, Junia, Euodia, and Syntyche), who are described approvingly as exercising religious leadership. Nothing in the Genesis creation narrative commands the woman to defer to Adam in matters pertaining to religion or God, commands her to look to Adam for her religious teaching, or prohibits her from exercising authority. Since there can be no transgression where there is no command, none of these can properly be regarded as her "transgression." Instead, Gen 1:26 gives them (plural) rule "over all the earth and over all the creatures," and 1:27 commands them (male and female) to subdue the earth (cf. 5:2).

---

68. Gen 2:17 confirms that God said both the introductory and final clauses of 3:3, so one should not assume that God could not also have said the middle clause, "and you must not touch it."
69. Hurley, *Biblical Perspective*, 216.

Not surprisingly in light of the lack of connection between Hurley's interpretation and the text of both Genesis and 1 Tim 2:14, he describes 2:14 as "cryptic words ... cryptic references to the early chapters of Genesis."[70] Rather than letting the emphasis of the verse guide him to focus on Eve's deception, he interprets it as a cryptic message that Eve transgressed by not deferring to Adam and draws from this that women by their created order are not to exercise religious leadership. In fact, not only does 1 Tim 2:13 – 14 not compare men in general to women in general or generalize from Adam and Eve to all people, it focuses on the unique status of Adam and Eve as "formed by God" and the awful consequences of Eve's deception.[71]

The text of 1 Tim 2:14 emphasizes the deception of Eve, providing a warning to Eves in Ephesus not to be similarly deceived by the false teachers or to spread their deception. As Satan deceived the woman leading to the fall, so Satan had already deceived some women in the Ephesian church (1 Tim 5:15). The example of Eve provides an excellent explanation and appropriate support for the command in verse 11 that women learn lest their deception lead to their fall from the faith. It directly supports the prohibition in verse 12, warning lest women teach their deception in the assembled church and threaten its fall.

This logical relationship between verses 11 – 12 and 13 – 14 supports the view that Paul restricted teaching by women because false teachers had deceived women in Ephesus. It also supports the most natural reading of the present tense "I am not permitting" in verse 12, namely, that these are temporary requirements in light of the influence of the false teaching among women in the Ephesian church. Eve's deception vividly illustrates the danger when a woman is deceived. Consequently, there is no need to attempt to find here a cryptic appeal to gender-based hierarchy established at creation.

---

70. Ibid., 214, 221. Cf. Moo, "What Does It Mean," *RBMW* 189, "Paul's reference to Eve in verse 14 is difficult"; Schreiner, "Dialogue," *WCA* 112, "the verse [1 Tim 2:14] is difficult."
71. Harris, "Eve's Deception," 347.

22

1 TIMOTHY 2:15:
SALVATION THROUGH "THE CHILDBIRTH"

P. C. Spicq found 1 Tim 2:15's affirmation of salvation through childbearing so "bizarre" that he considered it a non-Pauline gloss.[1] Verse
15 should be understood in its context as a direct contrast to the negative
statements about woman's deception and transgression in verse 14. Many
interpretations of this verse, however, ignore its grammatical and conceptual connection to its context following the deception and fall of Eve.
Some treat this as a prediction that if women lead a holy life they will be
protected from physical harm in childbirth[2] or that childbearing (however
broadly it is interpreted) is a "necessary accompaniment ... to salvation"[3]
for women.

Such interpretations are not only dubious factually and theologically,
they are unrelated to the argument of the passage. What does safety in
childbirth or childbirth as a means of woman's salvation have to do with
deception and fall? Furthermore, how are those fitting conclusions to Paul
not permitting women to "teach and assume authority over men"? Any
acceptable interpretation must answer these questions and be a natural
reading of the text.

---

1. P. C. Spicq, *Saint Paul: Les épîtres Pastorales* (EBib; 4th ed.; Paris: Gabalda, 1969), 382.
2. E.g., Moffatt's translation "women will get safely through childbirth"; NIV "women will be kept
    safe through childbirth."
3. Moo, "Rejoinder," 205, cf. the critique below, pp. 425–27. Cf. JB, "she will be saved by child-
    bearing."

WHAT DOES Σῴζω MEAN IN 1 TIMOTHY 2:15?

Immediately following the statement that the woman fell into transgression is the affirmation, "but she[4] shall be saved through the childbirth." Her salvation stands in contrast to the rupture in her relationship with God that occurred at the fall and so must indicate a renewal of that relationship. Coming on the heels of the reference to the fall, "she shall be saved" naturally refers to corresponding spiritual salvation. The passive of the verb points to salvation provided by another.[5] "The passive voice is probably a divine or theological passive, that is, God is the agent of salvation."[6] Its future tense points forward beyond Eve to the promised Savior.[7] Paul and the church in Ephesus believed that spiritual salvation was accomplished only through the incarnation and work of Christ. Unless 1 Tim 2:15 is the only exception, each of the twenty-nine occurrences of the verb σῴζω in the Pauline corpus refers to spiritual salvation from sin that comes through Christ.[8]

When Paul focuses on physical deliverance, he uses a different word, ῥύομαι, "to deliver" (e.g., Rom 15:30–31; 2 Cor 1:10–11; 2 Tim 3:11; 4:17,

---

4. This is singular, but many versions translate it as plural, including Amplified, Beck, CEV, Goodspeed, LB, NASB, NIV, Moffatt, Phillips, TNT, and Williams.
5. Knight, *Pastoral Epistles*, 147, cf. 144–49, supporting "the Childbirth" referring to Christ.
6. Porter, "Saved by Childbirth," 94.
7. So Knight, *Pastoral Epistles*, 147.
8. BDAG 982–83 lists every Pauline occurrence, including 1 Tim 2:15, as *"save/preserve from eternal death"*; even Rom 9:27 and 1 Cor 3:15 apply metaphors to eternal salvation. Cf. W. Foerster, *TDNT* 7:992, "In Paul σῴζω and σωτηρία are obviously limited quite intentionally to the relation between man and God." J. Schneider, "Redemption," *NIDNTT* 3:214, "Paul uses *sōzō* and *sōtēria* exclusively for the saving activity of God." Moo, "What Does it Mean," *RBMW* 192, σῴζω "elsewhere always refers to salvation, in the theological sense, in Paul." Marshall, *Pastoral Epistles*, 467, "σῴζω consistently refers to salvation from sin in the PE." J. E. Huther, "The Pastoral Epistles," in *Critical and Exegetical Commentary on the New Testament* (ed. Heinrich August Wilhelm Meyer; Edinburgh: T&T Clark, 1881), 133, "σωθήσεται is to be taken here in the sense which it continually has in the N.T." Schreiner ("Dialogue," *WCA* 115) with extensive bibliography affirms, "σῴζω always has the meaning of spiritual salvation in the Pastoral Epistles ... and the other Pauline writings." Porter, "Saved by Childbirth," 93–94, "The sense of 'be kept safe' must be rejected.... 1 Timothy 2:15 ... is virtually guaranteed a salvific sense." In contrast, Andreas J. Köstenberger ("Ascertaining Women's God-Ordained Roles: An Interpretation of 1 Timothy 2:15," *BBR* 7 [1997]: 126 n. 48), although acknowledging that 1 Cor 3:15 "is clearly eschatological," alleges that here "σῴζω is used to denote an escape through danger" rather than its obvious meaning "will be saved spiritually." He misinterprets what is clearly an analogy to spiritual salvation, "but as one escaping through the flames," as though it were the denotation of "will be saved." Similarly, although acknowledging that 2 Tim 4:18 "clearly has an ultimate eschatological reference point," which is the point of, "The Lord will ... save me to His heavenly kingdom," he gives the false impression that "will save" in this verse also conveys "safekeeping in this life," which is conveyed instead by the first verb of the sentence, "to rescue." None of his examples support his interpretation of σῴζω to mean "is preserved." All of them refer to ultimate spiritual salvation. Cf. Schreiner ("Dialogue," *WCA* 227 n. 232), who refutes Köstenberger's interpretation.

18a, which he specifically contrasts to spiritual salvation expressed by σῴζω in 2 Tim 4:18b), or the passive of χαρίζομαι, "to be restored" (Phlm 22). Similarly, each of the twelve occurrences of σωτήρ, each of the nineteen occurrences of σωτηρία, and both occurrences of σωτήριον and σωτήριος in the Pauline corpus refer to the Savior or salvation in a spiritual sense.

In only one of these passages (Phil 1:19) is there a reasonable likelihood that σωτηρία may carry a physical sense as well as its primary spiritual sense. Paul writes in 1:18b–21:

> I will continue to rejoice, for I know that through your prayers and the support of the Spirit of Jesus Christ, what has happened to me will turn out for my salvation [σωτηρία]. I eagerly expect and hope that I will in no way be ashamed, but will have courage so that now as always Christ will be exalted in my body, whether by life or by death. For to me, to live is Christ and to die is gain.

The primary basis for Paul's continuing to rejoice was not the expectation of his physical deliverance from prison, which he acknowledges to be in doubt in Phil 1:20, 21, and 27. Instead, he rejoices confidently in his spiritual salvation, just as he was confident that the Philippians who stand firm in the faith "will be saved—and that by God" (Phil 1:28). Since Paul prays for the salvation of others (e.g., Rom 10:1; 2 Cor 5:20; 2 Thess 1:11), it is not odd that he would associate his own perseverance to future salvation with the prayers of others.

The ultimate source of spiritual salvation is clearly expressed in Paul's following phrase in Phil 1:19, "through the support [ἐπιχορηγίας] of the Spirit of Jesus Christ." The closest parallel to this passage (Gal 3:5) expresses spiritual salvation by the phrase, "supplying [ἐπιχορηγῶν] you the Spirit of Jesus Christ." Paul explained the basis of his confidence in Phil 1:6, "He who began a good work in you will carry it on to completion until the day of Christ Jesus."

Since every other occurrence of the σῴζω word group in the Pauline corpus conveys the sense of spiritual salvation, there is a strong expectation that it carries that sense in 1 Tim 2:15 as well, particularly in light of its contrast to the fall. Apart from four instances in the Gospels where σῴζω refers to the healing of an infirmity, which does not fit as a possible meaning in 1 Tim 2:15, each of the other fifteen occurrences of the future passive of σῴζω in the NT denotes spiritual salvation.[9] The future passive of σῴζω in the NT has become such a stock expression of God's action (a "divine passive") in giving eternal salvation that, barring compelling contextual evidence to the contrary, this ought to be understood as its meaning in 1 Tim 2:15.

The closest and hence grammatically most natural subject of "she shall be saved" is "the woman" of 1 Tim 2:14, who is identified as "Eve" in verse 13. The shift from "Eve" to "the woman" to "she" adds to the natural association of Eve as representative of women in general. Paul's use of the singular verb "she shall be saved," in spite of its being modified by a subordinate clause using a plural verb ("if they continue"), confirms that Paul still has Eve in view. Paul, therefore, treats Eve here as representative of women in general.[10]

This confirms that Paul continued to have the Genesis account in mind as he wrote 1 Tim 2:15. Immediately following the statement of the woman's deception in Gen 3:13 is the curse on the serpent. This curse predicts that the seed of the woman will crush the serpent's head (Gen 3:15), a passage called the *protevangelium*, the Bible's first prediction of the promised seed that will overcome Satan[11] and the effects of the fall. Paul's

---

9. Healings: Matt 9:21 = Mark 5:28; Luke 8:50; John 11:12. Spiritual salvation: Matt 10:22 = 24:13; Mark 16:16; John 10:9; Acts 2:21; 11:14; 16:31; Rom 5:9, 10; 9:27; 10:9, 13; 11:26; 1 Cor 3:15. The analysis of Köstenberger agrees with this in "God-Ordained Roles," 126–27.

10. Schreiner ("Dialogue," WCA 117) supports this understanding, but p. 116 misrepresents the view that "the Childbirth" refers to Christ's birth, as though it must entail Mary as the subject of "she shall be saved."

11. Serpent terminology is interwoven throughout the fall narrative and provides a surface meaning about the tempter serpent and its punishment, but the description of the serpent points to a far more sinister reality than a particular snake or snakes in general, the ultimate tempter to evil, Satan. The tempter is called "the serpent" (הַנָּחָשׁ, with an article) each time he is identified (Gen 3:1, 2, 4, 13, 14), marking him as unique. He is said in 3:1 to be "more crafty than any of the animals of the field the LORD God had made," separating him from animals. It is only as a result of the curse of 3:14 that God tells him, "You will crawl on your belly and … eat dust all the days of your life," exposing his true nature as low down and dirty. This prophecy proves that the being that tempted Eve was unlike any other snake. This same being will not only have enmity with the woman but will himself, not some descendant, ultimately suffer defeat ("he will crush your head") by the predicted seed of the woman. In light of these factors and the picture throughout the OT and NT of Satan as the crafty tempter who will be overcome by the Messiah, "the serpent" evidently is Satan. The snake imagery reinforces his symbolism as sneaky and dangerous. In Gen 3:15 "I will put enmity between you and the woman" fits naturally as a reference to the enmity between Satan and Eve that must have accompanied the results of the fall, but to what does "I will put enmity between your seed and her seed" refer? Are snakes to be regarded as Satan's offspring? The close association of "seed" with descendants and the widespread enmity between snakes and humans does make this a natural reading, but no other part of Scripture hints that Satan had or could have had snakes as offspring. It is possible that "seed" here refers to a spiritual, not biological, reality as it does in Isa 53:10, where the "seed" of the Messiah is associated with those he justifies in 53:11. Here Satan's seed could be sin or

understanding of "the seed" elsewhere as referring to Christ[12] and his pairing in Rom 16:20: "The God of peace will soon crush Satan under your feet. The grace of our Lord Jesus Christ be with you" evidence his understanding of Gen 3:15 as its content demands, namely as a prediction that the seed of the woman will crush the head of the serpent. This prediction is the only reference to salvation in Gen 3:13–16, from which Paul is citing, and it is depicted in Genesis as the solution to the fall caused by the woman's deception. The natural implication, then, is that the salvation from the fall to which Paul appeals in 1 Tim 2:15 is that same salvation through the seed of the woman identified in Gen 3:15b.

The similarity between τεκνογονίας ("childbirth") in 1 Tim 2:15 and τέξῃ τέκνα ("you will give birth to children") in Gen 3:16 further supports the view that Paul still had the Genesis account in mind in 1 Tim 2:15.[13] The change in wording from "children" (Gen 3:16) to "the childbirth" (1 Tim 2:15) suggests, however, that it is the predicted salvation through the seed of Gen 3:15 that is in view, not childbearing in general. Furthermore, there is no reference to pain in 1 Tim 2:15 to correspond to Gen 3:16. Rather, "she shall be saved through the childbirth" associates the predicted salvation of 1 Tim 2:15 with the predicted salvation of Gen 3:15.[14]

---

sinners who carry out his evil desires. "Her seed" could refer to Eve's descendants or it could refer to the singular overcoming male descendant with whom her seed is identified in the next clause. "Seed" in Hebrew can refer to an individual descendant, as it does in Gen 4:25 referring to Seth, in 1 Sam 1:11 to Samuel, and in 2 Sam 7:12 to Solomon. These choices need not be mutually exclusive. As in parables and miracles, so too in prophecy, physical symbols may have a literal meaning that points to a more important spiritual meaning. "Seed" points to both a physical and a spiritual reality (the idolatry of Judah) in Isa 17:11 and in Ps 126:5–6, where it points to the prosperity of Zion; cf. BDB 282. Although it might seem trivial that a serpent may strike at a man's heel and the man might crush the serpent's head, it is a powerful picture of Satan's venom spewed out at the cross, which became the ultimate victory of Christ over Satan. Similarly, the enmity between humankind and snakes points to the enmity between Christ and Satan along with his legacy of sin. Cf. *Slavonic Life of Adam and Eve* 34:3, "Adam was not ignorant that the Lord would descend on earth and tread the devil under foot" (*APOT*, 2:135).

12. Cf. below, pp. 434–36.
13. Cf. I. Howard Marshall in collaboration with Philip H. Towner, *A Critical and Exegetical Commentary on the Pastoral Epistles* (ICC; Edinburgh: T&T Clark, 1999), 470 n. 204.
14. Thus, the RV text: "she shall be saved through her child-bearing"; Berkeley and New Berkeley: "through the child-bearing"; Berkeley margin: "saved through the birth of the Child"; Fenton: "she will be saved because of the child-bearing"; Amplified: "through the Child-bearing, that is, by the birth of the [divine] Child"; TNT text: "saved through the birth of the Child"; and similarly the texts of Young, Montgomery, and Godbey versions, the RSV margin: "by the birth of the child"; CEV margin: "saved by the birth of a child" (that is, by the birth of Jesus)"; NEB margin: "saved through the Birth of the Child"; Weymouth margin: "It is not improbable that the writer is thinking here primarily of the birth of Christ by Mary"; and the margins of the ASV and Knox. So also, the commentaries by Clarke, Ellicott, Fairbairn, Gurney, Hammond, Humphreys, Kent, Knight, Liefeld, Liddon, Lock, Oden, Rowland, H. von Soden, Wohlenberg, Wordsworth, and the studies by Thomas C. Geer, Jr., "Admonitions to Women

The Genesis narrative of Eve's creation, deception, the fall, and its consequences provided Paul with the perfect defense of his "not permitting a woman to teach and exercise self-assumed authority over a man." The terrible consequences of Eve's deception highlight the seriousness of the deception of women in Ephesus. Yet the story of Eve also offers women hope and dignity. Although women experience pain in childbirth as a result of the fall, a woman has given birth to the promised Seed who will destroy Satan and overcome the fall. Not only was woman the vehicle for the entry into the world of sin, death, and the power of Satan, she was also the vehicle for the entry into the world of the Savior who delivers people from sin and death. Paul highlights both the deception of woman leading to the fall and woman as the channel through whom the Savior came.

Thus, Paul's explanation of his prohibition of women teaching with self-assumed authority over men does not entail degradation of women but rather elevates woman to a privileged position that is far higher than anything offered by the false teachers: the promised seed of the woman came through Mary in the childbirth of the Savior. As Paul so often does, he brings the focus back to salvation through Christ, and he does so in a distinctive way that gives dignity to women. The promised Seed, who came through a woman, fulfills the deepest yearnings of women.

In summary, eight key factors confirm that 1 Tim 2:15 speaks about spiritual salvation:

1. Paul invariably uses σῴζω elsewhere for spiritual salvation.
2. The adversative δέ links 2:15 to 2:14 and requires that "she shall be saved" contrasts to and delivers from the fall. Only spiritual salvation contrasts to and delivers from the fall.
3. The singular subject in "she shall be saved" (1 Tim 2:15) confirms that Eve is still in view, and "shall be saved" points to the only

in 1 Tim. 2:8–15," in *Essays on Women in Earliest Christianity* (corrected and 2nd print.; ed. C. D. Osburn; Joplin, Mo.: College Press, 1995), 1:298–99; Alan Padgett, "Wealthy Women at Ephesus: I Timothy 2:8–15 in Social Context," *Int* 41 (1987): 29; Hilde Huizenga, "Women, Salvation and the Birth of Christ: A Reexamination of 1 Timothy 2:15," *SBT* 12 (1982): 17–26; P. Altfrid Kassing, "Das Heil der Mutterschaft," *Liturgie und Mönchtum* (1958): 39–63; Mark D. Roberts, "Women Shall Be Saved: A Closer Look at 1 Timothy 2:15," *TSF Bulletin* (1981): 4–7; Aída Dina Besançon Spencer, "Eve at Ephesus (Should Women Be Ordained as Pastors according to the First Letter to Timothy 2:11–15?)," *JETS* 17 (1974): 215–22; Williams, *Apostle Paul*, 113; and Clark, *Man and Woman*, 205–8. Cf. below, pp. 424–40.

reference to salvation in Eve's story, salvation through her seed in Gen 3:15. This follows, "the serpent deceived me, and I ate" in 3:13, just as "she shall be saved" in 1 Tim 2:15 follows, "the woman was deceived and became a transgressor" in 2:14. Her salvation, then, refers to the salvation through the woman's seed.

4. There is no reference to pain in 1 Tim 2:15 as would be expected if Paul were appealing simply to that result of the fall.

5. The "for" introducing 1 Tim 2:13–15 implies that these verses explain 2:12's prohibition of women teaching with self-assumed authority over men. A reference to physical safety in childbirth does not explain 2:12,[15] but spiritual salvation does, since teachers with self-assumed authority threatened the spiritual salvation of people in the Ephesian church (5:15).

6. Physical safety in childbirth is unrelated to Paul's central concern in 1 Timothy, which is false teaching.

7. Physical safety in childbirth is not conditioned by what follows in 1 Tim 2:15: faith, love, and holiness, but spiritual salvation is.

8. To interpret 2:15 to be about physical safety in childbirth insults believing women who miscarry, have complications, or die in childbirth. Their experience contradicts this interpretation. If this is what it means, it is a false prophecy.

Thus, the evidence overwhelmingly supports that "she shall be saved" refers to ultimate spiritual salvation, not merely that women will be kept "safe" in childbirth or "kept safe from seizing men's roles"[16] or "will escape (or be preserved) [from Satan]."[17]

The adversative δέ in verse 15 implies that the salvation will overcome the fall, and if the adversative includes the role of the subject as well, it implies an affirmation of the role of woman in salvation that counteracts

---

15. This is so whether v. 12 prohibits women assuming authority to teach men or their domineering teaching of men.
16. Hurley, *Biblical Perspective*, 223. Other weaknesses of his interpretation include: (1) It does not fit the contrast between the fall and salvation implied by "but she shall be saved"; (2) it does not fit the contrast between the woman's deception and salvation through the woman's seed in Gen 3:13–15; (3) "seizing men's roles" is not mentioned in this verse or elsewhere in this context or Genesis 3; (4) it must interpret "the childbirth" symbolically to encompass "embracing a woman's role"; (5) it interprets "if" as "should be accompanied by," contrary to its established meaning.
17. Köstenberger, "God-Ordained Roles," 142. Marshall (*Pastoral Epistles*, 468) critiques Köstenberger's view.

the role of woman in the fall.[18] Nothing corresponds as well as the woman's role in bringing Christ into the world. In contrast to the negative role of woman in the fall, 1 Tim 2:15 affirms the positive role of woman in salvation, giving birth to the Christ. As in Eden, so in Ephesus, the woman's deception (LXX: ἡ γυνή ... ἠπάτησεν) led her to turn away from God to follow Satan (cf. 1 Tim 5:15). "She shall be saved through the childbirth" in 1 Tim 2:15 reflects the key idea of Gen 3:15, that the seed of the woman will crush the serpent's head. Thus, both Gen 3:15 and 1 Tim 2:15 specify the role of woman in salvation, affirming her in a way that balances the criticism of her deception and fall.

Furthermore, the strife stressed in Gen 3:12–16, resulting from the deception of the first woman, is reflected in the strife in Ephesus, resulting from the deception of women there. The theme of 1 Tim 2 is peace without contention. This passage addresses strife in the church, caused by the influence of the false teachers over women. Just as Paul in ignorance received mercy (1 Tim 1:13–16), these women who were deceived could be saved. Similarly, their salvation comes through the promised Seed of the woman, just like all other believers, "if they abide in faith, love and holiness with propriety" (2:15). Thus, 1 Tim 2:11–15 attempts to bring deceived women back into grace and a godly life.

WHAT DOES Διά MEAN IN 1 TIMOTHY 2:15?

First Timothy 2:15 is one of seven passages in the NT, all but one in the Pauline corpus, where "saved" (σῴζω) occurs with "through" (διά): Acts 15:11; Rom 5:9; 1 Cor 1:21; 3:15; 15:2; Eph 2:8; 1 Tim 2:15. In all except 1 Cor 1:21, σῴζω is passive. In all except 1 Cor 3:15, where διά has a different construction (ὡς διά, that requires a comparison), διά identifies the means through which salvation comes. Διά is perfectly suited to express mediate or indirect agency.[19] For example, 1 Cor 15:2 states, "by [διά] this gospel you are saved."

The birth of Christ is the agency through which salvation has come. In Paul's writings "διά is often used with Christ in regard to our relation

---

18. In a similar way, Paul balances his criticism of women who disrespectfully let their hair down in 1 Cor 11:5–6, 10, with the affirmation of women in 11:11–12, also introduced by an adversative, "however" (πλήν).

19. Cf. Robertson, *Grammar*, 580–83, 820; Homer A. Kent Jr., *The Pastoral Epistles* (Chicago: Moody, 1982), 115–16, and cf. below, p. 425 with examples. This is one more example of Paul's distinctive expressions in the Pastoral Epistles.

to God,"[20] as in "peace with God through [διὰ τοῦ] our Lord Jesus Christ, through [δι'] whom we have gained access by faith into this grace" (Rom 5:1); "we will be saved through him [Christ, σωθησόμεθα δι' αὐτοῦ]" (5:9); "reign in life through the [διὰ τοῦ] one man, Jesus Christ" (5:17); "sons of God through [διὰ] the [τῆς] faith in Christ Jesus" (Gal 3:26); "salvation through [διὰ] our Lord Jesus Christ" (1 Thess 5:9). Διά followed by a reference to or about Christ using the genitive case (the case following διά in 1 Tim 2:15) is commonplace in Paul's letters.[21]

BDF §223 summarizes the typical meaning of διά with the genitive: " 'Through' of space, time, agent."[22] BAGD 179–80 identifies these same three: of place, of time, and of means, instrument, agency (+causal). There is nothing about space or time[23] in 1 Tim 2:15, but it refers quite naturally to Christ's childbirth as the means, instrument, or agency through which salvation came. Moule identifies διά with the genitive expressing "by means of" as "very common,"[24] and *TDNT* 2:66–69 discusses many examples.

Some interpret 1 Tim 2:15 as teaching that women are saved spiritually through bearing children or, if they are unable to bear children, by fulfilling their domestic role of nurturing children.[25] They say that women must fulfill a motherly role as a necessary work to be saved. Moo asks, "Why is it objectionable to view faithfulness to a God-ordained role as a ... necessary accompaniment ... to salvation?"[26] It is objectionable for four key reasons:

1. "Necessary accompaniment" is not a recognized meaning conveyed by διά.[27] If Paul had intended this he should have put "childbirth"

---

20. Robertson, *Grammar*, 583.
21. Rom 1:5, 8; 2:16; 5:1, 2, 9, 11, 17, 21; 7:4, 25; 8:37; 16:27; 1 Cor 1:10; 8:6; 15:21, 57; 2 Cor 1:5, 20; 3:4; 5:18; 10:1; Gal 1:1, 12; 2:16; 3:26; 6:14; Eph 1:5; 2:18; 3:12; Phil 1:11; Col 1:16, 20; 3:17; 1 Thess 4:2; 5:9; 2 Tim 1:10; Titus 3:6; Phlm 7.
22. Cf. also Robertson, *Grammar*, 581; Dana and Mantey, *Manual Grammar*, 101; BDF §223 (4) gives the translation equivalent for διά with the genitive, "by virtue of."
23. Porter ("Saved by Childbirth," 97) notes that convincing examples include temporal words, lacking here, and that "during the time of childbirth" is incompatible with a salvific sense.
24. Moule, *Idiom-Book*, 56–57, lists many examples. Both Spicq (*Épîtres pastorales*, 1:383) and Jürgen Roloff (*Der erste Brief an Timotheus* [EKKNT; Zürich: Benziger, 1988], 142 n. 167) appeal mistakenly to Moule to deny this use.
25. Porter, "Saved by Childbirth," 102, concludes that the author of 1 Timothy believed that woman's eschatological "salvation will come by the bearing of children."
26. Moo, "Rejoinder," 205; similarly, Grudem, EF 73–74; Jerome D. Quinn and William C. Wacker, *The First and Second Letters to Timothy: A New Translation with Notes and Commentary* (Grand Rapids: Eerdmans, 2000), 231.
27. BDAG 223–26 does not mention it. Schreiner ("Dialogue," WCA 117) correctly identifies διά as instrumental but inconsistently explains on the one hand on pp. 118–19, "This does not

(or "child rearing") along with "propriety" at the end of the sentence, not as that instrument "through" which woman will be saved.

2. If "bearing children" is a "necessary accompaniment" to salvation, then unmarried and barren women, even if due to their husband's sterility, are excluded from salvation. This interpretation also conflicts with 1 Tim 5:3–5's urging that widows without children receive special honor because of their hope in God and since they continue night and day in prayer. These widows put their hope in God and evidence it in their lives (1 Tim 5:5, 9–10), so they are surely saved. The salvation of childless women cannot have come through childbearing unless they bore children who preceded them in death. Moo and others who adopt this view have to expand the meaning of "childbearing" to something like "child rearing," for which LSJ and BDAG give no support.[28] Nowhere else does Paul use the term τεχνογονία inclusively. When Paul does use the verb τεχνογονέω in 1 Tim 5:14 in a context where he is encouraging domestic life choices for women, he does not stretch its meaning to cover child rearing. Rather, to convey a broader range of meaning he adds to it three other infinitives for this purpose: "to marry, to bear children, to manage their home, and to give the enemy no opportunity for slander." If Paul intended to identify nurture of children, he should have chosen a word that meant that, such as τεχνοτροφέω, as he did in 1 Tim 5:10.

3. Childbearing as a God-given requirement for women's salvation would place a special requirement for salvation on a specific category of persons. This objection applies even with Moo's interpretation of "childbearing" to include child rearing. On this view, all women have to rear children in order to be saved, but men do not have this requirement for salvation. There is no other instance in the NT where a particular category of persons is required to meet

---

mean that all women must have children in order to be saved ... [rather it is] evidence that the salvation already received is genuine," but on the other hand states on p. 120 that "conforming to her God-ordained role [is] ... necessary to obtain eschatological salvation [= necessary accompaniment]." He admits on p. 119 that on his view, "σωθήσεται is used rather loosely here, so that Paul does not specify in what sense women are saved by childbearing and doing other good works."

28. Cf. the criticism of Moo by Porter, "Saved by Childbirth," 95–96, and Schreiner, "Dialogue," WCA 117 n. 241.

standards for salvation that are not universal. Even if one tries to limit the meaning of Gal 3:28 to entering the status of salvation, at a bare minimum it teaches that all people without differentiation, women as well as men, experience salvation alike "through faith in Jesus Christ" (Gal 3:22, 23, 24, 25, 26), not through some additional "condition that women must also maintain,"[29] namely childbearing, however defined.

4. Making childbearing a "necessary accompaniment" to salvation is difficult, if not impossible, to reconcile with Paul's understanding of salvation by grace through faith apart from works.

In order to avoid the theological errors associated with childbearing as the means, instrument, or agency of salvation, some have appealed to Paul's occasional use of διά to introduce an attendant circumstance.[30] They interpret the verse: "She shall be saved through the circumstance of childbearing, if they continue in faith, and love and holiness with propriety." This interpretation faces three primary difficulties exemplified in Marshall's interpretation:[31]

1. Not all women bear children and so cannot fulfill this attendant circumstance for salvation. To relieve this problem, "childbearing" must be interpreted as though it meant "child rearing" or fulfilling a woman's proper domestic role as a nurturing mother, a meaning unsupported by lexicons or Paul's usage (cf. 2, above).

2. This interpretation does not fit the logic or the syntactical structure of the sentence.[32] Those who advocate this line of interpretation typically treat the circumstance of childbearing as though it were part of the "if" clause, namely, one of the conditions for salvation, not as part of the main clause,[33] since the "if" clause of

---

29. Moo, "Meaning and Significance," 73.
30. On this use of διά see BDAG 224, A.3.c. This interpretation is critiqued by Schreiner, "Dialogue," WCA 117; Porter, "Saved by Childbirth," 97. Payne, "Libertarian Women," 180–81, critiques Moo's suggestion that the διά may indicate "efficient cause."
31. Marshall, *Pastoral Epistles*, 467–70. See the critique of this view by Porter, "Saved by Childbirth," 97.
32. This is only avoided if Paul's otherwise universal use of σώζω for spiritual salvation is abandoned as follows: "she will be kept safe through childbirth if they continue in faith, and love and holiness with propriety." Although this makes syntactical sense, it simply is not true, since many devout believers have died in childbirth.
33. Although Marshall (*Pastoral Epistles*, 470) says that διά "expresses circumstances rather than instrument," in order to make his interpretation understandable, on p. 470 he describes a

1 Tim 2:15b does not make sense qualifying "she shall be saved through the circumstance of childbearing." Thus, if it had been Paul's intention to indicate an attendant circumstance using διά, he should have positioned it somewhere after the "if."

3. Since on this view 1 Tim 2:15 is addressing the domestic lifestyle that accompanies the salvation of Christian women, its subject "she" does not fit Eve. This disturbs the syntax in two ways. First, it appeals to a remote antecedent as the subject of "she," namely "woman," from 1 Tim 2:11 – 12 rather than the natural grammatical antecedent, "Eve," of 1 Tim 2:13 – 14. Second, since Eve is no longer in view, the justification for a change in number from singular, "she shall be saved," to plural, "if they continue," namely, that Eve is representative of women, no longer applies. Consequently, this view entails a breach of the grammatical rule that singular subjects should take singular verbs, which normally applies even if the singular subject is generic.[34] These factors make it highly unlikely that the διά in 1 Tim 2:15 is one of the rare occurrences where it introduces an attendant circumstance.

A few have interpreted the διά as concessive, "She will be saved even though she must bear children."[35] By this view Eve, the representative woman, will be saved even though, as a result of her sin, she experiences pain in childbirth. BDAG, BDF, LSJ, and Robertson, however, do not even mention this as a possible meaning of διά. Until analogous instances with this meaning are established,[36] preferably in the Pauline epistles, this must

---

woman's "fulfilling her domestic role" as a "condition" of her being saved, speaks of "the normativity of childbearing," and says that "women will still be saved by fulfilling their Christian duty in motherhood." "By," however, expresses instrumentality, not attendant circumstance, and Barrett (*Pastoral Epistles*, 56) states, "the rendering *motherhood* seems baseless except as a euphemism."

34. E.g., Robertson, *Grammar*, 403. Not one generic singular subject in 1 Cor 11:3 – 16 has a plural verb; all twenty-four of their verbs are singular, cf. 1 Tim 2:11. To solve this, some writers treat "they" as referring to a separate group of people such as a woman's children, as argued by J. H. Ulrichsen, "Noen bemerkninger til 1. Tim 2,15," *Norsk Teologisk Tidsskrift* [Oslo] 84.1 (1983): 19 – 25. Childbearing as an attendant circumstance accompanying salvation, however, is not something that would be conditioned by the actions of a woman's children or spouse.

35. E.g., E. F. Scott, *The Pastoral Epistles* (London: Hodder & Stoughton, 1936), 28. The view is rebutted by Porter, "Saved by Childbirth," 97; Schreiner, "Dialogue," WCA 117 and 228 n. 244; Douglas J. Moo, "Meaning and Significance," 71.

36. Marshall (*Pastoral Epistles*, 469) writes "for the construction cf. Acts 14.22; Rev 21.24." In Rev 21:24, however, διά cannot mean "despite," and Acts 14:22 fits the normal use of διά with verbs of motion, here "to enter," and so does not justify creating a new meaning for διά.

be regarded as baseless conjecture motivated by a desire to find a palatable meaning. In any event, this interpretation does not fit the argument of this passage and must treat childbirth as a hindrance to salvation, a view of the false teachers that Paul opposes.[37]

Since salvation comes only through Christ, it would seem incongruous for Paul to say that salvation comes "through" anything that is not integrally related to Christ. In fact, if 1 Tim 2:15 does not refer to salvation through Christ's childbirth, it would be the only occurrence of σῴζω + διά ("saved" + "through") in all of Paul's writing that does not point to Christ. Thus, by far the most common use of διά with the genitive, indicating agency and meaning "through," is also its most natural reading in 1 Tim 2:15.

FIRST TIMOTHY 2:15'S ARTICLE IN "THE CHILDBIRTH"

Robertson argues that the Greek "article always retain[s] something of the demonstrative force.... [It] aids in pointing out like an index finger.... Whenever the Greek article occurs, the object is certainly definite."[38] The question regarding 1 Tim 2:15 is whether the article is individualizing or generic. By far the most common use is described by BDAG 686, 2 ℵ: "In its individualizing use it focuses attention on a single thing or single concept." BDAG 686–87 states, "The individ. art. also stands before a common noun which, in a given situation, is given special attention as the only or obvious one of its kind.... The article takes on the idea of κατ᾽ ἐξοχήν 'par excellence' ... ὁ ἐρχόμενος *the one who is (was) to come* or *the coming one par excellence* = the Messiah."

Use of the article "par excellence," identifying its supreme manifestation, is widely recognized in the grammars.[39] Just as ὁ ἐρχόμενος identifies Jesus as "the coming one" in Matt 11:3 and Luke 7:19, so, too, his birth can be identified as τῆς τεκνογονίας, "the childbirth par excellence" through which salvation comes. Lock translates it "the great child-bearing" and notes many church fathers with this view.[40] Similarly, Luke, who was probably Paul's secretary for 1–2 Timothy, uses an article to specify Christ's

---

37. Cf. Huther, *The Pastoral Epistles*, 134.
38. Robertson, *Grammar*, 755–56, citing the same conclusions by Gildersleeve. Exceptions include abstract nouns.
39. E.g., BDF §252, citing ὁ προφήτης in John 1:21; 7:40; BDF §263; Wallace, *Grammar*, 222–23.
40. Cf. Lock, *The Pastoral Epistles*, 32–33; cf. above, pp. 439–40 on similar expressions in the church fathers.

birth in Luke 1:35, "the holy one to be born (τὸ γεννώμενον) will be called the Son of God," and in 1:42, "blessed is the child you will bear" [lit., "the fruit of your womb"].

The use of the article to make something specific that would otherwise be general is especially common in the Pastorals, as in "the mystery," "the faith," and "the teaching." Of the sixty-one occurrences of an article modifying a singular noun[41] in 1 Timothy, fifty-five are clearly individualizing,[42] one is clearly generic,[43] and five could be interpreted as either but are more likely individualizing.[44] Every one of the nine other occurrences in 1 Timothy that, like 1 Tim 2:15, has a prepositional phrase containing an article with a singular noun is individualizing.[45] First Timothy regularly adds an article to distinguish individualizing references from generic ones, as in "God our Savior" (2:3), "the devil" (3:7), and "the mystery" (3:9, 16).

Thus, based on the stylistic tendency of 1 Timothy, it is far more likely that the article in 1 Tim 2:15 identifies a specific childbirth, not childbirth in general. Indeed, if the combination of preposition + article + singular noun in 1 Tim 2:15 does not identify a specific childbirth, it would be the only such case in the entire book that is not individualizing. Porter grossly downplays the evidence by stating, "the article may be used to specify a particular item, and in fact does so on occasion in the pastoral epistles."[46]

---

41. This analysis was done by the present writer using the grammatical analysis of Barbara and Timothy Friberg, *Analytical Greek New Testament* (Grand Rapids: Baker, 1981), limiting the analysis to singular nouns since that is what occurs in 1 Tim 2:15, and excluding unrelated specialized uses of the article described by BDAG.

42. Thirty-two of these are translated "the" by the NIV: 1 Tim 1:5, 8, 10, 11, 14, 15, 17, 18; 2:6, 14; 3:2, 9, 16; 4:1, 1, 3, 13; 5:8, 16, 18, 18; 6:7, 10, 10, 12, 12, 13, 14, 15, 15, 19, 21. Fourteen are translated by the NIV using another individualizing term such as "this": 1 Tim 1:16, 18, 19; 4:9, 14, 16; 5:4, 12; 6:1, 2, 12, 14, 17, 20. Nine are left untranslated by the NIV, but in context are clearly individualizing, not generic. Five of these, 1 Tim 4:3; 5:4, 21; 6:1, 13, are with the name of God, ὁ θεός, which BDAG 686 2 ℵ identifies as individualizing. Two identify specifically quoted trustworthy sayings; the same clause is translated by the NIV in 1 Tim 4:9, "This is a trustworthy saying." Just as "the public reading of Scripture" in 1 Tim 4:13 refers to a specific activity in Christian worship, so, too, should "the preaching" and "the teaching" in the same verse.

43. 1 Tim 4:8.

44. Three of these refer to "godliness" and may be either generic or specifically Christian godliness: 1 Tim 4:8; 6:5, 6. In favor of specifically Christian godliness is that 3:16 has just defined "the mystery of godliness" as being found in Christ, that 4:7 contrasts "godliness" with "godless myths," and that 6:3 links godliness with "the sound doctrine of our Lord Jesus Christ." The "grace be with you" in 1 Tim 6:21 probably refers not to generic grace but, as in 1:14, "the grace of our Lord Jesus Christ." The fifth is "the childbirth" in 2:15.

45. 1 Tim 1:11, 15, 19; 6:7, 10, 12, 14, 17, 21.

46. Porter ("Saved by Childbirth," 92), who consequently concludes on p. 102 that the author of 1 Timothy believed that women's eschatological "salvation will come by the bearing of children."

BDAG 687, 2 ב, states about the article, "In its generic use it singles out an individual who is typical of a class, rather than the class itself."[47] Those who appeal to the generic use of the article in 1 Tim 2:15 have not shown how this verse appeals to an individual instance of childbearing as typical of its class. A further characteristic of the generic article is that it "comprehends a class as a single whole and sets it off in distinction from all other classes."[48] For instance, in the one clear instance of the generic article in 1 Timothy (4:8), "physical training" is set off in distinction from training in Christian godliness. Those who appeal to the generic use of the article in 1 Tim 2:15, however, have not shown how this article distinguishes childbearing from other classes. Instead, quite to the contrary, they have typically tried to encompass in the meaning of "childbearing" other issues such as child rearing.[49]

Thus, the generic use of the article is not only comparatively rare, the interpretations that appeal to it in 1 Tim 2:15 do not fit the characteristic features of generic use of the article. Consequently, the pervasive individualizing use of the article with singular nouns in 1 Timothy is also its most natural reading in 1 Tim 2:15.

THE MEANING OF "CHILDBIRTH"

Τεκνογονίας, from the words for "child" and "to be born,"[50] is a medical term specifically referring to childbirth or childbearing. There is probably no more appropriate or unambiguous noun in the Greek language than τεκνογονία to denote childbirth. Köstenberger gives evidence that

---

47. BDAG 687, 2 ב. Cf. Dana and Mantey, *Manual Grammar,* 144: "The principle of the generic article is the selection of a representative or normal individual," citing Gildersleeve.
48. Dana and Mantey, *Manual Grammar,* 144; cf. Robertson, *Grammar,* 757; Wallace, *Grammar,* 227–28.
49. E.g., Köstenberger, "God-Ordained Roles," 107–44. On pp. 141–42, he asserts "the generic nature of the reference indicated by the definite article." However, instead of then distinguishing childbearing from other activities, he alleges that "a general concept is in view, 'procreation.' ... One should view procreation as merely the core of the woman's responsibility that also entails, not merely the bearing, but also the raising of children, as well as managing the home." His interpretation also has against it the un-Pauline use of σώζω to mean "escape," the necessity of appealing to the rare use of a gnomic future, ellipsis of "from Satan," interpreting διά "under the condition of" (p. 142), giving a meaning for τεκνογονία, "procreation," with no prior support in Greek literature, and his dubious assumptions stated on p. 139 that "Christian women ... will escape or be kept safe from Satan, if they adhere to their God-given domestic role" and that "Eve's mistake [was] leaving her proper God-given realm." Fee, *1 and 2 Timothy, Titus,* 38, criticizes interpreting σώζω "kept safe": "it is nearly inconceivable that Paul would use the verb saved in an absolute way, as he does here, without some qualifier (e.g., 'from these errors')."
50. Groves, *Greek and English Dictionary,* 554.

the most natural meaning of each of the three occurrences of the noun τεχνογονία prior to Paul is "childbirth."[51] In Hippocrates' fifth century BC *Epistulae* 17.21 (105), childbirth (τεχνογονίην) is compared to weddings, festivals, and religious rites, and thus the term probably refers to childbirth as an event rather than the process of childbearing.[52] Its lack of an article corresponds to its nonspecific reference.

In Aristotle's fourth century BC *Hist. an.* 7.1.8 (p. 528a, 28), τεχνογονία is used in describing the ideal time when women are sufficiently mature for the giving of birth to children: "After thrice seven years the women have reached a favourable state for childbearing [πρὸς τὰς τεχνογονίας], while the men continue to improve."[53] The prior statement (p. 528a, 20–22), "Now the young females conceive quicker; but having conceived they have more trouble in childbearing [ἐν τοῖς τόκοις = bringing forth, birth]" makes it clear that τεχνογονία refers to the actual giving of birth, not the begetting or the process of bearing children. Furthermore, it is at birth when physical maturity is most important.[54] In this case, the presence of the article probably points to "the giving of birth" as a specific event as opposed to the process of childbearing.

In the third century BC, the Stoic philosopher Chrysippus, *Fragmenta Moralia* 611, wrote: "Submit to marriage and to childbirth [τεχνογονίαν] for its sake and [that of their] homeland, and ... endure for it, if necessary, both pain and death."[55] The reference to "both pain and death" implies that childbirth is in view. Furthermore, "for the sake of their homeland" implies the production of children, not just childbearing as a process. Its lack of an article again corresponds to its nonspecific reference.

---

51. Köstenberger, "God-Ordained Roles," 140–41. His evidence disproves Fee's allegation in *1 and 2 Timothy, Titus*, 38 that τεχνογονίας "has to do with the activity of 'bearing,' not with the noun 'birth' or 'child,'" which, unfortunately, is followed uncritically by Marshall, *Pastoral Epistles*, 468 n. 190.
52. So Köstenberger, "God-Ordained Roles," 140, "childbirths as events" and the translation "naissances d'enfants" in Littré, ed., *Oeuvres complètes d'Hippocrate* (Paris: Baillieère, 1839; repr. Amsterdam: Hakkert, 1973), 9:356–57.
53. Aristotle, *Hist. an.* 8–10.424–25 (D. M. Balme, LCL), following MSS P Da (Aa Ca read τεχνοποΐίας).
54. Köstenberger, "God-Ordained Roles," 141, also argues that it means "the physical giving of birth." If τεχνογονίας is a later reading, as Köstenberger thinks, it would probably put this usage nearer the time of Paul.
55. Köstenberger, "God-Ordained Roles," 140, citing a translation by Lawrence Lahey. Köstenberger's conjecture, repeated in Marshall, *Pastoral Epistles*, 468, that this use of τεχνογονίαν involves synecdoche entailing "married life and having children" ignores the reference to the risk of pain and death, which is clearly a reference to childbirth. This statement is not appropriate for the wider meaning he tries to read into it.

Galen, *De instrumento odoratus* 49 (second c. AD), Joannes Philoponus, *De opoifici mundi* 301 (sixth c. AD), and Simplicius, *Commentarius in Epicteti enchiridion* 96 (sixth c. AD) also use τεκνογονίας to denote the specific act of bearing children.[56] Schreiner is therefore incorrect to state that τεκνογονία refers not to "the result of birth but the actual birthing process."[57] Similarly, Marshall errs in stating that the term "does not mean 'the birth of a child.'"[58] All occurrences of this word prior to Paul focus on the event, not the process, of childbirth, and the key feature of the event is the resulting child.

The scarcity of occurrences of the noun τεκνογονία prior to Paul precludes a dogmatic answer to the question of whether it refers to childbirth in 1 Tim 2:15, as each instance identified by Köstenberger supports, or to the process of childbearing. Since, however, all identified occurrences of the noun up to the time of Paul refer to childbirth, the preferred reading in 1 Tim 2:15 should be, "She shall be saved through the childbirth."[59] Given the normal use of the article, this statement implies that a particular childbirth is the means through which salvation comes.[60] This fits the birth of Christ since this was the means through which salvation has come. In the unlikely eventuality that Paul intended to identify the process of childbearing, then "through the childbearing" would emphasize woman's role in the process of bringing salvation.

The meaning "childbirth" makes sense in this commentary on Gen 3:13–16 since 3:16 (NASB) states, "I will greatly multiply your pain in childbirth. In pain you shall bring forth children." The LXX gives even greater stress on the pain at childbirth: "I will greatly multiply your pains and your groanings. In pain you shall bring forth [τέξῃ] children." Both the verb "to give birth" (τίκτω) and the stress on pains and groanings make it clear that childbirth is in view, not childbearing as a drawn-out process. The gospel narratives repeatedly use the same verb τίκτω, "to give birth," to identify the birth of Jesus (Matt 1:21, 23, 25; 2:2; Luke 1:31; 2:6, 7, 11; cf. Rev 12:2, 4, 5, 13). They associate his birth with his saving work in Luke 2:11, "there has been born for you a Savior, who is Christ the Lord," and

---

56. Cf. Porter, "Saved by Childbirth," 96 and n. 28.
57. Schreiner, "Dialogue," WCA 116.
58. Marshall, *Pastoral Epistles*, 468 n. 190.
59. *Pace* BDAG 994, τεκνογονία ("the bearing of children").
60. Cf. Wallace, *Grammar*, 206–31, especially the "Monadic ('One of a Kind' or 'Unique' Article)" use, as in "*the* Christ," 223–24.

Matt 1:21, "She will give birth to a son, and you are to give him the name Jesus, because he will save his people from their sins." The name Jesus, given at his birth, identifies his saving work. Neither LSJ or BDAG lists a noun form of the verb τίκτω, so τεκνογονία was the natural term to use to denote childbirth.

In the Genesis passage, the promise of the seed that will overcome the serpent is sandwiched in between the reference to the woman's deception in 3:13 and God's prediction of the consequences of the fall on woman in 3:16, including "you will bring forth children [τέξῃ τέκνα] in pain." Paul's citation of both the deception and fall followed by his contrasting, "but she will be saved through the childbirth [διὰ τῆς τεκνογονίας]," makes it natural to associate "the childbirth" with the birth of the Christ, the seed of the woman.

Genesis 3:15 identifies a particular male descendant of the woman who will crush the head of the original serpent: "He [הוא singular masculine pronoun] will crush your head." The verb "he will crush you" (יְשׁוּפְךָ) also specifies a singular masculine subject and a singular masculine object. The LXX further supports a messianic understanding of Gen 3:15. Although the independent personal pronoun "he" (הוּא) occurs over one hundred times in the MT, Hamilton notes that this is the only one that the LXX translates literally with the masculine αὐτός. This is particularly noteworthy since "seed" (σπέρμα) is neuter, so Greek idiom should require the neuter instead.[61] The verb "you [the serpent] will strike him [the seed] (תְּשׁוּפֶנּוּ)" also specifies a singular masculine subject and a singular masculine object. This clause, then, restricts the meaning of "seed" in this instance to one particular descendant and highlights it as a specific prophecy.

Another distinctive feature of Gen 3:15 is its use of "her seed" (זַרְעָהּ). Hebrew typically identifies the seed of a man, as in "the seed of Abraham" or of Isaac, Jacob, or Aaron. In the Pentateuch, זֶרַע (LXX almost always = σπέρμα) is used seventy-four times to identify the seed of a man, but only three times to identify the seed of a woman. The close association of "seed" with men is evident in its use in Hebrew for semen (BDB 282 cites: Lev 15:16, 17, 18, 32; 18:20; 19:20; 22:4; Num 5:13). Quell notes that

---

61. Hamilton, *Genesis Chapters 1–17*, 199. Cf. R. A. Martin, "The Earliest Messianic Interpretation of Genesis 3:15," *JBL* 84 (1965): 425–27; Walter C. Kaiser Jr., *Toward an Old Testament Theology* (Grand Rapids: Zondervan, 1978): 36–37. Kaiser argues that the word "seed" is flexible enough to denote both a group of descendants and an individual who is representative of that group.

the bitter water testing in Num 5:28 uses the Niphʿal passive of the verb זרע: "she shall be provided with seed."[62] Similarly, the daughters of Lot determined to "preserve seed from our father (מֵאָבִינוּ)" (Gen 19:32, 34), specifying their father to be the source of the seed. In Lev 22:13, a childless woman is referred to as one to (ל) whom there is no seed. In Gen 38:8–9, it is the brother of the deceased who is commanded to "raise up seed for your brother."

There appear to be only two passages outside of Gen 3:15 in the Pentateuch where the noun "seed" is identified as belonging to a woman, and both use the expression "your seed." In Gen 16:10, it refers to Hagar's descendants, but the text explicitly states that Abram is responsible (16:2–5), so clearly "your seed" refers to her descendants through Abram. In 24:60, it refers to the descendants of Rebekah as a result of Isaac taking her as his wife (24:67). Genesis 3:15 is the only instance in the Pentateuch where "seed" has the feminine suffix: (זַרְעָהּ). Since the curse in 3:14–15 is addressed to the serpent, the verse would have made just as good sense if the seed had been identified as Adam's seed, "his seed" or "their seed" (with both human parents in view).

Thus, although there is no lexical reason why "her seed," if it meant "descendants," could not be used of a woman, the fact that *"her* seed" occurs nowhere else in the Pentateuch and is not demanded by the narrative itself makes its occurrence here noteworthy. In the christological context of the prediction of the serpent being overcome, "her seed" is uniquely appropriate since the Gospels teach that there was no male seed involved in Christ's birth. The expression "her seed" fits the virgin birth of Christ perfectly.[63] It is sufficiently exceptional in contrast to the usual association of seed with males that there is ample textual basis for regarding this as a Messianic prophecy, especially with the emphasis on the singular male seed overcoming "the" serpent in the context of hope in spite of the fall. Christ

---

62. *TDNT* 7:539. Cf. BDB 282, "semen virile … *she shall be made pregnant* with seed"; *HALOT* 1:282, "to be allowed to be impregnated." The verb זרע is also used of a woman conceiving in Lev 12:2.
63. Cf. C. F. Keil and F. Delitzsch, *Commentary on the Old Testament* (trans. James Martin; Grand Rapids: Eerdmans, n.d.), 1:10, 102. Fee's objection in *1 and 2 Timothy, Titus*, 38 that Jews do not interpret Gen 3:15 messianically does not remove the clear textual basis for this understanding. Those who recognize Jesus as the Messiah have a framework that facilitates recognition of Gen 3:15 as a messianic prediction.

is the singular seed of the woman, born of Mary with no human father, who through the cross and resurrection overcame Satan, crushing his head.

Did Paul regard Christ as the promised "seed" prophesied in Gen 3:15? In Gal 3:16 and 19 he argues, "The Scripture does not say 'and to seeds,' meaning many people, but 'and to your seed,' meaning one person, who is Christ ... the Seed to whom the promise referred." Three times in this passage Paul refers to Christ as the promised seed using the singular with an article, twice in Gal 3:16 (τῷ σπέρματι) and again in 3:19 (τὸ σπέρμα). Although this passage is about the seed of Abraham, the promised seed is linked to the fall: "the whole world is a prisoner of sin, so that what was promised, being given through faith in Jesus Christ, might be given to those who believe" (3:22). This passage goes on to affirm the oneness of male and female in Christ (3:28) and that Christ was "born of woman" (4:4).

Paul's references to Christ as "the seed of David" in Rom 1:3 and 2 Tim 2:8 show that he believed in the continuity of the promise of the Seed. Furthermore, Paul describes Christ as the one who reverses the effects of the fall in 1 Cor 15:21–26: "For since death came through a man, the resurrection of the dead comes also through a man. For as in Adam all die, so in Christ all will be made alive.... Then the end will come ... [after] he has put all his enemies under his feet. The last enemy to be destroyed is death."

Is there anything in the context of 1 Tim 2 that prepares the reader for an allusion to salvation through Jesus at the crucial time of fulfillment? Indeed, does this context even mention the Savior? Yes! Not only is this implicit in the use of "to save" (σῴζω) in 1 Tim 2:15, but 1 Tim 2:3–6 had just affirmed, "For this is good, and pleases God our Savior, who wants all people to be saved and to come to a knowledge of the truth. For there is one God and one mediator between God and human beings, the man Christ Jesus, who gave himself as a ransom for all people, the testimony given at the crucial time of fulfillment [καιρός]." Similarly, Titus 1:2–3 identifies "the hope of eternal life, which God, who does not lie, promised before the beginning of time, and at his appointed season [καιρός] he brought his word to light."

Paul specifically associates the birth of Jesus by a woman in Gal 4:4 as the crucial time of fulfillment: "But when the time had fully come, God sent his Son, born of woman [γενόμενον ἐκ γυναικός], born under the law, to redeem those under the law" (4:4–5).[64] "Born of a woman" is not essential to the sentence, but its inclusion proves that Paul regarded this as an important part of Christ being the promised seed (3:16, 19), who saves the world from its imprisonment to sin (3:22; 4:3). This same concern with salvation through the incarnation was also earlier introduced in 1 Tim 1:15, "Christ Jesus came into the world to save sinners," and is reiterated in 2 Tim 1:10 as reversing the fall: grace "has been revealed through the appearing [διὰ τῆς ἐπιφανείας] of our Savior, Jesus Christ, who has destroyed death."[65]

The normal mediatorial sense of διά,[66] "she shall be saved through the childbirth," fits the incarnation of Christ, the event through which the Savior came, the event that mediated salvation. It is not a "messianic typology."[67] Rather, "saved through the childbirth" parallels "saved through faith" and "saved through the gospel," both of which also literally mediate salvation to believers. It does not change this basic meaning if "the childbirth" is also viewed as a synecdoche representing the whole of the Christ event. The Pauline epistles repeatedly speak of the whole of Christ's work through a representative part[68] introduced with διά.[69]

Paul evidently chose the particular expression "the childbirth" (as opposed to simply "Christ") in order to highlight the positive role of woman in salvation and to counterbalance his immediately preceding citation of her negative role in the fall. This affirmation counters the common low view of woman because of her part in the fall (e.g., Sir 25:24). This fits Paul's pattern of balancing criticism of women with affirmation in this passage:

---

64. This redemption is for those described in Gal 4:3 as "under the basic principles of the world." In light of the description of these principles as "weak and miserable" in 4:9, this is a possible allusion to the elemental principles of sinful humanity as alienated from God through the fall; cf. Rom 5:18; 1 Cor 15:22 and this use of "the world" in Gal 6:14 and 2 Cor 7:10.

65. *Pace* Fee, *1 and 2 Timothy, Titus,* 38, "Paul nowhere else suggests that salvation is by the Incarnation." Schreiner, "Dialogue," *WCA* 116, repeats this error.

66. E.g., Robertson, *Grammar,* 567, 580–83; Wallace, *Grammar,* 368. Direct means, however, is more clearly conveyed by ὑπό, as its contrast with διά in Matt 1:22 shows; cf. Robertson, *Grammar,* 582.

67. *Pace* Köstenberger, "God-Ordained Roles," 118, 138. Richard N. Longenecker, *Paul, Apostle of Liberty* (New York: Harper & Row, 1964), 93, observes regarding Paul's statements about Adam and Eve, "The Apostle is not allegorizing; he is identifying. For him the experience of Adam was an historical reality."

68. E.g., "the cross" (Gal 5:11), "justified by his blood" (Rom 5:9), "saved by his life" (Rom 5:10), "saved through faith" (Eph 2:8).

69. E.g., "inheritance ... through [διά] a promise" (Gal 3:18), "reconciled through the [διὰ τοῦ] death of his Son" (Rom 5:10), "through the [διὰ τῆς] obedience of the one man the many will be made righteous" (5:19), "grace might reign through [διά] righteousness" (5:21), "through [διά] which [the gospel] you are saved" (1 Cor 15:2), and "he saved us through [διά] [the] washing of rebirth and renewal by the Holy Spirit, whom he poured out on us generously [διά] through Jesus Christ our Savior" (Titus 3:5–6).

"good deeds appropriate for women" in 1 Tim 2:10, "let woman learn" in 2:11, and "then Eve [was formed]" in 2:13.

The objection that "the childbirth" is too vague to be a reference to the incarnation does not take into account that this epistle is addressed to Timothy, a minister Paul trained. Timothy would have known Paul's theology of Christ as the second Adam counteracting the results of the fall.[70] Paul's writings are filled with OT allusions and affirmations that Christ is the fulfillment of OT prophecies. Ironically, some who affirm that Paul authored the Pastoral Epistles write as though they teach non-Pauline theology[71] or that one must not expect typical Pauline creative use of language in the Pastoral Epistles. They treat this vibrant letter as though it were a second-century product of fossilized Christianity.

There is ample precedent for expecting to find Paul's high Christology and creative use of language in the Pastoral Epistles. For example, 1 Tim 1:17 and 2:3–6 display a remarkable breadth of salvific vision, and Titus 2:3 contains a word coined to affirm women: "καλοδιδάσκολοι," teachers of what is excellent. The same vitality that created new meaning for expressions like "the body," "in Christ," "the seed," and "the coming" can use "the childbirth" to refer to Christ. If τεκνογονίας were unreadable in ancient texts of 1 Tim 2:15, readers would assume that it must have something to do with Christ: " ... will be saved through _____, if they continue in faith, love and holiness with propriety."

Some say Paul must be talking about childbirth because he wants young widows in Ephesus to marry and have children. Up to this point in the letter, however, there is no mention of marriage or having children. It is the "straightforward interpretation" of women being saved through childbirth that reads back into this passage material its recipient had yet to read. Paul did not prepare his addressee, Timothy, for a novel teaching that women will be saved through bearing children, but 1 Tim 2:3–6 does establish the central focus on Christ coming to save at the critical time. Paul's immediately prior statements in 2:14 about Eve's deception (citing Gen 3:13 ἡ γυνή ... ἠπάτησέν) and fall set the framework for

---

70. E.g., Rom 5:12–19; 1 Cor 15:21–22, 45–49. E. Earle Ellis, *Paul's Use of the Old Testament* (Grand Rapids: Baker, 1957), 125, calls Paul's Adam-Christ typology "the scaffolding for his doctrine of redemption."

71. E.g., Richard I. Pervo, "Social and Religious Aspects of the 'Western' Text," in *The Living Text: Essays in Honor of Ernest W. Saunders* (ed. Dennis E. Groh and Robert Jewett; New York: Univ. Press of America, 1985), 229–41 (esp. 239).

understanding the future salvation through "the childbirth." The singular "she will be saved" highlights continued reference to Eve's story, which highlights the promised seed of the woman who will overcome Satan (Gen 3:15).

Various early church fathers use the expression "the child-bearing" with an article to represent the incarnation. Ignatius, *Eph.* 19:1, written on the way to his martyrdom c. AD 110,[72] identifies the birth of Jesus as ὁ τοκετός, "the child-bearing": "hidden from the prince of this world were the virginity of Mary and her child-bearing and likewise also the death of the Lord—these three mysteries."[73] It was commonplace among the church fathers to compare the fall through Eve to the coming of the Savior through Mary.[74]

Even though it is not provable that any particular citation that closely parallels the logic of 1 Tim 2:14–15 was based on these verses, this seems probable both in Theophylact's identification of the childbirth (τεκνογονίαν) with "the birth of God" and Cramer's catena to an anonymous ancient author who identified the interpretation that "she shall be saved" through the one born through her, the Christ.[75] It is indisputable

---

72. J. B. Lightfoot, *The Apostolic Fathers* (London: Macmillan, 1891), 55.

73. Ibid., 67–68.

74. Justin Martyr (c. AD 153): "He became man by the Virgin, in order that the disobedience which proceeded from the serpent might receive its destruction in the same manner in which it derived its origin. For Eve, who was a virgin and undefiled, having conceived the word of the serpent, brought forth disobedience and death. But the Virgin Mary received faith ... the Holy Thing begotten of her is the Son of God ... by her He has been born" (*Dialogue with Trypho* 100; ANF 1:249); Tertullian (c. AD 160–220), "the ensnaring word had crept into her [Eve's] ear which was to build the edifice of death ... so that what was reduced to ruin by this sex, might by the selfsame sex be recovered to salvation. As Eve had believed the serpent, so Mary believed the angel. The delinquency which the one occasioned by believing, the other by believing effaced.... Mary, on the contrary, bare one who was one day to secure salvation.... God therefore sent down into the virgin's womb His Word ... it was necessary that Christ should come forth for the salvation of man, in that condition of flesh into which man had entered ever since his condemnation" (*de carne*, 41.17; ANF 3:536); Irenaeus, *Haer.* 3.22.4 (written c. AD 175–195) states, "Eve having become disobedient, was made the cause of death, both to herself and to the entire human race; so Mary ... became the cause of salvation ... both to herself and to the entire human race." Irenaeus, *Haer.* 5.19, using a similar construction, contrasts the fall through Eve to salvation through the Virgin Mary ("salvetur per virginem" SC 34, 380ff.); cf. similarly his *Demonstration* 33. Many other fathers contrasted the position of woman in the fall and in salvation: Origen, PG 13:1819; Cyril of Alexandria, PG 72:941; Hippolytus, GCS 1, 1, 354–55; Ambrose, PL 15:1843ff.; PL 16:327–29; Augustine, PL 38:1108; PL 40:186; Gregory the Great, PL 76:1194.

75. Theophylact: τινὲς δὲ οὐκ οἶδ᾽ ὅπως τεκνογονίαν ἐνόησαν τὴν τῆς θεοτόκου, and Cramer vii.22: ἄλλος φησίν· σώζεται τὸ γυναικεῖον γένος, καὶ πᾶσα δὲ ἡ τῶν ἀνθρώπων φύσις, διὰ τοῦ ἐξ αὐτῆς κατὰ σάρκα τικτομένου Χριστοῦ are cited in H. B. Swete, *Theodori Episcopi Mopsuesteni in Epistolas B. Pauli Commentarii. The Latin Version with the Greek Fragments* (2 vols.; Cambridge: Cambridge Univ. Press, 1882), 2:96.

that the early church had a keen interest in the contrast between the fall through Eve's deception and the coming of Christ through Mary to overcome Satan and reverse the effects of the fall. Thus, the conceptual framework for understanding "the childbirth" as a reference to the birth of Christ is evident in Paul's writings, in other books of the NT,[76] and throughout the early church fathers.

By affirming that God became incarnate through a woman, this passage ennobles all women and their role in childbirth. The christological interpretation gives a far deeper and theologically based affirmation of woman's role in childbirth than the interpretation that "childbearing" is a generic reference to a biological or sociological role. First Timothy 2:15 is not simply a call to a role; it is a call to the Savior. Mary's bearing of the Christ was the highest role any human has ever taken. It ennobles women and their role in childbirth in a way that dwarfs and counteracts the appeal of the false teachers and undermines their repudiation of marriage.

The Conditions of 1 Timothy 2:15 Fit Spiritual Salvation

In order to experience the salvation Christ provides, Eve's descendents must abide in faith. Paul uses the plural because he includes Eve's descendents in Eve, so named "because she would be the mother of all the living" (Gen 3:20), just as he includes "the many" in Adam in Rom 5:19. The grammatical shift from singular to plural is a direct reflection of the Genesis narrative's reference to the woman giving birth to children (plural τέκνα = בָּנִים) in 3:16 and so itself includes a shift from one representative woman to her descendents. Eve is representative, so the salvation that her seed will provide may apply both to her and to her offspring. Paul's use of "the childbirth" implies Mary's role at the culmination of that messianic line, the one through whom that messianic seed is born.

The implication of Mary inevitably expands the scope of those in view beyond Eve and adds to the appropriateness of the shift from singular to plural. In 1 Tim 2:9–15, Paul is specifically concerned with one segment of Eve's offspring: the deceived women in Ephesus. He encourages them by affirming woman's role in bearing the Savior but warns them that their

---

76. Besides the detailed treatments of Mary's miraculous birth of Christ in the Gospels, Rev 12:1–6 describes a woman who "gave birth to a son, a male child, who will rule all the nations" as a "great and wondrous sign."

salvation is contingent on their continuing in faith, love, and holiness with propriety. The verb "continue" can apply only to believers. If children were in view one would expect instead, "if they are brought to faith."[77] Nor would "continue" apply to unbelieving husbands. Consequently, "if they continue" most naturally applies to believers, and in particular, believing women in the Ephesian church.

The first condition for their spiritual salvation is that they continue in faith. Throughout this epistle, "faith" is centered on Christ, life in Christ, or one's membership in Christ.[78] The fact that their salvation is contingent on faith confirms that the salvation is spiritual, not physical. The second condition for their spiritual salvation is that they continue in love, the central defining mark of a Christian. The third is that they continue in holiness. Paul regards holiness[79] as an inevitable result of the work of the Holy Spirit. Salvation "through the childbirth," if it points to woman's role in bearing the Savior, perfectly fits these contingencies on faith, love, and holiness, but these do not fit the translations "safety" or "preservation" through childbirth.[80]

Paul adds "with propriety" to counteract socially unacceptable behavior here just as in 1 Tim 2:9 (cf. 1 Cor 11:3–16).[81] For women to assume for themselves teaching authority over men was disrespectful, not acting "with propriety." Paul calls women away from the allure of the false teachers and following after Satan to a life of propriety in Christ. In rejecting propriety, they were rejecting the salvation that Christ provided. Paul is not saying here that women are saved by being proper. Rather, they are saved by Christ, the incarnation, "the childbirth." But if they leave the faith, love, and holiness of Christ to follow the false teachers, they will no longer be continuing in the faith, but will jeopardize their salvation like the women who turned away to follow Satan (1 Tim 5:15). Paul is not advocating legalism to the women of Ephesus: bear children, be good. Instead, he is pointing them to ennobling life in Christ, who alone saves.

---

77. Marshall, *Pastoral Epistles*, 471.
78. Centered on Christ: 1 Tim 1:14; 2:5–7; 3:9, 13; 4:6; 5:11–12; life in Christ: 1:4, 5, 19; 4:12; 6:11–12; membership in Christ: 1:2, 19; 2:15; 3:9; 4:1; 5:8; 6:10, 12, 21.
79. This word occurs eight times in the Pauline corpus but only twice in the rest of the NT (Rom 6:19, 22; 1 Cor 1:30; 1 Thess 4:3, 4, 7; 2 Thess 2:13; 1 Tim 2:15; Heb 12:14; 1 Pet 1:2). This adds evidence for authorship by Paul.
80. Cf. J. L. Houlden, *The Pastoral Epistles I and II Timothy, Titus* (London: SCM, 1976), 72.
81. Cf. K. O. Sanders, "' … et liv som vinner respekt.' Et sentrait perspektiv på 1 Tim 2:11–15," *TTKi* 59 (Oslo, 1988): 2:97–108 (K. O. Sanders, "' … a Respectful Life': A Central Perspective in 1 Tim 2:11–15").

23

1 TIMOTHY 2:8 – 15: CONCLUSION

The central purpose of 1 Timothy is to counter false teaching in the church in Ephesus. Some women in the church in Ephesus were so influenced by false teaching they had "in fact already turned away to follow Satan" (5:15). Some were "idle and going about from house to house" and, like the false teachers (1:6; 6:20; 2 Tim 2:23), were speaking nonsense (φλύαροι 5:13) and "saying things they ought not" (5:13).

Consequently, Paul calls women to "good deeds" (2:10), and in order to counter their deception he commands, "Let women learn in quietness and all submission" (2:11). To stop the group most influenced by the false teachers from teaching in church assemblies (where men would be present), he adds, "I am not permitting a woman to teach and [in combination with this, as shown by Paul's typical use of οὐδέ] to assume authority over a man, but to be in quietness" (2:12). "To assume authority" is the only confirmed meaning of αὐθεντέω in Paul's day other than its component parts, "self-achieving." In contrast, there are no unambiguous instances of this word meaning "to have authority" until several centuries after Paul. Given this understanding, Paul prohibited women from doing exactly what the false teachers were doing, namely, assuming authority to teach in church assemblies.

Paul gives two reasons or explanations for this restriction on women assuming authority to teach men. First, it would typically convey disrespect to man, woman's source in creation, for Eve was taken out of Adam, who was formed first (2:13; 1 Cor 11:8, 12). Second, Eve's deception (2:14) epitomizes how serious the consequences can be when a woman is deceived by a false teacher and conveys the false teaching to a man.

Throughout this passage Paul repeatedly affirms women. He encourages women to engage in good works (2:9). He commands them to learn (2:11). He affirms for the first time in surviving literature that Eve, like Adam, was "formed" by God (2:13), in effect equalizing their status, as he did in 1 Cor 11:11–12. He affirms that it was through woman that "the childbirth" brought into the world Christ the Savior, through whom women experience salvation if they continue in faith, love, and holiness (2:15). "The childbirth" makes best sense in this context as a synecdoche referring to Jesus.

This exegesis argues that 1 Tim 2:12 does not support a universal prohibition of women teaching or having authority over men. Nothing in this passage states that women are inherently unsuited to teach or exercise authority over men in spiritual or any other matters. Nor does Paul universalize this particular prohibition for all churches and all times. This passage, therefore, does not conflict with the scriptural record of women in Paul's circle of ministry who, like Phoebe, Priscilla, Junia, Euodia, and Syntyche, held leadership positions in the church. Solid exegesis does not warrant using 1 Tim 2:8–15 as a blanket prohibition against women teaching in the church or holding positions of authority over men.

24

1 TIMOTHY 3:1–13 AND TITUS 1:5–9: MAY WOMEN BE OVERSEERS AND DEACONS?

If it were Paul's intention that women should forever be excluded from teaching and from positions of authority in the church, there is no more natural place in all his letters for him to have said so than in the immediately following passage listing requirements for overseers and deacons, 1 Tim 3:1–13. Unfortunately, practically all English versions of 1 Tim 3:1–13 and Titus 1:5–9 give the false impression that Paul uses masculine pronouns,[1] implying that these church leaders must be male. In Greek, however, there is not even one masculine pronoun or "men only" requirement for the offices of overseer and deacon in 1 Tim 3:1–12 or elder in Titus 1:5–9. The following analysis lays out evidence that women can fulfill the requirements for the church offices in 1 Tim 3:1–12 and Titus 1:5–9 and that none of these requirements excludes women from either office.

Some object that "one woman man" in 1 Tim 3:2, 12, and Titus 1:6 excludes women from being overseers, deacons, or elders. Most scholars, however, understand it to exclude polygamists[2] and probably also any man

---

1. The NIV and NAB insert 14 masculine pronouns into 1 Tim 3:1–12, the JB 13, the RSV 10, the NRSV 9, and the NASB 9, which also inserts "If any man" into 1 Tim 3:1, where there is no "man" in the Greek. The NIV adds, "Deacons, likewise are to be men," where there is no word for "men" in the Greek of 1 Tim 3:8. In 1 Tim 3:1–12 the NAB and NEB also add "man" or "men" four times, the JB three times, the RSV once. Only the CEV is faithful to the Greek in not adding a single masculine pronoun, "man" or "men" to either 1 Tim 3:1–12 or Titus 1:5–9.
2. E.g., Grudem, EF 80, with references to Josephus and rabbinic literature.

446 ᴏᴿ ᴍᴀɴ ᴀɴᴅ ᴡᴏᴍᴀɴ

not living in sexual fidelity to his wife.[3] So, for instance, Chrysostom's *Homily on 1 Tim 3:2* states, "This he does not lay down as a rule, as if he [an overseer] must not be without one [a wife], but as prohibiting his having more than one."[4] Consequently, "one woman man" functions as an exclusion of polygamists and probably adulterers, not a requirement that must describe every overseer. Presumably the reason Paul did not include "one man woman" in these passages is the same reason he did not include it with the other requirements for women deacons in verse 11. Polyandry was rare, if practiced at all in Ephesus, and husbands were regarded as more likely to be sexually unfaithful than their wives.

Some of Paul's descriptions of church leaders are requirements for all office holders; others are not, but instead describe specific categories of people as ineligible. Three other examples of exclusions involve children: "having children in subjection with all respect" (1 Tim 3:4), "ruling children and their own households well" (v. 12), and "having children who believe" (Titus 1:6). If these clauses about children are requirements for all overseers, deacons, and elders, then only married people with at least two children old enough to believe would be eligible. This was surely not Paul's intention. Paul implies that he is not married in 1 Cor 7:7, and he encourages single believers not to marry but to be devoted to the Lord in 1 Cor 7:27–28, 32–35. Consequently, if this were a requirement for all overseers and deacons, not even Paul, as single, would qualify to be an overseer or a deacon, even though his actions epitomize church oversight and he calls himself "διάκονος" seven times in his NT letters.[5]

Because Marshall misses the crucial distinction between required trait and exclusion and interprets "household" to imply "servants/slaves," he concludes from 1 Tim 3:12 ("managing children and household well") that "slaves are not envisaged as church leaders!" and "it is assumed that householders are appointed to the task of ἐπίσκοπος."[6] Yet Ignatius, who was strongly influenced by Paul and was martyred in the reign of Trajan (AD 98–117), in *Eph.* 1:3 identifies Onesimus (a slave name) as bishop of

---

3. A man having sexual relations with a woman other than his wife could hardly be called a "one woman man." Fidelity is almost certainly also entailed in the "one man woman" requirement in 1 Tim 5:9. It would be culturally irrelevant if it excluded only polyandry.
4. NPNF[1] 13:438.
5. 1 Cor 3:5; 2 Cor 3:6; 6:4; 11:23; Eph 3:7; Col 1:23, 25.
6. Marshall, *Pastoral Epistles*, 495, 479.

Ephesus, and Pliny *Ep.* 10.96 (AD 112) identifies "two female slaves, who were styled *deaconesses* (ministrae)"[7] whom he tortured. Paul's clause does imply the importance of leadership skills for church office, but it does not imply that being the manager of a household or of slaves is a requirement for church office.

Since "one woman man" is a set phrase that functions as an exclusion, any claim that a single word of it ("man") also functions separately as a requirement must posit a double meaning. This is not warranted by the context. It is bad hermeneutics to isolate a single word ("man") from a set phrase ("one woman man") that functions as an exclusion (of polygamists and probably adulterous husbands) and to elevate that single word to the status of an independent requirement (that all overseers be men).

Grudem is correct to recognize "one woman man" as an exclusion and so to conclude that "this expression is not intended to rule out a single man (such as Jesus or Paul) from being an elder,"[8] but he is self-contradictory in calling it a necessary qualification for office and misrepresents the text by adding "each" where there is none in the Greek of 1 Tim 3:12,[9] leading to his faulty conclusion that this is a "qualification that could not be true of women ... for a woman could not be a 'husband.'"[10] If Grudem is permitted to dismember "one woman man" and arbitrarily designate one word of it out of context as a new requirement, what is to keep one from isolating "one's own house" from "ruling one's own house well" (3:4 – 5) and designate home ownership or rule of a household as a new requirement for overseers? Moo, in contrast, acknowledges that this phrase need not exclude "unmarried men or females from the office ... it would be going too far to argue that the phrase clearly excludes women."[11]

Paul gives eight confirmations that "one woman man" does not exclude women:

---

7. William Melmoth, trans., *Pliny Letters*, 2:404 – 5 (LCL).
8. Grudem, *EF* 80.
9. Ibid., 263 n. 107, "Let deacons each be the husband of one wife." By adding "each," he treats this as a requirement for all, not an exclusion of some, and so contradicts his inclusion of single men.
10. Ibid., 263 n. 107; cf. p. 80, "elders had to be men."
11. Moo, "Rejoinder," 211, but his following assertion "it *does* suggest that Paul had men in mind while he wrote" applies properly only to Paul's having in mind the exclusion of particular men, not that he had in mind a requirement that all overseers must be men.

1. Paul affirms "anyone [τις] who desires the office of overseer desires a good work" (3:1, 5). Would Paul encourage women to desire an office, as these words do, if it were prohibited to them?

2. All seventeen requirements for elders in Titus 1:6–9, "called overseers," correspond to requirements in 1 Tim 3:1–7, six using identical words, including the two exclusions, "one woman man" and "having children" who do not discredit the faith.[12] Both lists come from the same author at approximately the same time. Consequently, one should interpret identical requirements in these two lists as having the same meaning. Titus 1:6 states that these qualifications apply to "anyone": "if anyone [τις] is above reproach." Several factors in Titus 1:6–9 confirm that "anyone" does not exclude women. This passage contains no specification that clearly excludes women, and this letter does not specify any restrictions on how women may minister. Thus, in Titus 1:6, "one woman man" excludes polygamists and adulterers and is not a requirement that elders be men. Consequently, the identical phrase in 1 Tim 3:2 should not exclude women either.

3. In the Greek of 1 Tim 3:1–12 and Titus 1:6–9, there is not even one masculine pronoun.

4. Since the natural reading of 3:11 is that women can be deacons,[13] Paul must not have intended the immediately following clause, "Deacons shall be one woman men" (3:12), to exclude women.[14] Since "one woman men" does not exclude women from the office of deacon, this same phrase should not exclude women from the office of overseer either.

5. Paul in Rom 16:1 calls Phoebe, "deacon of the church of Cenchrea,"[15] so he believed women can be deacons. Thus, he would not intend "one woman men" to exclude women as deacons.

---

12. Μιᾶς γυναικὸς ἄνδρα/ἀνήρ, σώφρονα, φιλόξενον, μὴ πάροινον, μὴ πλήκτην, τέκνα ἔχοντα/ ἔχων.

13. This is argued below, pp. 454–59.

14. Moo, "Rejoinder," 211, asserts without evidence, "it is probable that he specifically addresses the *male* deacon in v 12." The subject of v. 12, however, is the inclusive term for deacons and consists of only two exclusions, neither a requirement, and v. 13 clearly affirms all deacons.

15. Cf. above, pp. 61–62.

6. Throughout church history, deacon ministry has prepared people for overseer ministry. Since Paul includes women as deacons, one would expect that they could become overseers, too.

7. The office of overseer requires someone "able to teach."[16] Paul lays the foundation for women to fulfill this requirement by writing "Let them learn" in 1 Tim 2:11. Titus 2:3 shows that women can teach, for it urges women to be "teachers of what is excellent."

8. The qualifications for the office of overseer apply to women as well as to men. First Timothy mentions verbal or conceptual parallels to each of the overseer requirements in passages specifically regarding women. Close to half of these parallels use nearly identical terminology, most of the others use synonymous expressions, and the rest affirm the opposite of a forbidden characteristic. These show that in Paul's thinking at the time he writes this letter, these qualifications not only can, but in fact do, apply to women.

The first two columns in the following table identify the nine words or expressions that describe overseers and that are applied to women in nearly identical terminology in 1 Timothy. The third column lists the number of times each expression occurs in the Pauline corpus. The three columns on the far right of the table identify the probability of this happening for each word or expression based on their random distribution in the Pauline epistles, the Pastoral Epistles, or the combination of Paul's and Luke's writings. Which probability set best describes the vocabulary of the author(s) depends on whether or not Paul wrote the Pastoral Epistles or if Luke wrote it as Paul's scribe.

---

16. This does not require that all overseers teach or specialize in teaching. 1 Tim 5:17 states, "The elders who direct the affairs of the church well are worthy of double honor, especially those whose work is preaching and teaching."

Table: Nearly Identical Terminology Used of Women and of Overseers in 1 Timothy

Overseer Description	Nearly identical terminology about women in 1 Timothy	Pauline hits[17]	Pauline odds[18]	Pastorals odds[19]	Paul+Luke odds[20]
3:1 καλοῦ ἔργου	5:10 ἔργοις καλοῖς[21] (cf. 2:10)	8[22]	8/113	8/14	8/258
3:2 ἀνεπίλημπτον	5:7 ἀνεπίλημπτοι	3	3/113	3/14	3/258
μιᾶς γυναικὸς ἄνδρα	5:9 ἑνὸς ἀνδρὸς γυνή[23]	4	4/113	4/14	4/258
νηφάλιον	3:11 νηφαλίους	3	3/113	3/14	3/258
σώφρονα	2:9, 15 σωφροσύνης	12[24]	12/113	6/14	14[25]/258
κόσμιον	2:9 κοσμίῳ	2	2/113	2/14	2/258
3:4 σεμνότητος	3:11 σεμνάς	7	7/113	6/14	7/258
3:6 κρίμα	5:12 κρίμα	12	12/113	2/14	16[26]/258
3:7 μαρτυρίαν καλήν	5:10 καλοῖς μαρτυρουμένη	3	3/113	3/14	3/258

---

17. These figures are based on Moulton and Geden's *Concordance to the Greek Testament*.
18. These odds are calculated as follows: There are 36 lines of Greek text in the Nestle-Aland 27th edition explicitly about women in 1 Timothy (2:9–15; 3:11; 5:2–7, 9–16) out of a total of 4,070 lines in the NA[27] Pauline epistles. Therefore, these verses about women in 1 Timothy comprise almost exactly 1/113 of the Pauline epistles. Thus, the total occurrences of each expression divided by 113 gives the odds that in a random distribution throughout the Pauline epistles this expression would occur in the 36 lines of 1 Timothy explicitly about women.

The probability based on random distribution, of all of these words and expressions also occurring in the thirty-six lines of 1 Timothy explicitly about women is the product of each of the separate odds for the appropriate columns. The probability of this occurring in:

- the Pauline corpus is approximately five in one trillion (10^{12} = 1,000,000,000,000),
- the Pastoral Epistles is approximately six in one million (10^{6} = 1,000,000),
- Paul's + Luke's corpus is approximately two in ten quadrillion (10^{16} = 10,000,000,000,000,000).

The use of so much identical terminology in the verses explicitly about women in 1 Timothy is statistically so improbable that it makes sense that Paul deliberately described women with these words, presumably to show that women could and should fulfill these requirements. Moo writes that the statistical picture "would be meaningful only if calculated on the basis of the unique vocabulary of the Pastorals."[27] Statistical probability even for

---

19. Cf. n. 18. There are 516 lines in the NA[27] Pastoral Epistles. Therefore, these verses about women in 1 Timothy comprise approximately 1/14 of the Pastoral Epistles. Thus, the total occurrences of each expression in the Pastoral Epistles divided by 14 gives the odds that in a random distribution throughout the Pastoral Epistles this expression would occur in the 36 lines of 1 Timothy explicitly about women.

20. Cf. n. 18. There are 4,070 lines in the NA[27] Pauline epistles plus approximately 5,210 lines of Greek in Luke–Acts, for a total of approximately 9,280 lines in the Pauline epistles plus Luke–Acts. Therefore, these verses about women in 1 Timothy comprise approximately 1/258 of the Pauline epistles plus Luke and Acts. Thus, the total occurrences of each expression in the Pauline epistles plus Luke and Acts divided by 258 gives the odds that in a random distribution throughout the Pauline epistles plus Luke and Acts this expression would occur in the 36 lines of 1 Timothy explicitly about women.

21. Moo, "Rejoinder," 211, states that καλοῦ ἔργου, the good work of an overseer, is "not comparable" to the good works ἔργοις καλοῖς (5:10) of a woman. The latter is in the plural, but both refer to the same sorts of service and are expressed in the same Greek words, so there is no legitimate basis for excluding this parallel.

22. 1 Tim 3:1; 5:10, 25; 6:18; Titus 2:7, 14; 3:8, 14.

23. Moo, "Rejoinder," 211, states that "one woman man" is "not comparable" to "one man woman" (5:9). Almost all interpreters, however, regard both to exclude sexual infidelity, as did Theodore of Mopsuestia 2.161, "If she has lived in chastity with her husband, no matter whether she has had only one, or whether she was married a second time." Since both are nearly identical in meaning and form, it would not be proper to exclude them. They show that the moral requirement demanded of an overseer can be fulfilled by a woman. Since Paul encourages young widows to remarry, it is unlikely that he intends this to exclude remarried women. Cf. Marshall, Pastoral Epistles, 594.

24. All occurrences of the σώφρων group including: σωφρονέω, σωφρονίζω, σωφρονισμός, σωφρόνως, σωφροσύνη, and σώφρων.

25. Luke–Acts adds Luke 8:35 and Acts 26:25 to the Pauline occurrences of the σώφρων group.

26. Luke/Acts adds Luke 20:47; 23:40; 24:20 and Acts 24:25 to the Pauline occurrences of κρίμα.

27. Moo, "Rejoinder," 211. Is it correct, however, to regard the situation of the Pastorals as so unique? There are close parallels between the false teaching in Ephesus and Corinth. All of

just the Pastorals is approximately six in one million, so the evidence is still overwhelming.

The above table does not include the following borderline cases where only part of a word or phrase describing overseers is used regarding women in 1 Timothy: "managing house well" (3:4 οἴκου καλῶς προϊστάμενον) means the same as "to manage house" (5:14 οἰκοδεσποτεῖν). "Having children in subjection" (3:4 τέκνα ἔχοντα ἐν ὑποταγῇ) is entailed in "to bear children, to manage house" (5:14 τεκνογονεῖν, οἰκοδεσποτεῖν). "Not a neophyte" (3:6 μὴ νεόφυτον) uses the same root term as "refuse younger women" (5:11 νεωτέρας ... παραιτοῦ). "Not addicted to much wine" (3:3 μὴ πάροινον) is equivalent to women being "sober" (3:11 νηφαλίους) and to older women "not addicted to much wine" (Titus 2:3 μὴ οἴνῳ πολλῷ δεδουλωμένας). These and other conceptual parallels decrease even further the likelihood that these parallels are just coincidental. It appears that the author of 1 Timothy intended to make it undeniable that these qualifications of overseers not only can, but in fact do, apply to women.

Grudem argues that women cannot be overseers since "the New Testament never uses *proistēmi* to speak of women 'managing' or governing a household, but only of men."[28] Paul does, however, use the even stronger word οἰκοδεσποτεῖν (lit., "to be house despots") in 1 Tim 5:14 to call younger widows to marry and to rule their homes. Thus, Paul calls both men and women, including married women, to manage their homes well. He is not assigning roles based on gender or limiting the authority of women. Grudem's statement about only men governing a household is false; the NT never uses προΐστημι to identify a man specifically as governing a household. Even where this verb is used of the church, as in Rom 12:8, it is expressed in a way that could apply to men and women. The NIV conceals this by adding "man" and eight masculine pronouns where none occur in the Greek of Rom 12:6–8. No NT passage using the verb "to rule" (προΐστημι) excludes women. In fact, the only NT use of the noun

Paul's letters have a similar aim of building up Christians in the faith. Moo's insistence that statistical probabilities must be limited to the Pastoral Epistles seems to imply that the vocabulary of the Pastorals is so foreign to Paul's vocabulary elsewhere that it cannot be statistically compared to his other letters. Ironically, on p. 198 of his "Rejoinder," Moo expressed his frustration with those who restrict what constitutes evidence to only part of Scripture.

28. Grudem, *EF* 263 n. 107; cf. p. 80, "elders had to be men."

form of this verb describes a woman, Phoebe, in Rom 16:2, "she has been a προστάτις of many people, including me.[29]

Does Paul's prohibition in 1 Tim 2:12 introduce a limitation into the requirements for overseer that would not have been apparent from those requirements alone? This might be possible if there were not so much evidence for the interpretation of 1 Tim 2:12 argued above and if there were no control passage, Titus 1:6–9, that anchors the meaning of identical terms in these two parallel lists.[30] The error of letting one's interpretation of 1 Tim 2:12 override the normal meaning of "anyone" in 1 Tim 3:1 and its parallel in Titus 1:6 can be exemplified by applying the same logic to the restriction placed on teaching in Titus. It would be unwarranted to override the normal meaning of "anyone" in Titus 1:6 in order to exclude members of the circumcision group from the office of elder on the basis of the fact that "members of the circumcision group ... must be silenced" (Titus 1:10–11). Correspondingly, it is unwarranted to override the normal meaning of "anyone" in 1 Tim 3:1 and 5 in order to exclude women from the office of overseer (especially for all time) on the basis of a debatable interpretation of the restriction on women teaching in 1 Tim 2:12 (especially since its verb is first person singular present indicative).

Some object that the NT nowhere identifies by name any woman in the church as an overseer. But, apart from one reference to Christ as "the Overseer of your souls" (1 Pet 2:25), the term for "overseer" used here (ἐπίσκοπος) is never used with the name of any man, either. It is always used of overseers in general: Acts 20:28; Phil 1:1; 1 Tim 3:2; and Titus 1:7. Paul's calling Phoebe a προστάτις ("leader") in Rom 16:2 seems roughly equivalent to "overseer."[31]

Why didn't Paul state requirements for women overseers as he did for women deacons in 3:11? It is clear from 1 Tim 2:12–15 that Paul was concerned enough about the false teachers' deception of women in Ephesus that he prohibited the women in Ephesus from assuming authority to teach men. He probably did not want to encourage these women to become overseers prematurely because of the false teachers' influence on them[32] and

---

29. Cf. above, pp. 62–63.
30. Even if there were not parallel requirements in Titus 1:6, one ought to search for an interpretation of 1 Tim 2:12 that is in harmony with 1 Tim 3:1–13, such as the interpretation for which the previous chapters argue.
31. Cf. above, pp. 62–63.
32. Cf. above, pp. 299–304.

because of the spiritual influence overseers have through teaching.[33] If he had included a list of requirements for women overseers as he did for deacons in 3:11, he would have provided a specific mechanism for women to attain a position of authority from which they could promote false teaching. In that case, deceived women might have used such a list as a basis for demanding the office of overseer, from which they could spread false teachings.

Nevertheless, one can be confident on the basis of 1 Cor 11:5–13 that Paul was not opposed to women communicating prophetic messages. Furthermore, Paul commands that women learn in 1 Tim 2:11, thereby providing the foundation for them to prepare to teach. In fact, 3:1, "Anyone desiring the office of overseer desires a good work," encourages women to aspire to be overseers. Paul repeats "anyone" in 3:5 and includes parallels to each requirement for overseer specifically about women in 1 Timothy. He thereby shows that women can fulfill all the requirements for the office of overseer.

FIRST TIMOTHY 3:8–13: DEACONS

In the midst of Paul's next section about deacons is a list of requirements for "women." It begins, "Women [γυναῖκας], similarly, must be worthy of respect," using the feminine form of the identical qualification in verse 8, "Deacons, similarly, must be worthy of respect." Ancient interpreters nearly universally regarded verse 11 as identifying women in church office,[34] as do most modern scholars.

Romans 16:1 shows that the NT makes no distinction between "deacons" and "deaconesses," a word used in the church only later.[35] E. K. Simpson perceptively notes that because "deacon" applied to both men and women at that time, "there was no need to repeat the appellation in regard to deaconesses."[36] Hurley writes that in Greek the expression "woman deacons" would be clumsy and that the position of verse 11 in the middle of

---

33. This is implied since overseers were required to be "able to teach" (1 Tim 3:2).
34. E.g., Chrysostom, *Homily on 1 Tim 3:11*, states, "He is speaking of those who hold the rank of Deaconesses" (NPNF¹13.438). So, too, Pliny, *Ep.* 10.96–97 (written AD 112): "*duabus ancillae quae ministrae dicebantur*"; *Didaskalia* (third century); Canon 19 of the Council of Nicea (AD 323); *Apostolic Constitutions* 2.26; 3.15 (fourth century); and these individuals: Theodoret, Theodore of Mopsuestia, Oecumenius, Grotius. Most major versions give this understanding: e.g., ASV, CEV, JB, NAB, NRSV, REB, RSV, TNIV; also Amplified, JND, Fenton, Way, Weymouth, Williams.
35. Cf. above, pp. 61–62, and below, pp. 455–59.
36. E. K. Simpson, *The Pastoral Epistles: The Greek Text with Introduction and Commentary* (London: Tyndale, 1954), 56.

qualifications for deacons makes such an expression unnecessary to identify women deacons.[37] J. N. D. Kelly correctly notes that the absence of the later term "deaconess" points to the primitiveness of this letter and argues for the translation as the less technical term, "women deacons."[38]

Many interpreters assume that "similarly" in 3:11 introduces a separate category of church office to be differentiated from both overseers and deacons, but if that were the case, its position in the middle of the section on deacons would be extraordinarily clumsy. It is, therefore, more likely that verse 11 designates a group within the larger category of deacons, namely, deacons who are women. Accordingly, J. A. Robinson concluded, "at Ephesus the Order included deacons of either sex."[39] Verse 11 ensures that women fulfill the same qualifications as men.

Many versions,[40] however, translate verse 11, "In the same way their wives are to be...." Like the understanding "women deacons," this translation avoids inserting a new category of church office in the middle of the section on deacons, but it is doubtful for eleven reasons:

1. To make that idea clear Paul would have to add "of deacons," "their," or some other expression indicating their wives such as "having wives" (cf. "having children" in 3:4).[41]

2. "Women similarly" in verse 11 exactly parallels "Deacons similarly" in verse 8, and so, as in the former case, is most naturally read, "Similarly the qualifications for women deacons are...." The parallel structure and the word "similarly" implies something parallel to "Deacons similarly." Both instances of "similarly" join parallel sets of qualifications: for overseers, deacons, and women deacons. Each case identifies a church office followed by qualifications that apply directly to its office holders. If, however, "women" is translated "their wives," the verse would not be similar either in identifying a church office or in listing qualifications for those

37. Hurley, *Man and Woman*, 232; cf. also Kent, *The Pastoral Epistles*, 135–36.
38. J. N. D. Kelly, *A Commentary on the Pastoral Epistles: I Timothy II Timothy Titus* (HNTC; New York: Harper & Row, 1963), 83–84.
39. "Deacon and Deaconess," *Encyclopædia Biblica* 1:1039; cf. Jouette M. Bassler, *1 Timothy, 2 Timothy, Titus* (ANTC; Nashville: Abingdon, 1996), 70.
40. E.g., Beck, Berkeley, New Berkeley, ESV, Goodspeed, HCSB, KJV, LB, Moffatt, NEB, NIV, Phillips, TNT.
41. As argued by B. L. Blackburn, "The Identity of the 'Women' in 1 Tim. 3.11," in *Essays on Women in Earliest Christianity* (ed. C. D. Osburn; Joplin: College Press, 1993), 1:303–19; 308–9; Marshall, *Pastoral Epistles*, 493.

office holders themselves (women deacons). Everything else in 3:1–13 addresses church officials' qualifications; nothing else is about their wives. Reinforcing this parallel structure, both sentences, "Deacons, similarly" (vv. 8–9) and "Women, similarly" (v. 11), have no verb, but rather presuppose the reapplication of "it is necessary for ... to be" (δεῖ ... εἶναι) from verse 2. All these parallels would be broken if "women" did not identify a group whose qualifications for office follow.

3. If γυναῖκας in 3:11 refers to wives, it is hard to explain why there is no similar qualification for the wives of overseers since their position was more influential and had stricter requirements. It would be more important for church reputation for the overseers' wives to be worthy of respect. Its position does not permit it to refer to overseers' wives as well as deacon's wives.[42]

4. In order to avoid objection 2, those who argue that verse 11 refers to the wives of deacons typically describe these wives going along with their husbands to perform deacon functions for other women. If, however, these wives join their husbands in diaconal ministry, then they should be recognized as deacons, not just deacons' wives. Furthermore, if the only women who can serve are deacons' wives, this requirement would disqualify all single women, all women whose husbands are not deacons, and all otherwise qualified men whose wives do not qualify. Most of the gifted women willing to do these tasks were not married to deacons. Consequently, restricting "women" to "their wives" severely limits the pool of women and men eligible for this service. Such a reading is particularly awkward if the author is Paul since he makes it clear both in practice[43] and in principle (e.g., Gal 3:28; 1 Cor 11:11) that in Christ women have equal rights and privileges with men and since 1 Cor 7 encourages ministry by singles.

5. It would be strange for non-office holders to be required to meet practically identical qualifications, listed in the same order, as the qualifications for deacons listed in 3:8:

---

42. So Marshall, *Pastoral Epistles*, 493; *pace* John Calvin, *Calvin's Commentaries: The Second Epistle of Paul the Apostle to the Corinthians and the Epistles to Timothy, Titus and Philemon* (trans. T. A. Smail; Grand Rapids: Eerdmans, 1964), 229.
43. Cf. above, pp. 61–68.

3:8 Διακόνους ὡσαύτως σεμνούς (worthy of respect)	3:11 Γυναῖκας ὡσαύτως σεμνάς (worthy of respect)
μὴ διλόγους (not double tongued)	μὴ διαβόλους (not slanderous)
μὴ οἴνῳ πολλῷ προσέχοντας (not addicted to much wine)	νηφαλίους (sober)
μὴ αἰσχροκερδεῖς (not fond of dishonest gain)	πιστὰς ἐν πᾶσιν (trustworthy in every respect)

Being sober (νηφαλίους) is also the third overseer qualification, and, if anything, is more restrictive than the parallel in verse 8, so is more appropriate for a woman deacon than a deacon's wife. Similarly "trustworthy in every respect" is more demanding than "not fond of dishonest gain" and so, too, is more appropriate as a qualification for a woman deacon than for a deacon's wife.

6. The first requirement for overseers, deacons, and women (deacons) is that they hold public respect. "Worthy of respect" in both verses 8 and 11 is a requirement that is much more appropriate for people who act on behalf of the church than for their wives.

7. The statement about women in verse 11 is surrounded by other qualifications for deacons. If this is a reference to the wives of deacons, it is out of place at this point and should more logically have followed all the qualifications of the deacons themselves.[44]

8. If Paul did not condone women deacons, why did he refer to Phoebe as "deacon of the church in Cenchrea" in Rom 16:1? The church office term "deaconess" did not exist at that time, so interpreting 1 Tim 3:11 as identifying qualifications for deaconesses is anachronistic.

9. In addition to the many official-sounding titles Paul gives to his female colleagues in ministry, 1 Tim 5:3–11 lists qualifications for officially recognized "widows" under church support. Since verse 9 states that widows are "enrolled" into this position, it is

---

44. E.g., Hurley, *Man and Woman*, 230.

clear that it is a recognized church position. A qualified widow "continues night and day to pray" (v. 5) and is known for "showing hospitality to strangers, washing the feet of the saints, helping those in trouble and devoting herself to all kinds of good deeds" (v. 10).[45] Reference to "the saints" implies that their ministries were not limited to other women and makes it clear that Paul did intend at least these unmarried women to work for the church. Consequently, this reference to women deacons is not surprising. Even leading complementarians like Köstenberger, Schreiner, Hurley, Clark, and Grudem understand 1 Tim 3:11 to refer to women deacons.[46]

10. If women are excluded from the office of deacon, they are deprived both of the blessing given to deacons ("those who have served well gain an excellent standing and great assurance in their faith in Christ Jesus," 3:13) and of the opportunities the office affords to bless others. Such deprivation is not consistent with Paul's treatment of and statements about women elsewhere.

11. Most patristic commentators writing on this advocate female deacons.[47] Kevin Madigan and Carolyn Osiek cite sixty-one inscriptions and forty literary references to female deacons through the sixth century AD in the East, where the church in Ephesus was located.[48]

The natural reading, then, of 1 Tim 3:11 is that women are eligible to be deacons, with the same title (deacon, not deaconess) and same requirements as men. This was affirmed by Theodoret 3.656, Theodore of

---

45. Admittedly these are listed as qualifications in order to be put on the list to receive financial support, but the natural presumption, especially now that they are receiving support from the church, is that, as they are able, they will continue their lifelong pattern of service to the church.

46. Andreas J. Köstenberger, "Women in the Pauline Mission," in *The Gospel to the Nations: Perspectives on Paul's Mission* (ed. Peter Bolt and Mark Thompson; Leicester, England; Downers Grove, Ill.: InterVarsity Press, 2000), 229, and Köstenberger's review of Belleville's *Women Leaders and the Church: Three Crucial Questions*," *JETS* 44 (2001): 345. Thomas R. Schreiner, "The Valuable Ministries of Women in the Context of Male Leadership: A Survey of Old and New Testament Examples and Teaching," *RBMW* 209–24, 214. Hurley, *Man and Woman*, 229–231 argues cogently that 1 Tim 3:11 addresses women deacons. Clark, *Man*, 119–23. On April 13, 2005 in Blanchard Hall at Wheaton College Wayne Grudem affirmed that women can be deacons and that Phoebe was a deacon.

47. Kevin Madigan and Carolyn Osiek, eds., *Ordained Women in the Early Church: A Documentary History* (Baltimore: Johns Hopkins Univ. Press, 2005), 23ff.

48. Madigan and Osiek, *Ordained Women*, passim.

Mopsuestia 2.128, and the third century *Didascalia apostolorum* 3.12, and has been widely held throughout church history.[49]

CONCLUSION TO 1 TIMOTHY 3:1–13 AND TITUS 1:5–9

Paul specifically includes women in the church office of deacon (1 Tim 3:11). Similarly, he states that "anyone desiring the office of overseer desires a good work" in 3:1 and 5. The subject for those meeting the qualifications of elder and overseer according to Titus 1:6 is "anyone," which implies the eligibility of women to be overseers. "One woman man" excludes polygamists and probably adulterers from church office, but it must not be a requirement for all church officers since that would exclude unmarried men like Paul. Nowhere else in the qualifications for overseers, elders, or deacons in 1 Tim 3:1–12 or Titus 1:5–9 does Paul mention "man," "men," any masculine pronoun, or any expression that excludes women from church office. Moreover, 1 Timothy's use of similar expressions specifically regarding women that parallel each overseer qualification is strong evidence that Paul regards women as able to meet all the qualifications for overseers.

---

49.   Cf. the list of advocates of this view in Marshall, *Pastoral Epistles*, 493 n. 82.

CONCLUSION:
PAUL CONSISTENTLY
CHAMPIONS THE EQUALITY OF
MAN AND WOMAN IN CHRIST

To think that Paul must have had a restrictive attitude toward women's roles in ministry because of his rabbinic upbringing does not adequately weigh his primary guiding influences: the Holy Scriptures, the Holy Spirit, and Jesus, as well as the Mishnaic evidence of the actual sayings of Paul's teacher, Gamaliel. Unlike typical rabbinic treatment of women, Gamaliel's relaxing of restrictions on women anticipates the many clear affirmations of freedom and equality for women that Paul champions both in principle (e.g., Gal 3:28; 1 Cor 7:2–34; 1 Cor 11:10–12) and in practice as evidenced by the many women he affirms as colleagues in ministry (e.g., Rom 16:1–15). Paul repeatedly affirms the equal standing and privileges of women and men in the church and in marriage.

Only two passages in Paul's letters restrict what women may do in the church: 1 Cor 14:34–35 and 1 Tim 2:12. There is an exceptionally broad range of evidence that 1 Cor 14:34–35 is an interpolation not originally in the text of this letter. It reflects a common convention that women should be silent in public assemblies, a restriction counter to Paul's repeated affirmations in this chapter that the entire church should encourage or teach one another in worship. Someone probably wrote it in the margin of an early manuscript to counter the natural implications of Paul's affirmations in this chapter and in 1 Cor 11:5–15 of women's authority to pray and prophesy in church.

In 1 Tim 2:12, the one passage where Paul himself clearly restricts women's ministry in the church, his expression "I am not permitting" uses a verb that favors a present over a universal prohibition, particularly in this present indicative grammatical form. The only clearly established meaning of αὐθεντεῖν in Paul's day that makes sense in 1 Tim 2:12 is the one identified by BDAG, "to assume authority." The first established occurrence of the meaning "to exercise authority" is not until ca. AD 370. Consequently, 1 Tim 2:12 does not prohibit women from exercising authority over men. It only prohibits women from assuming for themselves authority over men that the church had not granted them. Furthermore, Paul's typical use of οὐδέ to join two elements to convey a single idea strongly supports that 1 Tim 2:12 gives only one prohibition: of women assuming authority for themselves to teach men. Paul's wording and the context of this passage show that it is a specific restriction to keep the only group he identifies as influenced by the false teachings, namely women, from taking authority into their own hands to teach in public gatherings of the church where men are present. He prohibits them from doing precisely what the false teachers had done. He does not prohibit women from teaching per se, nor does he prohibit women from being delegated authority in the church.

Some people interpret each of Paul's affirmations of women in practice and in principle one by one in isolation against the supposedly "clear" prohibition by Paul in 1 Tim 2:12 of women teaching or having authority over men. No matter how improbable or strained their particular interpretations, they argue that it is better to accept them than to deny the "clear" teaching of 1 Tim 2:12. Such arguments that treat each piece of opposing evidence in isolation are like a person caught in an avalanche thinking, "I will jump out of the way of each rock or clump of snow as it comes, and none of it will hit me." But in an avalanche the rocks and snow do not come in isolation. Just as the totality of the avalanche is inescapable, so the totality of the Scriptures' affirmations of women leading God's people is inescapable. To maintain the view that women must never teach or have authority over men, one must demonstrate that, given the entirety of the scriptural evidence, it is improbable that God ever authorized a woman to teach or to have authority over a man. Yet the biblical evidence against this is as strong as an avalanche.

To the degree my thirty-six years of research on this topic has led me to understand correctly the message God intends to communicate through his Word, I pray that this book will bring about a consensus on the primary exegetical issues that have divided the church on women's equal status and freedom to minister. Just as the church has come to unanimity in rejecting "separate but equal" rights for whites and blacks, I trust that this book will help bring a truly biblical unanimity to the church in rejecting the view that God established "separate but equal" leadership roles for men and women in the church. It is my prayer that one day soon the church with substantial unanimity will affirm that woman and man are not separate in status or privilege from one another in the Lord, but are, indeed, one in Christ.

SELECT BIBLIOGRAPHY

Thousands of other entries are in the complete bibliography at http://www.pbpayne.com. Note, too, that this select list excludes all commentaries and individual articles contained in books listed here.

Alexander, T. Desmond. "Further Observations on the term 'Seed' in Genesis." *TynBul* 48.2 (1997): 363–67.

Allison, Robert W. "Let Women be Silent in the Churches (1 Cor. 14:33b–36): What Did Paul Really Say, and What Did it Mean?" *JSNT* 32 (1988): 27–60.

Arichea, Daniel C. "The Silence of Women in the Church: Theology and Translation in 1 Corinthians 14.33b–36." *BT* (Technical Papers) 46 (1995): 101–12.

Arnold, Clinton E. "Jesus Christ: 'Head' of the Church (Colossians and Ephesians)." Pages 346–66 in *Jesus of Nazareth: Lord and Christ: Essays on the Historical Jesus and New Testament Christology*. Edited by Joel B. Green and Max Turner. Grand Rapids: Eerdmans, 1994.

Barth, Karl. *The Doctrine of Creation*. Edited by G. W. Bromiley and T. F. Torrance. Edinburgh: T&T Clark, 1960 [from vol. 3 of *Church Dogmatics*].

Bauckham, Richard. *Gospel Women: Studies of the Named Women in the Gospels*. Grand Rapids: Eerdmans, 2002.

Baum, Armin D. "Semantic Variation within the Corpus Paulinum: Linguistic Considerations concerning the Richer Vocabulary of the Pastoral Epistles." *TynBul* 59.2 (2008): 271–92.

Baumert, Norbert. *Woman and Man in Paul: Overcoming a Misunderstanding.* Translated by Patrick Madigan. Collegeville, Minn.: Liturgical Press, 1996.

Beck, J. R. "Is There a Head of the House in the Home? Reflections on Ephesians 5." *Journal of Biblical Equality* [Lakewood, Col.] 1 (December 1989): 61–70.

Beck, James R., and Craig L. Blomberg. *Two Views on Women in Ministry.* Counterpoints. Edited by Stanley N. Gundry. Grand Rapids: Zondervan, 2001.

Bedale, Stephan. "The Meaning of κεφαλή in the Pauline Epistles." *JTS* 5 NS (1954): 211–15.

BeDuhn, Jason D. "'Because of the Angels': Unveiling Paul's Anthropology in 1 Corinthians 11." *JBL* 118 (1999): 295–320.

Belleville, Linda L. "Ἰουνιαν ἐπίσημοι ἐν τοῖς ἀποστόλοις: A Re-examination of Romans 16.7 in Light of Primary Source Materials." *NTS* 51 (2005): 231–49.

———. *Women Leaders and the Church: Three Crucial Questions.* Grand Rapids: Baker, 2000.

Bilezikian, Gilbert G. *Beyond Sex Roles: What the Bible Says about A Woman's Place in Church and Family.* Grand Rapids: Baker, 1985 (2nd ed. 1987).

———. "Hermeneutical Bungee-Jumping: Subordination in the Godhead." *JETS* 30 (1997): 57–68.

———. "Hierarchist and Egalitarian Inculturations." *JETS* 30 (1987): 421–26.

———. *Subordination in the Godhead: A Re-emerging Heresy.* St. Paul, Minn.: Christians for Biblical Equality, 1993.

Blattenberger III, David E. *Rethinking 1 Corinthians 11:2–16 through Archaeological and Moral-Rhetorical Analysis.* Lewiston, N.Y.: Mellen, 1997.

Bloesch, Donald G. *Is the Bible Sexist? Beyond Feminism and Patriarchalism.* Westchester: Crossway, 1982.

Böhm, M. "Beobachtungen zur paulinischen Schriftrezeption und Schrift-argumentation im 1. Korintherbrief." *ZNW* 97 (2006): 207–34.

Boldrey, Richard, and Joyce Boldrey. *Chauvinist or Feminist? Paul's View of Women*. Grand Rapids: Baker, 1976 (formerly published as "Women in Paul's Life." *Trinity Studies* 2 [1972]: 1–36).

Boomsma, Clarence. *Male and Female, One in Christ: New Testament Teaching on Women in Office*. Grand Rapids: Baker, 1993.

Boucher, Madeleine. "Some Unexplored Parallels to 1 Cor 11.11–12 and Gal 3.28: The New Testament on the Role of Women." *CBQ* 31 (1969): 50–58.

Bowman, Ann L. "Women in Ministry: An Exegetical Study of 1 Timothy 2:11–15." *BSac* 149 (1992): 193–213.

Bristow, John Temple. *What Paul Really Said about Women*. San Francisco: Harper & Row, 1988.

Brooten, Bernadette J. "Junia: Outstanding among the Apostles (Romans 16:7)." Pages 41–144 in *Women Priests: A Catholic Commentary on the Vatican Declaration*. Edited by Leonard and Arlene Swidler. New York: Paulist, 1977.

Bruce, F. F. "One in Christ Jesus: Thoughts on Galatians 3:26–29." *Journal of the Christian Brethren Research Fellowship* [Wellington, New Zealand] 122 (1990): 7–10.

Brueggemann, Walter. "Of the Same Flesh and Bone: Gen. 2:23a." *CBQ* 32 (1970): 532–42.

Burer, Michael H., and Daniel B. Wallace. "Was Junia Really an Apostle? A Re-examination of Rom 16.7." *NTS* 47 (2001): 76–91.

Cerling, Charles Edward, Jr. "Women Ministers in the New Testament Church." *JETS* 19 (1976): 209–15.

Cervin, Richard S. "A Note Regarding the Name 'Junia(s)' in Romans 16.7." *NTS* 40 (1994): 464–70.

———. "Does Κεφαλή Mean 'Source' or 'Authority over' in Greek Literature? A Rebuttal." *TJ* 10 NS (1989): 85–112.

———. "ΠΕΡΙ ΤΟΥ ΚΕΦΑΛΗ: A Rejoinder." Unpublished. 1991 (39 pages).

Chadwick, John. "κεφαλή." Pages 177–83 in *Lexicographica Graeca: Contributions to the Lexicography of Ancient Greek*. Oxford: Clarendon, 1996.

Chilton, Bruce D., and Jacob Neusner. "Paul and Gamaliel." *BBR* 14.1 (2004): 1–43.

Clark, Stephen B. *Man and Woman in Christ: An Examination of the Roles of Men and Women in Light of Scripture and the Social Sciences*. Ann Arbor, Mich.: Servant, 1980.

Clines, David J. A. "What Does Eve Do to Help? and Other Irredeemably Androcentric Orientations in Genesis 1–3." Pages 1–22 in *What Does Eve Do to Help? and Other Readerly Questions to the Old Testament*. JSOTSup 94; Sheffield: JSOT Press, 1990.

Clouse, Bonnidell, and Robert G. Clouse, eds. *Women in Ministry: Four Views*. With contributions from Robert D. Culver, Susan Foh, Walter Liefeld, and Alvera Mickelsen. Downers Grove, Ill.: InterVarsity Press, 1989.

Collins, Jack. "A Syntactical Note (Genesis 3:15): Is the Woman's Seed Singular or Plural?" *TynBul* 48.1 (1997): 139–48.

Conn, Harvie. "Evangelical Feminism: Some Bibliographical Reflections on the Contemporary State of the 'Union.'" *WTJ* (1984): 104–24.

Cowles, C. S. *A Woman's Place? Leadership in the Church*. Kansas City: Beacon Hill, 1993.

Crain, Terrence Alexander. "The Linguistic Background to the Metaphoric Use of κεφαλη in the New Testament." B.D. Honours Thesis. Murdoch University, Australia, 1990.

Crüsemann, Marlene. "Irredeemably Hostile to Women: Anti-Jewish Elements in the Exegesis of the Dispute about Women's Right to Speak (1 Cor. 14.34–35)." *JSNT* 23 (2001): 19–36.

Cunningham, Loren, and David J. Hamilton with Janice Rogers. *Why Not Women? A Biblical Study of Women in Missions, Ministry, and Leadership*. Seattle: YWAM, 2000.

Davis, John D. *Genesis and Semitic Tradition*. New York: Scribner's, 1894.

Davis, John Jefferson. "Some Reflections on Galatians 3:28, Sexual Roles, and Biblical Hermeneutics." *JETS* 19 (1976): 201–8.

Dawes, Gregory W. *The Body in Question: Meaning and Metaphor in the Interpretation of Ephesians 5:21–33*. Leiden: Brill, 1998.

Delobel, Joël. "1 Cor 11:2–16: Towards a Coherent Explanation." Pages 369–89 in *L'apôtre Paul. Personnalité, style et conception du ministère*. Edited by A. Vanhoye. BETL 73. Leuven: Leuven University/Peeters, 1986.

Derrett, J. Duncan. "Religious Hair." Pages 170–75 in *Studies in the New Testament* 1. Leiden: Brill, 1977.

Dudrey, Russ. "'Submit Yourselves to One Another': A Socio-Historical Look at the Household Code of Ephesians 5:15–6:9." *ResQ* 41.1 (1999): 27–44.

Dunn, Peter W. "The Influence of 1 Corinthians on the Acts of Paul." Pages 438–54 in *Society of Biblical Literature 1996 Seminar Papers*. Atlanta: Scholars Press, 1996.

Edwards, Ruth B. *The Case for Women's Ministry*. London: SPCK, 1989.

Ellis, E. Earle. "Paul and His Co-Workers." *NTS* 17 (1970–71): 437–52.

———. "The Silenced Wives of Corinth (I Cor. 14:34–5)." Pages 213–20 in *New Testament Textual Criticism, Its Significance for Exegesis: Essays in Honour of Bruce M. Metzger*. Edited by Eldon Jay Epp and Gordon D. Fee. Oxford: Clarendon, 1981.

Epp, Eldon Jay. *Junia: The First Woman Apostle*. Minneapolis: Fortress, 2005.

Erickson, Millard J. *Who's Tampering with the Trinity? An Assessment of the Subordination Debate*. Grand Rapids: Kregel, 2009.

Evans, Mary J. *Woman in the Bible: An Overview of All the Crucial Passages on Women's Roles*. Downers Grove, Ill.: InterVarsity Press, 1983.

Fatum, Lone. "Image of God and Glory of Man: Women in the Pauline Congregations." Pages 56–137 in *Image of God and Gender Models in Judaeo-Christian Tradition*. Edited by K. E. Børresen. Oslo: Solum Forlag, 1991.

Fee, Gordon D. "The Cultural Context of Ephesians 5:18–6:9." *Priscilla Papers* 16.1 (2002): 3–8.

———. *God's Empowering Presence: The Holy Spirit in the Letters of Paul*. Peabody, MA: Hendrickson, 1994.

———. "Issues in Evangelical Hermeneutics, Part III: The Great Watershed—Intentionality & Particularity: I Timothy 2:8–15 as a Test Case." *Crux* 26 (1990): 31–37.

———. "Women in Ministry: The Meaning of 1 Timothy 2:8–15 in Light of the Purpose of 1 Timothy." *Journal of the Christian Brethren Research Fellowship* [Wellington, New Zealand] 122 (1990): 11–18.

Finger, R. H. "Phoebe: Role Model for Leaders." *Daughters of Sarah* [Chicago] 14.2 (1988): 5–7.

Fiorenza, Elisabeth Schüssler. "The Apostleship of Women in Early Christianity." Pages 135–40 in *Women Priests: A Catholic Commentary on the Vatican Declaration*. Edited by Leonard Swidler and Arlene Swidler. New York: Paulist, 1977.

———. *In Memory of Her: A Feminist Theological Reconstruction of Christian Origins*. New York: Crossroad, 1983.

———. "Missionaries, Apostles, Cowokers: Romans 16 and the Reconstruction of Women's Early Christian History." *Word and World* 6.4 (1986): 420–33.

———. "Women in the Pre-Pauline and Pauline Churches." *USQR* 33 (1978): 153–66.

Fitzmyer, J. A. "Another Look at ΚΕΦΑΛΗ in 1 Corinthians 11.3." *NTS* 35 (1989): 503–11.

———. "*Kephalē* in I Corinthians 11:3" *Int* 47.1 (1993): 52–59.

Fleming, Joy Elasky. *Man and Woman in Biblical Unity: Theology from Genesis 2–3*. St. Paul, Minn.: Christians for Biblical Equality, 1993.

Foh, Susan T. "What is the Woman's Desire?" *WTJ* 37 (1975): 376–83.

———. *Women and the Word of God: A Response to Biblical Feminism*. Philadelphia: Presbyterian and Reformed, 1979.

Ford, J. Massingberde. "Biblical Material Relevant to the Ordination of Women." *JES* 10 (1973): 669–94.

Foster, Lewis. "The Earliest Collection of Paul's Epistles." *BETS* 10 (1967): 44–55.

France, R. T. *Women in the Church's Ministry: A Text Case for Biblical Hermeneutics*. The Didsbury Lectures, 1995. Exeter: Paternoster, 1995.

Freedman, R. David. "Woman, A Power Equal to Man: Translation of Woman as a 'Fit Helpmate' for Man Is Questioned." *BAR* 9 (1983): 56–58.

Fuller, D. P. "Paul and Galatians 3:28," *TSF Bulletin* [Madison, Wisc.] 9.2 (1985): 9–13.

Gagnon, Robert A. J. *The Bible and Homosexual Practice: Texts and Hermeneutics*. Nashville: Abingdon, 2001.

Gasque, W. Ward. "The Role of Women in the Church, in Society, and in the Home." *Crux* 19.3 (1983): 3–9.

Gerstner, John, and David Scholer. *Is Women's Ordination Unbiblical?* Hamilton, Mass.: Current Affairs Committee, Gordon-Conwell, 1980.

Giles, Kevin. *Jesus and the Father: Modern Evangelicals Reinvent the Doctrine of the Trinity*. Grand Rapids: Zondervan: 2006.

———. "Jesus and Women." *Interchange* [Sydney] 19 (1976): 131–36.

———. "The Order of Creation and the Subordination of Women." *Interchange* [Sydney] 23 (1978): 175–89.

———. *The Trinity and Subordinationism: The Doctrine of God and the Contemporary Gender Debate*. Downers Grove, Ill.: InterVarsity Press, 2002.

———. *Women and Their Ministry: A Case for Equal Ministries in the Church Today*. East Malvern, Victoria, Australia: Dove, 1977.

Gill, David W. J. "The Importance of Roman Portraiture for Head-Coverings in 1 Corinthians 11:2–16." *TynBul* 44.2 (1993): 245–60.

Gombis, Timothy G. "A Radically New Humanity: The Function of the *Haustafel* in Ephesians." *JETS* 48 (2005): 317–30.

Gourgues, Michel, "Who Is Misogynist: Paul or Certain Corinthians? Note on 1 Corinthians 14:33b–36." Pages 117–24 in *Woman Also Journeyed with Him: Feminist Perspectives on the Bible*. Edited by Gérald Caron et al. Collegeville, Minn.: Liturgical Press, 2000.

Greenbury, James. "1 Corinthians 14:34–35: Evaluation of Prophecy Revisited." *JETS* 51 (2008): 721–31.

Grenz, Stanley J. "Anticipating God's New Community: Theological Foundations for Women in Ministry." *JETS* 38 (1995): 595–611.

————. "Theological Foundations for Male-Female Relationships." *JETS* 41 (1998): 615–30.

Grenz, Stanley J. with Denise Muir Kjesbo. *Women in the Church: A Biblical Theology of Women in Ministry.* Downers Grove, Ill.: InterVarsity Press, 1995.

Groothuis, Rebecca Merrill, *Good News for Women: A Biblical Picture of Gender Equality.* Grand Rapids, Baker, 1996.

Grudem, Wayne. *Biblical Foundations for Manhood and Womanhood.* Wheaton, Ill.: Crossway, 2002.

————. *Evangelical Feminism and Biblical Truth: An Analysis of More Than One Hundred Disputed Questions.* Sisters, Ore.: Multnomah, 2004. [EF]

————. "The Meaning of κεφαλή ('Head'): An Evaluation of New Evidence, Real and Alleged." *JETS* 44 (2001): 25–65.

————. "Prophecy—Yes, But Teaching—No: Paul's Consistent Advocacy of Women's Participation without Governing Authority." *JETS* 30 (1987): 11–23.

Gruenler, Royce Gordon. "The Mission-Lifestyle Setting of 1 Tim 2:8–15." *JETS* 42 (1998): 215–38.

Gundry-Volf, Judith M. "Gender and Creation in 1 Corinthians 11:2–16: A Study in Paul's Theological Method." Pages 151–71 in *Evangelium, Schriftauslegung, Kirche: Festschrift für Peter Stuhlmacher.* Edited by J. Ådna, S. J. Hafemann, and O. Hofius. Göttingen: Vandenhoeck & Ruprecht, 1997.

Harris, Timothy J. "Why Did Paul Mention Eve's Deception: A Critique of P. W. Barnett's Interpretation of I Timothy 2." *EvQ* 62 (1990): 335–52.

Hays, Richard B. "Paul on the Relation between Men and Women." Pages 46–59 in *The Moral Vision of the New Testament: Community, Cross, New Creation.* San Francisco: HarperSanFrancisco, 1996.

————. "Relations Natural and Unnatural: A Response to John Boswell's Exegesis of Romans 1." *JRE* 14.1 (1986): 184–215.

Hayter, Mary. *The New Eve in Christ: The Use and Abuse of the Bible in the Debate about Women in the Church.* London: SPCK, 1987.

Herter, H. "Effeminatus." *RAC* 2:620–50.

Hess, Richard S. "The Roles of the Woman and the Man in Genesis 3." *Them* 18 (1993): 15–19.

———. "Evidence for Equality in Genesis 1–3." *E–Quality* 7.3 (2008): 8–11.

Hestenes, Roberta, and Lois Curley, eds. *Women and Men in Ministry: Collected Readings.* Pasadena: Fuller Theological Seminary, 1980.

Hogan, Pauline Nigh. *"No Longer Male and Female": Interpreting Galatians 3.28 in Early Christianity.* Library of NT Studies 380. New York: T&T Clark, 2008.

Holmes, J. M. *Text in a Whirlwind: A Critique of Four Exegetical Devices at 1 Timothy 2.9–15.* JSNTSup 196; Studies in NT Greek 7. Sheffield: Sheffield Academic Press, 2000.

Hooker, Morna D. "Authority on Her Head: An Examination of 1 Cor XI.10." *NTS* 10 (1963–64): 410–16.

Horowitz, M. C. "The Image of God in Man: Is Woman Included?" *HTR* 72 (1979): 179–206.

Horrell, David G. *The Social Ethos of the Corinthian Correspondence: Interests and Ideology from 1 Corinthians to 1 Clement.* Studies of the New Testament and its World. Edinburgh: T&T Clark, 1996.

Howe, E. Margaret. *Women & Church Leadership.* Contemporary Evangelical Perspectives. Grand Rapids: Zondervan, 1982.

Hugenberger, G. P. "Women in Church Office: Hermeneutics or Exegesis? A Survey of Approaches to 1 Tim 2:8–15." *JETS* 35 (1992): 341–60.

Hull, Gretchen Gaebelein. *Equal to Serve: Women and Men in the Church and Home.* Old Tappan, N.J.: Revell, 1987.

Hurley, James B. "Did Paul Require Veils or the Silence of Women? A Consideration of 1 Cor. 11:2–16 and 1 Cor. 14:33b–36." *WTJ* 35 (1973): 190–220.

———. *Man and Woman in Biblical Perspective.* Leicester: Inter-Varsity Press, 1981; Grand Rapids: Zondervan, 1981.

Huttar, David, "ΑΥΘΕΝΤΕΙΝ in the Aeschylus Scholium." *JETS* 44 (2001): 615–25.

Isaksson, Abel. *Marriage and Ministry in the New Temple: A Study with Special Reference to Mt. 19:3–12 and 1 Cor. 11:3–16.* Translated by

N. Tomkinson et al. Acta Seminarii Neotestamentici Upsaliensis 24. Lund, Sweden: Gleerup, 1965.

Jenkins, Claude. "Origen on 1 Corinthians." *JTS* 10 (1909): 29–51.

Jewett, Paul K. *Man as Male and Female: A Study in Sexual Relationships from a Theological Point of View.* Grand Rapids: Eerdmans, 1975.

Johnston, Robert K. "The Role of Women in the Church and Home: An Evangelical Testcase in Hermeneutics." Pages 234–59 in *Scripture, Tradition, and Interpretation.* Edited by W. W. Gasque and W. S. LaSor. Grand Rapids: Eerdmans, 1978.

Kearsley, R. A. "Women in Public Life in the Roman East: Iunia Theodora, Claudia Metrodora and Phoebe, Benefactress of Paul." *TynBul* 50.2 (1999): 189–211.

Kee, Howard C. "The Changing Role of Woman in the Early Christian World." *ThTo* 49 (1992): 225–38.

Keener, Craig S. Paul, *Women and Wives: Marriage and Women's Ministry in the Letters of Paul.* Peabody, Mass.: Hendrickson, 1992.

———. "Women's Education and Public Speech in Antiquity." *JETS* 50 (2007): 747–59.

Kendrick, W. Gerald. "Authority, Women, and Angels: Translating 1 Corinthians 11.10." *BT* 46 (1995): 336–43.

Khiok-khng, Yeo. "Differentiation and Mutuality of Male-Female Relations in 1 Corinthians 11:2–16." *BR* 43 (1998): 7–21.

Klauck, Hans-J. *Ancient Letters and the New Testament: A Guide to Context and Exegesis.* Waco, Tex.: Baylor Univ. Press, 2006.

Knight III, George W. "ΑΥΘΕΝΤΕΩ in Reference to Women in 1 Timothy 2:12." *NTS* 30 (1984): 143–57.

———. *The Role Relationship of Men and Women: New Testament Teaching.* Chicago: Moody Press, 1977; rev. ed., 1985.

Köstenberger, Andreas J. "Ascertaining Women's God-Ordained Roles: An Interpretation of 1 Timothy 2:15." *BBR* 7 (1997): 107–44.

———. "Syntactical Background Studies to 1 Tim. 2:12 in the New Testament and Extrabiblical Greek Literature." Pages 156–79 in *Discourse Analysis and Other Topics in Biblical Greek.* Edited by S. Porter and D. A. Carson. JSNTSup 113. Sheffield: Sheffield Academic Press, 1995.

Köstenberger, Andreas J., Thomas R. Schreiner, and H. Scott Baldwin, eds. *Women in the Church: A Fresh Analysis of 1 Timothy 2:9–15.* Grand Rapids: Baker, 1995. [WCFA]

Köstenberger, Andreas J. and Thomas R. Schreiner, eds. *Women in the Church: An Analysis and Application of 1 Timothy 2:9–15.* 2nd ed. Grand Rapids: Baker, 2005. [WCA]

Kroeger, Catherine Clark. "The Apostle Paul and the Greco-Roman Cults of Women." *JETS* 30 (1987): 25–38.

———. "Toward an Understanding of Ancient Conceptions of 'Head,'" *Priscilla Papers* 20.3 (Summer 2006): 4–8.

Lampe, Peter. *From Paul to Valentinus: Christians at Rome in the First Two Centuries.* Trans. by Michael Steimnhauser. Edited by Marshall D. Johnson. Minneapolis: Fortress, 2003.

Levine, Amy-Jill, ed. *A Feminist Companion to Paul.* London: T&T Clark, 2004.

Levine, Lee I. "Women in the Synagogue." Pages 499–518 of *The Ancient Synagogue.* New Haven, Conn./London: Yale Univ. Press, 2000; 2nd ed. 2005.

Lewis, Jack P. "The Woman's Seed (Gen. 3:15)." *JETS* 34 (1991): 299–319.

Liefeld, Walter L. "Women and the Nature of Ministry." *JETS* 30 (1987): 49–61.

Lockwood, P. F. "Does 1 Corinthians 14:34–35 Exclude Women from the Pastoral Office?" *Lutheran Theological Journal* 30.1 (1996): 300–338.

Lösch, Stephan. "Christliche Frauen in Corinth (I Cor. 11,2–16)." *TQ* 127 (1947): 216–61.

Longenecker, Richard N. *New Testament Social Ethics for Today.* Grand Rapids: Eerdmans, 1984.

Longstaff, Thomas R. W. "The Ordination of Women: A Biblical Perspective." *ATR* 57 (1975): 316–27.

Lowe, Stephen D. "Rethinking the Female Status/Function Question: The Jew/Gentile Relationship as Paradigm." *JETS* 34 (1991): 59–75.

Luter, A. Boyd, "Partnership in the Gospel: The Role of Women in the Church at Philippi." *JETS* 39 (1996): 411–20.

Luttikhuizen, Gerard P., ed. *The Creation of Man and Woman*. Leiden: Brill, 2000.

Madigan, Kevin, and Carolyn Osiek, eds. *Ordained Women in the Early Church: A Documentary History*. Baltimore: Johns Hopkins Univ. Press, 2005.

Maier, Walter A. "An Exegetical Study of 1 Corinthians 14:33b–38." *CTQ* 55.2 (1991): 81–104.

Malcolm, Kari Torjesen. *Women at the Crossroads: A Path beyond Feminism and Traditionalism*. Downers Grove, Ill.: InterVarsity Press, 1982.

Manus, Chris Ukachukwu, "The Subordination of the Women in the Church: 1 Cor 14:33b–36 Reconsidered." *Revue Africaine de Théologie* [Kinshasa-Limete, Zaire] 8.16 (1984): 183–95.

Martin, Dale B. *The Corinthian Body*. New Haven, Conn.: Yale Univ. Press, 1995.

Martin, Troy, "Paul's Argument from Nature for the Veil in 1 Corinthians 11:13–15: A Testicle instead of a Head Covering." *JBL* 123 (2004): 75–84.

Martin, W. J. "1 Corinthians 11.2–16: An Interpretation." Pp. 231–41 in *Apostolic History and the Gospel: Biblical and Historical Essays Presented to F. F. Bruce*. Edited by W. W. Gasque and R. P. Martin. Exeter: Paternoster, 1970.

Massey, Preston T. "The Meaning of κατακαλύπτω and κατὰ κεφαλῆς ἔξων in 1 Corinthians 11.2–16." *NTS* 53 (2007): 502–23.

Meeks, Wayne A. "The Image of the Androgyne: Some Uses of a Symbol in Earliest Christianity." *HR* 13 (1974): 165–208.

Meier, John P. "On the Veiling of Hermeneutics (1 Cor 11:2–16)." *CBQ* 40 (1978): 212–26.

———. "*Presbuteros* in the Pastoral Epistles." *CBQ* 35 (1973): 323–45.

Mendell, Henry. "ΑΡΣΕΝΟΚΟΙΤΑΙ: Boswell on Paul" [unpublished detailed critique of John Boswell's exegesis of Rom 1:26–27].

Mercadante, Linda. *From Hierarchy to Equality: A Comparison of Past and Present Interpretations of 1 Cor. 11:2–16 in Relation to the Changing*

Status of Women in Society. Vancouver, B.C.: G.M.H. Books, Regent College, 1978.

Metzger, Bruce M. "A Reconsideration of Certain Arguments against the Pauline Authorship of the Pastoral Epistles." *ExpTim* 70 (1958–59): 91–94.

———. *A Textual Commentary on the Greek New Testament.* 2nd ed. Stuttgart: German Bible Society, 1994.

Mickelsen, Alvera, ed. *Women, Authority and the Bible.* Downers Grove, Ill.: InterVarsity Press, 1986.

Mickelsen, Berkeley, and Alvera Mickelsen. "The 'Head' of the Epistles." *Christianity Today* 25.4 (February 20, 1981): 20–23.

———. *Women and the Bible.* Downers Grove, Ill.: InterVarsity Press, 1985.

Moo, Douglas J. "1 Timothy 2:11–15: Meaning and Significance." *TJ* 1 NS (1980): 62–83.

———. "The Interpretation of 1 Tim. 2:11–15: A Rejoinder." *TJ* 2.2 (1981): 198–222.

Motyer, Steve. "Expounding 1 Timothy 2:8–15." *VE* 24 (1994): 91–102.

———. "The Relationship between Paul's Gospel of 'All One in Christ Jesus' (Galatians 3:28) and the 'Household Codes.'" *VE* 19 (1989): 91–102.

Moule, C. F. D. "The Problem of the Pastoral Epistles: A Reappraisal." *BJRL* 47 (1965): 430–52.

Mount, Christopher. "1 Corinthians 11:3–16: Spirit Possession and Authority in a Non-Pauline Interpolation." *JBL* 124 (2005): 313–40.

Munro, W. *Authority in Paul and Peter: The Identification of a Pastoral Stratum in the Pauline Corpus and 1 Peter.* SNTSMS 45; Cambridge: Cambridge Univ. Press, 1983.

———. "Women, Text and the Canon: The Strange Case of 1 Corinthians 14:33–35." *BTB* 18 (1988): 26–31.

Murphy-O'Connor, Jerome. "1 Corinthians 11:2–16 Once Again." *CBQ* 50 (1988): 265–74.

———. "Interpolations in 1 Corinthians." *CBQ* 48 (1986): 81–94.

———. "Sex and Logic in 1 Corinthians 11:2–16." *CBQ* 42 (1980): 482–500.

Ng, Esther Yue L. "Phoebe as *Prostatis*," *TJ* 25 NS (2004): 3–13.

Niccum, Curt. "The Voice of the Manuscripts on the Silence of Women: The External Evidence for 1 Cor 14.34–5." *NTS* 43 (1997): 242–55.

Odell-Scott, David W. "Editorial Dilemma: The Interpolation of 1 Cor 14:34–35 in the Western Manuscripts of D, G, and 88." *BTB* 30 (2000): 68–74.

———. "In Defense of an Egalitarian Interpretation of 1 Cor 14:34–36. A Reply to Murphy-O'Connor's Critique." *BTB* 17.3 (1987): 100–103.

———. "Let the Women Speak in Church: An Egalitarian Interpretation of 1 Cor. 14:33b–36." *BTB* 13.3 (1983): 90–93.

———. *A Post-Patriarchal Christology*. Altanta: Scholars Press, 1991.

Orr, W. F. "Paul's Treatment of Marriage in I Cor. 7." *Perspective* 8 (1967): 5–22.

Osborne, Grant R. "Hermeneutics and Women in the Church." *JETS* 20 (1977): 337–52.

Osburn, Carroll D. "ΑΥΘΕΝΤΕΩ (1 Timothy 2:12)." *ResQ* 25.1 (1982): 1–12.

Osburn, Carroll D., ed. *Essays on Women in Earliest Christianity*. 2 vols. Joplin, Mo.: College Press, 1993. 2nd printing, corrected, 1995.

Osiek, C., and D. L. Balch. *Families in the New Testament World: Household and House Churches*. Louisville: Westminster/John Knox, 1997.

Oster, Richard E. "Use, Misuse and Neglect of Archaeological Evidence in Some Modern Works on 1 Corinthians (1 Cor 7:1–5; 8:10; 11:2–16; 12:14–26)." *ZNW* 83 (1992): 52–73.

———. "When Men Wore Veils to Worship: The Historical Context of 1 Corinthians 11.4." *NTS* 34 (1988): 481–505.

Padgett, Alan. "The Scholarship of Patriarchy (on 1 Timothy 2:8–15): A Response to *Women in the Church*, eds. Köstenberger, Schreiner and Baldwin." *Priscilla Papers* 11.1 (1997): 24–29.

———. "The Significance of ἀντί in 1 Corinthians 11:15." *TynBul* 45 (1994): 181–87.

———. "Wealthy Women at Ephesus: I Timothy 2:8–15 in Social Context." *Int* 41.1 (1987): 19–31.

Paige, Terence. "The Social Matrix of Women's Speech at Corinth: The Context and Meaning of the Command to Silence in 1 Corinthians 14:33b–36." *BBR* 12.2 (2002): 217–42.

Panning, Armin J. "ΑΥΘΕΝΤΕΙΝ—A Word Study." *Wisconsin Lutheran Quarterly* 78 (1981): 185–91.

Pagels, Elaine. *Adam, Eve, and the Serpent.* London: Penguin, 1988.

Payne, Philip B. "1 Tim 2.12 and the Use of οὐδέ to Combine Two Elements to Express a Single Idea." *NTS* 54 (2008): 235–53.

———. "Distigmai Matching the Original Ink of *Codex Vaticanus*: Do They Mark the Location of Textual Variants?" Pages 191–213 in *Le manuscrit B de la Bible (Vaticanus gr. 1209): Introduction au fac-similé, Actes du Colloque de Genève (11 juin 2001), contributions supplémentaires.* Edited by Patrick Andrist. Prahins, Switzerland: Éditions du Zèbre, 2009.

———. "Fuldensis, Sigla for Variants in Vaticanus, and 1 Cor 14.34–5." *NTS* 41 (1995): 240–62.

———. "The Interpretation of I Timothy 2:11–15: A Surrejoinder." Part II of *What Does Scripture Teach about the Ordination of Women? Differing Views by Three New Testament Scholars.* Minneapolis: The Evangelical Free Church of America, 1986.

———. "Libertarian Women in Ephesus: A Response to Douglas J. Moo's Article, '1 Timothy 2:11–15: Meaning and Significance.'" *TJ* 2 NS (1981): 169–97.

———. "Ms. 88 as Evidence for a Text without 1 Cor 14.34–35." *NTS* 44 (1998): 152–58.

———. "The Originality of Text-Critical Symbols in Codex Vaticanus." *NovT* 42 (2000): 105–13.

———. "The Text-Critical Function of the Umlauts in Vaticanus, with Special Attention to 1 Corinthians 14.34–35: A Response to J. Edward Miller." *JSNT* 27 (2004): 105–12.

———. "Wild Hair and Gender Equality in 1 Corinthians 11:20–16." *Priscilla Papers* 20:3 (Summer 2006): 9–18.

Perriman, Andrew C. "The Head of a Woman: The Meaning of ΚΕΦΑΛΗ in 1 Cor. 11:3." *JTS* 45 (1994): 602–22.

———. *Speaking of Women: Interpreting Paul.* Leicester: Apollos, 1998.

————. "What Eve Did, What Women Shouldn't Do: The Meaning of ΑΥΘΕΝΤΕΩ in 1 Timothy 2:12." *TynBul* 44.1 (1993): 129–42.

Peterman, G. W. "Marriage and Sexual Fidelity in the Papyri, Plutarch and Paul." *TynBul* 50.2 (1999): 163–72.

Petzer, Jacobus H. "Reconsidering the Silent Women of Corinth — A Note on 1 Corinthians 14:34–35." *ThEv* (Pretoria) 26 (1993): 132–38.

Pierce, Ronald W., and Rebecca Merrill Groothuis. *Discovering Biblical Equality: Complementarity without Hierarchy*. Downers Grove, Ill.: InterVarsity Press, 2004.

————. "Evangelicals and Gender Roles in the 1990s: 1 Tim 2:8–15: A Test Case." *JETS* 36 (1993): 343–55.

Piper, John, and Wayne Grudem, eds. *Recovering Biblical Manhood and Womanhood: A Response to Evangelical Feminism*. Wheaton, Illinois: Crossway, 1991. [RBMW]

Porter, Stanley E., ed. *The Pauline Canon*. Leiden: Brill, 2004.

————. "What Does It Mean to Be 'Saved by Childbirth' (1 Timothy 2.15)?" *JSNT* 49 (1993): 87–102.

————. "Wittgenstein's Classes of Utterances and Pauline Ethical Texts." *JETS* 32 (1989): 85–97.

Ramsey, George W. "Is Name-Giving an Act of Domination in Genesis 2:23 and Elsewhere?" *CBQ* 50 (1988): 24–35.

Redekop, G. N. "Let the Women Learn: 1 Timothy 2:8–15 Reconsidered." *Studies in Religion/Sciences Religieuses* [Waterloo, Ont.] 19.2 (1990): 235–45.

Richardson, Peter. "From Apostles to Virgins: Romans 16 and the Roles of Women in the Early Church." *TJT* 2.2 (1986): 232–61.

Ridderbos, Herman. *Paul: An Outline of His Theology*. Grand Rapids: Eerdmans, 1975.

Ryrie, Charles Caldwell. *The Place of Women in the Church*. Chicago: Moody Press, 1958.

Saucy, Robert L. "Women's Prohibition to Teach Men: An Investigation into Its Meaning and Contemporary Application." *JETS* 37 (1994): 79–97.

Scanzoni, Letha, and Nancy Hardesty. *All We're Meant to Be: A Biblical Approach to Women's Liberation.* Waco, Tex.: Word, 1974.

Scholer, David M. "The Evangelical Debate over Biblical 'Headship.'" Pages 28–57 in *Women, Abuse, and the Bible.* Edited by Catherine Clark Kroeger and James R. Beck. Grand Rapids: Baker, 1996.

———. "Feminist Hermeneutics and Evangelical Biblical Interpretation." *JETS* 30 (1987): 407–20.

———. "Paul's Women Co-Workers in Ministry." *Theology, News and Notes* 42.1 (March 1995): 20–22.

———. "Women in the Church's Ministry: Does I Timothy 2:9–15 Help or Hinder?" *Daughters of Sarah* 16.4 (1990): 7–12.

Schultz, R. R. "A Case for 'President' Phoebe in Romans 16:2." *Lutheran Theological Journal* [North Adelaide, S. Australia] 24.3 (1990): 124–27.

———. "Romans 16:7: Junia or Junias?" *ExpTim* 98.4 (1987): 108–10.

Scroggs, Robin. "Paul and the Eschatological Woman." *JAAR* 40 (1972): 283–303.

———. "Paul and the Eschatological Woman: Revisited." *JAAR* 42 (1974): 532–37.

———. "Paul: Chauvinist or Liberationist?" *Christian Century* 15 (1972): 307–9.

Sherlock, C. H. "On God and Gender." *Interchange* [Sydney] 22 (1977): 93–104.

Sherlock, Peta. "Women and the Arguments from Creation." *Interchange* [Sydney] 20 (1976): 245–49.

Sigountos, James G., and Myron Shank. "Public Roles for Women in the Pauline Church: A Reappraisal of the Evidence." *JETS* 26 (1983): 283–95.

Snodgrass, K. "Paul and Women." *Covenant Quarterly* 34 (1976): 3–19.

Spencer, Aída Dina Besançon. *Beyond the Curse: Women Called to Ministry.* Nashville: Nelson, 1985.

———. "Eve at Ephesus (Should Women Be Ordained as Pastors according to the First Letter to Timothy 2:11–15?)." *JETS* 17 (1974): 215–22.

Stagg, Frank. "The Domestic Code and the Final Appeal, Ephesians 5.21–6.24." *RevExp* 76 (1979): 541–52.

Stendahl, Krister. *The Bible and the Role of Women: A Case Study in Herme-neutics.* Trans. by Emilie T. Sander. FBBS 15. Philadelphia: Fortress, 1966.

Strobel, August. "Schreiben des Lukas? Zum sprachlichen Problem der Pas-toralbriefe." *NTS* 15 (1968–69): 191–210.

Swartley, Willard M. *Slavery, Sabbath, War, and Women: Case Issues in Biblical Interpretation.* Scottdale, Pa.: Herald, 1983.

Swidler, Leonard. *Biblical Affirmations of Woman.* Philadelphia, Westmin-ster, 1979.

———. *Women and Ministry in the New Testament.* Ramsey, N.J.: Paulist, 1980.

———. *Women in Judaism: The Status of Women in Formative Judaism.* Metuchen, N.J.: Scarecrow, 1976.

Thiselton, Anthony C. "Realized Eschatology at Corinth." *NTS* 24 (1977–78): 510–26.

Thompson, Cynthia L. "Hairstyles, Head-Coverings, and St. Paul: Portraits from Roman Corinth." *Biblical Archaeologist* 51.2 (1988): 99–115.

Thorley, John. "Junia, a Woman Apostle." *NovT* 38 (1996): 18–29.

Thurston, Bonnie. *Women in the New Testament.* New York: Crossroad, 1998.

Torrance, Thomas F. *The Christian Doctrine of God: One Being, Three Per-sons.* Edinburgh: T&T Clark, 1996.

Trible, Phyllis. "Depatriarchalizing in Biblical Interpretation." *JAAR* 41 (1973): 30–48.

Trombley, Charles. *Who Said Women Can't Teach?* South Plainfield N.J.: Bridge, 1985.

Trompf, G. W. "On Attitudes toward Women in Paul and Paulinist Lit-erature: 1 Corinthians 11:3–16 and its Context." *CBQ* 42 (1980): 196–215.

Tucker, Ruth A. *Women in the Maze: Questions & Answers on Biblical Equality.* Downers Grove, Ill.: InterVarsity Press, 1992.

Tucker, Ruth A., and Walter Liefeld. *Daughters of the Church: Women and Ministry from New Testament Times to the Present.* Grand Rapids: Zondervan, 1987.

van de Jagt, Krijn A. "Women Are Saved through Bearing Children (I Timothy 2:11 – 15)." *BT* 39.2 (1988): 201 – 8.

Walker, William O., Jr. "The Burden of Proof in Identifying Interpolations in the Pauline Letters." *NTS* 33 (1987): 610 – 18.

———. *Interpolations in the Pauline Letters.* JSNTSup 213. Sheffield: Sheffield Academic Press, 2001.

Waltke, Bruce K. "The Role of Women in the Bible." *Crux* 31.3 (1995): 29 – 40.

Ward, R. B. "Musonius and Paul on Marriage." *NTS* 36.2 (1990): 281 – 89.

Warfield, Benjamin B. "The Biblical Doctrine of the Trinity." Pages 38 – 59 in *Biblical and Theological Studies.* Edited by S. G. Craig. Philadelphia: Presbyterian & Reformed, 1952.

Waters, Kenneth L., Jr. "Saved through Childbearing: Virtues as Children in 1 Timothy 2:11 – 15." *JBL* 123 (2004): 703 – 35.

Watson, Francis. "The Authority of the Voice: A Theological Reading of 1 Cor 11.2 – 16." *NTS* 46 (2000): 520 – 36.

Weeks, N. "Of Silence and Head Covering." *WTJ* 35 (1972): 21 – 27.

Westermann, Claus. *Creation.* Trans. by John J. Scullion. Philadelphia : Fortress, 1974.

———. *Genesis 1 – 11.* Trans. by John J. Scullion. Minneapolis: Augsburg, 1984; London: SPCK, 1984.

———. *The Genesis Accounts of Creation.* Philadelphia: Fortress, 1964.

Wiley, Tatha. *Paul and the Gentile Women: Reframing Galatians.* New York: Continuum, 2005.

Williams, Don. *The Apostle Paul and Women in the Church.* Ventura, Calif.: Regal, 1977.

Wilshire, Leland Edward. "The TLG Computer and Further Reference to ΑΥΘΕΝΤΕΩ in 1 Timothy 2.12." *NTS* 34 (1988): 120 – 34.

———. "The TLG Computer and Further Reference to AUTHENTEO in I Timothy 2:12 Revisited: A Reply to Paul W. Barnett and Timothy J. Harris." *EvQ* 65.1 (1993): 43 – 55.

Windisch, Hans. "Sinn und Geltung des apostolischen *Mulier taceat in ecclesia* (Die Frau schweige in der Gemeinde)." *Christliche Welt* (1930), cols. 411–25. [Continued under the title] "Noch einmal: *Mulier taceat in ecclesia*: Ein Wort zur Abwehr und zur Klärung." Ibid., cols. 837–40.

Winter, B. W. *Roman Wives, Roman Widows: The Appearance of New Women and the Pauline Communities.* Grand Rapids: Eerdmans, 2003.

———. "The 'New' Roman Wife and 1 Timothy 2:9–15: The Search for a *Sitz im Leben.*" *TynBul* 51 (2000): 285–94.

Wire, Antoinette Clark. *The Corinthian Women Prophets: A Reconstruction through Paul's Rhetoric.* Minneapolis: Fortress, 1990.

Witherington, Ben, III. "Rite and Rights for Women—Galatians 3:28." *NTS* 27 (1980–81): 593–604.

———. *Women and the Genesis of Christianity.* Edited by Ann Witherington. Cambridge: Cambridge Univ. Press, 1990.

———. *Women in the Earliest Churches.* SNTSMS 59. Cambridge: Cambridge Univ. Press, 1988.

Wolters, Al. "A Semantic Study of αὐθέντης and Its Derivatives." *Journal of Greco-Roman Christianity and Judaism* 1 (2000): 145–75.

Wolterstorff, Nicholas. "The Bible and Women: Another Look at the 'Conservative' Position." *Reformed Journal* 29 (1979): 23–26.

Zucker, Friedrich. "ΑΥΘΕΝΤΗΣ und Ableitungen." Pages 3–26 in *Sitzungsberichte der Sächsischen Akademie der Wissenschaften zu Leipzig. Philologish-historische Klasse.* Vol. 107, book 4. Berlin: Akademie-Verlag, 1962.

SIGNIFICANT HEBREW WORDS INDEX

SIGNIFICANT GREEK WORDS INDEX

Scripture Index

Subject Index

Author Index

A

Aalen, S., 320
Adams, A. W., 239
Adler, A., 362
Ådna, J., 169
Aeschylus, 35, 143, 155, 362, 370
Agosto, Efrain, 70
Albert, M., 153
Alexander of Alexandria, 251
Allison, D. C., 106
Allison, Robert W., 117, 224, 226, 256
Ambrose, 81, 146, 150–51, 439
Ambrosiaster, 137, 228, 253, 309
Ammonius Alexandrius, 387
Anatolius, 251
Andrist, Patrick, 232, 234, 245
Apollodorus, 143
Apollonius, 143, 177
Archelaus, 251
Aristarkhos, 233
Aristides, Aelius, 22, 34, 127, 143, 218, 252
Aristophanes, 143, 218
Aristotle, 19, 22, 32–33, 35, 122, 123, 128, 145, 218, 271, 279, 282, 432
Armstrong, David, 121
Armstrong, Gregory T., 42
Arndt, W. F., 13, 14, 377
Arnobius, 251
Arnold, Clinton E., 288
Artemidorus, Daldianus, 19, 122, 125, 126
Askwith, E. H., 296

Athanasius, 137
Athenaeus, 19, 143, 173
Athenagorus, 251
Augustine, 96, 151, 439
Azzai, Ben, 314

B

Babbitt, Frank C., 34, 141, 152, 158, 201, 218, 357
Bachmann, Philipp, 149
Back, James R., 210
Bailey, Derrick S., 143
Bailey, Kenneth E., 255
Balch, D. L., 226
Baldwin, Henry S., 19, 350, 361–63, 366–68, 370, 373–75, 377–79, 381–82, 385–89, 391–92, 399, 407
Ball, John, 403
Balsdon, J. P. V. D., 155, 160–61
Bammel, Caroline, 364
Bammel, Ernst, 370
Barnett, Paul W., 35, 297, 315, 316, 328, 362, 383
Barrett, C. K., 63, 118, 122, 127, 142, 183, 184, 209, 221, 222, 226, 248, 305, 329, 428
Barrett, David P., 66, 241
Barth, Karl, 42
Barth, Markus, 31, 34, 37, 38, 40, 127, 128, 274, 287, 288
Barton, S. C., 226
Basil, 137
Bassler, Jouette M., 177, 226, 455
Bauckham, Richard, 65, 66
Bauer, Walter, 13, 14, 251, 377

Baugh, S. M., 157, 314, 354
Baum, Armin D., 293
Baumgartner, W., 16
Beard, Mary, 142
Beardslee, W. A., 226
Beasley-Murray, G. R., 82
Beck, James R., 122, 149, 281
Beck, William F., 24
Bedale, Stephan, 117–18
BeDuhn, Jason D., 182
Behr, C. A., 34
Belleville, Linda L., 34, 39, 65, 66, 281, 337, 373, 458
Bell, H. I., 388
Bengel, Albert, 227, 228, 267
Berkowitz, Luci, 150, 361
Bernard, J. H., 329, 383
Betz, Han Dieter, 79, 93
Bilezikian, Gilbert G., 117, 120, 121, 133–34, 224
Billerbeck, P., 18
Bittlinger, Arnold, 226
Blass, F., 14
Blattenberger III, David E., 169
Blomberg, Craig L., 122, 149, 169, 182, 203, 210, 281, 325, 351, 356, 358
Boer, Æ., 381
Böhm, M., 169
Boice, James M., 88
Boll, Franz, 381
Bölting, Rudolf, 123
Bolt, Peter, 458
Boomsma, Clarence, 351
Boswell, John, 177
Bousset, Wilhelm, 226
Brawley, Robert L., 408

We want to hear from you. Please send your comments about this book to us in care of zreview@zondervan.com. Thank you.

ZONDERVAN.com/
AUTHORTRACKER
follow your favorite authors